SIXTH EDITION

Legal Research, Analysis, and Writing

Joanne Banker Hames
DeAnza Community College

Yvonne Ekern
Santa Clara University School of Law

330 Hudson Street, NY, NY 10013

Vice President, Portfolio Management: Andrew Gilfillan
Portfolio Manager: Gary Bauer
Editorial Assistant: Lynda Cramer
Senior Vice President, Marketing: David Gesell
Field Marketing Manager: Thomas Hayward
Product Marketing Manager: Kaylee Carlson
Senior Marketing Coordinator: Les Roberts
Director, Digital Studio and Content Production: Brian Hyland
Managing Producer: Cynthia Zonneveld
Content Producer: Ruchi Sachdev
Manager, Rights Management: Johanna Burke
Operations Specialist: Deidra Smith
Creative Digital Lead: Mary Siener
Managing Producer, Digital Studio: Autumn Benson
Content Producer, Digital Studio: Maura Barclay
Full-Service Management and Composition: iEnergizer Aptara®, Ltd.
Full-Service Project Manager: Manas Roy
Cover Design: StudioMontage
Cover Art (or Cover Photo): Photogl/Fotolia
Printer/Binder: LSC Communications
Cover Printer: LSC Communications
Text Font: 11/13 pt TimesLTPro

Acknowledgments of third-party content appear on page 539, which constitutes an extension of this copyright page.

Library of Congress Cataloging-in-Publication Data
Names: Hames, Joanne Banker, author. | Ekern, Yvonne, author.
Title: Legal research, analysis, and writing / Joanne Banker Hames, DeAnza Community College, Yvonne Ekern, Santa Clara University School of Law.
Description: Sixth edition. | Boston : Pearson, 2018. | Includes index.
Identifiers: LCCN 2016030175| ISBN 9780134559841 | ISBN 0134559843
Subjects: LCSH: Legal research—United States. | Legal composition.
Classification: LCC KF240 .H36 2018 | DDC 340.072/073—dc23 LC record available at https://lccn.loc.gov/2016030175

28 2022

ISBN 10: 0-13-455984-3
ISBN 13: 978-0-13-455984-1

Brief Contents

Contents

About the Authors

Joanne Banker Hames is an attorney and paralegal educator who has been actively involved in paralegal education since 1977. She is an instructor in and the former coordinator for the ABA-approved paralegal program at DeAnza Community College in Cupertino, California, as well as an adjunct instructor at Santa Clara University's School of Law. She earned her J.D. degree from Santa Clara University Law School and has been an active member of the California Bar since 1972. As an attorney, she has been involved in research and writing for legal memoranda and appellate briefs. Among the classes she teaches are Legal Research and Writing, Advanced Legal Research and Writing, Advanced Legal Research Using Westlaw, and Advanced Legal Research Using Lexis. She is the co-author of *Civil Litigation, Introduction to Law,* and *Constitutional Law: Principles and Practice.*

Yvonne Ekern is an Associate Clinical Professor of Law at Santa Clara University's School of Law and a full-time member of the Legal Analysis, Research, and Writing faculty. For seven years she was the chairperson of the West Valley College Paralegal Program (ABA approved). Prior to attending law school, she taught high school English and math in California and Missouri. She graduated from the University of Idaho School of Law in 1985. While working in criminal and family law offices, she taught part-time in several Silicon Valley paralegal programs. Among the classes she teaches are Legal Research and Writing, Advanced Legal Research and Writing, Appellate Advocacy, Advanced Legal Research and Writing Using Lexis, and Legal Analysis. She has over 25 years' teaching experience. She is the co-author of the texts *Introduction to Law* and *Constitutional Law: Principles and Practice.*

chapter **one**

INTRODUCTION TO LEGAL RESEARCH, WRITING, AND ANALYSIS

SKILL OBJECTIVES FOR CHAPTER 1

When you complete chapter 1, you should be able to

- Describe the role of a legal researcher.
- Explain the effect of federalism on legal publications.
- Describe the sources of U.S. law.
- Explain the difference between a primary and a secondary source of law.
- List the types of materials often found in law libraries.
- List the common features of law books.

CHAPTER OUTLINE

From the Desk of W. J. Bryan, Esq.

TO: Research Assistant
FROM: W. J. Bryan
RE: Our Client, Justin Meyers
DATE:

I'm sorry I won't be here to greet you personally on your first day of work. Unfortunately, I need to be in court today. I am leaving a file on your desk for you to review. The case relates to a new client, Justin Meyers. He is charged with murder. There may be a problem with the legality of a search and seizure, and we need to do more research into this matter. After you read the documents in the file, including statements from several individuals, please write a brief memorandum outlining the issues in the case.

You need to familiarize yourself with our office library. The firm has a legal library containing all state and federal cases and codes, as well as selected secondary source materials. I hope that all the books you need are available. You can access information on various free Internet sites, but these sites are sometimes unreliable. The firm maintains subscriptions to both Westlaw and Lexis but these sources are not free, and using them can be costly.

Just leave your memo on my desk and I will review it tomorrow morning.

1-1 INTRODUCTION

If you are a research assistant for W. J. Bryan working on the Meyers case, you must engage in legal research, analysis, and writing. You are asked to determine if Meyers's rights were violated. To do this, you first need to conduct legal research and locate laws dealing with police searches. You then need to read and analyze the law and apply it to the facts of the Meyers case. Your job is not complete, however, until you communicate your findings to Bryan in a written memorandum.

One of the most important skills for lawyers and paralegals is the ability to find and analyze the law and to communicate their findings, usually in writing. Many other professions also find legal research skills useful. Police officers, for example, often refer to code sections and case law in their jobs. Although this textbook is intended primarily for students pursuing a career as a legal professional, it provides a basic framework for legal research that any student should be able to follow. The subject matter of each chapter is introduced in a hypothetical factual scenario, found in a note from the desk of W. J. Bryan, Esq. As you go through the text, you will learn where and how laws are published, how to find the law, how to analyze a factual situation and apply the relevant legal principles, and how to communicate your findings to clients, other attorneys, and the court. You will also learn how to access legal information through the Internet and how to evaluate online information. At the end of each chapter are several practical research, analysis, and writing exercises. Some exercises can be completed with materials found in the text. Others require that you visit a law library or access the Internet. In addition to the exercises found at the end of the chapters, Appendixes A and B contain several hypothetical cases for research and writing assignments.

Preparing for Legal Research

As you develop your research skills, you will also develop your legal vocabulary. Initially, legal terminology may present problems for you. When you read cases, statutes, or other legal source material, you are reading material written by lawyers (or judges) for other lawyers. Many terms used in the law are not common in everyday language. Latin terminology is used to express some legal concepts. Many words that you *think* you understand have special meanings when used in a legal context. A ***legal dictionary*** is an essential tool that defines and explains legal terms. Another tool is a ***legal thesaurus***. This provides synonyms for legal terms. This is particularly helpful when you use an ***index***. Table 1-1 shows common legal terms used in case law. Review this list and see how many you understand without the use of a legal dictionary or thesaurus.

legal dictionary
A dictionary defining and explaining legal terms.

legal thesaurus
A book providing synonyms for legal words.

index
A list of words and phrases that reflects the topics covered in the book.

Legal Research and Law Practice

Although legal professionals and paraprofessionals spend considerable time studying the law before working in the field, they do not know the answer to every legal question. Even the most experienced lawyers must research the law. Laws change constantly. Legislatures routinely enact, amend, or repeal statutes. Courts decide new cases every day. Even constitutions are amended. When lawyers make legal arguments in court or give legal advice to clients, they must be certain about the current state of the law. Because laws are not the same throughout the various states, lawyers must be certain about the law in their jurisdiction. This often requires legal research.

The researcher's job starts with identifying the nature of the client's legal problem and researching laws related to that problem. It does not stop with just finding the law. The law must be analyzed in relation to the facts of the particular case and the results of the research and analysis explained, usually in written form, to the appropriate person. See Box 1-1. This person may be a client, another attorney, or a judge. Thus, the legal research process usually involves three steps—finding the law, analyzing the law, and then preparing a written explanation or argument based on the law.

TABLE 1-1 Legal Terminology

Affirm	Precedent
Appeal	Real party in interest
Appellant	Remand
Appellee	Respondent
Civil	Reverse
Criminal	*Stare decisis*
Defendant	Writ of certiorari
Motion for summary judgment	Writ of habeas corpus
Plaintiff	Writ of mandate

BOX 1-1 THE LEGAL RESEARCH PROCESS

- ✓ Identify factual question raised by the client's problem.
- ✓ Find law that applies to factual question.
- ✓ Analyze law in relationship to factual question.
- ✓ Communicate findings.

The Role of the Researcher

Only attorneys can give legal advice to clients. Therefore, if you are not an attorney, your legal research should be under the general supervision of an attorney, who must review the research before a client is advised of the findings.

As a research assistant, you may find yourself engaged in various responsibilities, including:

- Gathering or verifying the facts that raise a legal question
- Summarizing the facts
- Conducting legal research
- Summarizing relevant law
- Drafting legal memoranda
- Reviewing legal memoranda for technical requirements
- Checking the citations in memoranda
- Reviewing legal memoranda from opposing counsel

Whatever your responsibilities are, realize that the attorney always expects accuracy and thoroughness. The attorney often relies on your research when advising clients or when arguing matters in court. Even if your job responsibilities do not include working as a research assistant for an attorney, if you work in a law office, you often need to perform legal research for your own benefit. Legal research, analysis, and writing skills contribute greatly to your success in a law office.

The Writer's Corner

IRAC

How to Organize Most Legal Writing

At first, legal writing seems daunting. Questions of where to begin and how to begin can seem overwhelming. The good news is that most legal writing follows a very simple formula. At the core of a legal discussion or argument there are four absolutely necessary sections: the ISSUE, the RULE of law, the ANALYSIS/APPLICATION of the law to the facts of the case you are working on, and the CONCLUSION. (This formula is often referred to as the IRAC method.)

When you add a concise INTRODUCTION and a Statement of FACTS, you have the outline of most legal analysis.

Keep in mind that the reader needs the document organized such that it is easy to read. When drafting a document, simply adhere to this basic formula and the reader—your audience—will easily follow your logic.

Under this formula, the basic outline of most legal memoranda is:

Introduction
(concise overview for the reader)

Statement of Facts
(summary of all key facts and helpful explanatory facts)

Issue
(the legal question(s) to be analyzed under the applicable rule(s) of law)

Rule
(state and explain the rule(s))

Analysis/Application
(analyze/apply the rule(s) of law to the key facts)

Conclusion
(state the conclusion you reach after your analysis)

Remember—you take this approach with each issue. If your case involves three issues, you will go through this process three times.

As you study law notice how this is the formula for most legal writing, including case law decisions. Basic writing skills are also essential in legal writing. At the end of each chapter is an exercise to see if you can "write it right."

A Point to Remember

A nonlawyer, such as a paralegal or a law clerk, cannot give legal advice. To do so is the unauthorized practice of law and is unethical, not to mention illegal. Paralegals or clerks who do legal research should report their findings to a supervising attorney. All legal advice to a client must come from an attorney.

1-2 THE U.S. LEGAL SYSTEM

The ability to engage in effective legal research requires a basic understanding of the U.S. legal system. Several principles of government affect the way our laws are published and applied. One of the most important concepts is federalism. In the United States, government operates under a principle called ***federalism***, which means that separate governments, federal and state, regulate citizens. Each government makes its own laws. When researching an issue, you face different sets of laws for each state and for the federal government. A key feature of legal publications is that separate publications often exist for federal law and for that of each individual state. Even though some secondary sources attempt to discuss all laws, many legal publications (especially primary sources of law) contain law related only to a specific jurisdiction, that is, only federal law or only the law of one state. When you begin research, you save time, and are more accurate, if you focus on publications that contain the proper law. See Box 1-2. As you continue with your legal education, your ability to do this will improve.

federalism
A system of government in which the people are regulated by both federal and state governments.

Sometimes your research shows that both state and federal laws apply. For example, consider the Meyers case mentioned at the beginning of the chapter. In this case, the defendant is charged with the crime of murder. This is a state crime, and a state court will hear the case. However, the U.S. Constitution controls the question of the legality of a search that prohibits unreasonable searches and seizures. To complicate matters, the state in which Meyers resides may also have constitutional provisions regulating unreasonable searches by police. Researching this type of case can be difficult. Keep in mind that where a conflict exists between state and federal law, federal law controls. This is because of the "Supremacy Clause" of the Constitution (Article VI): "This Constitution, and the Laws of the United States which shall be made in Pursuance thereof … shall be the supreme Law of the Land; and the Judges in every State shall be bound thereby, any Thing in the Constitution or Laws of any State to the Contrary notwithstanding." When a state passes a law that conflicts with the Constitution, the U.S. Supreme Court has the power to declare that state law unconstitutional and unenforceable. Like the concept of federalism, the Supremacy Clause is important to legal research.

BOX 1-2 RESEARCH CHECKLIST

Before You Begin

- ✔ Review the factual situation.
- ✔ Determine whether federal law, state law, or both control the factual situation.
- ✔ Use research materials that contain the proper law.

1-3 SOURCES OF U.S. LAW

In both federal and state systems, laws come from the same types of sources. U.S. law is found in four sources: constitutions, statutes, administrative rules or regulations, and case law decisions. All governments, state and federal, have constitutions generally published in various sources. Other laws come from our legislatures, courts, and administrative agencies. Both the federal and state legislatures enact statutory laws, published in codes. Federal courts and state courts are responsible for case law found in case reporters. Administrative agencies exist on both federal and state levels from which we derive administrative rules or regulations.

Constitutional Law

The federal government and all states have constitutions, documents whose primary purpose is to establish the government and define its functions and obligations in relation to the people. The U.S. Constitution establishes and defines the role of the federal government and its relation to the people of the United States. The U.S. Constitution applies only to the federal government, unless expressly made applicable to individual states. Each state constitution establishes and defines the role of the state government and its relationship to citizens of that state. The various constitutions are published in numerous ways, often with the statutory law for the jurisdiction. The U.S. Constitution can be found with the U.S. Codes, and state constitutions are usually found with the state codes.

Statutory Law

Statutory law results from legislative action. The federal and state legislatures enact laws that are then sent to the chief executive (the president or the governor) for approval. After they are signed (or a veto properly overridden), the laws are organized and published in codes. The code for the United States is the *United States Code.* Legislatures also empower the courts to enact rules, known as *rules of court*, which govern practice in the courts. In addition, local governing bodies (cities and counties) enact laws, often known as *local ordinances* or *municipal codes.*

Administrative Regulations

In order for the government to perform all of its tasks, legislatures created various agencies to handle specific jobs. For example, Congress created the Securities and Exchange Commission (SEC) to handle corporate stock transactions. Agencies generally have the power to make necessary rules or regulations. These are *administrative regulations.* Administrative agencies exist in the federal government as well as in each state.

common law
Body of law developed through the courts.

precedent
The example set by the decision of an earlier court for similar cases or similar legal questions that arise in later cases.

stare decisis
"It stands decided"; another term for precedent.

Case Law

The English ***common law*** plays an important role in the U.S. legal system. Common law is based on the concept of ***precedent*** or ***stare decisis***, rather than an exhaustive system of written laws or rules. When parties have a legal problem, their dispute comes before a judge who decides the case. The decision becomes a precedent. Then, if the same type of factual dispute comes before a court in the future, the judge follows the decision of the first case. Although the federal government, as well as the states, has codified considerable law, precedent still plays an important role. U.S. courts have the role of interpreting other laws and applying these laws to different factual disputes. Case law results from selected decisions made by various *appellate* courts, including the U.S. Supreme Court. It does not come from trial court decisions. The concept of *stare decisis* is discussed in more detail in Chapter 3.

Relationship between Sources of Law

When you research an issue, you often find that more than one primary source of law applies. In the U.S. legal system, the courts have the power to interpret the U.S. Constitution, state constitutions, federal and state codes, and federal and state administrative regulations. See Box 1-3. Thorough research requires that when you find constitutional or statutory law (including administrative regulations), you must also determine if case law interprets these laws.

BOX 1-3 PRIMARY SOURCES OF LAW

Federal Law	State Law
U.S. Constitution	State constitution
U.S. Code	State codes
Federal administrative regulations	State administrative regulations
Federal cases	State cases

1-4 LEGAL PUBLICATIONS

Law is published in the same types of materials as any other information, that is, books, periodicals such as magazines or newspapers, and electronic media. Published law is either a ***primary source*** of law or a ***secondary source*** of law. The former is a work that contains the law, such as publications of constitutions, statutes, administrative regulations, and cases. Publications of statutes are sometimes called ***code books***. Publications of cases are ***case reporters***. Secondary sources of law are publications that explain or discuss the law (e.g., legal encyclopedias and journals). Secondary sources are helpful in finding and understanding the primary law. The goal of legal research is to find a primary source of law that controls your factual situation or answers your legal question.

Until recently, the term *law publication* referred to books or magazines. Today, a broader definition is necessary. Primary and secondary sources of law are published not only in books but also in electronic form. Today, many legal researchers rely heavily on the Internet, including fee-based services such as ***Lexis*** (Lexis Advance) and ***Westlaw***. These sites provide access to vast amounts of primary and secondary sources of law. The Internet provides access to numerous other fee-based and free sites containing legal information. *CD-ROM and DVD libraries* containing both primary and secondary sources are also available.

Two major publishers are responsible for many legal publications. These publishers are Thomson Reuters/West and Lexis Law Publishing, and they produce many materials in both print and electronic formats. Each of these publishers adds helpful editorial features to their legal publications to assist the researcher. As you proceed through this text, these features will be introduced and explained.

primary source
A work that contains the law.

secondary source
A tool used to help understand the law; one such tool is a legal encyclopedia that explains the law.

code books
Books that contain codes or statutes.

case reporters
Books that contain case decisions from the courts.

Lexis
A computer-assisted legal research service.

Westlaw
A computer-assisted legal research service.

1-5 THE LAW LIBRARY

Traditional Law Libraries

law library
A library that is dedicated to legal resource material.

One of the prerequisites to doing legal research is familiarity with the ***law library***, which is a library dedicated to legal resource material. Many law firms maintain their own law libraries. These libraries vary in size and content and may contain small collections of basic law books or extensive collections of legal research material. Some larger law firms even employ law librarians to maintain their libraries.

If you need a comprehensive legal library, you might use a county law library or that of a nearby law school. These libraries generally contain primary and secondary sources related to the laws of your state as well as materials related to the laws of the United States. Most likely, these libraries also contain primary and secondary sources concerning the laws of other states and of foreign nations. County law libraries are often open to the public. Law school libraries, on the other hand, may be available to you only if your law firm has a special arrangement with the school.

A Point to Remember

You should make every effort to become familiar with your firm's law library as soon as possible. Knowing what resources are immediately available can save you time and worry.

Types of Legal Materials

See Figure 1-1 for a list of the specific types of books found in most law libraries. Many law libraries also provide electronically stored information. Today legal

FIGURE 1-1 Types of Legal Materials

Case Reporters	Large sets of books containing written case decisions or opinions from state and federal courts
Code Books	Sets of books containing either federal or state statutory law organized in a topical order; may also contain copies of the federal or state constitution
Encyclopedias	Multivolume sets of books that explain the law; they are organized alphabetically by topic; some explain American law in general, others are limited to explanations of laws in a single state
Digests	Multivolume sets of books that act as a detailed topical index to case reporters; are organized topically and contain short summaries of cases
Looseleaf Service	A type of legal work, usually concerning a single legal topic (such as family law), where the written material is kept in a pull-apart binder. The material is continually updated. When laws are changed the publisher sends replacement pages to the subscribers of the service. Pages with the old law are removed and replaced with new pages that reflect the changes in the law
Treatises	Usually single books published on one legal subject
Form Books	Books containing forms that lawyers use to prepare legal documents; sometimes referred to as *practice books*
Legal Periodicals	Magazines, journals, and newspapers related to the practice of law; included are law reviews and journals published regularly by law schools

A Point to Remember

Most legal sources follow the general format of

Title

Volume

Book or reporter (abbreviated)

Page

Year

When you are looking at an unfamiliar citation, try to identify these elements. This will enable you to understand the various citations you come across in your legal studies.

GO TO: *The Bluebook*, Table 1

United States Constitution

The Fourteenth Amendment to the United States Constitution is written as follows:

U.S. Const. amend. XIV.

If you want to indicate a certain section of the Amendment you add: § 1

The full citation looks like this:

U.S. Const. amend. XIV, § 1.

GO TO: *The Bluebook*, Rule 11

The United States Code (Statutes)

The United States Code is cited in the following manner:

Number of Code Title	Code	Section Cited	Date
28	U.S.C.	§ 1291	(XXXX)

The proper cite is 28 U.S.C. § 1291 (XXXX).

GO TO: *The Bluebook*, Rule 12

State Codes (Statutes)

A statute citation must show

1. the numbers of the statutory topic,
2. the abbreviated name of the publication,
3. the specific statute or section of the statute, and
4. the year of the publication.

Examples

Ariz. Rev. Stat. Ann. § ## (XXXX)	Arizona Revised Statutes Annotated
Cal. Educ. Code § ## (XXXX)	California Education Code
Conn. Gen. Stat. § ## (XXXX)	Connecticut General Statutes
Ind. Code § ## (XXXX)	Indiana Code

GO TO: *The Bluebook*, Table 1

Legal citation rules are often complex. Each chapter in this text highlights an important aspect of these rules in a feature entitled "Citation Matters."

Online Research

The Internet provides access to a great deal of legal information, both free and fee based. Some of this information is useful and accurate. However, some information is outdated and inaccurate. Anyone can create and maintain his or her own web page, and legal information can be posted by anyone. Using a general search engine such as Google may lead you to unreliable sites. Be careful to evaluate the source of the information you locate. Always check to see who publishes the information you find and when it was last updated. One very reliable source is the law library website of the Library of Congress (http://www.loc.gov/law/index.php). This site provides extensive information about the U.S. legal system, as well as links to numerous sources of law. Here you will also find guides to the legislative and judicial processes of the United States (Link to Guide to Law Online).

It is impossible to provide a complete and accurate list of great legal research sites. However, this text suggests certain websites and provides tips to help you navigate the Internet successfully. In addition to the website discussed in this chapter, the following sites lead you to virtual libraries, where you can access different legal sources without cost.

http://www.gpo.gov/fdsys/
U.S. Government Publishing Office
www.law.cornell.edu
Legal Information Institute

For an online legal dictionary, go to the following website:
http://dictionary.law.com/

For an online guide to citing legal publications, go to the following website:
http://www.law.cornell.edu/citation/

An understanding of the U.S. legal system is important to the research process. To learn more about it, check the "educational resources" on http://www.uscourts.gov/.

CITATION MATTERS

WHY LEGAL CITATION MATTERS

The term *citation* refers to special information provided by the author of a document. A legal citation shows the reader the origin of the cited authority. Everyone is familiar with the use of quotations. When you use a quote, you must indicate the origin of the quote. Generally, the citation to the original material follows the quoted language. The same is true in legal writing, only we take it a bit further. Most legal writing informs or convinces. The best way to do that is to show the reader where the ideas originated, whether or not a quote is used.

Case law provides good examples of citation use in legal writing. Sometimes it seems as though every sentence has a citation following it. That can make reading legal material tedious and slow. But because legal citations alert the reader to the origin of the material, they are a critical element of legal writing. When a judge writes a decision in a case, that judge strives to explain the reasons for that decision. Often these reasons originate in previously decided cases, and citations to these cases are included.

When attorneys write legal memoranda, they must provide legal authority for the statements they make. Previous cases carry what we call a "weight of authority"—something that personal opinion does not carry. A court is not interested in personal opinions. It is interested in the legal authority that supports the opinion. Courts and other attorneys sometimes need to read the authorities that are cited in memoranda or briefs. It is essential, therefore, that citations be accurate.

In your legal writing, you should strive to cite carefully and completely. Appendix C provides a basic overview of citation. Read it carefully and begin to learn the basic rules of legal citation. Review the use of legal citations below:

> The United States Constitution guarantees the right to trial by jury in order to prevent oppression by the government. U.S. Const. amend. VI and XIV; *Duncan v. State of La.*, 391 U.S. 145, 194 (1968).

This sentence is a statement of law, not an opinion: "The United States Constitution guarantees the right to trial by jury in order to prevent oppression by the government." The writer shows his audience that the guarantee of a jury trial is found in the U.S. Constitution under Amendments Six and Fourteen. The citation to a U.S. Supreme Court case further supports this same statement. A period separated by a semicolon separates the two citations. The second sentence is a *citation sentence.*

The *name* of the case is *Duncan v. State of La.* The name of a case is italicized or underlined, never both.

This case is found in the United States Reports. *U.S.* is the proper abbreviation for the *official reporter* of U.S. Supreme Court case law.

This case is located in *volume* 391, and the *first page* of the case is 145. The writer also provided a "pinpoint cite" for the page in the case where the Court addresses the right to trial by jury. The pinpoint cite is to page 194.

The *year of the decision* is 1968. Notice that the year is placed at the end of the citation, and it must be placed in parentheses.

The citation manual used in the preparation of this text is *The Bluebook: A Uniform System of Citation* (Columbia Law Review Ass'n et al. eds., 20th ed. 2015).

CHAPTER **SUMMARY**

Legal research usually involves finding the law that applies to a specific factual question. Because lawyers must know the current law in their jurisdiction, even the most experienced legal practitioners do research before advising a client or arguing a matter before a court. Paralegals and law clerks often do legal research; indeed, many nonlegal professionals find this competency to be an important tool.

The total process of legal research involves identifying the factual issue, finding the law, applying the law to the factual situation, and communicating these findings. While paralegals and law clerks often perform the research, they should do so under the supervision of a lawyer. Accuracy and thoroughness are essential. Paralegals and other nonattorneys must be careful not to give legal advice to a client because to do so constitutes the unauthorized practice of law and is unethical and illegal.

Before you begin any legal research, you must understand the U.S. legal system. This system was founded on the principle of federalism, which means that two separate governments, federal and state, regulate citizens. The laws of each government are usually found in separate publications. When you research a factual issue, either federal or state law generally controls it, although at times both may apply. Determining which law applies to a factual question is one of the first decisions a researcher must make.

All laws, whether state or federal, are published in constitutions, statutes or codes, administrative regulations, and cases. Case law stems from the English common law, a system where laws developed through the courts and through case decisions. The common law was based on the concept of precedent or *stare decisis*, which means that once a court decided a factual dispute, the same factual dispute in the future had to be decided in the same way. In the United States, case law results from decisions from the appellate and supreme courts in the federal and state systems.

Legal publications include primary and secondary sources of the law. A primary source includes the law itself (constitutions, cases, statutes, and administrative regulations). Secondary sources, such as legal encyclopedias and journals, help explain and find the primary source of law. Legal publications are published in printed as well as in electronic formats.

Legal research is usually conducted in law libraries found in most law offices. Counties and law schools also maintain large law libraries. Materials there resemble materials found in any library. Law books contain many of the same features found in reference books, such as a table of contents and an index. In addition, many law books contain tables of cases, tables of statutes, and tables of abbreviations used in the book. Many books also include pocket part supplements that keep the work up to date.

TERMS TO **REMEMBER**

legal dictionary
legal thesaurus
index
federalism
common law
precedent
stare decisis
primary source
secondary source
code books
case reporters
Lexis
Westlaw
law library
table of contents
table of cases
table of statutes
table of abbreviations
pocket part
legal citations

QUESTIONS FOR **REVIEW**

1. Explain the process of legal research, analysis, and writing.
2. Discuss the various sources of U.S. law.
3. Explain the concept of federalism and how it affects legal research.
4. What are the primary sources of law in the United States?
5. What is the difference between a primary source of law and a secondary source of law?
6. What types of legal materials are found in law libraries?
7. Describe some of the common features of legal publications.

CAN YOU **FIGURE IT OUT?**

1. Refer to Figure 1-1, "Types of Legal Materials." One of the most famous cases decided by the U.S. Supreme Court is the case of *Miranda v. Arizona.* In which type of legal material would you expect to find that case? In which type of legal materials would you expect to find discussions or analysis of that case?
2. Refer to Figure 1-2, Westlaw screen. This screen contains general categories of materials (i.e., Federal Materials, State Materials, etc.) and sub-categories (i.e., Cases, etc.). In which general and sub-categories of material would you expect to find the case of *Miranda v. Arizona*? In which general categories would you expect to find discussions or analysis of that case?

TEST **YOURSELF** (Check Your Answers in Appendix G)

1. Using a legal dictionary, define the following terms: *en banc*, *petitioner*, and *per curiam*.
2. Are the following situations controlled by federal law, by state law, or by both?
   a. Jackson is arrested for possession of narcotics. The drugs were found after Jackson was stopped for speeding. The officer states that as he was writing a ticket for Jackson, the officer noted the smell of marijuana, ordered the driver out of the car, searched the vehicle, and found the drugs. Jackson is charged with possession of marijuana, a state crime. The case is filed in state court. Which law controls the case?
   b. Adams, a resident of Texas, is involved in an automobile accident with Brown, a resident of California. The accident is Adams's fault and Brown is injured. Brown wants to sue. The accident occurred in California. In which court should the lawsuit be filed, and which law should apply?
3. In Appendix F find the case of *Ohio v. Robinette*, a U.S. Supreme Court case dealing with the questions of federalism and how federal and state laws interact. Read the case and answer the following question: Did federal drug laws apply to this case? Why or why not?
4. Access the Law Library of Congress. Under the Guide to Law Online, link to U.S. Federal. Among the various sources on this page is a list of Legal Guides, the first of which is Guide to Law Online: Criminal Justice System. What are the names of the other legal guides?

TEST **YOURSELF**—WRITE IT RIGHT Effective Sentence Structure

Too often sentences are hard to follow, making a reader reread or pause to consider the meaning of the sentence. Sometimes sentences seem awkward or unclear because the words are not in the best order. The construction of most sentences should follow the format of: actor ➡ action ➡ object.

For example: Bobby kicked the ball.
actor ➡ action ➡ object

When we read just the "working words," the sentence says "Bobby kicked ball."

Consider this poor example: The ball was kicked by Bobby.
object ➡ action ➡ actor

When we read just the "working words," here the sentence says "ball kicked Bobby." This does not work.

Writers need to edit for this problem. When we read just the working words, readers should understand the meaning of the sentence.

Now, You Try It

(Check Your Answers in Appendix G)

Rewrite the following sentences to create the effective sentence structure of actor ➡ action ➡ object.

1. The game was won by the Blackhawks.
2. The puck was shot by Crosby.
3. The jury verdict was read by the Judge.
4. A response must, within 60 days after service of the order, be filed with the court.

CITATION **EXERCISES**

Using Section 1-7, answer the following questions.

1. What is missing from these citations?
   a. *Roe v. Wade*, 410 U.S. 113.
   b. *Marbury*, 5 U.S. 137 (1803).
   c. Brandenburg v. Ohio, U.S. 444.
2. Correct the following citations.
   a. Arizona Rev. Stat. Ann. § ## (year).
   b. Ariz. Rev Stat. Ann. ## (year).
   c. Conn General Stat § ## (year).
3. Correct the following citations.
   a. 28 USC Section 1291 (year).
   b. US Const Amend. XIV.

FROM **THE WRITER'S CORNER** How to Organize Most Legal Writing

1. What does IRAC stand for?
2. List the basic outline of most legal memoranda.

ASSIGNMENTS AND **EXERCISES**

Research Exercises

1. Using a legal dictionary, define the terms in Table 1-1.
2. Using a legal thesaurus, find different words for each of the terms in Table 1-1.
3. Visit the law library that you will use to do your legal research assignments. Locate the following legal sources:

   The United States Code

   A case reporter containing decisions from the U.S. Supreme Court

   Your state code

   Case reporters containing case law from your state

Review the list of common features of law books found in Box 1-4 earlier in this chapter. Which of these features is found in each of the legal sources listed here?

Analysis and Writing Assignments

4. Consider the following questions and state whether you would begin your research in state or federal sources.
   a. Can a client who filed bankruptcy five years ago file for bankruptcy again?
   b. If a person took $10,000 from an employer without permission but paid it back when discovered, could that person be charged with any crime?
   c. What are the elements of the crime of counterfeiting?
   d. Mary's boss told her that if she did not have sex with him, she would not get a raise. What are Mary's options?
   e. Terry is a word processor, and he developed carpal tunnel syndrome. Terry's doctor says it is a result of Terry's job. What rights does Terry have?

5. In Appendix F find the case of *Ohio v. Robinette*, a U.S. Supreme Court case dealing with the questions of federalism and how federal and state laws interact. Read the case and answer the following questions.
   a. What primary source of law is the Court interpreting in this case?
   b. Is there a conflict between the state and federal search and seizure laws in this case?
   c. If you were researching a similar search and seizure issue in your state, would you rely on the case of *Ohio v. Robinette* (a) if the issue revolved around your state's constitution or (b) if the issue revolved around the meaning of the U.S. Constitution?

Online Research Exercises

Review the websites listed in this chapter (in the "Online Legal Research" feature).

6. Which of these sources, if any, provide access to your state's constitution?
7. Which of these sources, if any, provide access to your state codes?
8. Which of these sources, if any, provide access to your state cases? If they do provide access to your state cases, for what years are cases provided?
9. Access the Law Library of Congress and find the Guide to Law Online. Which Guide would you link to for laws from your state?

CASE **PROJECT**

In-Class Small Group Work

Select one hypothetical case from those found in Appendix A. (Your instructor may assign a specific case.)

Read the facts carefully and make a list of all legal terms found in the factual scenario. Which of these terms appear in Table 1-1? Discuss the terms. List and explain those terms that are familiar to you. Make a list of those terms you do not recognize.

When you have access to a legal dictionary, define all legal terms found in the factual situation. Compare the dictionary definitions with your group's understanding of the terms.

chapter **two**

THE STARTING POINT: ANALYZING FACTS AND IDENTIFYING LEGAL ISSUES

SKILL OBJECTIVES FOR CHAPTER 2

When you complete chapter 2, you should be able to

- State and describe the three basic factual categories.
- Explain how to compare case law facts with a client's factual situation.
- Describe how to identify legal issues in a client's factual situation.
- Describe how to identify legal issues in a reported case law decision.
- Provide examples of good issue statements.

CHAPTER OUTLINE

From the Desk of W. J. Bryan, Esq.

To: Research Assistant
FROM: W. J. Bryan
RE: Meyers Matter
DATE:/OPEN

The office just received additional information on the Meyers murder case. We now have copies of the search warrant and a copy of the transcript from the grand jury hearing that resulted in Mr. Meyers's indictment for murder. The search warrant allows the police to search our client's house for drugs and drug paraphernalia. During their search, the police found and seized a bloody rag. Forensic evidence indicates that the blood belongs to a murder victim. Carefully read all the new documents, and identify and summarize all facts that are relevant to legality of the search and seizure. After you do that, try to find case law that will help our client.

2-1 INTRODUCTION

As described in the previous chapter, the legal research process consists of finding law, analyzing the law and the facts of your case, and communicating the results of your research and analysis to interested parties. This process usually begins with determining the important facts in your client's case and then identifying the legal question or issues in that case. This chapter discusses the importance of the facts and legal issues to the research process and provides some methods of analyzing the facts and identifying the issues.

At the beginning of the research process, a clear understanding of the facts involved in a client's situation is essential. No legal research is productive until the researcher acquires a good picture of the client's facts. A good client interview produces a factually rich picture of the events and people involved in the client's situation. Sometimes, additional interviews and investigation are necessary. Ascertain and place into perspective all relevant facts before beginning legal research. Students who are new to the law may be tempted to begin research projects prior to establishing a clear picture of the events involved in the case. This is a time-consuming error. Until the facts are well established, researching the law is impossible. Contrary to what one might initially think, the facts determine the area of law to be researched. Facts are found in many places: client interviews, witness interviews, relevant documents, depositions, and other discovery. A thorough understanding of the facts enables the researcher to focus on those most significant, thereby leading the researcher to pinpoint the relevant area of law.

2-2 UNDERSTAND AND ANALYZE THE FACTS

The attorney handling the Meyers case wants his research assistant to find case law that helps his client. In his note, Attorney Bryan gives an important instruction to his assistant. Identification of the relevant facts precedes researching the law. Research is usually undertaken as a direct result of a set of facts: The facts come first, and then the law is applied to those facts. The researcher must begin by categorizing or analyzing the known facts. Obviously, some are more important than others. Your subsequent research assists you in determining which ones are *most* relevant. There are three basic categories of facts:

- Relevant facts
- Explanatory facts
- Legally unimportant facts

Once you gather all of the known facts, the next step is to place them into one of these categories. However, determining relevant facts requires that the researcher have at least a general understanding of the legal principles governing the case. You cannot determine what facts are legally important if you are very unfamiliar with the law. For example, if you know nothing about the criminal law, you might not know whether the contents of a search warrant are important. If you are unfamiliar with the area of law, you must perform some general legal research first. Become familiar with the basic legal principles and then analyze your client's facts. As your research continues, you might also have to reevaluate how to categorize the facts.

Relevant Facts: Relevant facts are essential; do not ignore them. They are legally and factually important. There may be several ways to identify them in a factual situation: (1) remove the fact and ask yourself if it *significantly* changes the situation, and (2) change the fact and ask yourself if it *significantly* changes the situation. If either alters the fact situation, it is probably a relevant fact.
Explanatory Facts: Explanatory facts clarify the relevant facts. They enable the researcher to grasp the entire picture of the events by supplementing and explaining the relevant facts. They often provide color or depth of understanding to the situation.
Legally Unimportant Facts: Put aside legally unimportant facts during legal research. They play no real role in the legal situation. They do not belong in your written analysis of the case. There are several ways to identify them: (1) remove the fact and ask yourself if it significantly changes the situation, and (2) change the fact and ask yourself if it significantly changes the situation. If the answer to either question is "no, it does not alter the fact situation," the fact is probably legally unimportant.

2-3 SORT THE FACTS OF A CLIENT'S CASE

Categorizing your client's facts helps you focus your research. Remember from Chapter 1 that when you research you look for primary law (case law, statutory law, and constitutional law). Because of the rule of *stare decisis*, relevant case law includes cases where the courts have decided the same or similar factual questions. Relevant statutory law includes laws or rules applicable to your factual situation. In any event, identification of the relevant facts in your client's case is essential.

A Point to Remember

The relevant and explanatory facts are the focal points for the researcher. The key here is to recognize and put aside the legally unimportant facts. Sorting the facts enables you to zoom in on the relevant facts and highlight missing facts.

The ultimate sorting of the facts is best left to those trained in the law. Clients are often ill equipped to categorize facts. What is important to a client may be legally irrelevant. However, always let the client tell the entire story. Do not encourage a client to edit the facts. Sometimes facts that appear unimportant initially take on special significance as the litigation or the case moves forward.

2-4 COMPARE CASE LAW FACTS WITH YOUR CLIENT'S FACTS

If your research is focused on case law, you must compare your client's factual situation with those found in published cases. Before determining that specific cases apply to your client's situation, you must determine that the nature of the dispute or the issue is similar. The researcher looks for factually and legally similar cases to compare with the client's case. Identifying issues is addressed later in this chapter.

A process of comparison of relevant facts is a good starting place in the legal analysis process. Factual comparison usually takes place after the researcher clarifies the client facts and locates case law that may be applicable to the client's legal situation. The effective legal researcher works to locate ***case law*** that is as factually similar to the client facts as possible. Because our legal system is based on ***precedent***, the sorting and comparison of facts are essential ***legal analysis*** skills.

case law
A collection of reported cases.

precedent
The example set by the decision of an earlier court for similar cases or similar legal questions that arise in later cases.

legal analysis
The process of comparing and contrasting facts and legal issues.

SORTING THE FACTS

Consider the following factual situation.

Rimma was traveling at 40 miles per hour (mph) on a city street when Emerson, moving at 65 mph, ran into the back of Rimma's vehicle. Emerson's vehicle was a new black Jeep Cherokee. Rimma was driving a four-year-old green Volvo. Emerson did not notice that traffic was slowing and that Rimma's brake lights were on. Emerson was talking on a cell phone, and he was in a hurry to get to his office. He was returning from an appointment with his physician. Emerson took a strong sedative about 30 minutes prior to the accident. He has been under a great deal of stress recently. There was serious damage to Rimma's car. She was injured. Because of the accident, Rimma could not get to her job that evening, due to lack of transportation. Rimma is a 22-year-old exotic dancer. She had a contract for a special engagement that evening, which would have paid her $1,000.00. Emerson is an automobile salesperson. Your office represents Rimma in an action against Emerson.

It is not always clear in which category a particular fact belongs. What is most important is that you begin to sort them. You are not discarding them, only sorting them. As research continues, the researcher may move the facts from one category to another.

Sort the facts discussed here into the following three categories.

Relevant Facts

1. Emerson was driving under the influence of a narcotic.
2. Emerson was exceeding a safe driving speed under the conditions.
3. Emerson's vehicle struck Rimma's vehicle.
4. Rimma's vehicle was damaged because of Emerson's actions.
5. Rimma lost wages because of Emerson's actions.

Explanatory Facts

1. Emerson was hurrying while returning to his office.
2. Emerson was talking on his cellular phone.
3. Emerson was returning from a visit to his physician.
4. Emerson was traveling at 65 mph while Rimma slowed to 40 mph.
5. Emerson did not notice that traffic was slowing down and did not see Rimma's brake lights.

Legally Unimportant Facts (remember these facts will not be used, but they should be identified)

1. Rimma is an exotic dancer.
2. Emerson is a car salesperson.
3. Rimma's car is a green Volvo.
4. Emerson's car is a new black Jeep Cherokee.

The fact category for any given fact may change if the fact pattern is changed. For example: Does the fact pattern change if Emerson's car was malfunctioning and the accelerator was stuck? Does the fact pattern change if Rimma was traveling at 40 mph in a 65 mph zone and was legally intoxicated? Obviously, the answer to both questions is "of course that changes the situation." You can see that changes in the facts may change the overall factual analysis of the case.

Factual comparison at first may seem confusing and somewhat arbitrary. However, once you establish a process, the confusion dissolves. When you compare the client's facts with those of a reported case, look for the following:

- Factual similarities
- Factual unknowns
- Factual differences

	Client's Case	**Published Case**
Factual Similarities:		
Factual Unknowns:		
Factual Differences:		

This chart enables you to easily compare and contrast the facts of your client's case with those of a reported case. A good number of similarities of relevant facts indicate that the case *may* apply in your client's situation. Conversely, a good number of differences in the relevant facts indicate that the case *may not* apply. When there are significant gaps or unknown facts, the reported case probably does not apply to your client's case. As a legal researcher, you are looking for cases that are factually and legally very similar to the one you are researching.

2-5 LEGAL ISSUES

Once the client's factual situation is clear, you can consider what the issues may be. Ask yourself the following question as you begin each legal research assignment: Do I understand the client's problems? If the answer is yes, you are ready to attempt to identify the issues or problems presented by the client's facts. If you are unclear on the legal issues, ask your supervisor for guidance.

Legal issues are specific questions raised by the facts. Think of it this way: An incident occurs, and now you need to give the factual situation a legal label. Properly identifying these "legal labels" helps you locate relevant law. After careful review of a fact pattern, the legal researcher must begin to identify the area of law involved. Once this is known (e.g., contract law, tort law, or family law), identification of the issues must occur. Review the factual situation in the case of *Rimma v. Emerson* described earlier in this chapter. This case involves the general area of tort law. The issue is therefore related to tort law. In very general terms, a question raised by these facts is "Did Emerson commit a tort?" This question or issue is much too broad and will not help in your research. Specific identification of the issue and the relevant facts is essential. A specific area of law involved here is negligence, a part of tort law. However, asking "Was Emerson negligent?" is also too broad. The issue must be stated specifically in relationship to the facts of the case. A better way to state the issue might be "Was Emerson negligent when he drove his car on a city street at 65 mph while he was under the influence of drugs, and rear-ended a vehicle driven by Rimma, damaging the car and injuring Rimma?" This is a more complete issue statement. To ask simply "Was Emerson negligent?" is not enough; the facts are missing.

Another way to think of issues is that they are the questions the parties to a lawsuit bring to the court for resolution. The court resolves the legal issues. Sometimes issues are called ***questions presented***—meaning the questions presented to the court for resolution.

questions presented
A statement of the legal issue presented to the court for resolution.

2-6 IDENTIFY THE LEGAL ISSUES

Issues in Your Client's Case

Once ***pleadings*** are filed in a case, go to the pleadings and read about the causes of action involved to help establish the issues. ***Causes of action*** or ***affirmative defenses*** in pleadings contain the issues. For example, if you read the complaint filed by Rimma against Emerson, you would probably find a cause of action labeled "negligence." When you read this cause of action, you see that Rimma claims (1) that Emerson was driving his car on a public road, (2) that he drove negligently in that he was under the influence of drugs and was not paying attention to traffic, (3) that he rear-ended the vehicle driven by Rimma, and (4) that he caused damage to the car and injury to Rimma. In this type of civil lawsuit, one of the questions the court must decide is whether Emerson was negligent, if Rimma's claims are true. Let us look at this issue statement again: "Was Emerson negligent when he drove his car on a city street at 65 mph while he was under the influence of drugs, and rear-ended a vehicle driven by Rimma, damaging the car and injuring Rimma?" Note how the claims or allegations in a cause of action relate to the way a proper issue statement is phrased. Of course, not all legal issues relate to the existence of a cause of action. Sometimes procedural problems or questions of the admissibility of evidence may also be a legal issue in a case. If you are in doubt about the specific legal issue you are researching, always ask your supervisor for initial guidance. As with your analysis of relevant facts, your specific legal questions may change as you do more research and find out more about the relevant law.

pleadings
The formal, written allegations filed with the court by both sides to a lawsuit; claims and defenses are clearly set out so that both parties are placed on notice of the position of the opposing party.

causes of action
The basis upon which a lawsuit may be brought to the court.

affirmative defenses
Defenses raised by the defendant in the answer; reasons why the plaintiff should not recover even if all of the allegations of the complaint are true.

Issues in a Reported Case

Once you identify the issues in your client's case, you must look for case law dealing with the same issue and similar fact pattern. In reported cases, the court explains the legal issues. Usually, the issues are stated after the court explains the factual background of the case and the ***judicial history*** of the case. The court in some instances actually states "The first issue is ..." or "The question before this court involves... ." This is the clearest indication of the issue. Many cases involve more than one issue. The court usually indicates when it is moving from one issue to the next. The excerpt from the *Kyllo* case that follows provides a typical example of the way in which a court introduces issues.

judicial history
The legal (courtroom) history of a case.

In some cases, the Court makes it very easy to locate the issue. For example: "In this case, we consider whether the Fourth Amendment permits the seizure of contraband detected through a police officer's sense of touch during a protective patdown search." This is the first sentence written by the Court in *Minnesota v. Dickerson*, 508 U.S. 366 (1993). It precedes the facts and the judicial history. This is a good example of Justice White letting the reader know exactly what question the Court would answer. In *Bush v. Gore*, 531 U.S. 98 (2000) the opinion opens with: "The petition presents the following questions: whether the Florida Supreme Court established new standards for resolving Presidential election contests, thereby violating Art. II, § 1, cl. 2 of the United States Constitution and failing to comply with 3 U.S.C. § 5, and whether the use of standardless manual recounts violates the Equal Protection and Due Process Clauses." This is an example of an issue statement that contains several questions.

A Point to Remember

Case law instructs and guides the legal community. It is written not so much for the parties involved in the litigation as for those who will read it in search of case law relevant to their client's situation. The parties to the litigation are primarily concerned with the outcome of the case. The legal researcher is concerned with the legal reasoning or legal analysis provided by the court.

The Writer's Corner

An Issue Includes the Legal Question and the Key Facts

It can be tempting to state an issue as "Did the defendant commit robbery?"

This might be a good starting place in your research and analysis; however, you need more when you write an issue in a memorandum—predictive or persuasive.

Imagine saying to your supervisor: "The question is whether the defendant committed robbery." Your supervisor will simply look at you with a blank stare. This statement does not provide a basis for analysis of the question. It is fine as the starting place in your research and analysis. It is inadequate once it is placed into writing.

Your research will lead you to the following definition. The elements of robbery are:

1. the felonious taking
2. of the personal property of another
3. from their person or immediate presence
4. against their will
5. accomplished by means of force or fear.

Combination of these elements with the facts of a case might produce the following issue:

"Did the defendant commit robbery when he pushed the victim to the ground and grabbed her purse from her hand, while she was kicking at him and yelling for help?"

This is something the supervisor will understand. This question weaves the legal issue—robbery—with the key facts of the case.

Issues have two elements—legal and factual.

2-7 WRITING ISSUE STATEMENTS

An issue statement sets forth the legal question, and it provides the reader with the most significant facts. State the issue as a question. Remember, it is the question presented to the court for resolution.

For example, John is the second baseman of the Hidden Valley Ranger softball team. He is its best hitter. After striking out, he carelessly tosses the wooden bat 16 feet behind him, hitting and injuring Rachael, a 10-year-old spectator. The Rangers lost the final game of the season due to John's striking out.

elements
The components of a cause of action or of a statute.

Your initial research tells you that a cause of action for negligence has four ***elements***: (1) a duty on the part of the defendant to act in a safe manner, (2) breach of the duty to behave in a safe manner, (3) causation (of the injury or damage), and (4) damage to the plaintiff. On a very basic level, the question in the fact pattern above is this: "Was John negligent?" However, this question does not provide the reader with enough information. A better, more specific issue statement is this: "Was John negligent when he carelessly tossed a wooden baseball bat into the crowd injuring a spectator standing 16 feet away?" This question or issue statement provides the reader with a clear picture of what happened. By placing the most relevant facts into the issue, the reader may easily look at the four elements of negligence and decide whether the plaintiff makes a ***prima facie case*** for negligence.

prima facie case
On first view or on its face; for example, the plaintiff presented a strong *prima facie* case for establishing the negligence of the defendant.

Read the excerpt from the *Kyllo* case, looking for facts and issues.

CASE EXCERPT ***Kyllo v. United States***, 533 U.S. 27 (2001)

Justice Scalia delivered the opinion of the Court.

This case presents the question whether the use of a thermal-imaging device aimed at a private home from a public street to detect relative amounts of heat within the home constitutes a "search" within the meaning of the Fourth Amendment.

I

In 1991 Agent William Elliott of the United States Department of the Interior came to suspect that marijuana was being grown in the home belonging to petitioner Danny Kyllo, part of a triplex on Rhododendron Drive in Florence, Oregon. Indoor marijuana growth typically requires high-intensity lamps. In order to determine whether an amount of heat was emanating from petitioner's home consistent with the use of such lamps, at 3:20 a.m. on January 16, 1992, Agent Elliott and Dan Haas used an AgemaThermovision 210 thermal imager to scan the triplex. Thermal imagers detect infrared radiation, which virtually all objects emit but which is not visible to the naked eye. The imager converts radiation into images based on relative warmth—black is cool, white is hot, shades of gray connote relative differences; in that respect, it operates somewhat like a video camera showing heat images. The scan of Kyllo's home took only a few minutes and was performed from the passenger seat of Agent Elliott's vehicle across the street from the front of the house and also from the street in back of the house. The scan showed that the roof over the garage and a side wall of petitioner's home were relatively hot compared to the rest of the home and substantially

warmer than neighboring homes in the triplex. Agent Elliott concluded that petitioner was using halide lights to grow marijuana in his house, which indeed he was. Based on tips from informants, utility bills, and the thermal imaging, a Federal Magistrate Judge issued a warrant authorizing a search of petitioner's home, and the agents found an indoor growing operation involving more than 100 plants. Petitioner was indicted on one count of manufacturing marijuana, in violation of 21 U.S.C. § 841(a)(1). He unsuccessfully moved to suppress the evidence seized from his home and then entered a conditional guilty plea.

The Court of Appeals for the Ninth Circuit remanded the case for an evidentiary hearing regarding the intrusiveness of thermal imaging. On remand the District Court found that the Agema 210 "is a non-intrusive device which emits no rays or beams and shows a crude visual image of the heat being radiated from the outside of the house"; it "did not show any people or activity within the walls of the structure"; "[t]he device used cannot penetrate walls or windows to reveal conversations or human activities"; and "[n]o intimate details of the home were observed." Supp. App. to Pet. for Cert. 39-40. Based on these findings, the District Court upheld the validity of the warrant that relied in part upon the thermal imaging, and reaffirmed its denial of the motion to suppress. A divided Court of Appeals initially reversed, 140 F. 3d 1249 (1998), but that opinion was withdrawn and the panel (after a change in composition) affirmed, 190 F. 3d 1041 (1999), with Judge Noonan dissenting. The court held that petitioner had shown no subjective expectation of privacy because he had made no attempt to conceal the heat escaping from his home, *id.*,at 1046, and even if he had, there was no objectively reasonable expectation of privacy because the imager "did not expose any intimate details of Kyllo's life," only "amorphous 'hot spots' on the roof and exterior wall," *id.*, at 1047. We granted certiorari. 530 U.S. 1305 (2000).

II

The Fourth Amendment provides that "[t]he right of the people to be secure in their persons, houses, papers, and effects, against unreasonable searches and seizures, shall not be violated." "At the very core" of the Fourth Amendment "stands the right of a man to retreat into his own home and there be free from unreasonable governmental intrusion." *Silverman v. United States,* 365 U.S. 505, 511 (1961). With few exceptions, the question whether a warrantless search of a home is reasonable and hence constitutional must be answered no. *See Illinois v. Rodriguez,* 497 U.S. 177, 181 (1990); *Payton v. New York,* 445 U.S. 573, 586 (1980).

On the other hand, the antecedent question of whether or not a Fourth Amendment "search" has occurred is not so simple under our precedent. The permissibility of ordinary visual surveillance of a home used to be clear because, well into the 20th century, our Fourth Amendment jurisprudence was tied to common-law trespass. *See, e.g., Goldman v. United States,* 316 U.S. 129, 134-136 (1942); *Olmstead v. United States,* 277 U.S. 438, 464-466 (1928). Cf. *Silverman v. United States, supra,* at 510-512 (technical trespass not necessary for Fourth Amendment violation; it suffices if there is "actual intrusion into a constitutionally protected area"). Visual surveillance was unquestionably lawful because " 'the eye cannot by the laws of England be guilty of a trespass.' " *Boyd v. United States,*

116 U.S. 616, 628 (1886) (quoting *Entick v. Carrington,* 19 How. St. Tr. 1029, 95 Eng. Rep. 807 (K. B. 1765)). We have since decoupled violation of a person's Fourth Amendment rights from trespassory violation of his property, *see Rakas v. Illinois,* 439 U.S. 128, 143 (1978), but the lawfulness of warrantless visual surveillance of a home has still been preserved. As we observed in *California v. Ciraolo,* 476 U.S. 207, 213 (1986), "[t]he Fourth Amendment protection of the home has never been extended to require law enforcement officers to shield their eyes when passing by a home on public thoroughfares."

One might think that the new validating rationale would be that examining the portion of a house that is in plain public view, while it is a "search" despite the absence of trespass, is not an "unreasonable" one under the Fourth Amendment. *See Minnesota v. Carter,* 525 U.S. 83, 104 (1998) (*Breyer, J.,* concurring in judgment). But in fact we have held that visual observation is no "search" at all—perhaps in order to preserve somewhat more intact our doctrine that warrantless searches are presumptively unconstitutional. *See Dow Chemical Co. v. United States,* 476 U.S. 227, 234–235, 239 (1986). In assessing when a search is not a search, we have applied somewhat in reverse the principle first enunciated in *Katz v. United States,* 389 U.S. 347 (1967). *Katz* involved eavesdropping by means of an electronic listening device placed on the outside of a telephone booth—a location not within the catalog ("persons, houses, papers, and effects") that the Fourth Amendment protects against unreasonable searches. We held that the Fourth Amendment nonetheless protected Katz from the warrantless eavesdropping because he "justifiably relied" upon the privacy of the telephone booth. *Id.*, at 353. As Justice Harlan's oft-quoted concurrence described it, a Fourth Amendment search occurs when the government violates a subjective expectation of privacy that society recognizes as reasonable. *See id.*,at 361. We have subsequently applied this principle to hold that a Fourth Amendment search does *not* occur—even when the explicitly protected location of a *house* is concerned—unless "the individual manifested a subjective expectation of privacy in the object of the challenged search," and "society [is] willing to recognize that expectation as reasonable." *Ciraolo, supra,* at 211. We have applied this test in holding that it is not a search for the police to use a pen register at the phone company to determine what numbers were dialed in a private home, *Smith v. Maryland,* 442 U.S. 735, 743-744 (1979), and we have applied the test on two different occasions in holding that aerial surveillance of private homes and surrounding areas does not constitute a search, *Ciraolo, supra; Florida v. Riley,* 488 U.S. 445 (1989).

The present case involves officers on a public street engaged in more than naked-eye surveillance of a home. We have previously reserved judgment as to how much technological enhancement of ordinary perception from such a vantage point, if any, is too much. While we upheld enhanced aerial photography of an industrial complex in *Dow Chemical,* we noted that we found "it important that this is *not* an area immediately adjacent to a private home, where privacy expectations are most heightened," 476 U.S., at 237, n. 4 (emphasis in original).

2-8 SAMPLE CASE FILE

Figure 2-1 contains the instructions your teacher might provide with the sample case file shown in Figure 2-2. A case file contains the documents pertaining to a case. Each client has a case file. As a case moves forward, the file grows. Sometimes a client's case may require many physical files to organize and preserve all of the documents generated by the legal matter. The sample in Figure 2-2 shows the portion of the file that contains the documents relevant to a research project. Figure 2-2 also includes a memo from the assigning attorney and relevant documents.

You may come back to this research case file in the weeks ahead, when you are ready to create a research strategy and begin the research on this case file. You will notice that the dates are shown as 20XX; this allows your teacher to provide current dates for the case file.

FIGURE 2-1 Case File

CASE FILE

INSTRUCTIONS FOR BAYLOR OFFICE MEMORANDUM

For this assignment, you are to write a memorandum. This time, however, you are also doing the research for the memo. You will conduct your initial research using print resources. Once you find appropriate primary sources, you can download and/or read them online. Although we live in a technological world, attorneys still use print sources for research. Practice in this is essential to developing the skills you will need as an attorney. You must also "validate" any authority you use in your memo. (This means you must either "Shepardize" or Key Cite the authorities—this should be done online.)

Follow these instructions with the documents contained in your file. You have all you need to research, and now write the office memorandum for this project.

The memorandum will contain the following sections, unless your instructor assigns another format:

Statement of Facts
Questions Presented (Issues)
Argument
    Using a thesis paragraph
    Using topic sentences
    Using appropriate point headings
Conclusion

The educational goals of this assignment are:

1. To gain or improve the following skills:
    - Skill in research (federal sources)
    - Skill in validating sources
    - Skill in legal citation
    - Skill in organizing a multi-issue memorandum
    - Skill in synthesizing and explaining clearly a complex series of rules
    - Skill in analogical reasoning (contrasting favorably and distinguishing)
    - Skill in converting predictive writing to persuasive writing
2. To gain additional practice in the following skills, which you used in prior assignments:
    - Skill in identifying legal issues arising in a client's case
    - Skill in combining rules from statutes with rules from cases when writing a rule explanation

FIGURE 2-1 *(continued)*

- Skill in anticipating and responding to opposing arguments
- Skill in outlining the elements of legal rules
- Skill in thinking and writing in the classic IRAC paradigm: issue, rules, application, and conclusion
- Skill in drafting issue statements
- Skill in applying legal rules to the facts of a given case
- Skills in writing thesis paragraphs
- Skills in writing and using topic sentences and thesis statements in the context of a legal office memo

FIGURE 2-2 Memo to Research Associate

Memo to Research Associate

FROM: Assistant U.S. Attorney
TO: Research Associate
DATE: January 23, 20XX

RE: Potential Criminal Complaint (*United States v. Baylor*)

We recently received a file from the F.B.I. involving the commission of a credit card/access card fraud and need you to research some questions and prepare a memo. Very briefly, the case involves a young man who used ATM and credit cards belonging to his deceased mother. Unfortunately, this individual appears to have fled the country and prosecution against him at this time is unlikely. However, the investigation into this matter shows that the young man's girlfriend (Melyssa Baylor) willingly accepted and kept property acquired with the credit card and assisted her boyfriend in evading arrest. We will not file charges for receiving stolen property because we cannot establish that she knew the ring was stolen when she first accepted it. However, I would like to file charges against her for being an accessory after the fact. I am attaching a copy of an application for a search warrant in which the investigating F.B.I. agent details the facts of this case and his justification for searching the Baylor residence. Also attached is a copy of the search warrant and the return of the warrant. The return of the warrant lists the items found during the search of the Baylor residence.

Please review these documents and review the federal statutes dealing with accessory after the fact and credit card fraud. Do some preliminary research regarding our charging Ms. Baylor with being an accessory after the fact. There should be ample case law related to this issue, but it would be a good idea to get an overview of this offense by checking some sources such as Am. Jur. or A.L.R. (The federal jury instructions might also provide some help.) There may be many issues in this case. We will need to prove the elements of this offense as listed in the code. One of those elements requires that we prove that the underlying felony also occurred. At this point, please concentrate on the following questions:

1. Can we meet the requirement of the accessory statute requiring that the accused had knowledge that someone committed a federal offense?
2. Does it matter that we cannot find Baylor's boyfriend to arrest and prosecute him for the underlying felony?
3. Can we support the element of the underlying felony requiring that the property obtained by fraud be valued at $1,000 or more?

I scheduled a tentative meeting time early next week for us to discuss your preliminary findings. Until then, limit your research to the above questions. If you identify any other potential problems make a note of them, but do not spend time researching them. When we meet next week, we will discuss the issues.

FIGURE 2-2 *(continued)*

AO106 (Rev. 7/87) Affidavit for Search Warrant

UNITED STATES DISTRICT COURT

NORTHERN DISTRICT OF CALIFORNIA

In the Matter of the Search of
(Name, address or brief description of person, property or premises to be

The Person of Melyssa Baylor and
The Premises at 786 Hightower Drive, San Jose, California

APPLICATION AND AFFIDAVIT FOR SEARCH WARRANT

Case Number: cr-00897

I, Bryan Jergen being duly sworn depose and say:

I am a(n) Agent of the Federal Bureau of Investigation ___ and have reason to believe
Official Title

that ✓ on the person of or ✓ on the property or premises known as (name, description and/or location)

Melyssa Baylor and 786 Hightower Drive, San Jose, California

in the Northern District of California

there is now concealed a certain person or property, namely (describe the person or property to be seized)

a diamond ring, documentation related to the fraudulent purchase of said ring, documentation showing the location of one Benjamin Creighton

which is (state one or more bases for search and seizure set forth under Rule 41(b) of the Federal Rules of Criminal Procedure)

contraband and evidence of a crime

concerning a violation of Title 18 United States code, Section(s) 1029

The facts to support a finding of Probable Cause are as follows:

Included in the Statement of Probable Cause attached as an addendum hereto and incorporated by reference herein.

Continued on the attached sheet and made a part hereof: ✓ Yes No

[signature]
Signature of Affiant

Sworn to before me and subscribed in my presence,

November 25, 20XX at San Jose, California
Date City and State

CLARA DARROW, MAGISTRATE
Name and Title of Judicial Officer

[signature]
Signature of Judicial Officer

FIGURE 2-2 *(continued)*

Your affiant, Bryan Jergen, has been an agent with the Federal Bureau of Investigation (F.B.I.) for 11 years. For the past five years, I have been assigned to work in the unit investigating white collar crimes. Part of my responsibilities with that unit includes the investigation of credit card fraud. During the past five years, I have been involved in the investigation of over 100 cases involving credit card fraud. In approximately 80% of those cases, I was the lead investigator.

On November 15, 20XX, I was contacted by Martin Jankovich, an investigator employed by Citibank. I have worked with Investigator Jankovich in more than 15 investigations, including credit card fraud and bank robbery. He has always proved to be a reliable and thorough investigator and has always provided this department with reliable information. On November 15, 20XX, Investigator Jankovich informed me of an investigation he had conducted related to a suspected credit card fraud perpetrated by one Benjamin Creighton. He believes that Benjamin Creighton used the ATM card and Citibank Mastercard belonging to Terry Creighton, his mother, two days after her death. His investigation resulted in the following factual findings.

A review of records of Citibank showed that Terry Creighton maintained a checking account with Citibank as well as having a Citibank Mastercard. Terry Creighton was issued an ATM card for use with the checking account. Both the checking account and the credit card were in Terry Creighton's name alone. No one else was authorized to access the account or use the credit card. On July 26, 20XX, the ATM card was used to withdraw the sum of $758 from the checking account, bringing its balance to zero. In addition on the same date, the credit card was used to purchase an item of jewelry at Mario's Jewelers. The item price was $600 plus tax for a total of $648.00. Between August 2, 20XX, and August 5, 20XX, three checks were submitted to Citibank drawn against the checking account owned by Terry Creighton. The checks were signed by Ms. Creighton and dated July 20, 20XX. Although the checking account had no funds at the time the checks were presented for payment, the checks were paid pursuant to the "overdraft protection" covering Ms. Creighton's account. Regular credit card billing statements were sent to Ms. Creighton in August, September, and October of 20XX. No payment was received. Statements showing the balance owed on the overdraft protection were also sent during these months. No payment was received.

Employees of Citibank attempted to personally contact Ms. Creighton regarding the overdue accounts. In the course of such attempts, employees telephoned Ms. Creighton at numbers provided to Citibank by Creighton. These telephone numbers included both a home telephone and a work telephone number. The home telephone number was disconnected. Contact was made with individuals at the work telephone number on or about November 2, 20XX; Citibank was advised that Ms. Creighton had died suddenly on July 24, 20XX. Because of the usage of both the ATM card and credit card after July 24, 20XX, the matter was referred to Martin Jankovich, a bank investigator. Investigator Jankovich provided me with copies of business records from Citibank verifying the above information and I personally verified the contents of these records.

Investigator Jankovich stated that as soon as the matter was referred to him on November 2, 20XX, he again contacted Ms. Creighton's employer and spoke with Ellen Rivera, an employee believed to be a close friend of Terry Creighton. Ms. Rivera stated that Terry Creighton was divorced and lived with her 24-year-old son, Benjamin, in a rented home. Benjamin was the only known relative of Ms. Creighton. Ms. Creighton often complained about her son, who was unemployed and often in minor trouble with the law. Ms. Rivera did not know

FIGURE 2-2 *(continued)*

the specifics of his legal troubles. Ms. Rivera was able to provide Investigator Jankovich with a cellular phone number for Benjamin Creighton. She also told Investigator Jankovich that Ms. Creighton often spoke about a new girlfriend of her son. She had hoped that the girlfriend would "straighten out" her son. Ms. Creighton had mentioned that the young woman and her son had talked about marriage. The girlfriend's name was Melyssa Baylor. Ms. Rivera was also able to provide Investigator Jankovich with a photograph of Benjamin Creighton that Ms. Creighton had kept on her desk.

On or about November 5, 20XX, Investigator Jankovich contacted the owner of Mario's Jewelers regarding the Citibank Mastercard charge. After reviewing his records, Mario Battaglia, the owner of Mario's, recalled the transaction. The transaction involved the purchase of a diamond engagement ring. The purchaser of the ring had been in the store on several prior occasions with a young woman looking at rings. Mr. Battaglia described the purchaser as having physical characteristics similar to that of Benjamin Creighton. At this point, Investigator Jankovich showed Battaglia the photograph of Benjamin Creighton provided by Ellen Rivera and Battaglia positively identified him as the purchaser of the ring. Battaglia also stated that he sold the ring for $600 because he was closing his business. He gave the purchaser a written appraisal stating that the value of the ring was $1,200. Prior to the sale, the ring was offered at $1,050.00.

Investigator Jankovich then managed to locate contact information for Melyssa Baylor. On November 10, 20XX, he had a telephone conversation with her during which he inquired about the whereabouts of Benjamin Creighton. He also asked about the engagement ring. Ms. Baylor stated that Benjamin Creighton had stayed with her from August 15, 20XX, through October 30, 20XX, but that he had left on October 30, 20XX, and she had not heard from him since then. She denied any knowledge concerning the ring. She also denied that she had ever been in a jewelry store with Creighton looking at rings. After this conversation, Investigator Jankovich approached various neighbors of Ms. Baylor. One neighbor, Mildred Delmonico, told Investigator Jankovich that within the last week she had seen Melyssa wearing a diamond engagement ring.

At this point, Investigator Jankovich contacted the F.B.I. and the case was referred to this affiant. I obtained the California driver's license for Benjamin Creighton and compared the picture on the driver's license with the photo obtained from Ellen Rivera. The pictures appeared to be of the same individual. On November 17, 20XX, I contacted Ellen Rivera, Mario Battaglia, and Mildred Delmonico. They all confirmed the facts related to me by Investigator Jankovich. Mario Battaglia provided a further description of the ring. It was a round solitaire of approximately .4 carats, set in white gold.

Also on November 17, 20XX, I contacted Melyssa Baylor. After I identified myself as an agent of the F.B.I., she refused to have any discussion with me. For the past 17 months, Melyssa Baylor has lived at 786 Hightower Dr., San Jose, California.

Based on the foregoing and upon my experience, I believe that the diamond ring purchased by fraudulent use of a credit card is located at the premises at 786 Hightower Dr., San Jose, California. Because of its value, it is not likely that the parties have disposed of the ring. It is my opinion based on my experience that other indicia of the ring is also located on the premises including the appraisal and photographs. It is also my belief, based on my experience, that letters or other documentation indicating the present location of Benjamin Creighton are likely to be found on the premises.

Finding It Online

At times, we need information but we are not sure how to locate it. A library provides several options: the computerized filings of the library collection, the card catalog, and the librarian. The Internet also provides choices. Sometimes you want to perform a search but are not sure which sites lead to good information.

The following list represents some of the major search engines that lead to legal information. These search engines search many websites at one time and then provide you with a great many options. Caution: Practice writing your searches. A poorly written search results in a great deal of unwanted information or no information at all. A search with carefully chosen terms produces finely focused information. Choose your search terms only after you have identified the relevant facts and issues. A list of relevant facts and a statement of your issue will suggest search terms. Practice with creating searches is essential. Many search engines and websites provide help with how to use their site. Always check this information; you may be amazed at what is new since the last time you used the resource. Some search engines also provide opportunities for conducting "advanced searches." These features are often similar to search methods used in the legal databases of Westlaw and Lexis.

Two of the major search engines are:

Google—www.google.com
Yahoo!—www.yahoo.com

CITATION MATTERS

LEGAL DICTIONARIES

***THE BLUEBOOK*—RULE 15.8**

A legal dictionary requires a special citation form.

Conversion, Black's Law Dictionary (10th ed. 2014).

Seizure, Ballentine's Law Dictionary (3rd ed. 1969).

Dictionary Citation Analyzed

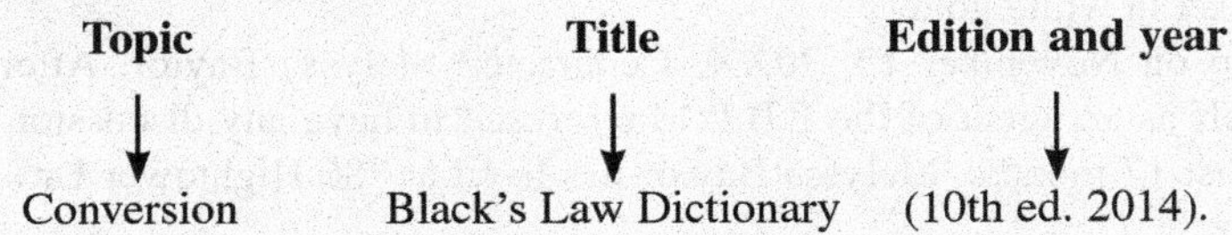

The *topic* is placed first.

The *title* of the dictionary follows the topic.

Place the edition in parentheses at the end of the citation sentence. There is a space between *10th* and the *ed.* There is also a space before the year.

A good legal dictionary is an essential research tool. All students of law need one. If you use a definition from the dictionary, you need to place a citation behind the definition.

Researchers also need a good legal thesaurus. Use these tools together. If you look up your term in both resources, you are much more likely to understand it. Law libraries make legal dictionaries and legal thesauri available. Acquire these resources for your personal use.

CHAPTER **SUMMARY**

The identification of relevant facts is an essential step in both reading the law and researching the law. Understanding the facts is the first step toward analysis of the legal problem. No research should begin until facts identified and understood. Categorize facts as relevant, explanatory, or legally unimportant. Once this categorization takes place, you are ready to determine the legal issues. Factual analysis arises in two frameworks. First, one must analyze the client's facts. The second involves categorizing the facts in a reported case. When you compare your client's facts with the facts in a reported case, look for similarities, unknowns (gaps), and differences. State legal issues as questions. A good issue statement contains a legal question surrounded by the relevant facts.

TERMS TO **REMEMBER**

case law
precedent
legal analysis
questions presented
pleadings
causes of action
affirmative defenses
judicial history
elements
prima facie case

QUESTIONS FOR **REVIEW**

1. Why is the client's factual situation important?
2. State and describe the three basic categories of facts.
3. Explain the process for factual comparison.
4. What is a legal issue?
5. How do you identify the issues in a case in which pleadings have been filed?
6. How do you identify the issues in a case in which no pleadings have been filed?
7. How do you identify the issues in a reported case?
8. What does a good issue statement contain?

CAN YOU **FIGURE IT OUT?**

1. Using the *Kyllo v. United States* case excerpt (located in this chapter), can you find the code section the petitioner was originally indicted under?

TEST **YOURSELF** (Check Your Answers in Appendix G)

Read Problem 9 in Appendix B—(*Speeker v. Oliver Wendell High School*) and the case of *Morse v. Frederick* in Appendix F.

(a) Create a chart of the relevant, explanatory, and legally unimportant facts for the *Speeker* fact pattern.
(b) What is the legal issue in the *Speeker* case?
(c) What was the legal issue in the *Morse v. Frederick* case?
Relevant Facts
Explanatory Facts
Legally Insignificant Facts

TEST **YOURSELF**—WRITE IT RIGHT Working Words and Glue Words

Not all words in a sentence carry the same weight. Some words are "working words" or words that convey important information. Other words are "glue words" or words that simply hold the sentence together, often making it grammatically correct. Writers want to use as few glue words as possible because they are of little value to the reader. One way to look at this is that writers want a large proportion of working words in all sentences.

In the following example, the working words are underlined:

The prosecutor cross-examined all witnesses.

Six words are used and five of them are working words. This proportion of working words to glue words works well. When we read just the working words, we easily understand the meaning of the sentence: "prosecutor cross-examined all witnesses."

Consider this poorly drafted sentence:

All witnesses were cross-examined by the prosecutor.

Eight words and again five of them are working words.

This proportion of working words to glue words does not work as well as the first example. In addition, when we read the working words in the original order, the meaning of the sentence is not clear: "all witnesses cross-examined prosecutor."

Now, You Try It

(Check your answers in Appendix G)

For each of the following sentences, (1) underline the working words and (2) rewrite the sentence to lower the proportion of glue words to working words. The words in the sentences may need to be placed in a more logical order.

1. The plan for the attack was created by Tomas.
2. The juvenile defendant was examined by the Judge.
3. There were three misstatements of fact in the lawyer's opening argument.
4. It has been three months since the office served the Request for Production of Documents.

CITATION **EXERCISES**

Using Appendix C and the inside front and back cover of this text, answer the following questions.

1. Using "State Case Law" in Appendix C, write the correct abbreviation for the following regional reporters—be careful to get the spacing right.
   a. South Western Reporter
   b. Atlantic Reporter
   c. Southern Reporter
2. Case names are ____________________________ or ______________________, but never both.
3. Most legal sources follow the general format of: [check the second point to remember in Appendix C]
4. What does the number 384 represent in this citation? *Miranda v. Arizona*, 384 U.S. 436 (1996).

FROM **THE WRITER'S CORNER**— An Issue Includes the Legal Question and the Key Facts

1. Issues have two elements—name them.
2. Explain what is missing from the following issue: "The question is whether the defendant was negligent."

ASSIGNMENTS AND **EXERCISES**

Analysis and Writing Exercises

1. Create a chart of relevant, explanatory, and legally unimportant facts for the *Kyllo v. United States* case.
2. State the issue in the *Kyllo v. United States* case. Remember to include the legal question and the key facts.
3. Read the documents in the Meyers case file found in Appendix A. Summarize the relevant and explanatory facts regarding the legality of the search and seizure of the bloody rag.
4. Consider the following hypothetical case: Ms. Grace Sanchez, your client, was recently dismissed from her position as Day Manager of Helman's, a large local department store. Ms. Sanchez is 64 years old. She was with the company for over 30 years. She began her career at Helman's as a clerk in the jewelry department. Ms. Sanchez believes Helman's dismissed her because she is approaching retirement age and they do not want to pay her a pension. Also, read the case of *Cancellier v. Federated Department Stores,* 672 F.2d 1312 (9th Cir. 1981), found in Appendix F.
   a. Create a chart of the relevant, explanatory, and legally unimportant facts for the Sanchez fact pattern.
   b. What is the legal issue in the Sanchez case?
   c. What was the legal issue in the *Cancellier* case?

Online Research Exercises

5. Review the facts and issues in the case of *Rimma v. Emerson* found earlier in the chapter. Using the search features on both Google and Yahoo, look for information about applicable law. From your search results, select two websites and summarize the information you find. For each website, identify who prepared the site and the date of the latest revision of the site.
6. Repeat the assignment in Question 1 for the Sanchez case.
7. Repeat the assignment in Question 1 for the Meyers case (the search and seizure issue).

CASE **PROJECT**

IN-CLASS SMALL GROUP WORK

Review the hypothetical case you selected in Chapter 1. Try to identify the relevant facts, explanatory facts, and legally unimportant facts. Also, try to identify the legal issues. Remember that this may change after you have researched the case.

chapter **three**

FINDING AND ANALYZING CASE LAW

CHAPTER OUTLINE

SKILL OBJECTIVES FOR CHAPTER 3

When you complete chapter 3, you should be able to

- List where case law may be located.
- Explain the purpose of case law.
- Explain the elements of a case law citation.
- List the print publications containing U.S. Supreme Court case law.
- Explain the differences between the official publication of U.S. Supreme Court case law and the unofficial publications of the same material.
- List other federal reporters.
- Explain the purpose of a regional reporter.
- List and define the components of a case.
- Compare and contrast the facts of a reported case with a client's factual situation.

From the Desk of W. J. Bryan, Esq.

To: Research Assistant
FROM: W. J. Bryan
RE: Our Client Justin Meyers
DATE:

The office needs to begin case law research in the Meyers case. Look for California and U.S. Supreme Court case law to support our client's position regarding the admissibility of the bloody handkerchief. Review the file before you begin. (The case file is found in Appendix A, Problem 1.) Please check with me if you need clarification. Create a list of the cases you locate and include a brief summary of each case on your list.

3-1 WHAT IS A CASE?

A case is a decision, sometimes called an opinion, written by a judge (the court). Judges write opinions designed to inform and instruct those who read the decisions. The parties to most litigation are interested in the outcome of the case. But they may not be interested in the court's legal reasoning, although on appeal that may be important.

In the course of legal research, we read case law to attempt to understand the factual and legal issues and a court's resolution of those issues. Judges rely on previous decisions, the Constitution, statutory law, and administrative regulations in rendering decisions and writing opinions. Judges are acutely aware that legal researchers read reported case law looking for opinions that may apply to their client's situation. That is why judges are so careful to provide detailed facts and lengthy analysis of the factual and legal issues. It is not enough for a court to state, "Plaintiff, you win; defendant, you lose."

The importance of case law is apparent when we recall that the U.S. legal system relies on precedent. The court must look to past decisions to aid it in making current decisions. Therefore, researchers must do the same to locate case law similar to the factual and legal situation being researched.

When you read a case decision, keep in mind that the decision usually comes from a panel of judges. At the appellate level, three justices hear and decide a case; at the Supreme Court level, nine justices hear and decide a case. In many instances, the decision of the court is not unanimous. One or more justices may disagree entirely with the decision. In such a case, that justice may write a dissenting opinion in which the justice explains his or her position. Sometimes one or more justices may agree with the ultimate result of the case but not with the reasoning of the majority. That justice may write a concurring opinion, an opinion in which the justice explains his or her reasoning. Although concurring and dissenting opinions are published with the majority opinion, they do not result in case law. Case law is found only in the majority opinion.

3-2 CASE CITATIONS

The name of the case is either italicized or underlined and placed at the beginning of any case law citation, which is arranged in the following format. The volume number is first, the abbreviation for the name of the reporter is next, and the page on which the case begins follows the reporter abbreviation. The year of the

FIGURE 3-1
Sample Case Citation

Marvin v. Marvin (1976) 18 Cal. 3d 660, 557 P. 2d.106, 134 Cal. Rptr. 815 or *Marvin v. Marvin,* 18 Cal. 3d 660, 557 P. 2d.106, 134 Cal. Rptr. 815 (1976)

decision is best placed at the very end of the citation, but some states prefer the year just after the name of the case (see Figure 3-1). If your state publishes a citation guide, confer with a supervisor about proper format for your office.

The year is always placed in parentheses. The *Uniform System of Citation* (*The Bluebook*) provides a comprehensive guide to proper citation format. Check your state citation rules for the proper placement of the year. Appendix C provides a Basic Citation Reference Guide.

A Point to Remember

When looking in a case reporter, check the very top of the first full page of the case for the proper case citation. This is the proper abbreviation of the case name. (See Figure 3-2.) *Illinois v. Gates,* 462 U. S. 213 (1983) is the accepted citation for this case. Usually, it is shorter than the full names of all of the parties. Compare the full names of the parties in the *Texas v. Johnson* case with the short version at the top of the page (Figures 3-3–3-5).

official citation
This is the citation to the official publication of case law for a particular jurisdiction (this is usually a government publication); the official citation includes the name of the case, volume number in which the case is located, the first page of the case, and the year of the decision.

secondary sources
Tools used to understand the law; one such tool is a legal encyclopedia, which explains the law.

style manual
A manual illustrating the proper citation format for a particular state.

primary authority
The resources that provide the actual law; laws are found in constitutions, statutes, case law, and some administrative materials.

decision
The formal written resolution of a case; it explains the legal and factual issues, the resolution of the case, and the law used by the court in reaching its resolution.

opinion
A decision is sometimes referred to as an opinion.

Sometimes, a case is reported in several publications. It is the same case, just different publishers. The ***official citation*** is always listed first; this is followed by the parallel (unofficial) citations. For example, the *United States Reports,* abbreviated as U.S., is the official reporter of all U.S. Supreme Court case law. There are, however, other publishers of all U.S. Supreme Court case law. Section 3-5 discusses this.

A Point to Remember

Sometimes in ***secondary sources*** the citations are incomplete. For example, the year may be omitted or the reporter abbreviation may differ from that suggested in the *Uniform System of Citation* or your state ***style manual***. Once the case is retrieved, you are able to complete and, if necessary, correct the citation.

3-3 OVERVIEW OF CASE LAW AND THE CONCEPT OF *STARE DECISIS*

Case law is ***primary authority***. Judges write cases. Once a case is presented to the court and the legal and factual issues are resolved, the judge writes a ***decision***, sometimes called an ***opinion***. This written decision is case law. At the state and federal levels, decisions are reported for many appellate and all supreme court cases. At the federal level, even some of the trial court cases are reported. Once you become familiar with case citations, you will know the level of the court deciding the case with just a glance at the reporter abbreviation in the case citation. Case law is based on the concept of ***stare decisis***, which means, "it stands decided." Case law is ***precedent***. This concept, which is the basis of English common law, means that once a court has decided a particular factual dispute, other courts should follow the same ruling when presented with the same facts. This provides stability and uniformity to the legal system. Case law in the United States follows this idea, with some qualifications:

stare decisis
"It stands decided"; another term for precedent.

precedent
The example set by the decision of an earlier court for similar case or similar legal questions that arise in later cases.

- First, *stare decisis* applies only to published case decisions that come from appellate or supreme courts. Decisions from trial courts, even when published, do not create case law that other courts must follow.
- Second, generally, *stare decisis* applies only to cases within the same jurisdiction. For example, if the California Supreme Court decides a case, that decision is not binding, in the other 49 states. Of course, if, in deciding a case, the U.S. Supreme Court interprets a federal law or the U.S. Constitution, that interpretation is binding in all states.

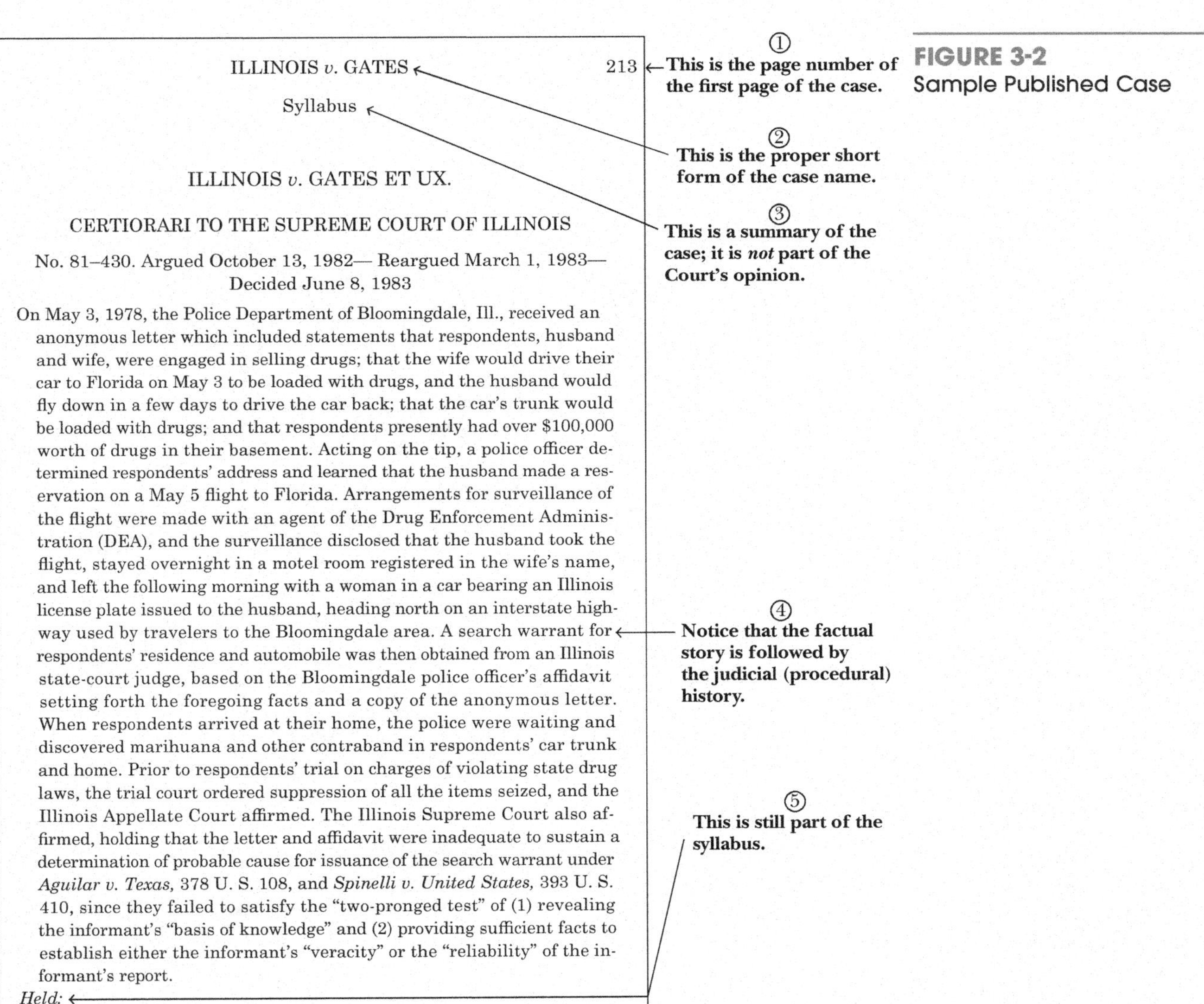
ILLINOIS *v.* GATES 213

Syllabus

ILLINOIS *v.* GATES ET UX.

CERTIORARI TO THE SUPREME COURT OF ILLINOIS

No. 81–430. Argued October 13, 1982— Reargued March 1, 1983— Decided June 8, 1983

On May 3, 1978, the Police Department of Bloomingdale, Ill., received an anonymous letter which included statements that respondents, husband and wife, were engaged in selling drugs; that the wife would drive their car to Florida on May 3 to be loaded with drugs, and the husband would fly down in a few days to drive the car back; that the car's trunk would be loaded with drugs; and that respondents presently had over $100,000 worth of drugs in their basement. Acting on the tip, a police officer determined respondents' address and learned that the husband made a reservation on a May 5 flight to Florida. Arrangements for surveillance of the flight were made with an agent of the Drug Enforcement Administration (DEA), and the surveillance disclosed that the husband took the flight, stayed overnight in a motel room registered in the wife's name, and left the following morning with a woman in a car bearing an Illinois license plate issued to the husband, heading north on an interstate highway used by travelers to the Bloomingdale area. A search warrant for respondents' residence and automobile was then obtained from an Illinois state-court judge, based on the Bloomingdale police officer's affidavit setting forth the foregoing facts and a copy of the anonymous letter. When respondents arrived at their home, the police were waiting and discovered marihuana and other contraband in respondents' car trunk and home. Prior to respondents' trial on charges of violating state drug laws, the trial court ordered suppression of all the items seized, and the Illinois Appellate Court affirmed. The Illinois Supreme Court also affirmed, holding that the letter and affidavit were inadequate to sustain a determination of probable cause for issuance of the search warrant under *Aguilar v. Texas,* 378 U. S. 108, and *Spinelli v. United States,* 393 U. S. 410, since they failed to satisfy the "two-pronged test" of (1) revealing the informant's "basis of knowledge" and (2) providing sufficient facts to establish either the informant's "veracity" or the "reliability" of the informant's report.

Held:

1. The question—which this Court requested the parties to address—whether the rule requiring the exclusion at a criminal trial of evidence obtained in violation of the Fourth Amendment should be modified so as, for example, not to require exclusion of evidence obtained in the reason-

FIGURE 3-2
Sample Published Case

FIGURE 3-2 (continued)

① **This is the volume number of the *United States Reports*.**

② **Pages 217–224 of this case present the material covered in the first section of the Syllabus.**

214 OCTOBER TERM, 1982

Syllabus 462 United States

able belief that the search and seizure at issue was consistent with the Fourth Amendment will not be decided in this case, since it was not presented to or decided by the Illinois courts. Although prior decisions interpreting the "not pressed or passed on below" rule have not involved a State's failure to raise a defense to a federal right or remedy asserted below, the purposes underlying the rule are, for the most part, as applicable in such a case as in one where a party fails to assert a federal right. The fact that the Illinois courts affirmatively applied the federal exclusionary rule does not affect the application of the "not pressed or passed on below" rule. Nor does the State's repeated opposition to respondents' substantive Fourth Amendment claims suffice to have raised the separate question whether the exclusionary rule should be modified. The extent of the continued vitality of the rule is an issue of unusual significance, and adhering scrupulously to the customary limitations on this Court's discretion promotes respect for its adjudicatory process and the stability of its decisions, and lessens the threat of untoward practical ramifications not foreseen at the time of decision Pp. 217–224.

2. The rigid "two-pronged test" under *Aguilar* and *Spinelli* for determining whether an informant's tip establishes probable cause for issuance of a warrant is abandoned, and the "totality of the circumstances" approach that traditionally has informed probable-cause determinations is substituted in its place. The elements under the "two-pronged test" concerning the informant's "veracity," "reliability," and "basis of knowledge" should be understood simply as closely intertwined issues that may usefully illuminate the common-sense, practical question whether there is "probable cause" to believe that contraband or evidence is located in a particular place. The task of the issuing magistrate is simply to make a practical, common-sense decision whether, given all the circumstances set forth in the affidavit before him, there is a fair probability that contraband or evidence of a crime will be found in a particular place. And the duty of a reviewing court is simply to ensure that the magistrate had a substantial basis for concluding that probable cause existed. This flexible, easily applied standard will better achieve the accommodation of public and private interests that the Fourth Amendment requires than does the approach that has developed from *Aguilar* and *Spinelli*, Pp. 230–241.

3. The judge issuing the warrant had a substantial basis for concluding that probable cause to search respondents' home and car existed. Under the "totality of the circumstances" analysis, corroboration of details of an informant's tip by independent police work is of significant value. Cf. *Draper v. United States*, 358 U. S. 307. Here, even standing alone, the facts obtained through the independent investigation of the Bloomingdale police officer and the DEA at least suggested that

mandatory authority
Case law that must be followed by a court.

binding authority
Another term for mandatory authority.

persuasive authority
Nonbinding case law that nevertheless is considered by a court.

- Third, *stare decisis* requires that courts follow case decisions of higher courts. For example, if a court of appeals decides a particular dispute, all of the trial courts within that jurisdiction must follow the decision. Other appellate courts in that jurisdiction do not have to follow the decision.

When a case is truly *stare decisis*, lower courts in the same jurisdiction must follow the decision. The case is ***mandatory authority***, sometimes called ***binding authority***. However, this does not mean that a court cannot consider published cases from other courts. In fact, many courts consider nonbinding case law when deciding an issue. ***Persuasive authority*** is nonbinding authority.

FIGURE 3-3
Texas *v.* Johnson, from U.S. Reports

TEXAS *v.* JOHNSON 397

Syllabus

TEXAS *v.* JOHNSON

CERTIORARI TO THE COURT OF CRIMINAL APPEALS OF TEXAS

No. 88–155. Argued March 21, 1989—Decided June 21, 1989

During the 1984 Republican National Convention in Dallas, Texas, respondent Johnson participated in a political demonstration to protest the policies of the Reagan administration and some Dallas-based corporations. After a march through the city streets, Johnson burned an American flag while protesters chanted. No one was physically injured or threatened with injury, although several witnesses were seriously offended by the flag burning. Johnson was convicted of desecration of a venerated object in violation of a Texas statute, and a State Court of Appeals affirmed. However, the Texas Court of Criminal Appeals reversed, holding that the State, consistent with the First Amendment, could not punish Johnson for burning the flag in these circumstances. The court first found that Johnson's burning of the flag was expressive conduct protected by the First Amendment. The court concluded that the State could not criminally sanction flag desecration in order to preserve the flag as a symbol of national unity. It also held that the statute did not meet the State's goal of preventing breaches of the peace, since it was not drawn narrowly enough to encompass only those flag burnings that would likely result in a serious disturbance, and since the flag burning in this case did not threaten such a reaction. Further, it stressed that another Texas statute prohibited breaches of the peace and could be used to prevent disturbances without punishing this flag desecration.

Held: Johnson's conviction for flag desecration is inconsistent with the First Amendment. Pp. 402–420.

(a) Under the circumstances, Johnson's burning of the flag constituted expressive conduct, permitting him to invoke the First Amendment. The State conceded that the conduct was expressive. Occurring as it did at the end of a demonstration coinciding with the Republican National Convention, the expressive, overtly political nature of the conduct was both intentional and overwhelmingly apparent. Pp. 402–406.

(b) Texas has not asserted an interest in support of Johnson's conviction that is unrelated to the suppression of expression and would therefore permit application of the test set forth in *United States v. O'Brien*, 391 U. S. 367, whereby an important governmental interest in regulating nonspeech can justify incidental limitations on First Amendment freedoms when speech and nonspeech elements are combined in the same course of conduct. An interest in preventing breaches of the peace is not implicated on this record. Expression may not be prohib-

FIGURE 3-3 (continued)

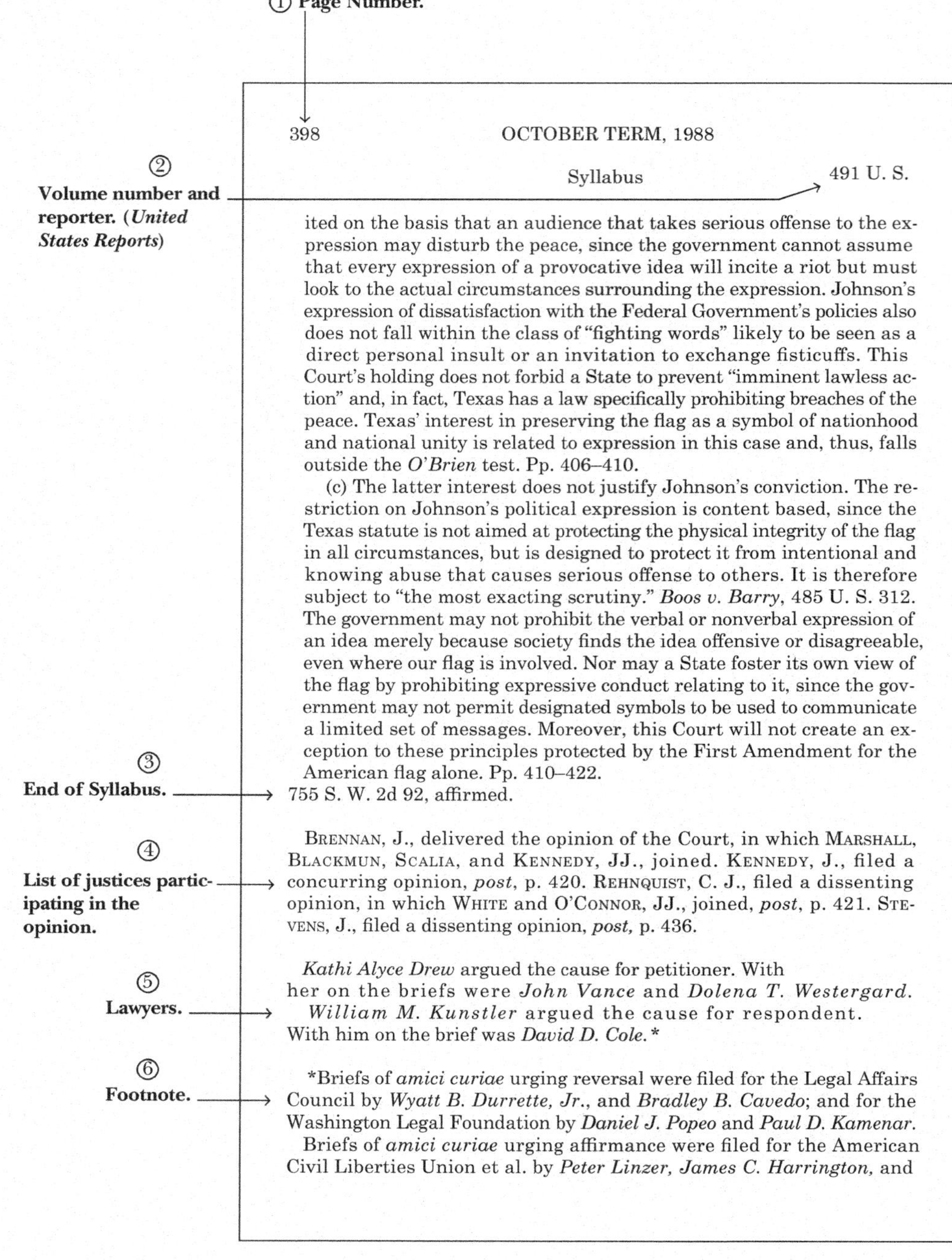

398 OCTOBER TERM, 1988

Syllabus 491 U. S.

ited on the basis that an audience that takes serious offense to the expression may disturb the peace, since the government cannot assume that every expression of a provocative idea will incite a riot but must look to the actual circumstances surrounding the expression. Johnson's expression of dissatisfaction with the Federal Government's policies also does not fall within the class of "fighting words" likely to be seen as a direct personal insult or an invitation to exchange fisticuffs. This Court's holding does not forbid a State to prevent "imminent lawless action" and, in fact, Texas has a law specifically prohibiting breaches of the peace. Texas' interest in preserving the flag as a symbol of nationhood and national unity is related to expression in this case and, thus, falls outside the *O'Brien* test. Pp. 406–410.

(c) The latter interest does not justify Johnson's conviction. The restriction on Johnson's political expression is content based, since the Texas statute is not aimed at protecting the physical integrity of the flag in all circumstances, but is designed to protect it from intentional and knowing abuse that causes serious offense to others. It is therefore subject to "the most exacting scrutiny." *Boos v. Barry*, 485 U. S. 312. The government may not prohibit the verbal or nonverbal expression of an idea merely because society finds the idea offensive or disagreeable, even where our flag is involved. Nor may a State foster its own view of the flag by prohibiting expressive conduct relating to it, since the government may not permit designated symbols to be used to communicate a limited set of messages. Moreover, this Court will not create an exception to these principles protected by the First Amendment for the American flag alone. Pp. 410–422.

755 S. W. 2d 92, affirmed.

BRENNAN, J., delivered the opinion of the Court, in which MARSHALL, BLACKMUN, SCALIA, and KENNEDY, JJ., joined. KENNEDY, J., filed a concurring opinion, *post*, p. 420. REHNQUIST, C. J., filed a dissenting opinion, in which WHITE and O'CONNOR, JJ., joined, *post*, p. 421. STEVENS, J., filed a dissenting opinion, *post*, p. 436.

Kathi Alyce Drew argued the cause for petitioner. With her on the briefs were *John Vance* and *Dolena T. Westergard*. *William M. Kunstler* argued the cause for respondent. With him on the brief was *David D. Cole*.*

*Briefs of *amici curiae* urging reversal were filed for the Legal Affairs Council by *Wyatt B. Durrette, Jr.*, and *Bradley B. Cavedo*; and for the Washington Legal Foundation by *Daniel J. Popeo* and *Paul D. Kamenar*.

Briefs of *amici curiae* urging affirmance were filed for the American Civil Liberties Union et al. by *Peter Linzer, James C. Harrington,* and

FIGURE 3-3 (continued)

TEXAS *v.* JOHNSON 399

397 Opinion of the Court

JUSTICE BRENNAN delivered the opinion of the Court.

After publicly burning an American flag as a means of political protest, Gregory Lee Johnson was convicted of desecrating a flag in violation of Texas law. This case presents the question whether his conviction is consistent with the First Amendment. We hold that it is not.

I

While the Republican National Convention was taking place in Dallas in 1984, respondent Johnson participated in a political demonstration dubbed the "Republican War Chest Tour." As explained in literature distributed by the demonstrators and in speeches made by them, the purpose of this event was to protest the policies of the Reagan administration and of certain Dallas-based corporations. The demonstrators marched through the Dallas streets, chanting political slogans and stopping at several corporate locations to stage "die-ins" intended to dramatize the consequences of nuclear war. On several occasions they spray-painted the walls of buildings and overturned potted plants, but Johnson himself took no part in such activities. He did, however, accept an American flag handed to him by a fellow protestor who had taken it from a flagpole outside one of the targeted buildings.

The demonstration ended in front of Dallas City Hall, where Johnson unfurled the American flag, doused it with kerosene, and set it on fire. While the flag burned, the protestors chanted: "America, the red, white, and blue, we spit on you." After the demonstrators dispersed, a witness to the flag burning collected the flag's remains and buried them in his backyard. No one was physically injured or threatened with injury, though several witnesses testified that they had been seriously offended by the flag burning.

Steven R. Shapiro; for the Christic Institute et al. by *James C. Goodale;* and for Jasper Johns et al. by *Robert G. Sugarman* and *Gloria C. Phares.*

① **Page number.**

② **The opinion begins here. All material before this is prefatory and *not* written by one of the justices.**

③ **Always pay attention to how the Court organizes the opinion.**

FIGURE 3-4
Texas *v.* Johnson, from Supreme Court Reporter

② This is the unofficial reporter citation for the *Supreme Court Reporter.*

③ Page number in the *Supreme Court Reporter.*

① This is the official citation for this case.

④ Case name.

⑤ In the West reporters, a key symbol is used to mark the end of one case and the beginning of the next case.

⑥ References to the *Lawyers' Edition* citation for this case, an unofficial reporter citation.

⑦ The beginning of the West editor's summary, an editorial enhancement.

491 U.S. 397 **TEXAS v. JOHNSON** **2533**
Cite as 109 S.Ct. 2533 (1989)

trial court originally sentenced the defendant only to the term of imprisonment. When the court realized its mistake five hours later, it recalled the defendant for resentencing and imposed the $100 fine as well. We held that the resentencing did not violate the defendant's rights under the Double Jeopardy Clause. There, as in *DiFrancesco*, the defendant could not argue that his *legitimate* expectation of finality in the original sentence had been violated, because he was charged with knowledge that the court lacked statutory authority to impose the subminimum sentence in the first instance. See 330 U.S., at 166, 167, 67 S.Ct., at 648, 649. See also *United States v. Arrellano–Rios*, 799 F.2d 520, 524 (CA9 1986) (stating that defendant can have no legitimate expectation of finality in an illegal sentence); *United States v. Edmondson*, 792 F.2d 1492, 1496, n. 4 (CA9 1986) (same).

Applying *DiFrancesco* and *Bozza* here, it seems to me respondent must prevail. There is no doubt that the court had *authority* to impose the 15–year sentence, and respondent therefore had a legitimate expectation of its finality. There are only two grounds on which that could possibly be contested: (1) that the court had authority to impose a 15–year sentence, but not *both* a 15–year sentence and life, or (2) that his legitimate expectation was not necessarily 15 years, but rather *either* 15 years (on the one sentence) *or* life (on the other sentence). But at least where, as here, the one sentence has been fully served, these alternative approaches to defining his legitimate expectation are ruled out by *Bradley*. There also it could have been said that the court had no authority to impose both the $500 fine and the six months' imprisonment; and there also it could have been said that the defendant's legitimate expectation was not necessarily a $500 fine, but either a $500 fine or six months' imprisonment. But we in effect rejected those approaches, holding that once the fine had been paid a subsequent proceeding could not replace[396] it with the alternative penalty. There is simply no basis for departing from that holding here.

The Double Jeopardy Clause is and has always been, not a provision designed to assure reason and justice in the particular case, but the embodiment of technical, prophylactic rules that require the Government to turn square corners. Whenever it is applied to release a criminal deserving of punishment it frustrates justice in the particular case, but for the greater purpose of assuring repose in the totality of criminal prosecutions and sentences. There are many ways in which these technical rules might be designed. We chose one approach in *Bradley*—undoubtedly not the only possible approach, but also not one that can be said to be clearly wrong. (The fact that it produces a "windfall" separates it not at all from other applications of the double jeopardy guarantee.) With technical rules, above all others, it is imperative that we adhere strictly to what we have stated the rules to be. A technical rule with equitable exceptions is no rule at all. Three strikes is out. The State broke the rules here, and must abide by the result.

For these reasons, I believe the Court of Appeals was correct to set aside respondent's life sentence. I would therefore affirm the judgment of the Court of Appeals, and respectfully dissent from the Court's disposition of this case.*

* I agree with the Court, *ante*, at 2527, n. 3, that the Court of Appeals erred in saying that the State could not resentence or retry respondent for a non-jeopardy-barred lesser included of-

491 U.S. 397, 105 L.Ed.2d 342

[397]**TEXAS, Petitioner**
v.
Gregory Lee JOHNSON.
No. 88–155.

Argued March 21, 1989.
Decided June 21, 1989.

Defendant was convicted in the County Criminal Court No. 8, Dallas County, John

FIGURE 3-4 (continued)

① **Reference to the volume and name of the reporter.**

② **End of editor's summary.**

③ **This is West digest topic and corresponding key numbers. These are editorial enhancements. These digest topics and key numbers are called *headnotes*.**

2534 **109 SUPREME COURT REPORTER** 491 U.S. 397

C. Hendrik, J., of desecration of venerated object, and he appealed. The Dallas Court of Appeals, Fifth Supreme Judicial District, 706 S.W.2d 120, Vance, J., affirmed, and defendant petitioned for discretionary review. The Texas Court of Criminal Appeals, 755 S.W.2d 92, Campbell, J., reversed and remanded, and certiorari was granted. The Supreme Court, Justice Brennan, held that: (1) defendant's act of burning American flag during protest rally was expressive conduct within protection of First Amendment, and (2) State could not justify prosecution of defendant based on interest in preventing breaches of peace or to preserve flag as symbol of nationhood and national unity.

Affirmed.

Justice Kennedy concurred and filed an opinion.

Chief Justice Rehnquist dissented and filed an opinion in which Justice White and Justice O'Connor joined.

Justice Stevens dissented and filed an opinion.

1. Constitutional Law ⚷90(1), 274.1(1)

Conduct may be sufficiently imbued with elements of communication to fall within scope of First and Fourteenth Amendments. U.S.C.A. Const.Amends. 1, 14.

2. Constitutional Law ⚷90.1(1)

In deciding whether particular conduct possesses sufficient communicative elements to bring First Amendment into play, it is necessary to determine whether there was an intent to convey a particularized message and whether likelihood was great that message would be understood by those who viewed it. U.S.C.A. Const. Amend. 1.

3. Constitutional Law ⚷90.1(1)

Any action taken with respect to American flag is not automatically expressive; rather, in characterizing such action for First Amendment purposes, Supreme Court considers context in which conduct occurred. U.S.C.A. Const.Amend. 1.

4. Constitutional Law ⚷90.1(2)

In prosecution for desecration of venerated object, defendant's burning of American flag as part of political demonstration that coincided with convening of political party and renomination of incumbent for President was expressive conduct subject to First Amendment protection. U.S.C.A. Const.Amend. 1; V.T.C.A., Penal Code § 42.09(a)(3).

5. Constitutional Law ⚷90(3)

Government generally has freer hand in restricting expressive conduct than it has in restricting written or spoken word, but it may not proscribe particular conduct because it has expressive elements; law directed at communicative nature of conduct must, like law directed at speech itself, be justified by substantial showing of need that First Amendment requires. U.S.C.A. Const.Amend. 1.

6. Constitutional Law ⚷90(1)

Principal function of free speech under our system of government is to invite dispute; it may indeed best serve its high purpose when it induces condition of unrest, creates dissatisfaction with conditions as they are, or even stirs people to anger. U.S.C.A. Const.Amend. 1.

7. Constitutional Law ⚷90.1(2)
United States ⚷5½

State's interest in preventing breaches of peace did not justify defendant's conviction for violation of Texas flag desecration

fense, see *Morris v. Mathews,* 475 U.S. 237, 106 S.Ct. 1032, 89 L.Ed.2d 187 (1986). Since it is undisputed, however, that the State has made no attempt to do that, that portion of the Court of Appeals' opinion was the purest dictum, and no basis for reversal of its judgment.

FIGURE 3-4 (continued)

491 U.S. 397 **TEXAS v. JOHNSON** **2535**
Cite as 109 S.Ct. 2533 (1989)

statute when he burned American flag as part of protest; no actual breach of peace occurred at time of flag burning or in response to flag burning, and mere potential for breach of peace could not serve to justify prosecution. U.S.C.A. Const. Amend. 1; V.T.C.A., Penal Code § 42.09(a)(3).

8. Constitutional Law ⇐90.1(2)

In prosecution for violation of Texas flag desecration statute based on defendant's burning of American flag during protest rally, state's asserted interest in preserving special symbolic character of American flag would be subject to the most exacting scrutiny since defendant's political expression was restricted by prosecution because of content and message he conveyed. U.S.C.A. Const.Amend. 1; V.T.C.A., Penal Code, § 42.09(a)(3).

9. Constitutional Law ⇐90(1)

If there is a bedrock principle underlying the First Amendment, it is that government may not prohibit expression of an idea simply because society finds idea itself offensive or disagreeable. U.S.C.A. Const. Amend. 1.

10. Constitutional Law ⇐90.1(2)

State of Texas could not justify criminal prosecution under flag desecration statute of defendant who burned American flag at protest rally based on interest in preserving flag as symbol of nationhood and national unity. U.S.C.A. Const.Amend. 1; V.T.C.A., Penal Code § 42.09(a)(3).

The Syllabus, provided by the *United States Reports*, follows the headnotes.

Syllabus *

During the 1984 Republican National Convention in Dallas, Texas, respondent Johnson participated in a political demonstration to protest the policies of the Reagan administration and some Dallas-based corporations. After a march through the city streets, Johnson burned an American flag while protesters chanted. No one was physically injured or threatened with injury, although several witnesses were seriously offended by the flag burning. Johnson was convicted of desecration of a venerated object in violation of a Texas statute, and a State Court of Appeals affirmed. However, the Texas Court of Criminal Appeals reversed, holding that the State, consistent with the First Amendment, could not punish Johnson for burning the flag in these circumstances. The court first found that Johnson's burning of the flag was expressive conduct protected by the First Amendment. The court concluded that the State could not criminally sanction flag desecration in order to preserve the flag as a symbol of national unity. It also held that the statute did not meet the State's goal of preventing breaches of the peace, since it was not drawn narrowly enough to encompass only those flag burnings that would likely result in a serious disturbance, and since the flag burning in this case did not threaten such a reaction. Further, it stressed that another Texas statute prohibited breaches of the peace and could be used to prevent disturbances without punishing this flag desecration.

Held: Johnson's conviction for flag desecration is inconsistent with the First Amendment. Pp. 2538–2548.

(a) Under the circumstances, Johnson's burning of the flag constituted expressive conduct, permitting him to invoke the First Amendment. The State conceded that the conduct was expressive. Occurring as it did at the end of a demonstration coinciding with the Republican National Convention, the expressive, overtly political nature of the conduct was both intentional and overwhelmingly apparent. Pp. 2538–2540.

* The syllabus constitutes no part of the opinion of the Court but has been prepared by the Reporter of Decisions for the convenience of the reader. See *United States v. Detroit Lumber Co.*, 200 U.S. 321, 337, 26 S.Ct. 282, 287, 50 L.Ed. 499.

FIGURE 3-4 (continued)

2536 109 SUPREME COURT REPORTER 491 U.S. 397

(b) Texas has not asserted an interest in support of Johnson's conviction that is unrelated to the suppression of expression and would therefore permit application of the test set forth in *United States v. O'Brien*, 391 U.S. 367, 88 S.Ct. 1673, 20 L.Ed.2d 672, whereby an important governmental interest in regulating nonspeech can justify incidental limitations on First Amendment freedoms when speech and nonspeech elements are combined in the same course of conduct. An interest in preventing breaches of the peace is not implicated on this record. Expression may not be prohibited398 on the basis that an audience that takes serious offense to the expression may disturb the peace, since the government cannot assume that every expression of a provocative idea will incite a riot but must look to the actual circumstances surrounding the expression. Johnson's expression of dissatisfaction with the Federal Government's policies also does not fall within the class of "fighting words" likely to be seen as a direct personal insult or an invitation to exchange fisticuffs. This Court's holding does not forbid a State to prevent "imminent lawless action" and, in fact, Texas has a law specifically prohibiting breaches of the peace. Texas' interest in preserving the flag as a symbol of nationhood and national unity is related to expression in this case and, thus, falls outside the *O'Brien* test. Pp. 2540–2542.

(c) The latter interest does not justify Johnson's conviction. The restriction on Johnson's political expression is content based, since the Texas statute is not aimed at protecting the physical integrity of the flag in all circumstances, but is designed to protect it from intentional and knowing abuse that causes serious offense to others. It is therefore subject to "the most exacting scrutiny." *Boos v. Barry*, 485 U.S. 312, 108 S.Ct. 1157, 99 L.Ed.2d 333. The government may not prohibit the verbal or nonverbal expression of an idea merely because society finds the idea offensive or disagreeable, even where our flag is involved. Nor may a State foster its own view of the flag by prohibiting expressive conduct relating to it, since the government may not permit designated symbols to be used to communicate a limited set of messages. Moreover, this Court will not create an exception to these principles protected by the First Amendment for the American flag alone. Pp. 2542–2548.

755 S.W.2d 92, (Tex.Cr.App.1988), affirmed.

BRENNAN, J., delivered the opinion of the Court, in which MARSHALL, BLACKMUN, SCALIA, and KENNEDY, JJ., joined. KENNEDY, J., filed a concurring opinion, *post*, p. 2548. REHNQUIST, C.J., filed a dissenting opinion, in which WHITE and O'CONNOR, JJ., joined, *post*, p. 2549. STEVENS, J., filed a dissenting opinion, *post*, p. 2556.

Kathi Alyce Drew, Dallas, Tex., for petitioner.

William M. Kunstler, New York City, for respondent.

⊥399Justice BRENNAN delivered the opinion of the Court.

After publicly burning an American flag as a means of political protest, Gregory Lee Johnson was convicted of desecrating a flag in violation of Texas law. This case presents the question whether his conviction is consistent with the First Amendment. We hold that it is not.

I

While the Republican National Convention was taking place in Dallas in 1984, respondent Johnson participated in a political demonstration dubbed the "Republican War Chest Tour." As explained in literature distributed by the demonstrators and

① Page 398, in the *United States Reports* begins here: "ited."

② ⊥399 indicates where page 399 in the *United States Reports* begins (official reporter).

③ The Court's opinion begins here.

FIGURE 3-5
Texas v. Johnson, from *Lawyers' Edition*

① The volume and reporter. (*Lawyers' Edition 2d*)

② Full name designation of parties. Look at the top of the next page for the proper short name of the case. Always cite the case using the short name.

③ Summary of the case written by an editor.

④ References to supplemental material available at the end of this volume.

⑤ The briefs filed with the Court are available to the researcher in *this* publication.

U.S. SUPREME COURT REPORTS 105 L Ed 2d

[491 US 397]
TEXAS, Petitioner

v

GREGORY LEE JOHNSON

491 US 397, 105 L Ed 2d 342, 109 S Ct 2533

[No. 88-155]

Argued March 21, 1989. Decided June 21, 1989.

Decision: Conviction of protester for burning American flag as part of political demonstration held to violate Federal Constitution's First Amendment.

SUMMARY

While the 1984 Republican National Convention was taking place in Dallas, Texas, a group of people staged a political demonstration in Dallas to protest the policies of the President of the United States, who was being nominated by the Convention for re-election, and of certain Dallas-based corporations. During the course of that demonstration, one of the protesters (1) accepted an American flag handed to him by a fellow protester, who had taken the flag from a pole outside one of the targeted buildings, (2) doused the flag with kerosene, and (3) set the flag on fire. While the flag burned, the protesters chanted, "America, the red, white, and blue, we spit on you." The protester who allegedly had burned the flag was subsequently prosecuted in a Texas trial court for that act and was convicted of violating a state statute which (1) prohibited the desecration of, among other things, a state or national flag, and (2) defined desecration as the physical mistreatment of such objects in a way which the actor knows will seriously offend one or more persons likely to observe or discover the act. Several witnesses testified that they had been seriously offended by the flag burning. The defendant protester appealed his conviction on the ground, among others, that the application of the state statute violated his right to freedom of speech under the Federal Constitution's First Amendment. In affirming the conviction, the Court of Appeals for the Fifth District of Texas at Dallas ruled that the defendant protester's flag burning constituted symbolic speech requiring First Amendment scrutiny, but concluded that the desecration statute nevertheless could be upheld as a legitimate and constitutional means of (1)

SUBJECT OF ANNOTATION

Beginning on page 809, infra

Supreme Court's views as to constitutionality of laws prohibiting, or of criminal convictions for, desecration, defiance, disrespect, or misuse of American flag

Briefs of Counsel, p 807, infra.

342

FIGURE 3-5 (continued)

① **Short name of case.**

TEXAS v JOHNSON

(1989) 491 US 397, 105 L Ed 2d 342, 109 S Ct 2533

② **List of all three citations to the *Texas v. Johnson* case.**

protecting the public peace, because acts of flag desecration are, of themselves, so inherently inflammatory that the state may act to prevent breaches of the peace, and (2) realizing the state's legitimate and substantial interest in protecting the flag as a symbol of national unity (706 SW2d 120). The Court of Criminal Appeals of Texas, however, held that the desecration statute as applied violated the defendant protester's First Amendment rights, because the statute (1) was too broad for First Amendment purposes as it related to breaches of the peace, and (2) was not adequately supported by the state's purported interest in preserving a symbol of unity; therefore, the court reversed the decisions below and remanded the case to the trial court with instructions to dismiss the information (755 SW2d 92).

On certiorari, the United States Supreme Court affirmed. In an opinion by Brennan, J., joined by Marshall, Blackmun, Scalia, and Kennedy, JJ., it was held that the conviction of the defendant protester was inconsistent with the First Amendment under the particular circumstances presented, because (1) the protester's conduct was sufficiently imbued with elements of communication to implicate the First Amendment, given that this flag burning was the culmination of a political demonstration and that the state conceded that the protester's conduct was expressive; (2) the state's interest in preventing breaches of the peace was not implicated on the record in this case, since (a) no disturbance of the peace actually occurred or threatened to occur because of the flag burning, (b) it cannot be presumed that an audience which takes serious offense at a particular expression is necessarily likely to disturb the peace, and (c) the flag burning does not fall within the small class of "fighting words" that are likely to provoke the average person to retaliation and thereby cause a breach of the peace; and (3) the state's asserted interest in preserving the flag as a symbol of nationhood and national unity does not justify the conviction, since (a) the attempted restriction on expression is content-based, and thus subject to the most exacting scrutiny, given that the flag-desecration statute is aimed not at protecting the physical integrity of the flag in all circumstances, but only against impairments that would cause serious offense to others, and is aimed at protecting onlookers from being offended by the ideas expressed by the prohibited activity, and (b) although the state has a legitimate interest in encouraging proper treatment of the flag, it may not foster its own view of the flag by prohibiting expressive conduct relating to it and by criminally punishing a person for burning the flag as a means of political protest.

Kennedy, J., concurred, expressing the view that the First Amendment compels the result reached in this case, regardless of how distasteful that result may be to the Justices who announce it, because the defendant protester's acts were speech in both the technical and the fundamental meaning of the Federal Constitution.

Rehnquist, Ch. J., joined by White and O'Connor, JJ., dissented, expressing the view that (1) the Texas statute is not invalid under the First Amendment as applied in this case, because (a) the American flag has come to be the visible symbol embodying our nation and is not simply another

343

③ **Page number.**

FIGURE 3-5 (continued)

idea or point of view competing for recognition in the marketplace of ideas, and (b) the public burning of the American flag in this case was no essential part of any exposition of ideas and had a tendency to incite a breach of the peace, for flag burning is the equivalent of an inarticulate grunt or roar that is most likely to be indulged in not to express any particular idea, but to antagonize others, and the statute thus deprived the defendant protester of only one rather inarticulate symbolic form of protest—a form of protest that was profoundly offensive to many—and left him with a full panoply of other symbols and every conceivable form of verbal expression to express his deep disapproval of national policy; and (2) the statute is not unconstitutionally vague or overbroad.

Stevens, J., dissented, expressing the view that (1) sanctioning the desecration of the flag will tarnish its value as a national symbol, a tarnish which is not justified by the trivial burden on free expression that is occasioned by requiring that alternative modes of expression be employed; (2) the flag-desecration statute does not prescribe orthodox views or compel any conduct or expression of respect for any idea or symbol; and (3) the defendant protester in this case was prosecuted not for his criticism of government policies, but for the method he chose to express those views, and a prohibition against that method is supported by a legitimate interest in preserving the quality of an important national asset.

FIGURE 3-5 (continued)

TEXAS v JOHNSON

(1989) 491 US 397, 105 L Ed 2d 342, 109 S Ct 2533

HEADNOTES

Classified to U.S. Supreme Court Digest, Lawyers' Edition

Constitutional Law §§ 934, 935, 960; Evidence § 419 — free speech — flag burning — provoking public disturbance — presumption

1a-1i. The conviction of a protester for burning an American flag, in violation of a state statute which prohibits the desecration of the flag and which defines desecration as physical mistreatment which the actor knows will seriously offend one or more persons likely to observe or discover the action, is inconsistent with the free speech guarantee of the Federal Constitution's First Amendment under the particular circumstances presented, where (1) the protester's conduct is sufficiently imbued with elements of communication to implicate the First Amendment, given that this flag burning was the culmination of a political demonstration protesting the policies of a President of the United States who was then being nominated for re-election in the city where the demonstration occurred, and the policies of various corporations based in

TOTAL CLIENT-SERVICE LIBRARY® REFERENCES

12 Am Jur 2d, Breach of Peace and Disorderly Conduct § 8; 16A Am Jur 2d, Constitutional Law §§ 507-511, 513, 514, 516; 35 Am Jur 2d, Flag §§ 3-5

USCS, Constitution, Amendment 1

US L Ed Digest, Constitutional Law §§ 934, 935, 960

Index to Annotations, Breach of Peace and Disorderly Conduct; Fighting Words; Flags; Freedom of Speech and Press

Auto-Cite®: Cases and annotations referred to herein can be further researched through the Auto-Cite® computer-assisted research service. Use Auto-Cite to check citations for form, parallel references, prior and later history, and annotation references.

ANNOTATION REFERENCES

Supreme Court's view as to the protection or lack of protection, under the Federal Constitution, of the utterance of "fighting words." 39 L Ed 2d 925.

The Supreme Court and the right of free speech and press. 93 L Ed 1151, 2 L Ed 2d 1706, 11 L Ed 2d 1116, 16 L Ed 2d 1053, 21 L Ed 2d 976.

What constitutes violation of flag desecration statutes. 41 ALR3d 502.

345

FIGURE 3-5 (continued)

that city, and given that the state conceded that the protester's conduct was expressive; (2) the interest in preventing breaches of the peace, asserted by the state as justifying the individual's conviction, is not implicated on the record in this case, because (a) no disturbance of the peace actually occurred or threatened to occur because of the flag burning, (b) the only evidence as to onlookers' reactions was the testimony of several persons who were seriously offended by the flag burning, (c) it cannot be presumed that an audience which takes serious offense at a particular expression is necessarily likely to disturb the peace, and (d) the flag burning does not fall within the small class of "fighting words" that are likely to provoke the average person to retaliation and thereby cause a breach of the peace; and (3) the state's asserted interest in preserving the flag as a symbol of nationhood and national unity does not justify the protester's conviction, since (a) the attempted restriction on expression is content-based, and thus subject to the most exacting scrutiny, given that the flag-desecration statute is aimed not at protecting the physical integrity of the flag in all circumstances, but only against impairments that would cause serious offense to others, and is aimed at protecting onlookers from being offended by the ideas expressed by the prohibited activity, and (b) although the state has a legitimate interest in encouraging proper treatment of the flag, it may not foster its own view of the flag by prohibiting expressive conduct relating to it and by criminally punishing a person for burning the flag as a means of political protest. (Rehnquist, Ch. J., and White, O'Connor, and Stevens, JJ., dissented from this holding.)

[See annotation p 809, infra]

Appeal § 1600; Constitutional Law § 960; Trial § 288 — free speech — flag burning — related speech — instruction on aiding and abetting — reversible error

2a, 2b. Although the jury, in the state court prosecution of a protester for burning the American flag—in violation of a state statute which makes it a crime to desecrate the flag, but does not on its face permit conviction for remarks critical of the flag or its referents—was instructed in accordance with the state's law of parties that a person is criminally responsible for an act committed by another if he or she solicits, encourages, directs, aids, or attempts to aid the other person to commit the offense with the intent of promoting or assisting the commission of the offense, this instruction could not have led the jury, in violation of the individual's rights under the Federal Constitution's First Amendment, to convict the protester solely for his words in leading chants denouncing the flag while it burned, where (1) this instruction was offered by the prosecution, because the individual's defense was that he was not the person who had burned the flag in question, (2) the instruction does not permit a conviction merely for the pejorative nature of the individual's words, and (3) the words themselves —"America, the red, white, and blue, we spit on you"—do not encourage the burning of the flag as the instruction seems to require; given the additional fact that the bulk of the prosecutor's argument, which mentioned that the individual had led this chant, was premised on the individual's culpability as a sole actor, it is too unlikely that the jury

FIGURE 3-5 (continued)

TEXAS v JOHNSON
(1989) 491 US 397, 105 L Ed 2d 342, 109 S Ct 2533

convicted the individual on the basis of this alternative theory for the conviction to be reversed on this ground.

Appeal § 732 — United States Supreme Court — review of state court decision — validity of state statute

3a, 3b. Although an individual who has been convicted in a state court of desecrating the American flag by burning it raises a claim that the state statute under which he was convicted violates on its face the free speech provisions of the Federal Constitution's First Amendment, the United States Supreme Court, in reviewing the individual's conviction on certiorari, will address only the alternative claim that the statute violates the First Amendment as applied to political expression like that engaged in by the individual—who allegedly burned the flag, to the accompaniment of the chant "America, the red, white, and blue, we spit on you," in the course of a demonstration protesting the policies of the incumbent President of the United States, who was then being nominated for a second term in the city where the demonstration was held, and of various corporations based in that city—because (1) although one violates the statute, according to its terms, only if one knows that one's physical mistreatment of the flag will seriously offend one or more persons likely to observe or discover this action, this does not necessarily mean that the statute applies only to expressive conduct protected by the First Amendment; (2) the prosecution of a person who had not engaged in expressive conduct would pose a different case; and (3) the case can be disposed of on narrower grounds.

Constitutional Law § 934 — free speech — regulation of expressive conduct

4. Under the Federal Constitution's First Amendment, the government generally has a freer hand in restricting expressive conduct than it has in restricting the written or spoken word, but it may not proscribe particular conduct because that conduct has expressive elements; a law directed at the communicative nature of conduct must, like a law directed at speech itself, be justified by the substantial showing of need that the First Amendment requires; in short, it is not simply the verbal or nonverbal nature of the expression, but the governmental interest at stake, that helps to determine whether a restriction on that expression is valid.

Appeal § 1662 — effect of decision on other grounds

5a, 5b. The United States Supreme Court—in reviewing on certiorari the state court criminal conviction of an individual who is charged with desecrating an American flag by burning it and who claims that his act was expressive conduct protected by the Federal Constitution's First Amendment—need not consider the individual's argument that the state's interest in preventing breaches of the peace, asserted as justifying the conviction, is related to the suppression of free expression in that the violent reaction to flag burnings feared by the state would be the result of the message conveyed by them, where the Supreme Court finds that this interest is not implicated on the particular facts of the case.

Constitutional Law § 934 — free speech — prosecution for expressive conduct

6. Under the Federal Constitu-

347

FIGURE 3-5 (continued)

tion's First Amendment, where a court is confronted with a case of prosecution for the expression of an idea through activity, the court must examine with particular care the interests advanced to support the prosecution.

Constitutional Law §§ 935, 960 — free speech — flag burning — audience reaction

7a, 7b. For purposes of the free speech clause of the Federal Constitution's First Amendment, there is no distinction of constitutional significance between (1) a state flag-desecration statute which is violated only when one physically mistreats the American flag in a way that he or she "knows" will offend others—so that a conviction for flag burning under that statute purportedly does not depend on onlookers' actual reactions, but on the actor's intent—and (2) a statute which depends on actual audience reaction.

[See annotation p 809, infra]

Constitutional Law § 935 — free speech — offensiveness

8. Under the Federal Constitution's First Amendment, the government may not prohibit the expression of an idea simply because society finds the idea itself offensive or disagreeable.

Constitutional Law §§ 925, 961 — freedom of speech and religion

9. Under the Federal Constitution, no official, high or petty, can prescribe what shall be orthodox in politics, nationalism, religion, or other matters of opinion or force citizens to confess by word or act their faith therein.

Constitutional Law § 934 — free speech — regulation — mode of expression

10. The rule, under the Federal Constitution's First Amendment, that the government may not prohibit expression simply because it disagrees with its message, is not dependent on the particular mode in which one chooses to express an idea.

SYLLABUS BY REPORTER OF DECISIONS

During the 1984 Republican National Convention, respondent Johnson participated in a political demonstration to protest the policies of the Reagan administration and some Dallas-based corporations. After a march through the city streets, Johnson burned an American flag while protesters chanted. No one was physically injured or threatened with injury, although several witnesses were seriously offended by the flag burning. Johnson was convicted of desecration of a venerated object in violation of a Texas statute, and a state court of appeals affirmed. However, the Texas Court of Criminal Appeals reversed, holding that the State, consistent with the First Amendment, could not punish Johnson for burning the flag in these circumstances. The court first found that Johnson's burning of the flag was expressive conduct protected by the First Amendment. The court concluded that the State could not criminally sanction flag desecration in order to preserve the flag as a symbol of national unity. It also held that the statute did not meet the State's goal of preventing breaches of the peace, since it was not drawn narrowly enough to encompass only those flag burnings that would likely result in a serious disturbance, and since the flag burning in this case

FIGURE 3-5 (continued)

TEXAS v JOHNSON
(1989) 491 US 397, 105 L Ed 2d 342, 109 S Ct 2533

did not threaten such a reaction. Further, it stressed that another Texas statute prohibited breaches of the peace and could be used to prevent disturbances without punishing this flag desecration.

Held: Johnson's conviction for flag desecration is inconsistent with the First Amendment.

(a) Under the circumstances, Johnson's burning of the flag constituted expressive conduct, permitting him to invoke the First Amendment. The State conceded that the conduct was expressive. Occurring as it did at the end of a demonstration coinciding with the Republican National Convention, the expressive, overtly political nature of the conduct was both intentional and overwhelmingly apparent.

(b) Texas has not asserted an interest in support of Johnson's conviction that is unrelated to the suppression of expression and would therefore permit application of the test set forth in United States v O'Brien, 391 US 367, 20 L Ed 2d 672, 88 S Ct 1673, whereby an important governmental interest in regulating nonspeech can justify incidental limitations on First Amendment freedoms when speech and nonspeech elements are combined in the same course of conduct. An interest in preventing breaches of the peace is not implicated on this record. Expression may not be prohibited on the basis that an audience that takes serious offense to the expression may disturb the peace, since the Government cannot assume that every expression of a provocative idea will incite a riot but must look to the actual circumstances surrounding the expression. Johnson's expression of dissatisfaction with the Federal Government's policies also does not fall within the class of "fighting words" likely to be seen as a direct personal insult or an invitation to exchange fisticuffs. This Court's holding does not forbid a State to prevent "imminent lawless action" and, in fact, Texas has a law specifically prohibiting breaches of the peace. Texas' interest in preserving the flag as a symbol of nationhood and national unity is related to expression in this case and, thus, falls outside the O'Brien test.

(c) The latter interest does not justify Johnson's conviction. The restriction on Johnson's political expression is content based, since the Texas statute is not aimed at protecting the physical integrity of the flag in all circumstances, but is designed to protect it from intentional and knowing abuse that causes serious offense to others. It is therefore subject to "the most exacting scrutiny." Boos v Barry, 485 US 312, 99 L Ed 2d 333, 108 S Ct 1157. The Government may not prohibit the verbal or nonverbal expression of an idea merely because society finds the idea offensive or disagreeable, even where our flag is involved. Nor may a State foster its own view of the flag by prohibiting expressive conduct relating to it, since the Government may not permit designated symbols to be used to communicate a limited set of messages. Moreover, this Court will not create an exception to these principles protected by the First Amendment for the American flag alone.

755 SW2d 92, affirmed.

Brennan, J., delivered the opinion of the Court, in which Marshall, Blackmun, Scalia, and Kennedy, JJ., joined. Kennedy, J., filed a concurring opinion. Rehnquist, C.J., filed a dissenting opinion, in which White and O'Connor, JJ., joined. Stevens, J., filed a dissenting opinion.

349

FIGURE 3-5 (continued)

① The Court's opinion begins here.

② Page 400 in the *United States Reports* begins here.

③ Courts do not always follow *The Bluebook* Citation Format.

U.S. SUPREME COURT REPORTS 105 L Ed 2d

APPEARANCES OF COUNSEL

Kathi Alyce Drew argued the cause for petitioner.
William M. Kunstler argued the cause for respondent.
Briefs of Counsel, p 807, infra.

OPINION OF THE COURT

[491 US 399]

Justice **Brennan** delivered the opinion of the Court.

[1a] After publicly burning an American flag as a means of political protest, Gregory Lee Johnson was convicted of desecrating a flag in violation of Texas law. This case presents the question whether his conviction is consistent with the First Amendment. We hold that it is not.

I

While the Republican National Convention was taking place in Dallas in 1984, respondent Johnson participated in a political demonstration dubbed the "Republican War Chest Tour." As explained in literature distributed by the demonstrators and in speeches made by them, the purpose of this event was to protest the policies of the Reagan administration and of certain Dallas-based corporations. The demonstrators marched through the Dallas streets, chanting political slogans and stopping at several corporate locations to stage "die-ins" intended to dramatize the consequences of nuclear war. On several occasions they spray-painted the walls of buildings and overturned potted plants, but Johnson himself took no part in such activities. He did, however, accept an American flag handed to him by a fellow protestor who had taken it from a flag pole outside one of the targeted buildings.

The demonstration ended in front of Dallas City Hall, where Johnson unfurled the American flag, doused it with kerosene, and set it on fire. While the flag burned, the protestors chanted, "America, the red, white, and blue, we spit on you." After the demonstrators dispersed, a witness to the flag burning collected the flag's remains and buried them in his backyard. No one was physically injured or threatened with injury, though several witnesses testified that they had been seriously offended by the flag burning.

[491 US 400]

Of the approximately 100 demonstrators, Johnson alone was charged with a crime. The only criminal offense with which he was charged was the desecration of a venerated object in violation of Tex Penal Code Ann § 42.09(a)(3) (1989).[1] After a trial, he was convicted, sentenced to one year in prison, and fined $2,000. The Court of Appeals for the Fifth District of Texas at Dallas affirmed Johnson's conviction, 706 SW2d 120 (1986), but the Texas Court of Criminal Appeals reversed, 755 SW2d 92

1. Tex Penal Code Ann § 42.09 (1989) provides in full:

"§ 42.09. Desecration of Venerated Object

"(a) A person commits an offense if he intentionally or knowingly desecrates:

"(1) a public monument;

"(2) a place of worship or burial; or

"(3) a state or national flag.

"(b) For purposes of this section, 'desecrate' means deface, damage, or otherwise physically mistreat in a way that the actor knows will seriously offend one or more persons likely to observe or discover his action.

"(c) An offense under this section is a Class A misdemeanor."

350

A Point to Remember

Dictum is reasoning or a comment by the court that is not essential to the outcome (the holding) of the decision. Dictum (the plural is dicta) is nonbinding on other courts. Sometimes courts make statements like "if this case involved state statutes rather than the federal statutes our analysis might involve considerations such as... ." This is an example of a court going beyond the analysis that is essential to the holding of the case before the court. Dictum is not in every case. Researchers need to be alert that dictum exists, but it is not necessary to read every case worrying about it. When a court uses dicta, it is usually obvious to the reader.

dictum
Reasoning or a comment by the court that is not essential to the outcome (the holding) of the decision. Dictum (the plural is dicta) is nonbinding on other courts.

Chief Justice Marshall said this about the difference between dictum and holding: "It is a maxim not be disregarded, that general expressions, in every opinion, are to be taken in connection with the case in which those expression are used. If they go beyond the case, they may be respected, but ought not to control the judgment in a subsequent suit when the very point is presented for decision. The reason of this maxim is obvious. The question actually before the court is investigated with care, and considered in its full extent. Other principles which may serve to illustrate it are considered in their relation to the case decided, but their possible bearing on all other cases is seldom completely investigated."

The Appeal Process

Because all case law comes from appellate courts, before reading case law you should be familiar with the appeal process (see Box 3-1). An appeal results when one party to an action is dissatisfied with the result and asks a higher court to review the trial. In general, in a civil case, either party has the right to appeal. In a criminal trial, however, only the defendant has the right to appeal because of the ***double jeopardy*** clause of the Constitution. An appeal usually takes place only after a final judgment in the trial court. Appellate rules are very technical, and the appeal process is very limited. However, in some instances, parties may seek appellate review from a higher court through proceedings known as writs. The courts hear petitions or requests for many types of writs, including:

double jeopardy
Clause in the U.S. Constitution that generally prevents the government from trying a person more than once for the same offense.

Petition for writ of mandate	A request that the appellate court order the lower court to do something or to refrain from doing something
Petition for writ of habeas corpus	A request that the court order the release of one who is imprisoned or otherwise confined

Case law can result from both appeals and petitions for writs. In rendering its decision, the appellate court can ***affirm*** the decision, ***reverse*** the decision, or reverse and ***remand*** the decision. When the court affirms the decision, it lets the lower court decision stand. When it reverses the case, it overturns or changes the lower court decision. When it reverses and remands the case, it overturns the lower court decision, but sends it back to the trial court for a retrial. In any case, the appellate court always renders a written decision in which it explains its reasons. It discusses the claims made by each of the parties and also reviews and analyzes the various primary legal authorities cited by the parties.

affirm
To uphold: in connection with an appeal to uphold the lower court's decision.

reverse
To change.

remand
To send back.

BOX 3-1 APPELLATE PROCESS AND CASE LAW

Process	Case law
Factual dispute is resolved at trial court. ↓	No case law results
Losing party files appeal in intermediate appellate court (exception: prosecutor in criminal case cannot appeal guilty verdict). ↓	
Appellate court reviews case and renders a written opinion.	Opinion becomes case law if published and if there is no further appeal.
Losing party can seek further review in highest state court (often by filing a petition for writ of certiorari). ↓	
High court has discretion to grant or deny review.	
If high court grants a hearing, it reviews actions of lower courts and renders a written opinion. ↓	Opinion becomes case law if final.
If the case contains a constitutional issue, the losing party can request a hearing in the U.S. Supreme Court.	
If the Court grants a hearing, it reviews state court actions and renders a written opinion.	Opinion becomes case law.

In the federal legal system and in many states, a supreme court also exists. This court plays a role in the appellate process. If a party is still not satisfied after a hearing in the appellate court, parties can petition the highest court in their legal system for a hearing. When a case is tried originally in the state courts, the parties can petition for a hearing in the U.S. Supreme Court if a federal issue is involved. Such a request is a *petition for a writ of certiorari*.

The basis for any appeal is a legal error. This means that the trial court did not follow the law. Often this stems from the trial judge's ruling regarding the admissibility of evidence or from the instructions given to the jury by the judge at the end of the trial. Legal errors can also stem from the court's ruling on various ***motions*** that attorneys make in the case. When you read case law, always be sure that you understand the nature of the proceedings in the trial court. If the appellate court describes unfamiliar procedures, be sure to use a dictionary or other resource.

motion
A request for an order from the court.

3-4 WHERE TO FIND CASE LAW

Cases are published by several publishers and may be located in a number of resources. Each state publishes, or arranges to have published, its appellate and supreme court cases. States such as New York, Texas, Florida, New Jersey, Washington, California, and many others publish their opinions in official publications of their case law. Other states arrange with the West Group to publish their case law in the appropriate ***regional reporters***. A concise guide to the appropriate resources is located in ***A Uniform System of Citation*** (*The Bluebook*). In addition to the traditional paper publications, state case law is available through the online legal databases of ***Lexis*** and ***Westlaw*** and on various CD-ROM products. Most state's official websites also provide this data. Increasing collections of state and federal case law are located at various sites on the Internet.

regional reporters
A set of published volumes of cases by courts in specific regions of the United States; for example, the *Pacific Reporter* or the *North Eastern Reporter*.

A Uniform System of Citation
A reference manual; it contains the rules for proper citation format; often called *The Bluebook*.

case law reporters
Sets of published volumes of cases decided by various courts.

Case Law Reporters

Case law reporters are books filled with decisions. They exist for most states; in addition, there are large sets of books known as *regional reporters* that publish selected case law from a geographical region of the United States. Section 3-6 discusses these reporters.

Lexis and Westlaw

Lexis and Westlaw are huge online legal databases. Use of these services is through contract with the publishers. Only persons trained to search in large legal databases should use these services. Case law is only one of the many resources they provide. Bloomberg Law is a relative newcomer. Bloomberg Law, like Lexis and Westlaw, offers a range of legal research options. All three of these databases are addressed in Chapter 10.

CD-ROM Products

Some publishers continue to offer case law on CD-ROM. These products often combine the ease of using books with the speed of using an online database.

Internet

There are many Internet sites for case law retrieval. Because the Internet is growing and changing at a rapid rate, it is difficult to offer a complete list of research sites. Some law schools continue to maintain consistently reliable websites. Many legal organization and commercial websites also provide access to federal and some state case law. The Law Library of Congress Guide to Law Online (http://www.loc.gov/law/help/guide.php) provides links to each state's judicial materials.One problem sometimes faced with using free Internet websites for research projects is that the cases may not identify page breaks that appear in the printed resources. Two commercial websites, however, do provide this information. Those sites are Google Scholar (http://scholar.google.com/) and Justia (https://www.justia.com/). Both of these sites provide access to extensive federal and state case law.

3-5 FEDERAL CASE LAW

Various federal case law reporters publish cases decided by federal courts. For example, U.S. Supreme Court cases are available in written format from several publishers.

parallel citations
Many case citations include references to unofficial publications as well as the official citation. These additional references are parallel citations; simply stated—you may find the exact case in more than one publication.

United States Supreme Court Case Law

This is a Supreme Court case citation with ***parallel citations***:

Meritor Sav. Bank, FSB v. Vinson, 477 U.S. 57, 106 S. Ct. 2399, 91 L. Ed. 2d 49 (1986)

United States Reports
Official publication of all United States Supreme Court case law; published by the federal government.

United States Reports

This is the official publication of all U.S. Supreme Court case law. The federal government publishes it. The proper citation format for the ***United States Reports*** is U.S. Figure 3-3 is the first page of the *Texas v. Johnson* case as it appears in the *United States Reports.*

Supreme Court Reporter

unofficial publication
Material not published by a government entity or a government designee.

editorial enhancements
Helpful information included in many unofficial publications; the enhancements assist the researcher to understand the material. Most official publications have little or no editorial enhancements.

digest topics
Topics included in an index (digest) to reported case law, arranged by subject.

key numbers
A research aid unique to the West Group materials; these numbers allow a researcher to quickly access specific material in a digest.

Supreme Court Reporter
Printed by West, this is an unofficial publication of all United States Supreme Court case law.

Lawyers' Edition
LexisNexis publishes this unofficial (nongovernment) printing of all U.S. Supreme Court case law.

Federal Reporter
The set containing all of the federal appellate decisions.

Federal Supplement
The set containing the cases argued and determined in the United States District Courts, the United States Court of International Trade, and the rulings of the Judicial Panel on Multidistrict Litigation.

Federal Rules Decisions
The set containing federal opinions, decisions, and rulings involving the Federal Rules of Civil Procedure and the Federal Rules of Criminal Procedure.

This is an ***unofficial publication*** of all Supreme Court case law. West, a Thomson Reuters business, publishes it. The cases are identical to those published in the *United States Reports*. The only differences are in the format in which the cases are published and the ***editorial enhancements***. The primary editorial enhancement worth noting in all West case reporter publications is the inclusion of ***digest topics*** and ***key numbers***. Chapter 8 explains digests. These tools enable the researcher to quickly and easily expand the research. The West publications are linked together using the digest topics and the key numbers. The proper citation format for the ***Supreme Court Reporter*** is S. Ct. Notice the different format of the *Supreme Court Reporter* publication of *Texas v. Johnson* (Figure 3-4) starting in the second column on page 46.

Lawyers' Edition

This is also an unofficial publication of all Supreme Court cases published by LexisNexis. Lawyers' Cooperative Publishing previously published it. The case law is identical to that in the *United States Reports* and the *Supreme Court Reporter*. Again, the differences involve format and editorial comments. The proper citation format for the ***Lawyers' Edition*** is L. Ed. Always be sure to include the edition of the report, for example, 91 L. Ed. 2d 49. Compare the *Lawyers' Edition* publication of *Texas v. Johnson* with the other versions. It is the same case; the differences lie in publication format and editorial enhancements. Over time, you will develop a preference for one publication over the other two. (See Figure 3-5.)

These are the three most common printed sources in which a researcher may locate all U.S. Supreme Court case law. The text of the opinion, what the justices wrote, is identical in each source. The differences are the editorial enhancements and the speed of publication. The official reporter, the *United States Reports,* is published later than all other reporters.

Other Federal Reporters

There are several reporters publishing federal case law. Of these, the ***Federal Reporter*** and the ***Federal Supplement*** are most important to the beginning legal researcher. The *Federal Reporter* publishes the U.S. Circuit court of appeals' opinions. The *Federal Supplement* includes cases from the U.S. district courts and some special courts.

Federal Reporter West's *Federal Reporter* is a set of federal appellate decisions. Because West publishes it, it uses the Key Number Digest System. There is also a specific digest for federal decisions. You will learn more about the Key Number Digest System and digests in general in Chapter 8.

Federal Rules Decisions West's ***Federal Rules Decisions*** collects federal opinions, decisions, and rulings involving the Federal Rules of Civil Procedure and the Federal Rules of Criminal Procedure.

Federal Supplement The *Federal Supplement* reports the cases argued and determined in the U.S. district courts (trial courts), the United States Court of International Trade, and the rulings of the Judicial Panel on Multidistrict Litigation. This is a very large set, also published by West. Decisions from the *Federal Supplement* are digested in the *Federal Digest*.

Specialized Reporters

West also publishes numerous ***specialized reporters***. For example, the *Military Justice Reporter* provides opinions of the United States Courts of Appeals for the Armed Forces and selected opinions of the Courts of Criminal Appeals. The *Bankruptcy Reporter* includes bankruptcy cases decided in the United States bankruptcy courts, the United States bankruptcy appellate panels, the United States district courts, the United States courts of appeals, and the Supreme Court of the United States.

specialized reporters
Collections of cases grouped by specific topics rather than by level of court or jurisdiction.

Lexis and Westlaw

All U.S. Supreme Court case law is located in either Lexis or Westlaw. These large legal databases make retrieval of case law fast and extremely simple. The researcher may locate a case by its name, its citation, or its facts and legal issues. Chapter 10 addresses Lexis and Westlaw.

Internet U.S. Supreme Court case law is readily available on the Internet. New sites appear rapidly; look for changes and additions to the sites you already frequent. Cornell Law School's Legal Information Institute offers U.S. Supreme Court decisions on the day the decision is handed down. Chapter 11 addresses Internet resources.

3-6 STATE CASE LAW

State and regional reporters publish state court cases. For example, in California, state cases are printed in the official reporters, *California Reports* (California Supreme Court case law) or *California Appellate Reports,* and in the unofficial reporter, *California Reporter*. In addition, selected cases are published in the regional reporter, the *Pacific Reporter*, which includes cases from a number of western states, including California. Therefore, in California and some other states, all cases are published in at least two reporters, and some are found in a third.

Regional Reporters

There are seven regional reporters, each of which covers the case law of a specific region of the United States. For example, the following states are included in the Pacific Region:

Alaska, Arizona, California, Colorado, Hawaii, Idaho, Kansas, Montana, Nevada, New Mexico, Oklahoma, Oregon, Utah, and Washington.

Official Reporters

Some states, such as Missouri, do not have a state ***official reporter***. For such states, *all* cases are reported in the appropriate regional reporter. These states contract with West to print all of their cases. In this way, the state avoids the expense and delay of a government publication. Other states print their own official reports. In these instances, West publishes only the state supreme court cases in the regional reporter.

official reporters
Sets of case law published by the government or the designee of the government.

Unofficial Reporters

unofficial reporters
Collections of printed decisions that are not government publications.

headnote
Editorial enhancement added to the front material of a case; useful summary of most of the legal topics addressed in the case.

Unofficial reporters are collections of printed decisions, usually from a specific state, that are not government publications and are not authorized by the government. The publisher cannot change the text of the decision, but it adds useful information, which often includes a short summary of the facts of the case, the legal issue, and the outcome. In addition, ***headnotes*** are added to assist the researcher to find additional case law on a given topic. For these reasons, researchers often find these unofficial reporters extremely helpful.

A Point to Remember

At first, the concept of headnotes may be confusing. However, as your research skills improve and the importance of a digest becomes clear, you will find headnotes to be an important research aid. Always read them and the summary provided by the editors; this information is designed to help you understand the case you are about to read. The information is there to provide focus. However, you may not quote from the editorial material. All quotes must originate within the actual opinion of the court.

Remember, wherever you locate the case, no matter who published it, the actual language in the decision is *identical* in every source. Go back and look at the *Texas v. Johnson* case. Once the opinion begins, the language is identical.

Other Sources

State case law is also available on Lexis and Westlaw. Increasingly, many cases are located on the Internet.

A Point to Remember

When performing legal research, one must be conscious of the jurisdiction in which the cause of action (the client's legal problem) arose. In general, if your client lives in Florida and the cause of action arose in Florida, your research usually takes place in the Florida codes, cases, and practice guides. Similarly, if the cause of action involves a federal issue, all research is performed in the federal research sources.

3-7 AN APPROACH TO READING A CASE

Most cases follow a similar format; this format becomes familiar as one reads more case law. Knowing what to expect and looking for the basic components of a case helps you to read a case once rather than repeatedly in a seemingly vain attempt to master the court's reasoning.

Components of a Case

Initially, some students find case law difficult to read and understand. Each case must be approached with a plan. Case law contains each of the following components.

Facts The key facts, provided by the court, are essential to the researcher. In legal research, one reads case law to locate those cases that are similar, factually and legally, to a client's case. Without the facts, no effective comparisons may take place. Many judges provide the reader with the facts at the very beginning of the case.

Judicial History The judicial history explains the prior proceedings—what happened in the lower court(s). This component is usually included early in the case.

Issues Issues are the legal questions before the reviewing court. Courts sometimes guide the reader with language such as "the question before this court is" or "at issue here is"—look for this type of help.

Rules Rules are the primary law relied upon by the court in the analysis or reasoning component of the case. Rules are found in primary law: the Constitution, statutes/codes, rules and regulations, and case law.

Analysis The analysis or reasoning component of most cases will be the longest section. It usually follows the facts, judicial history, and a basic statement of the issues. This component contains a discussion of the facts, issues, and appropriate rules or laws relied upon by the court in reaching its decision.

Conclusion The conclusion—the holding of the court—is the legal outcome of the case.

Many students of the law learn to read cases looking for issues, rules, analysis, and a conclusion. Known as the *IRAC method,* it prepares the researcher to effectively summarize or "brief" the case. Add the relevant facts and the basic judicial history and you have a complete summary.

Each paragraph of a case includes one or more of these six components: (1) judicial history, (2) facts, (3) issues, (4) rules, (5) analysis, and (6) conclusion. As you read, identify the components of every paragraph. This allows you to focus and sort out the case while you read, rather than going back and rereading. Some of the paragraphs contain more than one element; for example, paragraphs of analysis almost always contain rules/law and possibly some relevant facts.

Reading Topic Sentences—An Approach to Reading Case Law

In good writing, the author opens each paragraph with a topic sentence (or sometimes a transition sentence). These topic sentences let the reader know the basic content of the body of the paragraph. We do not read case law as we might a work of fiction. In fiction we expect to be surprised or even confused. This is not true of reading legal writing.

Before you sit down to read a case from start to finish, try this: Read nothing but the first sentence of each paragraph. Do not take notes; do not underline; just read the first sentences. In most instances, this provides a great overview of the case. Good writers lead us through their documents.

Locate the *Illinois v. Caballas* case found on page 68. When we try this with the 10 paragraphs in the *Illinois v. Caballas* case, this is what we read:

1. Illinois State Trooper Daniel Gillette stopped respondent for speeding on an interstate highway.
2. Respondent was convicted of a narcotics offense and sentenced to 12 years' imprisonment and a $256,136 fine.

3. The question on which we granted certiorari [citation omitted] is narrow: "Whether the Fourth Amendment requires reasonable, articulable suspicion to justify using a drug-detection dog to sniff a vehicle during a legitimate traffic stop."
4. Here, the initial seizure of respondent when he was stopped on the highway was based on probable cause, and was concededly lawful.
5. In the state-court proceedings, however, the judges carefully reviewed the details of Officer Gillette's conversations with respondent and the precise timing of his radio transmissions to the dispatcher to determine whether he had improperly extended the duration of the stop to enable the dog sniff to occur.
6. Despite this conclusion, the Illinois Supreme Court held that the initially lawful traffic stop became an unlawful seizure solely as a result of the canine sniff that occurred outside respondent's stopped car.
7. Official conduct that does not "compromise any legitimate interest in privacy" is not a search subject to the Fourth Amendment. [citation omitted]
8. Accordingly, the use of a well-trained narcotics-detection dog—one that "does not expose non-contraband items that otherwise would remain hidden from public view"—during a lawful traffic stop, generally does not implicate legitimate privacy interests. [citation omitted]
9. This conclusion is entirely consistent with our recent decision that the use of a thermal-imaging device to detect the growth of marijuana in a home constituted an unlawful search. [citation omitted]
10. The judgment of the Illinois Supreme Court is vacated, and the case is remanded for further proceedings not inconsistent with this opinion.

After reading only these 10 sentences, we have a good picture of the facts, the issue, some of the rules (law), and the outcome of the case. Now, we are ready to read the case. The second reading involves marking the case and taking margin notes.

A Method for Reading and Color Highlighting a Legal Decision

Reading case law and looking for rules often feel like looking for a needle in a haystack. Decisions may contain more than a simple, direct explanation of the court's opinion. A court may take the opportunity to show the flaws of the argument of one or both parties. In addition, a court may show distinctions or differences between the current proceedings and past decisions. It can be difficult to sort through all of this.

Color highlighting a case law decision may help you better visualize the various components of the case. You need, at least, four color highlighters. If you are working with a case online, your software will most likely allow you to highlight the text using this approach.

For example:

Pink: for facts

Blue: for the issue(s)

Green: for the rules (law) and the citation connected to the rules

Yellow: for the court's analysis

For the purposes of this process, you do not need to color the judicial history or the court's holding. In general, these sections are not difficult to identify.

First (pink): Shade all of the facts with the pink highlighter. The key facts are usually located near the beginning of the case. Courts often open with either the facts or the judicial history. Look for the information where the court is telling a story about people before trial. Above in *Caballas,* sentences 1 and 2 are factual.

Second (blue): Shade the issue. A court often helps the reader with sentences that begin with language similar to:

> The question before this Court is whether ... ; or
> The issue presented today is ... ; or
> This Court must decide whether ...

The word *whether* is often the best clue that the issue is about to make an appearance. The issue is often stated just after the facts and judicial history. Not all cases follow this pattern, but many well-written decisions do follow this format. Topic sentence number 3 in *Caballas* is the issue statement.

Third (green): First, shade each citation. Second, look at the sentence directly preceding the citation. Often this sentence contains a rule of law. The rule can stand alone. This means that the rule may be applied in many cases; it is not unique to the case before the court. Third, as you search for the rules or the rule of law relied upon by the court, look for statements that can stand alone, that is, statements that do not directly connect to the case under consideration. Notice that in the *Caballas* case topic sentence numbers 7 and 8 are rules that can stand alone (topic sentence number 9 contains the holding of a previous case and is not being used for its content here). The basic rules, in topic sentences 7 and 8, can be used in any number of situations.

Fourth (yellow): The most difficult information to identify may be the court's analysis. There are clues, however, for the reader. Paragraphs containing citations to law are usually paragraphs containing the court's analysis. When you see the green citations and the rules connected to those citations, you are probably looking at a paragraph containing the court's analysis. Think of the "analysis" as the court's reasoning or the court's explanation of the holding in the case. Courts want readers to understand how and why decisions are reached. The court cites, when applicable, to the constitution, statutes, rules and regulations, and case law. The court's analysis involves the application of the rule to the case before the court. The analysis is usually the long portion of any case. This includes the reasons the court did not hold for the other party. Topic sentence number 4 contains a statement of general analysis. At this point, you should not be surprised to find that the *Caballas* Court's analysis is generally found in the body of the paragraphs rather than in the topic sentences. Courts usually explain the rule of law, and then apply the rule of law.

After you complete this process, you should see a very colorful version of the case, one in which it is easy to identify the components you shaded with the color markers. To check yourself, the analysis paragraphs tend to be green and yellow. Fact paragraphs are mostly pink. Many times the blue-shaded issue opens an analysis paragraph. This is not an exact science, but it does provide a framework for reading and thinking about case law. In the *Caballas* example above, topic sentences 5 and 6 contain judicial history and topic sentence number 10 is the holding of the Court. After reading only the topic sentences, you are prepared to read and understand the case. You know the outcome of the case and some basic facts; now, you must read the case to understand *why* the Court reached the decision contained in topic sentence number 10.

A Point to Remember

It is not possible, nor is it prudent, to give only one label to each paragraph of a decision. But remember: Each paragraph must contain at least one of the six components listed above. Do not become frustrated if you find four elements in one paragraph. Rather, congratulate yourself on careful analysis.

The *Illinois v. Caballas* case follows. The margin notes identify the components of the case. Try using color highlighters as described previously to mark the text.

CASE 3-1 *Illinois v. Caballas*, 543 U.S. 405 (2004)

JUSTICE STEVENS delivered the opinion of the Court

1. Facts (what happened before court proceedings)
2. Judicial History (activity in lower court (s))
3. Issue (question before this Court—note that the Issue opens with the term "whether)"
4. Analysis (rules and citations to law are part of the Court's analysis)

Illinois State Trooper Daniel Gillette stopped respondent for speeding on an interstate highway. When Gillette radioed the police dispatcher to report the stop, a second trooper, Craig Graham, a member of the Illinois State Police Drug Interdiction Team, overheard the transmission and immediately headed for the scene with his narcotics-detection dog. When they arrived, respondent's car was on the shoulder of the road and respondent was in Gillette's vehicle. While Gillette was in the process of writing a warning ticket, Graham walked his dog around respondent's car. The dog alerted at the trunk. Based on that alert, the officers searched the trunk, found marijuana, and arrested respondent. The entire incident lasted less than 10 minutes.

Respondent was convicted of a narcotics offense and sentenced to 12 years' imprisonment and a $256,136 fine. The trial judge denied his motion to suppress the seized evidence and to quash his arrest. He held that the officers had not unnecessarily prolonged the stop and that the dog alert was sufficiently reliable to provide probable cause to conduct the search. Although the Appellate Court affirmed, the Illinois Supreme Court reversed, concluding that because the canine sniff was performed without any " 'specific and articulable facts' " to suggest drug activity, the use of the dog "unjustifiably enlarg[ed] the scope of a routine traffic stop into a drug investigation." 207 Ill. 2d 504, 510, 802 N.E.2d 202, 205, 280 Ill. Dec. 277 (2003).

The question on which we granted certiorari, 541 U.S. 972, 159 L. Ed. 2d 84, 124 S. Ct. 2219 (2004), is narrow: "Whether the Fourth Amendment requires reasonable, articulable suspicion to justify using a drug-detection dog to sniff a vehicle during a legitimate traffic stop." Pet. for Cert. i. Thus, we proceed on the assumption that the officer conducting the dog sniff had no information about respondent except that he had been stopped for speeding; accordingly, we have omitted any reference to facts about respondent that might have triggered a modicum of suspicion.

Here, the initial seizure of respondent when he was stopped on the highway was based on probable cause, and was concededly lawful. It is nevertheless clear that a seizure that is lawful at its inception can violate the Fourth Amendment if its manner of execution unreasonably infringes interests protected by the Constitution. *United States v. Jacobsen*, 466 U.S. 109, 124, 80 L. Ed. 2d 85, 104 S. Ct. 1652 (1984). A seizure that is justified solely by the interest in issuing a warning ticket to the driver can become unlawful if it is prolonged beyond the time reasonably required to complete that mission. In an earlier case involving a dog sniff that occurred during an unreasonably prolonged traffic stop, the Illinois Supreme Court held that use of the dog and the subsequent discovery of contraband were the product of an unconstitutional seizure. *People v. Cox,* 202 Ill. 2d 462, 782 N.E.2d 275, 270 Ill. Dec. 81 (2002). We may assume that a similar result would be warranted in this case if the dog sniff had been conducted while respondent was being unlawfully detained.

In the state-court proceedings, however, the judges carefully reviewed the details of Officer Gillette's conversations with respondent and the precise timing of his radio transmissions to the dispatcher to determine whether he had improperly extended the duration of the stop to enable the dog sniff to occur. We have not recounted those details because we accept the state court's conclusion that the duration of the stop in this case was entirely justified by the traffic offense and the ordinary inquiries incident to such a stop.

Despite this conclusion, the Illinois Supreme Court held that the initially lawful traffic stop became an unlawful seizure solely as a result of the canine sniff that occurred outside respondent's stopped car. That is, the court characterized the dog sniff as the cause rather than the consequence of a constitutional violation. In its view, the use of the dog converted the citizen–police encounter from a lawful traffic stop into a drug investigation, and because the shift in purpose was not supported by any reasonable suspicion that respondent possessed narcotics, it was unlawful. In our view, conducting a dog sniff would not change the character of a traffic stop that is lawful at its inception and otherwise executed in a reasonable manner, unless the dog sniff itself infringed respondent's constitutionally protected interest in privacy. Our cases hold that it did not.

Official conduct that does not "compromise any legitimate interest in privacy" is not a search subject to the Fourth Amendment. *Jacobsen,* 466 U.S., at 123, 80 L. Ed. 2d 85, 104 S. Ct. 1652. We have held that any interest in possessing contraband cannot be deemed "legitimate," and thus, governmental conduct that *only* reveals the possession of contraband "compromises no legitimate privacy interest." *Ibid.* "This is because the expectation that certain facts will not come to the attention of the authorities" is not the same as an interest in "privacy that society is prepared to consider reasonable." *Id.*, at 122, 80 L. Ed. 2d 85, 104 S. Ct. 1652 (punctuation omitted). In *United States v. Place,* 462 U.S. 696, 77 L. Ed. 2d 110, 103 S. Ct. 2637 (1983), we treated a canine sniff by a well-trained narcotics-detection dog as "*sui generis*" because it "discloses only the presence or absence of narcotics, a contraband item." *Id.*, at 707, 77 L. Ed. 2d 110, 103 S. Ct. 2637; see also *Indianapolis v. Edmond,* 531 U.S. 32, 40, 148 L. Ed. 2d 333, 121 S. Ct. 447 (2000). Respondent likewise concedes that "drug sniffs are designed, and if properly conducted are generally likely, to reveal only the presence of contraband." Brief for Respondent 17. Although respondent argues that the error rates, particularly the existence of false positives, call into question the premise that drug-detection dogs alert only to contraband, the record contains no evidence or findings that support his argument. Moreover, respondent does not suggest that an erroneous alert, in and of itself, reveals any

5. Analysis cont.

6. Analysis cont.

7. Analysis cont.

8. Analysis cont.

9. Analysis cont.

10. Holding (outcome of the case—this is sometimes called the "conclusion" but when a case is remanded this decision is not truly a *conclusion* to the case)

legitimate private information, and, in this case, the trial judge found that the dog sniff was sufficiently reliable to establish probable cause to conduct a full-blown search of the trunk.

Accordingly, the use of a well-trained narcotics-detection dog—one that "does not expose non-contraband items that otherwise would remain hidden from public view," *Place,* 462 U.S., at 707, 77 L. Ed. 2d 110, 103 S. Ct. 2637—during a lawful traffic stop, generally does not implicate legitimate privacy interests. In this case, the dog sniff was performed on the exterior of respondent's car while he was lawfully seized for a traffic violation. Any intrusion on respondent's privacy expectations does not rise to the level of a constitutionally cognizable infringement.

This conclusion is entirely consistent with our recent decision that the use of a thermal-imaging device to detect the growth of marijuana in a home constituted an unlawful search. *Kyllo v. United States*, 533 U.S. 27, 150 L. Ed. 2d 94, 121 S. Ct. 2038 (2001). Critical to that decision was the fact that the device was capable of detecting lawful activity—in that case, intimate details in a home, such as "at what hour each night the lady of the house takes her daily sauna and bath." *Id.*, at 38, 150 L. Ed. 2d 94, 121 S. Ct. 2038. The legitimate expectation that information about perfectly lawful activity will remain private is categorically distinguishable from respondent's hopes or expectations concerning the non-detection of contraband in the trunk of his car. A dog sniff conducted during a concededly lawful traffic stop that reveals no information other than the location of a substance that no individual has any right to possess does not violate the Fourth Amendment.

The judgment of the Illinois Supreme Court is vacated, and the case is remanded for further proceedings not inconsistent with this opinion.

It is so ordered.

The Chief Justice took no part in the decision of this case.

A Point to Remember

While you are learning to read case law effectively, make a copy of the case, highlight the components, and note in the margins the components found in each paragraph. This helps you to remain focused while you read.

Official and Unofficial Publications

When citing to case law, always cite to the official citation first; the parallel/unofficial citation follows the official. In most citation formats, the year follows the last parallel citation.

de-publish
In rare instances, a court will decide a case, write and release a decision, *but before it is published in the official reporter,* the court decides not to publish some or all of the case decision. A de-published case cannot be used as precedent.

A Point to Remember

Sometimes the unofficial publishers go to press so quickly that they publish cases a court later decides to ***de-publish*** in whole or in part. A de-published case is not case precedent. Always check to make sure that the case has an official citation. One good method to ensure that you do not miss a de-published case is to carefully *Shepardize* all cases you research. Chapter 9 covers *Shepardizing* in detail.

3-8 HOW TO USE CASE LAW

Compare and Contrast the Facts of a Reported Case with Your Client's Facts

The doctrine of precedent mandates that, when you use case law, you must show factual similarities between your client's situation and the case law found in your research.

> **First**
> Compare the facts of the cases you locate in your research with those of your client's situation. If both sets are similar, or easily analogous, the case *may* be considered precedent.
>
> **Second**
> Contrast the facts of the cases you research with those of your client's situation. Significant factual differences probably mean that the case should *not* be used in an attempt to support your client's position.

After comparison of the facts, compare the legal issues. Ask yourself: Are my client's problems the same as, or similar to, the problems in the case I located? If the answer is yes, the case *may* be considered precedent.

Consider the following fact pattern:

Our client Mr. Mark Thelle was arrested for possession of a large amount of marijuana. He was stopped on a local freeway because he was driving well below the speed limit. He was returning from the auto repair shop where he had work done on his brakes. After leaving the repair shop, he merged onto the freeway, but when he tried to accelerate to join traffic, his car started to slow down. He put his warning flashers on and headed for the first possible exit when a patrol car pulled him over. When the officer asked for his license, he just handed it over without trying to explain his situation. After about five minutes, while the officer was checking on his license, his partner exited the patrol car with his drug-detection dog. When the dog reached the back passenger door, he alerted. The officer opened the door and pulled out a duffle bag filled with bags of marijuana. Mr. Thelle was arrested for possession of an illegal substance. Based on the *Caballas* case, what advice is your firm likely to give Mr. Thelle?

The Writer's Corner

Make Positive Statements

A positive assertion is powerful. It is simple. It is effective.

The use of the word "not" interferes with making a definite assertion.

For example:

He was not employed.	vs.	He was unemployed.
He was not well.	vs.	He was ill.

When possible, use the positive form to express a negative thought.

For example:

not helpful	vs.	unhelpful
not important	vs.	unimportant

The Elements of Style suggests that placing a positive and a negative in opposition creates a better structure.

For example:

"**Ask not what** your country can do for you—**ask** what you can do for your country." John F. Kennedy

A Point to Remember

In legal research, never lose sight of the fact that you are researching on behalf of a client. The more you understand about the client's factual situation, the better you are able to focus the research.

Finding It Online

The major law schools often provide access to some case law. Try this site:

www.law.cornell.edu

This is only a starting place. Explore as your time permits.

You will also find court opinions on the following sites:

http://scholar.google.com/ (Google Scholar)
http://www.plol.org/ (Public Library of Law)
https://www.justia.com/ (Justia)
www.statelocalgov.net/index.cfm (directory to state court case law)

Searching for case law on the Internet is most likely to be successful if you are looking for U.S. Supreme Court cases, very recent cases, or cases of high interest. The very best sources of online accurate case law are Lexis and Westlaw. However, these are not free resources. You may visit their websites to read about their services and try some of their resources. There are other pay-per-view providers of case law. You see most of them advertised in legal newspapers, bar journals, and legal periodicals.

www.lexis.com
www.westlaw.com

CITATION MATTERS

UNITED STATES SUPREME COURT CASE LAW

***THE BLUEBOOK*—RULE 8**

Capitalize "Court" when referring to the U.S. Supreme Court.

The Court stated that all immigrants are entitled to due process (referring to the U.S. Supreme Court).

***THE BLUEBOOK*—RULE 10**

U.S. Supreme Court Case Law Citation Analyzed

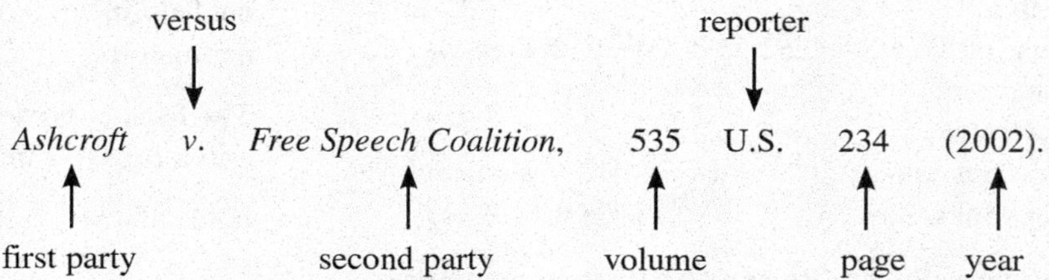

Place a period at the end of this *citation sentence*.

THE BLUEBOOK—TABLE 1 (T.1)

Cite to the *U.S. Reports* unless the official citation is not yet assigned. This is often the situation with very new cases. When there is no U.S. citation, cite to the *Supreme Court Reporter* (S. Ct.), *Lawyer's Edition* (L. Ed., L. Ed. 2d), or *United States Law Week* (U.S.L.W.), in that order of preference.

The *U.S. Reports* is the official reporter of U.S. Supreme Court case law. It is "official" because the federal government publishes it. The *Supreme Court Reporter*, *Lawyer's Edition*, and *United States Law Week* are all unofficial reporters of U.S. Supreme Court case law. That simply means the federal government does not publish these collections of U.S. Supreme Court case law. The *case law decisions* in these sets are identical. The differences are found in the editorial enhancements. Chapter 3 explains some of the features found in the unofficial publications. Take a trip to your local law library. Locate the following volumes.

491 U.S. 397
109 S. Ct. 2533
105 L. Ed. 2d 342

Open all of them to the first page of the *Texas v. Johnson* case. Remember, the first number is the volume number; the second number is the first page of the case. Notice that the prefatory material varies from one publication to the next. You may use any of these volumes during your research.

However, you must cite to the official publication (the U.S.). Notice that the unofficial publications indicate the page breaks for the *U.S. Reports*. That means it is not necessary to read the official publication because you can easily cite to it from the unofficial publications.

Look at Figure 3-4 on page 49. Notice that in the first column the word *prohibited* is broken with what looks like an upside-down T. It is breaking the word *prohibited*, and there is a number following *ited*. This shows that page 398, in the official reporter (U.S.), begins with "ited on the basis that… ."

Look at Figure 3-5 on page 50. Notice at the top just above the petitioner's name it says "[491 US 397]." This publication lets the reader know that the material following the bracketed citation is the beginning of page 397 in the official reporter. Remember, this allows the researcher may use the unofficial publications and still cite to the official publication.

A researcher may quote from material *in* the opinion. A researcher should never quote from anything added by a publisher. That material (the editorial enhancements) is there to help, but it is not part of the decision. Do not cite it.

OTHER FEDERAL REPORTERS

The *Federal Reporter* publishes the United States court of appeals cases for the Federal Circuits. This is an example of a *Federal Reporter* citation:

Free Speech Coalition v. Reno, 220 F.3d 1113 (9th Cir. 2000).

There is no space between the F. and 3d.

The *Federal Supplement* publishes the United States trial court cases for the federal districts. This is an example of a *Federal Supplement* citation:

EEOC v. Rotary Corp., 297 F. Supp. 2d 643 (N.D.N.Y. 2003).

There is a space between F. and Supp.

Table 1 (T.1) of *The Bluebook* lists other reporters of federal case law.

STATE CASE LAW

The Bluebook—*Rule 10*

The Bluebook—Table 1(T.1)

Cite to state case law in the same basic format that the U.S. Supreme Court cases are cited. In many instances, state case law is published in two or three reporters. Some states publish their own case law reporters; those are the official reporters.

Unofficial reporters also publish these cases. For example, in California, the state authorizes one publication of all California Supreme Court and appellate court cases. All California cases are also published in the *California Reporter* (unofficial). In addition, the California Supreme Court cases are included in the *Pacific Reporter*, the regional reporter for California (this is also an unofficial reporter). Be sure to check Table 1 to review the publications and proper abbreviations for the state case law you need to cite.

CHAPTER **SUMMARY**

Case law is primary authority. Attorneys argue cases before courts. Once the legal and factual issues are resolved by the court, the judge writes a decision, often called an *opinion*. The concept of *stare decisis*, or precedent, requires that courts look to what other courts in the same jurisdiction have done with the same or similar legal and factual issues.

Case law is published in large sets of books often referred to as *reporters*. Most states publish their own case law. In addition to the government publications (official reporter), several independent publishers (unofficial reporters) quickly add editorial enhancements and publish well ahead of the government publications. Case law is also easily located on Lexis, Westlaw, and other websites on the Internet.

Learning to cite the law properly is essential. Review of a style manual or the *Uniform System of Citation* is required of anyone citing to legal references. Many citations contain official and unofficial references. All citations must include the short name of the case followed by the volume, the abbreviation for the reporter, the number of the first page of the case, and the year of the decision.

All U.S. Supreme Court cases are published in three separate publications. The official reporter is the *United States Reports* (U.S.). The two unofficial reporters are the *Supreme Court Reporter* (S. Ct.) and the *Lawyers' Edition* (L. Ed.). Other federal case law is found in the *Federal Reporter, Federal Rules Decisions, Federal Supplement,* and various specialized reporters. The Internet is also a good resource for some federal case law.

The state government usually publishes state case law; this is the official reporter. There is also a regional reporter system, which breaks up the United States into geographic regions.

As you read a case, always focus on the six components of a decision: (1) facts, (2) judicial history, (3) issues, (4) rules, (5) analysis, and (6) conclusion. In your research, remain focused on the doctrine of precedent. When you use or cite case law, you must show factual similarities between your client's situation and the case law found in your research.

TERMS TO **REMEMBER**

official citation
secondary sources
style manual
primary authority
decision
opinion
stare decisis
precedent
mandatory authority
binding authority
persuasive authority
dictum
double jeopardy
affirm
reverse
remand
motion
regional reporters
Uniform System of Citation
Lexis
Westlaw
case law reporters
parallel citations
United States Reports
unofficial publication
editorial enhancements
digest topics
key numbers
Supreme Court Reporter
Lawyers' Edition
Federal Reporter
Federal Rules Decisions
Federal Supplement
specialized reporters
official reporters
unofficial reporters
headnote
de-publish

QUESTIONS FOR **REVIEW**

1. Discuss the importance of precedent or *stare decisis*.
2. What is a case law reporter?
3. Explain what is meant by "official citation."
4. Discuss the differences between the three publishers of U.S. Supreme Court case law.
5. What is a parallel citation?
6. Why will a researcher choose to read an unofficial reporter?
7. List, with brief explanations, the various publications of federal case law.
8. What is a regional reporter?
9. List, with brief explanations, the six components of a case.
10. Why is factual analysis so important?

CAN YOU **FIGURE IT OUT?**

1. Which reporter listed in the *Marvin v. Marvin* case citation in Figure 3-1 is the official cite?
2. State four highly relevant facts from *Illinois v. Caballas*.
3. State the factual similarities between the fact pattern in Section 3-8 and *Illinois v. Caballas*.

TEST **YOURSELF** (Check Your Answers in Appendix G)

1. Locate and cite the following U.S. Supreme court cases, including the name, official citation, and the year:

   549 U.S. 1181

   546 U.S. 470

   390 U.S. 400
2. Read the case of *Morse v. Frederick* in Appendix F. Compare the following facts of the Speeker case (Problem 9 in Appendix B) to the facts in *Morse*.
   a. Speeker and her family were attending a community-wide health fair at which the harmful nature of drugs was stressed.
   b. Speeker is a high school student who was promised extra credit by her teachers for attending the health fair.
   c. Speeker was suspended from school for holding a sign reading: Be compassionate, legalize marijuana for medical purposes!

TEST **YOURSELF**—WRITE IT RIGHT Use Short Sentences

Short sentences are the most effective sentences. They are also easy to read. One of a writer's goals should be to craft sentences that do not require re-reading. It is annoying when we must read a sentence more than once. Long sentences tax the reader's ability to stay focused on the meaning of the sentences. Making sure that a sentence has a reasonable proportion of *working words vs. glue words* and that the sentence follows the *actor → action → object format* is a very good start. In addition, we need to keep sentences short.

In legal writing, we need to inform and or persuade. This is best done using short, easy-to-understand sentences.

The following sentence is difficult to read:

> The defendant angered the officer when he slapped at the officer's hand and then reached for the officer's weapon that was at that time still holstered to his belt but then they both struggled for it and it went off injuring the officer's partner who was still standing back waiting to see what would happen next.

This is a 56-word sentence that reads poorly. It needs to be broken apart. For example:

> The defendant angered the officer. The defendant slapped at the officer's hand and he reached for the officer's weapon. The weapon was holstered to the officer's belt. They struggled for the weapon. During the struggle the weapon was fired. The officer's partner was injured while he was standing back during the struggle.

This uses 52 words and 6 sentences. This short sentence approach makes it easy for the reader to follow what happened. Sentences create breaks for the reader. These breaks are necessary if the reader is to easily understand the author's point.

Now, You Try It

(Check your answers in Appendix G)

Break the following sentences into groups of shorter sentences.

1. Here, it can be inferred that Smith would have formally adopted Kilmer earlier in his lifetime "but for" her husband's unwillingness to consent because spousal consent is required in the adoption process, Smith was legally estopped from formally adopting Kilmer.
2. Admittedly, her husband's unwillingness to consent does not alone satisfy the requirement that a legal barrier "must have continued throughout the joint lifetimes of the" claimant and deceased, *In re Joseph*, 17 Cal. 4th 203, 207 (1998); however, Smith was offered only a small window of opportunity to adopt Kilmer following her husband's death and her debilitating cancer, thus satisfying the but-for legal barrier requirement of Cal. Prob. Code section 6454.

CITATION **EXERCISES**

Use the Citation Matters feature in this chapter to answer these questions.

1. When it is appropriate to capitalize "Court"?
2. Which *Bluebook* rule explains U.S. Supreme Court case law citations?
3. What is meant by "unofficial citation"?
4. The *Federal Reporter* publishes:

FROM **THE WRITER'S CORNER** Make Positive Statements

1. Reword the following: He was not happy.
2. Reword the following: That is not important.
3. According to *The Elements of Style,* what makes the following quote effective? "Ask not what your country can do for you—ask what you can do for your country."

ASSIGNMENTS AND **EXERCISES**

Research Exercises

1. Locate the following U.S. Supreme Court cases, preferably in a library, in print. For each case, write the name of the case (the short form of the name), the official citation, and the year. Use the *Uniform System of Citation (Bluebook)* format:

   Gideon v. Wainwright, 372 U.S. 335 (1963).

   Cases to be located:

   491 U.S. 274

   387 U.S. 1

   367 U.S. 568

   384 U.S. 436

   471 U.S. 1
2. Locate and read *Kyllo v. United States*, 533 U.S. 27 (2001). Summarize the case using the components set forth in Section 3-7 of this chapter.

Analysis and Writing Assignments

3. Locate the following case: *Arizona v. Hicks*, 480 U.S. 321 (1980). Read and summarize the case using the components in Section 3-7.
4. Compare the facts of the Justin Meyers case with the facts of *Arizona v. Hicks*.

A Point to Remember

When you receive instructions, be sure to complete each part of the assignment. For example, under Analysis Assignments above, items 1 and 2 require the completion more than one task. In fact, several separate tasks are required: (1) read the *Hicks* case; (2) summarize the case; and (3) compare the facts of the Meyers case with the facts of the *Hicks* case.

Your completed written project should clearly set out the summary and the factual comparison. Avoid making your reader guess what is coming next. Use simple titles or headings (these are Point Headings). Make your written work very easy to follow. Always write for your audience.

Online Research Exercises

1. List at least two online locations where you can locate U.S. Supreme Court cases.
2. Locate the following cases online. For each case, provide the proper name of the case and the year. Following the citation, state the name of the justice who wrote the opinion. If there are concurrences or dissents, list the name of the justice and the type (concurrence or dissent) of opinion he or she wrote.
   a. 466 U.S. 109
   b. 462 U.S. 696
   c. 531 U.S. 32
   d. 533 U.S. 27

CASE **PROJECT**

In-Class Small Group Work

Review the hypothetical case you selected in Chapter 1. List the numerous case reporters that contain mandatory authority for the situation.

chapter **four**

HOW TO READ AND SUMMARIZE A CASE LAW DECISION

CHAPTER OUTLINE

SKILL OBJECTIVES FOR CHAPTER 4

When you complete chapter 4, you should be able to

- Explain the purpose of a case brief.
- List the components of a case brief.
- Describe the components of a case brief.
- Write a simple case brief (summary).
- Explain how to approach a daunting project systematically.

From the Desk of W. J. Bryan, Esq.

TO: Research Assistant
FROM: W. J. Bryan
RE: Our Client Justin Meyers
DATE:

Please read *Minnesota v. Dickerson* (copy attached) and brief it for me. This is a U.S. Supreme Court decision; I have not had time to get to this, and we need to be familiar with the legal reasoning in this case. For now, just read and brief the case. Later we will compare and contrast the *Dickerson* case with our client's facts in the Meyers situation.

4-1 PURPOSE OF A CASE BRIEF

Simply stated, a ***case brief*** is a short summary of a ***reported case***. It serves several purposes. Students of law write case briefs to summarize the cases they read for class in an effort to keep track of the large number of cases they are required to read and analyze. During legal research, case briefs serve to help the researcher keep track of the cases read and analyzed, and may serve as the foundation for legal arguments in ***trial briefs*** or other documents filed with the court. An attorney may hear about a case and ask a research assistant to read and brief or summarize the case. The overall purpose is to summarize the components of a case concisely.

case brief
A short summary of a reported case.

reported case
A published judicial decision.

trial brief
A document submitted to the court; the trial brief contains a statement of facts, the issues, the party's legal argument, and the conclusion.

Recall from Chapter 3 that case law informs and educates the legal community. When we focus on the purpose of case law, it is easier to understand the purpose of a case brief. A well-written case brief simplifies and condenses the reported case. Most case law is written in a basic, simple format using certain components. Once you realize that all cases contain the same or very similar components, the mystery of reading cases (decisions) begins to fade.

4-2 THE COMPONENTS OF A CASE BRIEF

A judge, writing to inform the legal community, has certain goals in every reported case. It is important that the reader of any case understand the following.

- Who are the parties?
- What happened in the lower court(s)—if the case is an appeal?
- What happened to bring these parties into court in the first place?
- What is the legal question before *this* court?
- What rules (primary law) did the court rely on in reaching its decision?
- How did the court analyze the facts in light of the legal question and the rules?
- How did the court resolve the dispute?

These questions lay the foundation for the components of a case brief.

A Point to Remember

Whenever possible, make a hard copy of the case you plan to brief. Note in the margins, for each paragraph, which component (or components) of the brief is included in that paragraph. This technique helps you focus as you read and provides organization as you begin writing the brief. Remember that highlighting the various components helps you visualize the different case components. Many computers utilize software that allows the user to make margins notes and highlight the text. If this works better for you, then a hard copy is not necessary.

These components may be divided into the following elements: name and citation of the case, judicial history, facts, issue(s), rule(s), analysis/reasoning, and holding.

Name and Citation of the Case

The name of the case, the citation, and the year are essential. Always provide the name and full citation of the case at the beginning of the case brief.

When you cite a U.S. Supreme Court case, you need only give the official citation. However, in a case brief you may want to include the full citation, including parallel citations. This way a reader may use any one of the three publications of U.S. Supreme Court case law. Many legal researchers prefer one publication over another.

Judicial History/Procedural History

The judicial history (sometimes referred to as the procedural history) explains how the case traveled through the courts. The reader of the brief needs to understand who sued whom and why. Let the reader know what happened in each of the courts. Consider using no more than one sentence for the outcome of each lower court. Avoid explaining why the courts made certain decisions. The focus of a case brief must be on what *this* reviewing court decides.

Facts

Include only the facts that are relevant to the court's reasoning and decision. Tell a story about what happened to bring these parties before the court. If possible, tell a story about people. Leave the legal terminology *out* of this section. In general, names are not helpful. The role of the person is helpful. For example, the roles, "nurse" and "patient," are often better than the names, Mr. Ross Shelty and Mr. Ronald Row. Ultimately, the reader needs to understand the role of the party, not the name.

Issue(s)

The issue is the question presented to *this* court for resolution. Each issue should be one sentence long and is best written as a question. Most cases have judicial history. This means that lower courts already adjudicated this case. The case you are briefing is probably an appeal of what the lower court decided. Many times the issue is stated in the format of "Did the lower court err when it held … ?" This issue asks: "Did the last court to hear this case make one or more mistakes in its resolution of the legal issues?" Many times courts (and legal writers) begin the issue statement with the word *whether* when this issue format is used, and there is no question mark at the end. Thus, the issue becomes a statement.

Rule(s)

The rules section is usually a listing of the laws the court relied on in the analysis or reasoning. This might include statutes, case law, articles or amendments from the Constitution, or other ***primary sources*** of the law. This section does not include every source discussed by the court, just the relevant primary sources. Each constitutional reference and statute, and the cases most relied upon by the court, should receive a very brief statement including the title of the constitutional reference, the topic of the statute, and the relevance of the case law cited. A separate rules section is not necessary when the brief writer includes the rules in the Analysis or Reasoning section.

primary sources
A work that contains the law.

Analysis or Reasoning

This is the lengthiest and the most important section of most case briefs. The analysis *incorporates* much of the information from the facts, issues, and rules into a focused discussion. This is an application of the rules of law to the facts of the case. If you are asked to read and brief a case for someone else, that person did not read the case. The reader must understand why the court resolved the issues as it did. This section never includes the writer's personal analysis or opinions. Think of the analysis as a summary of how the court analyzed the facts and issues. Notice the laws used or discussed by the court. All of this provides the court's ***rationale*** or reasoning supporting its ultimate holding or conclusion.

rationale
The reasoning or explanation for the court's ultimate resolution of the case.

Holding

The conclusion or ***holding*** is the court's answer to the issue or question presented and the action taken by the court. Each issue has an answer. It is easiest to list each issue with its answer. Keep this section short and to the point. This is not a discussion section.

holding
The legal principle to be taken from the court's decision.

A Point to Remember

A case brief does not include the writer's personal opinion. The brief is a summary of (1) what the court held and (2) why the court held as it did. There is no room for the pronoun "I" in a good case brief. Pay close attention to the facts stressed by the court. Notice when one or more facts are discussed at length or in more than one context. This is a clue for the reader that the court views these facts as relevant; they are essential to an overall understanding of the case.

Apply the notes-in-the-margin technique from Chapter 3 with the *Gideon v. Wainwright* case. As you read the case, locate the following:

The name and the citation of the case: Name of litigants and correct legal citation for this reported case.

The judicial history: What happened in the lower court(s)?

The facts: What happened to bring the parties before the Court?

The issues: What is the legal question before *this* Court?

The rules: What rules (primary law) did the court rely on in reaching its decision?

The analysis: How did the court analyze the facts in light of the legal question and the rules?

The holding/conclusion: How did the Court resolve the dispute?

When we look only at the topic sentences for *Gideon v. Wainwright,* the case condenses to this:

- Petitioner was charged in a Florida state court with having broken and entered a poolroom with intent to commit a misdemeanor.
- "The COURT: Mr. Gideon, I am sorry, but I cannot appoint Counsel to represent you in this case."
- "The DEFENDANT: The United States Supreme Court says I am entitled to be represented by Counsel."
- Put to trial before a jury, Gideon conducted his defense about as well as could be expected from a layman.
- The facts upon which Betts claimed that he had been unconstitutionally denied the right to have counsel appointed to assist him are strikingly like the facts upon which Gideon here bases his federal constitutional claim.
- "Asserted denial [of due process] is to be tested by an appraisal of the totality of facts in a given case."
- Treating due process as a "concept less rigid and more fluid than those envisaged in other specific and particular provisions of the Bill of Rights," the Court held that refusal to appoint counsel under the particular facts and circumstances in the *Betts* case was not so "offensive to the common and fundamental ideas of fairness" as to amount to a denial of due process.
- The Sixth Amendment provides, "In all criminal prosecutions, the accused shall enjoy the right … to have the Assistance of Counsel for his defense."
- We think the Court in *Betts* had ample precedent for acknowledging that those guarantees of the Bill of Rights, which are fundamental safeguards of liberty immune from federal abridgment, are equally protected against state invasion by the Due Process Clause of the Fourteenth Amendment.
- We accept *Betts v. Brady*'s assumption, based as it was on our prior cases, that a provision of the Bill of Rights, which is "fundamental and essential to a fair trial," is made obligatory upon the States by the Fourteenth Amendment.
- "We concluded that certain fundamental rights, safeguarded by the first eight amendments against federal action, were also safeguarded against state action by the due process of law clause of the Fourteenth Amendment, and among them the fundamental right of the accused to the aid of counsel in a criminal prosecution."
- And again in 1938 this Court said: "[The assistance of counsel] is one of the safeguards of the Sixth Amendment deemed necessary to insure fundamental human right of life and liberty… . The Sixth Amendment stands as a constant admonition that if the constitutional safeguards it provides be lost, justice will not 'still be done.' "
- In light of these and many other prior decisions of this Court, it is not surprising that the *Betts* Court, when faced with the contention that "one charged

with crime, who is unable to obtain counsel, must be furnished counsel by the State," conceded that "expressions in the opinions of this court lend color to the argument. . . . "

- "The right to be heard would be, in many cases, of little avail if it did not comprehend the right to be heard by counsel."
- The Court in *Betts v. Brady* departed from the sound wisdom upon which the Court's holding in *Powell v. Alabama* rested.
- The judgment is reversed and the cause is remanded to the Supreme Court of Florida for further action not inconsistent with this opinion.

A review of the topic sentences provides an excellent overview and introduction to the case. Notice how many of the six case components are touched upon in the topic sentences. You are now ready to read and fully understand *Gideon v. Wainwright.* Reading these 16 sentences, before reading the entire decision, is time well spent.

CASE 4-1 *Gideon v. Wainwright,* 372 U.S. 335 (1963)

SYLLABUS

Charged in a Florida State Court with a non-capital felony, petitioner appeared without funds and without counsel and asked the Court to appoint counsel for him; but this was denied on the ground that the state law permitted appointment of counsel for indigent defendants in capital cases only. Petitioner conducted his own defense about as well as could be expected of a layman; but he was convicted and sentenced to imprisonment. Subsequently, he applied to the State Supreme Court for a writ of *habeas corpus,* on the ground that his conviction violated his rights under the Federal Constitution. The State Supreme Court denied all relief.

Held

The right of an indigent defendant in a criminal trial to have the assistance of counsel is a fundamental right essential to a fair trial, and petitioner's trial and conviction without the assistance of counsel violated the Fourteenth Amendment. *Betts v. Brady,* 316 U.S. 455.

OPINION: MR. JUSTICE BLACK delivered the opinion of the Court.

Petitioner was charged in a Florida state court with having broken and entered a poolroom with intent to commit a misdemeanor. This offense is a felony under Florida law. Appearing in court without funds and without a lawyer, petitioner asked the court to appoint counsel for him, whereupon the following colloquy took place:

"The COURT: Mr. Gideon, I am sorry, but I cannot appoint Counsel to represent you in this case. Under the laws of the State of Florida, the only time the Court can appoint Counsel to represent a Defendant is when that person is charged with a capital offense. I am sorry, but I will have to deny your request to appoint Counsel to defend you in this case."

"The DEFENDANT: The United States Supreme Court says I am entitled to be represented by Counsel."

Put to trial before a jury, Gideon conducted his defense about as well as could be expected from a layman. He made an opening statement to the jury, cross-examined the State's witnesses, presented witnesses in his own defense, declined to testify himself, and made a short argument "emphasizing his innocence to the charge contained in the Information filed in this case." The jury returned a verdict of guilty, and petitioner was sentenced to serve five years in the state prison. Later, petitioner filed in the Florida Supreme Court this *habeas corpus* petition attacking his conviction and sentence on the ground that the trial court's refusal to appoint counsel for him denied him rights "guaranteed by the Constitution and the Bill of Rights by the United States Government." Treating the petition for *habeas corpus* as properly before it, the State Supreme Court, "upon consideration thereof" but without an opinion, denied all relief. Since 1942, when *Betts v. Brady*, 316 U.S. 455, was decided by a divided Court, the problem of a defendant's federal constitutional right to counsel in a state court has been a continuing source of controversy and litigation in both state and federal courts. To give this problem another review here, we granted *certiorari*. 370 U.S. 908. Since Gideon was proceeding *in forma pauperis*, we appointed counsel to represent him and requested both sides to discuss in their briefs and oral arguments the following: "Should this Court's holding in *Betts v. Brady*, 316 U.S. 455, be reconsidered?"

I.

The facts upon which Betts claimed that he had been unconstitutionally denied the right to have counsel appointed to assist him are strikingly like the facts upon which Gideon here bases his federal constitutional claim. Betts was indicted for robbery in a Maryland state court. On arraignment, he told the trial judge of his lack of funds to hire a lawyer and asked the court to appoint one for him. Betts was advised that it was not the practice in that country to appoint counsel for indigent defendants except in murder and rape cases. He then pleaded not guilty, had witnesses summoned, cross-examined the State's witnesses, examined his own, and chose not to testify himself. He was found guilty by the judge, sitting without a jury, and sentenced to eight years in prison. Like Gideon, Betts sought release by *habeas corpus*, alleging that he had been denied the right to assistance of counsel in violation of the Fourteenth Amendment. Betts was denied any relief, and on review this Court affirmed. It was held that a refusal to appoint counsel for an indigent defendant charged with a felony did not necessarily violate the Due Process Clause of the Fourteenth Amendment, which for reasons given the Court deemed to be the only applicable federal constitutional provision. The Court said:

"Asserted denial [of due process] is to be tested by an appraisal of the totality of facts in a given case. That which may, in one setting, constitute a denial of fundamental fairness, shocking to the universal sense of justice, may, in other circumstances, and in the light of other considerations, fall short of such denial." 316 U.S. at 462.

Treating due process as "a concept less rigid and more fluid than those envisaged in other specific and particular provisions of the Bill of Rights," the Court held that refusal to appoint counsel under the particular facts and circumstances in the *Betts* case was not so "offensive to the common and fundamental ideas of fairness" as to amount to a denial of due process. Since the facts and circumstances of the two cases are so nearly indistinguishable, we think the *Betts v. Brady* holding if left standing would require us to reject Gideon's claim that the Constitution guarantees him the assistance of counsel. Upon full reconsideration we conclude that *Betts v. Brady* should be overruled.

II.

The Sixth Amendment provides, "In all criminal prosecutions, the accused shall enjoy the right... to have the Assistance of Counsel for his defense." We have construed this to mean that in federal courts counsel must be provided for defendants unable to employ counsel unless the right is competently and intelligently waived. Betts argued that this right is extended to indigent defendants in state courts by the Fourteenth Amendment. In response the Court stated that, while the Sixth Amendment laid down "no rule for the conduct of the States, the question recurs whether the constraint laid by the Amendment upon the national courts expresses a rule so fundamental and essential to a fair trial, and so, to due process of law, that it is made obligatory upon the States by the Fourteenth Amendment." 316 U.S. at 465. In order to decide whether the Sixth Amendment's guarantee of counsel is of this fundamental nature, the Court in *Betts* set out and considered "relevant data on the subject ...afforded by constitutional and statutory provisions subsisting in the colonies and the States prior to the inclusion of the Bill of Rights in the national Constitution, and in the constitutional, legislative, and judicial history of the States to the present date." 316 U.S. at 465. On the basis of this historical data the Court concluded that "appointment of counsel is not a fundamental right, essential to a fair trial." 316 U.S. at 471. It was for this reason the *Betts* Court refused to accept the contention that the Sixth Amendment's guarantee of counsel for indigent federal defendants was extended to or, in the words of that Court, "made obligatory upon the States by the Fourteenth Amendment." Plainly, had the Court concluded that appointment of counsel for an indigent criminal defendant was "a fundamental right, essential to a fair trial," it would have held that the Fourteenth Amendment requires appointment of counsel in a state court, just as the Sixth Amendment requires in a federal court.

We think the Court in *Betts* had ample precedent for acknowledging that those guarantees of the Bill of Rights which are fundamental safeguards of liberty immune from federal abridgment are equally protected against state invasion by the Due Process Clause of the Fourteenth Amendment. This same principle was recognized, explained, and applied in *Powell v. Alabama*, 287 U.S. 45 (1932), a case upholding the right of counsel, where the Court held that despite sweeping language to the contrary in *Hurtado v. California*, 110 U.S. 516 (1884), the Fourteenth Amendment "embraced" those "fundamental principles of liberty and justice which lie at the base of all our civil and political institutions," even though they had been "specifically dealt with in another part of the federal Constitution." 287 U.S. at 67. In many cases other than *Powell* and *Betts*, this Court has looked to the fundamental nature of original Bill of Rights guarantees to decide whether the Fourteenth Amendment makes them obligatory on the States. Explicitly recognized to be of this "fundamental nature" and therefore made immune from state invasion by the Fourteenth, or some part of it, are the First Amendment's freedoms of speech, press, religion, assembly, association, and petition for redress of grievances. For the same reason, though not always in precisely the same terminology, the Court has made obligatory on the States the Fifth Amendment's command that private property shall not be taken for public use without just compensation, the Fourth Amendment's prohibition of unreasonable searches and seizures, and the Eighth's ban on cruel and unusual punishment. On the other hand, this

Court in *Palko v. Connecticut*, 302 U.S. 319 (1937), refused to hold that the Fourteenth Amendment made the double jeopardy provision of the Fifth Amendment obligatory on the States. In so refusing, however, the Court, speaking through Mr. Justice Cardozo, was careful to emphasize that "immunities that are valid as against the federal government by force of the specific pledges of particular amendments have been found to be implicit in the concept of ordered liberty, and thus, through the Fourteenth Amendment, become valid as against the states" and that guarantees "in their origin ... effective against the federal government alone" had by prior cases "been taken over from the earlier articles of the federal bill of rights and brought within the Fourteenth Amendment by a process of absorption." 302 U.S. at 324–325, 326.

We accept *Betts v. Brady's* assumption, based as it was on our prior cases, that a provision of the Bill of Rights which is "fundamental and essential to a fair trial" is made obligatory upon the States by the Fourteenth Amendment. We think the Court in *Betts* was wrong, however, in concluding that the Sixth Amendment's guarantee of counsel is not one of these fundamental rights. Ten years before *Betts v. Brady*, this Court, after full consideration of all the historical data examined in *Betts*, had unequivocally declared that "the right to the aid of counsel is of this fundamental character." *Powell v. Alabama*, 287 U.S. 45, 68 (1932). While the Court at the close of its *Powell* opinion did by its language, as this Court frequently does, limit its holding to the particular facts and circumstances of that case, its conclusions about the fundamental nature of the right to counsel are unmistakable. Several years later, in 1936, the Court reemphasized what it had said about the fundamental nature of the right to counsel in this language:

"We concluded that certain fundamental rights, safeguarded by the first eight amendments against federal action, were also safeguarded against state action by the due process of law clause of the Fourteenth Amendment, and among them the fundamental right of the accused to the aid of counsel in a criminal prosecution." 297 U.S. 233, 243–244 (1936).

And again in 1938 this Court said:

"[The assistance of counsel] is one of the safeguards of the Sixth Amendment deemed necessary to insure fundamental human rights of life and liberty.... The Sixth Amendment stands as a constant admonition that if the constitutional safeguards it provides be lost, justice will not 'still be done.' " *Johnson v. Zerbst*, 304 U.S. 458, 462 (1938). To the same effect, *see Avery v. Alabama*, 308 U.S. 444 (1940), and *Smith v. O'Grady*, 312 U.S. 329 (1941).

In light of these and many other prior decisions of this Court, it is not surprising that the *Betts* Court, when faced with the contention that "one charged with crime, who is unable to obtain counsel, must be furnished counsel by the State," conceded that "expressions in the opinions of this court lend color to the argument.... " 316 U.S. at 462–463. The fact is that in deciding as it did—that "appointment of counsel is not a fundamental right, essential to a fair trial"—the Court in *Betts v. Brady* made an abrupt break with its own well-considered precedents. In returning to these old precedents, sounder we believe than the new, we but restore constitutional principles established to achieve a fair system of justice. Not only these precedents but also reason and reflection require us to recognize that in our adversary system of criminal justice, any person haled into court, who is too poor to hire a lawyer, cannot be assured a fair trial unless counsel is provided for him. This seems to us to be an obvious truth. Governments, both state and federal, quite properly spend vast sums of money to establish machinery to try defendants accused of crime. Lawyers to prosecute are everywhere deemed essential to protect the public's interest in an orderly society. Similarly, there are few defendants charged with crime, few indeed, who fail to hire the best lawyers they can get to prepare and present their defenses. That government hires lawyers to prosecute and defendants who have the money hire lawyers to defend are the strongest indications of the widespread belief that lawyers in criminal courts are necessities, not luxuries. The right of one charged with crime to counsel may not be deemed fundamental and essential to fair trials in some countries, but it is in ours. From the very beginning, our state and national constitutions and laws have laid great emphasis on procedural and substantive safeguards designed to assure fair trials before impartial tribunals in which every defendant stands equal before the law. This noble ideal cannot be realized if the poor man charged with crime has to face his accusers without a lawyer to assist him. A defendant's need for a lawyer is nowhere better stated than in the moving words of Mr. Justice Sutherland in *Powell v. Alabama:*

"The right to be heard would be, in many cases, of little avail if it did not comprehend the right to be heard by counsel. Even the intelligent and educated layman has small and sometimes no skill in the science of law. If charged with crime, he is incapable, generally, of determining for himself whether the indictment is good or bad. He is unfamiliar with the rules of evidence. Left without the aid of counsel he may be put on trial without a proper charge, and convicted upon incompetent evidence, or evidence irrelevant to the issue or otherwise inadmissible. He lacks both the skill and knowledge adequately to prepare his defense, even though he have a perfect one. He requires the guiding hand of counsel at every step in the proceedings against him. Without it, though he be not guilty, he faces the danger of conviction because he does not know how to establish his innocence." 287 U.S. at 68–69.

The Court in *Betts v. Brady* departed from the sound wisdom upon which the Court's holding in *Powell v. Alabama* rested. Florida, supported by two other States, has asked that *Betts v. Brady* be left intact. Twenty-two States, as friends of the Court, argue that Betts was "an anachronism when handed down" and that it should now be overruled. We agree.

The judgment is reversed and the cause is remanded to the Supreme Court of Florida for further action not inconsistent with this opinion.

Reversed.

4-3 HOW TO WRITE A CASE BRIEF

Each component should be set forth as a separate section of the case brief. Paragraphs explaining the component follow each section heading. The analysis, or reasoning, section combines or synthesizes much of what is included in the facts, issues, and rules sections. Again, think of this as an application of the rule of law to the fact of the case. As a writer, you may detect that there is a certain degree of redundancy in a completed case brief.

A brief or summary of the *Gideon* case might look like this:

Gideon v. Wainwright, **372 U.S. 335 (1963)**

Judicial History
The trial court denied Gideon's request for appointment of defense counsel. As a result of this denial, he conducted his own defense. The jury found him guilty. The Florida State Supreme Court denied Gideon's request for relief.

Facts
Gideon was charged with breaking and entering a poolroom. He appeared for trial without counsel. He asked the court to appoint counsel for him; his request was denied. Gideon conducted his own defense.

Issues

1. Were Gideon's rights under the Fourteenth Amendment violated when, as an indigent defendant in a state criminal trial, he was denied assistance of counsel?
2. Should *Betts v. Brady* be overruled? (This issue was raised by the Court. Both parties were asked to argue this issue.)

Rules
Fourteenth Amendment: Due Process Clause
Sixth Amendment: "In all criminal prosecutions, the accused shall enjoy the right ... to have the Assistance of Counsel for his defense."
Betts v. Brady, 316 U.S. 455 (1942): "appointment of counsel is not a fundamental right, essential to a fair trial... ." (*Betts* is reconsidered by the Court in *Gideon* and overruled.)
Powell v. Alabama, 287 U.S. 45 (1932): the right to counsel is fundamental and essential to a fair trial. (Followed in *Gideon.*)

Analysis
The facts of the *Gideon* case are very similar to the facts of the *Betts v. Brady* case. The *Betts* case held that "a refusal to appoint counsel for an indigent defendant charged with a felony did not necessarily violate the due process clause of the Fourteenth Amendment." The Court overruled *Betts v. Brady*. Relying on the Sixth Amendment, the Court held that "counsel must be provided for defendants unable to employ counsel unless the right is competently and intelligently waived." The fundamental safeguards of liberty are protected by the due process clause of the Fourteenth Amendment. The Sixth Amendment guarantee of counsel is one of these fundamental safeguards. The Court cites the sound wisdom upon which the *Powell v. Alabama* case was decided. In *Powell,* the Court explained that a criminal defendant needs the "guiding hand of counsel at every step in the proceedings against him."

Conclusion
The judgment of the Florida State Supreme Court was reversed. The cause was remanded to the Florida courts for "further action not inconsistent with this opinion." *Betts v. Brady* was overruled.

This is only one approach to briefing the *Gideon* case. No two people will write exactly the same brief, and the actual format for the brief may differ, but the information contained generally falls into the categories set forth in this sample brief. The following case brief contains the same basic information, but it is arranged differently.

Gideon v. Wainwright, 372 U.S. 335 (1963)

Facts

Gideon was charged with breaking and entering a poolroom. He appeared for trial without counsel. He asked the court to appoint counsel for him; his request was denied. Gideon conducted his own defense. The jury found him guilty. The Florida State Supreme Court denied Gideon's request for relief.

Issues

1. Were Gideon's rights under the Fourteenth Amendment violated when, as an indigent defendant in a state criminal trial, he was denied assistance of counsel?
2. Should *Betts v. Brady* be overruled? (This issue was raised by the Court. Both parties were asked to argue this issue.)

Holding

The judgment of the Florida State Supreme Court was reversed. The cause was remanded to the Florida courts for "further action not inconsistent with this opinion." *Betts v. Brady* was overruled.

Rationale

The facts of the *Gideon* case are very similar to the facts of the *Betts v. Brady*, 316 U.S. 455 (1942) case. The *Betts* case held that "a refusal to appoint counsel for an indigent defendant charged with a felony did not necessarily violate the due process clause of the Fourteenth Amendment." The Court overruled *Betts v. Brady*. Relying on the Sixth Amendment, the Court found that "counsel must be provided for defendants unable to employ counsel unless the right is competently and intelligently waived." The fundamental safeguards of liberty are protected by the due process clause of the Fourteenth Amendment. The Sixth Amendment guarantee of counsel is one of these fundamental safeguards. The Court cites the sound wisdom upon which the *Powell v. Alabama*, 287 U.S. 45 (1932) case was decided. In *Powell*, the Court explained that a criminal defendant needs the "guiding hand of counsel at every step in the proceedings against him."

A Point to Remember

Some cases include concurring opinions and dissenting opinions. Include a section explaining the concurrence or dissent only if there is something of importance that the reader needs to know. Read *Minnesota v. Dickerson*. Take notes on the judicial history, facts, issues, rules, analysis, and conclusion/holding. Color highlight the six components of a case to help you visualize the patterns in the decision.

CASE 4-2 *Minnesota v. Dickerson*, 508 U.S. 366 (1993)

JUSTICE WHITE delivered the opinion of the Court.

In this case, we consider whether the Fourth Amendment permits the seizure of contraband detected through a police officer's sense of touch during a protective patdown search.

I

On the evening of November 9, 1989, two Minneapolis police officers were patrolling an area on the city's north side in a marked squad car. At about 8:15 p.m., one of the officers observed respondent leaving a 12-unit apartment building on Morgan Avenue North. The officer, having previously responded to complaints of drug sales in the building's hallways and having executed several search warrants on the premises, considered the building to be a notorious "crack house." According to testimony credited by the trial court, respondent began walking toward the police but, upon spotting the squad car and making eye contact with one of the officers, abruptly halted and began walking in the opposite direction. His suspicion aroused, this officer watched as respondent turned and entered an alley on the other side of the apartment building. Based upon respondent's seemingly evasive actions and the fact that he had just left a building known for cocaine traffic, the officers decided to stop respondent and investigate further.

The officers pulled their squad car into the alley and ordered respondent to stop and submit to a patdown search. The search revealed no weapons, but the officer conducting the search did take an interest in a small lump in respondent's nylon jacket. The officer later testified:

"As I pat-searched the front of his body, I felt a lump, a small lump, in the front pocket. I examined it with my fingers and it slid and it felt to be a lump of crack cocaine in cellophane." Tr. 9 (Feb. 20, 1990).

The officer then reached into respondent's pocket and retrieved a small plastic bag containing one fifth of one gram of crack cocaine. Respondent was arrested and charged in Hennepin County District Court with possession of a controlled substance.

Before trial, respondent moved to suppress the cocaine. The trial court first concluded that the officers were justified under *Terry v. Ohio*, 392 U.S. 1, 20 L. Ed. 2d 889, 88 S. Ct. 1868 (1968), in stopping respondent to investigate whether he might be engaged in criminal activity. The court further found that the officers were justified in frisking respondent to ensure that he was not carrying a weapon. Finally, analogizing to the "plain-view" doctrine, under which officers may make a warrantless seizure of contraband found in plain view during a lawful search for other items, the trial court ruled that the officers' seizure of the cocaine did not violate the Fourth Amendment:

"To this Court there is no distinction as to which sensory perception the officer uses to conclude that the material is contraband. An experienced officer may rely upon his sense of smell in DWI stops or in recognizing the smell of burning marijuana in an automobile. The sound of a shotgun being racked would clearly support certain reactions by an officer. The sense of touch, grounded in experience and training, is as reliable as perceptions drawn from other senses. 'Plain feel,' therefore, is no different than plain view and will equally support the seizure here." App. to Pet. for Cert. C-5.

His suppression motion having failed, respondent proceeded to trial and was found guilty. On appeal, the Minnesota Court of Appeals reversed. The court agreed with the trial court that the investigative stop and protective patdown search of respondent were lawful under *Terry* because the officers had a reasonable belief based on specific and articulable facts that respondent was engaged in criminal behavior and that he might be armed and dangerous. The court concluded, however, that the officers had overstepped the bounds allowed by *Terry* in seizing the cocaine. In doing so, the Court of Appeals "decline[d] to adopt the plain feel exception" to the warrant requirement.469 N.W.2d 462, 466 (1991).

The Minnesota Supreme Court affirmed. Like the Court of Appeals, the State Supreme Court held that both the stop and the frisk of respondent were valid under *Terry*, but found the seizure of the cocaine to be unconstitutional. The court expressly refused "to extend the plain view doctrine to the sense of touch" on the grounds that "the sense of touch is inherently less immediate and less reliable than the sense of sight" and that "the sense of touch is far more intrusive into the personal privacy that is at the core of the Fourth Amendment." 481 N.W.2d 840, 845 (1992). The court thus appeared to adopt a categorical rule barring the seizure of any contraband detected by an officer through the sense of touch during a patdown search for weapons. The court further noted that "even if we recognized a 'plain feel' exception, the search in this case would not qualify" because "the pat search of the defendant went far beyond what is permissible under *Terry*."*Id*. at 843, 844, n.1. As the State Supreme Court read the record, the officer conducting the search ascertained that the lump in respondent's jacket was contraband only after probing and investigating what he certainly knew was not a weapon. *See id*., at 844.

We granted certiorari, 506 U.S. 814 (1992), to resolve a conflict among the state and federal courts over whether contraband detected through the sense of touch during a patdown search may be admitted into evidence. We now affirm.

II

A

The Fourth Amendment, made applicable to the States by way of the Fourteenth Amendment, *Mapp v. Ohio*, 367 U.S. 643, 6 L. Ed. 2d 1081, 81 S. Ct. 1684 (1961), guarantees "the right of the people to be secure in their persons, houses, papers, and effects, against unreasonable searches and seizures." Time and again, this Court has observed that searches and seizures " 'conducted outside the judicial process, without prior approval by judge or magistrate, are *per se* unreasonable under the Fourth Amendment—subject only to a few specifically established and well delineated exceptions.' " *Thompson v. Louisiana*, 469 U.S. 17, 19–20, 83 L. Ed. 2d 246, 105 S. Ct. 409 (1984) *(per curiam)* (quoting *Katz v. United States*, 389 U.S. 347, 357, 19 L. Ed. 2d 576, 88 S. Ct. 507 (1967) (footnotes omitted)); *Mincey v. Arizona*, 437 U.S. 385, 390, 57 L. Ed. 2d 290, 98 S. Ct. 2408 (1978); *see also United States v. Place*, 462 U.S. 696, 701, 77 L. Ed. 2d 110, 103 S. Ct. 2637 (1983). One such exception was recognized in *Terry v. Ohio*, 392 U.S. 1, 20 L. Ed. 2d 889, 88 S. Ct. 1868 (1968), which held that "where a police officer observes unusual conduct which leads him reasonably to conclude in light of his experience that criminal activity may be afoot ... ," the officer may briefly stop the suspicious person and make "reasonable inquiries" aimed at confirming or dispelling his suspicions. *Id*., at 30; *see also Adams v. Williams*, 407 U.S. 143, 145–146, 32 L. Ed. 2d 612, 92 S. Ct. 1921 (1972).

Terry further held that "when an officer is justified in believing that the individual whose suspicious behavior he is investigating at close range is armed and presently dangerous to the officer or to others," the officer may conduct a patdown search "to determine whether the person is in fact carrying a weapon." 392 U.S. at 24. "The purpose of this limited search is not to discover evidence of crime, but to allow the officer to pursue his investigation without fear of violence... ." *Adams, supra*, at 146. Rather, a protective search—permitted without a warrant and on the basis of reasonable suspicion less than probable cause—must be strictly "limited to that which is necessary for the discovery of weapons which might be used to harm the officer or others nearby." *Terry, supra*, at 26; see also *Michigan v. Long*, 463 U.S. 1032, 1049, 77 L. Ed. 2d 1201, 103 S. Ct. 3469, and 1052, n.16 (1983); *Ybarra v. Illinois*, 444 U.S. 85, 93–94, 62 L. Ed. 2d 238, 100 S. Ct. 338 (1979). If the protective search goes beyond what is necessary to determine if the suspect is armed, it is no longer valid under *Terry* and its fruits will be suppressed. *Sibron v. New York*, 392 U.S. 40, 65–66, 20 L. Ed. 2d 917, 88 S. Ct. 1889 (1968).

These principles were settled 25 years ago when, on the same day, the Court announced its decisions in *Terry* and *Sibron*. The question presented today is whether police officers may seize nonthreatening contraband detected during a protective patdown search of the sort permitted by *Terry*. We think the answer is clearly that they may, so long as the officers' search stays within the bounds marked by *Terry*.

B

We have already held that police officers, at least under certain circumstances, may seize contraband detected during the lawful execution of a *Terry* search. In *Michigan v. Long, supra*, for example, police approached a man who had driven his car into a ditch and who appeared to be under the influence of some intoxicant. As the man moved to reenter the car from the roadside, police spotted a knife on the floor-board. The officers stopped the man, subjected him to a patdown search, and then inspected the interior of the vehicle for other weapons. During the search of the passenger compartment, the police discovered an open pouch containing marijuana and seized it. This Court upheld the validity of the search and seizure under *Terry*. The Court held first that, in the context of a roadside encounter, where police have reasonable suspicion based on specific and articulable facts to believe that a driver may be armed and dangerous, they may conduct a protective search for weapons not only of the driver's person but also of the passenger compartment of the automobile. 463 U.S. at 1049. Of course, the protective search of the vehicle, being justified solely by the danger that weapons stored there could be used against the officers or bystanders, must be "limited to those areas in which a weapon may be placed or hidden." *Ibid.* The Court then held: "If, while conducting a legitimate *Terry* search of the interior of the automobile, the officer should, as here, discover contraband other than weapons, he clearly cannot be required to ignore the contraband, and the Fourth Amendment does not require its suppression in such circumstances." *Id.* at 1050; accord, *Sibron*, 392 U.S. at 69–70 (WHITE, J., concurring); *id.*, at 79 (Harlan, J., concurring in result).

The Court in *Long* justified this latter holding by reference to our cases under the "plain-view" doctrine. *See Long, supra*, at 1050; *see also United States v. Hensley*, 469 U.S. 221, 235, 83 L. Ed. 2d 604, 105 S. Ct. 675 (1985) (upholding plain-view seizure in context of *Terry* stop). Under that doctrine, if police are lawfully in a position from which they view an object, if its incriminating character is immediately apparent, and if the officers have a lawful right of access to the object, they may seize it without a warrant. *See Horton v. California*, 496 U.S. 128, 136–137, 110 L. Ed. 2d 112, 110 S. Ct. 2301 (1990); *Texas v. Brown*, 460 U.S. 730, 739, 75 L. Ed. 2d 502, 103 S. Ct. 1535 (1983) (plurality opinion). If, however, the police lack probable cause to believe that an object in plain view is contraband without conducting some further search of the object—*i.e.*, if "its incriminating character [is not] 'immediately apparent,'" *Horton, supra*, at 136—the plain-view doctrine cannot justify its seizure. *Arizona v. Hicks*, 480 U.S. 321, 94 L. Ed. 2d 347, 107 S. Ct. 1149 (1987).

We think that this doctrine has an obvious application by analogy to cases in which an officer discovers contraband through the sense of touch during an otherwise lawful search. The rationale of the plain-view doctrine is that if contraband is left in open view and is observed by a police officer from a lawful vantage point, there has been no invasion of a legitimate expectation of privacy and thus no "search" within the meaning of the Fourth Amendment—or at least no search independent of the initial intrusion that gave the officers their vantage point. *See Illinois v. Andreas*, 463 U.S. 765, 771, 77 L. Ed. 2d 1003, 103 S. Ct. 3319 (1983); *Texas v. Brown, supra*, at 740. The warrantless seizure of contraband that presents itself in this manner is deemed justified by the realization that resort to a neutral magistrate under such circumstances would often be impracticable and would do little to promote the objectives of the Fourth Amendment. *See Hicks, supra*, at 326–327; *Coolidge v. New Hampshire*, 403 U.S. 443, 467–468, 469–470, 29 L. Ed. 2d 564, 91 S. Ct. 2022 (1971) (opinion of Stewart, J.). The same can be said of tactile discoveries of contraband. If a police officer lawfully pats down a suspect's outer clothing and feels an object whose contour or mass makes its identity immediately apparent, there has been no invasion of the suspect's privacy beyond that already authorized by the officer's search for weapons; if the object is contraband, its warrantless seizure would be justified by the same practical considerations that inhere [*sic*] in the plain-view context.

The Minnesota Supreme Court rejected an analogy to the plain-view doctrine on two grounds: first, its belief that "the sense of touch is inherently less immediate and less reliable than the sense of sight," and second, that "the sense of touch is far more intrusive into the personal privacy that is at the core of the Fourth Amendment," 481 N.W.2d at 845. We have a somewhat different view. First, *Terry* itself demonstrates that the sense of touch is capable of revealing the nature of an object with sufficient reliability to support a seizure. The very premise of *Terry*, after all, is that officers will be able to detect the presence of weapons through the sense of touch and *Terry* upheld precisely such a seizure. Even if it were true that the sense of touch is generally less reliable than the sense of sight, that only suggests that officers will less often be able to justify seizures of unseen contraband. Regardless of whether the officer detects the contraband by sight or by touch, however, the Fourth Amendment's requirement that the officer have probable cause to believe that the item is contraband before seizing it ensures against excessively speculative seizures. The court's second concern—that touch is more intrusive into privacy than is sight—is inapposite in light of the fact that the intrusion the court fears has already been authorized by the lawful search for weapons. The seizure of an item whose identity is already known occasions no further invasion of privacy. *See Soldal v. Cook County*, 506 U.S. 56, 66, 121 L. Ed. 2d 450, 113 S. Ct. 538 (1992); *Horton, supra*, at 141; *United States v. Jacobsen*, 466 U.S. 109, 120, 80 L. Ed. 2d 85, 104 S. Ct. 1652 (1984). Accordingly, the suspect's privacy interests are not advanced by a categorical rule barring the seizure of contraband plainly detected through the sense of touch.

III

It remains to apply these principles to the facts of this case. Respondent has not challenged the finding made by the trial court and affirmed by both the Court of Appeals and the State Supreme Court that the police were justified under *Terry* in stopping him and frisking him for weapons. Thus, the dispositive question before this Court is whether the officer who conducted the search was acting within the lawful bounds marked by *Terry* at the time he gained probable cause to believe that the lump in respondent's jacket was contraband. The State District Court did not make precise findings on this point, instead finding simply that the officer, after feeling "a small, hard object wrapped in plastic" in respondent's pocket, "formed the opinion that the object ... was crack ... cocaine," App. to Pet. for Cert. C-2. The District Court also noted that the officer made "no claim that he suspected this object to be a weapon," *id.* at C-5, a finding affirmed on appeal, *see* 469 N.W.2d at 464 (the officer "never thought the lump was a weapon"). The Minnesota Supreme Court, after "a close examination of the record," held that the officer's own testimony "belies any notion that he 'immediately' " recognized the lump as crack cocaine. *See* 481 N.W.2d at 844. Rather, the court concluded, the officer determined that the lump was contraband only after "squeezing, sliding and otherwise manipulating the contents of the defendant's pocket"—a pocket which the officer already knew contained no weapon. *Ibid.*

Under the State Supreme Court's interpretation of the record before it, it is clear that the court was correct in holding that the police officer in this case overstepped the bounds of the "strictly circumscribed" search for weapons allowed under *Terry*. *See Terry*, 392 U.S. at 26. Where, as here, "an officer who is executing a valid search for one item seizes a different item," this Court rightly "has been sensitive to the danger ... that officers will enlarge a specific authorization, furnished by a warrant or an exigency, into the equivalent of a general warrant to rummage and seize at will." *Texas v. Brown*, 460 U.S. at 748 (STEVENS, J., concurring in judgment). Here, the officer's continued exploration of respondent's pocket after having concluded that it contained no weapon was unrelated to "the sole justification of the search [under *Terry:*] ... the protection of the police officer and others nearby." 392 U.S. at 29. It therefore amounted to the sort of evidentiary search that *Terry* expressly refused to authorize, *see id.*, at 26, and that we have condemned in subsequent cases. *See Michigan v. Long*, 463 U.S. at 1049, n.14; *Sibron*, 392 U.S. at 65–66.

Once again, the analogy to the plain-view doctrine is apt. In *Arizona v. Hicks*, 480 U.S. 321, 94 L. Ed. 2d 347, 107 S. Ct. 1149 (1987), this Court held invalid the seizure of stolen stereo equipment found by police while executing a valid search for other evidence. Although the police were lawfully on the premises, they obtained probable cause to believe that the stereo equipment was contraband only after moving the equipment to permit officers to read its serial numbers. The subsequent seizure of the equipment could not be justified by the plain-view doctrine, this Court explained, because the incriminating character of the stereo equipment was not immediately apparent; rather, probable cause to believe that the equipment was stolen arose only as a result of a further search—the moving of the equipment—that was not authorized by a search warrant or by any exception to the warrant requirement. The facts of this case are very similar. Although the officer was lawfully in a position to feel the lump in respondent's pocket, because *Terry* entitled him to place his hands upon respondent's jacket, the court below determined that the incriminating character of the object was not immediately apparent to him. Rather, the officer determined that the item was contraband only after conducting a further search, one not authorized by *Terry* or by any other exception to the warrant requirement. Because this further search of respondent's pocket was constitutionally invalid, the seizure of the cocaine that followed is likewise unconstitutional. *Horton*, 496 U.S. at 140.

IV

The judgment is affirmed.

Case Questions

1. Summarize the facts in the *Dickerson* case.
2. What are the legal issues?
3. Which rules/law did the Court rely upon most?

4-4 ANALYSIS AND THE CASE BRIEF

The brief or summary of a reported case is only the starting point. The legal researcher reads law looking for primary law that contains rules and explanations that are applicable to a client's situation. When you begin serious research, you are armed with the facts of your client's case. These facts provide the initial foundation for your research and your research plan or strategy. The facts help the researcher identify and articulate the legal issues involved in the client's case. Always attempt to identify the most relevant facts involved in your client's situation. After research and analysis, the most important facts become clear.

When researching, you search for primary law containing facts that are similar to the facts of your client's case. In Chapter 2 you learned to separate facts into the following categories:

- **Relevant:** These are the key facts of the case—some might say the case "turns" on these facts.
- **Explanatory:** These facts help the reader understand the overall situation.
- **Legally unimportant:** These facts have no legal significance.

After categorizing the facts of a case you researched, you are ready to compare and contrast the facts of the reported decision with those of your client's situation. This process of comparing the facts of a client's case with those of a reported case is an essential analytical skill. As you begin the comparison process, be sure to look for the following:

- **Similarities:** *Significant* similarities may mean that the decision's reasoning and holding should be applied in your client's case.
- **Differences:** *Significant* differences may mean that the reasoning and holding of the decision should not be applied to your client's case.
- **Unknowns (gaps):** When there are few or no points of significant comparison, the reasoning and holding are not applicable to your client's case.

Section 2-4 in Chapter 2 suggests creating a small chart to help organize the facts so that they are easily analyzed. The creation of this picture, this visual, can be helpful.

The following document is a first draft of a brief for the case of *Kaupp v. Texas*. The reader provided proofreading corrections and editorial comments. The second brief is the revised version of the brief. Over time, this is the sort of proofreading and editing we must do on our *own* writing.

Kaupp v. Texas, 538 U.S. 626 (2003)

combine and shorten, this is explanatory material not key facts

what was said?—it is important

not helpful

Facts

Disappearance of a girl led police to question her half brother and his friend, Robert Kaupp. Confession to murder from the half brother implicated Kaupp in the crime. After failing to obtain a warrant, several officers went to Kaupp's house at 3 a.m. and instructed him to go with them. The officers handcuffed Kaupp and transported him, shoeless and in his underwear, to the crime scene then the sheriff's headquarter for questioning. Shortly after being interrogated Kaupp admitted to taking part in the crime, but not causing the fatal wound.

do you find this awkward?

Procedural Context

Petitioner Kaupp was convicted of murder following a hearing where his alleged illegally obtained confession was admitted as evidence. Kaupp was convicted after motion to suppress his confession was denied. The State Court of Appeals affirmed the conviction, and the Court of Criminal Appeals of Texas denied discretionary review. The U.S. Supreme Court granted writ of *certiorari.*

this does not explain what happened—there are no key facts, go back to the first sentence of the case, can you work with it to create this issue?

Issue

Whether Kaupp's confession was obtained illegally when his Fourth and Fourteenth Amendment rights were violated.

think about your use of tense here

Holding

Kaupp's confession is to be suppressed under the due process of the Fourth Amendment and Fourteenth Amendment.

from being?

Rule

The Fourth Amendment prohibits an illegally obtained confession to be used against a criminal defendant. This rule applies to state courts through the Due Process Clause of the Fourteenth Amendment.

you need to weave in the case law cited by the Court in its reasoning

cite to law

no—name the case and use the citation

you need to cite the case here

best term?

cite to law

'[w]e

unclear

cite to law? and where is the holding?

Analysis

When involuntary seizure of a person is so invasive that it is comparable to an arrest, the police must have probable cause or judicial authorization for it to be legal. According to the test derived from a U.S. Supreme Court opinion, the Fourth and Fourteenth Amendments are invoked "when police conduct communicates to a reasonable person that he is not at liberty to ignore the police and go about his business." Circumstances of Kaupp's seizure fall within the meaning of the Fourth and Fourteenth Amendments, all of which indicate an arrest, thus required probable cause or judicial authorization to be legal. Threatening presence of several officers at 3 a.m. and being told "we need to go and talk" do not to a reasonable person suggest that refusal is an option. Kaupp's obedient "[o]kay" reply is not consent, and not resisting arrest does not waive of his Fourth Amendment right. Being removed from his house, in handcuffs and underwear only, to the police station further transforms this into a seizure of detention under the Fourth Amendment. Kaupp was arrested before giving his confession and because the State did not have probable cause, established precedent requires his confession to be suppressed unless it was an act of free will.

The following document is the second draft of the *Kaupp v. Texas* brief. This shows a significant improvement. Notice that the author truly edited the document, making major changes.

***Kaupp v. Texas*, 538 U.S. 626 (2003)**

Judicial History

The trial court denied Kaupp's motion to suppress his confession. He was convicted. The State Court of Appeals affirmed this decision. The Court of Criminal Appeals of Texas denied discretionary review. The U.S. Supreme Court granted certiorari.

Facts

A 14-year-old girl was murdered. Her half-brother (19 years old) and 17-year-old Kaupp were together on the day of the girl's disappearance. Officers questioned both young men. The brother confessed that he stabbed his half-sister. He also implicated Kaupp in the crime. Detectives tried unsuccessfully to obtain a warrant for Kaupp's arrest. Nevertheless at least five law enforcement officers went to Kaupp's house at approximately 3 a.m. At least three officers woke the boy with a flashlight and stated that they needed to talk. He was handcuffed and led to the police car wearing boxers and a T-shirt. Nothing on the records shows that the boy was made aware that he was free to decline going with the officers. He was then led to the scene of the crime and brought to an interrogation room at the Sheriff's office. While there he was told of the brother's confession. Eventually he admitted to having some part in the crime.

Issue

Was the confession obtained from Kaupp after he was awakened at 3:00 a.m., handcuffed, placed in a police car half-naked, driven to the scene of a crime, and then interrogated at the police station the fruit of an illegal arrest?

Analysis

Under the Fourth Amendment a confession "obtained by exploitation of an illegal arrest" may not be used against a criminal defendant. *Brown v. Illinois*, 422 U.S. 590, 605 (1975). A seizure of the person within the meaning of the Fourth and Fourteenth Amendments occurs when, "taking into account all of the circumstances surrounding the encounter, the police conduct would have communicated to a reasonable person that he was not at liberty to ignore the police presence and go about his business." *Florida v. Bostick*, 501 U.S. 429, 437 (1998). The Court has never sustained against a Fourth Amendment challenge the involuntary removal of a suspect from his home to a police station and his detention for investigative purposes absent probable cause or judicial authorization. *Hayes v. Florida*, 470 U.S. 811, 815 (1980). Kaupp did not struggle with a cohort of deputy sheriffs but that is not a waiver of Fourth Amendment protection. Even "an initially consensual encounter can be transformed into a seizure of detention within the meaning of the 4th Amendment." *INS v. Delgado*, 466 U.S. 210, 215 (1984). Because Kaupp was arrested before he was questioned, and because the State did not even claim that the sheriff's department had probable cause to detain him at that point, precedent requires suppression of a confession unless that confession was "an act of free will sufficient to purge the primary taint of unlawful invasion." *Wong Sun v. U.S.*, 371 U.S. 471, 486 (1963)

Holding

The judgment of the State Court of Appeals was vacated, and the case was remanded for further proceedings not inconsistent with this opinion.

The Writer's Corner

Avoid Shortcuts

Writers sometimes forget about the audience (the reader). In legal writing, we write to inform and to persuade. Do not use initials for the names of businesses, schools, or organizations, unless you are certain that the reader will easily recognize your meaning. The best rule is to write out the names in full early in the document. Give the reader a chance to become familiar with the cast of characters.

You can see the problem below:

Example: Robert Smith worked for GM for 20 years.

The reader does not know what GM means. One reader might guess General Motors and another might guess General Mills; both may be wrong. Introduce the full names early on. Once the reader is comfortable with the cast of characters, abbreviations and shortened names are appropriate. No reader likes to wade through sentences burdened with too many abbreviations. Shortcuts are annoying.

Example: The BNA addressed this in the LRT plan. The IRS chose to ignore the problem in the RTS plan.

This might make sense to the writer who is familiar with the cast of characters and the facts. To the average reader, this does not make sense. Readers find these shortcuts annoying.

4-5 AN APPROACH TO A DAUNTING PROJECT

Briefing cases is often part of a larger research project. Sometimes this larger project is daunting. If so, try the following approach.

1. Reread the ***directions***. Ask yourself:
   Do I fully understand what I was asked to do?
   If not, get clarification.
   Do I have a mental picture of the document I must create?
   If not, get an example.
   Do I have a deadline?
   Do I have special instructions?
2. Begin the project *only* after framing clear answers to the preceding questions.
3. Begin the project in a ***logical fashion***.
   Create an outline of the material to be covered. Leave plenty of space between the sections. Do this on the word processor. In this way, the project officially begins.
   Fill in the outline with key words and phrases.
   Make a separate list of problem areas.
   Identify the easy parts of the project.
   Consider doing these portions first.
   Identify the difficult part of the project.
   Create a special approach for this part of the project.
4. Choose one section of the project and begin writing. Do not worry about spelling, grammar, consistency, or anything else at this point. Just get your ideas on paper. You will proofread and edit later. Remember, your computer software will do much of this simple proofing for you.
5. Complete one section before you move on to another section of the project. Try to accomplish closure of small portions of the project. This will serve you well in the workplace. Because it is easy to show your supervisor small portions of a project, the supervisor has the opportunity to see that you are organized and proceeding in a logical fashion.
6. Consider this: Will placing material into a chronology help you? Will the chronology help the reader? If it helps you, do it in an effort to get your ideas on paper. If a chronology will not be particularly helpful to the reader, do not use it in the final copy.

A chronology may help the writer sort out a large number of facts or events. Creation of a "list" is often helpful. This list probably does not belong in the final written product, but it is a good outlining tool during the drafting stage.

As you look at a long, often very detailed list, you often see where you may combine facts or events. Or you may see a pattern emerge.

For example: If you have a series of judicial events, think about lumping them into a time frame, or addressing the happenings at each court level, *or* saying "Petitioner's various motions to re-open the case were repeatedly denied" *or* "Defendant's motions were heard favorably in the appellate court, but the State Supreme Court was not so lenient. . . . "

Remember, not all judicial events are equal in importance; even the number of hearings or trials may not be significant. In a summary, the writer cannot possibly cover everything in the original document and therefore must make choices based on knowledge and analytical skill. Such choices are learned through practice.

7. If you are summarizing a document, is there a specific format or order in which it is written?

   If there is a specific format or order, adopt it if possible.

   Until you fully understand the document, you will not be able to create an effective summary.

   Ask yourself the following questions:

      On what does the author of the document focus?

      On what does the author spend the most time?

      What seems most critical to the author of the document? (*not* what do *you* think is most important?)

   Follow the lead of the original document.

8. Remember, a summary should *reflect* the original. Think about this. A summary synthesizes or condenses the original document.
9. Avoid creating confusion. We are often our own worst enemies.
10. Go back to the directions. Are you still focused?

    Have you done what you were asked to do?

    Is your document clear and concise?

    Is it in the appropriate format?

    When is the deadline?

11. At this point, put your draft away for 24 to 48 hours. Just let it sit; avoid even thinking about it.
    a) Print a copy.
    b) Get out a bright color pen (felt pen edits are hard to ignore).
    c) Reread the directions (yes, again).
    d) Start reading at the beginning, marking as you go.
    e) Proofread for simple errors (spelling, grammar, etc.).
    f) Proofread for passive voice (use active voice, if possible).
    g) Proofread for long sentences (count the words!).
    h) Edit for topic sentences (make sure you have them).
    i) Edit for format consistency.
    j) Edit for internal consistency.
    k) Edit for vagueness.
    l) Edit for redundancy.
12. At this point, all sorts of potential changes (improvements) are identified. Make the necessary corrections and put the document aside. You are done. Going over and over a document is not realistic. Of course, we all strive for some degree of perfection, but the sheer reality of the working world often precludes perfection in all aspects of every project. Remember: Sometimes our changes are just changes, not improvements. You can over think and over edit your work.
13. Closure is a good thing!

Finding It Online

There are a growing number of large, inclusive showcases on the web. These mega search engines search groups of other search engines. The following sites represent only two of the more successful mega search engines.

www.hg.org
www.dogpile.com

A caution: Searching a large group of search engines is a great idea and often works reasonably well. However, remember, the form in which you write a search for one site or search engine may vary from others. This variation could cause you to miss otherwise available information. Sometimes valuable information may not be retrieved because not all of the search engines used by these inclusive showcases are able to understand or properly assimilate the search request. When you do not retrieve appropriate data, you should try again. Change your search terms and target reliable search engines.

Writing case briefs is an essential task in law school. As a result, many law schools provide explanations and examples of case briefs for students. To search for examples of various case briefs, use the general search engines listed above. Compare the results you obtain from each of these sites. Also try the popular search engines, Google and Bing and search for sample case briefs or briefing cases. Again, compare your results. Also, try searching www.youtube.com for "briefing cases."

Remember that there are many different formats used to brief cases. If you are asked to prepare a brief for your class, be sure to follow your instructor's directions.

CITATION MATTERS

QUOTATIONS

***THE BLUEBOOK*—RULE 5**

Quotations are an important part of legal writing. When you quote, you *must* alert the reader that you are using quoted language. This means, in most instances, you need quotation marks. A citation must follow a quote. This citation lets the reader know where the borrowed material originated.

Quotations of 50 words or more are *blocked* and no quotation marks are used. A blocked quote is single spaced and slightly indented on the left and right margins. The citation that follows a blocked quote is placed on the line below the last line of the blocked quote, and it is drawn all the way over to the left margin. Good examples are included under *The Bluebook* Rule 5.

Example of a blocked quote:

> The *Ferber* case upheld a prohibition on the distribution and sale of child pornography, as well as its production, because these acts were "intrinsically related" to the sexual abuse of children in two ways. *New York v. Ferber*, 458 U.S. 747, 759 (1982). First, as a permanent record of a child's abuse, the continued circulation itself would harm the child who had participated. *See id.* Second, because the traffic in child pornography was an economic motive for its production, the State had an interest in closing the distribution network.

Id. at 760.

Quotes of 49 words or fewer are placed in quotation marks, but not set off from the remainder of the text. Place periods and commas inside the quotation marks. Place other punctuation inside the quotation marks *only* if it is part of the quoted excerpt.

CHAPTER **SUMMARY**

A case brief is a summary of a reported case. Briefs serve many purposes: Some are written as a reminder for the writer, others for someone who did not read the case. A good case brief simplifies and condenses the reported case. It must be broken down into components that enable the reader to follow the information easily. The most common components of a case brief are (1) name of the case, (2) judicial history, (3) facts, (4) issues, (5) rules, (6) analysis or reasoning, and (7) conclusion or holding. Making notes in the margin while reading the case is an effective method of initial summarization. Color highlighting the components of the case is also helpful in acquiring a good understanding of the case.

Analysis of your client's situation involves placing facts into categories. Facts should be categorized as (1) relevant, (2) explanatory, and (3) legally unimportant. Then you can compare and contrast them.

A daunting project requires advance planning. A logical approach to the project saves time and helps the writer create the structure of the document early in the drafting process. Editing your own work is a skill you should work on with every document you produce.

TERMS TO **REMEMBER**

case brief
reported case
trial brief
primary sources
rationale
holding

QUESTIONS FOR **REVIEW**

1. Discuss the various uses of case law briefs.
2. What is the purpose of a case brief?
3. What questions lay the foundation for the components of a case brief?
4. List and explain the components of a case brief.
5. What clues might a court provide as to which facts are most important?
6. When comparing facts, what categories help in the compare and contrast process?

CAN YOU **FIGURE IT OUT?**

1. Use your citation manual to define the following.

   Cf.
   Id. at 847
   Cert. Denied
2. What is the first page of the *Miranda v. Arizona* case in the official reporter (United States Reports—U.S.)? (Refer to box on page 80)
3. What is the first page of the *Miranda v. Arizona* case in the *Supreme Court Reporter*? (Refer to box on page 80.)

TEST **YOURSELF** (Check Your Answers in Appendix G)

1. Complete the following components of a brief of *Morse v. Frederick* (Appendix F).

   Judicial History (what happened in the lower courts?)
   Issue(s) (what is the question before *this* Court?)
   Rules (a list here is fine—but the list should include the citation and the actual rule applied by the Court)
   Conclusion (what is the decision of the Court?)

TEST **YOURSELF**—WRITE IT RIGHT Keep It Simple, Use Tabulation

Sentences are hard to understand (or follow) when there is a long list of information in the sentence. One tool that helps is tabulation, this is sometimes called a laundry list. We do not want to over use this sort of tool, but it can be helpful.

Consider this federal statutory language:

> Whoever, under color of any law, statute, ordinance, regulation, or custom, willfully subjects any person in any State, Territory, Commonwealth, Possession, or District to the deprivation of any rights, privileges, or immunities secured or protected by the Constitution or laws of the United States, or to different punishments, pains, or penalties, on account of such person being an alien, or by reason of his color, or race, than are prescribed for the punishment of citizens, shall be fined under this title or imprisoned not more than one year, or both; or an attempt to commit aggravated sexual abuse, or an attempt to kill, shall be fined under this title, or imprisoned for any term of years or for life, or both, or may be sentenced to death.

This sentence is 127 words long and it is very hard to understand. There is just too much information in this one sentence. In order to better understand the sentence, and to use it in your legal writing, you could *tabulate* the sentence.

For example:

Whoever, under color of any law, statute, ordinance, regulation, or custom

- willfully subjects any person in any State, Territory, Commonwealth, Possession, or District
- to the deprivation of any rights, privileges, or immunities secured or protected by the Constitution or laws of the United States
- or to different punishments, pains, or penalties, on account of such person being an alien, or by reason of his color, or race, than are prescribed for the punishment of citizens
- shall be fined under this title
- or imprisoned not more than one year, or both

This is easier to read. You can also think of this a pulling the statutory language into the various elements.

Now, You Try It

(Check your answers in Appendix G)

Use tabulation to make this 116-word statutory sentence easier to read:

> Every person who, under color of any statute, ordinance, regulation, custom, or usage, of any State or Territory or the District of Columbia, subjects, or causes to be subjected, any citizen of the United States or other person within the jurisdiction there of to the deprivation of any rights, privileges, or immunities secured by the Constitution and laws, shall be liable to the party injured in an action at law, suit in equity, or other proper proceeding for redress, except that in any action brought against a judicial officer for an act or omission taken in such officer's judicial capacity, injunctive relief shall not be granted unless a declaratory decree was violated or declaratory relief was unavailable.

CITATION **EXERCISES**

Use Appendix C and the Citation Matters feature in this chapter to answer these questions.

1. Which *Bluebook* rule explains the use of quotations?
2. Explain what a blocked quote is and when it is used.
3. Are quote marks used with a blocked quotation?

FROM THE **WRITER'S CORNER:** Avoid Shortcuts

1. In legal writing, we write to ________________ and to ________________.
2. Explain what is wrong with this sentence: "The DEA was not in communication with the DOD or the CIA before speaking with MI6."

ASSIGNMENTS AND **EXERCISES**

RESEARCH EXERCISES

1. Find the *Terry v. Ohio*, 392 U.S. 1 (1968) case in your local law library. Search for the two unofficial reporters that also publish this case. Cite them. (*Hint:* You are looking for the Supreme Court Reporter—S. Ct. and the Lawyer's Edition—L. Ed.)
2. Find the *Map v. Ohio*, 367 U.S. 643 (1961) case. Summarize the facts of this case.

ANALYSIS AND WRITING ASSIGNMENTS

3. Write a brief of the *Minnesota v. Dickerson* case. Use the six components of a case brief.
4. Compare and contrast the Meyers case with the *Dickerson* case. Identify and discuss the factual similarities, differences, and gaps. Discuss whether the *Dickerson* precedent should apply to the Meyers case.
5. Consider the following situation: Our client, Mr. Nguyen, was arrested three weeks ago under the following circumstances: Mr. Nguyen rents one-half of a duplex on North 15th Street. Apparently, Mr. Nguyen's residence was under surveillance for several days prior to the arrest that took place three weeks ago. The police received a tip that large numbers of automatic weapons were being sold out of Mr. Nguyen's residence. The officers believe that the sale and purchase of the weapons is gang related. A search warrant was obtained for the residence several hours prior to the arrest. Two uniformed officers, armed with a properly executed search warrant, approached the residence while other officers positioned themselves around the duplex. As the officers stepped onto the porch, Mr. Nguyen's brother opened the front door; upon seeing the officers, he began to yell over his shoulder and retreated into the home. Without announcing their intent or purpose, five officers rushed the doors of the duplex at that time. The front and back doors were broken down and the officers entered the duplex. Many weapons were seized and our client was arrested. Apply the *Richards v. Wisconsin* decision to Mr. Nguyen's situation. Write a short memorandum explaining the application of the *Richards* precedent to the Nguyen situation. *Richards v. Wisconsin*, 520 U.S. 385 (1997) is printed in Appendix F.
6. Reread the *Illinois v. Caballas* case found in Chapter 3. Complete the missing sections (facts, analysis, holding) of the following case brief. Be sure to review the redrafted (second) *Kaupp* brief in Section 4-5.

Judicial History

Respondent Caballas was charged with possession of cannabis in the Illinois state court. In the trial court, he moved to suppress the cannabis and the motion was denied. Subsequently, he was convicted and appealed the conviction. The Illinois appellate court affirmed the conviction. The Illinois Supreme Court heard the Respondent's appeal and reversed the conviction. The State of Illinois filed a petition for writ of *certiorari* to the U.S. Supreme Court and the Court granted a hearing.

Facts

Issue(s)

Does the Fourth Amendment require reasonable, articulable suspicion to justify using a drug-detection dog to sniff a vehicle during a legitimate traffic stop, where the vehicle stop is not unreasonably prolonged?

Rules

1. Fourth Amendment to U.S. Constitution—right to be free from unreasonable search or seizures.
2. *People v. Cox*, 202 Ill. 2d 462, 270 Ill. Dec. 81, 782 N.E.2d 275 (2002): Contraband discovered through a dog sniff that occurred during an unreasonably prolonged traffic stop was the product of an unconstitutional seizure.
3. *United States v. Jacobsen*, 466 U.S. 109, 124, 104 S. Ct. 1652, 80 L. Ed. 2d 85 (1984): A seizure that is lawful at its inception can violate the Fourth Amendment if its manner of execution unreasonably infringes interests protected by the Constitution.
4. *United States v. Place*, 462 U.S. 696, 103 S. Ct. 2637, 77 L. Ed. 2d 110 (1983): The use of a well-trained narcotics-detection dog during a lawful traffic stop generally does not implicate legitimate privacy interests.

Analysis

Conclusion

ONLINE **RESEARCH EXERCISES**

7. Try the following search on Google: seizing evidence not listed in a search warrant. Summarize the information in the first few "hits." Did you find any information that might be helpful in the Meyers case regarding the bloody handkerchief found and seized by the police?
8. Using a site such as www.findlaw.com search for cases and other information on illegal police searches, explain your online research results.

chapter **five**

CONSTITUTIONS, STATUTES, AND ADMINISTRATIVE REGULATIONS

SKILL OBJECTIVES FOR CHAPTER 5

When you complete chapter 5, you should be able to

- Describe the various parts of the U.S. Constitution.
- Explain how federal statutory law is enacted.
- Identify and contrast the various publications of the United States Code.
- Find a section of the *United States Code* with a citation to the *United States Code* (U.S.C.), the *United States Code Service* (U.S.C.S.), or the *United States Code Annotated* (U.S.C.A.).
- Use a pocket part supplement.
- Discuss the differences between the *Code of Federal Regulations* and the *United States Code.*
- Find administrative regulations and rules of court.
- Use an index to locate applicable constitutional or statutory law.
- Locate legislative materials found on the freely accessible Internet.

CHAPTER OUTLINE

From the Desk of W. J. Bryan, Esq.

To: Research Assistant
FROM: W. J. Bryan
RE: Our Client, Justin Meyers
DATE:

After reading the cases you found for the Meyers case, I decided that the bloody handkerchief and our client's subsequent statements in the patrol car were illegally obtained. I need to make a proper motion in court to have this evidence suppressed. First, we need to check both the U.S. and California state constitutions for additional law regarding illegal searches and interrogations. You have already found some helpful cases, but if you check the case annotations for the constitutions you might find more cases. State codes deal with procedures for search warrants and we should check this. Pay attention to the case annotations as well as the language of the code. Finally, we need to review any procedural requirements for the motion we will be filing. Check both the state codes and rules of court for this. Since this case is in state court, there is no need to check procedural rules for the federal court.

5-1 INTRODUCTION

Although the legal system in the United States relies heavily on common law principles, case law is not the only source of law in this country. Constitutions, statutes, and administrative regulations are primary sources as well. The U.S. legal system relies on these various rules and regulations. Unlike case law, these rules are created before disputes arise. They are in place and provide guidelines to parties *before* a dispute arises. When disputes arise between parties, courts first look to constitutional provisions, statutory law, or administrative regulations in deciding how to resolve the dispute. If appropriate law exists, the court must apply it to the factual dispute. In applying these sources, courts also consider case law that interprets the law. These interpretations are *stare decisis* or binding precedent under appropriate circumstances. (Review Chapter 3 for the requirements for *stare decisis* to apply.)

Constitutions, statutory law, and administrative regulations are published in numerous print resources by both the government publishing office and private commercial publishers. Thomson Reuters (West) and LexisNexis (Lexis) publish many of these materials, along with case reporters and secondary source materials. West and Lexis also provide access to all of this material on their online databases. However, the use of free Internet resources for this type of research is becoming more popular and more effective. In part this is because the government provides access to almost all of its legislative publications. In addition to providing the law itself, some of the online resources offer tools or features to help in searching the material. This chapter discusses constitutions and statutory and administrative materials in both print and electronic formats.

5-2 CONSTITUTIONS

The U.S. Constitution, the supreme law of the land, provides the framework for the establishment of the federal government. It describes governmental powers and the limits of that power. The U.S. Constitution also sets out rights that people have in relationship to the federal government. This part of the Constitution is the ***Bill of Rights***.

Bill of Rights
First 10 amendments to U.S. Constitution.

The Constitution has three main parts:

- The preamble
- The articles
- The amendments

The preamble briefly sets forth the purpose of the constitution. Seven articles, some of which are divided into sections and clauses, provide the framework for the federal government. For example, consider the following excerpt from Article II of the Constitution:

ARTICLE II

Section 1

Clause 1: The executive Power shall be vested in a President of the United States of America. He shall hold his Office during the Terms of four Years and, together with the Vice President, chosen for the same Term, be elected, as follows …

Clause 2: Each State shall appoint, in such Manner as the Legislature thereof may direct a Number of Electors, equal to the whole Number of Senators and representatives to which the State may be entitled in the Congress: but no Senator or Representative, or Person holding an Office of Trust or Profit under the United States, shall be appointed Elector.

The amendments are changes or additions to the original Constitution. The first 10 amendments are known as the Bill of Rights. At present there are 27 amendments. In some publications, the amendments are referred to as articles. Knowing the article or amendment number allows a researcher to easily locate a specific provision in the Constitution.

The U.S. Constitution is published in numerous print sources. It is published as a single pamphlet and in connection with other works, including the *United States Code Annotated* and *United States Code Service*, which are discussed later in this chapter. For legal researchers, these publications are important for two reasons. First, the Constitution is ***indexed*** with the Code. This enables researchers to locate appropriate provisions of the Constitution when researching a specific topic. Second, it is published in an ***annotated*** format. In an annotated format, the publisher provides not only the exact text of the Constitution but also references to cases that interpret the Constitution. See Figure 5-1 for an example of an annotated Constitutional provision.

index
A list of words and phrases that reflect the topics covered in the book.

annotated
A brief summary of a statute or a case added to explain or clarify.

The U.S. Constitution is easily found online. In addition to services such as Lexis or Westlaw, any general search engine will direct you to numerous publications available through the Internet.

Each state has a constitution. Like the U.S. Constitution, state constitutions are published either separately or with the state codes. They are also found on the Internet, generally through the state's official homepage.

FIGURE 5-1 Annotated Constitution (Preamble) as Published in U.S.C.A.

① **Preamble to Constitution** →

② **Editorial enhancement** →

③ **Annotations** →

(Notes of Decision) →

PREAMBLE

WE THE PEOPLE of the United States, in Order to form a more perfect Union, establish Justice insure domestic Tranquility, provide for the common defence, promote the general Welfare, and secure the Blessings of Liberty to ourselves and our Posterity, do ordain and establish this CONSTITUTION for the United States of America.

WESTLAW ELECTRONIC RESEARCH

WESTLAW supplements your legal research in many ways, Westlaw allows you to

- update your research with the most current informantion
- expand pyour library with additional resources
- retrieve current, comprehensive history citing references to a case with KeyCite

For more information on using Westlaw to supplement your research, see the Westlaw Electronic Research Guide, which follows the explanation

NOTES OF DECISIONS

Formation of more perfect Union 3
Nature and function of Preamble 1
Ordainment and establishment of Constitution 6
Promotion of general welfare 4
Securing of liberty 5
United States of America 7
We the People 2

PREAMBLE

1. Nature and function of Preamble

The Preamble can never be resorted to, to enlarge the powers confided to the general government and can never be the legitimate source of any implied power, when otherwise drawn from the Constitution; its true office is to expound the nature, extent, and application of the powers actually conferred by the Constitution and not substantively to create them. U.S. v. Boyer, W.D.Mo.1898, 85 F. 425.

2. We the People

In our system, while sovereign powers are delegated to the agencies of government, sovereignty itself remains with the people, by whom and for whom all government exists and acts. Yick Wo v. Hopkins, U.S.Cal.1886, 6 S.Ct. 1064, 118 U.S. 356, 30 L.Ed. 220.

The Constitution of the United States was made by, and for the protection of, the people of the United States. League v. De Young, U.S.Tex.1850, 52 U.S. 185, 11 How. 185, 13 L.Ed. 657.

The Constitution was ordained and established by the people of the United States for themselves, for their own government and not for the government of the individual states; the people of the United States framed such a government for the United States as they supposed best adapted to their situation and best calculated to promote their interests. Lessee, U.S.Va.1816, 14 U.S. 304, 4 L.Ed. 97, 1 Wheat. 304.

Under the Constitution we see the people acting as sovereigns of the whole country; and in the language of sovereignty, establishing a constitution by which it was their will that the state governments should be bound, and to which the state constitutions should be made to conform. Chisholm v. Georgia, U.S.Ga. 1793, 2 U.S. 419, 2 Dall. 419, 1 L.Ed. 440.

3. Formation of more perfect Union

The separate governments of the separate states, bound together by the Articles of Confederation alone, were not sufficient for the promotion of the general welfare of the people in respect to foreign nations, or for their complete protection as citizens of the confederated states; for this reason, the people of the United States, "in order to form a more perfect union, establish justice, insure domestic tranquillity, provide for the common defense, promote the general welfare, and secure the blessings of liberty" to themselves and their posterity, ordained and established the government of the United States, and defined its powers by a Constitution, which they adopted as its fundamental law and made its rule of action. U.S. v. Cruikshank, U.S.La.1875, 92 U.S. 542, 2 Otto 542, 23 L.Ed. 588.

The Federal Constitution created not a confederacy of states, but a government of individuals assumed that the govern-

FIGURE 5-1 (continued)

Barron v. City of Baltimore, U.S.Md. 1833, 32 U.S. 243, 7 Pet. 243, 8 L.Ed. 672.

The Constitution emanated from the people, and was not the act of sovereign and independent states. M'Culloch v. State, U.S.Md.1819, 17 U.S. 316, 4 L.Ed. 579, 4 Wheat. 316.

The Constitution of the United States was ordained and established not by the states in their sovereign capacities, but emphatically, as the preamble of the Constitution declares, by "the people of the United States; there can be no doubt that it was competent to the people to invest the general government with all the powers which they might deem proper and necessary, to extend or restrain these powers according to their own good pleasure, and to give them a paramount and supreme authority. Martin v. Hunter's ment and the Union which it created, and the states which were incorporated into the Union, would be indestructible and perpetual; as far as human means could accomplish such a work, it intended to make them so. White v. Hart, U.S.Ga. 1871, 80 U.S. 646, 20 L.Ed. 685, 13 Wall. 646.

The Constitution of the United States established a government, and not a league, compact, or partnership, and it was constituted by the people. Legal Tender Cases, U.S.Tex.1870, 79 U.S. 457, 20 L.Ed. 287, 12 Wall. 457. See, also, U.S., v. Cathcart, C.C.Ohio 1864, 1 Bond 556, 25 Fed.Cas. No. 14,756.

The union of the states began among the colonies, and grew out of common origin, mutual sympathies, kindred principles, similar interests, geographical relations, and received definite form, and character, and sanction from the Articles

A Point to Remember

State constitutions should always be reviewed when researching a constitutional question. Remember that when you research an issue controlled by the Bill of Rights, your state constitution may give an individual more rights than he or she has under the U.S. Constitution. If this is the case, your research must focus on your state constitution and on cases that interpret your state constitution, as well as on the U.S. Constitution.

5-3 FEDERAL STATUTORY LAW

Enactment of Statutory Law

In the U.S. system of government, legislative bodies have the power to make laws. These are ***statutory laws***. Unlike case law, statutory law is not enacted to resolve a specific factual dispute. Instead, legislative bodies make rules or laws that apply to society in general. Statutory law governs many aspects of our lives, including traffic, domestic relations, criminal and civil liability, corporate operation, immigration, homeland security, environment, and the financial industry. Statutory law comes from federal, state, and local governing bodies.

statutory law
Law enacted through the legislative process.

Federal statutory law includes those laws enacted by the U.S. Congress. Congress meets for two-year terms, with each separate term given a number. For example, the Congress for the years 2015 through 2016 is referred to as the *114th Congress*. Each year of Congress constitutes a separate session. One of the primary responsibilities of each Congress is the enactment of new legislation, which consists of the following steps.

Legislation Proposed All federal laws begin with a proposal, known as a ***bill***.

bill
Proposed legislation.

Bill Introduced The bill is introduced into either the House of Representatives or the Senate and immediately assigned a number. This number is preceded by "H.R." if the bill is introduced into the House of Representatives, or "S" if the bill is introduced into the Senate. The bill retains this number throughout the legislative process. These numbers are important when researching the ***legislative history*** of any statute. Legislative histories are discussed later in this chapter.

legislative history
The proceedings that relate to a bill before it becomes law.

Bill Referred to Committee After the introduction of the bill, it is referred to the appropriate committee for consideration. Both the House and the Senate have a number of standing committees that concentrate on certain matters. Once the bill is referred, the proper committee reviews and discusses the proposal, sometimes holding public hearings on the bill. If a committee looks favorably on a bill, it prepares a committee report with its recommendations and analysis of the bill.

Vote by Legislators If a report is issued, the whole house then considers the bill and votes on it. If it receives a majority vote of approval, it is passed and sent to the other house.

Action by Other House When referred to the other house, the bill goes through much the same process again. If the bill is amended or changed, a joint conference from both houses may convene to work out differences. Both houses must approve the same bill before submission to the president. Once passed by both houses, the bill moves to the president for approval.

Executive Action The president has the power to approve or to veto the bill. If the president does nothing with the bill, it is deemed approved after ten days unless Congress should adjourn within that ten-day period. If this happens, the bill is considered vetoed (pocket veto). If the president vetoes a bill, it can still be enacted as law if a two-thirds majority of each house votes to override the veto.

A more detailed description of the enactment of laws is found at https://www.congress.gov/legislative-process.

Initial Publication of Statutes

Laws enacted by Congress are categorized as either public laws or private laws. ***Public laws*** are those that concern the general public. For example, read the following selection from Public Law 111-15 dealing with the "bailout" legislation following the recent economic crisis.

public laws
Laws enacted by Congress that affect the public in general.

Public Law 111-15

111th Congress

An Act

To amend the Emergency Economic Stabilization Act of 2008 (division A of Public Law 110-343) to provide the Special Inspector General with additional authorities and responsibilities, and for other purposes. >

Be it enacted by the Senate and House of Representatives of the United States of America in Congress assembled, >

SECTION 1. SHORT TITLE.

This Act may be cited as the "Special Inspector General for the Troubled Asset Relief Program Act of 2009".

SECTION 2. AUDIT AND INVESTIGATION AUTHORITIES.

Section 121 of the Emergency Economic Stabilization Act of 2008 (division A of Public Law 110-343) > is amended—

(1) in subsection (c), by adding at the end the following:
"(4) (A) Except as provided under subparagraph (B) and in addition to the duties specified in paragraphs (1), (2), and (3), the Special Inspector General shall have the authority to conduct, supervise, and coordinate an audit or investigation of any action taken under this title as the Special Inspector General determines appropriate.
"(B) Subparagraph (A) shall not apply to any action taken under section 115, 116, 117, or 125."; and
(2) in subsection (d)—
(A) in paragraph (2), by striking "subsection (c)(1)" and inserting "subsection (c)(1) and (4)"; and
(B) by adding at the end the following:
"(3) The Office of the Special Inspector General for the Troubled Asset Relief Program shall be treated as an office included under section 6I(3) of the Inspector General Act of 1978 (5 U.S.C. App.) relating to the exemption from the initial determination of eligibility by the Attorney General."

Private laws are those that concern single individuals or groups. Private laws usually deal with matters such as naturalization or settlement of a claim by the government.

private laws
Laws enacted by Congress that affect only selected individuals.

After a bill completes the legislative process and is signed by the president (or a veto is properly overridden), the law is labeled as either a public law or a private law and assigned a number. The number includes the number of the Congress and the chronological number of the bill. Thus, the first public law enacted by the 111th Congress is identified as Public Law 111-1. Remember that, at this point, the legislation has two numerical references: the original number of the bill (i.e., H.R. 1234) and the public or private law number assigned after passage.

As each law is passed, it is published by the government in pamphlet form, known as a ***slip law***. At the end of each session of Congress, all of these laws are published in a book referred to as the *Statutes at Large*. The *Statutes at Large* publishes laws in chronological order. They are not organized according to topic or subject matter. As a result, the *Statutes at Large* is extremely difficult to research. In order to alleviate this problem, federal statutes are codified (put into codes). A ***code*** is an organization by subject matter of all of the public laws found in statutes. Because of the way Congress works, it is common for one statute to contain many different kinds of laws that end up in different code sections. In recent years, when *Statutes at Large* is published, it contains margin references to the codes where the section of the statute will be included. See Figure 5-2 for a sample of a law found in the *Statutes at Large*. Note the different code sections affected by the one statute.

slip law
First publication of a law; usually in pamphlet form.

code
A topical organization of statutes.

Thus, before a law finds it way into the *United States Code*, it goes through several numerical designations. See Box 5-1 for the history of one code section, 50 U.S.C. § 403-4b.

FIGURE 5-2 Pages from Statutes at Large, Volume 108, Pages 1970 and 1971

PUBLIC LAW 103-322—SEPT. 13, 1994 108 STAT. 1970

Note two references to same law.

"(1) for murder, by death or life imprisonment, or a fine of not more than $250,000, or both; and for kidnapping, by imprisonment for any term of years or for life, or a fine of not more than $250,000, or both;".

(13) GENOCIDE. —Section 1091(b)(1) of title 18, United States Code, is amended by striking " a fine of not more than $1,000,000 or imprisonment for life," and inserting ", where death results, by death or imprisonment for life and a fine of not more than $1,000,000, or both;".

(14) CARJACKING.—Section 2119(3) of title 18, United States Code, is amended by striking the period after "both" and inserting ", or sentenced to death."; and by striking ", possessing a firearm as defined in section 921 of this title, and inserting ", with the intent to cause death or serious bodily harm". (b) CONFORMING AMENDMENTTO FEDERAL AVIATION ACT OF 1954.—Chapter 465 of title 49, United States Code, is amended—

(1) in the chapter analysis by striking "Death penalty sentencing procedure for aircraft piracy" and inserting "Repealed"; and

(2) by striking section 46503.

SEC. 60004. APPLICABILITY TO UNIFORM CODE OF MILITARY JUSTICE. 18 USC 3591 note

Chapter 228 of title 18, United States Code, as added by this title, shall not apply to prosecutions under the Uniform Code of Military Justice (10 U.S.C. 801).

SEC. 60005. DEATH PENALTY FOR MURDER BY A FEDERAL PRISONER.

(a) IN GENERAL. —Chapter 51 of title 18, United States Code, is amended by adding at the end the following new section:

"§ 1118. Murder by a Federal prisoner

"(a) OFFENSE. —A person who, while confined in a Federal correctional institution under a sentence for a term of life imprisonment, commits the murder of another shall be punished by death or by life imprisonment.

"(b) DEFINITIONS.—In this section—

"'Federal correctional institution' means any Federal prison, Federal correctional facility, Federal community program center, or Federal halfway house.

"'murder' means a first degree or second degree murder (as defined in section 1111).

"'term of life imprisonment' means a sentence for the term of natural life, a sentence commuted to natural life, an indeterminate term of a minimum of at least fifteen years and a maximum of life, or an unexecuted sentence of death.".

(b) TECHNICAL AMENDMENT.—The chapter analysis for chapter 51 of title 18, United States Code, is amended by adding at the end the following new item:

"1118. Murder by a Federal prisoner.".

SEC. 60006. DEATH PENALTY FOR CIVIL RIGHTS MURDERS.

(a) CONSPIRACY AGAINST RIGHTS.—Section 241 of title 18, United States Code, is amended by striking the period at the end of the last sentence and inserting ", or may be sentenced to death.".

(b) DEPRIVATION OF RIGHTS UNDER COLOR OF LAW.—Section 242 of title 18, United States Code, is amended by striking the period at the end of the last sentence and inserting ", or may be sentenced to death.".

This section amends 18 USC § 242.

FIGURE 5-2 (continued)

108 STAT. 1970 PUBLIC LAW 103-322—SEPT. 13, 1994

(c) FEDERALLY PROTECTED ACTIVITIES.— Section 245(b) of title 18, United States Code, is amended in the matter following paragraph (5) by inserting ", or may be sentenced to death" after "or for life".

(d) DAMAGE TO RELIGIOUS PROPERTY; OBSTRUCTION OF THE FREE EXERCISE OF RELIGIOUS RIGHTS. —Section 247(c)(1) of title 18, United States Code, is amended by inserting ", or may be sentenced to death" after "or both".

SEC. 60007. DEATH PENALTY FOR THE MURDER OF FEDERAL LAW ENFORCEMENT OFFICIALS.

Section 1114 of title 18, United States Code, is amended by striking "punished as provided under sections 1111 and 1112 of this title," and inserting "punished, in the case of murder, as provided under section 1111, or, in the case of manslaughter, as provided under section 1112."

Drive-By Shooting Prevention Act of 1994. 18 USC 36 note.

SEC. 60008. NEW OFFENSE FOR THE INDISCRIMINATE USE OF WEAPONS TO FURTHER DRUG CONSPIRACIES.

(a) SHORT TITLE.—This section may be cited as the "Drive-By Shooting Prevention Act of 1994".

(b) IN GENERAL.—Chapter 2 of title 18, United States Code, is amended by adding at the end the following new section:

BOX 5-1 NUMERICAL HISTORY OF A CODE SECTION

Public Law 108-458	The initial publication of the law in pamphlet format
118 Stat. 3661 (Volume 118 of the *Statutes at Large,* page 3661)	The publication of the law at the end of the session of Congress, along with all public laws enacted during the same session; laws are published in chronological order
50 U.S.C. §403-4b (Title 50 of the *United States Code*, section 403-4b)	The publication of the law in the *United States Code* where laws are topically organized

5-4 *UNITED STATES CODE*

The *United States Code* contains a consolidation of the general and permanent laws of the United States arranged topically. (Private laws are not included in the code.) The laws are organized according to subject matter in 50 separate title headings. For example, all laws regarding bankruptcy are arranged under the general topical heading of bankruptcy or Title 11 (see Table 5-1 for a list of subject matter headings). The general topics are arranged alphabetically. However, the titles are officially referred to numerically rather than by the topical name. Titles are further divided into sections. Each section is a separate law. Laws are referred to and cited by title and section.

For example, if you refer to the code section at the beginning of the chapter, you say, "Title 18, section 242 of the *United States Code*." Of course, in speaking, lawyers often refer to the various codes by their more popular names, such as the Bankruptcy Code. The code books, and some online sites, contain popular name indexes so that researchers can find code sections by their common or popular name.

TABLE 5-1 Topic Headings for *United States Code* and Administrative Regulations (*Code of Federal Regulations*)

U.S. Code	*Code of Federal Regulations*
1. General Provisions	1. General Provisions
2. The Congress	2. The Congress (reserved)
3. The President	3. The President
4. Flag and Seal, Seat of Government, and the States	4. Accounts
5. Government Organization and Employees	5. Administrative Personnel
6. Domestic Security	6. Homeland Security
7. Agriculture	7. Agriculture
8. Aliens and Nationality	8. Aliens and Nationality
9. Arbitration	9. Animals and Animal Products
10. Armed Forces	10. Energy
11. Bankruptcy	11. Federal Elections
12. Banks and Banking	12. Banks and Banking
13. Census	13. Business Credit and Assistance
14. Coast Guard	14. Aeronautics and Space
15. Commerce and Trade	15. Commerce and Foreign Trade
16. Conservation	16. Commercial Practices
17. Copyrights	17. Commodity and Securities Exchange
18. Crimes and Criminal Procedure	18. Conservation of Power and Water Resources
19. Customs Duties	19. Customs Duties
20. Education	20. Employees' Benefits
21. Food and Drugs	21. Food and Drugs
22. Foreign Relations and Intercourse	22. Foreign Relations
23. Highways	23. Highways
24. Hospitals and Asylums	24. Housing and Urban Development
25. Indians	25. Indians
26. Internal Revenue Code	26. Internal Revenue
27. Intoxicating Liquors	27. Alcohol, Tobacco Products, and Firearms
28. Judiciary and Judicial Procedure	28. Judicial Administration
29. Labor	29. Labor
30. Mineral Lands and Mining	30. Mineral Resources
31. Money and Finance	31. Money and Finance: Treasury
32. National Guard	32. National Defense
33. Navigation and Navigable Waters	33. Navigation and Navigable Waters
34. Navy (eliminated by the enactment of Title 10)	34. Education
35. Patents	35. Panama Canal (reserved)
36. Patriotic and National Observances, Ceremonies, and Organizations	36. Parks, Forests, and Public Property
37. Pay and Allowances of the Uniformed Services	37. Patents, Trademarks, and Copyrights

TABLE 5-1 (continued)

U.S. Code	*Code of Federal Regulations*
38. Veterans' Benefits	38. Pensions, Bonuses, and Veterans' Relief
39. Postal Service	39. Postal Service
40. Public Buildings, Property, and Works	40. Protection of the Environment
41. Public Contracts	41. Public Contracts and Property Management
42. The Public Health and Welfare	42. Public Health
43. Public Lands	43. Public Lands: Interior
44. Public Printing and Documents	44. Emergency Management and Assistance
45. Railroads	45. Public Welfare
46. Shipping	46. Shipping
47. Telegraphs, Telephones, and Radiotelegraphs	47. Telecommunications
48. Territories and Insular Possessions	48. Federal Acquisition Regulations System
49. Transportation	49. Transportation
50. War and National Defense	50. Wildlife and Fisheries

In researching statutory law, legal researchers generally search the codes rather than the *Statutes at Large*. This is because the organization and indexing make the codes much easier to use. When statutory law is organized and put into appropriate codes, differences between the language of the statute and the language of the code occasionally occur. The law is the language that was approved by Congress. To eliminate confusion, Congress enacted several code titles as law. This allows researchers to rely on the code rather than the difficult-to-use *Statutes at Large*. Once approved, the code, rather than the statute at large, becomes the law and is called ***positive law***. Code titles not reenacted are considered *evidence* of what the law is. That means that you can cite the code sections to a court.

positive law
Codes that were enacted into law by Congress.

Legislative Histories

Once in a while, a legal dispute arises regarding the meaning of a particular code section. When this happens in connection with a factual dispute, the court is called upon to interpret the code section. The court gives great weight to the ***legislative intent*** behind the law. The legislative intent is what the legislature intended to accomplish by passing the law. While no one can absolutely prove what was in the minds of all the legislators when the law was enacted, various documents help the court make this determination. The original language of the bill and changes made to that language often provide evidence of intent. Transcripts of committee hearings and transcripts of debates on the bill also help.

legislative intent
The purpose of the legislature in passing a law.

Rather than seeking the originals of these records, a researcher can use *United States Code and Congressional and Administrative News* (U.S.C.C.A.N.) (a Thomson Reuters/West publication). This contains the legislative history of statutes, federal regulations, and court rules. It contains bills in their original format, changes, and committee hearings and discussions. Determining the meaning of any code section is more involved than simply looking at legislative intent. Chapter 6 discusses this in more detail.

BOX 5-2 COMMON FEATURES OF AN ANNOTATED CODE

- History of law
- Cross-reference to similar laws
- References to secondary authorities
- References to case decisions

A researcher can also conduct a legislative history using online materials. The Library of Congress website provides the researcher with an overview of the process as well as links to key government websites (such as the Government Publishing Office) that provide access to important legislative materials used in conducting a legislative history. (See http://www.loc.gov/law/help/leghist.php.)

United States Code Publications

There are three main print publications of the Unites States Code: the *United States Code,* published by the Government Publishing Office; the *United States Code Annotated,* published by Thomson Reuters (West); and the *United States Code Service,* from LexisNexis. The *United States Code* (abbreviated U.S.C.) contains only the statutory language of the code, as well as limited historical information and cross-references. It does not provide any references to cases or secondary source material related to the code section. On the other hand, both *United States Code Annotated* (abbreviated U.S.C.A.) and the *United States Code Service* (abbreviated U.S.C.S.) are annotated editions of the code. An annotated version of a code contains references to cases that interpret the code section along with references to other legal sources that explain the code section. The publisher adds annotations that are not part of the Code. These annotations assist the researcher. See Figures 5-3 and 5-4 for examples of an unannotated and annotated code section.

There is, however, one difference between the *United States Code Annotated* and the *United States Code Service*. The U.S.C.A. uses the exact language found in the *United States Code*. The U.S.C.S. uses the exact language found in the *Statutes at Large*. In most cases, this presents no problem to the researcher, who can usually use either source. All versions of the United States Code can be found online. The U.S.C.A. is available on the Westlaw website. The U.S.C.S is available on the Lexis website and the U.S.C. is available through the website for the government publishing office https://www.gpo.gov/. The U.S.C. is also available online through numerous government, commercial, and educational websites.

Pocket Part Supplements

pocket part supplement
A removable supplement; includes all changes or additions to the material contained in the hard-bound volume.

repeal
To undo; to declare a law no longer in effect.

amend
To change.

Laws change every year, and code publications must be kept up to date to reflect these changes. Rather than replacing the numerous volumes of the code each year, ***pocket part supplements*** are used in print publications to reflect any changes to the code. Pocket part supplements are replaced each year. When a code is ***repealed*** or ***amended***, that change is found in the pocket part supplement. In annotated codes, the pocket part supplement also contains the latest cases to interpret the statute. Thus, even if a code section has not changed, you must check the pocket part supplement to see if any recent case decisions affect the interpretation of the law. Occasionally, supplemental material becomes too voluminous for a

FIGURE 5-3 U.S.C. (United States Code)

U.S. Code provides amendments and cross annotations but no case decisions.

Note amendment from Pub. L 103–322 (Figure 5-2).

CHAPTER 13—CIVIL RIGHTS

Sec.	
241.	Conspiracy against rights.
242.	Deprivation of rights under color of law.
243.	Exclusion of jurors on account of race or color.
244.	Discrimination against person wearing uniform of armed forces.
245.	Federally protected activities.
246.	Deprivation of relief benefits.
247.	Damage to religious property; obstruction of persons in the free exercise of religious beliefs.
248.	Freedom of access to clinic entrances.

AMENDMENTS

1994—Pub. L. 103–322, title XXXIII, § 330023(a)(1), Sept. 13, 1994, 108 Stat. 2150, substituted "Freedom of access to clinic entrances" for "Blocking access to reproductive health services" in item 248.

Pub. L. 103–259, § 4, May 26, 1994, 108 Stat. 697, added item 248.

1988—Pub. L. 100–690, title VII, § 7018(b)(2), Nov. 18, 1988, 102 Stat. 4396, struck out "of citizens" after "rights" in item 241.

Pub. L. 100–346, § 3, June 24, 1988, 102 Stat. 645, added item 247.

1976—Pub. L. 94–453, § 4(b), Oct. 2, 1976, 90 Stat. 1517, added item 246.

1968—Pub. L. 90–284, title I, § 102, Apr. 11, 1968, 82 Stat. 75, added item 245.

§ 241. Conspiracy against rights

If two or more persons conspire to injure, oppress, threaten, or intimidate any person in any State, Territory, or District in the free exercise or enjoyment of any right or privilege secured to him by the Constitution or laws of the United States, or because of his having so exercised the same; or

If two or more persons go in disguise on the highway, or on the premises of another, with intent to prevent or hinder his free exercise or enjoyment of any right or privilege so secured—

They shall be fined under this title or imprisoned not more than ten years, or both; and if death results from the acts committed in violation of this section or if such acts include kidnapping or an attempt to kidnap, aggravated sexual abuse or an attempt to commit aggravated sexual abuse, or an attempt to kill, they shall be fined under this title or imprisoned for any term of years or for life, or both, or may be sentenced to death.

(June 25, 1948, ch. 645, 62 Stat. 696; Apr. 11, 1968, Pub. L. 90–284, title I, § 103(a), 82 Stat. 75; Nov. 18, 1988, Pub. L. 100–690, title VII, § 7018(a), (b)(1), 102 Stat. 4396; Sept. 13, 1994, Pub. L. 103–322, title VI, § 60006(a), title XXXII, §§ 320103(a), 320201(a), title XXXIII, § 330016(1)(L), 108 Stat. 1970, 2109, 2113, 2147.)

HISTORICAL AND REVISION NOTES

Based on title 18, U.S.C., 1940 ed., § 51 (Mar. 4, 1909, ch. 321, § 19, 35 Stat. 1092).

Clause making conspirator ineligible to hold office was omitted as incongruous because it attaches ineligibility to hold office to a person who may be a private citizen and who was convicted of conspiracy to violate a specific statute. There seems to be no reason for imposing such a penalty in the case of one individual crime, in view of the fact that other crimes do not carry such a severe consequence. The experience of the Department of Justice is that this unusual penalty has been an obstacle to successful prosecutions for violations of the act.

Mandatory punishment provision was rephrased in the alternative.

Minor changes in phraseology were made.

AMENDMENTS

1994—Pub. L. 103–322, § 320201(a), substituted "person in any State" for "inhabitant of any State" in first par.

Pub. L. 103–322, §§ 320103(a)(1), 330016(I)(L), amended section identically, substituting "They shall be fined under this title" for "They shall be fined not more than $10,000" in third par.

Pub. L. 103–322, § 320103(a)(2)–(4), in third par., substituted "results from the acts committed in violation of this section or if such acts include kidnapping or an attempt to kidnap, aggravated sexual abuse or an attempt to commit aggravated sexual abuse, or an attempt to kill, they shall be fined under this title or imprisoned for any term of years or for life, or both" for "results, they shall be subject to imprisonment for any term of years or for life".

Pub. L. 103–322, § 60006(a), substituted ", or may be sentenced to death." for period at end of third par.

1988—Pub. L. 100–690 struck out "of citizens" after "rights" in section catchline and substituted "inhabitant of any State, Territory, or District" for "citizen" in text.

1968—Pub. L. 90–284 increased limitation on fines from $5,000 to $10,000 and provided for imprisonment for any term of years or for life when death results.

CROSS REFERENCES

Action for neglect to prevent, see section 1986 of Title 42, The Public Health and Welfare.

Conspiracy to commit offense or to defraud United States, see section 371 of this title.

Conspiracy to interfere with civil rights, see section 1985 of Title 42, The Public Health and Welfare.

Proceedings in vindication of civil rights, see section 1988 of Title 42.

§ 242. Deprivation of rights under color of law

Whoever, under color of any law, statute, ordinance, regulation, or custom, willfully subjects any

FIGURE 5-4 U.S.C.S. (United States Code Service)

Evidence of victims' reactions to cross-burning, including photographs of security measures they took afterwards and son's testimony he began to sleep with baseball bat, was admissible, since it was probative of defendant's intent under 18 USCS §§ 241 and 844. United States v Magleby (2001, CA10 Utah) 241 F3d 1306.

73. —Sufficiency

Evidence that defendants resorted to acts which are not constitutionally protected, including bottle throwing, brandishing knives and verbally threatening, in order to prevent black persons from using public park was sufficient to prove violation of 18 USCS § 241. United States v McDermott (1994, CA8 Iowa) 29 F3d 404.

Evidence was sufficient to prove that defendant intended to threaten victims of cross burning with physical violence, where he made racial derogatory statements while constructing cross and testified at trial that his purpose was to scare victims so they would move out of town, in addition to which victim testified that she and her children felt physically threatened. United States v Pospisil (1999, CA8 Mo) 186 F3d 1023, reh en banc, den (1999, CA8) 1999 US App LEXIS 22128.

Evidence was sufficient to convict defendant of conspiring to violate 18 USCS § 241, despite fact that he did not directly participate in cross burning, where on afternoon of cross burning men waited to discuss defendant's altercation with victim until defendant arrived, defendant not only knew about, discussed, and encouraged action but initiated it, defendant was informed when mission was accomplished, and his credibility was suspect. United States v Whitney (2000, CA 10 Kan) 229 F3d 1296, 2000 Colo J C A R 5742.

Jury could infer that defendant intended to oppress, threaten, and intimidate victims in free exercise of their federal right to occupy property, where he, understanding meaning of burning cross to general public, had placed one in their yard. United States v Magleby (2001, CA10 Utah) 241 F3d 1306.

Juvenile delinquents are guilty beyond reasonable doubt of violation of 18 USCS § 241, where they were all active members of skinhead group New Dawn Hammerskins, which desecrated several Jewish temples and vandalized car of Jewish teacher, because U.S. has proven that defendants had specific intent to interfere with federal right of Jewish inhabitants to hold and use property. United States v Three Juveniles (1995, DC Mass) 886 F Supp 934.

75. Instructions

In prosecution of police officers for alleged use of excessive force in making arrests, jury instructions did not constructively amend indictment, which could be read in due process terms, whereas instruction alleged Fourth Amendment violation, since proof was same and defendants' substantial rights were not affected; instructions adequately distinguished specific intent and violation of constitutional rights as elements of proof. United States v Reese (1993, CA9 Cal) 2 F3d 870, 93 CDOS 5642, 93 Daily Journal DAR 9617, petition for certiorari filed (Oct 28, 1993) and (among conflicting authorities noted in United States v Lilly (CA1) 1994 US App LEXIS 69).

District court did not err in instructing jury that, while victim's reaction to cross-burning was not conclusive evidence of defendant's intent in burning cross in yard of Afro-American, it could be considered as some evidence of it. United States v Hartbarger (1998, CA7 Ind) 148 F3d 777, 49 Fed Rules Evid Serv 783, reh en banc, den (1998, CA7 Ind) 1998 US App LEXIS 177724.

District court properly instructed jury that victims' reactions to cross-burning could be considered by trier of fact as relevant evidence of defendant's intent under 18 USCS § 241. United States v Magleby (2001, CA10 Utah) 241 F3d 1306.

Same code as U.S.C. but features are added

§ 242. Deprivation of rights under color of law

Whoever, under color of any law, statute, ordinance, regulation, or custom, willfully subjects any person in any State, Territory, Commonwealth, Possession, or District to the deprivation of any rights, privileges, or immunities secured or protected by the Constitution or laws of the United States, or to different punishments, pains, or penalties, on account of such person being an alien, or by reason of his color, or race, than are prescribed for the punishment of citizens, shall be fined under this title or imprisoned not more than one year, or both; and if bodily injury results from the acts committed in violation of this section or if such acts include the use, attempted use, or threatened use of a dangerous weapon, explosives, or fire, shall be fined under this title or imprisoned not more than ten years or both; and if death results from the acts committed in violation of this section or if such acts include kidnapping or an attempt to kidnap, aggravated sexual abuse, or an attempt to commit aggravated sexual abuse, or an attempt to kill, shall be fined under this title, or imprisoned for any term of years or for life, or both, or may be sentenced to death.

(As amended Sept. 13, 1994, P. L. 103-322, Title VI, § 60006(b), Title XXXII, Subtitle A, § 320103(b), Subtitle B, § 320201(b), Title XXXIII, § 330016(1)(H), 108 Stat. 1970, 2109, 2113, 2147; Oct. 11, 1996, P. L. 104-294, Title VI, §§ 604(b)(14)(B), 607(a), 110 Stat. 3507, 3511.)

CRIMES

HISTORY; ANCILLARY LAWS AND DIRECTIVES

Amendments:

1994. Act Sept. 13, 1994, substituted "person in" for "inhabitant of", substituted "such person" for "such inhabitant", and inserted ", or may be sentenced to death".

Section 320103(b), as amended by Act Oct. 11, 1996 (effective on 9/13/94, pursuant to § 604(d) of such Act, which appears as 18 USCS § 13 note), inserted "from the acts committed in violation of this section or if such acts include the use, attempted use, or threatened use of a dangerous weapon, explosives, or fire", inserted "from the acts committed in violation of this section or if such acts include kid-

FIGURE 5-4 (continued)

napping or an attempt to kidnap, aggravated sexual abuse, or an attempt to commit aggravated sexual abuse, or an attempt to kill, shall be fined under this title, or", substituted "imprisoned" for "shall be subject to imprisonment", and inserted ", or both".

Section 330016(1)(H) of such Act substituted "under this title" for "not more than $1,000". 1996, Act Oct 11, 1996 (effective on 9/13/94, pursuant to § 604(d) of such Act, which appears at 18 USCS § 13 note) (amended § 320103(b) of Act Sept. 13, 1994, which amended this section.

Such Act further substituted "any State, Territory, Commonwealth, Possession, or District" for "any State, Territory, or District".

CROSS REFERENCES

Sentencing Guidelines for the United States Courts, 18 USCS Appx §§ 2H1.1, 2H2.1.

Publisher added features or enhancements to code

RESEARCH GUIDE

Federal Procedure:
12 Fed Proc L Ed, Evidence § 33:209.

Am Jur:
15 Am Jur 2d, Civil Rights §§ 205–215.
29 Am Jur 2d, Evidence § 441.

Immigration:
1 Immigration Law and Procedure (Matthew Bender rev. ed.), Aliens' Rights, Privileges and Liabilities § 6.02.
6 Immigration Law and Procedure (Matthew Bender rev. ed.), Procedure in Deportation Cases § 72.03.
8 Immigration Law and Procedure (Matthew Bender rev. ed.), Judicial Review § 104.11.

Annotations:
Validity, construction, and application of 18 USCS §§ 241 and 242 (and similar predecessor provisions), providing criminal liability for conspiring to deprive, or depriving, person of civil rights—Supreme Court cases. 137 L Ed 2d 1091.

Law Review Articles:
To serve and protect: police civil liability. 41 Fed B News & June 1994.
Fink; Rohr. Scylla and Charybdis: charting a course for law enforcement officers caught between 42 U.S.C. § 1983 and 18 U.S.C. §§ 241 and 242. 41 Fed B News & J, June 1994.

INTERPRETIVE NOTES AND DECISIONS

I. IN GENERAL

1. Generally

There is no private right of action under either 18 USCS § 242 or 18 USCS § 1385. Robinson v Overseas Military Sales Corp. (1994, CA2, NY) 21 F3d 502, 64 BNA FEP Cas 638, 64 CCH EPD ¶ 42973.

6. Construction, generally

Criminal liability may be imposed under 18 USCS § 242 for deprivation of federal constitutional right only if, in light of pre-existing law, unlawfulness under Constitution is apparent; where unlawfulness is apparent, constitutional requirement of fair warning of § 242 liability is satisfied; single standard for fair warning does not point a single level of specificity, for (1) in some circumstances, as when earlier case expressly leaves open whether general rule applies to conduct at issue, very high degree of prior factual particularity may be necessary, while (2) in other instances, general constitutional rule already identified in decisional law may apply with obvious clarity to conduct in question, even though conduct has not previously been held unlawful. United States v Lanier (1997, US) 137 L Ed 2d 432, S Ct 1219, 97 CDOS 2350, 97 Daily Journal DAR 4168, 10 FLW Fed S 388.

7. Relationship with other laws

General terms of 18 USCS § 242 incorporate constitutional law by reference, in lieu of describing specific conduct forbidden, and thus, neither statute nor good many of its constitutional references delineate range of forbidden conduct with particularity.

8. Civil liability

Former federal employee's 18 USCS §§ 242 and 371 claims against federal judges were dismissed because it was impermissible to bring private cause of action under those statutes. Rockefeller v United States Court of Appeals Office (2003, DC Dist Col) 248 F Supp 2d 17.

II. ELEMENTS OF CRIME

10. Deprivation of rights protected by Federal Constitution or laws

Test of whether officers violated arrestees' or detainees' Fourth Amendment rights by use of excessive force—as distinct from determination of specific intent—is objective one. United States v Reese (1993, CA9 Cal) 2 F3d 870, 93 CDOS 5642, 93 Daily Journal DAR 9617, petition for certiorari filed (Oct 28, 1993) and (among conflicting authorities noted in United States v Lilly (CA1) 1994 US App LEXIS 69). United States v Lanier (1997, US) 137 L Ed 2d 432, 117 S Ct 1219, 97 CDOS 2350, 97 Daily Journal DAR 4168, 10 FLW Fed S 388.

Because 18 USCS § 242 is merely criminal analog of 42 USCS § 1983, and because Congress intended both statutes to apply similarly in similar situations, civil precedents are equally persuasive in criminal context. United States v Mohr (2003, CA4 Md) 318 F3d 613.

Double jeopardy does not bar federal prosecution of former police officer for violation of 18 USCS § 242, where he allegedly used excessive force and assaulted person while attempting to arrest him, even though he was found guilty of criminally negligent homicide in state trial, because (1) § 242 and state crime require proof of different elements and (2) doctrine of dual sovereignty allows federal indictment charging conduct that was previously subject of state prosecution. United States v Livoti (1998, SD NY) 8 F Supp 2d 246.

pocket part supplement. When this happens, a separately bound volume known as a *bound supplement* is produced. Periodically, new editions of the code are published.

Online Publications

The *United States Code Annotated* and *United States Code Service* are available through the Westlaw and Lexis websites, respectively. These retain most of the features available in the print versions and are updated routinely without the need for pocket part supplements. The unannotated code is found on numerous websites as described later in this chapter.

For a review of federal statutory research material see Box 5-3.

> BOX 5-3 FEDERAL STATUTORY RESEARCH MATERIAL
>
> - *Slip Laws:* publication of a single statute in pamphlet form
> - *Statutes at Large:* cumulative chronological publication of laws enacted by Congress during a congressional session
> - *United States Code:* topical organization of public statutory law
> - *United States Code Annotated:* topical organization of public statutory law with references to related legal materials
> - *United States Code Service:* topical organization of public statutory law with references to related legal materials

5-5 STATE STATUTORY LAW

Statutory law is enacted by all state legislatures and then codified. Because state governments are largely patterned after the federal government, the legislative process is similar.

Publication of state laws is similar to that of federal law. In general, statutes are published first as slip laws. At the end of the state congressional session, all laws are published in chronological fashion in works similar to the *Statutes at Large*. Although differences exist from state to state in what these works are called, they are often referred to as ***session laws***. Finally, state laws are organized and arranged topically in a code and can generally be found both in print and online.

session laws
Laws from state legislatures, published in chronological order.

Differences exist from state to state regarding the names of the codes. In some states, individual codes are assigned separate names and are cited by those names, for example, California Penal Code §187. On the other hand, some states follow the federal pattern and refer to the codes only by the state name and section number. Citation manuals, such as the *Bluebook*, explain how state codes are cited. In addition, like the federal codes, state codes are published in both annotated and unannotated form. State codes in print form are kept up to date by the use of pocket part supplements.

In addition to publications that contain the entire state code, many publishers produce books containing selected titles from the total code, for example the state's penal code. These are particularly useful to lawyers or paralegals who specialize in an area of law and want easy access to frequently needed codes. However, these are usually not annotated and not supplemented. Instead, each year a new volume is published and the old volume is discarded.

5-6 LOCAL ORDINANCES

The right to make laws belongs not only to federal and state governments but also to local governing bodies. These municipal or county laws, sometimes called ordinances or codes, are not as widely published as state and federal codes. Generally, they can be located in the local county law library or in the local public libraries. Many local ordinances are now online and accessible through the website for the local government.

5-7 ADMINISTRATIVE REGULATIONS

Much of the work of the federal government is accomplished through the creation of boards or agencies, known as *administrative agencies*. These agencies are empowered by Congress to make rules or regulations to carry out their functions. As administrative rules and regulations are adopted, they are printed in the *Federal Register*. The *Federal Register* is a daily government publication (except for weekends and holidays) that keeps the public informed of actions taken by administrative agencies. Included in the publication are the following:

1. Enacted or amended rules or regulations
2. Proposed rules
3. Notices of administrative hearings
4. Presidential proclamations

Like the *Statutes at Large,* the *Federal Register* is a chronological organization of rules and notices and therefore difficult to use.

In order to allow easier access to administrative rules, like the statutes, the administrative rules or regulations are topically organized in the *Code of Federal Regulations* (abbreviated C.F.R.). This code is organized in a manner similar to the *United States Code*. There are 50 titles, whose topics closely parallel the topics of the 50 titles of the *United States Code*. See Table 5-1 for a comparison of the title topics.

A major difference between the *Code of Federal Regulations* and the *United States Code* is how the laws are updated. The *United States Code* is updated with pocket part supplements. The *Code of Federal Regulations* is not. Checking the current state of administrative regulations is a cumbersome process. You must use a separate publication titled "LSA—List of CFR Sections Affected." This monthly update of federal regulations explains if any section of the *Code of Federal Regulations* was changed the Government Publishing Office. The LSA only tells you *if* the section was changed. It refers you to the *Federal Register* where you can see *what* the change is.

The *Federal Register,* the *Code of Federal Regulations,* and the "List of Sections Affected" can be accessed online through the website for the Government Publishing Office.

Because states have administrative agencies, administrative rules and regulations are also found at the state level. These can usually be located through the state's official website.

BOX 5-4 ADMINISTRATIVE REGULATIONS—RESEARCH MATERIAL

- *Code of Federal Regulations:* topical organization of federal administrative regulations
- *LSA—List of Sections Affected:* publication containing list of all administrative regulations that have changed
- *Federal Register:* monthly publication of all changes and proposed changes to administrative regulations

5-8 COURT RULES

rules of court
Procedural rules adopted by all courts regulating practice in the court.

Congress gives the courts the right to make rules for practice within the courts. These are known as court rules or ***rules of court***. The federal court has adopted several rules for practice in the federal courts, including the following.

Federal Rules of Civil Procedure
Federal Rules of Bankruptcy Practice
Federal Rules of Evidence
Federal Rules for Appellate Procedure
Federal Rules of Criminal Procedure

local rules of court
Procedural rules adopted by an individual court for practice in that specific court.

The rules of court are published with the codes. The Federal Rules can also be accessed online through numerous sources including the website for the U.S. Courts at http://www.uscourts.gov/RulesAndPolicies.aspx. In addition to the rules of court that apply in all federal courts, each court is allowed to adopt its own ***local rules of court***. These local rules are generally found on the website for the specific court.

State courts also have state rules of court as well as local rules of court for individual courts. You will probably find state rules of court with your state codes. A local law library should have copies of the local rules of court. The reference desk usually keeps the local rules of court. You also find most local rules of court on the websites for the individual courts.

5-9 UNIFORM LAWS AND MODEL CODES

uniform laws
Similar laws that are enacted by the legislatures of different states (i.e., Uniform Commercial Code); intended to create uniformity in the law.

model codes
A collection of sample laws; created for the states to adopt in whole or in part; helps to create uniformity in law.

Because each state makes its own laws, a number of differences exist in the law from state to state. In order to promote more uniformity among the states, representatives from the states draft proposed laws known as ***uniform laws*** and ***model codes***. The most noted uniform law is the Uniform Commercial Code, a code that regulates contracts for the sale of goods. There are over 175 proposed uniform laws. A uniform law or model code, however, is *not* law in any state unless it was enacted by the state's legislature. West (*Uniform Laws Annotated*) publishes the uniform laws and model codes in an annotated form. These books closely resemble other code books. The case annotations to uniform laws come from all jurisdictions. To read more about uniform codes and to see the uniform laws your state has adopted, go to http://www.uniformlaws.org/, the website for the National Conference of Commissioners on Uniform State Laws. The Legal Information Institute also has online information about uniform laws.

When researching statutory law, you must refer to your state's code and not the uniform law or model code. If your state has enacted a uniform law or model code, you can check the annotations in the uniform laws to find case law that controls your factual situation. Remember, however, if you find a case and it does not come from your state, it is only persuasive authority.

5-10 FINDING CONSTITUTIONAL PROVISIONS, STATUTORY LAW, ADMINISTRATIVE REGULATIONS, AND RULES OF COURT

Using a Citation

Print Resources. If you are using a print source, locating a constitutional provision, code section, or rule of court when you have the citation is an easy task. Consider the following citations:

U.S. Const. art. II, § 1, cl. 1
18 U.S.C. § 242

Locating the constitutional provision listed above requires only that you locate a copy of the U.S. Constitution. Since all of the parts of the Constitution are labeled, you simply look for Article II, Section 1, clause 1. Refer to Figure 5-5.

Locating the citation to a section of the *United States Code* is also straightforward. Although the code consists of several volumes, the outside binding clearly identifies the code sections contained in each volume. To find this citation, first look for the volume containing Title 18, then for the volume also containing Section 242. The same is true if you use the *United States Code Annotated* or the *United States Code Service*.

Online Resources. If you are using an online source rather than a print source, your research task is probably even easier. Online sources for the code use the same citations as the print sources. Some online sources provide an easy template for finding specific code sections.

Using an Index

Print Resources. A more difficult research problem is locating the *proper* law when you have a factual situation or problem and are looking for an answer to the problem in constitutional or statutory law. A number of different methods can be used to do this. Probably the most common way when searching print sources is to use the index found at the end of the code. The print versions of *United States Code,* the *United States Code Annotated,* and the *United States Code Service* all contain descriptive word indexes that refer the reader to relevant code sections. A code index is an alphabetical list of words describing topics or subjects found in the codes. Using an index effectively requires that you identify all words related to your research question. A legal dictionary and thesaurus can help. See Figure 5-6 for an example of a page from the index to the *United States Code.* Note the alphabetical arrangement of the list and the references to the title and section numbers of the code. Since the code publications are arranged numerically by title number and then by section number, you can easily locate the code sections found in the index.

FIGURE 5-5
Excerpt from U.S. Constitution

CONSTITUTION OF THE UNITED STATES OF AMERICA—1787[1]

① ← Preamble

WE THE PEOPLE of the United States, in Order to form a more perfect Union, establish Justice, insure domestic Tranquility, provide for the common defence, promote the general Welfare, and secure the Blessings of Liberty to ourselves and our Posterity, do ordain and establish this Constitution for the United States of America.

②ARTICLE I. ← Articles

SECTION 1. All legislative Powers herein granted shall be vested in a Congress of the United States, which shall consist of a Senate and House of Representatives.

SECTION 2. [1]The House of Representatives shall be composed of Members chosen every second Year by the People of the several States, and the Elector in each State shall have the Qualifications requisite for Electors of the most numerous Branch of the State Legislature.

[2]No Person shall be a Representative who shall not have attained to the Age of twenty five Years, and been seven Years a Citizen of the United States, and who shall not, when elected, be an Inhabitant of that State in which he shall be chosen.

[3]Representatives and direct Taxes shall be apportioned among the several States which may be included within this Union, according to their respective Numbers, which shall be determined by adding to the whole Number of free Persons, including those bound to Service for a Term of Years, and excluding Indians not taxed, three fifths of all other Persons.[2] The actual Enumeration shall be made within three Years after the first Meeting of the Congress of the United States, and within every subsequent Term of ten Years, in such Manner as they shall by Law direct. The Number of Representatives shall not exceed one for every thirty Thousand, but each State shall have at Least one Representative; and until such enumeration shall be made, the State of New Hampshire shall be entitled to chuse three, Massachusetts eight, Rhode-Island and Providence Plantations one, Connecticut five, New-York six, New Jersey four, Pennsylvania eight, Delaware one, Maryland six, Virginia ten, North Carolina five, South Carolina five, and Georgia three.

[4]When vacancies happen in the Representation from any State, the Executive Authority thereof shall issue Writs of Election to fill such Vacancies.

SECTION 4. The President, Vice President, and all civil Officers of the United States, shall be removed from Office on Impeachment for, and Conviction of, Treason, Bribery, or other high Crimes and Misdemeanors.

ARTICLE II.

SECTION 1.

CLAUSE 1: The executive Power shall be vested in a President of the United States of America. He shall hold his Office during the Term of four Years, and, together with the Vice President, chosen for the same Term, be elected, as follows

CLAUSE 2: Each State shall appoint, in such Manner as the Legislature thereof may direct a Number of Electors, equal to the whole Number of Senators and representatives to which the State may be entitled in the Congress: but no Senator or Representative, or Person holding an Office of Trust or Profit under the United States, shall be appointed an Elector.

CLAUSE 3: The Electors shall meet in their respective States, and vote by Ballot for two Persons, of whom one at least shall not be an Inhabitant of the same State with themselves. And they shall make a List of all the Persons voted for, and of the Number of Votes for each; which List they shall sign and certify, and transmit sealed to the Seat of the Government of the United States, directed to the President of the Senate. The President of the Senate shall, in the Presence of the Senate and House of Representatives, open all the Certificates, and the Votes shall then be counted. The Person having the greatest Number of Votes shall be the President, if such Number be a Majority of the whole Number of Electors appointed; and if there be more than one who have such Majority, and have an equal Number of Votes, then the House of Representatives shall immediately chuse by Ballot one of them for President; and if no Person have a Majority, then from the five highest on the List the said House shall in like Manner chuse the President. But in chusing the President, the Votes shall be taken by States, the Representation from each State having one Vote: A quorum for this Purpose shall consist of a Member or Members from two thirds of the States, and a Majority of all the States shall be necessary to a Choice. In every Case, after the Choice of the President, the Person having the greatest Number of Votes of the Electors shall be the Vice President. But if there should remain two or more who have equal Votes, the Senate shall chuse from them by Ballot the Vice President.

CLAUSE 4: The Congress may determine the Time of chusing the Electors, and the Day on which they shall give their Votes; which Day shall be the same throughout the United States.

CLAUSE 5: No Person except a natural born Citizen, or a Citizen of the United States, at the time of the Adoption of this Constitution, shall be eligible to the Office of the President; neither shall any Person be eligible to that Office who shall not have attained to the Age of thirty five Years, and been fourteen Years a Resident within the United States.

CLAUSE 6: In Case of the Removal of the President from Office, or of his Death, Resignation, or Inability to discharge the Powers and Duties of the said Office *(See Note 9)* the Same shall devolve on the Vice President, and the Congress may by Law provide for the Case of Removal, Death, Resignation or Inability, both of the President and Vice President,

FIGURE 5-6 Index to Code

18 U.S.C. § 242 contains the terms "under color of law" and "deprivation of civil rights."

Online Resources. The Westlaw and Lexis databases contain an index to the *United States Code*. However, versions of the *United States Code* on government, commercial, or educational sites often do not have an index. However, many of these do allow a "keyword" search. This type of search resembles the index search method. Special capabilities of computer searching make the index unnecessary.

Popular Name Tables

In addition to topical indexes, the various print editions of the code contain popular name tables. When laws are passed, many of them have popular names, such as "Civil Rights Act of 1968." By checking this name in the table of popular names, you learn the proper citation and are able to find the law. (See Figure 5-7.) In addition to indexes, statutory law can be located using secondary sources. Chapters 7 and 8 discuss this. In addition, a general search engine, such as Google, will often identify the code section with a popular name.

Regardless of the method you use to locate relevant statutory law, always be sure to check for any pocket part supplement for current law.

Legislative materials on the Internet are discussed in Section 5-11 of this chapter. Online searching in general is discussed in more detail in Chapters 10 and 11. When using an online version of statutory law, you will not find pocket part supplements. Official versions of the *United States Code* as well as Westlaw and Lexis provide updated versions of the code. However, sometimes you may access websites with older versions of the law. Always verify the date of publication for any law you find on websites.

Finding Administrative Regulations and Rules of Court

Finding a particular topic in the *Code of Federal Regulations* is similar to finding a topic in the *United States Code*. That is, words or phrases describing the topic are located in an index. The index then directs you to appropriate titles and sections of the regulations. Verifying that the law is current, however, cannot be done as it is with the codes. Unfortunately, the *Code of Federal Regulations* is not regularly supplemented with pocket part supplements. Checking for revisions or changes is a two-step process. First, refer to the "LSA—List of CFR Sections Affected," a monthly publication listing regulations that have changed and telling you where to find the change in the *Federal Register*. This publication is both in print format and online. However, a daily update is available only online. Second, refer to the *Federal Register* to see how the regulation was changed.

Since rules of court are generally published with the codes, finding these are similar to finding the codes. They can be located by citation or through an index or secondary source. They can also be located on the court's website.

5-11 LEGISLATIVE MATERIALS ON THE INTERNET

The Internet is a valuable resource for locating legislative materials. You will find not only the law itself, but numerous congressional publications and documents. Information is located on government, education, and commercial websites. This section focuses on locating legislative materials on government websites. (Some other websites are described in Chapter 11.) Also, because of the variety of websites, a list of relevant sites with the URLs is found in this chapter's feature, Online Research.

FIGURE 5-7 Popular Name Index

18 U.S.C. § 242 is popularly called "Civil Rights Act of 1968." If you know that, you check the popular name and it refers you to 18 U.S.C. § 242 among other code sections.

Civil Liberties Act Amendments of 1992

Pub. L. 102–371, Sept. 27, 1992, 106 Stat. 1167

Civil Obedience Act of 1968

Pub. L. 90–284, title X, Apr. 11, 1968, 82 Stat. 90 (Title 18, §§ 231–233)

Civil Relief Act (Soldiers and Sailors)

See Soldiers' and Sailors' Civil Relief Acts of 1918 and 1940

Civil Rights Acts

See Title 42, §§ 1971 et seq., 1981 et seq.

Apr. 9, 1866, ch. 31, 14 Stat. 27

May 31, 1870, ch. 114, 16 Stat. 140

Feb. 28, 1871, ch. 99, 16 Stat. 433

Apr. 20, 1871, ch. 22, 17 Stat. 13

Mar. 1, 1875, ch. 114, §§ 3–5, 18 Stat. 336, 337

Civil Rights Act of 1957

Pub. L. 85–315, Sept. 9, 1957, 71 Stat. 634 (Title 28, §§ 1343, 1861; Title 42, §§ 1971, 1971 note, 1975–1975e, 1995)

Pub. L. 86–383, title IV, § 401, Sept. 28, 1959, 73 Stat. 724

Pub. L. 86–449, May 6, 1960, titles IV, VI, 74 Stat. 89, 90

Pub. L. 87–264, title IV, Sept. 21, 1961, 75 Stat. 559

Pub. L. 88–152, § 2, Oct. 17, 1963, 77 Stat. 271

Pub. L. 88–352, title V, July 2, 1964, 78 Stat. 249

Pub. L. 90–198, § 1, Dec. 14, 1967, 81 Stat. 582

Pub. L. 91–521, Nov. 25, 1970, 84 Stat. 1356

Pub. L. 92–64, Aug. 4, 1971, 85 Stat. 166

Pub. L. 92–496, Oct. 14, 1972, 86 Stat. 913

Pub. L. 94–292, § 2, May 27, 1976, 90 Stat. 524

Pub. L. 95–132, § 2, Oct. 13, 1977, 91 Stat. 1157

Pub. L. 95–444, §§ 2–7, Oct. 10, 1978, 92 Stat. 1067, 1068

Pub. L. 96–81, §§ 2, 3, Oct. 6, 1979, 93 Stat. 642

Pub. L. 96–447, § 2, Oct. 13, 1980, 94 Stat. 1894

Civil Rights Act of 1960

Pub. L. 86–449, May 6, 1960, 74 Stat. 86 (Title 18, §§ 837, 1074, 1509; Title 20, §§ 241, 640; Title 42, §§ 1971, 1974–1974e, 1975d)

Civil Rights Act of 1964

Pub. L. 88–352, July 2, 1964, 78 Stat. 241 (Title 28, § 1447; Title 42, §§ 1971, 1975a–1975d, 2000a et seq.)

Pub. L. 92–261, §§ 2–8, 10, 11, 13, Mar. 24, 1972, 86 Stat. 103–113

Pub. L. 92–318, title IX, § 906(a), June 23, 1972, 86 Stat. 375

Pub. L. 93–608, § 3(1), Jan. 2, 1975, 88 Stat. 1972

Pub. L. 94–273, § 3(24), Apr. 21, 1976, 90 Stat. 377

Pub. L. 95–251, § 2(a)(11), Mar. 27, 1978, 92 Stat. 183

Pub. L. 95–555, § 1, Oct. 31, 1978, 92 Stat. 2076

Pub. L. 95–598, title III, § 330, Nov. 6, 1978, 92 Stat. 2679

Pub. L. 95–624, § 5, Nov. 9, 1978, 92 Stat. 3462

Pub. L. 96–191, § 8(g), Feb. 15, 1980, 94 Stat. 34

Pub. L. 100–259, § 6, Mar. 22, 1988, 102 Stat. 31

Pub. L. 102–166, title I, §§ 104, 105(a), 106–108, 109(a), (b)(1), 110(a), 111, 112, 113(b), 114, Nov. 21, 1991, 105 Stat. 1074–1079

Pub. L. 102–411, § 2, Oct. 14, 1992, 106 Stat. 2102

Pub. L. 103–382, title III, § 391(q), Oct. 20, 1994, 108 Stat. 4024

Civil Rights Act of 1968

Pub. L. 90–284, Apr. 11, 1968, 82 Stat. 73–92 (Title 18, §§ 231–233, 241, 242, 245, 1153, 2101, 2102; Title 25, § 1301 et seq.; Title 28, § 1360 note; Title 42, §§ 1973j, 3533, 3535, 3601 et seq.)

Pub. L. 93–265, Apr. 12, 1974, 88 Stat. 84

Pub. L. 93–383, title VIII, § 808(b), Aug. 22, 1974, 88 Stat. 729

Pub. L. 100–430, §§ 4, 5, 6(a), (b)(1), (2), (c)–(e), 7–10, 15, Sept. 13, 1988, 102 Stat. 1619–1636

Pub. L. 101–511, title VIII, § 8077(b), (c), Nov. 5, 1990, 104 Stat. 1892

Civil Rights Act of 1991

Pub. L. 102–166, Nov. 21, 1991, 105 Stat. 1071

Pub. L. 102–392, title III, § 316, Oct. 6, 1992, 106 Stat. 1724

Pub. L. 103–50, § 1204(a), July 2, 1993, 107 Stat. 268

Pub. L. 103–283, title III, § 312(f)(1)–(3), July 22, 1994, 108 Stat. 1446

Civil Rights Attorney's Fees Awards Act of 1976

Pub. L. 94–559, Oct. 19, 1976, 90 Stat. 2641 (Title 42, §§ 1981 note, 1988)

Civil Rights Commission Act of 1978

Pub. L. 95–444, Oct. 10, 1978, 92 Stat. 1067 (Title 42, §§ 1975 note, 1975b–1975e)

Civil Rights Commission Act of 1983

Pub. L. 98–183, Nov. 30, 1983, 97 Stat. 1301 (title 42, § 1975 et seq.)

Pub. L. 101–180, § 2, Nov. 28, 1989, 103 Stat. 1325

Pub. L. 102–167, §§ 2–5, Nov. 26, 1991, 105 Stat. 1101

Pub. L. 102–400, § 2, Oct. 7, 1992, 106 Stat. 1955

Pub. L. 103–419, § 2, Oct. 25, 1994, 108 Stat. 4338

Civil Rights Commission Amendments Act of 1994

Pub. L. 103–419, Oct. 25, 1994, 108 Stat. 4338

A Point to Remember

When you use a general search engine to locate legislative materials, you sometimes retrieve documents in a "pdf" format. This is especially true when searching for court rules. Be sure to check the dates on these documents. They may not be current.

Constitutions

The U.S. Constitution can be located on the Internet on several freely accessible websites. Numerous commercial and educational websites provide access to the Constitution. In some instances, these sites provide a link to a congressionally produced version of the Constitution containing an analysis of the various provisions and references to important cases interpreting the document. This is known as *Constitution of the United States of America: Analysis and Interpretation*, sometimes referred to as the *Constitution Annotated.* This version can be located on the website of the U.S. Congress, the Law Library of Congress, or the Government Publishing Office (FDsys). (See Finding It Online for a list of URLs.) See Figure 5-8 for the title page of the Constitution. This version of the Constitution is helpful to researchers because it can be searched and it contains an analysis of the various articles and amendments as well as references to Supreme Court cases interpreting the provisions.

State constitutions are also generally accessible through the official website for the state. The Law Library of Congress (Guide to Law Online) also provides links through the general link, "States and Territories." See Figure 5-8.

FIGURE 5-8 Constitution Annotated (Online)

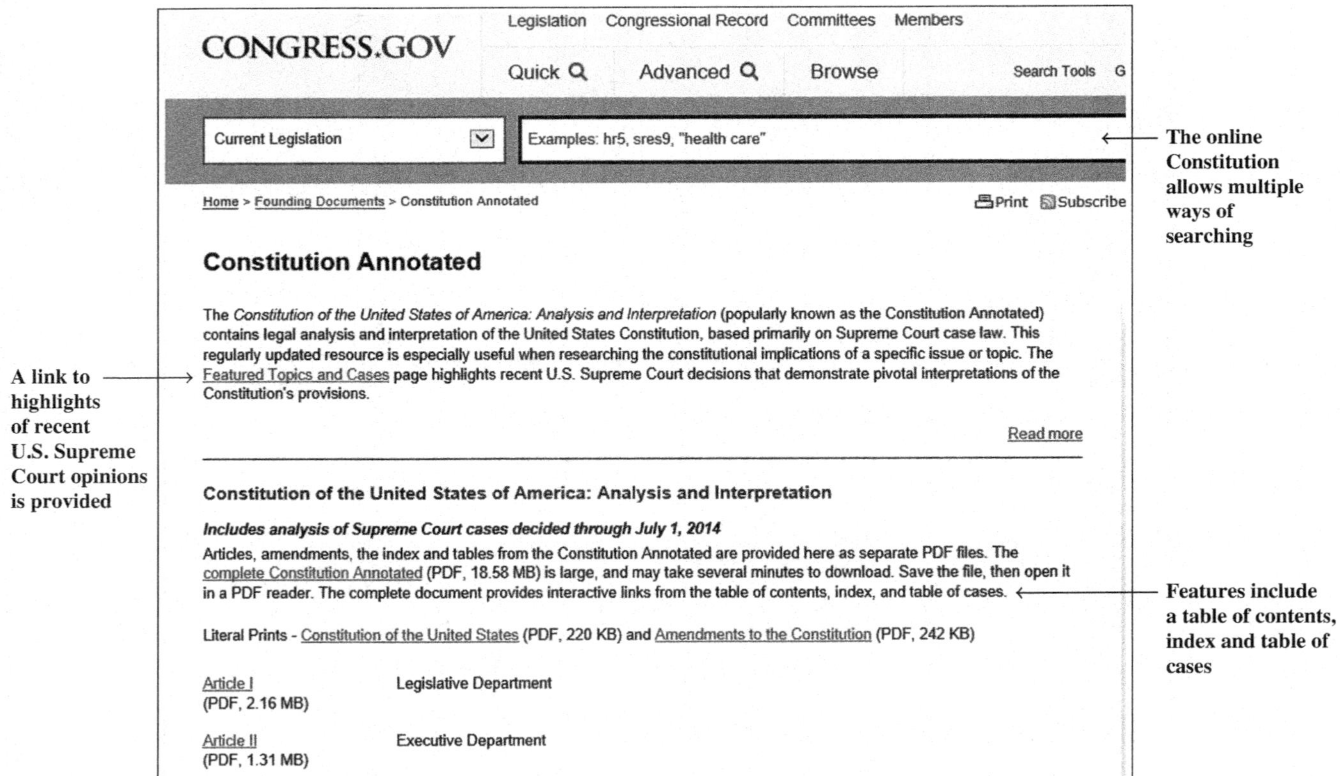

CONGRESS.GOV

Legislation Congressional Record Committees Members

Quick Advanced Browse Search Tools

Current Legislation | Examples: hr5, sres9, "health care"

Home > Founding Documents > Constitution Annotated

Print Subscribe

Constitution Annotated

The *Constitution of the United States of America: Analysis and Interpretation* (popularly known as the Constitution Annotated) contains legal analysis and interpretation of the United States Constitution, based primarily on Supreme Court case law. This regularly updated resource is especially useful when researching the constitutional implications of a specific issue or topic. The Featured Topics and Cases page highlights recent U.S. Supreme Court decisions that demonstrate pivotal interpretations of the Constitution's provisions.

Read more

Constitution of the United States of America: Analysis and Interpretation

Includes analysis of Supreme Court cases decided through July 1, 2014

Articles, amendments, the index and tables from the Constitution Annotated are provided here as separate PDF files. The complete Constitution Annotated (PDF, 18.58 MB) is large, and may take several minutes to download. Save the file, then open it in a PDF reader. The complete document provides interactive links from the table of contents, index, and table of cases.

Literal Prints - Constitution of the United States (PDF, 220 KB) and Amendments to the Constitution (PDF, 242 KB)

Article I (PDF, 2.16 MB) — Legislative Department

Article II (PDF, 1.31 MB) — Executive Department

Codes

The *United States Code* is accessible through several sources, including the websites of the Law Library of Congress and the Government Publishing Office. This code was prepared by the House of Representatives and has several search features to help the researcher. Refer to Figure 5-9A and you see that you can locate a code section with the citation or you can conduct a basic or advanced search. The site provides help for conducting advanced searches. See Figure 5-9B. In addition to the general search functions, other features also help the researcher, including a popular name table. Refer to Figure 5-9C.

State codes are also generally accessible through the Internet, generally through the legislative sites for the state. The Law Library of Congress (Guide to Law Online) provides links through general link "States and Territories." The website for the U.S. Congress also provides links.

FIGURE 5-9A United States Code (Online)

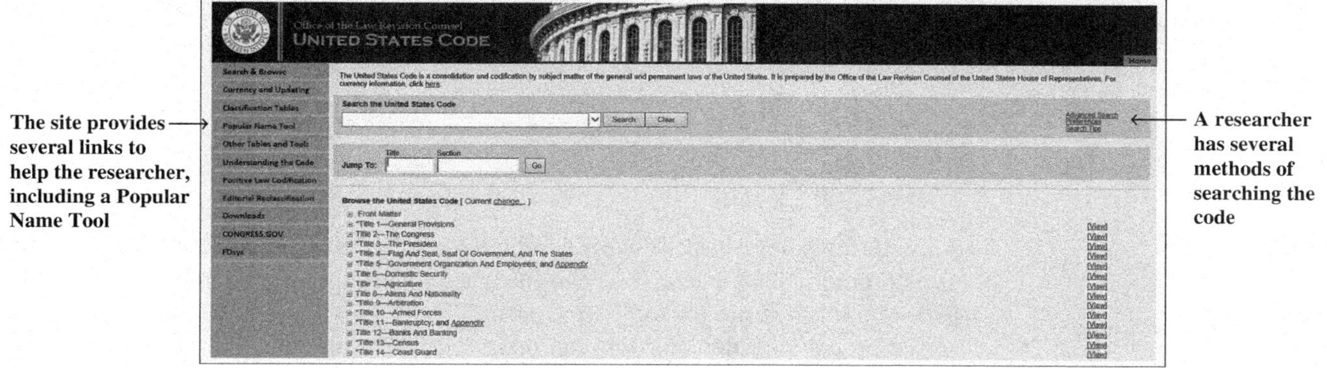

FIGURE 5-9B United States Code (Advanced Search Online)

Office of the Law Revision Counsel
UNITED STATES CODE
Search & Browse
Currency and Updating
Classification Tables
Popular Name Tool
Other Tables and Tools
Understanding the Code
Positive Law Codification
Editorial Reclassification
Downloads
CONGRESS.GOV
FDsys
ADVANCED SEARCH OPTIONS
Search in version: Current
General Search Terms:
Search In: Title Section
+ Also Search In...
Search For: Within: All Fields
+ Also Search For...
Search Clear
Search for references to: Title Section Search Clear
Developmental Deep Reference Searching
Search for references to: Title Section Subsec./Par./Subpar./Etc. Search Clear

Advanced search options allow more precision in searching

FIGURE 5-9C United States Code (Search Tips)

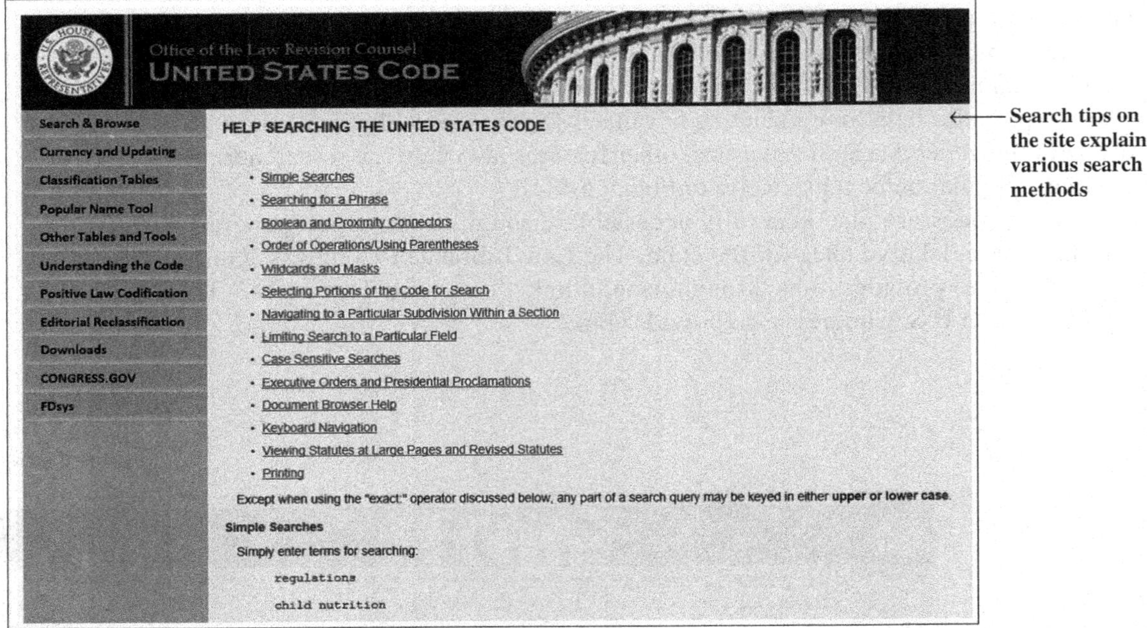

Rules of Court

As with other legislative materials, the Federal Rules of Court are found on several commercial websites. You can find the government publication of the Federal Rules on the website for the U.S. Courts.

Some state rules of court can be accessed through the Law Library of Congress (Guide to Law Online—"states and territories"). State rules of court are often found on a state's judicial website. Local rules of court are generally found on the specific court's website.

Administrative Regulations

The Code of Federal Regulations can be accessed through the U.S. Government Publishing Office Federal Digital System. Refer to Figure 5-10. The government also provides an electronic version of the code. State regulations can usually be accessed through the state's website.

Miscellaneous Legislative Materials

Numerous legislative publications are available on the GPO's Federal Digital System, including the Federal Register. Refer to Figure 5-10. The Federal Register also has a separate government-sponsored website.

Searching the GPO's Federal Digital System

As described above, numerous legislative materials can be accessed through the Government Publishing Office Federal Digital System (FDsys.) See Figure 5-10A for a list of these materials. The site permits different ways of searching. Researchers can conduct a simple, key word search, using the general search box on the home page. Using a variety of connectors, such as "and" or "or", researchers can create a more complex search query to produce better results. The site also allows one to search by citation. Using the search features on the site is not always easy. However, tutorials for searching as well as a "help" link provide extensive information about searching. See Figures 5-10A and 5-10B.

FIGURE 5-10A FDsys (Federal Digital System Online)

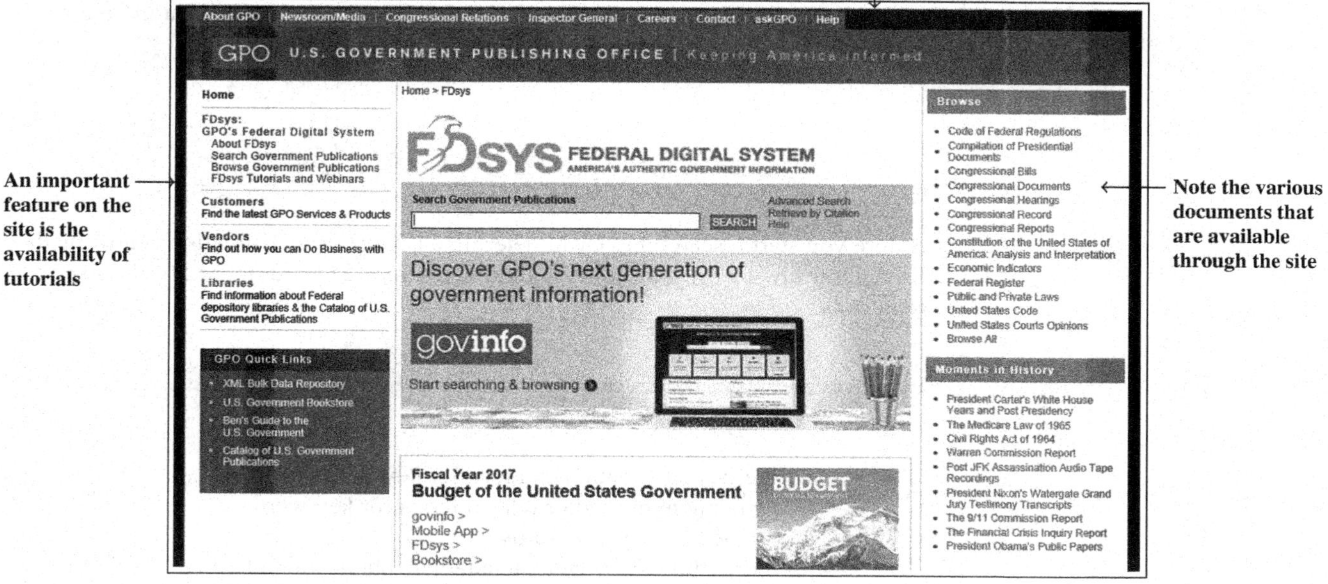

FIGURE 5-10B FDsys Search Help

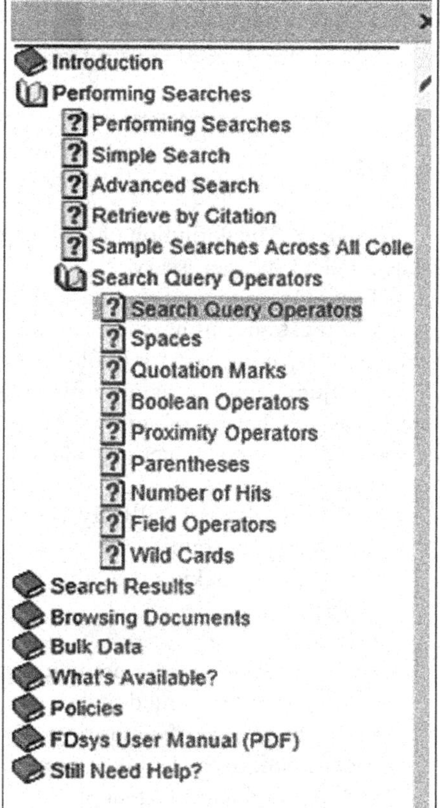

At some point in time, the Government Publishing Office plans on replacing the current FDsys website. A version of that replacement can be accessed at https://www.govinfo.gov/about.

A Point to Remember

Indexes are prepared by the publishers of the works and differ from edition to edition. If you are not successful in one index, check another.

If you are using an online version of the code, you may find that there is no index. Chapters 10 and 11 discuss search methods for online resources.

A Point to Remember

Before you start researching, try to determine if your factual situation is governed by federal law or by state law. Federal and state laws are generally published separately.

BOX 5-5 RESEARCH CHECKLIST: FINDING THE CODES

- Analyze factual situation and identify key words or terms.
- Consider synonyms and/or related terms for key words.
- Check index to code for words or terms.
- If unsuccessful, check index to alternate publication of code.
- Read code section.
- Check pocket part and any bound supplement.

The Writer's Corner

Lists Are Helpful

There are times when nothing beats a good list. Some statutes use long sentences that are difficult to understand. *Example:*

While doing research on a case involving robbery, you might locate this:

"Robbery is the taking of personal property from the person of another against his will, by either force or threat of force."

This definition uses several elements. Once you decide to use this definition in your legal analysis, it might help to set it up as an easy-to-read list:

Robbery is:

- The taking of personal property
- From the person of another
- Against his will,
- By force or
- By threat of force.

Example: The definition of espionage is more complicated and a list is necessary.

"Espionage is knowingly and willfully communicating, furnishing, transmitting, or otherwise making available to an unauthorized person, or publishing, or using in any manner prejudicial to the safety or interest of the United States, or for the benefit of any foreign government to the detriment of the United States, any classified information."

Espionage is:

- Knowingly and willfully communicating, furnishing, transmitting, or
- Otherwise making available to an unauthorized person, or
- Publishing, or
- Using in any manner prejudicial to the safety or
- Interest of the United States, or
- For the benefit of any foreign government to the detriment of the United States,
- Any classified information.

Finding It Online

Federal, state, and local statutory and regulatory materials are easily located on the Internet. Remember, however, that most free Internet sources do not contain annotations, such as case notations. Also remember to carefully check the date of any statutory or legislative material found on the Internet. The following is a list of Web sites for locating statutory and regulatory information on government Web sites:

Federal Resources

Annotated Constitution	https://www.congress.gov/constitution-annotated/
	https://www.loc.gov/law/help/guide/federal.php
	https://www.gpo.gov/fdsys/
US. Codes	http://uscode.house.gov/
	https://www.gpo.gov/fdsys/
	https://www.loc.gov/law/help/guide/federal.php
Code of Federal Regulations	www.ecfr.gov
	https://www.gpo.gov/fdsys/
Federal Rules of Court	http://www.uscourts.gov/rules-policies
Miscellaneous legislative materials	https://www.gpo.gov/fdsys/
	https://www.federalregister.gov/

State resources

	https://www.loc.gov/law/help/guide/states.php
	https://www.congress.gov/state-legislature-websites

CITATION MATTERS

UNITED STATES CONSTITUTION AND UNITED STATES CODE

***THE BLUEBOOK*—RULE 11**

This is the correct format for a citation to the Fourteenth Amendment to the United States Constitution:

U.S. CONST. amend. XIV.

United States Constitution Citation Analyzed

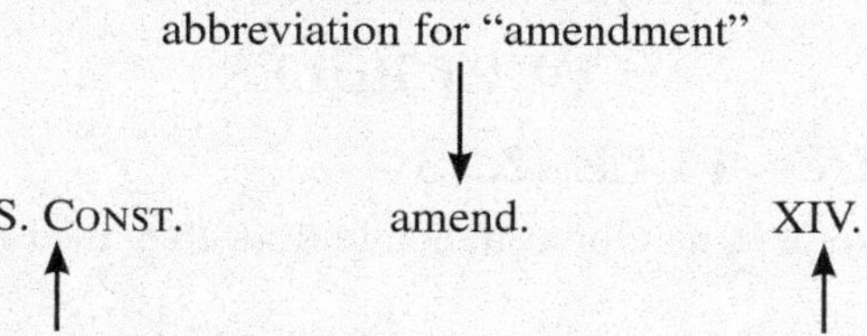

Other examples:

U.S. CONST. amend. XIV, § 2.

U.S. CONST. art. I, § 9, cl. 2.

(continued)

When you refer to one of the constitutional amendments, it is best to use the number spelled out. The number and the term amendment are capitalized, for example "Fourteenth Amendment." (In litigation documents Constitution can be abbreviated as Const.—Rule B11)

THE UNITED STATES CODE

THE BLUEBOOK—RULE 12

18 U.S.C. § 242 (2000)

Occupational Safety and Health Act (OSHA) of 1970, 29 U.S.C. § 651 (1988 & Supp. V 1993)

The *United States Code* (U.S.C.) is the official federal code. There are two popular unofficial federal codes. They are the *United States Code Service* (U.S.C.S.) and the *United States Code Annotated* (U.S.C.A.). You should cite to the official code when possible.

United States Code Citation Analyzed

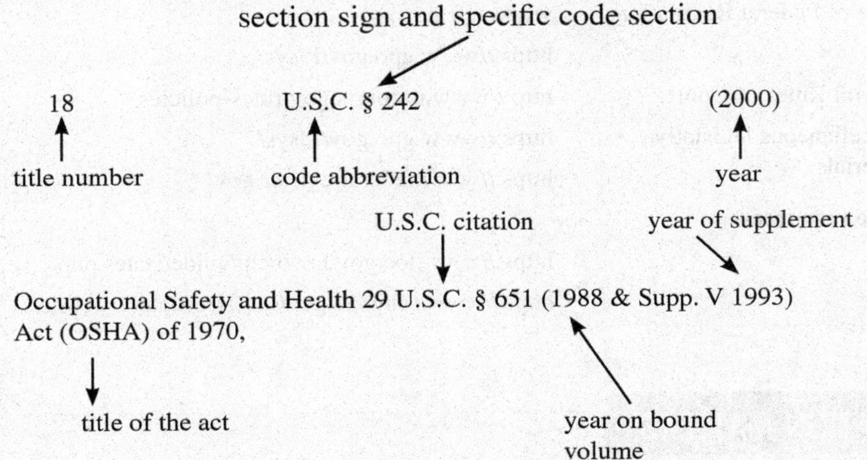

The Bluebook rules for citing the *United States Code* are detailed and complex. However, between Rule 12 and Table 1 (T.1), most situations are covered.

STATE CODES

THE BLUEBOOK—RULE 12

The Bluebook—Table 1 (t.1)

State codes are cited in much the same way the federal codes are cited. Each state has its own code. Each state has a specific format and special abbreviations. Look up the state in Table 1; review the examples.

COURT RULES

THE BLUEBOOK—RULE 12.9.3

This is the correct format for a citation to Rule 26 of the Federal Rules of Civil Procedure:

FED. R. CIV. P. 26

This is the correct format for a citation to Rule 6 of the Federal Rules of Criminal Procedure:

FED. R. CRIM. P. 6

This is the correct format for a citation to Rule 301 of the Federal Rules of Evidence:

FED. R. EVID. 301

CHAPTER SUMMARY

In addition to case law, primary law is found in constitutions, statutes or codes, administrative regulations, and court rules. All of these sources exist on the federal and state level. The U.S. Constitution, the supreme law of the land, can be located in numerous print and online sources, including publications of the *United States Code*. In these sources, the Constitution is indexed. The Constitution published with the annotated codes is also annotated, containing references to cases interpreting the various constitutional provisions or amendments.

Laws enacted by legislative bodies are *statutory laws*. Federal statutory law results from action by the U.S. Congress. Congress enacts both public laws and private laws. Public laws affect the general population. Private laws affect only named individuals or groups. When federal statutory law is enacted, it is first published in a pamphlet form and is known as *slip law*. At the end of each session of Congress, all of the public laws are published in chronological order in *Statutes at Large* and then topically organized and published as a code known as the *United States Code*. The *United States Code* is also published in an annotated form by two private publishers: West, which publishes the *United States Code Annotated*, and LexisNexis, which now publishes the *United States Code Service*. In an annotated format, the codes contain references to other legal resources, including cases that help with understanding the code. All print codes are indexed and kept up to date by the use of pocket part supplements. The *United States Code* appears on several websites. Although it is not indexed, many sites allow for a keyword search. Online versions of the codes are generally updated but do not use pocket part supplements. All states have statutory law found in state codes. Many local governments enact statutory law often known as *municipal ordinances* or *codes*.

Federal administrative agencies, created by Congress, often enact rules or regulations to carry out their functions. They are authorized by Congress to make these rules. Administrative rules or regulations are first published in the *Federal Register*, a monthly publication of the U.S. government. The regulations are topically organized and published in the *Code of Federal Regulations*. Courts are empowered by Congress to make rules for practice within the courts. These are known as *rules of court* and are published with the *United States Code*. States also have administrative regulations and rules of court.

Finding sections of the Constitution, codes, administrative regulations, or court rules requires that you know the citation. The citation can be found by analyzing your factual situation and identifying topics and key words. In print resources, those terms are then checked in a general index, which gives you the citation you need to find the law.

Legislative materials are generally accessible through the Internet and can be found on government, education, and commercial websites. An important source for legislative information is the website for the Government Publishing Office (Federal Digital System), known as FDsys. Other government agencies also have websites with legislative information. In some instances, the material can be searched by key word, by citation, or by advanced search queries.

TERMS TO REMEMBER

Bill of Rights
index
annotated
statutory law
bill
legislative history
public laws
private laws
slip law
code
positive law
legislative intent
pocket part supplement
repeal
amend
session laws
rules of court
local rules of court
uniform laws
model codes

QUESTIONS FOR REVIEW

1. What are the three parts of the U.S. Constitution?
2. Where will you find publications of the U.S. Constitution?
3. Describe the steps in the enactment of statutory law.
4. What do the following abbreviations mean?
   a. H.R. 346
   b. S. 123
   c. Public Law 104–398
5. What is a slip law?
6. What is contained in the *Statutes at Large?*
7. What are the similarities and differences among the *United States Code*, the *United States Code Annotated*, and the *United States Code Service?*
8. Explain the concept of positive law.
9. What is the importance of a pocket part supplement?

10. Describe the *Federal Register*, the *Code of Federal Regulations*, and "LSA—List of Sections Affected."
11. What are court rules?
12. How do you find a code section if you do not have the citation?
13. Explain how the Internet affects legislative research.

CAN YOU **FIGURE IT OUT?**

1. Refer to Figure 5-1 (Annotated Constitution). Does the preamble to the Constitution give powers to the federal government? Give the source of your answer.
2. Refer to Figure 5-2.
   a. Give the *Statutes at Large* citation for Public Law 103-322.
   b. Give the citation for the code sections affected by Public Law 103-322.
3. Refer to Figure 5-3.
   a. What is the number of the Public Law from the 103rd Congress that amended 18 U.S.C. §241?
   b. What is the year of this amendment?
4. Refer to Figure 5-4. Give a citation to a 1998 case that discusses 18 U.S.C.S. § 242.
5. Refer to Figure 5-6.
   a. What is the main topic indexed in this figure?
   b. Look at the subtopic "Desegregation." Under this, it states, "Public education, post, this heading." What does this mean?
   c. Look under the subtopic "Counselors." Here it states, "Attorneys and counselors, generally, ante, this heading." What does this mean?
   d. Look at the subtopic "Courts of Appeals." Here it says, "this index." What does this mean?
   e. What code section deals with obstruction of court orders?
6. Refer to Figure 5-7. Give the Public Law number and *Statutes at Large* citation for the Civil Rights Attorneys Fee Awards Act of 1976.

TEST **YOURSELF** (Check Your Answers in Appendix G)

Using either a print or online resource:

1. Find and summarize 6 U.S.C.A. § 111.
2. Find and summarize Fed. R. Civ. P. 61.
3. Find and summarize U.S. Const. art. 2 § 4.
4. Which *United States Code* section defines a criminal street gang?
5. Which Federal Rule of Civil Procedure describes the types of pleadings and motions for federal courts?

TEST **YOURSELF**—WRITE IT RIGHT Use a Short Introduction

Use a simple Introduction when writing to an audience who may not be familiar with your topic or who may need a something short to jog her memory.

There are times when a two- or three-sentence Introduction helps the reader get focused. This may, at first, seem unnecessary but consider this: You are asked to prepare a document and three weeks later that document is completed and you send it along to your supervisor for review. Your supervisor has not been thinking about this project. It is helpful to provide a concise reminder.

For example:

Introduction [for a supervisor]: You requested that I research the statute of limitations in the Cline matter. Under the current code we have another 54 days to file our claim for damages.

Introduction [for a court]: The Defendant files this Motion for Reconsideration in response to this court's ruling on December 5, 2016. The Defendant now has knowledge of new financial matters relevant to his case.

NOW, YOU TRY IT

(Check your answers in Appendix G)

1. You are asked to prepare a summarization of a deposition. You have completed that summary and you are preparing to send the document to your supervisor. It has been at least several weeks since you were asked to prepare the summary. The client is Adams; he owns a small store and he believes that the City is charging him fees that are unwarranted. The fees connect to his use of the sidewalk in front of his small café. You feel like the client has a good case based on the information in the deposition.

   Write an Introduction [to the supervisor] for the deposition summary.

CITATION **EXERCISES**

Use Appendix C and the Citation Matters feature in this chapter to answer these questions.

1. In a citation to the United States Constitution, what is the correct abbreviation for "amendment"?
2. In a citation to the *United States Code*, what is the correct abbreviation for the code?
3. State the *Bluebook* rule and the table that explain and show the correct format for citations to state codes.
4. State the correct citation for the Federal Rules of Evidence number 301.

FROM THE **WRITER'S CORNER** (Lists Are Helpful)

1. "Some statutes use ________ ____________________ that are difficult to understand."
2. Rewrite the following sentence as a list. "The plaintiff must prove that the defendant owed a duty of due care, that the duty was breached, that the defendant was the actual or proximate cause of the plaintiff's injuries."

ASSIGNMENTS AND **EXERCISES**

RESEARCH EXERCISES

Using Print or Online Sources, Answer the Following:

1. Find the following sections of the law. Summarize each in your own words.
   (a) 18 U.S.C. § 6002
   (b) 2 U.S.C. § 192
   (c) 11 U.S.C. § 541
2. Using the *United States Code*, answer the following questions and cite the source of your answer.
   (a) Who are the members of the National Council on the Arts?
   (b) Can a court award costs and attorney fees to successful litigants in a copyright infringement case?
   (c) Can one place an advertisement on the U.S. flag in Washington, D.C.?
   (d) Can a state impose income tax on retirement income of an individual who is not a resident or domicile of that state?
   (e) Which governmental entity or entities have the right to regulate the importation of honeybees into the United States? Why is it regulated? What is the punishment for unlawful importation?
   (f) When is failure to pay child support a federal crime?
   (g) Using a popular name table, find the Home Health Care and Alzheimer Disease Amendment of 1990. Where is this found in the *United States Code*? Is this a public law or a private law? How do you know?
3. Using an annotated *United States Code*, answer the following.
   (a) What code section makes it a crime for anyone to desecrate the flag? How has the Supreme Court considered this statute? Give the name and citation of a Supreme Court case or cases.
   (b) What is the punishment for counterfeiting? Review annotations in the U.S.C.S. and answer the following questions, providing full case citations using *The Bluebook*.
      1. Can states also have counterfeiting laws?
      2. Is it counterfeiting to insert a black-and-white photocopy of a $1 bill into a coin change machine?
4. Using a print or online version of the United States Constitution, answer the following questions.
   (a) What does U.S. CONST. art. IV, § 1 provide?
   (b) What does U.S. CONST. art. 1, § 2, cl.2 provide?
   (c) What does U.S. CONST. amend. XXV provide?
   (d) How often must Congress assemble, and when does the meeting begin? Give the authority for your answer.
   (e) Who has the power of impeachment? Give the authority for your answer.
5. Use a print or online source for rules of court and the *Code of Federal Regulations* to answer the following.
   (a) Summarize the following.
      1. Fed. R. Civ. P. 56
      2. Fed. R Crim. P. 6
      3. 27 C.F.R. § 555.180
   (b) Which federal rule sets out the requirement for the use of interrogatories in civil cases?
   (c) Can a deposition be used in a criminal case in federal court? Cite your authority.

ANALYSIS AND WRITING ASSIGNMENTS

6. Review the Meyers case. Assume that charges were brought against Meyers in your state court and you are asked to find the procedure for suppressing evidence

in that court. Create a list of terms that you might check in an index to the state codes or rules of court to begin this research task.

7. Read the code section cited in Research question 1(a) above. When can a witness not claim a right to self-incrimination?

Online Research Exercises

Access the website for the government publishing office, http://www.gpo.gov/fdsys/.

8. Access the version of the U.S. Constitution containing analysis and interpretation.
   (a) What right does the Seventh Amendment establish?
   (b) Does the right mentioned in the Seventh Amendment generally apply in state courts? Cite cases to support your answer.
   (c) Conduct a keyword search for due process. Which constitutional amendments expressly refer to this term?
9. Using any of the relevant websites listed in the chapter, find the following code sections and give the title of each:
   (a) 21 U.S.C. § 801
   (b) 15 U.S.C. § 1172
   (c) 42 U.S.C. § 3543
   (d) 8 C.F.R § 232.2
   (e) 6 C.F.R § 25.9
   (f) Federal Rules of Evidence 802

CASE **PROJECT**

Research federal and/or state codes for your Appendix A hypothetical case. List any relevant code sections and give a short summary of any code sections you find. List all terms that you checked in the index to the codes.

In-Class Small Group Work

Compare the research findings for your hypothetical case. Discuss the approaches you took to find the codes.

chapter **six**

STATUTORY AND CONSTITUTIONAL ANALYSIS

SKILL OBJECTIVES FOR CHAPTER 6

When you complete chapter 6, you should be able to

- Explain the relevance of the concept of federalism to constitutional analysis.
- Determine whether the U.S. Constitution or a state constitution applies to a factual situation arising under state law.
- Explain why it is helpful to outline statutory language.
- Discuss the importance of reviewing case law that interprets code provisions.
- Explain how legislative history affects statutory interpretation.
- List the four steps used in the IRAC approach in analyzing statutory law.
- Analyze a code section by identifying and outlining the statutory requirements or elements.
- Analyze a factual situation controlled by statutory law using the IRAC method.

CHAPTER OUTLINE

From the Desk of W. J. Bryan, Esq.

TO: Research Assistant
FROM: W. J. Bryan
RE: Our Client, Justin Meyers
DATE:

I am starting to outline the argument for my motion to suppress evidence in the Meyers case. I know you have located and read applicable constitutional provisions, statutes, and cases. I agree with your conclusion that Meyers's Fourth Amendment rights were violated, but would like to hear your explanation of how and why the Fourth Amendment applies to the Meyers case. We need to include that explanation in our motion to suppress the bloody handkerchief.

6-1 INTRODUCTION

In Chapter 5, you read about the Constitution and the different types of statutory law and administrative regulations. You also learned how to locate this type of law. However, researching constitutions, statutes, and administrative regulations requires more than merely locating the law, just as researching case law requires more than just finding a case. Researchers must understand and be able to explain how the law applies to a client's factual situation. This requires legal analysis.

As you read in Chapter 2, all legal analysis starts with identifying your client's legal issue and relevant facts. If your research produces case law, you start by comparing your client's factual situation with the facts of the cases you find. If your client's factual situation and issue are the same as that in the cases, and the cases are controlling in your jurisdiction, then the holdings or rules of law found in the cases apply to your case. However, legal analysis involving constitutions, statutes, and administrative rules and regulations is different. Unlike case law, these sources of law contain general rules that are not stated in reference to a specific factual situation.

After identifying your client's issue and key facts, you should begin constitutional or statutory analysis by examining the language of the law. Administrative regulations are analyzed in the same way. In both instances, your research and analysis are not complete until you consider cases that interpret the law. In this chapter, you see how to analyze statutory and constitutional laws.

6-2 CONSTITUTIONAL ANALYSIS

Article VI of the U.S. Constitution states that the Constitution is the supreme law of this land. "This Constitution, and the Laws of the United States which shall be made in Pursuance thereof … shall be the supreme Law of the Land; and the Judges in every State shall be bound thereby, any Thing in the Constitution or Laws of any State to the Contrary notwithstanding." It is therefore important to determine if a matter is controlled by any provision in the Constitution.

Many of the words and phrases found in the Constitution are not precise and are subject to various interpretations. Consider phrases such as "unreasonable search and seizure," "due process," and "equal protection." When faced with a research problem requiring interpretation and analysis of any provision in the U.S. Constitution, you must research case law that interprets that provision. The U.S. Supreme Court has the final say on what the U.S. Constitution means.

Constitutional research and analysis, however, sometimes presents an additional consideration. Many constitutional research problems deal with an individual's constitutional rights under the Bill of Rights (the first 10 amendments) and under the Due Process and Equal Protection Clauses of the Fourteenth Amendment. Consider the Meyers case. Recall from earlier chapters that local police searched Meyers's residence pursuant to a search warrant. Meyers was suspected of drug dealing. During the search, officers found and seized a bloody handkerchief. This evidence leads to criminal charges of murder against Meyers. These charges are filed in a state court. Meyers's attorney decides to make a motion to suppress the evidence of the bloody handkerchief on the grounds that it was an unreasonable search and seizure and violated the safeguards found in the Fourth Amendment to the U.S. Constitution. You are asked to help with the research.

You are faced with an important initial research question here. Should you begin your research in state sources or in federal sources? This is a state crime prosecuted in a state court. In all probability, this state has a state constitutional provision also regulating the area of search and seizure. However, the U.S. Constitution gives all individuals certain rights. Should your research focus on the state constitution and state cases or on the U.S. Constitution and Supreme Court cases? Recall that one of the first steps in legal analysis of constitutional (and statutory) law requires that you determine that a law applies to your case. In the Meyers case, therefore, you must determine whether federal or state constitutional law applies. This requires that you understand the concept of federalism and the relationship between state and federal governments.

Federalism—The Relationship between Federal and State Governments

In the United States, government operates under a principle called federalism. ***Federalism*** means that two separate governments regulate citizens: federal and state. The federal government has *limited* power over all 50 states. State governments have power only within their state boundaries. In addition, states cannot make laws that conflict with the laws of the federal government.

Because there are areas of ***concurrent jurisdiction***, conflicts sometimes exist between federal laws and state laws. Where a conflict exists, federal law controls because of the ***Supremacy Clause*** of the Constitution. When a state passes a law that conflicts with the Constitution, the U.S. Supreme Court has the power to declare the state law unconstitutional and unenforceable.

However, the fact that both state and federal governments regulate an area does not necessarily create a conflict. For example, if a defendant kidnaps a victim and takes the victim across state lines, both federal and state laws are violated and the defendant could be tried in either the state or federal court (or both) for the crime. Furthermore, in this situation the federal court has no priority over the state court.

In determining if a conflict between state and federal law exists, a particular problem arises in the area of criminal procedure. If an individual is arrested for a state crime, such as murder, that individual is tried in the state courts. States may formulate their own procedural rules and safeguards for this process. However, states are also bound by the Fourteenth Amendment to the Constitution, which provides in part, "nor shall any State deprive any person of life, liberty, or property, without due process of law." The U.S. Constitution does not set out specific rights that states must respect. Rather, it sets out a *minimum standard* that all states must follow, that is, due process. The Supreme Court decides what due process means. However, remember that it is a minimum standard. States can

federalism
A system of government in which the people are regulated by both federal and state governments.

concurrent jurisdiction
Jurisdiction or power exercised by two different entities.

Supremacy Clause
Clause in the U.S. Constitution providing that the U.S. Constitution is the supreme law of the land.

grant more rights to criminal defendants and not be in conflict with federal law. On the other hand, once the Supreme Court sets forth a specific minimum standard, states cannot take away a right. States may make laws in this area as long as those laws do not violate due process.

A conflict does not necessarily exist just because the state and federal rules differ. When you research such a problem, you must read Supreme Court cases to determine the minimum standard. You must then review state cases to determine how the state constitution has been interpreted. If the state constitution affords more rights, it controls. If it affords fewer rights, then the U.S. Constitution and the cases decided by the U.S. Supreme Court control.

A Point to Remember

Where conflicts exist between federal and state laws, the federal law controls. However, not all differences result in a conflict. Do not assume that federal law always controls. In determining if a difference results in a conflict, first determine if the federal law preempted the area of law. If it has, then the federal law controls. If the federal law has not preempted the area, then read the federal law carefully to determine its meaning. You must understand the federal law to determine if a conflict exists in the state law.

The Writer's Corner

"Place Yourself in the Background"

Mr. William Strunk, Jr., and Mr. E. B.White in *The Elements of Style* advise you to "place yourself in the background." That is excellent advice. They suggest we should write such that the focus is on the substance and sense of the written material.

Many writers want to be part of the substance and sense of the writing. In legal writing, that is rarely appropriate.

Avoid telling your audience what *you* think. Instead, explain the facts as they occurred. State the legal issue. Explain the rule of law. Explain the application of the rule of law to the facts. Reach conclusions based on the application of the law to the facts. This is a sound approach to legal analysis and legal writing.

Avoid the use of the pronoun "I" and the phrase "I think"—there is little use in legal writing for the pronoun "I." The audience rarely cares what the writer thinks. The focus is on what the law says and how that law can be applied to a client's facts.

Terms to avoid:

I

we

our

my

Edit your written work for these terms. Place yourself in the background.

6-3 ANALYZING STATUTES AND REGULATIONS

Determine if a Law Applies

Just as with constitutional law, before analyzing a statute or regulations, you must first determine that the law applies to your client's factual situation. Sometimes the words of the statute answer this question. Other times, you find clues in the organization of the laws. For example, a rule setting forth motion procedures found in the Federal Rules of Criminal Procedure would not apply to a motion made in a civil case. Sometimes only part of a statute or regulation applies. Codes and rules are sometimes written to cover numerous types of factual situations. For example, consider Rule 4 of the Federal Rules of Civil Procedure—the rule that establishes the methods of serving a civil complaint in a lawsuit. This rule is very long and consists of several subparts. The titles of some of the subparts are the following:

e. Serving an Individual within a Judicial District of the United States.
f. Service upon Individuals in a Foreign Country.
g. Serving a Minor or an Incompetent Person.
h. Serving a Corporation, Partnership, or Association.
i. Serving the United States, Its Agencies, Corporations, Officers, or Employees.
j. Serving a Foreign, State, or Local Government.

Under each of these subparts are directions for service of the complaint and summons. If you were asked to find the rules for serving a corporation doing business within the United States, you would read and follow the procedures found in subsection (h), not those found in any of the other subsections.

Outline Statutory or Regulatory Language

After identifying a client's issue and relevant facts, and after you determine that a statute or rule applies to your facts, legal analysis requires that you determine the meaning of the relevant law. This is not always easy. Unfortunately, statutory language is often cumbersome and confusing. Understanding statutory law requires that you read the law carefully. Although different types of code sections require different approaches to analysis, outlining the language of the law is usually helpful. For example, in researching the procedure for making a motion to suppress evidence, the research associate working on the Meyers case might find a state law similar to Rule 47 of the Federal Rules of Criminal Procedure, which provides the following.

Rule 47. Motions and Supporting Affidavits

a. ***In General.*** A party applying to the court for an order must do so by motion.
b. ***Form and Content of a Motion.*** A motion—except when made during a trial or hearing—must be in writing, unless the court permits the party to make the motion by other means. A motion must state the grounds on which it is based and the relief or order sought. A motion may be supported by affidavit.
c. ***Timing of a Motion***. A party must serve a written motion—other than one that the court may hear ex parte—and any hearing notice at least seven days before the hearing date, unless a rule or court order sets a different period. For good cause, the court may set a different period upon ex parte application.
d. ***Affidavit Supporting a Motion.*** The moving party must serve any supporting affidavit with the motion. A responding party must serve any opposing affidavit at least one day before the hearing, unless the court permits later service.

(As amended Apr. 29, 2002, eff. Dec. 1, 2002; Mar. 26, 2009, eff. Dec. 1, 2009.)

Outlining this rule protects you from missing an essential step in the procedures. An outline of this section might look something like the following:

A. Form and Content of the Motion
   1. Must be in writing, unless court says otherwise
   2. Must state the grounds for the motion

3. Must state the relief requested
4. Must be supported by affidavits

B. Timing of Service
   1. Seven days service of written notice required
   2. Court can set different time by order or by court rule

C. Supporting and Opposing Affidavits
   1. Affidavits supporting motion must be served with motion
   2. Affidavits opposing motion must be served one day prior to court hearing
   3. Court can permit later service

Rather than setting forth procedures to be followed, many statutes establish rights, liabilities, and obligations. This type of statute usually identifies requirements that must be met before the rights, liabilities, or obligations arise. For example, consider the federal statute making it a crime to be an "accessory after the fact." The code (18 U.S.C. § 3) provides:

> Whoever, knowing that an offense against the United States has been committed, receives, relieves, comforts or assists the offender in order to hinder or prevent his apprehension, trial or punishment, is an accessory after the fact.

By outlining the section, the researcher knows that a violation of this law occurs only when all of the following elements are met:

1. A person knows that an offense against the United States was committed
2. That person receives, relieves, comforts, or assists the offender
3. Aid was given in order to hinder or prevent the apprehension, trial or punishment of the offender.

In many instances, outlining and analyzing a statute is not a simple task. For example, consider Research Problem 4 in Appendix A, *The Rambeaux Matter*. This case arises from a traffic stop made by an off-duty police officer who was still in uniform. Individuals in the vehicle claim that the officer used excessive force during the stop and made racial slurs. The federal prosecutor is considering filing criminal charges against the officer for a civil rights violation under 18 U.S.C. § 242. That section provides:

> Whoever, under color of any law, statute, ordinance, regulation, or custom, willfully subjects any person in any State, Territory, Commonwealth, Possession, or District to the deprivation of any rights, privileges, or immunities secured or protected by the Constitution or laws of the United States, or to different punishments, pains, or penalties, on account of such person being an alien, or by reason of his color, or race, than are prescribed for the punishment of citizens, shall be fined under this title or imprisoned not more than one year, or both; and if bodily injury results from the acts committed in violation of this section or if such acts include the use, attempted use, or threatened use of a dangerous weapon, explosives, or fire, shall be fined under this title or imprisoned not more than ten years, or both; and if death results from the acts committed in violation of this section or if such acts include kidnapping or an attempt to kidnap, aggravated sexual abuse, or an attempt to commit aggravated sexual abuse, or an attempt to kill, shall be fined under this title, or imprisoned for any term of years or for life, or both, or may be sentenced to death.

As with the statute dealing with an accessory after the fact, this statute creates criminal liability if certain requirements are met. These are sometimes called ***statutory requirements*** or sometimes the statutory elements. In this statute, the connectors ("and" and "or") between the elements are important. By outlining the code section, the researcher determines that the law requires the following elements before any criminal responsibility exists:

statutory requirements
Various requirements or elements of a statute that must be met before the statute applies to a situation.

1. Someone must act under color of law ***and***
2. Act willfully ***and***
3. Deprive another of rights granted under the Constitution *or* the laws of United States
4. ***Or*** subject another to different punishments, pains or penalties, ***and*** do this because of race ***or*** color ***or*** because of being an alien.

To analyze a statute, you must pay close attention to all "connectors" and "qualifiers" such as *shall, and, or, except, unless,* and *provided that.* These tell you if all or only some of the elements or requirements must be met before a statute applies to a set of facts.

Before listing the elements of a statute, you should identify the research issue or question. The elements in the previous list answer the question "When does basic criminal responsibility occur?" If your question is different, your analysis is different. For example, suppose your research question is "What is Rambeaux's potential punishment?" To answer this question, you must include the punishment described in the statute.

Outlining a statute or regulation is only one step in the process of analysis. Words or phrases in statutes and regulations are sometimes unclear or ambiguous. Solving these ambiguities or uncertainties is the job of the researcher. This is done in different ways.

Review Case Law That Interprets Code or Regulatory Provisions

If case law explains a statute or regulation and that case law is controlling law in the jurisdiction, the rule of ***stare decisis*** requires that the court's interpretation be followed. Consider again the Rambeaux case and the criminal liability statute. A number of questions arise depending on the facts of the case. For example, what does the phrase "under color of any law" mean? Does it include a police officer? What if Rambeaux is off duty at the time of the shooting? Is he still acting under color of law? To answer these questions, it is necessary to see how the courts interpret the statute. One way to find relevant cases is to examine the notes of decision found in an annotated code, such as the United States Code Annotated or United States Code Service. Look at Figure 6-1 containing some of the case notes following 18 U.S.C.S. § 242. Looking at these case notes, you see that case law provides interpretations of the code. Of course, you cannot rely on reading only the annotation. You must read the entire case.

stare decisis
"It stands decided"; another term for *precedent.*

A Point to Remember

When using a print resource, always check the pocket part or bound supplement. Even if a code section was not amended, new case decisions may add to the interpretation of the statute.

FIGURE 6-1 18 U.S.C.S. § 242
Source: Reprinted with permission of LexisNexis.

18 USCS § 242, n 9 CRIMES & CRIMINAL PROCEDURE

lowing elements must be established by government, namely: (1) that defendants' acts must have deprived someone of right secured or protected by Constitution or laws of United States; (2) that defendants' illegal acts must have been committed under color of law; (3) that person deprived of his rights must have been inhabitant of state, territory, or district; and (4) that defendants must have acted willfully. United States v Shafer (1974, DC Ohio) 384 F Supp 496.

Elements of offense under 18 USCS § 242 are (1) that action was taken under color of state law, (2) wilfully to deprive rights protected by Constitution and laws of United States, (3) from inhabitant of any state of United States. United States v Fleming (1975, ED Mo) 399 F Supp 77, revd on other grounds (1975, CA8 Mo) 526 F2d 191, cert dismd (1976) 423 US 1082, 47 L Ed 2d 93, 96 S Ct 872.

10. Deprivation of rights protected by Federal Constitution or laws

Predecessor of 18 USCS § 242 making it federal offense wilfully to deprive any person under color of law of any rights, privileges, or immunities secured or protected by Constitution and laws of United States, does not come into play merely because law under which officer purports to act is violated, but is applicable only when some one is deprived of Federal right by such action. Screws v United States (1945) 325 US 91, 89 L Ed 1495, 65 S Ct 1031, 162 ALR 1330.

Both 18 USCS § 241, which makes conspiracy to interfere with citizen's free exercise or enjoyment of any right or privilege secured to him by Constitution or laws of United States federal offense, and 18 USCS § 242, which makes it federal offense wilfully to deprive any person under color of law of same rights, include, presumably, all of Constitution and laws of United States. United States v Price (1966) 383 US 787, 16 L Ed 2d 267, 86 S Ct 1152 (ovrld on other grounds by Adickes v S. H. Kress & Co. (1970) 398 US 144, 26 L Ed 2d 142, 90 S Ct 1598) as stated in Gresham Park Community Organization v Howell (1981, CA5 Ga) 652 F2d 1227.

Federal court had jurisdiction where defendant was charged with depriving named person of rights and privileges under Constitution of United States, even though acts of defendants also violated laws of state. Williams v United States (1950, CA5 Fla) 179 F2d 656, affd (1951) 341 US 97, 95 L Ed 774, 71 S Ct 576.

18 USCS § 242 is concerned only with deprivation of rights guaranteed by federal law or Constitution. United States v O'Dell (1972, CA6 Tenn) 462 F2d 224.

Once due process right has been defined and made specific by court decisions, right is encompassed by 18 USCS § 242. United States v Hayes (1979, CA5 Tex) 589 F2d 811, reh den (1979, CA5 Tex) 591 F2d 1343 and cert den (1979) 444 US 847, 62 L Ed 2d 60, 100 S Ct 93.

Acts done under color of state law do not violate federal law if only local rights are involved, since constitutional right must be violated before federal law is involved. Arkansas use of Temple v Central Surety & Ins. Corp. (1952, DC Ark) 102 F Supp 444.

11. Illegal act committed under color of law, generally

Predecessor to 18 USCS § 242 required actions under color of state law. United States v Powell (1909) 212 US 564, 53 L Ed 653, 29 S Ct 690.

It is immaterial, for purposes of predecessor to 18 USCS § 242, whether acts committed under color of state law are authorized by state law. Guinn v United States (1915) 238 US 347, 59 L Ed 1340, 35 S Ct 926.

Misuse of power, possessed by virtue of state law and made possible only because wrongdoer is clothed with authority of state law, is action taken "under color of" state law, within meaning of predecessor of 18 USCS § 242 making it offense to deprive inhabitant of state of his constitutional rights "under color of" any law. United States v Classic (1941) 313 US 299, 85 L Ed 1368, 61 S Ct 1031, reh den (1941) 314 US 707, 86 L Ed 565, 62 S Ct 51 and (ovrld on other grounds by Monell v Department of Social Services (1978) 436 US 658, 56 L Ed 2d 611, 98 S Ct 2018, 17 BNA FEP Cas 873, 16 CCH EPD ¶ 8345) as stated in Scott v Rosenberg (1983, CA9 Cal) 702 F2d 1263, cert den (1984) 465 US 1078, 79 L Ed 2d 760, 104 S Ct 1439, later proceeding (1984, CA9 Cal) 739 F2d 1464, 39 FR Serv 2d 1295 and later proceeding (1984, CA9 Cal) 746 F2d 1377.

Question was not whether state law had been violated but whether inhabitant of state had been deprived of federal right by one who acted under color of any law. Screws v United States (1945) 325 US 91, 89 L Ed 1495, 65 S Ct 1031, 162 ALR 1330.

Phrase "under color of any statute, ordinance, regulation, or custom" should be accorded same construction in both 18 USC § 242, which provides for criminal punishment of, and Rev Stat § 1979 (42 USC § 1983), which gives right of action against, person who, "under color of" state law, subjects another to deprivation of any rights, privileges, or immunities secured by Federal Constitution. Monroe v Pape (1961) 365 US 167, 5 L Ed 2d 492, 81 S Ct 473 (ovrld on other grounds by Monell v Department of Social Services (1978) 436 US 658, 56 L Ed 2d 611, 98 S Ct 2018, 17 BNA FEP Cas 873, 16 CCH EPD ¶ 8345) and (ovrld on other grounds by Ingraham v Wright (1977) 430 US 651, 51 L Ed 2d 711, 97 S Ct 1401) as stated

452

Annotations from Main Volume and Supplement.

FIGURE 6-1 (continued)

CRIMES **18 USCS § 242, n 16**

identically in four other provisions of Title 18, namely, 18 USCS §§ 831, 1365(h)(4), 1515(a)(5, 1864(d)(2), as (A) cut, abrasion, bruise, burn, or disfigurement; (B) physical pain; (C) illness; (D) impairment of a/the function of bodily member, organ, or mental faculty; or (E) any other injury to body, no matter how temporary. United States v Bailey (2005, CA1 Mass) 405 F3d 102.

10. Deprivation of rights protected by Federal Constitution or laws

Test of whether officers violated arrestees' or detainees' Fourth Amendment rights by use of excessive force—as distinct from determination of specific intent—is objective one. United States v Reese (1993, CA9 Cal) 2 F3d 870, 93 CDOS 5642, 93 Daily Journal DAR 9617, cert den (1994) 510 US 1094, 127 L Ed 2d 220, 114 S Ct 928 and (criticized in United States v Farrow (1999, CA6 Ohio) 198 F3d 179, 1999 FED App 409P).

11. Illegal act committed under color of law, generally

Government need not prove that police officers who allegedly used excessive force acted for ostensible government purpose rather than for personal reasons, since their acts were committed "under color of law." United States v Reese (1993, CA9 Cal) 2 F3d 870, 93 CDOS 5642, 93 Daily Journal DAR 9617, cert den (1994) 510 US 1094, 127 L Ed 2d 220, 114 S Ct 928 and (criticized in United States v Farrow (1999, CA6 Ohio) 198 F3d 179, 1999 FED App 409P).

Evidence was sufficient to show that town's mayor was acting "under color of law" when he invoked real or apparent power of his office to allegedly make continuing sexual abuse of two minor children possible in violation of 18 USCS § 242 because evidence established that mayor threatened minor children (and their mother/aunt) by invoking his "special authority" as mayor to undertake retaliatory action, and he used his authority to cause victims to submit to repeated abuse, by causing victims to fear that he would use his mayoral power to harm them if they reported abuse. United States v Giordano (2006, CA2) 442 F3d 30.

12. —Miscellaneous

Off-duty police officer who admitted to beating prisoner in city jail, using his official authority to get prisoner out of jail cell in order to attack him, and threatening to arrest prisoner every time he saw him in future was guilty of violating 18 USCS § 242 under color of state law, even though he was off-duty at time and his motivation was personal. United States v Colbert (1999, CA8 Mo) 172 F3d 594.

Convictions of police officer, drug dealer, and his associate for conspiracy to violate 18 USCS § 241 and violation of 18 USCS §§ 242, 1512 regarding murder of individual who filed complaint against police officer were for conduct "under color of state law," where officer abused his official power to access police station, police car, and police radio to plan, execute, and cover up murder, and his codefendants jointly engaged with him in these prohibited actions. United States v Causey (1999, CA5 La) 185 F3d 407, cert den (2000) 530 US 1277, 147 L Ed 2d 1010, 120 S Ct 2747 and cert den (2000) 530 US 1277, 147 L Ed 2d 1010, 120 S Ct 2747 and cert den (2000) 530 US 1277, 147 L Ed 2d 1010, 120 S Ct 2747 and (criticized in United States v Guadalupe (2005, CA3 Pa) 2005 US App LEXIS 5155).

Court affirmed defendant's conviction for felonious deprivation of civil rights under color of law in violation of 18 USCS § 242; where defendant was in uniform and on duty and victim was in custody at jail, even if defendant did not participate in victim's arrest and victim was not in defendant's custody, there was sufficient evidence that defendant acted "under color of law" when he punched and kneed victim in face. United States v Christian (2003, CA7 Ind) 342 F3d 744, 62 Fed Rules Evid Serv 55, cert den (2004) 540 US 1126, 157 L Ed 2d 927, 124 S Ct 1095.

14. Willfulness; intent

In determining whether police officers assigned to special drug task force had specific intent to use excessive force in arresting and detaining individuals, it was not necessary to prove that they knew their conduct was unlawful. United States v Reese (1993, CA9 Cal) 2 F3d 870, 93 CDOS 5642, 93 Daily Journal DAR 9617, cert den (1994) 510 US 1094, 127 L Ed 2d 220, 114 S Ct 928 and (criticized in United States v Farrow (1999, CA6 Ohio) 198 F3d 179, 1999 FED App 409P).

In order to convict under 18 USCS § 242, government must show that defendant had particular purpose of violating protected right made definite by rule of law or recklessly disregarded risk that he would violate such right; government does not need to show that defendant knowingly violated any right. United States v Johnstone (1997, CA3 NJ) 107 F3d 200 (criticized in United States v Farrow (1999, CA6 Ohio) 198 F3d 179, 1999 FED App 409P).

"Willfulness" under 18 USCS § 242 essentially requires that defendant intended to commit unconstitutional act without necessarily intending to do that act for specific purpose of depriving another of constitutional right; in other words, to act "willfully" in § 242 sense, defendant must intend to commit act that results in deprivation of established constitutional right as reasonable person would understand that right. United States v Bradley (1999, CA7 Ill) 196 F3d 762.

Evidence that defendant, police officer, released defendant's police dog on another suspect at later date was probative of willfulness by suggesting that, at least on one other occasion, defendant used dog in reckless disregard of another's right to be free from excessive force and was admissible under FRE 404(b), and was not unduly prejudicial under FRE 403 merely because it was pointed out that suspect was African-American; defendant's conviction under 18 USCS § 242 was affirmed. United States v Mohr (2003, CA4 Md) 318 F3d 613, 60 Fed Rules Evid Serv 906.

Actions of 400-pound correctional officer in stepping on prison inmate's penis on 3 separate occasions were subjectively wanton and malicious, violating inmate's Eighth Amendment rights and satisfying subjective element of conviction of criminal deprivation of rights under color of law pursuant to 18 USCS § 242, since there was no need for application of force used, there was no threat reasonably perceived by officer given that inmate was in his cell, and officer made no effort to temper severity of his forceful response. United States v Walsh (1998, WD NY) 27 F Supp 2d 186, subsequent app (1999, CA2 NY) 194 F3d 37.

III. RIGHTS AND PRIVILEGES SECURED OR PROTECTED

16. Freedom from unlawful arrest

Criminal liability may be imposed on commanding police officer who failed to prevent use of excessive

157

These annotations are in a pocket-part supplement. Note the newer cases.

Even if you think that the words of a statute are clear and that your facts obviously fit the language of the statute, your research should include case law. If courts have applied a particular code section to a factual situation that parallels your factual dispute, this gives added support to your analysis.

Some code sections contain numerous case notes. To facilitate searching lengthy notes, you often find a topical list of terms preceding the actual case notes. These lead you to case notes that are relevant to your search. See Figure 6-2.

Review Other Code Sections

Sometimes terms used in one code section are defined in another section of the same code. For example, Title 6 of the *United States Code* deals with the Homeland Security Organization. One of the first sections within that title, section 101, provides definitions of several terms that apply in the chapter. See Box 6-1 for a copy of that code section. Note the numerous terms that are defined.

FIGURE 6-2 List of Terms Preceding Case Notes

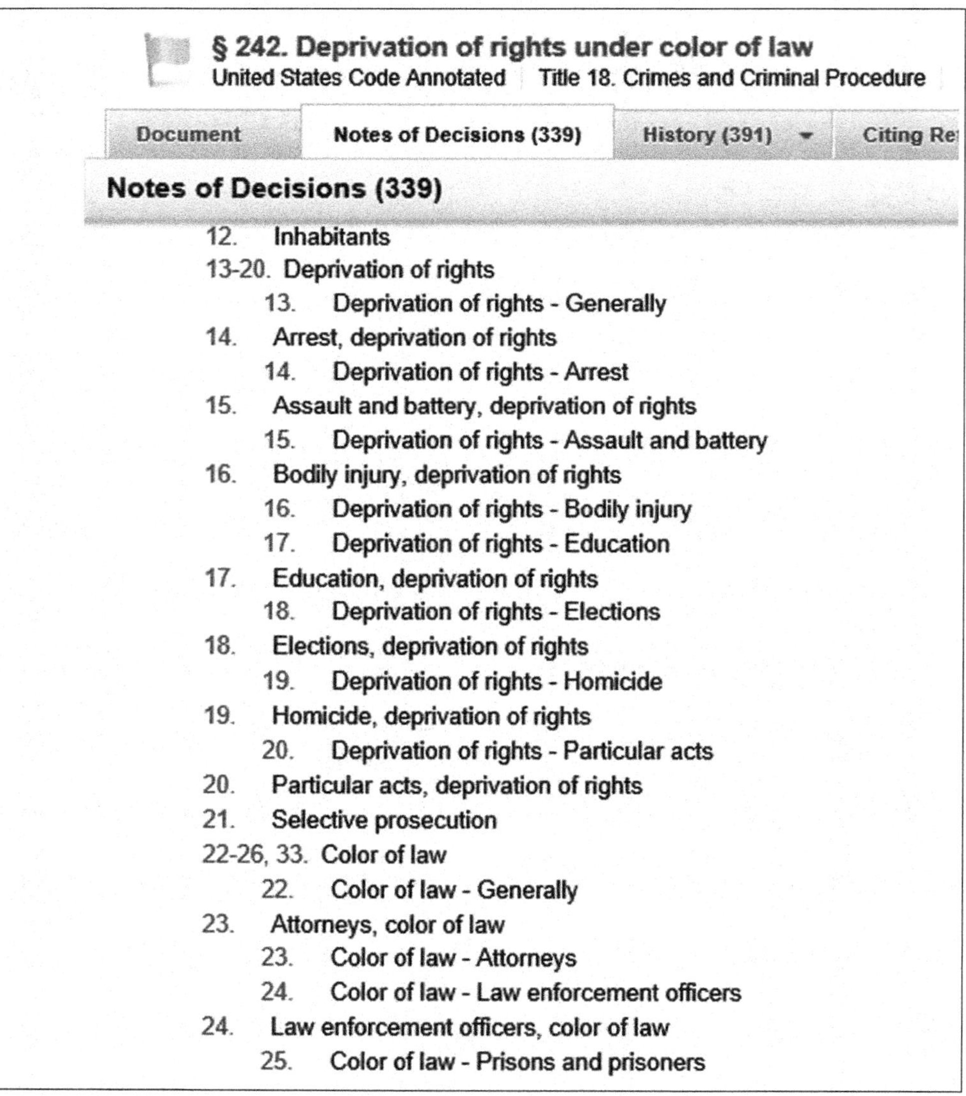
§ 242. Deprivation of rights under color of law
United States Code Annotated Title 18. Crimes and Criminal Procedure

Document | Notes of Decisions (339) | History (391) | Citing Re

Notes of Decisions (339)

12. Inhabitants
13-20. Deprivation of rights
 13. Deprivation of rights - Generally
14. Arrest, deprivation of rights
 14. Deprivation of rights - Arrest
15. Assault and battery, deprivation of rights
 15. Deprivation of rights - Assault and battery
16. Bodily injury, deprivation of rights
 16. Deprivation of rights - Bodily injury
 17. Deprivation of rights - Education
17. Education, deprivation of rights
 18. Deprivation of rights - Elections
18. Elections, deprivation of rights
 19. Deprivation of rights - Homicide
19. Homicide, deprivation of rights
 20. Deprivation of rights - Particular acts
20. Particular acts, deprivation of rights
21. Selective prosecution
22-26, 33. Color of law
 22. Color of law - Generally
23. Attorneys, color of law
 23. Color of law - Attorneys
 24. Color of law - Law enforcement officers
24. Law enforcement officers, color of law
 25. Color of law - Prisons and prisoners

In addition, many codes provide general rules to aid in the interpretation of the language of the code. For example, the following are two basic rules to help us understand the language of the statute.

1. Statutes are to be read as promoting the common law.
2. Particular or specific provisions control over general statements.

BOX 6-1 6 U.S.C. § 101

In this chapter, the following definitions apply:

1. Each of the terms "American homeland" and "homeland" means the United States.
2. The term "appropriate congressional committee" means any committee of the House of Representatives or the Senate having legislative or oversight jurisdiction under the Rules of the House of Representatives or the Senate, respectively, over the matter concerned.
3. The term "assets" includes contracts, facilities, property, records, unobligated or unexpended balances of appropriations, and other funds or resources (other than personnel).
4. The term "critical infrastructure" has the meaning given that term in section 5195c(e) of Title 42.
5. The term "Department" means the Department of Homeland Security.
6. The term "emergency response providers" includes Federal, State, and local governmental and nongovernmental emergency public safety, fire, law enforcement, emergency response, emergency medical (including hospital emergency facilities), and related personnel, agencies, and authorities.
7. The term "executive agency" means an executive agency and a military department, as defined, respectively, in sections 105 and 102 of Title 5.
8. The term "functions" includes authorities, powers, rights, privileges, immunities, programs, projects, activities, duties, and responsibilities.
9. The term "intelligence component of the Department" means any element or entity of the Department that collects, gathers, processes, analyzes, produces, or disseminates intelligence information within the scope of the information sharing environment, including homeland security information, terrorism information, and weapons of mass destruction information, or national intelligence, as defined under section 401a(5) of Title 50, except—
   - **A.** the United States Secret Service; and
   - **B.** the Coast Guard, when operating under the direct authority of the Secretary of Defense or Secretary of the Navy pursuant to section 3 of Title 14, except that nothing in this paragraph shall affect or diminish the authority and responsibilities of the Commandant of the Coast Guard to command or control the Coast Guard as an armed force or the authority of the Director of National Intelligence with respect to the Coast Guard as an element of the intelligence community (as defined under section 401a(4) of Title 50.)
10. The term "key resources" means publicly or privately controlled resources essential to the minimal operations of the economy and government.

BOX 6-1 (CONTINUED)

11. The term "local government" means—

A. a county, municipality, city, town, township, local public authority, school district, special district, intrastate district, council of governments (regardless of whether the council of governments is incorporated as a nonprofit corporation under State law), regional or interstate government entity, or agency or instrumentality of a local government;

B. an Indian tribe or authorized tribal organization, or in Alaska a Native village or Alaska Regional Native Corporation; and

C. a rural community, unincorporated town or village, or other public entity.

12. The term "major disaster" has the meaning given in section 5122(2) of Title 42.

13. The term "personnel" means officers and employees.

14. The term "Secretary" means the Secretary of Homeland Security.

15. The term "State" means any State of the United States, the District of Columbia, the Commonwealth of Puerto Rico, the Virgin Islands, Guam, American Samoa, the Commonwealth of the Northern Mariana Islands, and any possession of the United States.

16. The term "terrorism" means any activity that—

A. involves an act that—

i. is dangerous to human life or potentially destructive of critical infrastructure or key resources; and

ii. is a violation of the criminal laws of the United States or of any State or other subdivision of the United States; and

B. appears to be intended—

i. to intimidate or coerce a civilian population;

ii. to influence the policy of a government by intimidation or coercion; or

iii. to affect the conduct of a government by mass destruction, assassination, or kidnapping.

17. A. The term "United States," when used in a geographic sense, means any State of the United States, the District of Columbia, the Commonwealth of Puerto Rico, the Virgin Islands, Guam, American Samoa, the Commonwealth of the Northern Mariana Islands, any possession of the United States, and any waters within the jurisdiction of the United States.

B. Nothing in this paragraph or any other provision of this chapter shall be construed to modify the definition of "United States" for the purposes of the Immigration and Nationality Act [8 U.S.C.A. § 1101 et seq.] or any other immigration or nationality law.

18. The term "voluntary preparedness standards" means a common set of criteria for preparedness, disaster management, emergency management, and business continuity programs, such as the American National Standards Institute's National Fire Protection Association Standard on Disaster/Emergency Management and Business Continuity Programs (ANSI/NFPA 1600).

Watch Your Dates

When both statutory law and case law control a factual dispute, differences may exist between the two sources of law. When this happens, you must check the dates of the statute and the case. To determine whether the statute or the case applies, use the following guidelines:

1. If the issue is constitutional, then the case probably controls, regardless of the dates, unless the Constitution was amended.
2. If a statute is passed after a case is decided, that statute probably controls over the case, unless the issue is constitutional.
3. If there is a constitutional amendment after a case decision, then the constitutional amendment controls.

Read Box 6-2, this sets out the development of the law in California regarding the liability of bar owners and social hosts for furnishing too much alcohol to someone who injures another.

Legislative History

Another source used to aid in statutory interpretation is the legislative history of the statute. The legislative history helps the researcher determine the intent of the legislature in passing the law. A bill goes through several stages before becoming law. At each step there are records of what happened. These records include copies of the bill with deletions, additions, and changes noted. They might include transcripts of hearings and discussions on the bill. Rather than seeking the originals of these records, you can use a source such as *United States Code and*

BOX 6-2 ANALYZING CHANGES IN THE LAW—STATUTES AND CASES

Reconciling Statutes and Case Law

Research Question: Is a person who furnishes alcohol to another liable to a third person who is injured by an intoxicated individual to whom alcohol was furnished?

Research Findings: Prior to 1971, common law was followed. Common law provides that there is no liability on the part of the one who furnishes alcohol because that person is not the proximate cause of the injuries.

> 1971—State Supreme Court decides that the common law rule should not be followed as to commercial providers of alcohol (bars) and that they should be liable to third persons who are injured by one to whom alcohol was provided.
>
> 1978—State Supreme Court extends rule of liability to noncommercial providers of alcohol.
>
> 1978—State legislature amends statutes, expressly abrogates above holdings of State Supreme Court, and provides that commercial and noncommercial providers of alcohol to intoxicated persons are not the proximate cause of injuries suffered by a third person injured by the intoxicated individual.

Based on the above case and statute, how would you answer the research question?

Answer:

Here, the statute eliminating liability of bars and other providers of alcohol was enacted after the California Supreme Court decision. Because this case does not involve any constitutional issue, the statute controls, not the case.

Congressional and Administrative News (U.S.C.C.A.N.). This contains the legislative history of statutes, federal regulations, and court rules. It contains bills in their original format, changes, and committee hearings and discussions. See Figure 6-3 for an example of the contents of U.S.C.C.A.N.

FIGURE 6-3 Sample Page from U.S.C.C.A.N.

OKLAHOMA CITY NATIONAL MEMORIAL ACT OF 1997

PUBLIC LAW 105–58, see page 111 Stat. 1261

Dates of Consideration and Passage

Senate: July 31, 1997

House: September 23, 1997

Cong. Record Vol. 143 (1997)

Senate Report (Energy and Natural Resources Committee)
No. 105–71, July 30, 1997
[To accompany S. 871]

House Report (Resources Committee)
No. 105–316, October 8, 1997
[To accompany H.R. 1849]

The Senate Report is set out below.

SENATE REPORT NO. 105–71

[page 1]

The Committee on Energy and Natural Resources,to which was referred the bill (S. 871) to establish the Oklahoma City National Memorial as a unit of the National Park System; to designate the Oklahoma City Memorial Trust, and for other purposes,having considered the same, reports favorably thereon without amendment and recommends that the bill do pass.

PURPOSE OF THE MEASURE

The purpose of S. 871 is to establish the Oklahoma City National Memorial as a unit of the National Park System and to establish the Oklahoma City Memorial Trust and to manage the Memorial.

BACKGROUND AND NEED

One hundred and sixty-eight Americans lost their lives and many more were injured on April 19, 1995, when a bomb was detonated at the Alfred P. Murrah Federal Building in Oklahoma City, Oklahoma. This tragedy constitutes the worst domestic terrorist incident in American history.

This legislation would create a memorial at the site of the Murray Federal Building in Oklahoma City on 5th Street, between Robinson and Harvey Streets and would also include the sites of the Water Resources Building and Journal Record Building.

Concepts for the memorial were solicited through a design competition that included 624 design submissions from all 50 states and 23 foreign countries. The design that was selected was created by Hans-Ekkehard Butzer, Torrey Butzer and Sven Berg, a German-based design team. The design includes 168 chairs in the Murrah Building footprint, a water element designed to reflect spirit of change, a survivor tree, envisioned to reflect hope and "gates of time" on each end of Fifth Street that focus the visitor's attention on memorial inscriptions and the other elements of the memorial. Torrey Butzer of the German team states, "We watched Oklahomans and the world respond to this terrible tragedy from afar. This is our way of giving something to honor the victims, survivors and the heros. This design will tell the story of all of us changed forever."

The memorial established pursuant to this Act would serve not only as a monument to those who died and were injured in the bombing on April 19th, but also as a symbol of the galvanization of 'assistance, courage and good will shown by local citizens and Americans across the country in their outpouring of aid following the incident.

The Oklahoma City National Memorial will be designated as a unit of the National Park System. It will be placed under the charge of a wholly-owned government corporation, to be known as the Oklahoma City National Trust (Trust). The Trust will be governed by a nine-member Board of Directors (Board) which will have the authority to appoint an executive director and other key staff. Interim staff are authorized for two years to assist in the development of the memorial. Permanent National Park service staff and the ability to retain staff from other Federal agencies are also provided for by this measure on a reimbursable basis.

S. 871 authorizes $5 million in Federal funds for construction and maintenance, but stipulates that any Federal expenditures must be matched by non-Federal funds, dollar for dollar. It is expected that matching fund sources will include the Oklahoma State legislature and private donations.

FIGURE 6-3 (continued)

LEGISLATIVE HISTORY

S. 871 was introduced June 10, 1997 by Senators Nickles and Inhofe and was referred to the Committee on Energy and Natural Resources. The Subcommittee on National Parks, Historic Preservation and Recreation held a hearing in Oklahoma City on July 3, 1997 and in Washington, D.C. on July 17, 1997.

COMMITTEE RECOMMENDATIONS AND TABULATION OF VOTES

The Committee on Energy and Natural Resources, in open business session on July 30, 1997, by a unanimous vote of a quorum present, recommends that the Senate pass S. 871 without amendment.

The rollcall vote on reporting the measure was 20 yeas, 0 nays, as follows:

YEAS	NAYS
Mr. Murkowski	
Mr. Domenici	
Mr. Nickles	
Mr. Craig	
Mr. Campbell[1]	
Mr. Thomas	
Mr. Kyl	
Mr. Grams	
Mr. Smith	
Mr. Gorton	
Mr. Burns[1]	
Mr. Bumpers	
Mr. Ford	
Mr. Bingaman[1]	
Mr. Akaka	
Mr. Dorgan	
Mr. Graham	
Mr. Wyden	
Mr. Johnson	
Ms. Landrieu[1]	

[1]Indicates voted by proxy.

SECTION-BY-SECTION ANALYSIS

Section 1 entitles the bill the "Oklahoma City National Memorial Act of 1997."

Section 2 sets forth Congressional findings and purpose. The purpose of the bill is to establish the Oklahoma City National Memorial as a unit of the National Park System and to further establish how the memorial will be developed and managed.

Section 3 defines certain terms in the bill.

Section 4(a) establishes the Oklahoma City National Memorial (Memorial) and further establishes the Memorial as a unit of the National Park System.

Subsection (b) references the official boundary map for the memorial and authorizes the Oklahoma City National Memorial Trust (the Trust) to make boundary revisions when necessary.

Section 5(a) establishes a wholly owned government corporation to be known as the Oklahoma City National Memorial Trust.

Section (b)(1) sets forth the membership of the Board of Directors (Board) for the Trust. The 9-member Board shall consist of the Secretary of the Interior (Secretary) or his designee and 8 additional members appointed by the President, but selected from lists of nominees submitted by the Governor of Oklahoma, the Mayor of Oklahoma City and the Oklahoma delegations from the United States House of Representatives and Senate. This section also directs that the President is to appoint the Board members within 90 days after the date of enactment.

Paragraph (b)(2) sets the terms of Board members at 4 years and limits consecutive terms to 8 years. The section also staggers the first series of appointments, with two members serving for 2 years and two members serving a term of 3 years.

Paragraph (b)(3) directs that 5 members shall constitute a quorum.

Paragraph (b)(4) directs that the Board shall organize itself in a manner it deems most appropriate and that members shall not receive compensation, but may be reimbursed for actual and necessary travel and subsistence associated with Trust duties.

Paragraph (b)(5) establishes that Board members will not be considered Federal employees except for the purposes of the Federal Tort Claims Act, the Ethics in Government Act and provisions of titles 11 and 18 of the United States Code.

6-4 APPLYING STATUTORY LAW TO A FACT PATTERN

Statutory or regulatory analysis is not complete until you *explain* how a particular code section or rule controls your factual situation. When you explain a position, you should use the general IRAC approach in much the same way you do in using case law. (Review Chapters 2 to 4.) The IRAC approach consists of the following:

1. Stating your **I**ssue
2. Explaining and discussing the **R**ule or Rules of law that apply
3. **A**nalyzing the situation by applying the law to your facts
4. Reaching a **C**onclusion

The *issue* is the question you are researching. The discussion of the *rules of law* starts with the relevant code section. Elements or requirements of the code section should be stated and explained. If any cases contain relevant interpretation of the statutory law, that is also part of the rules of law. The *analysis* consists of applying your facts to the language of the law. If there are relevant cases, then you must also compare your facts with the facts of any relevant cases. The *conclusion* is the answer to your research question. Any factual situation may contain more than one issue. Each issue is analyzed separately using the IRAC approach. Consider the Rambeaux case mentioned earlier in the chapter. Assume you are working with the following facts.

Randy Rambeaux made a routine traffic stop on an automobile because the driver failed to signal when making a right-hand turn. The occupants of the vehicle were two Latino males in their late teens. According to the occupants, the following events occurred. Rambeaux approached the car and ordered the two out of the car. When the occupants asked why, Rambeaux opened the driver's door, and with his weapon drawn and pointed directly at the driver, again ordered them out of the car. After the driver exited the vehicle, Rambeaux struck him on the head with the gun and, according to the two occupants, said, "Why don't you guys go back where you belong? This country is for Americans." The driver maintains that he did nothing to provoke the attack.

You are asked to research whether Rambeaux is criminally responsible under 18 U.S.C. § 242. This is an issue. The rule of law in this case starts with the relevant code section, 18 U.S.C. § 242. The analysis begins by identifying the elements or requirements of the code section and then matching each element with the relevant facts. This should be done initially in an outline or table format. See Box 6-3 for an example of a table listing the statutory requirements of 18 U.S.C. § 242 and the related facts.

A complete analysis requires that you find and discuss case law that interprets this code section. For example, suppose in the Rambeaux case that Rambeaux was off duty when the incident occurred. Under such circumstances, whether he was acting under color of authority is questionable, and case law should be researched. This research might lead you to the case of *United States v. Tarpley*, 945 F.2d 806 (5th Cir. 1991). The *Tarpley* case discusses the meaning of color of law and helps to answer the question of whether an off-duty police officer acts under color of law. The case is found later in this chapter. After researching applicable case law you should revise your analysis outline or table. It should then look something like the table in Box 6-4.

BOX 6-3 STATUTORY REQUIREMENTS OF 18 U.S.C. § 242 AND THE RELATED FACTS

Requirements of 18 U.S.C. § 242	Application to Client Facts
1. Accused must act under color of authority.	Rambeaux is a police officer, performing a police function, that is, a traffic stop.
2. The action must be willful.	The incident was intentional, not accidental.
3. The action must either deprive a person of civil rights or impose different punishment or penalties because of race, and so on.	Rambeaux violated the Fourth Amendment to the Constitution: unreasonable arrest. Rambeaux beat the suspect; his comments about "going back" and "Americans" suggest racial bias.

BOX 6-4 STATUTORY ELEMENTS, CASE LAW INTERPRETATIONS, AND FACTUAL APPLICATIONS

Requirements of 18 U.S.C. § 242	Case Law Interpretation of Statutory Provisions	Application to Client Facts
1. Accused must act under color of authority.	*U.S. v. Tarpley*: Police officer was acting under color of law rather than as jealous husband where air of official authority pervaded entire assault incident.	Rambeaux is a police officer, performing a police function, that is, a traffic stop. The stop had the air of official authority.
2. The action must be willful.	(Here you include cases that discuss the meaning of willful.)	The incident was intentional, not accidental.
3. The action must either deprive a person of civil rights or impose different punishment or penalties because of race, and so on.	(Here you include cases defining "civil rights" or the meaning of "punishment, penalties or pains.")	Rambeaux violated the Fourth Amendment to the Constitution: unreasonable arrest. Rambeaux beat the suspect; his comments about "going back" and "Americans" suggest racial bias.

After outlining the statutory requirements, determining the meaning of these requirements by examining case law, and then applying each element to your facts, you can reach a conclusion. The conclusion should answer the question you are researching. In this case, the conclusion tells whether Rambeaux violated the statute.

Your analysis is not complete until you communicate your findings in an appropriate manner. Subsequent chapters in this text describe the various types of documents used to accomplish this. However, Box 6-5 illustrates a preliminary draft of a statutory analysis using the IRAC method. Be sure to read the *Tarpley* case before reading Box 6-5. See Box 6-6 for statutory analysis checklist.

CASE 6-1 *United States v. Tarpley,* 945 F.2d 806 (5th Cir. 1991)

A deputy sheriff appeals his conviction for violations of 18 U.S.C. §§ 241 and 242, which prohibit the deprivation of rights secured by the Constitution and laws of the United States under color of law. We find sufficient evidence to show that the defendant acted under color of law and conspired with another in doing so, and affirm.

I.

This is what happened, in the light most favorable to the government. In 1988, William Tarpley, deputy, Collingsworth County Sheriff's police force, learned of a past affair of his wife, Kathryn and Kerry Lee Vestal. Tarpley devised a plan to lure Vestal to the Tarpley home for the purpose of assaulting him.

Tarpley had his wife call Vestal and tell him that she had separated from her husband and that she wanted him to come pick her up. On the day that Vestal was to arrive, Tarpley and another deputy, Michael Pena, made a pair of "sap gloves" in his office at the sheriff's station. These are gloves with rubber hosing filled with metal or lead shot attached to the fingers. Tarpley told Pena that he planned to have his wife call her boyfriend over and then use the sap gloves on him.

That evening, Tarpley parked his patrol car behind the house of another deputy so as not to alert Vestal that he was at home. When Vestal arrived at the Tarpley residence, Mrs. Tarpley opened the door and pulled him into the house. Mr. Tarpley immediately tackled Vestal and hit him repeatedly in the head. He also inserted his service pistol in Vestal's mouth. He told Vestal that he was a sergeant on the police department, that he would and should kill Vestal, and that he could get away with it because he was a cop. He repeated "I'll kill you. I'm a cop. I can." As he continued to beat and threaten Vestal, Mrs. Tarpley may have been taking pictures of the encounter. Tarpley then had his wife telephone the sheriff's station and ask Pena to come to their house. She did, and when Pena arrived, Tarpley introduced him to Vestal as a fellow sergeant from the police department. Pena confirmed Tarpley's claims that Tarpley had shot people in the past.

Eventually, Tarpley let Vestal go, chasing him out of the house with threats to kill him if he reported the incident. Pena then gave Vestal his keys, and Vestal drove away, but not before Tarpley smashed the headlights on Vestal's truck. Pena and the Tarpleys followed Vestal in Pena's squad car until Vestal had left town. Pena also apparently radioed for another officer to meet up with them and that police car also followed Vestal to the edge of town.

A federal grand jury indicted Tarpley and Pena and "another individual known to the grand jury" for conspiracy to injure and oppress Vestal in the exercise of his constitutional rights, as well as willfully subjecting Vestal to a deprivation of his constitutional rights, in violation of 18 U.S.C. §§ 241 and 242. Jointly tried, Pena was acquitted on both counts and Tarpley was convicted on both counts. Defense counsel later learned that during the trial one of the jurors spoke with the juror's daughter, a legal secretary, about the difficulty he had understanding the nature of a conspiracy charge. There was also evidence that the juror's daughter had in turn contacted a lawyer about the matter. The district court held a hearing concerning these events at which both the lawyer and the juror's daughter testified. The court determined that no extrinsic evidence had reached the jury and that further investigation was not required.

Tarpley now appeals his conviction to this court.

II.

Tarpley was convicted of violating two statutes, both of which require that an individual act "under color of law." 18 U.S.C. §§ 241 and 242. Tarpley argues that the jury's finding that he acted "under color of law" was insufficiently supported by the evidence produced at trial. In reviewing the sufficiency of the evidence, this court "must view the evidence in the light most favorable to the verdict to determine whether any rational trier of fact could have found each element of the crime beyond a reasonable doubt." *United States v. Berisha*, 925 F.2d 791, 795 (5th Cir. 1991).

The Supreme Court has in two famous cases explained the concept of "under color of law." In *United States v. Classic*, 313 U.S. 299, 326 (1941), the court stated that "misuse of power, possessed by virtue of state law and made possible only because the wrongdoer is clothed with the authority of state law, is action taken 'under color of' state law." In *Screws v. United States*, 325 U.S. 91, 111 (1944), the court reaffirmed the classic formula and stated more simply that "under 'color' of law means under 'pretense' of law." The court in *Screws* also observed that "acts of officers who undertake to perform their official duties are included whether they hew to the line of their authority or overstep it." *Id.* However, "acts of officers in the ambit of their personal pursuits are plainly excluded."

This court and other courts of appeals have made clear that whether a police officer is acting under color of law does not depend on duty status at the time of the alleged violation. *Delcambre v. Delcambre*, 635 F.2d 407 (5th Cir. 1981) (*per curiam*); *Layne v. Sampley*, 627 F.2d 12, 13 (6th Cir. 1980). Nor does *Screws* mean that if officials act for purely personal reasons, they necessarily fail to act "under color of law." *Brown v. Miller*, 631 F.2d 408 (5th Cir. 1980); *United States v. Davila*, 704 F.2d 749 (5th Cir. 1983). Rather, *Screws* held simply that individuals pursuing private aims and not acting by virtue of state authority are not acting under color of law purely because they are state officers. *Brown*, 631 F.2d at 411. Tarpley argues that there is no evidence that he "misused power possessed by virtue of state law" or that his actions were "made possible only because" he was "clothed with state authority." According to Tarpley, he was acting as a jealous husband, not as a police officer. He assaulted Vestal in his own home under circumstances in which it was clear that the motive for his attack was the extra-marital affair. That he told Vestal that he was a police officer, the argument continues, does not suggest that he was purporting to act under official authority. He never threatened to arrest Vestal. Vestal already knew he was a cop.

We are not persuaded. There was sufficient evidence in the record from which a rational juror could conclude that Tarpley was acting under color of law. Tarpley did more than simply use his service weapon and identify himself as a police officer. At several points during his assault of Vestal, he claimed to have special authority for his actions by virtue of his official status. He claimed that he could kill Vestal because he was an officer of the law. Significantly, Tarpley summoned another police officer from the sheriff's station and identified him as a fellow officer and ally. The men then proceeded to run Vestal out of town in their squad car. The presence of police and the air of official authority pervaded the entire incident. Under these circumstances, we are unwilling to say that no rational juror could find that Tarpley acted under color of law.

III.

The defendant also contends that he cannot be convicted on the conspiracy count after his alleged co-conspirator, Pena, was acquitted in the same proceeding. *The United States v. Klein*, 560 F.2d 1236, 1242 (5th Cir. 1977), *cert. denied*, 434 U.S. 1073 (1978), for the proposition that the conviction of only one defendant in a conspiracy prosecution will not be upheld if all other alleged co-conspirators are acquitted. Although this has long been the rule in this Circuit, *see, e.g., Herman v. United States*, 289 F.2d 362, 368 (5th Cir.1961); *United States v. Sheikh*, 654 F.2d 1057, 1062 (5th Cir. 1981), its continuing validity has recently come into question. We need not address this issue in this case, however, because there was a third potential co-conspirator not acquitted. The indictment alleged that "Tarpley and Pena, and another individual known to the grand jury, conspired to injure, threaten, oppress, and intimidate Kerry Vestal." The evidence is sufficient to support a conspiracy between Tarpley and this other individual, namely his wife. Mrs. Tarpley phoned Vestal and convinced him to come to the Tarpley home. She pulled Vestal into the house and apparently took pictures while her husband beat him. She contacted Pena at her husband's bidding and accompanied the two men as they followed Vestal out of town.

This court has held that even when named co-conspirators are acquitted, a person can be convicted of conspiring with unnamed individuals as long as the indictment refers to these individuals and the evidence supports their complicity. *United States v. Price*, 869 F.2d 801, 805 (5th Cir. 1989). It is also clear that "private persons, jointly engaged with state officials in the prohibited action, are acting 'under color' of law for purposes of the statute." *United States v. Price*, 383 U.S. 787, 794 (1996); *Adickes v. S.H. Kress & Co.*, 398 U.S. 144, 152 (1970).

IV.

The defendant argues next that the district court erred in its investigation of juror misconduct by failing to allow him to question the jurors or by failing to conduct its own voir dire. He relies on *United States v. Phillips*, 664 F.2d 971 (5th Cir.), *cert. denied*, 457 U.S. 1136 (1981), for the proposition that "any off-the-record contact with a jury is presumptively prejudicial and the Government bears a heavy burden of proving that such contact did not affect the jury; if the Government cannot meet this burden, a new trial is required." He argues that the government failed to carry its burden and that the district court effectively shifted the burden to him. We review the district court's decision not to grant a new trial for an abuse of discretion. *United States v. Sedigh*, 658 F.2d 1010, 1014 (5th Cir. 1981), *cert. denied*, 455 U.S. 921 (1982).

The defendant's argument is without merit. The district court here followed established procedure for addressing allegations of juror misconduct. This court has held that "the trial court should investigate the asserted impropriety to determine initially if and what extrinsic factual matter was disclosed to the jury." *Sedigh*, 658 F.2d at 1014. When the allegations remain speculative, the trial court need not inquire further. *Id.*

The district court in this case held a hearing at which the juror's daughter and the lawyer with whom she spoke testified. The juror's daughter testified that although her father had expressed uncertainty as to whether the crime of conspiracy required that both co-conspirators be convicted, she did not express any opinion on the matter. When she asked a lawyer about it, he told her that any communication with a juror on such issues was improper, and the juror's daughter had no further contact with the juror until after the verdict was rendered. The district court found that this testimony indicated beyond a reasonable doubt that extrinsic evidence was not disclosed to the jury. Consequently, further investigation was not required. The district court acted in accordance with standard procedures and did not abuse its discretion.

It is true that if the defendant had been able to demonstrate as a threshold matter that improper communication of extrinsic information had likely occurred, further investigation might have been required. *See United States v. Forrest*, 620 F.2d 446, 457–58 (5th Cir. 1980) (describing a two-part process under which voir dire is required upon a threshold showing of likely communication of extrinsic material). However in this case, the district court found that no extrinsic information had reached the jury. Contrary to defendant's assertions, it is not sufficient to trigger the requirement of further investigation that a juror have had contact with an outside source of information. Rather, the defendant must show "that extraneous prejudicial material had likely reached the jury." *Forrest*, 620 F.2d at 458. This showing was not made in the present case.

V.

Finally, the defendant argues that several sentences in the jury instructions were misleading. The standard for their review is "'whether the court's charge, as a whole, is a correct statement of the law and whether it clearly instructs the jurors as to the principles of law applicable to the factual issues confronting them.'" *United States v. Stacey*, 896 F.2d 75, 77 (5th Cir. 1990) [citations omitted].

Defendant's objections to the length and repetition in the jury instructions are without merit. Evaluated as a whole, the court's instructions stated the law. AFFIRMED.

BOX 6-5 STATUTORY ANALYSIS

Under the facts presented, Rambeaux probably committed a criminal offense as defined in 18 U.S.C. § 242. This section makes it a federal crime for anyone acting under color of authority to deprive any person of a constitutional right or to subject a person to different punishments, pains, or penalties because of that person's race or color. The requirements for a criminal conviction under this code section are that the individual:

Issue
(The issue is found in the first sentence.)

1. Act under color of law;
2. Act willfully;
3. Deprive someone of his constitutional rights; *or*
4. Impose different punishments, pains, or penalties because of the person's race or color.

Rules
(Here you set out the statutory requirements and rules of law from cases.)

BOX 6-5 (CONTINUED)

Police officers act under color of law when they are in the performance of their duties, unless they act for purely personal reasons. *United States v. Tarpley,* 945 F.2d 806, 809 (5th Cir. 1991).

In the *Tarpley* case, defendant Tarpley, a deputy sheriff, learned of a past affair between his wife and another individual, Vestal. Tarpley assaulted Vestal by inserting his service revolver in Vestal's mouth and told him that he could get away with it because he was a police officer. Tarpley also enlisted the aid of another sheriff's deputy to threaten Vestal. When they finally released Vestal, the officers followed him in a police vehicle. Tarpley was arrested and charged with violating 18 U.S.C. § 242. He was found guilty and appealed, claiming that he was not acting under color of law because he was off duty at the time of these events. The court of appeals found that even though he was off duty, he was still acting under color of law because "the air of official authority pervaded the entire incident." *Tarpley,* 945 F.2d at 809.

Analysis
(Here you apply the language of the statute to your facts. You also compare facts of relevant cases to your client's facts.)

In this case, Rambeaux's actions satisfy all the requirements of 18 U.S.C. § 242. Even though Rambeaux was off duty at the time of the incident, he acted under color of law. This incident, like that in *Tarpley,* was pervaded with the air of official authority. Rambeaux, like the defendant in *Tarpley,* used his police authority in acting. Rambeaux was doing what police officers routinely do—stopping traffic offenders. He was acting on behalf of the state, attempting to enforce state laws. Thus, Rambeaux was acting under color of law, meeting the first element of the statute.

All of the actions in this case were clearly willful. Rambeaux knew what he was doing and intended to do what he did. This was no accident. [At this point, bring in case law that interprets the word *willful.*] Thus, the second element is met.

In making this traffic stop, Rambeaux violated the constitutional rights of the driver. The Constitution guarantees that all persons have the right to be free from unreasonable searches and seizures. In this case, Rambeaux made a traffic stop and in doing this "seized" the persons in the vehicle, even if only temporarily. While Rambeaux may have been justified in making the stop, his conduct during this seizure was clearly unreasonable. The use of physical force such as occurred here is not allowed in simple traffic stops where the offender neither uses any force nor threatens the officer with any the use of force. [At this point, refer to case law that describes what force is constitutionally permissible during a traffic stop.] Thus, the third element of the statute is met.

In addition to violating the victim's constitutional rights, the evidence also suggests that Rambeaux subjected him to different punishment or pain because of the victim's race. Rambeaux used unnecessary force, subjecting the victim to pain. While it may be difficult to prove racial motivation, the facts do suggest its existence. According to the witnesses, Rambeaux made the statement, "Why don't you guys go back where you belong? This country is for Americans." This is strong evidence that Rambeaux's actions were racially motivated, also fulfilling the third requirement of the statute. [At this point discuss case law that interprets this element of the statute.]

Conclusion

The facts of this case support the conclusion that Rambeaux violated the federal law.

BOX 6-6 STATUTORY ANALYSIS CHECKLIST

- Determine if statute applies.
- Outline statutory language, listing the elements or requirements of the law.
- Note the meaning of connectors, such as *and, or,* etc.
- Determine meaning of statutory terms by referring to other code sections, case law, or legislative histories.
- Apply statutory law to factual situation using IRAC method.

6-5 THE INTERNET AND LEGISLATIVE ANALYSIS

An important step in any legislative analysis is reviewing any cases that may have interpreted the legislative provision. In privately published, annotated versions of the law, case notes appear providing the researcher with relevant cases. In general, however, this information is not found in freely accessible versions of the law. One noted exception is the Constitution Amended, discussed in the prior chapter. This version of the U.S. Constitution contains explanations of the various articles and amendments to the Constitution as well as references to relevant U.S. Supreme Court cases. See Figure 6-4 for an example.

Another important source for legislative analysis is the legislative history. The federal legislative history is found on the Federal Digital System (FDsys) of the U.S. Government publishing office. On this site, you can access congressional reports and other documents. See Figure 6-5.

Your state may also provide similar information on its legislative website. To locate your state site, use the link provided at <https://www.congress.gov/state-legislature-websites>

Library of Congress also provides assistance in conducting a legislative history. The library site provides detailed steps in conducting a legislative history and identifies relevant documents to be searched. The site is located at <http://www.loc.gov/law/help/leghist.php>

See Figure 6-6 Library of Congress—Legislative History

Finding It Online

The Internet provides access to many legal documents containing examples of statutory legal analysis. The following sites are valuable resources for sample documents:

http://www.justice.gov/ The website for the Department of Justice contains numerous briefs and memoranda. Reading these documents will help develop your analytic skills. To find the documents, go to the homepage and search for "public documents." (The pages for the Civil Rights and Antitrust Divisions contain numerous documents.)

http://www.supremecourt.gov/ The website for the U.S. Supreme Court provides a link to merits, briefs, and transcripts of oral arguments for cases heard by the Court.

http://supreme.lp.findlaw.com/supreme_court/briefs/index.html Findlaw publishes many of the briefs filed by the parties for Supreme Court cases.

AUTHENTICATED U.S. GOVERNMENT INFORMATION GPO

FIGURE 6-4 Constitution of the United States of America: Analysis and Interpretation (2014)

BEARING ARMS

SECOND AMENDMENT

A well regulated Militia, being necessary to the security of a free State, the right of the people to keep and bear Arms shall not be infringed.

IN GENERAL

Test For over 200 years, despite extensive debate and much legislative action with respect to regulation of the purchase, possession, and transportation of firearms, as well as proposals to substantially curtail ownership of firearms, there was no definitive resolution by the courts of just what right the Second Amendment protects. The Second Amendment is naturally divided into two parts: its prefatory clause ("A well regulated Militia, being necessary to the security of a free State") and its operative clause ("the right of the people to keep and bear Arms shall not be infringed"). To perhaps oversimplify the opposing arguments, the "states' rights" thesis emphasized the importance of the prefatory clause, arguing that the purpose of the clause was to protect the states in their authority to maintain formal, organized militia units. The "individual rights" thesis emphasized the operative clause, so that individuals would be protected in the ownership, possession, and transportation of firearms.[1] Whatever the Amendment meant, it was seen as a bar only to federal action, not state[2] or private[3] restraints.

[1] A sampling of the diverse literature in which the same historical, linguistic, and case law background shows the basis for strikingly different conclusions includes: Staff of Subcomm. on the Constitution, Senate Committee on the Judiciary, 97th Congress, 2d Sess., The Right to Keep and Bear Arms (Comm. Print 1982); Don B. Kates, Handgun Prohibition and the Original Meaning of the Second Amendment (1984); Gun Control and the Constitution: Sources and Explorations on the Second Amendment (Robert J. Cottrol ed., 1993); Stephen P. Halbrook, That Every Man Be Armed: The Evolution of a Constitutional Right (1984); Symposium, *Gun Control*, 49 Law & Contemp. Probs. 1 (1986); Sanford Levinson, *The Embarrassing Second Amendment*, 99 Yale L.J. 637 (1989); Joyce Lee Malcolm, To Keep and Bear Arms: The Origins of an Anglo-American Right (1994); Glenn Harlan Reynolds, *A Critical Guide to the Second Amendment*, 62 Tenn. L. Rev. 461 (1995); William Van Alystyne, *The Second Amendment and the Personal Right to Bear Arms*, 43 Duke L.J. 1236 (1994); Symposium, *Symposium on the Second Amendment: Fresh Looks*, 76 Chi.-Kent L. Rev. 3 (2000).

[2] Presser v. Illinois, 116 U.S. 252, 265 (1886). *See also* Miller v. Texas, 153 U.S. 535 (1894); Robertson v. Baldwin, 165 U.S. 275, 281–82 (1897). The non-application of the Second Amendment to the states was reaffirmed in Quilici v. Village of Morton Grove, 695 F.2d 261 (7th Cir. 1982), *cert. denied*, 464 U.S. 863 (1983).

[3] United States v. Cruikshank, 92 U.S. 542 (1876).

1361

Browse

- Code of Federal Regulations
- Compilation of Presidential Documents
- Congressional Bills
- Congressional Documents
- Congressional Hearings
- Congressional Record
- Congressional Reports
- Constitution of the United States of America: Analysis and Interpretation
- Economic Indicators
- Federal Register
- Public and Private Laws
- United States Code
- United States Courts Opinions
- Browse All

Documents such as Congressional Bills, Documents, Hearings, Record and Reports help with preparing a legislative history.
Also relevant is the Federal Register

FIGURE 6-5 List of searchable documents on FDsys

FIGURE 6-6 Library of Congress—Legislative History

CITATION MATTERS

CAPITALIZATION

THE BLUEBOOK—Rule 8

In titles and headings, capitalize the first word, the word following a colon, and all other words except articles, prepositions of four or fewer letters, and conjunctions of four or fewer letters. Capitalize nouns referring to groups or people only when they identify specific groups, persons, government offices, or government bodies or groups:

the President
Congress
the Agency
the FBI

CITATION MATTERS (Continued)

Capitalize *act* only when referring to a specific act:

Labor Management Relations Act
the Act

Capitalize *circuit* only when used with the circuit number:

the Ninth Circuit

Capitalize *code* only when referring to the *specific* code:

the 1956 and 1962 Codes

Capitalize *constitution* only when naming a constitution in full and when referring to the U.S. Constitution. Always capitalize components of the United States Constitution when using them in textual sentences:

Fourteenth Amendment
Supremacy Clause
Article I, Section 8, Clause 17 of the Constitution

However, this is the proper capitalization in a *citation:*
U.S. Const. art I, & § 8, cl. 17

Capitalize *judge* only when using the name of a specific justice or judge, or when referring to a United States Supreme Court Justice:

Judge Murphy
Justice Marshall
the Justice (used as a reference to a United States Supreme Court Justice)

CHAPTER **SUMMARY**

Unlike case law, statutory law, administrative regulations, and constitutions contain general rules intended to apply to many different factual situations. Therefore, legal analysis based on these sources differs from analysis based on case law. Analyzing a legal question based on these sources requires that you determine the meaning of the law. When researching constitutional law, you must determine whether the state constitution or the U.S. Constitution governs the situation. Statutory and regulatory analysis requires that you outline relevant provisions of the law by identifying the elements, sometimes referred to as *statutory requirements*. The various elements are applied to the facts of the case. Where the meaning of a word or phrase is unclear, you should review other statutory law, case law, or legislative history. A written analysis of a statute, administrative regulation, or constitution should follow the IRAC method. State the issue, provide the rule, apply the rule to your facts, and reach a conclusion.

TERMS TO **REMEMBER**

federalism
concurrent jurisdiction
Supremacy Clause
statutory requirements
stare decisis

QUESTIONS FOR **REVIEW**

1. How do you determine whether the U.S. Constitution or a state constitution applies to a factual situation arising under state law?
2. How does statutory analysis differ from case law analysis?
3. What is meant by *statutory requirements*?
4. List the steps in analyzing a statute or administrative regulation.
5. What sources can you consult to determine the meaning of a statute, administrative regulation, or constitutional provision?

CAN YOU **FIGURE IT OUT?**

1. The following abbreviations appear in the case found in this chapter. What do they mean?

   per curiam

   Id.

   Cert. Denied

2. Refer to Figure 6-1.
   a. Can excessive force be the basis of an action under 18 U.S.C. § 242? Cite a case for your answer.
   b. How does the court define "willfulness" in *United States v. Bradley?*
   c. Does 18 U.S.C. § 242 require that the defendant be acting for a governmental rather than personal purpose? Cite a case for your answer.

3. Refer to Box 6-1. Does the phrase *local government* include a school district? Cite the section of the law that applies.

4. Refer to Figure 6-3.
   a. Who introduced the bill that led to the Oklahoma City National Memorial Act of 1997?
   b. What is the purpose of this Act?
   c. On what dates was the bill passed in both the Senate and the House of Representatives?

TEST **YOURSELF** (Check Your Answers in Appendix G)

1. Read the following code section and list the statutory requirements for a copyright:

   Subject matter of copyright: In general

   a. Copyright protection subsists, in accordance with this title, in original works of authorship fixed in any tangible medium of expression, now known or later developed, from which they can be perceived, reproduced, or otherwise communicated, either directly or with the aid of a machine or device. Works of authorship include the following categories:
      1. literary works;
      2. musical works, including any accompanying words;
      3. dramatic works, including any accompanying music;
      4. pantomimes and choreographic works;
      5. pictorial, graphic, and sculptural works;
      6. motion pictures and other audiovisual works;
      7. sound recordings; and
      8. architectural works.

   b. In no case does copyright protection for an original work of authorship extend to any idea, procedure, process, system, method of operation, concept, principle, or discovery, regardless of the form in which it is described, explained, illustrated, or embodied in such work.

   (17 U.S.C. § 102)

2. a. Read the following code section and list the statutory requirements for a conspiracy:

   Conspiracy to commit offense or to defraud United States

   If two or more persons conspire either to commit any offense against the United States, or to defraud the United States, or any agency thereof in any manner or for any purpose, and one or more of such persons do any act to effect the object of the conspiracy, each shall be fined under this title or imprisoned not more than five years, or both.

   If, however, the offense, the commission of which is the object of the conspiracy, is a misdemeanor only, the punishment for such conspiracy shall not exceed the maximum punishment provided for such misdemeanor.

   (18 U.S.C. § 371)

   b. Assume that H and W file bankruptcy and agreed between themselves to hide their assets from the trustee in bankruptcy. In fact they did hide the assets. Assume that concealing assets from a trustee is a federal offense. Have they committed a conspiracy? Explain.

TEST **YOURSELF**—WRITE IT RIGHT Use Short Paragraphs

Readers find long paragraphs difficult to read. We all give a big mental sigh when we see a paragraph that fills an entire page. These large paragraphs are too simply dense. In legal writing, we write to inform and/or persuade. That means we need to write with the reader's needs and preferences in mind. Sometimes we can break a long paragraph with a *transition word or phrase*. Examples of such words or phrases are: furthermore, in addition, on the other hand, here, and moreover.

The paragraph below is too long.

Mr. Reed suffered second-degree burns to his face, neck, and chest after an unexplained fire started during a routine bur hole drainage operation on March 22, 2016. Discharge Instructions. It is unclear how the fire started. Both the surgeon and anesthesiologist, who spoke with Mrs. Reed on the day of the surgery, were unable to explain the cause of the fire. The only source of heat during the procedure was the tip of a small tool (called a bovie) used to cauterize blood vessels. Although neither the surgeon nor the anesthesiologist attributed the fire to the tool, they both discussed it while attempting to explain the fire to Mrs. Riordan. Following the surgery, Mr. Reed was transferred to the ICU for six days for treatment for his burns. Discharge Instructions. About a week after the surgery, when Mr. Reed regained lucidity, his general surgeon informed him of the surgery room fire and subsequent burns. Mr. Reed then spent the next 16 days as an inpatient for ongoing wound care of his burn injuries. Discharge Instructions. In all, Mr. Reed, a married 39-year-old painter, was an inpatient at El Camino Hospital for 23 days for what his surgeon initially described as a routine surgery. Recently, Mr. Reed consulted with a new plastic surgeon for the scars. Although the plastic surgeon did not explicitly state the burns were the result of negligence, she suggested Mr. Riordan seek legal counsel. The Record is unclear about treatment between his discharge from the hospital on April 13, 2016, and his recent visit with the new plastic surgeon.

When this paragraph is broken into three shorter paragraphs it is much easier to read.

Mr. Reed suffered second-degree burns to his face, neck, and chest after an unexplained fire started during a routine bur hole drainage operation on March 22, 2016. Discharge Instructions. It is unclear how the fire started. Both the surgeon and anesthesiologist, who spoke with Mrs. Reed on the day of the surgery, were unable to explain the cause of the fire. The only source of heat during the procedure was the tip of a small tool (called a bovie) used to cauterize blood vessels. Although neither the surgeon nor the anesthesiologist attributed the fire to the tool, they both discussed it while attempting to explain the fire to Mrs. Riordan.

Following the surgery, Mr. Reed was transferred to the ICU for six days for treatment for his burns. Discharge Instructions. About a week after the surgery, when Mr. Reed regained lucidity, his general surgeon informed him of the surgery room fire and subsequent burns. Mr. Reed then spent the next 16 days as an inpatient for ongoing wound care of his burn injuries. Discharge Instructions. In all, Mr. Reed, a married 39-year-old painter, was an inpatient at El Camino Hospital for 23 days for what his surgeon initially described as a routine surgery.

Recently, Mr. Reed consulted with a new plastic surgeon for the scars. Although the plastic surgeon did not explicitly state the burns were the result of negligence, she suggested Mr. Riordan seek legal counsel. The Record is unclear about treatment between his discharge from the hospital on April 13, 2016, and his recent visit with the new plastic surgeon.

Now, You Try It

(Check your answers in Appendix G)

Break the following long paragraph into a series of shorter paragraphs:

Our client, Jill Thompson, is a 16-year-old girl charged as an accessory to murder. As a result of her initial custodial interrogation, the police were able to locate the crime scene and ultimately link Jill to the murder through physical evidence. Police discovered a body located in a ditch and investigation revealed animosity and fights between Jill's boyfriend and the decedent. Jill's boyfriend revealed to police that he and Jill were at the mall together the night of the decedent's death. The following morning, an officer questioned Jill in the Principal's office during school. The doors to the officer remained locked throughout the interrogation session. Jill explicitly stated that she wanted to return to class and that she wanted to call her parents. The officer did not allow Jill to call her parents. The officer told Jill that if she did not cooperate, she could "go down to juvenile hall." Jill was allowed to use a restroom that was within eyesight of the Principal's office. After locating the crime scene following Jill's interrogation, the police discovered physical evidence linking Jill and her boyfriend to the murder. Police arrested Jill after her boyfriend stated that she was present when the killing occurred. Jill begged the police officers to allow her parents to accompany her as she was being arrested but the officers refused her request. She requests that the court grant her a motion to suppress all of the statements she made to law enforcement officers.

CITATION **MATTERS**

Use Appendix C and the Citation Matters feature in this chapter to answer these questions.

1. Capitalize "judge" only when:
2. Capitalize "circuit" only when:
3. Capitalize "constitution" only when:

FROM THE WRITER'S CORNER: Place yourself in the background

1. List four terms you should avoid in your legal writing.

2. "We should write such that the focus is on the ______________ and ______________ of the written material.

ASSIGNMENTS AND EXERCISES

Analysis and Writing Assignments

1. Read 42 U.S.C. § 1983 and list the elements or requirements for finding a person liable for civil damages under this code section:

42 U.S.C. § 1983

Every person who, under color of any statute, ordinance, regulation, custom, or usage, of any State or Territory or the District of Columbia, subjects, or causes to be subjected, any citizen of the United States or other person within the jurisdiction thereof to the deprivation of any rights, privileges, or immunities secured by the Constitution and laws, shall be liable to the party injured in an action at law, suit in equity, or other proper proceeding for redress, except that in any action brought against a judicial officer for an act or omission taken in such officer's judicial capacity, injunctive relief shall not be granted unless a declaratory decree was violated or declaratory relief was unavailable. For the purposes of this section, any Act of Congress applicable exclusively to the District of Columbia shall be considered to be a statute of the District of Columbia.

2. Read the following code section:

Robbery defined: Robbery is the felonious taking of personal property in the possession of another, from his person or immediate presence, and against his will, accomplished by means of force or fear.

a. Complete the following list of the statutory elements.

1. felonious taking
2. personal property
3.
4.
5.
6.

b. Analyze the following factual situation and determine if the defendant committed a robbery.

Defendant points a gun at a victim and tells him to hand over his wallet. The victim does and defendant opens the wallet, looks inside, sees it is empty, and throws it on the ground.

Begin your analysis by completing the following chart.

Elements of Statute	Factual Application
1. Felonious taking ⟶	1. D told V to and V does
2. Personal property ⟶	2. A wallet is personal property
3.	
4.	
5.	
6.	

c. Using the same chart and the same statute, analyze the following facts:

1. X and Y were engaged. X gave Y his grandmother's ring as an engagement ring. They break up and X wants the ring back. Y refuses. X threatens Y, and Y gives back the ring.

2. X steals a saxophone from a store. A security guard from another establishment chases and is threatened.

3. D and V know each other. He drugs her coffee. When she passes out, he steals her jewelry.

3. Read the following code section:

Subject to this division, the father and mother of a minor child have an equal responsibility to support their child in the manner suitable to the child's circumstances.

The duty of support imposed herein continues as to an unmarried child who has attained the age of 18 years, is a full-time high school student, and who is not self-supporting, until the time the child completes the 12th grade or attains the age of 19 years, whichever occurs first.

a. Outline the statutory requirements for a parent to be responsible for supporting a child who is 18 years of age.

b. Consider the following facts: Jeffrey turned 18 four months ago. He is a senior in high school, living at home, and will graduate in two months. He has a part-time job at a local fast-food restaurant and earns approximately $400 per month, most of which he spends on his car and entertainment. He is not married. Apply the code section to these facts, using the outline format found in Box 6-3. Are his parents obligated to support him? If so, for how long?

4. Read the following language from 18 U.S.C. § 1105:

Whoever—assaults, kidnaps, or murders, or attempts or conspires to kidnap or murder, or threatens to assault, kidnap or murder a member of the immediate family of a United States official, a United States judge, a Federal law enforcement officer, with intent to impede, intimidate, or interfere with such official, judge, or law enforcement officer while engaged in the performance of official duties, or with intent to retaliate against such official, judge, or law enforcement officer on account of the performance of official duties, shall be punished as provided in subsection (b). As used in this section, the term "immediate family member" of an individual means—

a. his spouse, parent, brother or sister, child or person to whom he stands in loco parentis; or
b. any other person living in his household and related to him by blood or marriage;

Now consider the following facts: Judge Thomas Merkins, a United States District Court Judge, sentenced James Oakley to a lengthy prison term for a drug-related offense. Oakley's father, John, outraged at the sentence, vowed to get even with the judge. He hired two thugs to attack the judge's son-in-law. Police officials learned of this before any attack occurred. The judge's daughter and son-in-law are temporarily living with the judge. Consider if John Oakley can be punished under 18 U.S.C. § 115. Before reaching your conclusion, do the following.

a. Outline the statutory elements or requirements under 18 U.S.C. § 115 for any person to be punished under the section.
b. Prepare a statutory analysis of the facts in outline form, relating appropriate statutory language to relevant facts. (See Box 6-3.)
c. Determine if there are any ambiguities or uncertainties that necessitate further research. If so, explain what research steps you would take.

5. Read the following amendments to the U.S. Constitution:

Amendment V:

No person shall be held to answer for a capital, or otherwise infamous crime, unless on a presentment or indictment of a Grand Jury, except in cases arising in the land or naval forces, or in the Militia, when in actual service in time of War or public danger; nor shall any person be subject for the same offence to be twice put in jeopardy of life or limb; nor shall be compelled in any criminal case to be a witness against himself, nor be deprived of life, liberty, or property, without due process of law; nor shall private property be taken for public use, without just compensation.

Amendment XIV:

All persons born or naturalized in the United States and subject to the jurisdiction thereof, are citizens of the United States and of the State wherein they reside. No State shall make or enforce any law which shall abridge the privileges or immunities of citizens of the United States; nor shall any State deprive any person of life, liberty, or property, without due process of law; nor deny to any person within its jurisdiction the equal protection of the laws.

a. List all terms in these amendments that could be considered ambiguous.
b. Keeping in mind that the Bill of Rights (the first 10 amendments) applies only to the federal government, analyze the following factual situations in relation to the Fifth and Fourteenth Amendments. Prepare an outline of the appropriate constitutional language related to the relevant facts (Box 6-3) and answer the specific questions asked.
   1. Financial support of elementary schools in Washington, D.C., that are predominantly composed of minority students is substantially less than the support given to elementary schools that are not minority-based.
      a. Is there a potential violation of the Fifth Amendment?
      b. Is there a potential violation of the Fourteenth Amendment?
      c. Are there any issues or questions you would want to research further? If so, list those questions and identify the sources you would consult.
   2. A regional planning commission in the Lake Tahoe area imposed a three-year moratorium on all building near the lake. Jones, who owned lake-view property, was unable to build and therefore unable to use his land. He claimed that the government should compensate him for his property.
      a. Does Jones have any potential claims under the Fifth Amendment?
      b. Does Jones have any potential claims under the Fourteenth Amendment?
      c. Are there any issues or questions you would want to research further? If so, list those questions and identify the sources you would consult.
   3. Write an analysis of the Rambeaux situation regarding Rambeaux's civil liability under 42 U.S.C. § 1983. Follow the example in Box 6-5.
   4. Assume that you work as a research assistant for the attorney handling the Meyers case. In researching the codes you find the following: **Penal Code section 1538.5. (a)** (1) A defendant

may move for the return of property or to suppress as evidence any tangible or intangible thing obtained as a result of a search or seizure on either of the following grounds:

(A) The search or seizure without a warrant was unreasonable.

(B) The search or seizure with a warrant was unreasonable because any of the following apply:

- **i** The warrant is insufficient on its face.
- **ii** The property or evidence obtained is not that described in the warrant.
- **iii** There was not probable cause for the issuance of the warrant.
- **iv** The method of execution of the warrant violated federal or state constitutional standards.
- **v** There was any other violation of federal or state constitutional standards.

Write a short paragraph explaining how this code section applies to the motion to suppress the bloody handkerchief in the Meyers case.

Online Research Exercises

6. Access a copy of the U.S. Constitution that contains analysis and interpretation. (This is available on several websites.) Review the annotations to the Fourth Amendment. Locate and cite any cases that might help with the Meyers case. Explain how or why the cases help.

7. Using an online source (such as Google Scholar or www.law.cornell.edu), locate and read *Robinson v. Shell Oil Company*, 519 U.S. 337 (1997). Explain the steps that the Court went through in interpreting the term *employee*.

CASE **PROJECT**

In-Class Small Group Work

In Chapter 5, you researched one of the hypothetical situations in Appendix A to determine what statutory law applied. Taking your results,

a. identify the elements of any statutes,

b. write an outline of the statutory elements and the facts.

Individual Work

Write a statutory analysis using the facts of the hypothetical situation.

chapter **seven**

SECONDARY SOURCES

CHAPTER OUTLINE

SKILL OBJECTIVES FOR CHAPTER 7

When you complete chapter 7, you should be able to

- Describe and use the common features of secondary source materials.
- Research a legal question using legal encyclopedias.
- Research a legal question using the *American Law Reports*.
- Evaluate the advantages and disadvantages of using treatises and periodicals to research a legal issue.
- Describe the features of a looseleaf service and explain its purpose.
- Explain the relevance and limitations of the *Restatement of Law* as a research tool.
- Explain why C.L.E. materials, form books, and pattern jury instructions are useful research tools.

From the Desk of W. J. Bryan, Esq.

TO: Research Assistant
FROM: W. J. Bryan
RE: Our Client, Justin Meyers
DATE:

Yesterday, a pretrial conference was held in the Meyers case and the judge ordered us to file all pretrial motions within the next 30 days. We need to file a motion to suppress the bloody handkerchief. I think we also have grounds to suppress statements Meyers made to the police while they were transporting him to jail. Review the Grand Jury Transcript and Search Warrant and conduct some preliminary research concerning our basis for making this motion to suppress. Write a brief memo summarizing your findings. Try to find a treatise that deals exclusively with criminal procedure but if you do not find one, try a legal encyclopedia. Either of these should give you a good overview of the law.

7-1 INTRODUCTION

Usually, the goal of legal research is to find primary law that controls a factual dispute or question. As you saw in previous chapters, you can locate constitutional provisions and relevant code sections by using the index to the codes. You can locate case law through the case notes in an annotated code. However, there are other, and often easier, ways to find all the relevant law.

To facilitate the legal research process, many publishers produce works generally known as *secondary sources*. A ***secondary source of law*** is not the law itself. It is someone's interpretation or explanation of the law. However, most secondary sources provide references or citations to the ***primary source of law***. Using secondary sources in the initial research process is very helpful because it provides an overview of the relevant area of law and enables you to identify the key facts and legal issues of the research problem. Once you identify the precise issue, a secondary source leads you to the relevant primary law. If both statutory law and case law apply to a situation, the secondary source refers you to each. Secondary sources include multivolume works, single books, and periodicals. Some are available on CD-ROM, and many are available through online services such as the Lexis or Westlaw databases. Because secondary sources are generally published commercially, and therefore subject to copyright protection, most are not available freely on the Internet. This chapter covers some of the more common types of secondary sources used by legal professionals

secondary source of law
Tool we use to help us understand the law; one such tool is a legal encyclopedia that explains the law.

primary source of law
A work that contains the law itself.

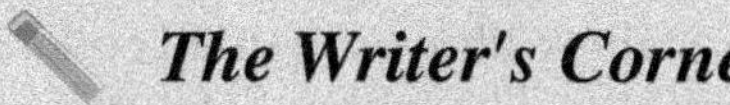

The Writer's Corner

Quotations

Place short quotes in quotation marks. Use double quotation marks around all quotations under fifty words (see *Bluebook* rule 5). To show a quote within a quote, use single quote marks around the interior quote.

Quotes of 50 or more words must be "blocked." Indent the quote on the right and left and use single spacing. Do not use quotation marks with these longer quotes. Place commas and periods inside the quotation marks.

Place square brackets around things you change or add in a quotation.

Example: "The burden of proof in Smith's case is . . . ." (citation to case follows here)

(continued)

You might not want to use the party name in your document. You may replace "Smith's" with "[the defendant's]."

"The burden of proof in [the defendant's] case is . . . ."

An ellipsis shows that you omitted something from the quote. An ellipsis is three periods separated by spaces. Be sure to leave a space before and after the ellipsis. Do not use an ellipsis to open a quote. When an ellipsis is used at the end of a quote, it needs a fourth period.

Example: "A homeowner is liable for damages when (1) the owner fails to acquire appropriate insurance or . . . (4) the owner fails to call for inspections . . . ."

Use a colon to introduce long quotations.

Be cautious about the amount of quoted language used in any document. Too many quotes may make the document difficult to read.

A Point to Remember

A secondary source is someone's interpretation of the primary law. It is not the law, and you should never rely on a secondary source as authority. You should always read the primary law and cite to it.

7-2 FEATURES OF SECONDARY SOURCE MATERIALS ACCESSED IN PRINT FORM

Finding specific information in secondary source materials is facilitated by several editorial features added to the text materials. Most secondary source materials accessed in print have some, if not all, of the following features. Secondary sources accessed online often do not have these research features, with the exception of a table of contents. Search methods for online searches are discussed in Chapters 10 and 11.

- **Descriptive Word Index**—An alphabetized list of words or phrases describing subjects discussed in the text. The index directs you to the page or section in the text where the material is covered; it is usually located at the end of the secondary source material. Multivolume works often contain separate volumes located at the end of the set containing the index. By identifying key words in your research problem, you are able to check these terms in an index and find the appropriate sections in the secondary source. See Figure 7-1.
- **Table of Contents**—A detailed list of topics covered in the text that precedes the text material. This is organized in the same order as the material appears in the text; similar and related topics are usually grouped together. A table of contents provides an overview of the material covered.
- **Table of Statutes Cited**—A list of statutes or codes discussed in the text. This is usually arranged alphabetically by the name of the code and then numerically within each titled code. If the code has no name, it is arranged numerically. The table of statutes tells you where in the text material the code section is found. If you know of a code section that applies to your research problem, you can check the table of statutes cited to find a section of the text in which the code section is cited. See Figure 7-2.
- **Table of Cases Cited**—A list of cases cited in the text material, arranged alphabetically by the plaintiff's name; sometimes also arranged alphabetically by the defendant's name. This table normally provides the case citation and a reference to the page or section in the text material where the case appears; sometimes called "Plaintiff/Defendant Index" or "Defendant/Plaintiff Index." See Figure 7-3.

- **Table of Abbreviations**—A list of all abbreviations used in the text, including those used for case reporters and other legal sources. This is an important feature to check because many secondary sources do not use standard or approved abbreviations for legal sources.
- **Preface**—A description of the contents and purpose of the material; often contains an explanation of how to use the material.
- **Parallel Reference Tables**—Tables included in works that are published in more than one series or edition. These tables show the reader how to find in the new editions material contained in the original editions.
- **Pocket Part Supplement**—Many print versions of secondary sources are supplemented in the way that codes are, that is, with pocket part supplements. (Online versions of secondary sources incorporate supplemental material with the initial publication.)

FIGURE 7-1 *American Jurisprudence 2d*, Index Page

AMERICAN JURISPRUDENCE 2d

SHERIFFS, POLICE, AND CONSTABLES—Cont'd
Defects and irregularities
arrests, defective or improper, **Sheriffs § 49**
levy on property, below
surety's liability on official bonds, below
Defenses
generally, **CrimLaw § 290; Sheriffs § 61-66**
amercement, **Sheriffs § 114**
answers, **Sheriffs § 124**
bonds, defenses of sureties, **Sheriffs § 71**
failure to levy process, **Sheriffs § 65**
failure to make return, **Sheriffs § 66**
governmental immunity, **Sheriffs § 62**
indemnity, **Sheriffs § 96**
instructions to officer, **Sheriffs § 63**
justification under writ, **Sheriffs § 64**
official bonds, defenses of sureties in actions on, **Sheriffs § 71**
return, failure to make, **Sheriffs § 66**
Definitions, **Sheriffs § 1-6**
Delay
levy on property, **Sheriffs § 48**
return or execution of process, **Sheriffs § 48**
Demand
actions against officers, demand or notice of, **Sheriffs § 100**
license, demand for display of, **Autos § 112**
Deputies
generally, **Sheriffs § 6**
actions against officer for wrongful acts of deputy
generally, **Sheriffs § 54-60**
arrest, acts in connection with, **Sheriffs § 58**
civil rights, deprivation of, **Sheriffs § 59**
damages, **Sheriffs § 149**
execution, defective, **Sheriffs § 57**
failure to supervise, train, or discipline deputy, **Sheriffs § 56**
imprisonment, acts in connection with, **Sheriffs § 58**
levy, defective, **Sheriffs § 57**
motor vehicles, operation of, **Sheriffs § 60**
pleadings, **Sheriffs § 121**
presumptions and burden of proof, **Sheriffs § 132**
return, defective, **Sheriffs § 57**
sale, defective, **Sheriffs § 57**
statutory provisions, **Sheriffs § 55**
surety's liability on official bonds, below
appointment, **Sheriffs § 13**
elections, **Sheriffs § 13**
imputed negligence. Actions against

SHERIFFS, POLICE, AND CONSTABLES—Cont'd
Deputies—Cont'd
officer for wrongful acts of deputy, above in this group
powers and duties, **Sheriffs § 32**
property rights in office, **Sheriffs § 17**
surety's liability on official bonds, below
United States Marshals (this index)
vicarious liability. Actions against officer for wrongful acts of deputy, above in this group
Directions from traffic officers, **Autos § 887**
Disbursements, **Sheriffs § 44**
Discovery (this index)
Discretion, **Sheriffs § 31**
Documentary evidence, police records and reports, generally, **Evidence § 1158, 1316, 1360-1362**
Drugs and narcotics, **DrugsEtc § 194**
Elections
generally, **Sheriffs § 12**
deputy sheriffs, **Sheriffs § 13**
Elevators, **Elevators § 28**
Eligibility, **Sheriffs § 7-11**
Embezzlement, criminal liability for, **Sheriffs § 155**
Escape, Prison Breaking, and Rescue (this index)
Evidence
generally, **Sheriffs § 125-139**
admissibility of evidence, **Sheriffs § 125-129**
documentary evidence, **Evidence § 1158, 1316, 1360-1362**
habit or routine practice (rule 406), **Evidence § 40**
levy, wrongful, **Sheriffs § 129**
misconduct, effect of exclusionary rule in deterring, **Evidence § 590**
presumptions and burden of proof, below
removal from office, **Sheriffs § 28**
return as evidence, **Sheriffs § 127, 128**
search for defendant as showing flight, **Evidence § 533**
seizure of property, **Sheriffs § 126**
weight and sufficiency of evidence, **Sheriffs § 139**
Exclusion of evidence, deterring misconduct, **Evidence § 590**
Execution of process
generally, **Sheriffs § 39**
actions against officers
generally, **Sheriffs § 47**
delay, **Sheriffs § 48**
deputy, liability for defective levy by, **Sheriffs § 57**
failure to execute process, below in this group
limitation of actions, **Sheriffs § 118**
omissions, **Sheriffs § 48**

SHERIFFS, POLICE, AND CONSTABLES—Cont'd
Execution of process—Cont'd
actions against officers—Cont'd
surety's liability on official bonds, **Sheriffs § 90**
civil arrest, defective, improper, or failure to make, **Sheriffs § 49**
deputy, liability for defective levy by, **Sheriffs § 57**
failure to execute process
civil arrest, defective, improper, or failure to make, **Sheriffs § 49**
damages, **Sheriffs § 143**
pleadings, **Sheriffs § 122**
presumptions and burden of proof, **Sheriffs § 133**
omissions. Failure to execute process, above in this group
sale of property, below
surety's liability on official bonds, **Sheriffs § 90**
Expenses, **Sheriffs § 44**
Expiration of term of office, **Sheriffs § 37**
Explosions and Explosives (this index)
Extraterritorial powers, **Sheriffs § 36**
Failure of officer to sign as principal, **Sheriffs § 72**
Failure to enforce laws, **Sheriffs § 46**
Failure to execute process. Execution of process, above
Failure to make civil arrest, **Sheriffs § 49**
Failure to make levy. Levy on property, below
Failure to make return. Return of process, below
Failure to pay over money, liability of sureties on official bonds, **Sheriffs § 81**
Failure to safeguard property, presumptions and burden of proof, **Sheriffs § 135**
Failure to supervise, train, or discipline deputy, **Sheriffs § 56**
Fair Labor Standards Act (this index)
False returns, damages, **Sheriffs § 147**
Federal Bureau of Investigation (FBI) (this index)
Federal Employers' Liability and Compensation Act (FELCA) (this index)
Federal marshals. **United States Marshals** (this index)
Federal Tort Claims Act (this index)
Fees, **Sheriffs § 43**
Force and violence
Assault and Battery (this index)
Obstruction of Justice (this index)
Fraud and deceit, false returns, damages, **Sheriffs § 147**
Fugitives, testimony as to search for defendant, **Evidence § 533**
Governmental immunity, **Sheriffs § 62**
Home rule, **MuncCorp § 119**
Identification materials. **Police Identification**

For assistance using this Index, call 1-800-328-4880

288

To find general information about a police officer's failure to enforce laws, go to the Topic "Sheriffs" in Am. Jr. 2d and read section 46.

Instead of looking under "SHERIFFS AND POLICE" go to "United States Marshals" in the index.

FIGURE 7-2 Table of Statutes Cited

AMERICAN JURISPRUDENCE 2d

UNITED STATES CODE ANNOTATED—Continued

18 U.S.C.A.	Sec.
210	BRIBERY: 2
211	BRIBERY: 2, 15
212	BRIBERY: 2
213	BRIBERY: 2
215	BANKS: 431; BRIBERY: 2
215(a)(1)	BANKS: 433
215(a)(2)	BANKS: 433
215(d)	BANKS: 433
216	LABOR: 1918; PUBLICOFF: 378, 379, 384
216(b)	PUBLICOFF: 319, 415, 417
216(c)	PUBLICOFF: 415
224	EXTORTION: 120
224(a)	BRIBERY: 22
224(b)	BRIBERY: 22
224(c)(1)	BRIBERY: 22
224(c)(2)	BRIBERY: 22
224(c)(3)	BRIBERY: 22
228	COMMERCE: 41; DESERTION: 1, 29, 32
228(a)	DESERTION: 32
228(a)(1)	DESERTION: 32
228(a)(2)	DESERTION: 32
228(a)(3)	DESERTION: 27, 32
228(c)(1)	DESERTION: 32
228(c)(2)	DESERTION: 32
228(d)	DESERTION: 32
228(e)(1)	DESERTION: 32
228(e)(2)	DESERTION: 32
228(e)(3)	DESERTION: 32
232(5)	EXPLOS: 5
232(5)(A)	EXPLOS: 5
232(5)(B)	EXPLOS: 5
232(5)(C)	EXPLOS: 5
241	CIVILRGHTS: 197, 199 to 204; ELECTIONS: 458; GRANDJURY: 32; INVOLSERV: 4
242	ALIENS: 1841; CIVILRGHTS: 90, 205 to 215; EVIDENCE: 441
245	CIVILRGHTS: 216 to 222
245(a)(1)	CIVILRGHTS: 219
245(a)(2)	CIVILRGHTS: 219
245(b)	CIVILRGHTS: 216, 218, 221, 222, 521; EVIDENCE: 439
245(b)(1)	CIVILRGHTS: 216
245(b)(2)	CIVILRGHTS: 216
245(b)(2)(B)	CIVILRGHTS: 222

18 U.S.C.A.	Sec.
245(b)(2)(C)	JOBDISCRIM: 2802
245(b)(2)(E)	CIVILRGHTS: 521
247	ARSON: 4
248	ABORTION: 96, 109, 115; COMMERCE: 41; INJUNCTION: 82
248(a)	ABORTION: 75, 83, 114, 122
248(a)(1)	ABORTION: 83, 114
248(a)(3)	ABORTION: 83
248(b)	ABORTION: 122
248(c)(1)(A)	ABORTION: 114
248(c)(1)(B)	ABORTION: 114
248(c)(2)(A)	ABORTION: 115
248(c)(2)(B)	ABORTION: 115
248(c)(3)(A)	ABORTION: 115
248(c)(3)(B)	ABORTION: 115
248(d)	ABORTION: 97
248(e)(4)	ABORTION: 99
248(e)(5)	ABORTION: 100
285	FALSEPR: 10, 87
286	FALSEPR: 81
287	FALSEPR: 80; FEDTAXENF: 1198, 1215
288	FALSEPR: 87; POST: 92, 93, 100
289	FALSEPR: 87; VETERANS: 147, 149
290	FALSEPR: 87
291	FALSEPR: 87
292	FALSEPR: 87
331	MONEY: 60
332	EMBEZZLE: 6, 67
333	MONEY: 60
334	BANKS: 431
336	MONEY: 32
341 et seq.	CARRIERS: 34
342	ALIENS: 22
351	HOMICIDE: 2
371	ABDUCTION: 16, 46; ALIENS: 1569; ATTNYS: 93; BANKRUPTCY: 417; BROKERS: 26; CONSPIRACY: 1, 15, 45; CORAMNOBIS: 8; ELECTIONS: 458; FEDTAXENF: 1198, 1215; MILITARY: 151; OBSTRUCT: 4; RECEIVSTOL: 38, 39, 45; ROBBERY: 99; SECURITIES: 1731; SEDITION: 12, 20, 38, 42; WELFARE: 41
401	BAIL: 159; CONTEMPT: 29, 44, 55, 62, 65, 118, 126, 147, 173, 196, 203, 206; JOBDISCRIM: 2797; LABOR: 3530; OBSTRUCT: 5
401(1)	CONTEMPT: 29, 50

178

18 U.S.C.A § 242 is mentioned in several Am. Jur. 2d topics and sections; it is mentioned in section 1841 of the topic Aliens, Sections 90 and 205 to 215 of the topic Civil Rights and section 441 of the topic Evidence.

FIGURE 7-3 Cases Cited in *A.L.R. Federal*

CASES CITED IN ALR FEDERAL

Urquhar v Lockham (1983. ED Ark) Hi F Supp 1334
75 ALR Fed 9, § 26

Urrutia. In re (1990. DC Puerto Rico) 137 BR 563
140 ALR Fed 1. § 43, 45

Urrutia v United States (1956. CA5 Fla) 253 F2d 501
38 ALR Fed 617, § 3, 4

Ursic v. Bethlehem Mines. 719 F.2d 670. 4 Employee Benefits Cas. (BNA) 2297, 14 Fed. R. Evid. Serv. 395 (3d Cir. 1983)
172 ALR Fed 571.§ 4

Urtz v. Callahan. 965 F. Supp. 324, Soc. Sec. Rep. Serv. 605. Unempl. Ins. Rep. (CCH) 1 157808 (N.D.N.Y. 1997)
165 ALR Fed 203. § 3-5, 9, 10, 20, 24. 25, 28, 31

Urwyler v Reecc (1987. ED Cal) 87-1 USTC P 9298. 59 AFIR 2d 87-843
99 ALR Fed 700. § 4, 10

Urwyles v United States (1989. ED Cal) 90-1 USTC P 50016. 71A AFTR 2d 93-3338
117 ALR Fed 75, § 16, 18, 34

Ury v Santee (1969. ND Ill) 303 F Supp 119
66 ALR Fed 750.§ 6. 12

U.S. v. 1,380,09 Acres of Land. More or Less. Situated In Caldwell Parish. State of La. 574 F.2d 238 (5th Cir. 1978)
172 ALR Fed 507, § 24

U.S. v. 2,116 Boxes of Boned Beef, Weighing Approximately 154.121 Pounds. 726 F.2d 1481 (10h Cir. 1984)
173 ALR Fed 465. §7. 10

U.S. v. 2,200 Paper Back Books. 565 F2d 366 (9th Cir. 1977)
172 ALR Fed 239.§ 3

U.S. v. 4.18 Aces of Land. More or Less. in Idaho County. State of Idaho. 542 F.2d 786 (9th Cir. 1976)
172 ALR Fed 507.§ 2. 4

U.S. v. 5.553.30 Acres of Land. More or Less, in Concordia Parish. State of La.. 451 F. Supp. 220 (W.D. La. 1978)
172 ALR Fed 507, § 5

U.S. v. 12 200-Foot Reels of Super 8mm. Film. 413 U.S. 123. 93 5. Ct. 2665. 37 L. Ed. 2d 500 (1973)
172 ALR Fed 239,§ 2

U.S. v. 25,000 Magazines, Entitled "Revue", 254 F. Supp. 1014 (D. Md. 1906)
172 ALR Fed 239.§ 3

U.S. v. 31 Photographs, 156 F. Supp. 350 (S.D.N.Y. 1957)
172 ALR Fed 239. § 3,5

U.S. v 35 MM. Moiion Picture Film "Language of Love". 432 F.2d 703 (2d Cir. 1970)
172 ALR Fed 239. § 4

U.S. v. 40.00 Acres of Land. More or Less. in Henry County. Mo.. 427 F. Supp. 434 (W.D. Mo. 1976)
172 ALR Fed 507, § 6

U.S. v. 122.00 Acres of Land, More or Less. Located in Koochiching County. Minn.. 856 F.2d 56 (8th Cir. 1988)
172 ALR Fed 307. § 4, 10

U.S. v. 127.295 Copies of Magazmes, More or Less, Entitled "Amor" 295 F. Supp. 1186 (D. Md. 1968)
172 ALR Fed 239. § 3

U.S. v. 243.538 Acres of Land. More or Less. In Maui County, State of Hawaii. 509 F. Supp. 981 (D. Haw. 1981)
172 ALR Fed 507, § 4. 10, 15. 16, 20, 21,28

U.S. v. 359.73 Acres of Land. Situated in Crenada and Yalobusha Counties. State of Miss.. 704 F.2d 800. 20 Env't. Rep. Cas. (BNA) 1025 (5th Cir. 1983)
172 ALR Fed 507. §2

U.S. v. 341.45 Acres of Land. More or Less. Located in the County of St. Louis. State of Minn., 751 F.2d 924 (8th Cir. 1984)
172 ALR Fed 507. §2

U.S. v. 410.69 Acres of Land. More or Less in Escambia County, State of Fla.. 608 F.2d 1073 (5th Cir. 1979)
171 ALR Fed 507. § 4

U.S. v. 431.60 Acres of Land. More or Less. in Richmond County, State of Ga., 355 F. Supp. 1093 (S.D. Ga. 1973)
172 ALR Fed S07. §2, 10, 15, 26, 28

U.S. v. 640.00 Acres of Land, More or Less, In Dade County. State of Fla., 756 F.2d 842 (11th Cir. 1985)
172 ALR Fed 507. §2

U.S. v. 1500 Cases. More or Less. etc., 249 F.2d 382 (7th Cir. 1957)
173 ALR Fed 465, § 7, 10

U.S. v. A Motion Picture Film Entitled "1 Am Curious-Yellow". 404 F.2d 196 (2d Cir. 1968)
172 ALR Fed 239. § 4

U.S. v. Abod. 770 F.2d 1293 (5ih Cir. 19851
173 ALR Fed 613, § 2. 4,5,9

U.S. v. ACB Sales se Service. Inc., 590 F. Supp. 561 (D. Ariz. 1984)
173 ALR Fed 223. § 7

U.S. v. Adler. 52 F.3d 20 (2d Cir (995)
173 ALR Fed 667. § 3

U.S. v. Ailsworth. 948 F. Supp. 1135 ,0. Kan. 1996)
173 ALR Fed 1.§ 61

U.S. v. Al-Cantara 973 F. 2d 1256 (4th Cir. 1992)
173 ALR Fed 613,§ 9

U.S. v. Alessi 618 F.2d 466. 7 Fed. R. Evid. Serv. 909 (2d Cir. 1980)
173 ALR Fed 613,§ 9

U.S. v. Alexander. 48 F.3d 1477. 41 Fed. R. Evid. Serv. 774 (9th Cir. 1995)
173 ALR Fed 1, § 24

U.S. v. Alkim. 925 F.2d 541 (2d Cir 1991)
172 ALR Fed 109. § 3-S. 18

U.S. v. American Cyanamid Co., 427 F, Supp. 859. 1 Fed. R. Evid. Serv. 672 (S.D.N.Y. I977)
173 ALR Fed 1. § 28

U.S. v. American Tel. and Tel. Co., 316 F. Supp. 1237. 8 Fed. R. Evid. Serv. 893 (D.D.C. 1981)
173 ALR Fed 1. § 26, 28, 46, 95

U.S. v. American Tel. and Tel. Co., 1981-1 Trade Cas. (CCH) 63933, 1981 WL 2047 (D.D.C 1981)
173 ALR Fed 1, § 7, 95

U.S. v. Ames Sintering Co., 927 F.2d 232 (6th Cir. 1900)
172 ALR Fed 109. § 3

U.S. v. Antelope. 430 U.S. 641, 97 S. Ct. 1393.51 L. Ed. 2d 701 (1977)
172 ALR Fed 1.§ 2, 23

U.S. v. Ardoin, 19 F.3d 177. 73 A.F.T.R.2d 94-1799. 73 .VF.T.R.Sd 94-2432 (5th Cir. 1994)
173 ALR Fed 667. § 4

U.S. v. Armstrong. 517 U.S. 456. 116 S. Ct. 1430. 134 L. Ed. 2d 687 (1996)
172 ALR Fed 1, § 26

U.S. v. Articles of Food Clover Club Potato Chips. 67 F.R.D. 419 (D. Idaho 1975)
173 ALR Fed 465., § 10

U.S. v. Atkins. 558 F.2d 133. 2 Fed. R. Evid. Serv. 296 (3d Cir. 1977)
173 ALR Fed 1, § 6

U.S. v. Atkins. 618 F.2d 366. 6 Fed. R. Evid. Serv. 166 (5th Cir. 1980)
173 ALR Fed 1, § 57

U.S. v. Azure. 801 F.2d 336. 21 Fed. R. Evid. Serv. 801 (8th Cir. 1986)
173 ALR Fed I. § 64

U.S. v. Azure. S45 F.2d 1503. 25 Fed. R. Evid. Serv. 1053 (6th Cir. 1988)
173 ALR Fed 1.§ 64

U.S. v. Bachsian. 4 F.3d 796. 39 Fed. R. Evid. Serv. 1091 (9th Cir. 1993)
I73 ALR Fed 1.§ 3. 7. 22

U.S. v. Bailey. 581 F.2d 341. 3 Fed. R. F.vid. Serv. 371 (3d Cir. 1978)
173 ALR Fed 1.§ 5, 6

U.S. v. Bailin. 1990 WL 114741 (N.D. III. 1990)
172 ALR Fed 109. § 5

U.S. v. Bajakajian. 524 U.S. 321. 118 S. Ct. 2028. 141 L Ed. 2d 314. 172 ALR. Fed. 705 (1993)
172 ALR Fed 389, § 3, 5-7. 12

U.S. v. Balfany. 965 F.2d 575. 35 Fed. R. Evid. Serv. 990 (8th Cir. 1992)
173 ALR Fed 1.§ 64

U.S. v. Banner. 226 F. Supp. 904. 64-1 U.S. Tax Cas. (CCH) 9264. 13 A.F.T.R.2d 579 (N.D.N.Y. 1963)
173 ALR Fed 465. § 27. 28

U.S. v. Barnes. 12 M.J. 614 (N.M.C.M.R. 1961)
173 ALR Fed 1.§ 71

U.S. v. Barnes. 586 F.2d 1052. 3 Fed. R. Evid. Serv. 1278 (5th Cir. 1978)
173 ALR Fed 1.§ 57

U.S. v. Barrett. 8 F.3d 1296. 38 Fed. R. Evid. Serv. 198 (8th Cir. 1993)
173 ALR Fed 1.§ 67

U.S. v. Barrett. 598 F. Supp. 469 (D. Me. 1984)
173 ALR Fed 1, § 4, 39

U.S. v. Barretto. 708 F. Supp. 577. 39-2 U.S. Tax Cas. (CCH) § 9046. 64 A.F.T.R.2d 89-5623 (S.D.N.Y. 1989)
173 ALR Fed 465.126

U.S. v. Bell. 86 F.3d 1164 (9th Cir. 1996)
173 ALR Fed 1.160

U.S. v. Beltran. 761 F.2d 1.18 Fed. R. Evid. Serv. 40 (1st Cir. 1985)
I73 ALR Fed 1. § 83

For assistance, call 1-800-328-4880

465

***U.S. v. Ames Sintering Co*, is cited in section 3 of the article starting on page 109 in volume 172 of A.L.R. Fed.**

7-3 LEGAL ENCYCLOPEDIAS: *AMERICAN JURISPRUDENCE 2D* AND *CORPUS JURIS SECUNDUM*

legal encyclopedia
A collection of legal information arranged alphabetically by topic; a secondary source of the law.

Nonlegal encyclopedias are multivolume works containing thorough discussions of a variety of subjects arranged alphabetically. ***Legal encyclopedias*** are multivolume works containing comprehensive and thorough discussions of a variety of *legal* topics arranged alphabetically. For example, you might find such broad topics as "aliens and citizens," "arrest," "civil rights," "job discrimination," "federal courts," "negligence," "space law," and "computers and the Internet." Each broad topic is divided into many specific subtopics. For example, under the general topic of "aliens and citizens," you find such subtopics as "immigration laws" and "ports of entry to the United States; border crossings." In addition to a discussion and analysis of legal principles, each article in the encyclopedia refers you to relevant primary sources of law.

Two major legal encyclopedias cover the entirety of U.S. law. These are *American Jurisprudence 2d* (Am. Jur. 2d) and *Corpus Juris Secundum* (C.J.S.). These encyclopedias discuss topics of both state and federal law. Other encyclopedias are state specific, covering only the law of that particular state. Print versions of encyclopedias are generally kept current with pocket part supplements.

Using Legal Encyclopedias

Because material in a legal encyclopedia is organized by general topic, the first step in using a legal encyclopedia is to identify that topic for your specific research question. Fortunately, all encyclopedias contain descriptive word indexes to help you do this. For example, suppose the question you are researching is as follows: "Does a police officer who uses excessive force in making an arrest incur criminal or civil liability under federal law?" At this point, you should proceed as follows.

1. Go to the index found at the end of the set of books.
2. Identify key terms or words to check in the index. Do this by reviewing the known facts. For example, since your research question relates to police officers, you might check for the word *police*. Other key words for this research question might include *excessive force* or *arrest*. When you locate the word *police,* the index directs you to another phrase in the index, "Sheriffs and Police." When you locate this phrase in the index, you find several subtopics. See Figure 7-1 for a portion of this index topic.
3. Review the subtopics found under the main topic. Some of the subtopics will lead you directly to a specific article in the encyclopedia. For example, the subtopic "Failure to Enforce Laws" directs you to section 46 of the general topic Sheriffs and Police. (It is abbreviated as Sheriff in the index.) Other subtopics direct you to other parts of the index. Eventually, you will be directed to an article and section in the encyclopedia.

A Point to Remember

If you have trouble finding the right term in an index, go back to your problem and make a list of all key words. If necessary, use a legal thesaurus.

When you read an encyclopedia article, consider the issues of mandatory and persuasive authority discussed in earlier chapters. Both *Am. Jur. 2d* and *C.J.S.* provide cites to authorities in many different states. If the topic is one that is controlled by state law, first look for authorities from your state, as only these are binding. Other authorities are persuasive. Also, always check the pocket part supplement for any changes or additions to the law. Remember to check the pocket part supplement to the index. Sometimes new topics or subtopics are added to reflect changes in the law. If you access these sources through Westlaw or Lexis, you will not need to use a separate supplement. See Box 7-1.

For an example of an encyclopedia article from *American Jurisprudence 2d*, see Figure 7-4.

FIGURE 7-4
Text Material, Am Jur 2d

70 Am Jur 2d SHERIFFS, POLICE, AND CONSTABLES § 155

Volume 70 of *American Jurisprudence 2d* page 343, section 155; the main topic here is "SHERIFFS, POLICE AND CONSTABLES."

his deputy's failure to make return of an execution within the time required by statute.[64]

If a deputy is negligent in the performance of his duties in regard to the notification, the mode of conducting sale, the title to be given the purchaser, and the return of his precept, the principal is liable to persons injuriously affected.[65] Constables and sheriffs have also been held liable for false returns made by deputies,[66] but the plaintiffs alleging that a deputy sheriff had made a false return of service have the burden of establishing that service of civil process was within the deputy's authority.[67]

§ 155. Acts in connection with arrest or imprisonment

A sheriff may be liable for the wrongful acts of his deputy in making an arrest,[68] including alleged violations of the suspect's civil rights,[69] using excessive force to capture persons committing a crime,[70] and escaping prisoners,[71] or for false imprisonment,[72] where such acts are done by virtue of his office as deputy and within the scope of his authority. For the act to have that character, it must have been done under a warrant or under circumstances which authorized the deputy to make an arrest without warrant. If the deputy makes an arrest in any other way it is not authorized by law and is consequently his individual, and not his official, act. But where the deputy acts under a warrant and abuses that process in making the arrest, the sheriff will be liable.[73] An arrest made in any other way is not authorized by law and

Cases and other supporting authorities are cited in footnotes.

64. Rogers v Anderson (Tenn) 580 SW2d 782.

65. Sexton v Nevers, 37 Mass 451.

66. Houser v Hampton, 29 NC 333.

Under a statute providing that the official acts of a deputy sheriff shall be deemed to be those of the sheriff himself, the sheriff alone, and not the deputy, is liable for a deputy's failure to take bail from a person arrested on civil process or for his false return that he has taken bail. Liability may not exist, however, where the plaintiff has directed the deputy not to take bail. Ordway v Bacon, 14 Vt 378.

67. Karr v Dow (App) 84 NM 708, 507 P2d 455, cert den 84 NM 696, 507 P2d 443.

68. Miles v Wright, 22 Ariz 73, 194 P 88, 12 ALR 970.

Practice Aids.—Complaint in action against deputy, sheriff, and sheriff's surety for wounding by sheriff's deputy. 22 Am Jur Pl & Pr Forms (Rev) Sheriffs, Police, and Constables, Form 133.

Police Misconduct Litigation—Plaintiff's Remedies. 15 Am Jur Trials 555 §§ 21–25.

69. § 156.

70. Widow stated cause of action against sheriff for death of husband killed in exchange of gun fire between sheriff 's deputies and fleeing felons who had taken husband as hostage where complaint alleged that sheriff's deputies were negligent in failing to engage in proper police practices. in engaging in close pursuit and thus placing husband's life in jeopardy, and in failing to retreat despite fact that husband's life was endangered. Michel v Hometown Super Markets, Inc. (La App 4th Cir) 352 So 2d 357.

71. Andry v Orleans (La App 4th Cir) 309 So 2d 814, later app (La App 4th Cir) 358 So 2d 334 (holding that under a statute providing that no sheriff nor his surety shall be liable for any act or tort committed by one of his deputies beyond the amount of the bond or limits of liability insurance furnished by the deputy sheriff, unless the deputy sheriff in the commission of the said tort acts in compliance with a direct order of, and in the personal presence of, the sheriff, at the time the act or tort is committed, a sheriff would not be liable individually for excessive force allegedly used by his deputy sheriff to apprehend a prisoner during an escape attempt, but a cause of action existed against the sheriff in his official capacity).

As to means permissible in recapturing prisoners, generally, see 27 Am Jur 2d Escape, Prison Breaking, and Rescue § 26.

72. Abbott v Cooper. 218 Cal 425, 23 P2d 1027.

73. Miles v Wright, 22 Ariz 73, 194 P 88, 12 ALR 970; Ivy v Osborne, 152 Tenn 470, 279 SW 384.

343

American Jurisprudence 2d and *Corpus Juris Secundum* are available in print and online through the Westlaw and/or Lexis databases.

BOX 7-1 USING ENCYCLOPEDIAS

(*American Jurisprudence 2d* and *Corpus Juris Secundum*)

✔ Review your research question and identify:
  - General legal topic
  - Specific legal topic
  - All descriptive words

✔ Look up descriptive words in the index to locate the proper encyclopedia topic.

✔ Retrieve the alphabetically arranged volume containing the relevant topic.

✔ Read the article and make note of primary law from your jurisdiction.

✔ Check pocket part supplement for updates.

7-4 AMERICAN LAW REPORTS

American Law Reports (*A.L.R.*) and *American Law Reports Federal* (*A.L.R. Fed.*) are other important secondary sources used by legal researchers. *American Law Reports* covers American law as found in the various states, and *American Law Reports Federal* covers federal law. Like encyclopedias, *American Law Reports* provides citations to primary law from all states. You must, therefore, consider the issues of mandatory and persuasive authorities in relying on cases cited within the annotations.

In print format, *A.L.R.* contains both leading cases and articles or annotations discussing and analyzing the legal issues raised in those cases. The online versions, found on both Westlaw and Lexis, contain only the annotations. (The cases are available online through other sources.) Figure 7-5 shows a portion of an annotation from *A.L.R. Fed. 2d.*

American Law Reports was first published in 1919 and is currently in its seventh edition or series. The various series are referred to as *A.L.R.*, *A.L.R. 2d*, *A.L.R. 3d*, *A.L.R. 4th*, *A.L.R. 5th*, *A.L.R. 6th*, and *A.L.R. 7th*. The federal series is in its third series and is known as *A.L.R. Fed. A.L.R. Fed. 2d.*, and *A.L.R. Fed 3d.*

The legal topics that form the basis of each article in *American Law Reports* are much more specific than those found in encyclopedias. For example, look at the title of the annotation reprinted in Figure 7-5. This article deals with one issue involving the war on terror. Articles in encyclopedias tend to be much more expansive in coverage. A second major difference between *A.L.R.* and encyclopedias is the arrangement of topics. *A.L.R.* does not arrange alphabetically. Rather, the arrangement is dependent on the date of the case law that leads to the article.

Using *A.L.R.*

The easiest way to find an article is to use the general *A.L.R. Index*. This is a cumulative word index that covers all *A.L.R.* and *A.L.R. Fed. series*. The index refers you to specific articles. In addition to the index, *A.L.R.* contains a digest covering all of the topics found in the various *A.L.R.* and *A.L.R. Fed.* series. The digest organizes all law alphabetically into more than 400 legal topics. To use the digest, you must first identify the proper legal topic. One advantage of the digest over the index is that the digest refers to other secondary sources.

FIGURE 7-5 *A.L.R.* Annotation as it appears on Westlaw

16 A.L.R. Fed. 2d 257
Admissibility of Evidence Procured by Torture or Alleged Torture—Global Cases

16 A.L.R. Fed. 2d 257 (Originally published in 2007)

American Law Reports
ALR Federal 2d
The ALR databases are made current by the weekly addition of relevant new cases.

Admissibility of Evidence Procured by Torture or Alleged Torture—Global Cases

Kurtis A. Kemper, J.D.

The admissibility of a confession or other statement (including a statement procured by torture or alleged torture) in judicial proceedings depends on whether it was made voluntarily. In U.S. v. Abu Ali, 395 F. Supp. 2d 338, 16 A.L.R. Fed. 2d 683 (E.D. Va. 2005), the defendant moved to suppress certain statements he made to Saudi Arabian authorities, claiming, inter alia, that the statements were inadmissible because he was tortured and the statements in question were involuntary. Denying the motion based on a finding that the government demonstrated by a preponderance of the evidence that any incriminating statements made by the defendant were voluntary and admissible, the court recognized its solemn duty to uphold the human rights guarantees of United States Constitution and those international documents on human rights to which the United States is a signatory. Note also that the United Kingdom House of Lords in A v. Secretary of State for the Home Department, 2005 WL 3299089 (HL 2005), held broadly that it would give a very clear negative answer to the question of whether evidence obtained by torturing another human being may lawfully be admitted against a party to proceedings in a British court, irrespective of where, by whom, or on whose authority the torture was inflicted. This annotation collects and analyzes those global cases which have considered the admissibility of evidence procured by torture or alleged torture.

TABLE OF CONTENTS

ARTICLE OUTLINE

FIGURE 7-5 (continued)

INDEX

[index terms omitted]

Table of Cases

[case citations omitted]

I. Preliminary Matters

§ 1. Scope

This annotation collects and analyzes the state and federal cases from the United States, as well as cases reported in the English language from the United Kingdom and the former and present British Commonwealth countries, in which the courts discussed the admissibility of evidence procured by torture or alleged torture.[FN1]

Some opinions discussed in this annotation may be restricted by court rule as to publication and citation in briefs; readers are cautioned to check each case for restrictions. A number of jurisdictions may have rules, regulations, constitutional provisions, or legislative enactments directly bearing upon this subject. These provisions are discussed herein only to the extent and in the form that they are reflected in the court opinions that fall within the scope of this annotation. The reader is consequently advised to consult the appropriate statutory or regulatory compilations to ascertain the current status of all statutes discussed herein.

§ 2. Summary and comment

According to the United States Supreme Court, it is axiomatic that a defendant in a criminal case is deprived of due process if his or her conviction is founded, in whole or in part, on an involuntary confession, without regard for the truth or falsity of the confession.[FN2] It was recognized by an English court, in an often cited case decided in 1783, that "A confession forced from the mind by the flattery of hope or by the torture of fear comes in so questionable a shape, when it is to be considered as evidence of guilt, that no credit ought to be given to it."[FN3]

All *A.L.R.* articles have similar features. Each article contains the following:

1. **Table of Contents** describes what you will find in the annotation.
2. **Research References** refers you to other legal resources that are related to your topic.
3. **Research Sources** lists the sources used in compiling the article; later series include the ***electronic search query*** used by authors of the article as well as West Digest Key Numbers; the electronic search query is used to find information on Westlaw and Lexis databases. This is discussed in Chapter 10.
4. **Article Descriptive Word Index** helps you locate treatment of specific subjects within the article.
5. **Jurisdictional Table of Cited Statutes and Cases** lists by jurisdiction all cases and statutes cited in the article.
6. **Scope** states exactly what is covered in the article.
7. **Related Annotations** lists other *A.L.R.* articles that are closely related.
8. **Summary and Comment** summarizes the substantive part of the article.
9. **Practice Pointers** hints to the best way to handle a case within the scope of the article.
10. **Substantive Sections** discusses the legal topic thoroughly.

electronic search query Words that constitute a search request when using electronically stored data, that is, information on the Internet or on a CD-ROM.

When you use an *A.L.R.* article, always check to see if the article was updated or ***supplemented***. The publishers update the articles by providing references to new cases and statutes that deal with the topic. In print form, the various series of *A.L.R.* are supplemented as follows:

supplemented Kept up to date.

A.L.R. (first series)	*A.L.R. Blue Book of Supplemental Decisions*
A.L.R. 2d	*A.L.R. 2d Later Case Service*
A.L.R. 3d through *7th*	Pocket part supplements

In addition to checking if your article was supplemented, check if the article was ***superseded***. In some cases, the law changes so often that an older article is no longer valid or helpful. As a result, a new article is written, superseding the prior article. The last volume of the *A.L.R. Index* contains an annotation history table that provides this information. In an online format, supplements are incorporated with the main article. See Box 7-2.

superseded Replaced.

BOX 7-2 USING *A.L.R.* OR *A.L.R.FED.*

- ✔ Determine if research question is one of state law or federal law.
- ✔ Review research question and identify descriptive words.
- ✔ Check general *A.L.R. Index* or *Digest* for a citation to an article if the question is one of state law.
- ✔ Check *A.L.R. Fed. Index* or *Digest* for a citation to an article if the question is one of federal law.
- ✔ Find appropriate article(s).
- ✔ Identify primary law from your jurisdiction.
- ✔ Check the pocket part supplement (or other supplement for early editions).
- ✔ Check the history of annotations table for superseded articles.

The publishers of *A.L.R.* offer some online features for users. Some of these features can be viewed even by nonsubscribers. Review the website http://west.thomson.com/alr. This site provides information from earlier series of *A.L.R.*

A Point to Remember

Remember that an *A.L.R.* article is a secondary source. Do not cite it to a court as your only authority. Always give the court references to primary law.

7-5 TREATISES

treatise
Either one book or a multivolume series of books dealing with one legal topic.

hornbook
Name given to books published by West that are a type of treatise; commonly used by law students.

Nutshell Series
Condensed versions of hornbooks.

A ***treatise*** is a publication covering a single legal topic, usually written by a legal scholar or practicing attorney who specializes in that area of law. It contains a thorough discussion and explanation of the law and provides cites to primary authority. Treatises may be a single volume or a multivolume set. Some are updated regularly, but others may never be supplemented. A well-known class of treatises is published by West and is known as the ***hornbook*** series. These books are written primarily for law students but are useful to anyone. Hornbook series books are also often published in a condensed version called the ***Nutshell Series***.

Using a Treatise

If there is a treatise relating to your research question (and there probably is), you can locate it in a law library by checking the library catalog. The catalog contains an alphabetical listing of legal topics and a list of all books relating to that topic that can be found in the library. Most treatises contain an index at the end of the book that is designed to help you locate your specific research issue. In using a treatise, be particularly careful to check the copyright date of the book, especially if there is no pocket part supplement. Some treatises found in law libraries are outdated. See Box 7-3.

BOX 7-3 USING A TREATISE

- ✔ Identify the legal topic.
- ✔ Check the library catalog.
- ✔ Check the copyright date on the treatise.
- ✔ Determine if the treatise is supplemented.
- ✔ Use the index to find the specific topic.

7-6 PERIODICALS

periodical
Legal material, published at regular intervals, consisting of magazines, journals, and law reviews.

law review
A type of legal periodical published by law schools containing articles on different legal topics.

Numerous legal magazines and journals (***periodicals***) are published. Many professional associations publish magazines. For example, the American Bar Association publishes a monthly magazine, *The American Bar Journal*. Selected articles from the magazine are published online at abajournal.com. The state bar associations also publish regular magazines or journals for their members. Magazines containing articles on legal topics are published for paralegals, for example, *Paralegal Today*. National and local paralegal associations may also publish regular newsletters. Often, these newsletters contain articles on current legal topics.

One very important type of periodical publication is a ***law review***. A law review is a publication from a law school. It contains scholarly articles by noted legal authorities, usually on current legal issues. It may also contain shorter articles written by law students. Most law schools publish law reviews at regular intervals. A law review article can be an excellent research source. If your research issue is the subject of a law review article, you will find a thorough discussion of the law, including references to numerous primary authorities. The major disadvantage of law review articles (or most periodical literature) is that they are not supplemented or updated.

Guides to Periodicals

Popular indexes to legal periodicals include: *Current Law Index* (and its web based version *LegalTrac*), *Legal Resource Index,* and *Index to Legal Periodicals and Books*. These indexes allow you to find information by subject matter or by author. They contain references to more than 1,000 different sources from the United States and several foreign jurisdictions. By visiting the website <http://www.hwwilsoninprint.com/index_legal.php>, you can see sample pages from the Index to Legal Periodicals and Books. See Box 7-4.

BOX 7-4 USING PERIODICALS

- ✔ Identify the legal topic or author.
- ✔ Check an index for topic or author.
- ✔ Locate the periodical.
- ✔ Check current status of the law.

7-7 LOOSELEAF SERVICES

The term ***looseleaf service*** is used to describe a type of secondary research material that is published in a binder format rather than as a bound book. Material concerning an area of law is printed on unbound, or "loose," pages and assembled in a binder. The purpose of these services is to allow frequent supplementation of the material without the use of the traditional pocket part supplement. As changes occur in the law, subscribers to the looseleaf service are sent the changes. These are printed on replacement pages for the binder. The subscribers remove the old page and replace it with a new page reflecting the current law.

looseleaf service
Legal material published in a binder format, regularly supplemented with replacement pages.

Looseleaf services are commonly used for areas of law regulated by administrative rules or regulations. Recall from Chapter 5 that finding the latest updates for administrative regulations is a cumbersome process if you rely on the official publications. Looseleaf services are secondary sources that provide this information. Major publishers of looseleaf services include Commerce Clearing House (CCH) and Bureau of National Affairs (BNA).

A Point to Remember

When replacement pages are sent to a looseleaf service subscriber, a preface page is included indicating the date of the latest page revisions. If you are responsible for updating the books, always file this page. If you are using the book, always check the date to make sure that the material is current.

7-8 RESTATEMENTS OF THE LAW

In reading case law, you have undoubtedly come across references to the "Restatement." This is a multivolume work compiled by the American Law Institute and is the result of the efforts of well-known and respected legal scholars. U.S. law is largely the result of English common law. However, because of many court decisions and legislative changes, some of those principles evolved and changed. The Restatement is a "statement" of the many principles of U.S. law as those principles exist today. The work is organized by legal topic, and each is known accordingly, for example, the *Restatement (Third) of Property* and the *Restatement (Second) Contracts*. The principles of law found in the Restatement look very similar to code sections. They are often followed by comments and examples. It is important to remember that the Restatement is *not* primary law. The statements of law found here may or may not reflect the law in your state. However, this is a well-respected source, and it is often quoted by judges in written opinions. The Restatement and the comments are especially helpful when the law of your state is not clear. In such an instance, referring to the Restatement can help. However, remember this is only persuasive authority, not mandatory. See Figure 7-6 for sample pages from the *Restatement (Second) of Torts*.

7-9 MISCELLANEOUS RESOURCES

Continuing Legal Education Books and Materials

practice books
Books for use in federal and state legal practice; these often contain discussions of an area of law and provide forms needed for practice in that legal area.

For practicing attorneys and paralegals, the most important and widely used research sources are often found in books and materials directed toward specific areas of legal practice. These are often referred to as ***practice books***. Practice books are published for a variety of legal subjects, both federal and state. The main function of these books is to help the practicing attorney (or paralegal) by providing a combination of substantive law, procedural rules, and relevant forms. In addition to these practice books, practicing attorneys also rely on material provided to them at various continuing legal education (C.L.E.) conferences. These materials are often assembled in a binder and generally consist of new laws, recent cases, and sample documents. Recent conferences provide this material electronically. Many lawyers also subscribe to newsletters to keep them current with legal issues related to their area of practice. Numerous practice books and C.L.E. material are also published by the Practicing Law Institute (P.L.I.), a nonprofit group that also sponsors seminars and webinars in various practice areas. More information about this group and its publications can be seen on its website at http://www.pli.edu/content.

Form Books

Form books are another type of research tool that lawyers and their assistants frequently utilize. The main purpose of these books, of course, is to provide sample forms or templates for lawyers to follow. However, form books are a valuable secondary source of the law. In addition to containing sample forms, many form books provide explanations of the law related to the use of the form, including references to the controlling primary law. Form books are often multivolume sets and are published for practice in the federal courts as well as for practice in state courts.

forms of pleading and practice
Form books containing forms for use in connection with litigation.

There are two major types of comprehensive form books: those that contain forms for use in connection with a lawsuit and those for use in connection with business or personal transactions. Forms for use in connection with lawsuits are often called ***forms of pleading and practice***. In forms of pleading and practice,

FIGURE 7-6 *Restatement (Second) of Torts*

to inflict, as where his assailant is standing on the brink of a cliff or on a girder of a steel building under construction so that the actor should realize that the other's instinctive reaction to his threatening gesture may cause a serious fall. If such is the case, the actor may not be privileged even to threaten to inflict a harm which under ordinary circumstances he would be privileged to inflict, and certainly is not privileged to threaten a greater harm. It is frequently a matter for the jury to determine, under proper instructions, whether the privilege exists in such a case.

§ 71. Force in Excess of Privilege

If the actor applies a force to or imposes a confinement upon another which is in excess of that which is privileged,

(a) the actor is liable for only so much of the force or confinement as is excessive;

(b) the other's liability for an invasion of any of the actor's interests of personality which the other may have caused is not affected;

(c) the other has the normal privilege stated in this Topic to defend himself against the actor's use or attempted use of excessive force or confinement.

See Reporter's Notes.

Comment on Clause (a):

a. While the actor is liable to another for any force or confinement which he applies or imposes upon the other which is in excess of that which he is privileged to impose, he is not liable for so much of the force or confinement as he is privileged to apply or impose, and so he does not become a "trespasser ab initio" by his abuse of his privilege.

b. While it is usually difficult to separate the harm done by the excess of force, it can sometimes be done, as where a confinement is continued longer than is necessary to prevent the commission of a battery. Where no such separation can be made, the actor is held liable for all of the harm inflicted by the use of the excessive force.

FIGURE 7-6 (continued)

Ch. 4 SELF-DEFENSE § 71

Illustrations:

1. A inflicts an offensive contact upon B, and threatens to continue it. Being stronger than A, B could easily prevent a continuance of the contact by seizing and holding A, and does so. B then unnecessarily strikes A in the face, breaking A's nose. B is not liable for holding A, but is subject to liability to A for the broken nose.

2. A inflicts an offensive contact upon B, and threatens to continue it. B could easily prevent the continuance of the contact by striking A a light blow. Instead he strikes a heavy blow, which breaks A's nose. B is subject to liability to A for the blow and the harm done.

Comment on Clause (b):

c. If the actor applies a force to or imposes a confinement upon another which is in excess of that which is privileged, the other's liability for an invasion of any of the actor's interests of personality which the other may have caused is not affected. In such a case, the actor and the other have cross actions against one another; the actor for the "assault." "battery," or "false imprisonment" which the other committed before the actor abused his privilege by using excessive force, the other for the excess of force used by the actor. The other's violation of the actor's right is entirely independent of the actor's abuse of his privilege. So far from being caused by the actor's misconduct, the violation of the actor's right gives the privilege which he abuses. There is, therefore, no reason why the actor's misconduct should exonerate the other's independent violation of his right, nor should the actor be penalized for his abuse of his privilege by a forfeiture of his right of action which preceded and was the occasion for his abuse. The liability to answer for his excess of force is both a sufficient punishment for the actor's abuse of his privilege and a sufficient deterrent to such misconduct.

Illustration:

3. Under the circumstances given in Illustration 1, while B is liable to A for the harm which he has caused to A by the excess of force which he used in self-defense, A is subject to liability to B for the offensive contact which he has inflicted upon B.

transaction forms
Form books containing forms for use in connection with business and personal transactions.

you find sample complaints, responsive pleadings, motions, and other litigation forms. Forms for use in business or personal transactions are often called ***transaction forms***. In transaction form books, you find forms such as sample articles of incorporation, partnership agreements, and wills.

Pattern Jury Instructions

jury instructions
Statements of the law read to the jury at the end of trial.

At the end of any jury trial, the judge must tell the jury what law applies to the evidence presented during trial. These statements of law are called ***jury instructions***. Judges do not create new instructions every time they preside over a trial. Instead, they consult books containing approved statements of law or jury instructions,

BOX 7-5 COMMON SECONDARY SOURCES

- ✔ *American Jurisprudence 2d*
- ✔ *Corpus Juris Secundum*
- ✔ *American Law Reports*
- ✔ Legal treatises
- ✔ Legal periodicals and law reviews
- ✔ Looseleaf services
- ✔ Restatements of the Law
- ✔ C.L.E. materials
- ✔ Form books
- ✔ Pattern jury instructions

referred to as *pattern jury instructions* or *model jury instructions*. Using these books, the judge and the attorneys develop a set of instructions to give the jury. However, the court is not limited to these approved jury instructions, and sometimes the judge or the attorneys write specific instructions for a case.

Books containing jury instructions can be valuable research tools for two reasons. First, each jury instruction provides a reference to the primary law from which it is taken. Second, unlike many other sources, these statements of law are written in easy-to-understand language because they are written for jurors, not lawyers. For example, if a defendant is charged with a crime, a relevant jury instruction will set forth the law, generally listing the elements or requirements of the law. It will also provide references to some primary law that relates to the instruction.

Pattern jury instructions exist for practice in the state and federal courts. They are published by private publishers or in some cases provided on a court's website by the court itself. Almost every federal circuit court of appeals provides model jury instructions on its website. Like the private publications, these model jury instructions explain the law in easy-to-understand language and also provide cites to some relevant primary law.

The Legal Dictionary and Legal Thesaurus

A legal dictionary and a legal thesaurus are essential tools for any legal researcher. A legal dictionary contains definitions of legal words and phrases. Because legal vocabulary is often unique, a beginning researcher can be very confused without the help of a legal dictionary. There are many legal dictionaries available for researchers. The most famous, and probably the most comprehensive, is *Black's Law Dictionary*. A legal thesaurus provides synonyms and antonyms for legal words. This tool is invaluable in helping you use an index to legal source material. A work that is somewhat similar to a legal dictionary is *Words and Phrases*. This set, published by West, contains numerous legal terms as they are defined in court opinions.

Box 7-5 is a list of several common secondary sources.

7-10 THE INTERNET AND SECONDARY SOURCES

Most of the secondary sources described in this chapter are traditional research tools that have been used by legal researchers for many years. Because they are privately published, most are not freely available online. However, they are generally available through the Westlaw and/or Lexis services. Some secondary sources are also located on Bloomberg Law (usually related to different aspects of business law).

There are some exceptions, however. Some periodicals, including some law reviews, are available through the Law Library of Congress, <http://www.loc.gov/law/help/guide/federal/lawreviews.php>. Some law schools also offer limited access to their law reviews through their websites. See Figure 7-7.

Google Scholar, a feature of Google, also allows you to search for law reviews and legal journals. This feature generally permits you to find a law review or journal about a specific legal topic. In some cases, you can access the full text of the article. In other cases, you access only a summary or introduction to the article; and to access the full text, you must pay a fee. See Figure 7-8.

Also available through the Internet are model or pattern jury instructions for many courts, usually found on the court website. These instructions provide not only a summary of a point of law, but often provide citations to relevant law. See Figure 7-9 for a sample instruction. To see a complete set of model jury instructions, go to <http://www3.ce9.uscourts.gov/jury-instructions/>.

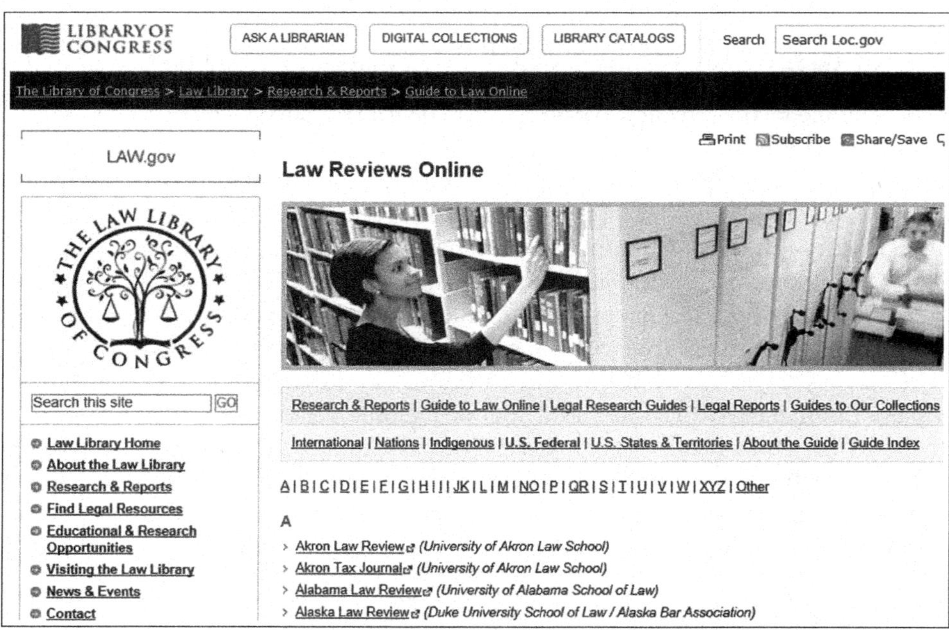

FIGURE 7-7 Library of Congress Law Reviews Online

FIGURE 7-8 Google Scholar

Although the traditional secondary sources are not freely available, you will find countless websites that provide extensive legal information. Some of this information is reliable, but some is questionable. You must use great care in relying on legal information that is freely available on the Internet. Popularity does not guarantee reliability. When using any online source, carefully consider the reliability and the date of the information. Relying on this information alone is dangerous. If this information cites primary authority—sometimes it does—you should read the primary law. This subject is discussed in more detail in Chapter 11.

Finding It Online

Some reliable websites do provide some secondary source information. Law school library websites are often valuable. (Always check for the *.edu* in the URL.) Review http://www.law.cornell.edu/.

Law librarians sometimes host valuable websites. One such site is http://www.nocall.org/.

Another popular website is Findlaw for Legal Professionals http://lp.findlaw.com/

FIGURE 7-9 Model Jury Instruction

9.1 SECTION 1983 CLAIM—INTRODUCTORY INSTRUCTION

The plaintiff brings [his] [her] claim[s] under the federal statute, 42 U.S.C. § 1983, that provides that any person or persons who, under color of state law, deprives another of any rights, privileges, or immunities secured by the Constitution or laws of the United States shall be liable to the injured party.

← **This is the instruction that is read to the jury**

Comment

See 42 U.S.C. § 1983.

The Committee notes that in the past decisions of the Supreme Court and the Ninth Circuit used the phrases "under color of law" and "under color of state law" interchangeably. *Compare, e.g., Livadas v. Bradshaw*, 512 U.S. 107, 132 (1994), and *Azer v. Connell,* 306 F.3d 930, 935 (9th Cir.2002) (using phrase "under color of law"), *withNelson v. Campbell*, 541 U.S. 637, 643 (2004), and *Meyers v. Redwood City*, 400 F.3d 765, 770 (9th Cir.2005) (using phrase "under color of state law").

← **These are references to law that supports the instruction. This is not read to the jury.**

Because recent Ninth Circuit case authority more frequently uses the phrase "under color of state law," rather that "under color of law," the Committee uses the phrase "under color of state law."*See Planned Parenthood Ariz., Inc. v. Betlach*, 727 F.3d 960, 966 (9th Cir.2013) ("Section 1983 creates a federal remedy against anyone who, under color of state law, deprives ?any citizen of the United States ... of any rights, privileges, or immunities secured by the Constitution and laws.");*OSU Student Alliance v. Ray*, 699 F.3d 1053, 1061 (9th Cir.2013) (using phrase "color of state law"); *Tsao v. Desert Palace, Inc.*, 698 F.3d 1128, 1138 (9th Cir.2012) (same); *Hall v. City of L.A.*, 697 F.3d 1059, 1068 (9th Cir.2012) (same).

CITATION MATTERS

SECONDARY RESOURCES

THE BLUEBOOK—RULES 15, 16, 17, AND 18

Books, Periodical Materials, and Other Secondary Sources

Rules 15 through 18 provide numerous examples for citation format for secondary sources. Set out below are common examples. If you cannot find an example of the exact source you need to cite, find a very similar resource and follow the general format for that citation.

EXAMPLES

15 Am. Jur. 2d *Civil Rights* § 18 (1983) (legal encyclopedia)

23 C.J.S. *Contracts* § 33 (1977) (legal encyclopedia)

William B. Johnson, Annotation, *Use of Plea Bargain or Grant of Immunity as Improper Vouching for Credibility of Witness in Federal Cases,* 76 A.L.R. Fed. 409 (1986). (The *Bluebook* example for the American Law Reports citation format.)

CHAPTER SUMMARY

Secondary sources are research tools that contain discussions and explanations of the primary law. They direct the researcher to the primary law by providing citations to relevant cases, statutes, and constitutional provisions. There are different types of secondary sources, but many have some, if not all, of the following features: descriptive word indexes, tables of contents, tables of statutes cited, tables of cases cited, tables of abbreviations, prefaces, parallel reference tables, and pocket part supplements.

One important type of secondary source is the legal encyclopedia. *American Jurisprudence 2d* and *Corpus Juris Secundum* are two national legal encyclopedias. In these works, hundreds of legal topics are arranged alphabetically. The encyclopedias contain discussions and explanations of those topics with references to relevant primary law. These books are updated with pocket part supplements. Some states have specific encyclopedias for legal topics in their jurisdictions.

Another important type of secondary source is *American Law Reports* (*A.L.R.*). The publishers of *American Law Reports* publish annotations dealing with the legal issues of newly published cases. The annotations contain extensive discussions of the issues as well as references to other relevant primary law. *A.L.R.* annotations are now supplemented with pocket part supplements. Occasionally, because of extensive changes in the law, an annotation is superseded rather than supplemented.

Secondary source material also includes treatises and a variety of legal periodicals, including law reviews. These materials may not be supplemented.

Looseleaf services consist of material found in binders and often relate to areas of law controlled by administrative regulations. These materials are supplemented frequently by revised replacement pages.

The Restatements of Law are well-respected legal sources that discuss and explain the current state of U.S. law. References to primary law from all states are included. Although frequently cited in judicial opinions, the Restatement is not primary law.

Practice books and C.L.E. materials are valuable resources for practicing attorneys. Form books are another valuable research tool for lawyers. Form books are found in comprehensive multivolume sets containing forms either for use in the courts (forms of pleading and practice) or for use in business or personal matters (transaction forms). Forms may be found in single-topic works, often referred to as *practice books*. Many form books provide not only sample forms but explanations of the law related to the forms and reference the controlling primary law.

Also important are pattern jury instructions. These contain short, concise statements of law written for nonlawyers. Books containing pattern jury instructions reference the primary law from which the instruction was taken.

A legal dictionary and a legal thesaurus are essential tools for researchers. Legal dictionaries explain legal words and phrases. A legal thesaurus provides synonyms and antonyms for legal words and phrases.

Traditional secondary sources are generally not found online for free because they are private publications. However, they can generally be located on the Westlaw or Lexis databases. Free legal information on the Internet must always be carefully evaluated by a researcher for accuracy and timeliness.

TERMS TO **REMEMBER**

secondary source of law
primary source of law
legal encyclopedia
electronic search query
supplemented
superseded
treatise
hornbook
Nutshell Series
periodical
law review
looseleaf service
forms of pleading and practice
transaction forms
practice books
jury instructions

QUESTIONS FOR **REVIEW**

1. What is the purpose of a secondary source of law?
2. Describe some of the common features of secondary sources.
3. What is a legal encyclopedia?
4. How do you use a legal encyclopedia?
5. Describe the contents of *American Law Reports.*
6. How is *A.L.R.* kept up to date?
7. How does a treatise differ from a legal encyclopedia or *A.L.R.*?
8. What is a law review?
9. Why are pattern jury instructions a useful research tool?
10. What is the Restatement?

CAN YOU **FIGURE IT OUT?**

1. Refer to Figure 7-1. In which *Am. Jur. 2d* article (title and section) will you find a discussion of governmental immunity?
2. Refer to Figure 7-2. In which *Am. Jur. 2d* article (title and section) will you find a discussion of 18 U.S.C.A. § 332?
3. Refer to Figure 7-4.
   a. Cite a case for the proposition that a sheriff may be liable for the wrongful acts of his deputy in making an arrest of an escaping prisoner.
   b. Where would you find a form for a complaint in an action against peace officers for wounding a prisoner?
4. Refer to Figure 7-5. In which section of this *A.L.R.* article do you find a discussion of cases in which physical torture of defendants resulted in admissible statements?
5. Refer to Figure 7-6. What does *Restatement (Second) Torts* § 71 (a) provide?

TEST **YOURSELF** (Check Your Answers in Appendix G)

1. Find and cite the section in *American Jurisprudence 2d* that discusses the constitutionality of rent control.
2. Find and cite an article in *A.L.R. Fed.2d* dealing with border searches of a traveler's laptop computer, or related equipment.
3. Using Google Scholar, search for a 1970 Harvard Law Review Article, "Federal Regulation of Cable Television: The Visible Hand." Who were the authors? Read the abstract of the article. How many cable channels do the authors predict?
4. Locate the criminal jury instructions for the Eighth Circuit Court of Appeals (http://juryinstructions.ca8.uscourts.gov/) What is the title of instruction 2.07?

TEST **YOURSELF**—WRITE IT RIGHT Know When to Use a Citation

In legal writing it is especially important that you cite to the sources you use. We cite when we borrow words and when we borrow ideas. Citations let the reader know what law you rely upon in your legal analysis. Use citations when you (1) quote, (2) assert a legal principal, and (3) refer to the content of an authority.

Notice the use of citations below—they are all placed in bold here to make them easier to locate. We do not place citations in bold in our legal writing.

DISCUSSION

1. Equitable adoption is established upon proof beyond a reasonable doubt of a decedent's unequivocal intent to pursue a formal adoption. Hames's intent to adopt Grimes was evidenced by (1) her initiation of adoption paperwork under the guidance of counsel and (2) the long-standing mutuality of a parent–child relationship forming an implied "contract-to-adopt."

The doctrine of equitable adoption in California requires "clear and convincing" evidence of a decedent's intent to legally adopt a claimant. **Cal. Prob. Code § 6455 (West 2016).** As **Cal. Prob. Code section 6455** is silent as to the particular elements of equitable adoption, the courts utilize an "agreement-plus-conduct analysis" to evaluate the decedent's intent. ***In Re Estate of Ford*, 32 Cal. 4th 160, 168 (2004).**

Here, Hames's attempt to complete adoption paperwork serves as "clear, cogent, and convincing," ***Ford*, 32 Cal. 4th at 173** evidence of her objective intent to legally adopt. Hames's attorney maintains that she initiated the paperwork soon after the death of her husband and immediately before becoming incapacitated by the cancer that took her life. It can thus be reasonably inferred that Hames would have completed the adoption process had she been in fair health. Using the rationale applied in ***Ford*,** therefore, Hames's legal actions satisfy the requirement that a claimant must demonstrate the existence of some direct expression, on the decedent's part, of an intent to adopt." ***Id.* at 171.**

In addition, Hames's subjective intent to adopt is unavoidable as her overt acts during the entirety of her relationship with Grimes "establish the existence of a contract of adoption and ... part performance thereof." ***Rivolo*, 194 Cal. App. 2d 773, 777 (1961).** First, Hames repeatedly stated her desire to adopt Grimes and did so "every few months." Second, Grimes was accepted and treated as a natural child, creating a "mutual recognition of a parent and child relationship." ***Mingo v. Heckler*, 745 F.2d 537, 539 (9th Cir. 1984).** Third, Hames also provided for all of Grimes' personal and financial needs in addition to including him in holiday cards under the greeting: "From the Hames." As such, Hames "publicly acknowledge[d] the adoptee as [her] child," ***Ford*, 32 Cal. 4th at 168**, on multiple occasions.

Now, You Try It

(Check your answers in Appendix G)

Note where citations should be placed in the following paragraphs.

A person commits fraud in relation to access devices when he knowingly effects transactions, using access cards issued to other another person, to obtain payment or property with an aggregate value of at least $1,000, within a one-year period, if such transactions affect foreign commerce. Alternatively, the person commits the offense by using unauthorized access devices to obtain anything of value aggregating at least $1,000 within a one-year period. An unauthorized access device is one that is "lost, stolen, expired, revoked, canceled, or obtained with intent to defraud." An access device is a card or other means of account access that may be used to obtain money or things of value, or to initiate transfers of funds. Conviction may result in imprisonment for not more than 15 years for a first-time offender. Conviction may result in imprisonment for not more than 10 years for a first-time offender.

The state may meet the statutory requirement of $1,000 by aggregating the values of payment or property obtained in different transactions, as long as the transactions constitute violations of the same statutory provisions.

CITATION **EXERCISES**

Use Appendix C and the Citation Matters feature in this chapter to answer these questions.

1. List the *Bluebook* rules that address books, periodical materials, and other secondary sources.
2. Correct this citation: 15 Am Jur. 2d Civil Rights Section 18(1983).
3. Correct this citation: 23 CJS Contracts §33 (1977).
4. Remember, spacing between the components of each is important. There are spacing problems in Exercises 2 and 3.
5. What is the abbreviation for the *American Law Reports*?

FROM THE **WRITER'S CORNER**—QUOTATIONS

1. "Quotes of 50 or more words must be ___________."
2. What is an ellipsis, and when should it be used?

ASSIGNMENTS AND **ACTIVITIES**

Research Exercises

Part One: Using Encyclopedias: *American Jurisprudence 2d*

For each of the following, answer the questions and cite to the section in *Am. Jur. 2d* where you found the answer.

1. Can a state impound a lost animal, considering it to be abandoned? Cite case authority for your answer.
2. What is the monetary liability of credit card owners for unauthorized use of their credit card? Cite statutory authority for your answer.
3. Can a child who is born illegitimate, but later legitimized, inherit from the natural father?
4. What is the test to determine whether a game is one of chance or one of skill?

5. Susan knowingly makes a false statement of fact under penalty of perjury. Later Susan changes the story to the truth. Does this excuse the perjury? What is the controlling federal statute?
6. Can a company that does interstate business refuse to hire a woman as vice president? Cite the controlling case.
7. Does the doctrine of *res ipsa loquitur* apply to test-firing of rockets by the federal government?
8. John married his cousin but believed that the marriage was void. After separating from his cousin, John later married Jill without obtaining a divorce from his first wife. Is John guilty of bigamy? Cite the controlling case.

Part Two: Using *A.L.R.*

9. Cite an *A.L.R.* annotation dealing with liability of property owners for injury caused by failure of an elevator to level at the floor.
10. What is the subject of the annotation found at 6 *A.L.R. 2d* 391? What issue is discussed in § 2 of this article?
11. Find and cite an *A.L.R.* annotation in *A.L.R. 4th* dealing with state laws that require a person who requests a jury trial in a civil case to pay costs associated with the jury.
12. Find and cite an *A.L.R.* annotation in *A.L.R. Fed.* dealing with the complexity of civil action as affecting the Seventh Amendment right to trial by jury.
13. What is the purpose of the annotation found at 24 *A.L.R. Fed.* 940? What is meant by the phrase "comity of nation" as used in the article?
14. Find and cite an *A.L.R.* annotation involving undue influence and nontestamentary gifts to clergymen, spiritual advisors, or the church.
15. Find and cite an *A.L.R.* annotation dealing with injury or property damage caused by lightning as a basis of tort liability.

Part Three: Periodicals and Law Reviews

16. Cite a 2007 law review article in the *Columbia Law Review* discussing the case of *Hamdan v. Rumsfeld*.
17. Find and cite a 1994 article in the *U.C.L.A. Law Review* dealing with lunar mining.
18. Find and cite an article in the *American Bar Association Journal* dealing with the legal aspects of artificial insemination.

Part Four: Restatement

19. Where in the *Restatement Second* do you find a section dealing with undue influence by a third person rendering a transaction voidable at the request of the victim where the other contracting party knew of the undue influence?
20. Where in the *Restatement Second* is negligence defined? What does comment "d" provide?

Part Five: State Research

21. Find out if your state has a state-specific encyclopedia. If so, what is its title and who is the publisher?
22. Identify at least one secondary source in your state that covers state law in general.
23. Identify at least three law reviews published in your state.
24. Find out if your state bar association publishes a journal. If so, what is its title?

Analysis and Writing Assignments

25. Read the portion of the *A.L.R.* annotation found in Figure 7-5 and write a paragraph summarizing the material.
26. Access the website abajournal.com. Summarize any recent article found online.
27. Review Research Problems 1, 2, and 3 in Appendix B. Assume that you are starting to research these questions in a secondary source such as an encyclopedia or treatise. For each fact pattern, create a list of words or phrases that you might search for in a descriptive word index.

Online Research Exercises

28. Select a Research Fact Pattern from Appendix B. Using any website listed in the chapter, conduct preliminary research. Write a summary of your findings, including references to any primary law.
29. Conduct an online search of law schools in your state. Do any of these offer law reviews online?
30. Access the following website: http://www.loc.gov/law/help/guide/federal/lawreviews.php. Here you find links to several law reviews.
    (a) Select law reviews from one law school and list the titles of the articles found within one volume of the publication.
    (b) Read and summarize one article found in a law review. (Hint: *Akron Law Review* provides full articles online.)

CASE **PROJECT**

Using the same case that you researched in previous chapters, find and cite articles in appropriate encyclopedias, periodicals, and the *A.L.R.* that relate to the issue. Read the articles and note cases and statutes that might apply to these issues. Write a brief summary of the articles and list cases and statutes that you should read. Read the cases and statutes and take notes.

In-Class Small Group Work

Discuss and compare the secondary sources that you found. Explain the various features of the secondary source works that helped you find relevant law.

chapter **eight**

DIGESTS

CHAPTER OUTLINE

SKILL OBJECTIVES FOR CHAPTER 8

When you complete chapter 8, you should be able to

- Explain the relationship between case reporters and digests.
- Explain how headnotes are organized in a digest.
- Describe the West topic and key number system.
- Describe the West digest system.
- Use a descriptive word index in a digest to locate case law.
- Use a headnote from a case to find similar cases in a digest.
- Describe online search methods for the Westlaw, Lexis Advance, and Bloomberg Law databases that utilize the digest concept.

From the Desk of W. J. Bryan, Esq.

TO: Research Assistant
FROM: W. J. Bryan
RE: Our Client, Justin Meyers
DATE:

Your preliminary research in the Meyers case has been very helpful. I think the *Dickerson* case is especially relevant. Please keep looking and see if you can find any similar cases. You might try looking in a digest.

8-1 INTRODUCTION

In addition to the secondary sources described in Chapter 7, an important legal resource to help you find case law is a ***digest***. Unlike legal encyclopedias, *American Law Reports,* and treatises, digests do not explain or discuss the law. Nor do they refer you to constitutional or statutory law. Digests are a multivolume special index to case reporters and are published by both West and LexisNexis to accompany their case reporters.

digest
An index to reported cases, arranged by subject; a short summary of cases is provided.

Digests contain hundreds of legal topics arranged alphabetically. However, unlike descriptive word indexes, each topic in a digest is followed by various case headnotes that relate to the topic. Although digests are found in print format, the concept behind digests plays an important role in finding cases on the Westlaw and Lexis Advance databases, as well as on the newer subscription-based site, Bloomberg Law. This chapter discusses digests and how the digest concept influences online case searching.

8-2 HEADNOTES AND TOPICS

Digests are based on the headnotes that precede the cases. Recall from Chapter 3 that when cases are published in case reporters, the publishers add many features, including ***headnotes***. The headnotes are brief statements of the legal principles found in the case. Each legal principle is assigned a topic name and number. Because many cases deal with the same or similar subjects, many different cases found in the same reporter system contain the same headnote topic and number. In addition, because one case may contain a discussion of several legal topics, each case often has many different headnote topics and numbers. Review Figures 8-1 and 8-2. Here you see headnotes to the case, *Minnesota v. Dickerson* in both the *Supreme Court Reporter* and the *Lawyer's Edition.* Note the different headnote topics found in the different reporter publications of the same case. Also, note that each reporter has many different headnotes for the same case.

headnotes
Editorial enhancement added to the front material of a case; a useful summary of most of the legal topics addressed in the case.

In a digest, headnotes from different cases that contain the same topic names and numbers are combined and organized alphabetically by topic name. Topic numbers further organize the headnotes. Refer to Figure 8-3 to see pages from the West digest for the *Supreme Court Reporter.* Note that this figure contains the same topic and key number as is found in Figure 8-1, the *Supreme Court Reporter* publication of *Dickerson.* Note how other cases involving the same topic are also referenced. Using the digest as a research tool enables you to locate cases containing the same legal principles as the *Dickerson* case. Also, compare the topics and key numbers in this digest to the headnotes in Figure 8-2. Figure 8-2 shows headnotes from the LexisNexis publication of Supreme Court cases (*Lawyer's Edition*). Note how the topics and sections for these headnotes do not match the topics and sections in the West digest.

FIGURE 8-1 *Supreme Court Reporter* Headnotes

2130 113 SUPREME COURT REPORTER 508 U.S. 365

I respectfully dissent and would affirm the judgment of the Court of Appeals.

508 U.S. 366, 124 L.Ed.2d 334

$\lfloor_{366}$MINNESOTA, Petitioner,

v.

Timothy DICKERSON.

No. 91–2019.

Argued March 3, 1993.

Decided June 7, 1993.

Defendant's motion to suppress seizure of crack cocaine from defendant's person was denied by the District Court, Hennepin County, and defendant appealed. The Minnesota Court of Appeals, 469 N.W.2d 462, reversed. The State appealed. The Minnesota Supreme Court, 481 N.W.2d 840, affirmed. The State's petition for certiorari was granted. The Supreme Court, Justice White, held that: (1) police may seize nonthreatening contraband detected through the sense of touch during protective patdown search so long as the search stays within the bounds marked by *Terry*, and (2) search of defendant's jacket exceeded lawful bounds marked by *Terry* when officer determined that the lump was contraband only after squeezing, sliding and otherwise manipulating the contents of the defendant's pocket, which officer already knew contained no weapon.

Affirmed.

Justice Scalia filed a concurring opinion.

The Chief Justice filed an opinion concurring in part and dissenting in part, in which Justice Blackmun and Justice Thomas joined.

1. Criminal Law ⚷1134(3)

Defendant's constitutional challenge to validity of patdown search was not moot even though, under Minnesota law, diversionary sentence would not be considered a conviction; there was possibility of reinstatement of the record of the charges in subsequent state or federal proceedings that would carry collateral legal consequences. U.S.C.A. Const.Amend. 4; M.S.A. § 152.18.

2. Arrest ⚷63.5(9)

A *Terry* protective search—permitted without a warrant and on basis of reasonable suspicion less than probable cause—must be strictly limited to that which is necessary for the discovery of weapons which might be used to harm the officer or others nearby. U.S.C.A. Const.Amend. 4.

3. Arrest ⚷63.5(9)

If the *Terry* protective search goes beyond what is necessary to determine if the suspect is armed, it is no longer valid and its fruits will be suppressed. U.S.C.A. Const. Amend. 4.

4. Arrest ⚷63.5(9)

Police officers may seize nonthreatening contraband detected during a patdown search for weapons so long as the officer's search stays within the bounds marked by *Terry*. U.S.C.A. Const.Amend. 4.

Headnote from *Supreme Court Reporter* Publication *Minnesota v. Dickerson.* See how this figure relates to Figure 8-3.

5. Searches and Seizures ⚷47.1, 49

Under "plain-view" doctrine, if police are lawfully in a position from which they view an object, if its incriminating character is immediately apparent, and if the officers have lawful right of access to the object, they may seize it without a warrant, but if the police lack probable cause to believe that an

ion circulated, hardly deserves acknowledgment, let alone comment. I had thought that this was a court of justice and that a criminal defendant in this country could expect to receive a genuine analysis of the constitutional issues in his case rather than the dismissive and conclusory rhetoric with which Kevin Taylor is here treated. I adhere to my derided "constitutional stew."

FIGURE 8-2 *Lawyers' Edition* Headnotes

U.S. SUPREME COURT REPORTS 124 L Ed 2d

nal defendant's suffering collateral legal consequences from a sentence already served precludes a finding of mootness with respect to appellate review of such defendant's case.

Appeal § 1662 — mootness — dismissal of charges against defendant

4a, 4b. A live controversy remains in a case before the United States Supreme Court, on certiorari to review a decision by a state's highest court, where an accused was found guilty on a state drug possession charge, but such charge was dismissed after the accused was sentenced to probation under a diversionary sentencing statute, and therefore such case is not moot, where reinstatement of the record of the charge against the accused—by way of its use in (1) determining the merits of subsequent proceedings against the accused, and (2) calculating the accused's criminal history category in the event of a subsequent federal conviction—would carry collateral legal consequences.

Search and Seizure § 25 — necessity of warrant

5. Searches and seizures conducted outside the judicial process, without prior approval by judge or magistrate, are per se unreasonable under the Federal Constitution's Fourth Amendment, subject to only a few specifically established and well-delineated exceptions.

Search and Seizure § 11.5 — brief stop of suspicious person

6. Where a police officer observes unusual conduct which leads the officer reasonably to conclude in light of the officer's experience that criminal activity may be afoot, the officer may, under the Federal Constitution's Fourth Amendment, briefly stop the suspicious person and make reasonable inquiries aimed at confirming or dispelling the officer's suspicions.

Evidence § 681; Search and Seizure §§ 11.5, 25 — patdown search for weapons — scope — fruits where invalid — necessity of warrant

7. When a police officer is justified in believing that the individual whose suspicious behavior the officer is investigating at close range is armed and presently dangerous to the officer or to others, the officer may, under the Federal Constitution's Fourth Amendment, conduct a patdown search to determine whether the person is in fact carrying a weapon; such protective search—permitted without a warrant and on the basis of reasonable suspicion less than probable cause—must be strictly limited to that which is necessary for the discovery of weapons which might be used to harm the officer or others nearby; if the protective search goes beyond what is necessary to determine if the suspect is armed, the search is no longer valid and its fruits will be suppressed.

Search and Seizure §§ 2.7, 25 — plain-view doctrine — necessity of warrant

8a, 8b. Under the "plain-view" doctrine, police officers may seize an object without a warrant if (1) the officers are lawfully in a position from which they view the object, (2) the object's incriminating character is immediately apparent, and (3) the officers have a lawful right of access to the object; if contraband is left in open view and is observed by a police officer from a lawful vantage point, there has been no invasion of

FIGURE 8-3 West *Supreme Court Digest*

12 S Ct D—49 **SEARCHES & SEIZURES** ⚷47.1

For references to other topics, see Descriptive-Word Index

It is essential predicate to any valid warrantless seizure of incriminating evidence under plain-view doctrine that police officer not violate Fourth Amendment in arriving at place from which evidence could be plainly viewed. U.S.C.A. Const.Amend. 4.

Horton v. California, 110 S.Ct. 2301, 496 U.S. 128, 110 L.Ed.2d 112.

To justify warrantless seizure of item in plain view, not only must item be in plain view, its incriminating character must be immediately apparent. U.S.C.A. Const.Amend. 4.

Horton v. California, 110 S.Ct. 2301, 496 U.S. 128, 110 L.Ed.2d 112.

To justify warrantless seizure of item in plain view, not only must police officer be lawfully located in place from which object can be plainly seen, but he or she must also have lawful right or access to object itself. U.S.C.A. Const.Amend. 4.

Horton v. California, 110 S.Ct. 2301, 496 U.S. 128, 110 L.Ed.2d 112.

Seizure of object in plain view does not involve intrusion on privacy. U.S.C.A. Const. Amend. 4.

Horton v. California, 110 S.Ct. 2301, 496 U.S. 128, 110 L.Ed.2d 112.

U.S.Cal. 1986. Mere fact that individual has taken measures to restrict some views of his activities does not preclude police officer's observations from public vantage point where he has right to be and which renders activities clearly visible. U.S.C.A. Const.Amend. 4.

California v. Ciraolo, 106 S.Ct. 1809, 476 U.S. 207, 90 L.Ed.2d 210, rehearing denied 106 S.Ct. 3320, 478 U.S. 1014, 92 L.Ed.2d 728.

U.S.Dist.Col. 1968. Objects falling in plain view of officer who has right to be in position to have that view are subject to seizure and may be introduced in evidence. U.S.C.A.Const. Amend. 4.

Harris v. U. S., 88 S.Ct. 992, 390 U.S. 234, 19 L.Ed.2d 1067.

U.S.Fla. 1980. Even though some circumstances—for example, if the results of a private search are in plain view when materials are turned over to the government—may justify the government's reexamination of the materials, the government may not exceed the scope of the private search unless it has the right to make an independent search. (Per Mr. Justice Stevens, with one Justice joining, two Justices concurring in part and in the judgment, and the one Justice concurring in the judgment.)

Walter v. U.S., 100 S.Ct. 2395, 447 U.S. 649, 65 L.Ed.2d 410, on remand U.S. v. Sanders, 625 F.2d 1311.

U.S.Ill. 1992. Absent consent or warrant, "plain view" seizures can be justified only if they meet probable cause standard and if they are unaccompanied by unlawful trespass because, in the absence of a privacy interest notwithstanding, seizure would obviously invade owners' possessory interests. U.S.C.A. Const. Amend. 4.

Soldal v. Cook County, Ill., 113 S.Ct. 538, 506 U.S. 56, 121 L.Ed.2d 450, on remand 986 F.2d 1425, on remand 1993 WL 199050.

Plain view doctrine merely reflects application of Fourth Amendment's central requirement of reasonableness of law governing seizures of property. U.S.C.A. Const.Amend. 4.

Soldal v. Cook County, Ill., 113 S.Ct. 538, 506 U.S. 56, 121 L.Ed.2d 450, on remand 986 F.2d 1425, on remand 1993 WL 199050.

If officers' presence in home itself entailed violation of Fourth Amendment, no amount of probable cause to believe that item in plain view is incriminating evidence will justify its seizure. U.S.C.A. Const.Amend. 4.

Soldal v. Cook County, Ill., 113 S.Ct. 538, 506 U.S. 56, 121 L.Ed.2d 450, on remand 986 F.2d 1425, on remand 1993 WL 199050.

U.S.Ill. 1983. Plain view doctrine authorizes seizure of illegal or evidentiary item visible to a police officer whose access to item has some prior Fourth Amendment justification and who has probable cause to suspect that item is connected with criminal activity. U.S.C.A. Const.Amend. 4.

Illinois v. Andreas, 103 S.Ct. 3319, 463 U.S. 765, 77 L.Ed.2d 1003.

U.S.Md. 1932. Search of garage and seizure of whisky without warrant after officers smelled whisky odor and saw cardboard cases through small opening held unreasonable. U.S.C.A. Const.Amend. 4.

Taylor v. U.S., 52 S.Ct. 466, 286 U.S. 1, 76 L.Ed. 951.

U.S.Minn. 1993. Under "plain-view" doctrine, if police are lawfully in a position from which they view an object, if its incriminating character is immediately apparent, and if the officers have lawful right of access to the object, they may seize it without a warrant, but if the police lack probable cause to believe that an object in plain view is contraband without conducting some further search of the object, i.e., if its incriminating character is not immediately apparent, the "plain-view" doctrine cannot justify its seizure. U.S.C.A. Const.Amend. 4.

Minnesota v. Dickerson, 113 S.Ct. 2130, 508 U.S. 366, 124 L.Ed.2d 334.

Note the reference to *Minnesota v. Dickerson* and citations to several other cases. Compare this to headnote 5 in Figure 8-1.

TABLE 8-1 Comparison of Headnotes from Different Case Reporters

Supreme Court Reporter Headnote	*Lawyer's Edition* Headnote
1. Criminal Law 1134(3) Defendant's constitutional challenge to validity of patdown search was not moot even though, under Minnesota law, diversionary sentence would not be considered a conviction; there was possibility of reinstatement of the record of the charges in subsequent state or federal proceedings that would carry collateral legal consequences. U.S.C.A. Const.Amend. 4; M.S.A. § 152.18	**Appeal § 1662—mootness—criminal case** 3a, 3b. The possibility of a criminal defendant's suffering collateral legal consequences from a sentence already served precludes a finding of mootness with respect to appellate review of such defendant's case.

A Point to Remember

Each publisher uses topics that *it* selects. Thus, the same legal principle may be identified by different topic names in different publications. You must use a digest connected to the specific reporter from which you take a headnote.

In assigning a topic to the headnotes, the editors of case reporters use lists of topics previously created. Figure 8-4 shows a partial list of topics used by Thomson Reuters (West). Other publishers use different terms. If you refer to Figure 8-1, you see that the topic of headnote number 1, "Criminal Law," deals with the issue of "mootness." Compare this to headnote number 3 in Figure 8-2. Here, a similar legal principle is found in the topic "Appeal." See Table 8-1.

8-3 WEST DIGESTS

Thomson/West, a major publisher of case reporters, publishes numerous digests. A comprehensive digest system from West, the American Digest System, covers annotations to *all* state and federal cases. Other West digests contain case annotations to U.S. Supreme Court cases, to selected state cases, to federal district court and appellate court cases, and to cases found in various specialty court reporters.

Like other West publications, the West digests use the ***topic and key number*** system. In selecting its digest topics, West started with seven main divisions of law: persons, property, contracts, torts, crimes, remedies, and government. More than 400 topics are now created under these categories. (Refer to Figure 8-4 for a partial list of these topics.) The topics describe different aspects of U.S. law. Each topic is then divided into more specific subjects that are assigned a number, called a key number. For example, one general topic used by West is "Searches and Seizures." One specific section of this topic deals with police executing a search warrant and seizing evidence not identified in the warrant. This section is assigned the key number 49. In print versions of the case reporters, the headnote number is preceded by a key symbol. (Refer to Figure 8-1.) On Westlaw, headnotes sometimes have a different appearance:

topic and key number
System used by West to integrate its various primary and secondary resource materials.

Topic and Key Number in Print Version	Online Numerical Equivalent
Search and Seizure 🔑 49	349 k 49

FIGURE 8-4 West's Key Number System: Alphabetical List of Digest Topics

OUTLINE OF THE LAW

Digest Topics are arranged for your convenience by Seven Main Divisions of Law. Complete alphabetical list of Digest Topics with topic numbers follows this section.

---

1. PERSONS
2. PROPERTY
3. CONTRACTS
4. TORTS
5. CRIMES
6. REMEDIES
7. GOVERNMENT

1. PERSONS

RELATING TO NATURAL PERSONS IN GENERAL

Civil Rights
Dead Bodies
Death
Domicile
Food
Health
Holidays
Intoxicating Liquors
Names
Seals
Signatures
Sunday
Time
Weapons

PARTICULAR CLASSES OF NATURAL PERSONS

Absentees
Aliens, Immigration, and Citizenship
Chemical Dependents
Children Out-of Wedlock
Convicts
Indians
Infants
Mental Health
Slaves
Spendthrifts

PERSONAL RELATIONS

Adoption
Attorney and Client
Child Custody
Child Support
Executors and Administrators
Guardian and Ward
Husband and Wife
Labor and Employment
Marriage
Parent and Child
Principal and Agent
Workers' Compensation

ASSOCIATED AND ARTIFICIAL PERSONS

Associations
Beneficial Associations
Building and Loan Associations
Clubs
Colleges and Universities
Corporations
Exchanges
Joint-Stock Companies and Business Trusts
Limited Liability Companies
Partnership
Religious Societies

PARTICULAR OCCUPATIONS

Accountants
Agriculture
Antitrust and Trade Regulation
Auctions and Auctioneers
Aviation
Banks and Banking
Bridges
Brokers
Canals
Carriers

IX

The American Digest System The largest digest available to researchers is the *American Digest System,* published by West. This digest system is based on the headnotes found in case reporters in the West reporter system and is a topical arrangement of headnotes of *all* state and federal cases published in any of the national reporters. The American Digest System, first published at the end of the 1800s, includes case references to every state and dates back to 1658! When first published, it consisted of 50 volumes and was called the ***Century Digest***. The *Century Digest* contains case annotations for the years 1658 to 1896. After the publication of the *Century Digest,* West updated the set with the publication of ***Decennial Digests***. As the name suggests, these digests were published every 10 years and are known as *First Decennial Digest, Second Decennial Digest,* and so on. These are now published every five years and are referred to as *Part I* and *Part II* of that *Decennial Digest.* Each *Decennial Digest* contains case annotations for the 10-year period it serves and consists of many volumes.

Century Digest
Part of the American Digest System; contains case annotations for the years 1658 to 1896.

Decennial Digest
Updates to the *Century Digest,* published every five years.

A Point to Remember

Each *Decennial Digest* is *not* a cumulative supplement of case annotations. It covers only a 10-year period.

In addition to the *Century Digest* and the *Decennial Digests,* the American Digest System contains a set known as the ***General Digest***. This set contains volumes that update the latest *Decennial Digest.*

General Digest
Updates to the *Decennial Digest.*

State Digests West publishes digests for cases from most states. In addition, digests are available for the regional reporters: *Atlantic Reporter, Pacific Reporter, North Western Reporter,* and *South Western Reporter.*

Federal and Supreme Court Digests West digests exist for cases published in federal reporters. The *United States Supreme Court Digest* is tied to the *Supreme Court Reporter* and contains annotations to U.S. Supreme Court cases. West's *Federal Practice Digest* contains references to published federal district court, court of appeals, and Supreme Court cases. Earlier editions of the *Federal Practice Digest* are known as the *Federal Digest* and *Modern Federal Practice Digest.*

Specialty Digests Digests also exist for certain special case reporters. Examples include West's *Bankruptcy Digest* and *United States Court of Claims Digest.* See Box 8-1 for an overview of the West digest system.

BOX 8-1 WEST DIGEST SYSTEM

The American Digest System

Century Digest (1658 through 1896)
Decennial Digest (10-year increments beginning in 1897)
General Digest (updates to *Decennial Digest*)
Supreme Court Digest
Federal Practice Digest
Atlantic Digest
North Western Digest
Pacific Digest
South Eastern Digest
State Digests
Specialty Digests

BOX 8-2

If You Are Using This Case Reporter:	Then Use This Digest:
Lawyers' Edition	*Supreme Court Digest, Lawyers' Edition*
Supreme Court Reporter	*United States Supreme Court Digest*
Federal Reporter	*Federal Practice Digest*
Atlantic Reporter	*Atlantic Digest*
North Western Reporter	*North Western Digest*
Pacific Reporter	*Pacific Digest*
South Eastern Reporter	*South Eastern Digest*
Any West Reporter	*American Digest*

8-4 OTHER DIGESTS

LexisNexis offers a digest to accompany its case reporter, *United States Supreme Court Cases, Lawyers' Edition.* This is known as the *United States Supreme Court Reports Digest, Lawyers' Edition.* (This case reporter and digest were previously published by Lawyers Cooperative Publishing Company.) The organization and features of this digest are similar to the West digest. The topic names, however, differ.

State-specific digests, accompanying state reporters, are also published. See Box 8-2 for a list of case reporters and corresponding digests.

8-5 USING DIGESTS

A digest is most effectively used in legal research once you find a case dealing with your research issue. (Using an encyclopedia or other secondary source helps you do this.) Once a case is found, identify the headnote or headnotes dealing with your issue. At this point, take the topic and number of the headnote, go to the appropriate digest, and find the topic and number. There you find references to other cases dealing with the same issue.

Although not recommended, digests can be used as a starting point in your research. All digests contain descriptive word indexes just like other secondary sources. Once you review and analyze your research question, you can identify key words or phrases that are likely to be found in a ***descriptive word index***. This index will help you identify the topic and number that is relevant to your research.

descriptive word index
An alphabetical listing of words describing the topics contained in a book or set of books; refers the researcher to the volume and page where the topic is discussed.

When using a digest, check the latest updates or supplements. Digests might be supplemented by bound volumes, pocket part supplements, or supplemental pamphlets. In addition, when using a digest, you must check what years are covered in the particular series you are using. Later series of digests are not usually cumulative. For example, if you use the *Federal Practice Digest 4th,* you will see that it does not contain references to cases that were summarized in *Federal Practice Digest 3d.* This information is found in the ***prefatory material*** and should always be checked.

prefatory material
Material found in the front of a book or set of books describing such matters as the purpose of the book and directions for using the book.

One special and very helpful feature found in digests is the table of cases. This table alphabetically lists all cases found in the digest by both the plaintiff's name and the defendant's name. Thus, if you know only a case name, you can find the citation.

See Boxes 8-3 and 8-4 for a checklist for using digests.

BOX 8-3 USING DIGESTS

Starting with a Known Case

- ✔ Identify headnotes relevant to your issue.
- ✔ Note the topic and number of those headnotes.
- ✔ Find the digest corresponding to the case reporter.
- ✔ Locate the topic and number in the digest.
- ✔ Note citations to other cases under the topic and number.
- ✔ Read the other cases.

BOX 8-4 USING DIGESTS

Starting with Issues or Facts, but No Known Cases

- ✔ Identify key words in facts and issues.
- ✔ Locate key words in the descriptive word index.
- ✔ Identify the proper topic and numbers from the index.
- ✔ Locate the topic and number in the digest.
- ✔ Note the case citations under the topic and number.
- ✔ Read the cases.

8-6 LEXIS ADVANCE, WESTLAW, BLOOMBERG LAW, AND DIGESTS

Neither Lexis Advance nor Westlaw provides direct access to the digests. However, Westlaw does allow a "key number" search. Additionally, the digest concept of finding cases, that is, finding cases with similar headnotes, affects search features on both Lexis Advance and Westlaw. These online legal databases provide features that allow the researcher to perform digest-type searches. Because of the increased power of online searching, using these features often produces better search results than using the digest in its print format. Cases reported in both Lexis Advance and Westlaw contain headnotes to all cases with topics and subtopics. Bloomberg Law, a relatively new database, provides headnotes for many, but not all, cases. In these legal databases, the researcher can use the headnotes to find additional cases with the same headnote topics and subtopics by simply linking from the headnote.

Lexis Advance

To see how the digest concept is used on Lexis Advance, refer to Figure 8-5, which shows a Lexis headnote from *Minnesota v. Dickerson.* Note the topics assigned to the headnote.

To retrieve cases with similar headnotes in Lexis Advance, the researcher can link from the headnote topics and will find other cases that have the same headnote.

Westlaw

Westlaw utilizes its key number system for headnotes. By linking to either the key number (110k1134.26—Figure 8-6A) or the topic ("mootness" in

FIGURE 8-5 LexisNexis Headnote from Minnesota v. Dickerson

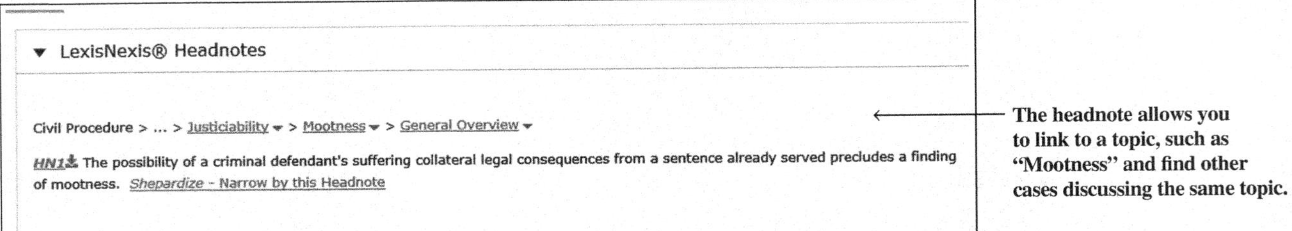

FIGURE 8-6A *Minnesota v. Dickerson*, Westlaw Headnote

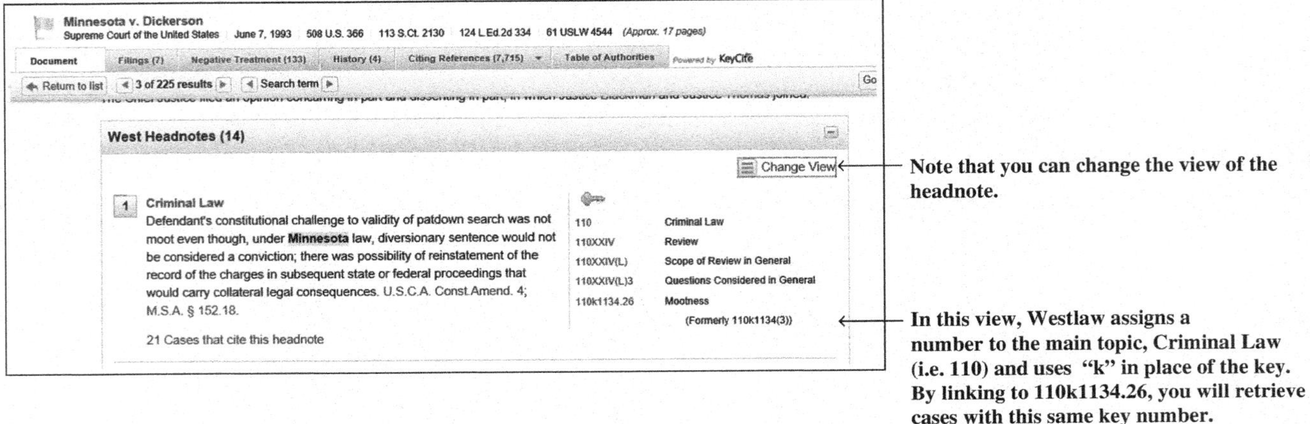

FIGURE 8-6B Westlaw Headnotes

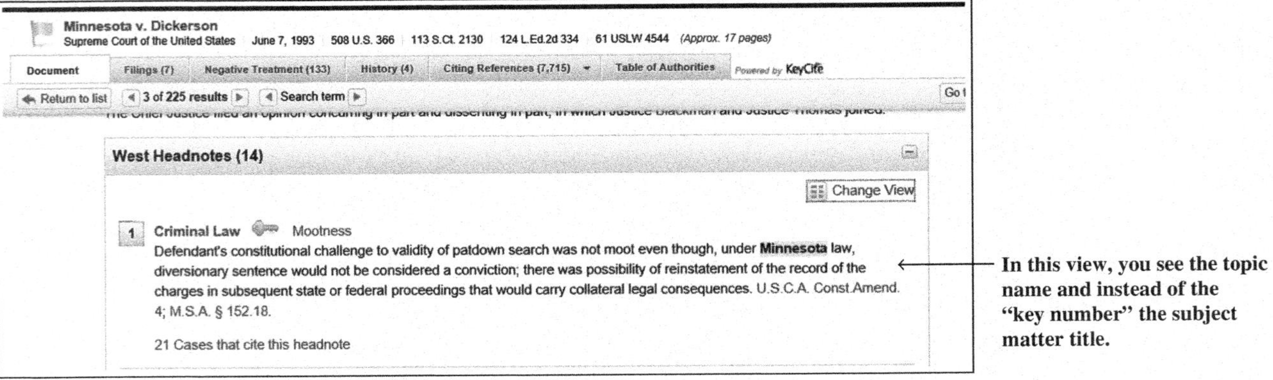

Figure 8-6B), you will retrieve cases that contain the same headnote topic and key number. Looking at the figures, see that you can also retrieve cases that cite this headnote.

An additional feature on Westlaw utilizes the data found in the West digest system. The "KeySearch" feature allows you to browse several topics selected by

FIGURE 8-7A Westlaw Key Number Search

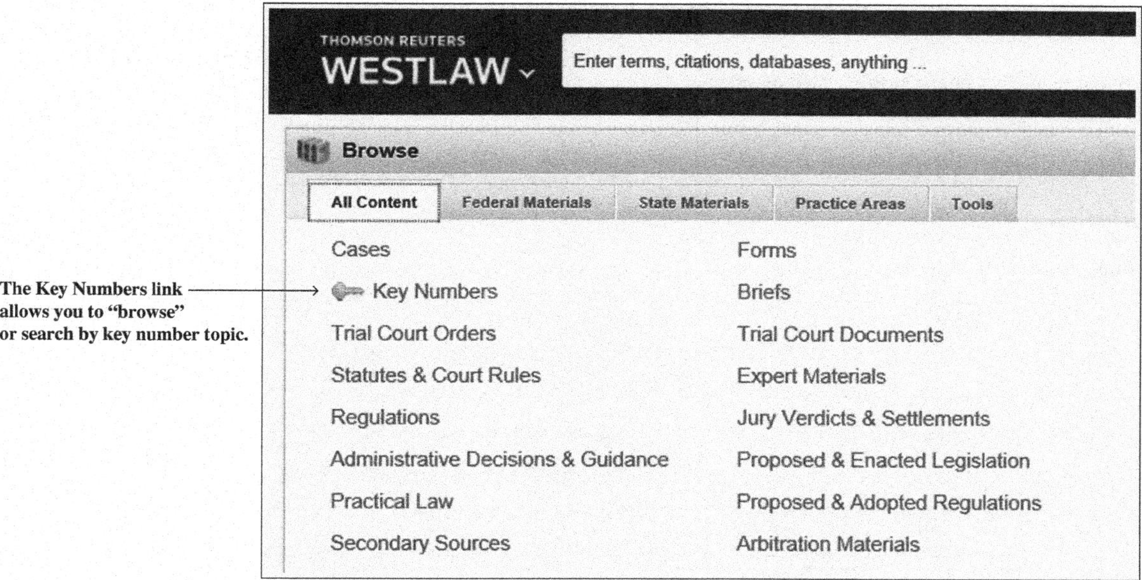

FIGURE 8-7B Key Number Search

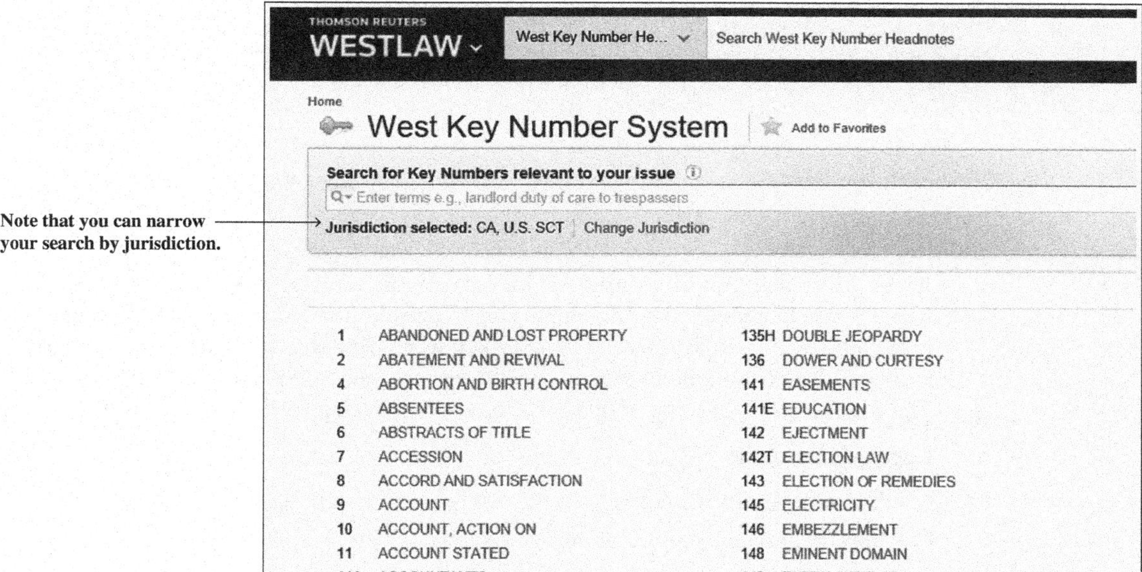

West and based on their digest topics, although the topics are not identical. See Figures 8-7A and 8-7B.

Bloomberg Law

Bloomberg Law is a relatively new subscription-based platform where a researcher can find case law. Many of the cases contain headnotes written by in-house editors. These headnotes are categorized topically in ways similar to the headnotes found in Lexis Advance and Westlaw. The headnotes are categorized by topic and number.

The Writer's Corner

Use the Active Voice

In general, active voice is the best choice. Active voice uses fewer words than the passive voice.

Active Voice: Amy threw the ball.

Passive Voice: The ball was thrown by Amy.

These two sentences mean the same thing. Notice that the active voice sentence is shorter.

In the active voice example, Amy is the subject (the actor), and she kicks the ball. In the passive voice sentence, the ball is the subject, and it is acted upon.

There are three *working words* and only one *noise word* (see the Writer's Corner in Chapter 9) in the active voice sentence. The passive voice example uses three *working* and three *noise words*. Readers prefer short, easy-to-understand sentences.

Active Voice	Passive Voice
Amy threw the ball.	The ball was thrown by Amy.
Amy throws the ball.	The ball is thrown by Amy.
Amy will throw the ball.	The ball will be thrown by Amy.
Amy has thrown the ball.	The ball has been thrown by Amy.
Amy had thrown the ball.	The ball had been thrown by Amy.
Amy will have thrown the ball.	The ball will have been thrown by Amy

When you edit your writing, look for "had," "had been," "has," and "has been." These words often indicate passive voice. Again, notice the number of *working versus noise words* in the passive voice sentences.

When we read only the *working words* in the active voice sentences, we understand the meaning.

Active: Amy threw ball

This is not true when we read only the *working words* in the passive voice sentences.

Passive: Ball thrown Amy

The point of the sentence should be obvious even when only the *working words* are read.

Finding It Online

An essential step in using digests is identifying the topic. If you have not already found a case headnote on point, identifying a digest topic first requires that you analyze your research questions and identify key words that can be located in a descriptive word index. A dictionary and a legal thesaurus help you identify relevant terms. The following websites provide access to these two valuable tools:

Legal Dictionaries

http://dictionary.law.com/

http://dictionary.findlaw.com/

Dictionaries

http://www.merriam-webster.com/ (Webster)

www.onelook.com (links to dozens of dictionaries)

Thesaurus

www.thesaurus.com/

http://www.merriam-webster.com/

You can also find information about using headnotes to search in "help" and "tutorial" information provided by Westlaw, Lexis Advance, and Bloomberg Law on their websites. This information does not require that you access the databases and is available to anyone.

A digest is a unique legal resource, and not available on the Internet without access to Westlaw or Lexis Advance. Free websites containing reported cases often allow the researcher to search by topic. However, this does not produce the same precise results as a digest.

CITATION MATTERS

BOOKS

***THE BLUEBOOK*—RULE 15**

Rule 15 explains how books, pamphlets, and treatises should be cited in legal documents. In general, cite the following in this order:

a. Volume number
b. Name of author
c. Title
d. Page number
e. Edition (if the publication is past its first edition)
f. Year of the publication (usually located on the back of the title page)

Review the following examples:

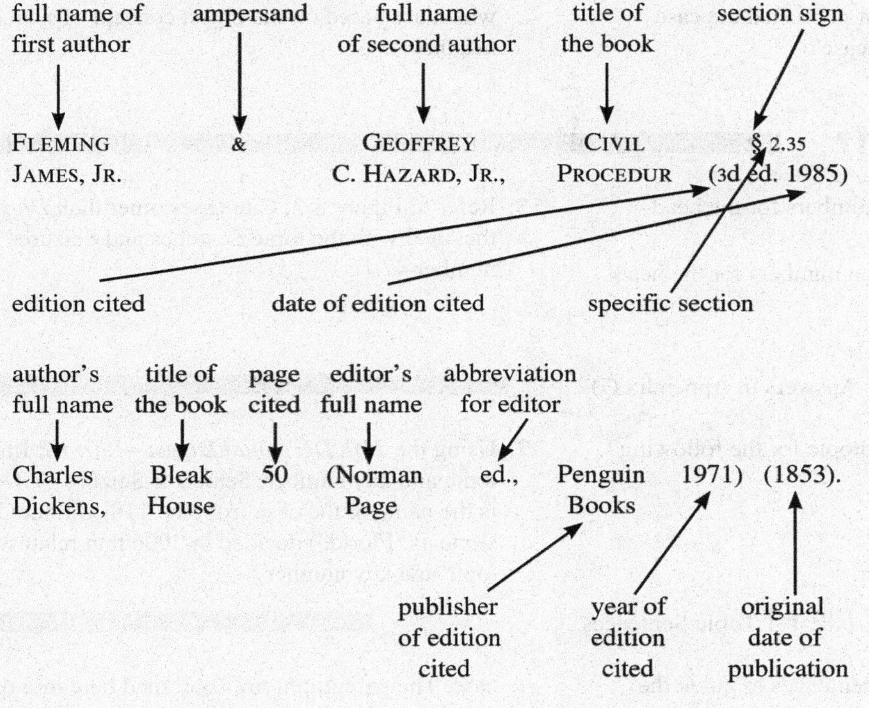

CHAPTER **SUMMARY**

An important research tool used to find case law is the digest. A digest is an alphabetical arrangement of topics found in headnotes with references to the cases where the headnotes are found. The publishers of the various case reporters publish digests corresponding to the case reporters. You can use a digest to find case law if you already have one case that relates to your issue or if you have identified key words from your facts and issues. If you have a known case, you note the appropriate headnotes, locate them in the digest that accompanies the case reporter you are using, and then find other cases on the same topic. If you do not have a known case, check the key terms in the descriptive word index. The index directs the researcher to various topics in the digest.

Although online services of Lexis Advance and Westlaw do not provide direct access to the digest, both contain features that allow the researcher to perform digest-type searches. On both sites, the researcher can link from the headnote of one case to similar headnotes in other cases. In addition, Westlaw offers the Key Number database. Searching this database allows the researcher to search all of the West topics and key numbers.

TERMS TO **REMEMBER**

digest
headnotes
topic and key number
Century Digest
Decennial Digest
General Digest
descriptive word index
prefatory material

QUESTIONS FOR **REVIEW**

1. What is a digest?
2. How are headnotes organized in a digest?
3. Describe the West topic and key number system.
4. How do key numbers in print sources differ from key numbers in Westlaw?
5. If you have a known case and are using a digest to find more cases, why is it important to use the digest published by the company that published the case reporter where you found the case?
6. What types of cases are found in West's American Digest System?
7. What is a table of cases, and why is it useful?
8. How do you use a digest if you do not have any case law related to your issue?
9. How are digests kept up to date?
10. Describe features on Lexis Advance and Westlaw, which are based on the digest concept of searching headnotes.

CAN YOU **FIGURE IT OUT?**

1. List the legal topics and key numbers for the headnotes found in Figure 8-1.
2. List the legal topics and section numbers for the headnotes found in Figure 8-2.
3. Refer to Figure 8-3. Cite cases other than *Dickerson* that deal with the topic Searches and Seizures and key number 47.1.

TEST **YOURSELF** (Check Your Answers in Appendix G)

1. What is the specific digest subtopic for the following?
   a. Child Custody 🔑 558
   b. Federal Courts 🔑 198
   c. Negligence 🔑 1085
2. Using the *11th Decennial Digest—Part III,* find the topic and key number, Search & Seizure 47.1. What is the name of the case from the 11th Circuit Court of Appeals (Florida) decided in 2006 that relates to this topic and key number?

TEST **YOURSELF**—WRITE IT RIGHT Topic Sentences

Well-written documents use topic sentences to guide the reader. Most readers carefully read the first sentence in every paragraph. The first sentence should alert the reader to the topic of the paragraph. If we look at a document and cut and paste the topic sentences into a list, that list should become a rough outline of the topics of the paragraphs.

Now, You Try It

(Check your answers in Appendix G)

1. The material below contains seven paragraphs. This is a Summary of an Argument in the *Morse v. Frederick* case. The paragraphs are combined here into one long paragraph. Locate the topic sentences and underline them.

SUMMARY OF ARGUMENT

In reversing the district court's grant of summary judgment in favor of the Juneau School Board and Deborah Morse, the Ninth Circuit embraced an unduly narrow reading of this Court's teachings with respect to the free speech rights of public school students. To make very bad matters profoundly worse, the court below fashioned an approach to qualified immunity doctrine that conflicts with this Court's precedents and is dangerously unsettling to thousands of public school educators and administrators across the country. The Ninth Circuit was doubly wrong. In its teachings with respect to student speech principles, this Court has consistently recognized that public educational institutions possess "special characteristics" that profoundly shape the contextually-sensitive contours of Free Speech doctrine. From its watershed decision in *Tinker,* 393 U.S. 503, through its subsequent decisions in *Fraser,* 478 U.S. 675, and *Kuhlmeier,* 484 U.S. 260, this Court has both protected nondisruptive political speech by students, while respectfully deferring to school administrators' judgments in cabining expression that is inconsistent with the educational function of public schools. In its First Amendment analysis, the Ninth Circuit fundamentally misconceived the nature and scope of the mission of public education in this country—as elucidated by this Court in both *Fraser* and *Kuhlmeier*. At the same time, it wildly enlarged the ambit of purportedly political speech. In doing so, the court of appeals substituted its unforgivingly libertarian worldview for the considered judgment of school officials (and school boards) in seeking, consistent with Congress' statutory mandate, to foster and encourage a drug-free student lifestyle. Frederick's banner display not only radically changed the subject from the Olympic Torch Relay ceremony to illegality-promoting, distracting banter, his message itself lay far outside the province of *Tinker*-protected political expression. To the contrary, as Chief Judge Sedwick rightly concluded, the banner's ambiguous but obtrusive message fell comfortably within the ambit of Fraser's focus on promoting appropriate norms of discourse and civility. *Kuhlmeier* likewise supports the school authorities' decision to just say no to respondent's whimsically drug-focused message, inasmuch as the banner—if left undisturbed—could have told not only the high school student body but the larger community that drug-use promotion is openly tolerated within the local public high school. Nothing in law or logic, much less common sense, requires such an extravagant result. The Ninth Circuit also strayed from this Court's qualified immunity jurisprudence, as embodied in decisions such as *Saucier v. Katz,* 533 U.S. 194 (2001). The court of appeals' conclusion that Deborah Morse, a paradigmatic conscientious educator and administrator, should face a potentially ruinous award for money damages, by virtue of her enforcement actions directed against respondent, cries out for the Court's muscular disapprobation. As a threshold matter, for reasons already adumbrated, the court of appeals fell into error as a matter of substantive First Amendment law. With that foundation removed, the edifice of potential personal liability for money damages entirely collapses. Even assuming arguendo, however, that Principal Morse was in constitutional error in enforcing the School Board's anti-drug-message policies, the Ninth Circuit was still mistaken in its articulation and application of qualified immunity principles. Under this Court's objective test, immunity doctrine provides a shield from civil damages suits unless "it is obvious that no reasonably competent officer would have concluded" that the actions at issue were constitutional at the time they were undertaken. *Malley v. Briggs,* 475 U.S. 335, 341 (1986). Principal Morse abundantly satisfies that objective standard. Responsible for maintaining order and proper decorum at a celebratory gathering of more than 1,000 high school students, the principal was confronted with a flagrant, inherently disruptive violation of a written school policy proscribing pro-illegal-drug messages. She responsibly took the appropriate action to ensure that the Olympic Torch Relay event was not further disrupted by Frederick's pro-drug banner. Nor does the fact that Frederick was not physically on school grounds at the time of the banner display exempt him from school discipline. At the pivotal moment when engaging in his expressive conduct, Frederick was a student participating in a school activity during school hours. A reasonable principal could well have believed that enforcing a well-established policy against promoting illegal substances at a non-classroom school activity was entirely lawful, and indeed required by School Board mandate. By doing so, the principal acted entirely reasonably. Accordingly, her conduct should, under this Court's body of qualified immunity jurisprudence, be fully immunized from judicial condemnation.

Type up the seven topic sentences into a list. You should have a good overview of the seven paragraphs in the Summary of the Argument.

CITATION **EXERCISES**

Use Appendix C and the Citation Matters feature in this chapter to answer these questions.

1. Which *Bluebook* rule addresses citations for books?
2. Choose a book and write the correct legal citation for use in legal documents (not for use in law reviews).

FROM **THE WRITER'S CORNER** Use the active voice

1. "Active voice uses ____________ words than the ____________."
2. Rewrite the following sentence: "The dog has been seen by Susan."

ASSIGNMENTS AND **ACTIVITIES**

RESEARCH EXERCISES

1. Using the *10th Decennial Digest—Part I,* answer the following.
   a. Cite a case in which Dannon Yogurt is a defendant.
   b. What is the specific topic of Patents 16.29?
      i What is the name of a New York federal case, found in this section, that deals with a patent from the United Kingdom?
      ii Locate the case described in "a." What case headnote corresponds to this digest entry?
   c. Using the descriptive word index, which civil rights section deals with arrest as a deprivation of constitutional rights?
2. Using the *11th Decennial Digest—Part II,* answer the following.
   a. Find the topic and key number, Searches and Seizures 47.1.
      i Give the name and citation for a Ninth Circuit Federal case decided in 2003 that is related to this issue.
      ii Give the name and citation for a 2004 case from Rhode Island regarding this issue.
   b. Assume that you are researching the following question, "Is it a violation of the freedom of speech to prohibit students from saying prayers at a high school graduation ceremony?" Use the descriptive word index to find digest topics that cover this issue. Answer the following.
      i What topics and key numbers provide case law relevant to the following topic: freedom of speech generally in schools?
      ii What topics and key numbers provide case law relevant to the following topic: prayers at graduation ceremonies?

ANALYSIS ASSIGNMENTS

3. Select one research problem from Appendix B and read it carefully. Identify which of the seven main divisions of law in Figure 8-4 apply to the situation.

ONLINE RESEARCH EXERCISES

4. Access the following site: http://www.law.cornell.edu/supct/index.html. Search archived Supreme Court opinions by topic.
   a. If you are searching for cases similar to ***Minnesota*** *v. Dickerson,* which topics would you select? (Consider the headnote topics you saw in Figures 8-1 and 8-2.)
   b. Select a topic and then search for more cases dealing with the specific area of plain view searches? What did you find?
5. Perform an advanced "Google" search for legal digests. Limit your search to documents in a Microsoft PowerPoint format. What did you find?
6. If you have access to Westlaw, do the following:
   Access *Hamdi v. Rumsfeld,* 542 U.S. 507, 124 S.Ct. 2633 (2004).
   a. What is the specific topic and key number for the first West headnote?
   b. What is the most cited case for the legal topic found in the first headnote?
7. If you have access to Lexis, do the following:
   Access *Hamdi v. Rumsfeld,* 542 U.S. 507, 159 L. Ed. 2d (2004).
   a. What is the topic of headnote 1?
   b. Click on "More Like This Headnote" and check for Supreme Court cases only. How many cases did you retrieve?

CASE **PROJECT**

Using the same case that you researched in Chapters 1 through 7, check the appropriate digest for topics relating to the issues. Begin by making a list of terms to check in the descriptive word index to the digest. Make a list of relevant digest topics and cases. Read the cases and take notes.

chapter **nine**

VALIDATING YOUR RESEARCH: USING *SHEPARD'S*, KEYCITE, AND OTHER CITATORS

SKILL OBJECTIVES FOR CHAPTER 9

When you complete chapter 9, you should be able to

- Explain the purpose of a citator.
- List the types of authorities that can be Shepardized.
- Shepardize a case using print and online resources.
- Explain the difference between the history of the case and the treatment of the case.
- Explain how *Shepard's* uses headnote numbers.
- Shepardize a statute using print and online resources.
- KeyCite case law and other legal authorities.
- Discuss the differences between *Shepard's* online and other online citators.
- Identify citators other than *Shepard's* and KeyCite.
- Cite check a document.

CHAPTER OUTLINE

From the Desk of W. J. Bryan, Esq.

TO: Research Assistant
FROM: W. J. Bryan
RE: Our Client, Justin Meyers
DATE:

Attached is a draft of the memorandum of points and authorities that I plan to file in support of our motion to suppress evidence in the Meyers case. Please check all the cases cited in the memo to verify that they are still good law. Also, check all cites in the document and correct any citation problems.

9-1 INTRODUCTION TO CITATORS

U.S. law is in a constant state of change. Although case law is founded on the concept of *stare decisis,* courts occasionally overrule or modify prior case law to meet the needs of justice in a changing society. Statutory law likewise undergoes changes. Statutes are commonly amended and repealed or given new interpretations by courts. Sometimes courts declare that statutes are unconstitutional and therefore unenforceable. Your research is never complete until you verify that your authorities are still ***good law***.

good law
Law that is still in effect or valid and can be cited as authority.

Determining that an authority is good law requires the use of special research material. Case reporters and code books do not provide complete, up-to-date information on the cases and codes found in the books. When you read a case in a case reporter, you cannot tell if that case was overruled or criticized in later cases. Published codes provide better information, but even they are not totally up to date. While most codes contain pocket part supplements, these supplements are replaced only once a year. Because most legislative changes take effect at the beginning of the year rather than when they are enacted, supplementing once a year is usually sufficient to provide the latest statutory language. However, some legislation is considered to be "emergency legislation" and takes effect immediately. This is not found in a yearly supplement. Furthermore, if you rely on case notes in an annotated code, you may miss important new relevant case law.

validate
To verify that an authority is still good law.

citators
Research materials used to update or "validate" legal authorities.

The research materials used to update or ***validate*** legal authorities are known as ***citators***, the most familiar of which is *Shepard's Citations. Shepard's* is available in print and online through Lexis Advance. Westlaw provides a citator on its database—KeyCite. Bloomberg Law also provides a citator, BCite. One free website, Google Scholar, offers a feature allowing the researcher to see how cases have been cited ("How cited"). However, unlike the commercial databases, this does not analyze subsequent case law. It only identifies the law.

9-2 SHEPARD'S CITATIONS

Shepardize
To check the validity of a citation in one of the *Shepard's* citations.

cited authority
The authority you are Shepardizing.

citing authority
Authorities you are referred to when you Shepardize.

Shepard's Citations is a popular collection that researchers use to validate their research. When you use any *Shepard's* citator to check a legal citation, you are ***Shepardizing*** your authority. The legal citation you are Shepardizing is the ***cited authority***. New law found when Shepardizing is referred to as the ***citing authority***. While *Shepard's* is most commonly used to check case law, it is also used to check other authorities, such as constitutions, statutory law, administrative regulations, selected law review articles, *A.L.R.* annotations, court rules, and approved jury instructions. *Shepard's* includes specialized citators for areas of law such as bankruptcy and patents. See Box 9-1.

The primary reason for Shepardizing any authority is to verify that the law found is still good law. However, *Shepard's* provides such extensive information regarding the cited authority that it can be used as a research tool. Citations to other cases and secondary authorities often help the researcher.

BOX 9-1 YOU CAN SHEPARDIZE THESE FEDERAL AND STATE AUTHORITIES

Case law
Statutory law
Constitutions
Administrative regulations
Selected law reviews and *A.L.R.*s
Court rules
Approved jury instructions

Shepard's Case Citators in Print

Until the advent of Lexis, attorneys relied on the print version of Shepard's. Because of the numerous abbreviations and manner of supplementing, the print versions were somewhat difficult to navigate. Although print versions are still used, most lawyers prefer to use Shepard's online. In fact, many attorneys and libraries have discontinued subscriptions to the print version, relying on the online service.

Shepard's includes separate case citators for cases from different courts. For federal cases, *Shepard's* publishes the following:

- *Shepard's United States Citations* for Shepardizing U.S. Supreme Court cases
- *Shepard's Federal Citations* for Shepardizing federal district court and appellate court decisions (*Federal Supplement* and *Federal Reporters*)

In addition, *Shepard's* publishes citators for each of the regional reporters as well as citators for state case reporters.

Cases listed in *Shepard's* are organized first by reporter and series then numerically by volume and page number of the case. See Figure 9-1 for an example of a page from a *Shepard's* case citator in print. On this page, you see *Shepard's* reports for three cases found in volume 316 of the *U.S. Reports.* The three cases start on pages 447, 450, and 455. (Note how all reports include citations to other authorities.)

A Point to Remember

When you use a state-specific case citator, you can only Shepardize cases (cited authorities) from the selected jurisdiction. However, citing authorities may be from all jurisdictions.

Because case citators are published for all major case reporters, researchers are able to Shepardize a case with either the official citation or a parallel citation. It is advisable to Shepardize all citations to the same case, though, because citing authorities are different, especially secondary authorities. (This is not the case if you Shepardize online.)

FIGURE 9-1 Shepard's United States Reports

Vol. 316 **UNITED STATES REPORTS**

75McL527
65MnL80
80MnL1451
83MnL1224
85MnL1437
72NwL26
57TxL540
64TxL12
77TxL167
60VaL197
83YLJ433
85YLJ45
94LE377n
94LE378n
47LE851n
171AR773n
171AR788n
16ARF429n

—447—
National Broad-casting Co. v United States
1942
(86LE1586)
(62SC1214)
s) 319US190
s) 44FS688
s) 47FS940
cc) 316US407
Cir. 7
95FS669
97CR840
80MnL1451
94LE377n
94LE378n
47LE851n
171AR773n
171AR788n

—450—
American Chicle Co. v United States
1942
(86LE1591)
(62SC1144)
s) 315US793
s) 41FS537
s) 94CCL699
493US140
505US73
Cir. 1
61FS1016
Cir. 2
158F2d161
306F2d827
199FS458
199FS466
Cir. 3
181F2d405
Cir. 4
205F2d342
Cir. 5
562F2d978
Cir. 6
151F2d1000
229F2d698
400F2d823
270FS939
Cir. 7
160FS328
Cir. 8
266F2d69
69F3d1407
Cir. 9
172FS938
Cir. 10
80FS344
Cir. DC
707F2d561
Cir. Fed.
856F2d172
CCPA
j) 359F2d885
ClCt
36FedCl 33
38FedCl 667
CtCl
375F2d838
530F2d869
620F2d855
f) 47FS119
e) 48FS358
55FS624
60FS469
f) 97CCL262
e) 99CCL570
99CCL571
101CCL743
104CCL122
179CCL610
208CCL579
223CCL430
4TCt216
18TCt12
24TCt637
29TCt271
36TCt282
58TCt911
59TCt74
66TCt356
77TCt63
89TCt776
90TCt1306
100TCt11
103TCt470
104TCt729
107TCt337
Ala
503So2d303
Mass
378Mas273
391NE263
Okla
780P2d668
PR
74PRR922
SoC
233SoC48
103SE427
78CR1659
92HLR1646
122PaL348
153AR1189n
12A2363n
12A2368n
12A2370n
12A2371n

—455—
Betts v Brady
1942
(86LE1595)
(62SC1252)
s) 315US791
317US24
317US276
321US115
j) 322US495
322US602
324US46
324US764
324US768
325US95
325US97
326US326
327US85
329US665
j) 332US83
332US137
j) 332US140
j) 332US141
333US281
333US656
333US659
333US660
333US666
333US676
j) 333US677
j) 333US679
334US684
j) 334US685
334US730
334US739
335US441
337US780
c) 337US782
339US661
339US666
342US64
342US179
d) 348US9
348US108
349US391
350US118
j) 351US36
354US77
355US159
j) 356US83
d) 357US441
j) 357US442
358US636
361US246
j) 361US255
j) 363US704
j) 364US275
365US117
q) 365US119
j) 365US208
j) 366US158
368US459
369US517
q) 369US519
q) 369US520
370US908
372US337
o) 372US339
372US348
e) 372US349
372US478
j) 375US3
q) 378US6
j) 378US26
j) 378US407
q) 379US80
q) 380US414
j) 381US512
381US590
j) 381US616
384US469
e) 385US399
385US564
q) 386US43
j) 388US172
q) 389US134
395US794
q) 395US795
c) 405US484
j) 405US485
q) 407US31
q) 407US65
408US287
q) 411US788
j) 419US255
422US807
j) 422US844
q) 440US371
j) 440US378
q) 452US25
j) 452US35
466US656
469US394
q) 492US12
j) 492US21
499US34
509US109
q) 510US273
q) 511US493
j) 511US738
523US850
j) 4LE292
q) 159LE507
j) 80SC315
q) 124SC2514
9FRD348
24FRD79
33FRD424
33FRD438
33FRD454
38FRD463
39FRD284
Cir. 1
181F2d602
d) 191F2d965
203F2d935
204F2d362
96FS707
f) 101FS165
f) 105FS529
111FS418
123FS443
124FS37
141FS606
332FS834
377FS1341
432FS115
q) 253FS2d33
Cir. 2
e) 137F2d1010
190F2d253
221F2d629
d) 250F2d354
263F2d943
292F2d323
303F2d885
d) 313F2d460
315F2d866
j) 319F2d318
330F2d304
q) 330F2d310
j) 330F2d315
332F2d891
q) 333F2d610
398F2d985
q) 465F2d121
j) 611F2d421
694F2d22
e) 709F2d168
113FS920
171FS561
177FS507
184FS282
184FS542
200FS907
205FS514
209FS530
210FS277
f) 210FS279
212FS880
212FS928
214FS646
219FS153
e) 219FS266
q) 219FS268
261FS400
q) 327FS546
Cir. 3
130F2d657
175F2d254
203F2d426
203F2d806
224F2d508
224F2d512
f) 310F2d724
j) 310F2d735
e) 329F2d858
q) 334F2d529
355F2d313
j) 359F2d947
j) 430F2d469
752F2d921
j) 782F2d455
994F2d1016
74FS848
81FS870
81FS871

22

① The reporter and volume number appear at the top of the page.

② Here you find *Shepard's* analysis of *Betts v. Brady*, 316 U.S. 455 (1942). Parallel citations are found in other parts of *Shepard's*. This is the cited authority.

③ All of the following cases are the citing authority. These cases all cite *Betts v. Brady*.

The Writer's Corner

Placement of Words in a Sentence

In the last Writer's Corner, we looked at a sentence using too many words *and* with the words out of order. In general, writers strive to place the working words (the words of value in the sentence) in the following order:

ACTOR to ACTION to OBJECT

Example:

"The defendant's motion to suppress the evidence was denied by the trial judge."

When we read only the working words, the sentence should make sense. Obviously, it needs the noise (or glue) words to be complete, but the reader can easily understand the sentence.

If one reads the working words from the previous example, the sentence says:

"Defendant's motion suppress evidence denied trial judge."

Improvement:

The trial judge denied the defendant's motion to suppress the evidence.

The working words then read like this:

"Trial judge denied defendant's motion suppress evidence."

The sentence is now in the **ACTOR to ACTION to OBJECT** format.

Example:

"The ball was kicked by Bobby."

Working words:	"ball	kicked	Bobby"
	OBJECT	ACTION	ACTOR

Improvement:

Bobby	kicked	the	ball.
ACTOR	ACTION		OBJECT

A Point to Remember

When you Shepardize a case, you must check all parallel cites to obtain references to all citing authorities.

Analyzing Information Once you find a case in *Shepard's*, you must analyze or interpret your findings. Shepardizing a case provides two types of information concerning your case (the cited case): the history of the case and the treatment of the case. The history of the case provides the published background of the *same* case you are checking. If you are Shepardizing a U.S. Supreme Court case, *Shepard's* provides the cite to published opinions of the same case from lower courts. If you are Shepardizing an appellate court case, *Shepard's* tells you if a higher court has granted a hearing. The treatment of the case provides citations to *other* authorities mentioning your case. In some instances, by the use of short abbreviations preceding the cite, *Shepard's* tells you how these other authorities viewed your case. Some of the more important facts that *Shepard's* tells you are whether a case was:

- Overruled by a subsequent case
- Criticized by a subsequent case
- Approved by a subsequent case
- Questioned by a subsequent case
- Cited in the dissent of a subsequent case

Shepard's also tells you if a case was cited in *A.L.R.* or law review articles. See Figure 9-2 for an illustrative page from *Shepard's* showing the various case treatments and corresponding abbreviations.

FIGURE 9-2
Shepard's Case Analysis Abbreviations

CASE ANALYSIS–ABBREVIATIONS

HISTORY OF CASES

cc	(Connected Case)	The citing case is related to the case you are *Shepardizing*, arising out of the same subject matter or involving the same parties.
m	(Modified)	On appeal, reconsideration or rehearing, the citing case modifies or changes in some way, including affirmance in part and reversal in part, the case you are *Shepardizing*.
r	(Reversed)	On appeal, reconsideration or rehearing, the citing case reverses the case you are *Shepardizing*.
S	(Superseded)	On appeal, reconsideration or rehearing, the citing case supersedes or is substituted for the case you are *Shepardizing*.
s	(Same Case)	The citing case involves the same litigation as the case you are *Shepardizing*, but at a different stage of the proceedings.
US reh den	(Rehearing Denied)	The citing order by the United States Supreme Court denies rehearing in the case you are *Shepardizing*.
US reh dis	(Rehearing Dismissed)	The citing order by the United States Supreme Court dismisses rehearing in the case you are *Shepardizing*.
v	(Vacated)	The citing case vacates or withdraws the case you are *Shepardizing*.

TREATMENT OF CASES

c	(Criticized)	The citing opinion disagrees with the reasoning/result of the case you are *Shepardizing*, although the citing court may not have the authority to materially affect its precedential value.
ca	(Conflicting Authorities)	Among conflicting authorities as noted in cited case
d	(Distinguished)	The citing case differs from the case you are *Shepardizing*, either involving dissimilar facts or requiring a different application of the law.
e	(Explained)	The citing opinion interprets or clarifies the case you are *Shepardizing* in a significant way.
f	(Followed)	The citing opinion relies on the case you are *Shepardizing* as controlling or persuasive authority.
h	(Harmonized)	The citing case differs from the case you are *Shepardizing*, but the citing court reconciles the difference or inconsistency in reaching its decision.
j	(Dissenting Opinion)	A dissenting opinion cites the case you are *Shepardizing*
L	(Limited)	The citing opinion restricts the application of the case you are *Shepardizing*, finding its reasoning applies only in specific limited circumstances.
o	(Overruled)	The citing case expressly overrules or disapproves the case you are *Shepardizing*.

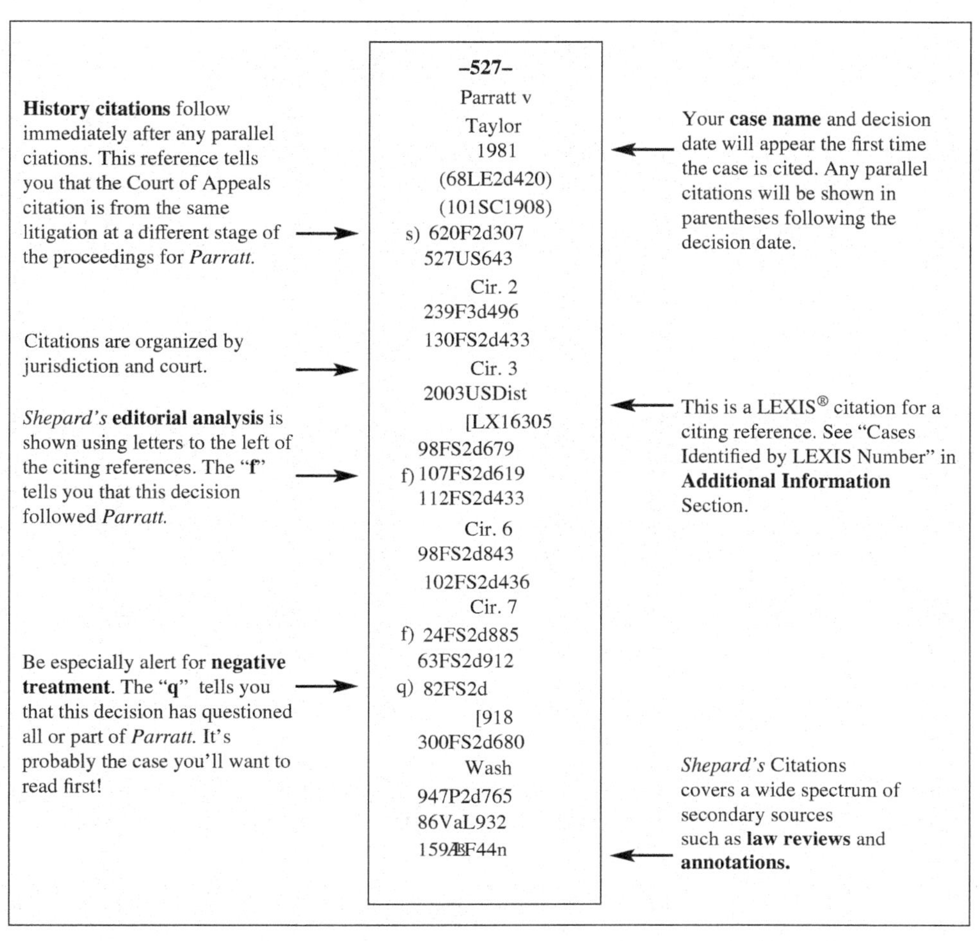

FIGURE 9-3 Shepard's Illustrative Citations

When you Shepardize a case using *Shepard's* in print, you also find the following:

- The first time a case appears in *Shepard's,* you see the case name.
- The first time a case appears in *Shepard's,* you find parallel citations in parentheses at the beginning of the citations.
- References to authorities are chronological (oldest cases first) within the following categories: U.S. Supreme Court cases, federal court cases, state court cases, and secondary sources. Citing references are not listed in order of importance.

See Figure 9-3 for an illustration from *Shepard's* case citations showing this.

A Point to Remember

If you see the following abbreviations, stop:

"o" (overruled): If a case was overruled, you cannot use the case as authority. This means it is no longer good law. However, sometimes only part of a case is overruled. You can use the case if your issue is not overruled.

"Grtd" (hearing granted): If a hearing was granted in a higher court, you cannot use your citation as authority. It is not a final decision. If the higher court has issued a published opinion, you can use that cite.

"c" (criticized): If a case was criticized, you can still use it as authority, but it would be better to find other authorities following your decision.

"q" (questioned): If a case was questioned, you can still use it as authority, but it would be better to find other authorities following your decision.

"r" (reversed): If a case was reversed by a higher court, you cannot cite it.

"S" (superseded): The decision in the case was superseded or replaced by another decision. Do not cite it.

"v" (vacated): Your case is no longer law. Do not cite it.

A Point to Remember

When a case is cited by numerous authorities, you must read the list of *all* of the citing authorities carefully. A citing authority overruling your case may appear in the middle of several pages of citations. Other than the abbreviation "o," nothing distinguishes this cite. Examine Figure 9-1. Note the placement of the overruling case for *Betts v. Brady*. Also, see Box 9-2.

BOX 9-2 SHEPARDIZING CASE LAW: INFORMATION PROVIDED

- ✔ Parallel cites for the cited authority
- ✔ Cites to the same case (if there are prior or subsequent reported decisions in the same action)
- ✔ Cites to all other cases discussing your citation
- ✔ Description of how other cases have considered your case citation
- ✔ Cites to selected secondary sources discussing your citation

Abbreviations *Shepard's* in print relies heavily on the use of abbreviations. The cited and citing references are abbreviated in a way that is unique to *Shepard's*. In describing the history and treatment of a particular case, one- or two-letter abbreviations are used. Often, although not always, the abbreviation is the first letter of the word. Each volume of *Shepard's* contains tables of abbreviations for cited cases, citing cases, history of the case, and treatment of the case.

Headnotes When an opinion in any case is written, the court often discusses different points of law within the opinion. For example, a court might discuss issues relating to the hearsay rule of evidence and the tort of strict liability in the same case. Cases that later cite to this case might be citing it because of what the court said about the hearsay rule or because of what it said about strict liability. When Shepardizing, your only concern might be to verify that what the court said about strict liability is still good law. How other courts have viewed this court's interpretation of hearsay might be irrelevant to you. *Shepard's* helps you to make this type of distinction by using the headnote numbers from your cited authority (the case you are Shepardizing). For example, consider the following citing authority: 128F2d^{10}1013. The number 10 tells you that this case discusses the point of law found in headnote 10 of the Shepardized case.

A Point to Remember

Each publisher of case reporters uses different headnotes and headnote numbers. The headnotes referred to when you Shepardize a *Lawyers' Edition* cite relate only to those headnotes found in the *Lawyers' Edition* publication of the case. When you Shepardize parallel cites, be sure not to confuse headnote numbers.

Updating *Shepard's* legal researchers expect *Shepard's* to be as current as possible. In order to ensure that this happens, *Shepard's* in print is continually supplemented. When you Shepardize, you must check all books containing references to your cited authority. Normally, this includes the following:

1. The main citator. This maroon-colored volume indicates on the spine what years it covers. Sometimes there is more than one volume.
2. A cumulative supplement (a red-covered paperback).
3. An annual or semiannual supplement (a gold-covered paperback).
4. An express update (a blue-covered paperback).

Shepard's helps you recognize what books and supplements you need to check by printing on the cover "What your library should contain . . . ." Before you Shepardize any authority, you must be sure that you have all the relevant books and supplements. (Most often the problem you will encounter in a library is that the librarians failed to remove a supplement that was replaced. This will not cause any serious research problems for you, although it might lead you to check more books than necessary.) In addition to the print material, *Shepard's* offers a Daily Update Service that allows users of the print materials to contact *Shepard's* editorial support by telephone for updated information.

A Point to Remember

If you are Shepardizing a relatively new case, it might not appear in the main citator. Always pay attention to the date of any case being Shepardized and start the Shepardizing process with the volume that first covers that time period. You can tell if you are in the right book if you see the case name and parallel cites for the case, as these appear only the first time the cite is mentioned.

If you use all of the *Shepard's* supplements that are in print, you are still missing recent case decisions. For that reason, and for ease of use, *Shepard's* Citation Service on the Lexis Advance website is widely used.

Shepard's Statutory Citators in Print

In addition to its case citators, *Shepard's* publishes citators that allow you to Shepardize constitutions, statutes or codes, and administrative rules or regulations, including the *Code of Federal Regulations*. These citators are similar to case citators in many respects. When you Shepardize this type of material, you find information about the history of the law, that is, if it was amended or repealed. You also find citations to cases and secondary authorities that discuss the law. See Box 9-3. The terms and abbreviations *Shepard's* uses to describe the treatment of statutory law differ from the terms used to describe the treatment of cases. See Figure 9-4 for a list of these abbreviations and Figure 9-5 for an example of a page from a statutory citator. Like *Shepard's* case citators, statutory citators are available in print and online through Lexis Advance.

BOX 9-3 SHEPARDIZING STATUTORY LAW: INFORMATION PROVIDED

- Whether the statute was amended or repealed
- Cites to case law discussing the statute
- Description of how case law considered the statute
- Cites to selected secondary sources discussing the citation

FIGURE 9-4 Shepard's Statutory Analysis and Abbreviations

ANALYSIS OF STATUTES, RULES, REGULATIONS AND ORDERS–ABBREVIATIONS

LEGISLATIVE

A	(Amended)	The citing reference, typically a session law, amends or alters the statute you are *Shepardizing*.
Ad	(Added)	The citing reference, typically a session law, adds new matter to the statute you are *Shepardizing*.
E	(Extended)	The citing reference extends the scope of, or the time period specified in, the statute you are *Shepardizing*.
L	(Limited)	The citing reference refuses to extend the provisions of the statute you are *Shepardizing*.
R	(Repealed)	The citing reference, typically a session law, repeals or abrogates the statute you are *Shepardizing*.
Re-en	(Re-enacted)	The citing reference, typically a session law, re-enacts the statute you are *Shepardizing*.
Rn	(Renumbered)	The citing reference, typically a session law, renumbers the statute you are *Shepardizing*.
Rp	(Repealed in Part)	The citing reference, typically a session law, repeals or abrogates in part the statute you are *Shepardizing*.
Rs	(Repealed & Superseded)	The citing reference, typically a session law, repeals and supersedes the statute you are *Shepardizing*.
Rv	(Revised)	The citing reference, typically a session law, revises the statute you are *Shepardizing*.
S	(Superseded)	The citing reference, typically a session law, supersedes the statute you are *Shepardizing*.
Sd	(Suspended)	The citing reference, typically a session law, suspends the statute you are *Shepardizing*.
Sdp	(Suspended in Part)	The citing reference, typically a session law, suspends in part the statute you are *Shepardizing*.
Sg	(Supplementing)	The citing reference, typically a session law, supplements the statute you are *Shepardizing*,
Sp	(Superseded in Part)	The citing reference, typically a session law, supersedes in part the statute you are *Shepardizing*.

JUDICIAL

C	(Constitutional)	The citing case upholds the constitutionality of the statute, rule or regulation you are *Shepardizing*.
cr	(Criticized)	The citing opinion criticizes the statute, rule or regulation you are Shepardizing in some significant way, although the citing court may not have the authority to materially affect its precedential value.
DG	(Decision for Gov't)	The citing decision holds for the Government in a dispute concerning the Code section you are *Shepardizing*.

FIGURE 9-4 (continued)

DGp	(Decision for Gov't in Part)	The citing decision holds in part for the Government in a dispute concerning the Code section you are *Shepardizing*.
DT	(Decision for Taxpayer)	The citing decision holds for the taxpayer in a dispute concerning the code section you are *Shepardizing*.
DTp	(Decision for Taxpayer in Part)	The citing decision holds in part for the taxpayer in a dispute concerning the code section you *are Shepardizing*.
f	(Followed)	The citing opinion expressly relies on the statute, rule or regulation you are *Shepardizing* as controlling authority.
i	(Interpreted)	The citing opinion interprets the statute, rule or regulation you are *Shepardizing* in some significant way, often including a discussion of the statute's legislative history.
j	(Dissenting Opinion)	A dissenting opinion cites the statute, rule or regulation you are *Shepardizing*.
na	(Not Applicable)	The citing opinion expressly finds the statute, rule or regulation you are *Shepardizing* inapplicable to the legal or factual circumstances of the citing case.
rt	(Retroactive/ Prospective)	The citing opinion discusses retroactive or prospective application of the statute, rule or regulation you are *Shepardizing*.
U	(Unconstitutional)	The citing case declares unconstitutional the statute, rule or regulation you are *Shepardizing*.
Up	(Unconstitutional in Part)	The citing case declares unconstitutional in part the statute, rule or regulation you are *Shepardizing*.
V	(Void or Invalid)	The citing case declares void or invalid the statute, rule, regulation or order you are *Shepardizing* because it conflicts with an authority that takes priority.
Va	(Valid)	The citing case upholds the validity of the statute, rule, regulation or order you are *Shepardizing*.
Vp	(Void or Invalid in Part)	The citing case declares void or invalid part of the statute, rule, regulation, or order you are *Shepardizing* because it conflicts with an authority that takes priority.

SPECIAL SYMBOL FOR CONCURRING OPINIONS

~	(Concurring Opinion)	A concurring opinion cites the statute, rule or regulation you are *Shepardizing*.

SPECIAL SYMBOL FOR CALIFORNIA CASES

The citing case is of questionable precedential value because review or rehearing has been granted by the California Supreme Court and/or the citing case has been ordered depublished pursuant to Rule 976 of the California Rules of Court. (Publication status should be verified before use of the citing case in California.)

SPECIAL SYMBOL FOR DATES OF UNITED STATES CODE AND CFR PROVISIONS

* followed by a year refers to the United States Code or CFR edition, when year is cited.
△ followed by a year indicates the date of the citing reference, when year is not cited.

FIGURE 9-5 Shepard's Statutory Citator Page

UNITED STATES CODE 198? and 1994 Eds. TITLE 18 § 700

857F2d523
937F2d461
945F2d1075
969F2d775
9F3d68
11F3d120
22F3d942
C 40F3d1000
59F3d940
661FS723
789FS346
918FS1383
Cir. 10
799F2d619
53F3d1108
64F3d1515
79F3d994
814FS1528
149FRD647
Cir. 11
905F2d352
907FS402
§ 666 (a)
Cir. 2
4F3d108
Cir. 4
874F2d217
Cir. 5
841F2d575
930F2d1091
987F2d1136
659FS834
687FS1049
727FS1069
C 816FS1136
Cir. 6
63F3d463
Cir. 7
957F2d1393
982F2d1105
Cir. 10
53F3d1110
§ 666 (a) (1)
Cir. 6
63F3d462
66F3d129
§ 666 (a) (1) (A)
Cir. 2
979F2d936
55F3d723
784FS63
Cir. 5
987F2d1137
80F3d1055
C 816FS1134
Cir. 6
966F2d186

Cir. 9
11F3d121
40F3d1001
§ 666 (a) (1) (A) (1)
Cir. 3
990F2d101
Cir. 5
727FS1070
Cir. 6
63F3d462
66F3d127
§ 666 (a) (1) (A) (2)
Cir. 5
727FS1070
Cir. 6
63F3d462
Cir. 9
40F3d1001
§ 666 (a) (1) (B)
Cir. 2
996F2d18
4F3d104
37F3d849
57F3d172
73F3d485
795FS1268
809FS1002
809FS1010
833FS204
Cir. 3
938F2d443
10F3d981
Cir. 5
841F2d577
987F2d1137
80F3d1055
Cir. 6
966F2d188
Cir. 7
913F2d1259
46F3d27
Cir. 9
937F2d463
§ 666 (a) (2)
Cir. 1
983F2d1153
Cir. 2
909F2d63
996F2d19
4F3d104
42F3d99
57F3d169
57F3d172
784FS63

794FS530
842FS1535
913FS704
Cir. 4
11F3d430
Cir. 5
889F2d1369
687FS1048
781FS1183
C 816FS1134
Cir. 7
777FS1397
Cir. 10
36F3d946
Cir. 11
C 907FS402
§ 666 (b)
Cir. 2
986F2d33
4F3d104
55F3d729
784FS63
794FS530
913FS705
Cir. 3
874F2d180
938F2d443
Cir. 4
11F3d434
Cir. 5
841F2d574
846F2d968
889F2d1369
930F2d1091
987F2d1136
659FS834
687FS1048
727FS1070
C 816FS1137
Cir. 6
63F3d462
Cir. 8
977F2d1232
Cir. 9
857F2d521
937F2d463
11F3d121
40F3d1000
§ 666 (c)
Cir. 2
979F2d936
C 987F2d896
996F2d21
4F3d104
651FS1035
815FS619
913FS711
Cir. 5
987F2d1137

727FS1072
C 816FS1137
Cir. 6
63F3d465
Cir. 7
868F2d936
Cir. 8
915FS1477
Cir. 9
11F3d121
40F3d1000
Cir. 10
799F2d619
§ 666 (d)
Cir. 2
4F3d109
Cir. 9
857F2d523
Cir. 10
799F2d620
§ 666 (d) (1)
Cir. 2
851FS508
Cir. 3
990F2d101
Cir. 9
40F3d1001
§ 666 (d) (2)
Cir. 2
913FS707
Cir. 5
987F2d1137
727FS1070
Cir. 9
857F2d523
Cir. 10
799F2d620
§ 666 (d) (3)
Cir. 10
799F2d620
§ 666 (d) (4)
Cir. 2
851FS508
Cir. 4
11F3d434
Cir. 9
857F2d523
969F2d775
Cir. 10
799F2d620
§ 666 (d) (5)
Cir. 2
897FS113

Cir. 6
63F3d463
§ 667
Ad 98St2149
§ 687
487US255
101LE237
108SC2373
§ 688
122LE222
113SC865
§ 700 et seq.
Cir. 1
531F2d1087
§ 700
Ad 82St291
394US604
459US949
Up 496US312
22LE592
74LE207
U 110LE292
129LE520
89SC1372
103SC267
U 110SC2406
114SC2461
128FRD300
136FRD238
Cir. DC
445F2d226
511F2d1312
U 731FS1125
Cir. 1
343FS165
397FS263
Cir. 2
324FS1278
Cir. 3
765FS188
Cir. 4
313FS49
317FS138
322FS593
Cir. 5
479F2d1177
Cir. 8
C 897F2d918
Cir. 9
462F2d96
C 302FS1112
U 731FS416
790FS221
Cir. 11
758F2d1481
560FS546
105LE812n
105LE816n

41A3504n
§ 700 (a)
415US582
491US427
496US314
39LE617
105LE369
U 110LE293
94SC1251
109SC2551
U 110SC2407
Cir. DC
445F2d226
C 454F2d972
Cir. 2
324FS1278
385FS167
Cir. 5
479F2d1179
407FS497
Cir. 9
C 462F2d96
Cir. 11
739F2d571
571FS1025
§ 700 (a) (1)
496US317
U 110LE295
U 110SC2409
Cir. DC
U 731FS1125
Cir. 9
U 731FS417
§ 700 (a) (2)
496US317
U 110LE295
U 110SC2409
Cir. DC
U 731FS1125
Cir. 9
U 731FS417
§ 700 (b)
496US314
U 110LE294
U 110SC2407
Cir. DC
445F2d226
U 731FS1125
Cir. 9
C 462F2d96
U 731FS417
§ 700 (c)
394US598
22LE588
89SC1369
Cir. 4
322FS585

521

A Point to Remember

Shepard's provides excellent explanations of how to use its resources along with complete tables of abbreviations. This information is found in the preface if you are using *Shepard's* in print and in the "Help" menu on the online service. You can also find out more about *Shepard's* by visiting the website at http://law.lexisnexis.com/shepards.

For a summary of Shepardizing in print, see Box 9-4.

BOX 9-4 SHEPARDIZING IN PRINT

- ✔ Note the citation to be Shepardized.
- ✔ Locate all relevant *Shepard's* volumes, including supplements and advance sheets.
- ✔ Check "What your library should contain ..." on the cover of supplements.
- ✔ Locate the first appearance of your authority in *Shepard's*.
- ✔ Check your citation in all supplements and advance sheets.
- ✔ Interpret or analyze your findings.
- ✔ Review the tables of abbreviations in the front of books, if necessary.
- ✔ If Shepardizing case law, repeat this process with all parallel cites.

Shepard's Citators on Lexis Advance

Shepard's Online is much easier to use than *Shepard's* in print and offers many advantages. Some of these advantages include the following:

- Information is current, so there is no need to check supplements or updates.
- Information provided under all parallel citations is the same, so a case must be checked only once.
- Negative information, such as overruling, is highlighted at the beginning.
- Citing information can be displayed selectively (i.e., only negative treatment).
- Treatment of the case is explained in normal terminology rather than abbreviations.
- Hyperlinks to citing authorities are provided.
- *Shepard's* can be accessed by hyperlinking from the Lexis Advance online version of the case.

Because of the numerous advantages and greater reliability of information, *Shepard's* Online is by far the preferred method of Shepardizing a case or other authority.

On Lexis Advance, *Shepard's* can be accessed in different ways. On a search bar at the top of the home screen, users can go directly to *Shepard's* with a citation. See Figure 9-6. Alternatively, a researcher can access *Shepard's* from any case or code section. A *Shepard's* signal advising or warning the researcher of the Shepard results appears near the top of the screen. A researcher will generally see either a red "stop sign" or a yellow "caution" sign. These signs appear if there is any negative treatment of the case. (If you use your cursor to "hover" over any sign, you will see an explanation of the sign.) A red stop sign with a case means that at least one point of law in the case is no longer good law. Often it means that the case was overruled. A yellow caution sign means the case has received negative treatment from another case. A red stop sign near a code section means that at some time the section was either repealed or found unconstitutional. This does not always mean the law is no longer valid, as the law may have been amended to correct the problem. See Figure 9-7.

> **A Point to Remember**
>
> You should never rely solely on the Shepard's signal. It is always important to read the law itself.

Rather than using the abbreviations that you see in Shepard's in print, when you access Shepard's on Lexis Advance, for cases you will see full terms such as "overruled" or "questioned." For code sections, you will see terms such as "unconstitutional." An additional online feature is the ability to focus or narrow the Shepard's result by categories, such as jurisdiction, headnote, or date. This cannot be

FIGURE 9-6 Lexis Advance Homepage Showing Lexis Access

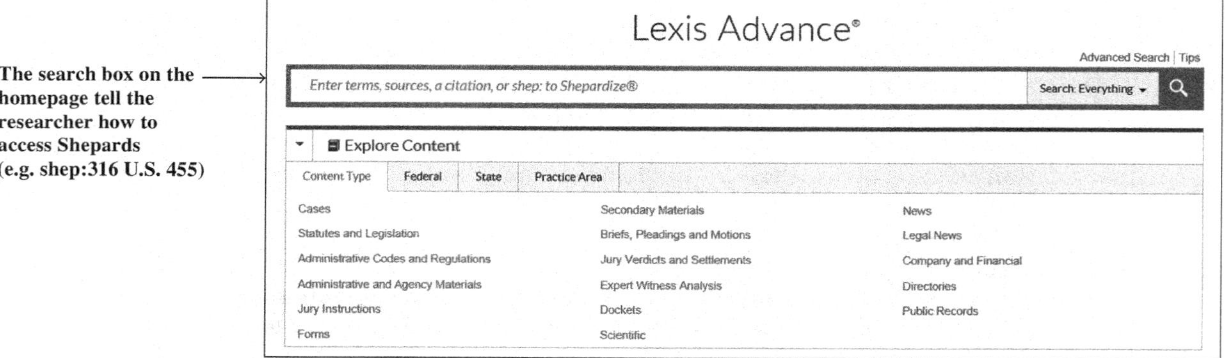

FIGURE 9-7 Lexis Advance Shepard's Case Signal

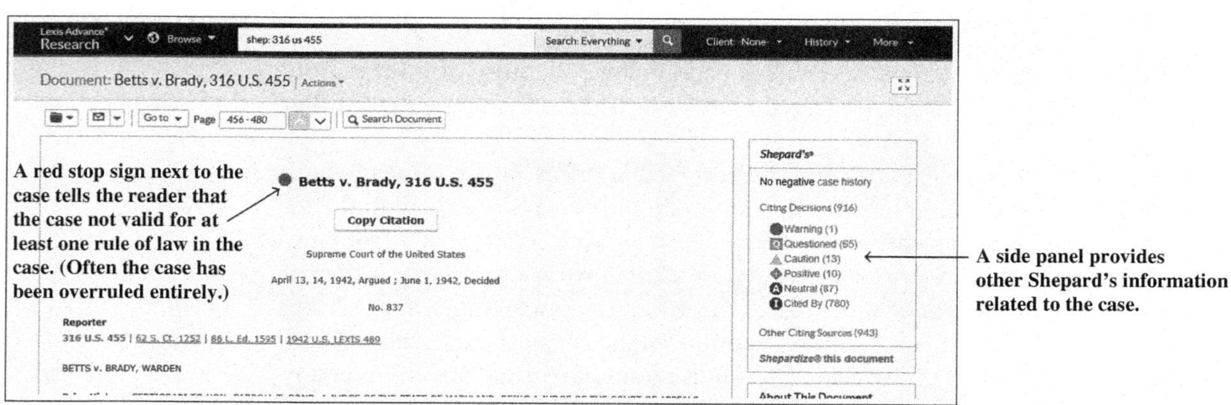

done with Shepard's in print. Another unique feature to the online case Shepard's is the "table of authorities." You can use this feature to see a list of all the authorities referenced by the court in its decision. See Figure 9-8A and 9-8B.

Although Shepard's has traditionally been primarily a "citator" used to validate research, many of the online features make it a valuable research tool. The ease of hyperlinking to other law found on a Shepard's results page makes it easy to locate other law. In addition, the following features also contribute to its value as a research tool:

- ✔ Ability to narrow or focus results to a specific jurisdiction
- ✔ Ability to narrow or focus case results to points of law in specific headnotes
- ✔ Ability to narrow or focus case results by type of result
- ✔ The table of authorities with case results that provides past cases relied upon by the court

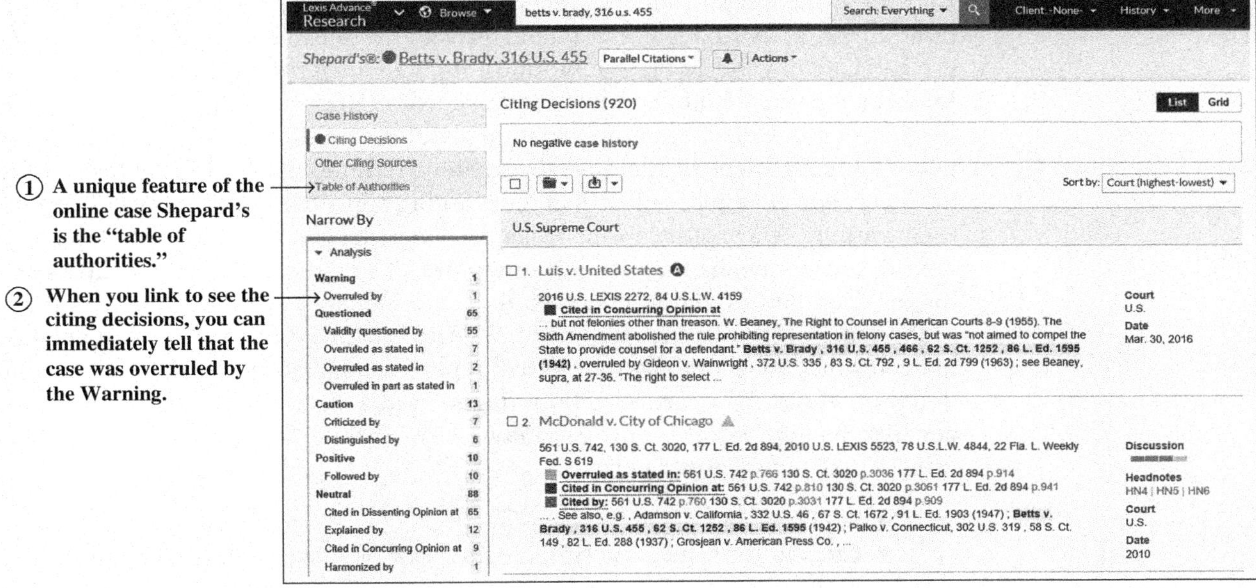

FIGURE 9-8A Lexis Advance Shepard's Case Report

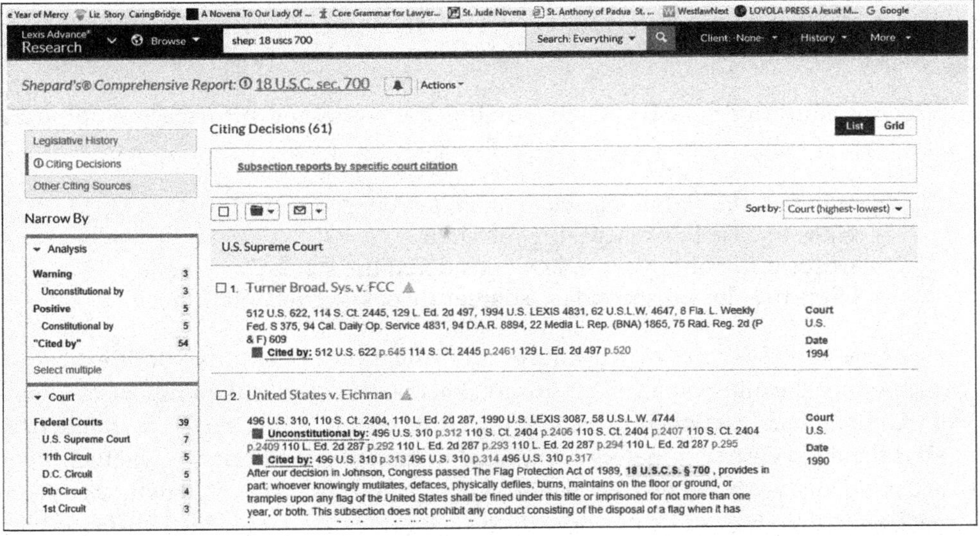

FIGURE 9-8B Lexis Advance Shepard's Statutory Report for 18 U.S.C. sec. 700

See Box 9-5 for a checklist for Shepardizing online.

BOX 9-5 SHEPARDIZING ONLINE

- ✔ Note the citation to be Shepardized and access Lexis Advance.
- ✔ Use the search bar to access *Shepard's* results for the citation or access the case or other authority and link to the Shepard's signal.
- ✔ Use the "Help" feature, if necessary.
- ✔ Analyze or interpret the results.

9-3 KEYCITE

KeyCite is the citator found on the Westlaw website. KeyCite is not available in print. Since *Shepard's* is not available through the Westlaw site, researchers must use KeyCite to validate legal authorities. As with *Shepard's,* you can use KeyCite to check a case, statute, administrative decision, or regulation to determine if it is still good law. The basic information about the validity of any legal authority is the same on *Shepard's* and KeyCite. Some terminology and icons may differ, however. For example, rather than the warning signs used on *Shepard's,* KeyCite uses warning "flags" to alert the researcher to problems with the case. A red flag next to a case means that at least one point of law discussed in the case is no longer good law. A yellow flag next to a case indicates some negative treatment of the case, but the case is still good law. A red flag next to a statute or regulation indicates that the statute was amended, repealed, superseded, or held unconstitutional in whole or in part. A yellow flag next to a statute or regulation warns of negative history, but it is still good law. Also, as with *Shepard's,* the researcher using KeyCite for cases can find:

- Parallel cites
- Cites to the same case (if there are prior or subsequent reported decisions in the same action)
- Cites to all other cases discussing your citation
- Description of how other cases have considered your case citation
- Cites to selected secondary sources discussing your citation
- A table of authorities for cases and other authorities used within the court opinion.

For statutory law, KeyCite provides the following information about the citation:

- Whether the statute has been amended or repealed
- Cites to case law discussing the statute
- Description of how case law considered the statute
- Cites to selected secondary sources discussing the citation

One added feature of KeyCite is an evaluation of the citing authorities (the cases citing the cite you are KeyCiting). This is reflected in the number of "depth of treatment bars" assigned to each of the citing cases. In this way, a researcher can tell if the cited case was merely mentioned in the citing authority or whether it was discussed and analyzed in great detail. (One bar indicates the cited authority is just mentioned, two bars indicate some discussion, three stars indicate substantial discussion, and four bars indicate extensive discussion. See the "bars" in Figure 9-10.)

As with Shepard's, KeyCite can be accessed in different ways. Once you are signed on to the Westlaw database, you can enter the citation in the search box, preceded with kc: (See Figure 9-9). Alternatively, when you access a case or statute, you can link from any KeyCite warning flag to the full KeyCite analysis. See Figures 9-9, 9-10, and 9-11 for KeyCite as viewed on Westlaw.

Enter the citation in the search box, preceded by kc, and you will go to KeyCite for the case.

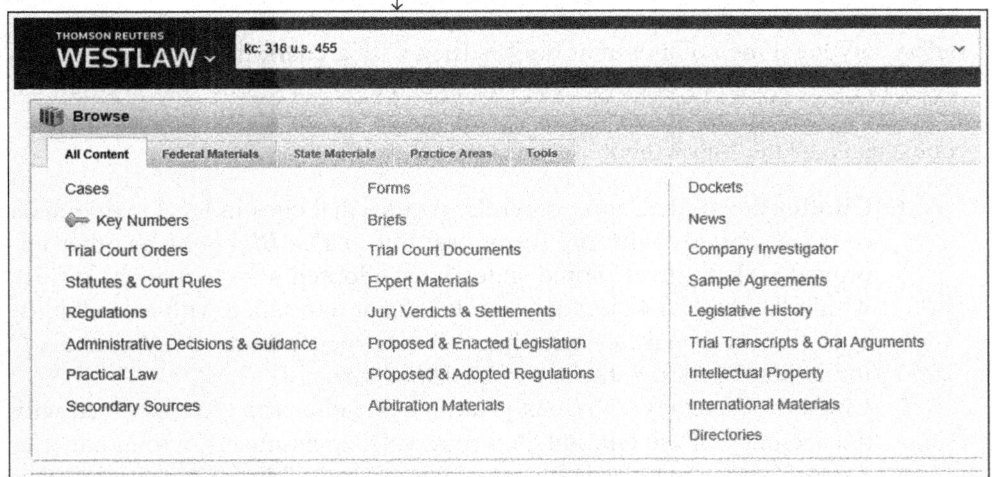

FIGURE 9-9 Westlaw Start Page

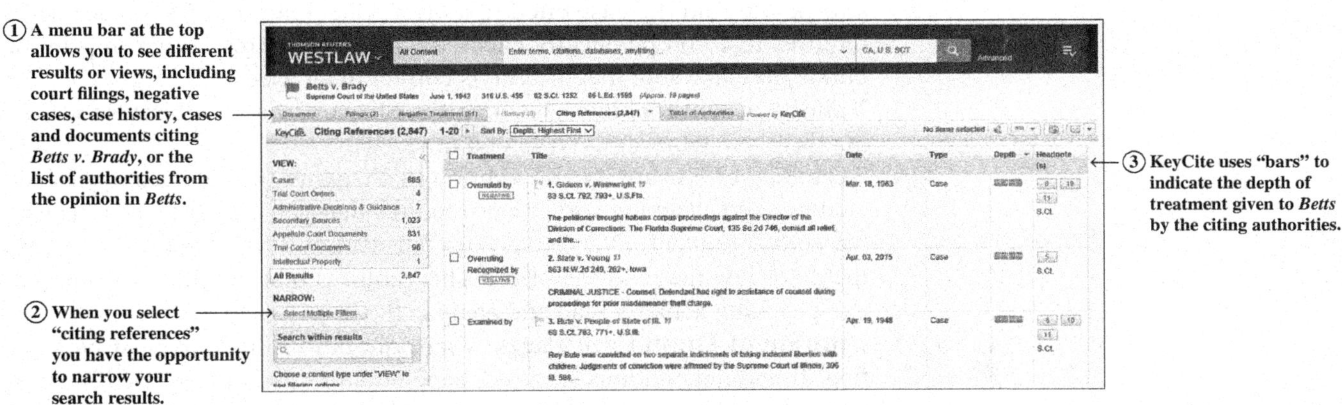

FIGURE 9-10 Westlaw KeyCite Case Results

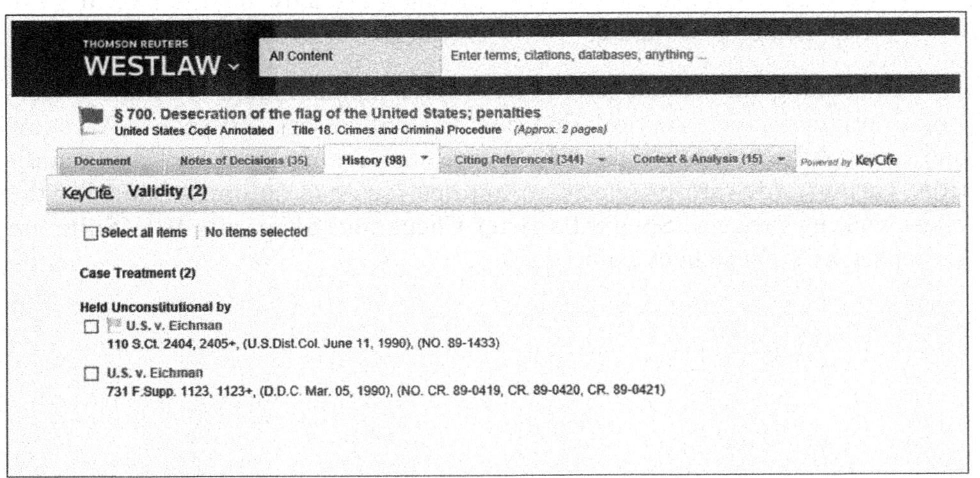

FIGURE 9-11 Westlaw KeyCite Statutory Results.

9-4 BCITE

Bloomberg Law allows researchers to conduct citation analysis for cases with its unique BCite feature. Researchers can see the direct history of the case, how the case has been cited by other cases and related legal documents, and a table of authorities for the case. The feature can be accessed from the case by linking on a menu bar near the top of the screen or a side panel.

9-5 CITE CHECKING A DOCUMENT

Before any legal memorandum or brief is filed with a court, the document is normally reviewed and all citations are checked. This task is one that is often assigned to a research assistant such as a paralegal or law clerk. When a document is "cite checked," the following items must be verified.

1. **Citation Format:** Courts generally require that cites in legal memoranda or briefs comply with the format set out in *The Bluebook* or other approved style manual. Some states have adopted a style manual for use within the state. All citations in a document to be filed with a court must be reviewed to make certain they are in proper format. (See Appendix C for an introduction to the use of *The Bluebook.*)
2. **Citation Accuracy:** Obviously, attorneys and courts are concerned with the accuracy of the citation. A wrong volume number, a wrong page, or a wrong series in a case cite can make it impossible for a judge or other attorney to find the case cited in a brief. Checking for citation accuracy requires that you physically check the primary source, either in print or online, to make sure that the cite is correct in all aspects.
3. **Validity of Authorities:** This involves Shepardizing or otherwise verifying the cited authority is still good law.
4. **Accuracy of Authority:** In addition to checking for the accuracy of the citation, cite checking sometimes requires that you check the accuracy of the authority itself. Does a case or code section really support the statements of law made in the brief? This requires that the person doing the cite checking actually read and analyze the law.
5. **Citation of Quotation:** Pages where quotations appear must be verified. If parallel citations are used, page numbers must be verified in those citations.
6. **Accuracy of Quotations:** Quotations must also be checked for accuracy. Any language quoted in a brief must match exactly the language found in a quoted case or statute.

It is a long and tedious job to cite check a memorandum or brief by referring to original sources entirely in print. The online services, such as Westlaw and Lexis Advance, can make this a much easier and quicker task. In addition, various software programs or applications can automate much of the cite-checking process. Shepard's Brief Check and Shepard's BriefSuite are examples, as is Westcheck.com.

Finding It Online

Extensive information about *Shepard's* can be found at the following:

http://www.lexisnexis.com/shepards/

http://www.lexisnexis.com/en-us/home.page (search for "shepards")

Information about KeyCite can be found at:

http://legalsolutions.thomsonreuters.com/law-products/support/

Look for brochures, user guides, or online tutorials. Also, search the sites for information regarding software downloads that can be used to automatically cite check documents. Lexis and Thomson frequently change specific URLs. If you have difficulty finding information about the products try searching Google for "lexis shepards citations" or "Westlaw keycite".

If you can access either Westlaw or Lexis Advance, use the "Help" features to learn more about using KeyCite or *Shepard's*.

Additional information about BCite can be found at:

http://about.bloomberglaw.com/
Look for Product Features.

Some of these sites also provide free trial subscriptions.

CITATION MATTERS

INTRODUCTORY SIGNALS

***THE BLUEBOOK*—RULE 1.2**

The purpose of a signal is to alert the reader to something. Signals are used to show support, suggest a comparison, indicate a contradiction, and indicate background materials. These signals must be italicized. However, when a signal is used as a verb in a sentence, it is not italicized.

Examples of signals used to show *support*:

- ***No signal*** —indicates the cited authority (a) directly states the proposition, (b) shows the source of quoted language, or (c) identifies the authority cited in the text.

- ***E.g.,*** —is used to show that the cited material states the proposition presented in the sentence; other materials also state the same proposition, but a citation to them is not helpful or is not necessary. This signal is often used in combination with other signals, for example: *See, e.g.,*.

- ***See*** —is used instead of "no signal" when the proposition presented is not *exactly* stated by the authority cited, but it clearly follows from it. This signal alerts the reader that there is an *inferential step* between the proposition and the cited authority.

- ***See also*** —is used to show that the cited authority is additional support for the proposition presented.

- ***Cf.*** —is used when the writer needs the reader to understand that the cited authority provides material that is analogous with the main proposition.

Example of a signal used to suggest a *comparison*:

- ***Compare*** —is used to show that comparison of the authorities offers support for the proposition presented. Parenthetical explanations often follow these authorities.

Examples of signals that indicate a *contradiction*:

- ***Contra*** —is used to show that the cited authority *states* the contrary of the proposition.
- ***But see*** —is used to show that the cited authority *supports* a position that is contrary to the writer's main position.

Example of a signal that indicates *background material*:

- ***See generally*** —is used to show that the cited authority offers background information related to the proposition.

Example of a signal used as a *verb*:

- *See Wisconsin v. Mitchell,* 508 U.S. 476 (1993). (*See* used as a signal.)
- See *Wisconsin v. Mitchell,* 508 U.S. 476 (1993) for an explanation of what made the statute at issue unconstitutionally overbroad. (*See* used as a verb.)

CHAPTER **SUMMARY**

Citators are a type of legal research material that allows the researcher to determine if certain legal authorities are still good law. Citators lead the researcher to additional authorities dealing with the same legal issues. The most well-known citators are published by *Shepard's. Shepard's* publishes citators for all jurisdictions and for many different types of legal authorities, including cases, constitutions, statutes, and selected secondary sources. *Shepard's* is available in print and online. An alternative citator, KeyCite, is available online through Westlaw. KeyCite has many of the same features as *Shepard's.* Researchers often use citators to help cite check a memorandum or brief that is to be filed with the court. In addition to checking whether an authority is still good law, cite checking requires that one check citation format, citation accuracy, accuracy of the authority, and accuracy of quotations.

TERMS TO **REMEMBER**

good law
validate
citators
Shepardize
cited authority
citing authority

QUESTIONS FOR **REVIEW**

1. What is a citator?
2. What types of authorities can be Shepardized?
3. What information is found in *Shepard's* case citators?
4. What is the difference between cited authority and citing authority?
5. If a case has parallel cites, is it necessary to Shepardize all cites? Explain.
6. What is the difference between the history of the case and the treatment of the case?
7. How does *Shepard's* use headnote numbers in its case citators?
8. What are some of the differences between *Shepard's* in print and *Shepard's* online?
9. What is KeyCite?
10. What must a person do to cite check a document?

CAN YOU **FIGURE IT OUT?**

1. Refer to Figures 9-1 and 9-2. Find the case of *Betts v. Brady*.
   a. What is the cite for the U.S. Supreme Court case to overrule *Betts v. Brady?*
   b. Do any cases in the *Federal Reporter 2d* from the Third Circuit cite this case in dissenting opinions?
   c. What are the reporter citations for all the cases Shepardized on this page?
2. Refer to Figure 9-5.
   a. Find 18 U.S.C. § 700. What has the U.S. Supreme Court said about this section?
   b. Give the *Lawyers' Edition* cite for a case to discuss 18 U.S.C. § 700 (c).

TEST **YOURSELF** (Check Your Answers in Appendix G)

1. Shepardize *United States v. Bramblett,* 348 U.S. 503 (1955). Answer the following questions.
   a. What are the parallel cites?
   b. What are the lower court citations for this case?
   c. Give all parallel cites for the case that overruled *Bramblett.*
   d. What is the full name of the *Bramblett* case?
   e. What is the citation for the case from the Eighth Circuit that questioned *Bramblett?*
   f. What is the citation for an *A.L.R.* annotation where the case is mentioned?
2. Shepardize and identify the problem with the following case: *Bowers v. Hardwick,* 478 U.S. 186 (1986).

TEST **YOURSELF**—WRITE IT RIGHT Turning Facts into a Statement of Facts

Telling a story (using facts well) can be a challenge. One must consider order, relevance, importance, and how much the reader needs to know. In general, we do not write a Statement of Facts until we understand the law that will be applied to the facts. It is only then that the writer knows which facts are legally relevant. Also, the purpose of the document containing the Statement of Facts helps to set up if the statement should be simply informative or if it should be persuasive. For now, let's consider the informative Statement of Facts. After a client interview, you know the following:

1. Your client, Ms. Janice Farmer, was injured when she tripped.
2. She was walking on Main Street, Sunny Valley, ID, when she tripped on a piece of raised concrete.
3. Her knee required surgery, and she may undergo a second related surgery soon.
4. It was a cloudy day but there was a lot of glare, so she wore dark sunglasses.
5. She was wearing flip flops.
6. She did not see a city sign advising her to avoid this part of the sidewalk.
7. She was on her phone when she tripped.
8. A business owner came out to help her and called for medical help.
9. This business owner told her several people had tripped right there in the last month, and that is why the sign said to avoid that part of the side walk.

The relevant state code section says, in pertinent part, that a city is responsible for maintenance of its sidewalks. Once a city is alerted to a dangerous condition, the city must take action to repair or secure the area in question.

The Statement of Facts might look like this:

> Ms. Janice Farmer injured her knee when she tripped and fell over a piece of raised concrete, on Main Street, Sunny Valley, ID. The City had posted the area with a sign advising pedestrians to avoid that part of the sidewalk. Ms. Farmer did not see this sign.
>
> Ms. Farmer was wearing flip flops and talking on her cell phone when the trip occurred. A local business owner came to her assistance after her fall. He said that others had tripped in this same location and that is why the city put up the warning sign.
>
> Ms. Farmer has undergone one surgery and may face a follow-up surgery soon.

Now, You Try It

(Check your answers in Appendix G)

Client Facts:

1. Your client, Ralph Smith, was injured when a City bus struck him.
2. Mr. Smith has a broken hip and a broken arm.
3. He has medical bill he cannot pay.
4. He may need more surgery.
5. He needs physical therapy.
6. The bus turned on a red light.
7. The bus did not stop before making the turn.

8. Mr. Smith says he stepped out when the "walk" signal came on—it indicated he has 25 seconds to cross the street.
9. He remembers seeing the seconds change to 21 just before the bus struck him.

The Law: negligence is a tort. To prove negligence, Mr. Smith must prove that the bus driver (1) had a duty to drive safely, (2) breached that duty, (3) caused the accident, and (4) injured Mr. Smith.

Write the Statement of Facts.

CITATION **EXERCISES**

Use Appendix C and the Citation Matters feature in this chapter to answer these questions.

1. What is the purpose of a signal?
2. Which *Bluebook* rule explains introductory signals?
3. List and define or explain each of the signals listed in the Citation Matters feature in this chapter.

FROM THE **WRITER'S CORNER** Placement of Words in a Sentence

1. Good writers strive to place the working words in what order?
2. Rewrite this sentence: The roast was carved by Richard.

ASSIGNMENTS AND **ACTIVITIES**

Research Exercises

1. Shepardize the case at 279 U.S. 263.
   a. What is the case name?
   b. What are the parallel cites?
   c. Give all the parallel cites for the case that overruled it.
   d. Give the cite of a case from the Ninth Circuit that harmonized with the cite.
   e. Give the cite to a *Stanford Law Review* that mentioned the case.
2. Shepardize 18 U.S.C. § 242.
   a. Give the citations for the *Statutes at Large* in which this section was amended.
   b. Give the citation for the U.S. Supreme Court case in volume 515 of the *U.S. Reports* that mentions this section.
   c. Give the cites for California cases that list this section as questionable precedent.
3. All of the following contain problems—Shepardize and identify the problem.
   a. *Ford Motor Co. v. Department of Treasury of Indiana,* 323 U.S. 459 (1945).
   b. *Penry v. Lynaugh,* 492 U.S. 302 (1989).
   c. Walton *v. Arizona,* 497 U.S. 639 (1990).
   d. *Ohio v. Roberts,* 448 U.S. 56 (1980).
   e. Va. Code Ann. § 18.2-423.

Analysis Assignments

4. Review Boxes 9-2 and 9-3. What information would be helpful in using *Shepard's* as a research tool? Explain.

Online Research Exercises

5. If you can access KeyCite or *Shepard's*, answer the following:
   a. 514 U.S. 549
      i What is the name of this case?
      ii Why is there a warning sign for this case?
      iii Is the case still good law?
   b. 18 U.S.C. § 922 (q)
      i When was this law last amended?
      ii What is the name of the 2005 U.S. Supreme Court case to cite this statute in a dissenting opinion?
   c. Using Google Scholar (http://scholar.google.com/), locate *Betts v. Brady* (316 U.S. 455). Locate and click on the link "How cited." Describe the result list. Without reading any of the cases cited, can you determine if the case was overruled?

CASE **PROJECT**

1. Shepardize any cases and statutes that you found previously in working on the case project. Have any cases been overruled? Make a list of any cases that question or criticize your cases. Read these.

IN-CLASS SMALL GROUP WORK

a. In small groups cite check the following Memorandum of Points and Authorities for format. Refer to Appendix C for proper citation format.

b. Using Westlaw, Lexis Advance, or the library, check each cite for accuracy. (You can also try using free online case databases, such as Google Scholar or Justia.) Also check each quotation for accuracy.

ATLAS INSURANCE COMPANY,	)	
A corporation,	)	
Plaintiff,	)	No. 12345
	)	
v.	)	MEMORANDUM OF POINTS &
	)	AUTHORITIES
SAVAGE RIDER, et al.	)	
Defendants	)	

Facts

The defendant was involved in a motor vehicle accident on June 23 of the previous year with an uninsured vehicle. Defendant Rider was operating a motorcycle owned by his roommate Motorcycle Murphy. This vehicle was not covered by insurance either. However, Rider did have a policy of automobile insurance, which policy is the subject of this lawsuit. The insurance policy in question covers Rider while he is operating another vehicle, as long as that vehicle is not owned by a "member of his household."

From the deposition testimony, it is clear that Rider and Murphy had a typical roommate relationship. They shared rent on an apartment. However, they each led their own social lives and had their own friends. Murphy in fact had a girlfriend and spent much of his time with her, away from the apartment. Meals were seldom shared by the defendant and his roommate.

Issue

Are roommates, who are unrelated and live separate lives, "members of the same household" under the exclusion provision of an insurance policy?

Argument

1. A "HOUSEHOLD" REQUIRES A FAMILIAL BOND, NOT JUST A JOINT RESIDENCE

In their complaint, plaintiffs state that the basis of the controversy is the fact that Savage Rider was driving a vehicle owned by a member of his household. The courts in various jurisdictions, including California, have clearly held that the mere fact that two persons reside under the same roof does not make them members of the same household. Rather a more familial or social bond is required. See *Island v. Fireman's Fund Indemnity Co.,* 30 C.2d 540 at 547–8. As the Supreme Court has stated, "Persons who dwell together as a family constitute a 'household'." *Arthur v. Morton* 112 U.S. 495, 500.

A case on point with the one here is *Bartholet v. Berkness* (Minn.), 189 N.W. 2d 410. In this case, the court held that two unmarried and unrelated men, dwelling in the same living quarters and sharing expenses but having separate and independent social lives, were not members of the same household. And in a Texas case, the court stated:

> A rather unreasonable and ridiculous result follows from an attempt to ascribe to the term "household" in the phrase under consideration the meaning of a building or structure, or to ascribe to the term resident a meaning which would embrace any and all persons who sleep within or take meals at such structure … .
>
> This court reached the conclusion that similar use of the term "household" connoted a "family" or a group of persons who habitually reside under one roof and form one domestic circle.

State Farm Mutual Automobile Insurance Company v. Walker (1960, Tex. Civ. App.) 334 S.W.2d 458, 463–464. *See also Giakares v. Kincade* (1961. Mo.) 330 S.W.2d 633 wherein a grandmother was held not to be a member of the same household as her grandchildren even though living under the same roof.

2. ANY AMBIGUITY IN THE INSURANCE POLICY MUST BE INTERPRETED AGAINST THE INSURANCE COMPANY AND IN FAVOR OF THE INSURED

Clearly, in the common, ordinary meaning of the words, as well as by judicial interpretation of them, "members or residents of the same household" must have more of a relationship than just "roommates." At most in the case at hand plaintiffs could contend that there is some ambiguity as to the meaning of the words. However, even if that were true, plaintiff could not prevail. It is a cardinal rule that where any ambiguity exists in an insurance policy it must be resolved in favor of the policy holder, not the insurance company. *Island v. Fireman's Fund Indemnity Co.,* 184 Pac. 153 at 159. *See also Juzefsky v. Western Cas. & Surety Co.,* 324 Pac. 2d 929.

3. DEFENDANT AND HIS ROOMMATE ARE NOT MEMBERS OF THE SAME HOUSEHOLD FOR PURPOSES OF THE INSURANCE POLICY

Defendant and his roommate should not be considered members of the same household. The purpose of an exclusionary provision in an insurance policy such as the one here is to avoid multiple coverage of several vehicles owned by members of the same family, who, by their close intimacy, might be expected to use each other's vehicles without hindrance and with or without the permission of another, thus increasing the liability of the insurer without benefit or added premium. The facts of this case show that the defendant, Rider, and his roommate, Murphy, led very separate and independent lives. Murphy's vehicle was not made freely available for Rider's use. In fact, Rider had only used it once, the day of the accident. Further, the motorcycle was generally kept at the house of Murphy's parents. In addition, there was no way that Rider could have obtained insurance for the motorcycle, as he had no insurable interest therein.

Conclusion

The objectives of the exclusionary provisions would not be properly served by applying the exclusion to the instant case. Judgment should be entered in favor of defendant.

chapter **ten**

INTRODUCTION TO LEXIS ADVANCE, WESTLAW, AND BLOOMBERG LAW

SKILL OBJECTIVES FOR CHAPTER 10

When you complete chapter 10, you should be able to

- List the steps the researcher should follow when preparing to research on either Lexis Advance or Westlaw.
- Distinguish Boolean searching from natural language searching.
- Discuss the benefits of full-text searching.
- Identify the types of materials on Lexis Advance and Westlaw.
- Explain the various ways to access and retrieve documents on Lexis Advance and Westlaw.
- Develop a search query for a legal research question.
- Explain the benefits and concerns associated with the use of Lexis Advance or Westlaw.

CHAPTER OUTLINE

From the Desk of W. J. Bryan, Esq.

TO: Research Assistant
FROM: W. J. Bryan
RE: Our Client, Justin Meyers
DATE:

Attached is a copy of the memorandum of points and authorities to be filed in support of our motion to suppress evidence in the Meyers case. Before filing it, I want to be sure we are complying with all of the local rules of court. Please check these rules for me. You can probably find the rules of court on the court's website or on Lexis Advance or Westlaw.

There is a second matter I want you to research. Motions in criminal cases are heard by only two judges in the local court, Judge Susan Templeton or Judge R. J. Guzman. Please see what you can find out about them. You can do a judicial profile on Westlaw.

10-1 INTRODUCTION

In Chapters 1 through 9, you read about the case reporters, code books, and various other materials used by legal researchers. For many years, these materials were available only in print. As a result, if lawyers wanted quick and easy access to the law, they maintained substantial legal libraries in their offices. The alternative was to complete their legal research at a law school or county law library. Modern technology and the Internet provide another alternative. Fee-based websites such as those provided by LexisNexis and Thomson Reuters/West and numerous free websites provide access to both federal and state law. Lawyers are no longer required to keep hundreds, or in some cases thousands, of volumes of legal books in their offices. Nor are they limited to standard library hours in which to accomplish their research. Furthermore, these online sources offer search methods and capabilities that are impossible using traditional methods of legal research. In addition to the Internet, many print sources are available on disk (either CD or DVD). This format allows attorneys to store voluminous materials in small spaces and provides the enhanced capabilities of computer search methods.

Because online databases and disks are accessed with a computer, searching materials in these formats is often referred to as ***computer-assisted legal research (CALR)***. The computer adds a great deal of flexibility and convenience to the research process. It also gives the researcher access to many materials not otherwise available. On the other hand, CALR is not without its difficulties.

computer-assisted legal research (CALR)
Legal research done with the use of a computer; includes the use of CD-ROM, online services such as Lexis Advance and Westlaw, the Internet, and intranets.

While it is beyond the scope of this text to discuss every source and every search feature found on Lexis Advance and Westlaw (previously called WestlawNext), this chapter provides an introduction to the major fee-based legal websites. This chapter also briefly discusses a third database, Bloomberg Law. (Detailed explanations of all features of these programs are available from Westlaw, Lexis, and Bloomberg on their websites and is available without cost.) Chapter 11 discusses the use of the free Internet for legal research.

10-2 PREPARING TO SEARCH

If you are using an online source such as Lexis Advance or Westlaw, you must prepare to research just as you do when researching materials in print. This is even more important when researching on a fee-based service where you may be charged for the time you spend on the service. Unless you have a citation to a specific legal resource, your research process for using these databases will be more precise if it includes the following steps.

- Understand your research assignment.
- Review all available facts.
- Identify all key facts.
- Identify legal issues.
- List words describing your key facts and legal issues.
- Consider synonyms, antonyms, and variations of all words listed.
- Consider the relationship among the words (i.e., should two or more words appear in the same sentence, the same paragraph, etc.).
- Develop your search question.
- Choose the type of material to be searched (i.e., federal or state cases or codes).

As with all legal research, adequate preparation will make your research much more efficient and successful. Review Box 10-1.

BOX 10-1 PROCEDURE FOR ONLINE SEARCHING

✔ Determine contents of available databases.
✔ Identify the proper jurisdiction.
✔ Identify database(s) containing the relevant source of law (case law, codes, etc.).
✔ Identify relevant words and phrases.
✔ Formulate search query.
✔ Review results.
✔ Validate results.

10-3 FULL-TEXT SEARCHING ON LEXIS ADVANCE AND WESTLAW

One major advantage of websites provided by Lexis Advance and Westlaw is the ability to do a ***full-text search***. Full-text searching involves searching the text of the legal material rather than relying on an index. For example, full-text searching of case law means searching the actual opinions of all cases found in the database in which you are working. When searching case law in print form, you are not able to do this. You need to use a digest, an annotated code, or some secondary source to lead you to a case.

Lexis Advance and Westlaw utilize common search methods. To conduct a search, you first formulate a search ***query***. A search query consists of ***key words*** that relate to your research question. There are different ways to formulate or phrase your search question. One is by using ***Boolean*** logic, referred to as *terms and connectors*. The other is by phrasing your question in a normal question format or simply using the key words without connectors. This is sometimes called a "natural language" or "keyword" search. In the original versions of Lexis Advance and Westlaw (lexis.com and Westlaw Classic), researchers often relied on "terms and connectors" for most precise searches, although "natural language" or keyword searching was available. Both Lexis Advance and Westlaw also utilize these search methods, although the default search is a simple keyword or natural language search. Refer to Figure 10-1, showing a Lexis Advance search box.

full-text search
Legal research method utilized in computer-assisted legal research, in which all documents in a database are searched for certain words.

query
Words that constitute a search request when using CD-ROM or online materials.

key words
Words that describe important aspects of a research question.

Boolean
A special logic used in computerized legal research; utilizes the use of connective words.

FIGURE 10-1 Lexis Advance Search Screen

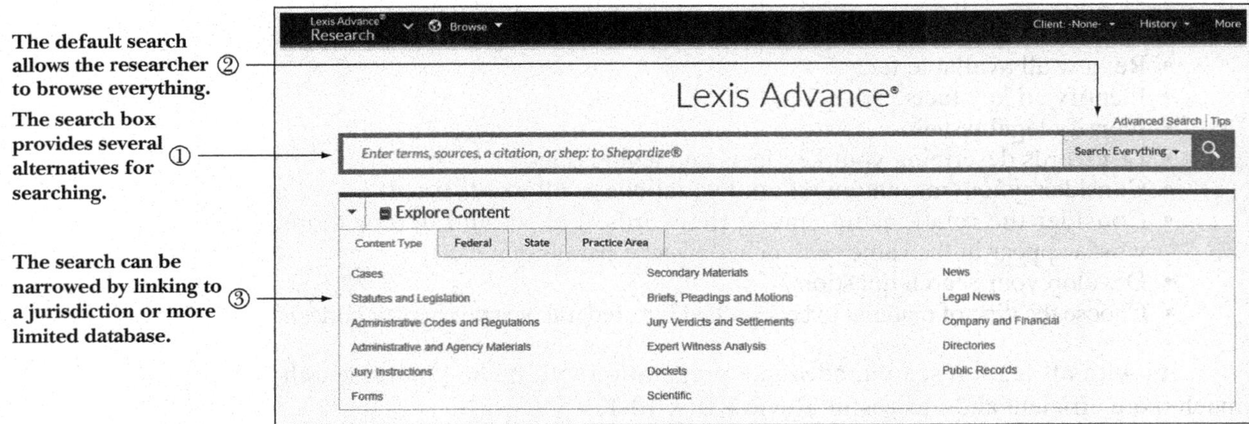

Natural Language/Keyword Searching

A natural language search involves using plain English to formulate a search. A keyword search is similar but consists only of the key words. In Lexis Advance and Westlaw, this type of search is the default.

Consider the following hypothetical situation:

> While on a routine traffic patrol on neighborhood streets, police officer Paul Patterson observed a speeding vehicle. The officer used his lights and siren to signal the driver to stop. Instead of stopping, the driver increased his speed in an attempt to flee. Officer Patterson gave chase. As he did, the driver increased his speed even more. A chase ensued in which both the driver and the officer exceeded 100 mph. Eventually, the driver lost control of his vehicle and hit a pedestrian who was crossing the street in a crossway. The pedestrian was seriously injured and sued not only the driver of the vehicle but also the police officer and the police department.

A natural language search for this search question might read:

Is a police department liable for damages suffered by a bystander during a high-speed automobile chase involving a police officer?

Note how similar this natural language search is to a statement of the issue in the case. (Review Chapter 2.)

You might also simply use key words:

Police
Liability
Pedestrian
Injured
Vehicle
Chase

Both Lexis Advance and Westlaw have powerful search engines that produce relevant search results with a key word search. However, many researchers feel that they obtain more precise results if they formulate a terms and connectors search query.

Terms and Connectors (Boolean Searching)

Boolean searching allows you to search the full text of primary and secondary sources of material by searching for specified combinations of words in a document. This is done by using connective words or ***connectors*** between key words. Key words are generally descriptive nouns, adjectives, or verbs. Words such as *a, the, of, when,* or *where* should not be included in a Boolean search query. (Sometimes these are called "noise" or "stop" words.) The most common connectors are the words *and* and *or.* One disadvantage of the terms and connectors search is that the search produces very precise results. You see results that match your search exactly.

connectors
Words such as *and* or *or* used in a search query to show the relationship between key words or terms.

Using a Boolean search method to find case law, you must formulate a query or search terms consisting of words or phrases you expect to see in cases dealing with a similar situation. You must then join these words with the proper connectors.

In a Boolean search for the hypothetical just described, you would identify the same key words as listed previously. In a Boolean search, you still want to find cases that contain all of these key concepts. However, when judges write court opinions, they may use different words and terms to explain similar concepts. For example, based on this hypothetical you want cases dealing with vehicle chases. A judge might describe this as a "car" chase or an "automobile" chase. Unfortunately, when you use a terms and connectors search, the computer searches literally. It does not search for synonyms or alternative terms. Therefore, you must expand your keyword list to include other words. In addition to "vehicle," you need to include synonyms such as "car" and "automobile." It is also possible that some of your initial key words might need to be expanded to include alternative descriptive words. For example, the hypothetical describes the injured party as a pedestrian. But prior cases dealing with similar situations might have described the injured party as a "bystander" or a "third party."

A related problem with creating a list of key words is that sometimes a word has several variations. For example, *automobile* might be referred to as *auto. Injure* might appear in a case as *injure, injury, injured,* or *injurious,* and the word *woman* might appear in a case as *women.* (Both Lexis Advance and Westlaw automatically search for normal plurals of words but not where the basic word changes.) Lexis Advance and Westlaw utilize features that allow you to include variations of words in your search without having to include each and every variation. The first is the "root expander." By placing an exclamation point (!) at the end of a word, every variation of the "root" word is included in the search. Thus, "injur!" produces results with *injure, injury, injured,* and *injurious.* Both databases also allow the use of a universal character, the asterisk (*) to substitute as a letter within a word. Thus, "wom*n" results in searches for *women* and *woman.*

Once you decide on your key words, you must join these terms with the proper connectors. Connectors establish the relationship of words to one another within the documents to be searched. For example, using the connector *and* between *police* and *bystander* indicates that the researcher is looking for documents containing both *police* and *bystander.* Using the connector *or* between the words *car* or *auto!* indicates that the researcher is looking for documents with either the word *car* or *auto* (and because the root extender was used, the researcher is also looking for *car* or *auto* or *automobile*).

The Lexis Advance and Westlaw databases recognize several "connectors." These are often called "proximity connectors" because they specify how close the key words are to one another in the document. For example, a search such as "police /s bystander" indicates that the key words, *police* and *bystander,* must appear within the same sentence. A list of common connectors for both Lexis Advance and Westlaw is found in Box 10-2.

Using proximity connectors in addition to the *and* and *or* might result in the following search query:

Police /s liab! and bystander /s (hurt or injur!) and (car or auto!) /p chase

Note that in this search some words are enclosed in parentheses. This ensures that the connector before the parenthesis will apply to all terms enclosed within the parentheses.

Both Lexis Advance and Westlaw provide help features to assist you in formulating a query.

Although a researcher can construct a Boolean search using appropriate terms and connectors, both Lexis Advance and Westlaw provide an "advance search" template to facilitate this. See Figure 10-2 for the advanced search screen from Lexis Advance and Figure 10-3 for the advanced search screen from Westlaw.

BOX 10-2 CONNECTORS AND EXPANDERS ON LEXIS ADVANCE AND WESTLAW

Lexis Advance	**Westlaw**	
And	&, and	Finds documents containing all key words connected by *and* or &
Or	A space, or	Finds documents containing either key word
w/n, /n	/n	Finds documents with key terms separated by the specified number of words; that is, "search /3 unreasonable" would retrieve documents where the word search appears within three words of the term *unreasonable*
not w/n		Finds documents where two words do not occur within a specified range
pre w/n	+n, +p, +s	Finds documents where one term appears *before* another term within a specified number of words (pre w/n or +n), within the same paragraph (+p), or within the same sentence (+s)
w/p, /p	/p	Finds documents where two key words appear in the same paragraph
not w/p		Finds documents where two key words do not appear in the same paragraph
w/seg		Finds documents where two key words appear in the same segment
not w/seg		Finds documents where two key words do not appear in the same segment
w/s, /s	/s	Finds documents where two terms appear in the same sentence
not w/s		Finds documents where two terms do not appear in the same sentence
and not	%	Finds documents with the first term but not the second

FIGURE 10-2 Lexis Advance, Advanced Search Template

Lexis Advance®
Research
Browse
Advanced Search | Actions
Home / Advanced Search

Enter terms, sources, a citation, or shep: to Shepardize®

Search Everything | Select a specific content type

Terms
All of these terms
Enter just keywords to run as Natural Language. To run as Terms & Connectors, choose a co
Add
Any of these terms
Enter just keywords to run as Natural Language. To run as Terms & Connectors, choose a co
Add
This exact phrase
Enter just keywords to run as Natural Language. To run as Terms & Connectors, choose a co
Add
Exclude these terms
Enter just keywords to run as Natural Language. To run as Terms & Connectors, choose a co
Add

Document Segments/Fields
While these segments apply to the majority of documents, they may not apply to all documents.
Date
All available dates
Date values will not appear in the search box but will be added to your search. date formats
Citation
Title
Search
Clear

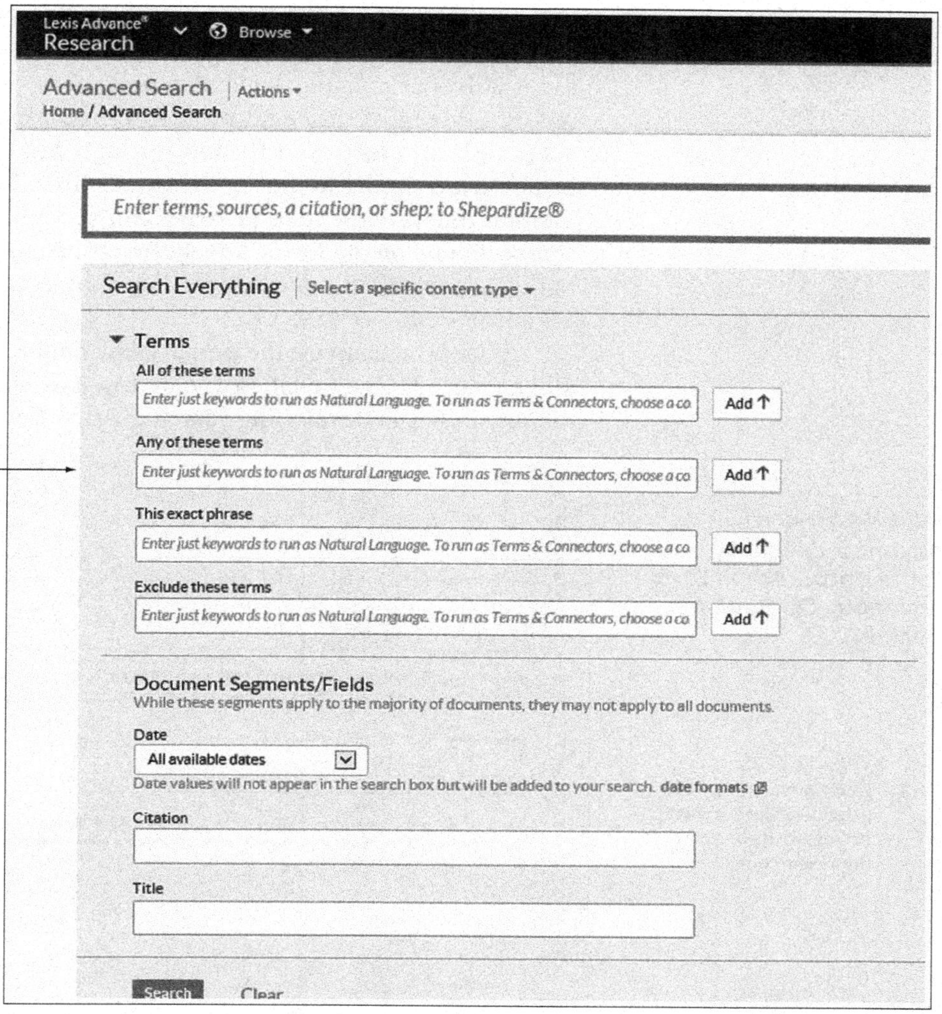

In this template, the researcher provides the "terms," but Lexis Advance has provided the "connectors." ①

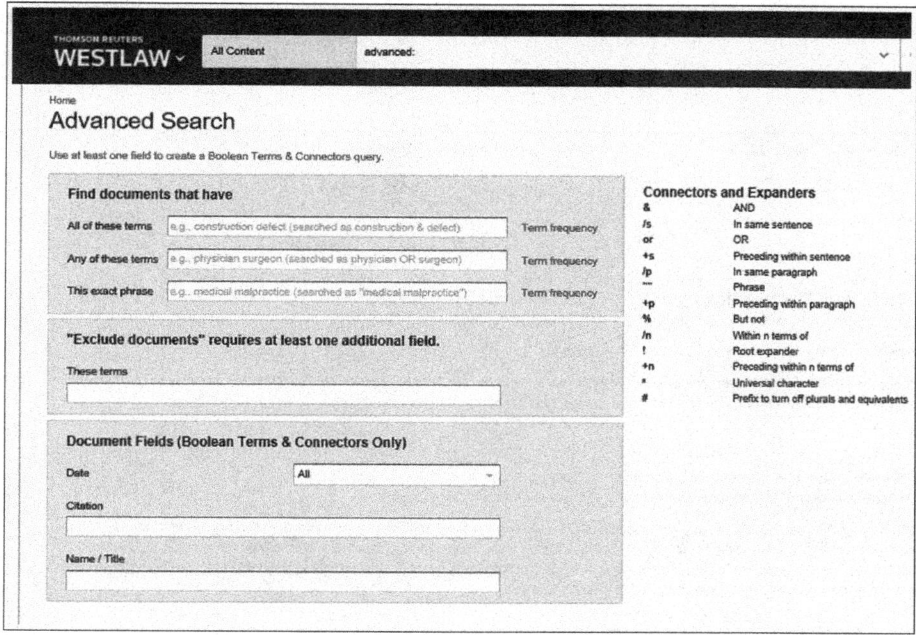

FIGURE 10-3 Westlaw Advanced Search Screen

The Westlaw advanced search template is similar to the one in Lexis Advance. Symbols for connectors and expanders are provided, but not necessary in using the template.

10-4 LEXIS ADVANCE SOURCES

Lexis Advance contains legal materials, news and business materials, and public records. Many of the legal print resources discussed in previous chapters are accessible in electronic format through this service. Legal materials on the database are similar to the legal materials found in a traditional law library. These include federal and state primary and secondary sources of law. Many of the sources found on the Lexis Advance website are published in print by LexisNexis, but the site also has materials published by others, including works published by Thomson Reuters (West.)

Like print sources, the primary law on the Lexis Advance website is editorially enhanced. Cases contain core terms, case summaries, and headnotes, to assist the researcher in developing search queries. See Figures 10-4 and 10-5. In some

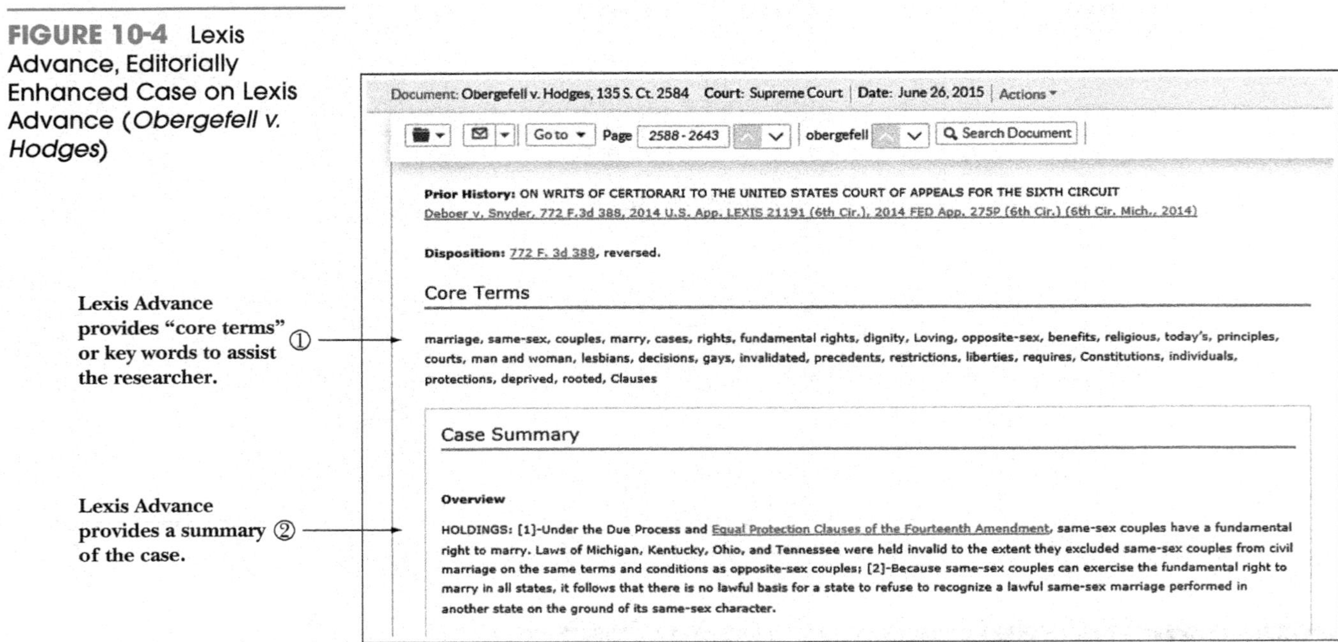

FIGURE 10-4 Lexis Advance, Editorially Enhanced Case on Lexis Advance (*Obergefell v. Hodges*)

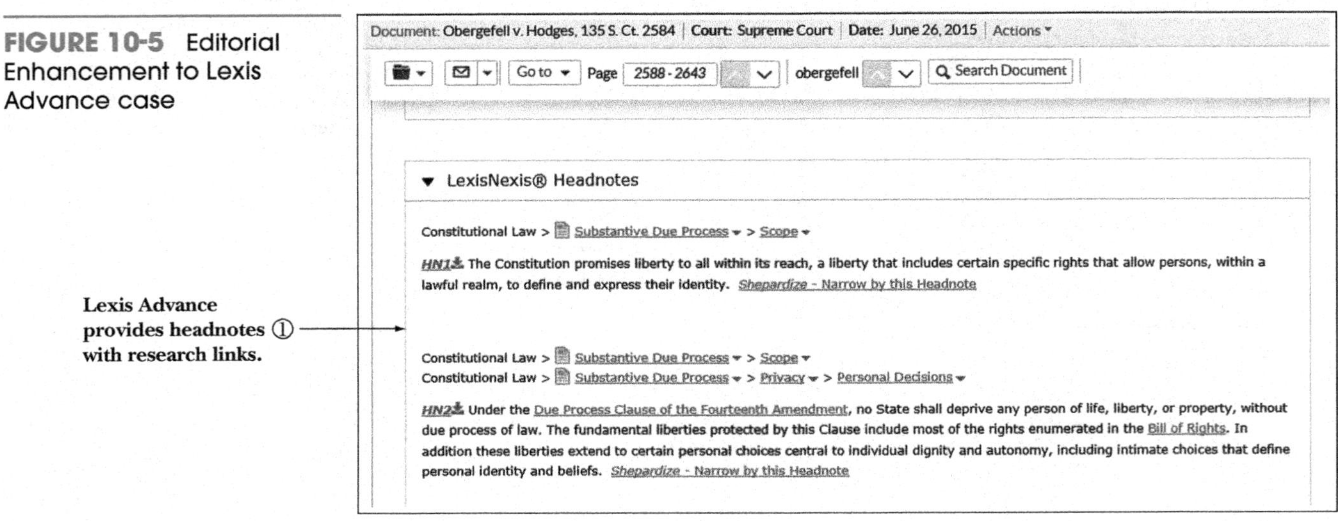

FIGURE 10-5 Editorial Enhancement to Lexis Advance case

instances, the Lexis Advance database allow the researcher to view a PDF copy of the print version of the case.

The online codes are annotated, containing case summaries that interpret the code section. Links to the cases are provided. Unlike the print versions of codes, you do not need to rely on pocket part supplements for updating. On Lexis Advance, you see the U.S. Codes and annotations from the United States Code Service, the Lexis print publication.

Also, unlike researching in print sources, when you research primary law on Lexis Advance, you are often given more than just the law. This is an annotated version of the code, so case notes are included. You also see a link to *Shepard's*. To be able to navigate the code, buttons at the top of the code section ("next" and "previous") allow you to go the following or prior code section with ease. See Figure 10-6.

The secondary sources available through Lexis Advance are comprehensive. Traditional legal encyclopedias, such as *American Jurisprudence Second,* and multiple treatises and journals, including law reviews, are also found.

One of the most important databases on Lexis Advance is the *Shepard's Citator* system. The Lexis Advance website is the only online database that provides access to *Shepard's.*

Shepard's was discussed in Chapter 9.

In addition to primary and secondary law, on Lexis Advance, you will find news sources, business resources, selected court documents including pleadings and motions, and public records. Major newspapers throughout the United States are included, as are many magazines and journals. Business information, including financial data and SEC filing information, is available. Public records include selected court records of criminal and civil cases, real estate title records, and business filings.

See Box 10-3 for a list of some of the materials found on Lexis Advance.

A point to remember: Even though the Lexis Advance database contains extensive materials, a subscription to Lexis Advance does not automatically give one access to all materials. Subscribers generally have access to, and pay for, limited materials.

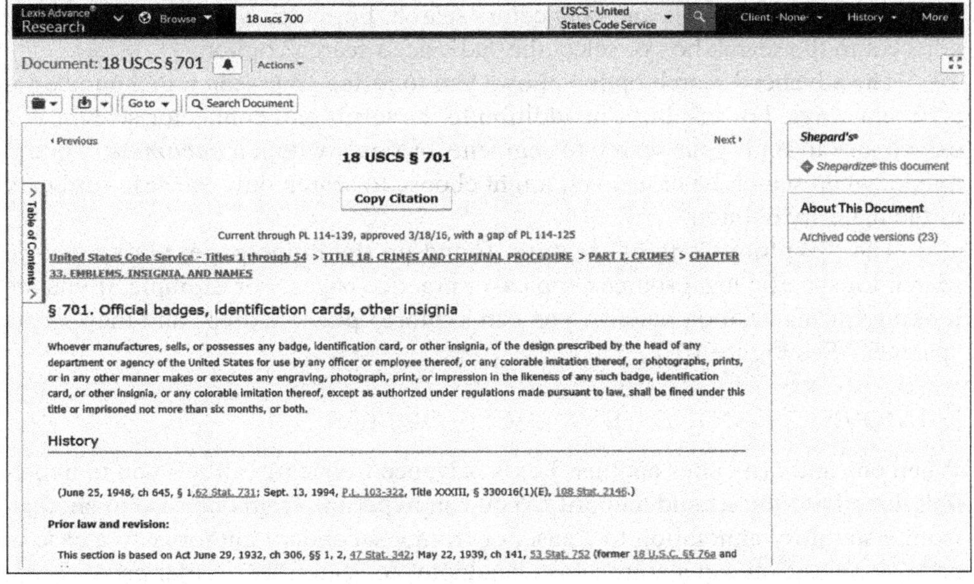

FIGURE 10-6 Lexis Advance Statutory View (18 U.S.C.S. §700)

BOX 10-3 MATERIALS ON LEXIS ADVANCE

Primary Law	Secondary Sources	Public Records and News Sources
U.S. Constitution	Encyclopedias *(Am. Jur. 2d)*	Business information
U.S. Code	*A.L.R.*	Real property information
Federal cases	Treatises	Court records
Code of Federal Regulations	Practice books	Legal news publications
Federal Rules	Form books	Worldwide general news publications
State constitutions	Law reviews and journals	
State codes	The Restatement	
State cases		
State administrative regulations		
Selected international laws		

10-5 SEARCHING AND RETRIEVING DOCUMENTS ON LEXIS ADVANCE

Searching on Lexis Advance

The home page on Lexis Advance provides a single search box for accessing documents. The home page also allows the researcher to search by "browsing" or to link to an "advanced search" screen. Refer back to Figure 10-1.

Using the single search box, you can choose to "search everything" or you can narrow your search by jurisdiction, category, practice area, or by favorite materials (see Figure 10-1). The search itself can consist of a citation or key words. You can also use a terms and connectors search. For help, click on "search tips" adjacent to the search box or select the "advanced search" option.

document
An identifiable item located in a database; can refer to a case or a single code section.

The advanced search option allows you to refine your search in a number of different ways. For instance, in addition to the terms and connector search, you can choose to limit your search to segments or fields within a ***document***. For example, when searching cases, you might choose to search only the case summary or the majority opinion.

The "Explore Content" feature, found on the home page, allows you to search for specific legal sources, topics, or practice pages. For example, if you are looking for material on patents, you can explore "practice area" and then locate "patents." See Figure 10-7.

Retrieving Documents by Hyperlinking

When one authority cites another, Lexis Advance frequently allows you to hyperlink directly to the second authority. You can hyperlink from one case to another, from a statutory annotation to a case, or from a secondary authority to a case or code section. You can also use case headnotes to search for similar cases. Lexis

FIGURE 10-7 Lexis Advance, Explore Content

Here, the researcher has first selected "Practice Area." The researcher can ① now select a specific area of practice to explore.

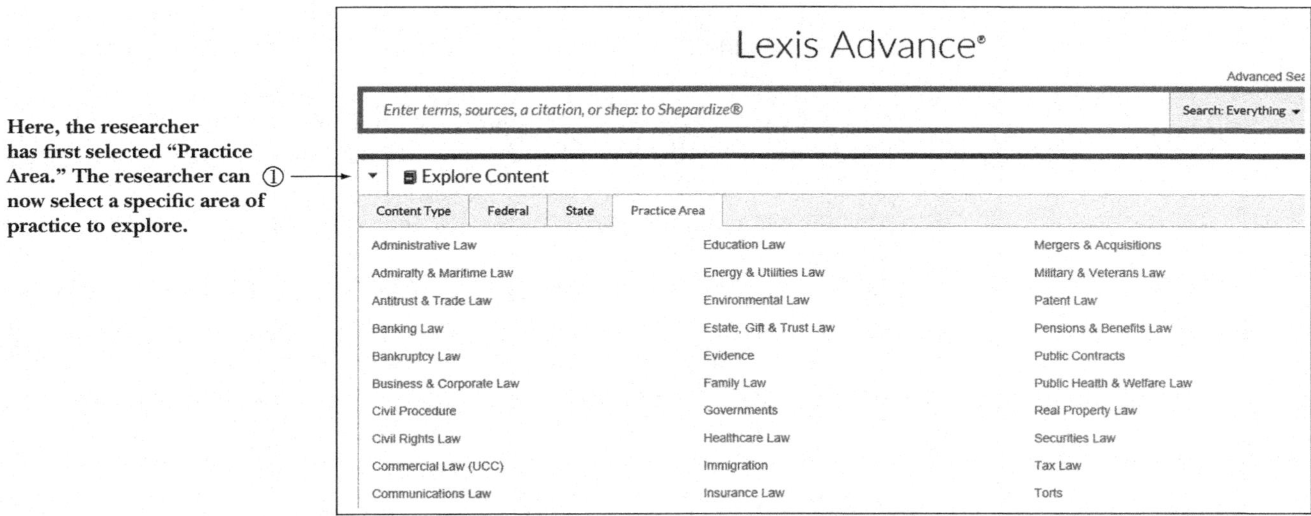

Advance has features that allow you to retrieve cases with similar headnotes simply by following links.

Retrieving Documents Using Tables of Contents

Locating codes and secondary sources is sometimes done by browsing the table of contents. The researcher can either browse the full table of contents or conduct a word search within the table of contents. This method of searching often provides narrower results than a full-text search and is therefore more efficient. When you access the appropriate code or secondary source, you will find a link to the table of contents. (Although not all secondary sources have a table of contents available.) Refer back to Figure 10-6.

Other Features of Lexis Advance

Star Pagination Documents found online are not paginated in the same way as print resources. Since citing to specific language in a case requires a page citation (pinpoint cite), Lexis Advance, like other online services, uses a feature called star pagination to tell the reader where page breaks occur in the print versions of a case. Citations to the various publications of this case appear as follows:

478 U.S. 186 *; 106 S. Ct. **;

92 L.Ed. 2d 140 ***; 1986 U.S. LEXIS 123

The asterisks (*) following each reporter are used throughout the case to indicate where page breaks occur in the specific reporter and the number of the pages. Thus, when you see [145 ***] within the text of the document, you know that you would now be reading page 145 of the *Lawyer's Edition* version of the case.

Copy Citation This feature allows you to copy a section from the document and paste it into a word-processed document. By using this feature, the pinpoint (page) citation for the copied material is automatically included.

Folders An important research tool added to Lexis Advance is the "folder" found within the "My Workspace" tab. Folders allow you to save documents, including cases, for easy retrieval. For a period of time, you can retrieve documents from your folder without any additional search fee. Within the folder feature, you can also add notes regarding your research. Folders can also be shared with others.

History Lexis Advance keeps track of your searches, and you can access this by accessing the "History." This is found on the home search page. Refer to Figure 10-1, and look at the top of the screen.

Mobile Apps Mobile apps for Lexis Advance are available for both the iPad and iPhone.

Tutorials and Help Lexis Advance has many other features not mentioned here, and new features are continually added. Fortunately, online tutorial user guides explain the numerous features and offer research tips. A subscription to the Lexis service is not needed to access the tutorials. The website also has excellent "help" features that can be accessed from within the database.

10-6 WESTLAW DATABASES

The materials found on Westlaw are similar to the source materials found on Lexis Advance, although Westlaw refers to its materials as "databases" rather than "sources." Although the terminology differs, as with Lexis Advance, on Westlaw, the researcher has access to primary law, numerous secondary sources, public records, litigation documents, and news sources. Codes, constitutions rules, and regulations are annotated. (On Westlaw, you see the U.S. Code Annotated, the West publication.) Case law contains case summaries and headnotes. A practical resource on Westlaw is a feature that allows you to do "profiles" of attorneys, judges, and experts. See Figure 10-8, Westlaw screen showing selected databases.

10-7 SEARCHING AND RETRIEVING DOCUMENTS ON WESTLAW

Searching on Westlaw

As with Lexis Advance, searching or retrieving documents on Westlaw can be accomplished in a variety of ways. Westlaw uses its own search engine to simplify search process. The home page contains one search box that allows the research to search by citation, by name, by key words, or by a Boolean search. The advanced search, which can be linked from the home page, provides a template for a terms and connector search. Before running a search, the researcher must choose a jurisdiction for the search. The site provides many options here. You can search for something as broad as "all state and federal" or as limited as "1st Circuit." You must also choose the type of database you want to search. You have options in selecting the type of documents to be retrieved, but the site allows the researcher to retrieve all documents of any nature ("all content"). With this type of search, you receive a list of the categories of documents retrieved (e.g., cases, statutes, and secondary sources). The researcher can then decide to limit the search to specific types of materials. See Figures 10-8 and 10-9. Also see Box 10-4.

FIGURE 10-8 Westlaw Start Page

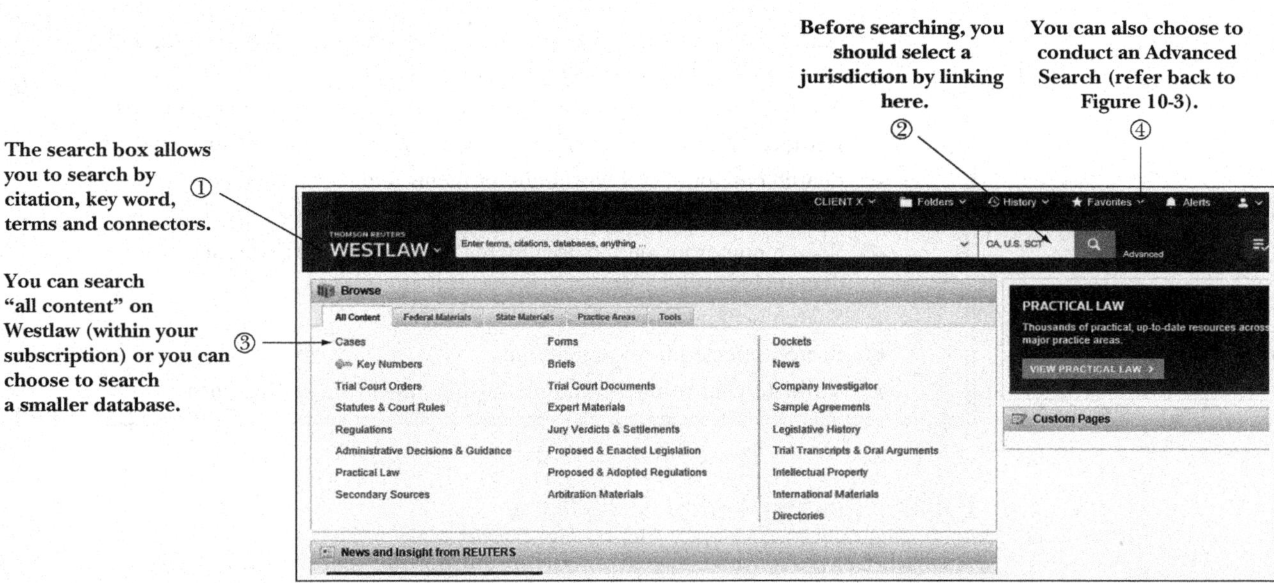

FIGURE 10-9 All Content Search Results on Westlaw

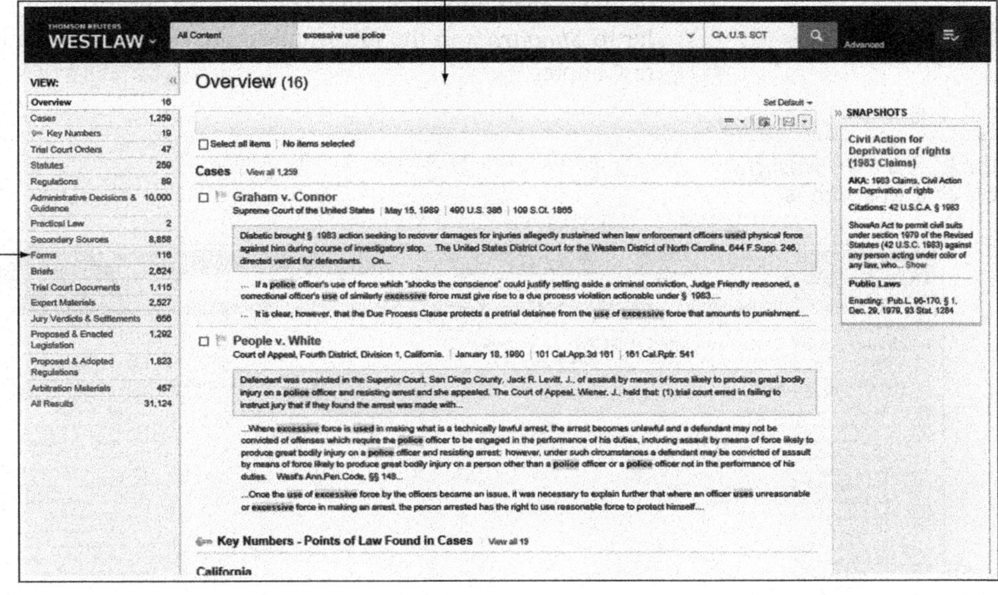

BOX 10-4 LEXIS ADVANCE AND WESTLAW ALLOW YOU TO

- ✔ Search full text of case law and codes for specific words and phrases.
- ✔ Search numerous secondary sources (e.g., encyclopedias, *A.L.R.*, and law reviews) for specific words and phrases.
- ✔ Search tables of contents for codes and numerous secondary sources.
- ✔ Retrieve documents (cases, codes, and secondary sources) with a citation.
- ✔ Search case opinions written by or mentioning specific justices.
- ✔ Search for cases within certain dates.
- ✔ Search numerous public documents (e.g., corporate and real estate documents).
- ✔ Search general news articles.
- ✔ Search selected foreign materials.
- ✔ Validate your research findings (using *Shepard's* or KeyCite)

Other Features of Westlaw

As with Lexis Advance, Westlaw offers numerous features to aid the researcher. The following are some examples, but the site contains many additional helpful features.

Indexes and Tables Westlaw provides easily accessible indexes for codes and selected secondary sources as well as tables of contents and popular name tables. The statutory indexes allow researchers to locate relevant code sections in the same way they do when using print resources. Simply select "Statute and Rules" from the categories on the homepage (see Figure 10-1). If you select the U.S. Code Annotated, you will see the screen in Figure 10-10.

Key Number Searching One of the unique features of West publications—key numbers—can be used as a basis for searching. This feature was discussed in Chapter 8.

KeyCite Rather than *Shepard's,* Westlaw provides a service called KeyCite to check the validity of legal sources. As described in Chapter 9, KeyCite is similar to *Shepard's* in the information provided. KeyCite is discussed in more detail in Chapter 9.

FIGURE 10-10 Westlaw: Tools and Resources

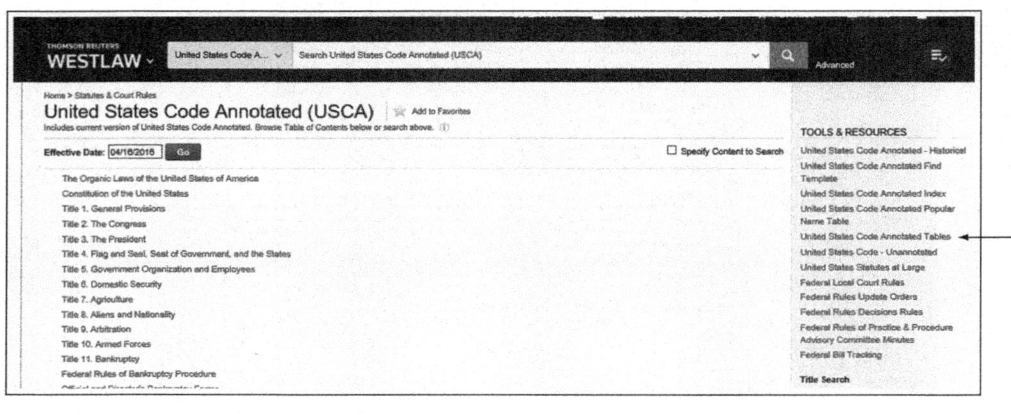

Star Pagination Like Lexis Advance, Westlaw also uses star pagination to indicate pages in the printed reporters. Westlaw also has a feature similar to "copy with cite." This feature allows you to copy selected text with a reference to the page cites in the printed versions of the case.

Folders Westlaw provides a folders feature similar to that on Lexis Advance.

History The history of your prior searches is kept by Westlaw and accessible to you by a link on the homepage.

Copy with Cite When you highlight text in a document, Westlaw assumes you want to copy the material and you see a "pop up" menu allowing you to copy the material with the citation, including page cite.

Tutorial information Westlaw also provides several helpful user guides and pamphlets, which can be downloaded without cost from its website, as well as online tutorials. You need not be a subscriber to access these aids.

A Point to Remember

When conducting a Boolean search, check the website "help" features for a list of connectors that can be used. These features change from site to site and are not interchangeable.

For a summary of the benefits of Lexis Advance and Westlaw, see Box 10-4.

To find more information about Westlaw, check http://west.thomson.com/Westlaw/.

10-8 SEARCH POSSIBILITIES AND PROBLEMS WITH LEXIS ADVANCE AND WESTLAW

CALR opens search possibilities that do not exist with materials in print. Websites such as Lexis Advance and Westlaw are often able to publish cases online the same day a decision is handed down, eliminating the need to search advance sheets or slip opinions. Full-text searching does not require the researcher to rely on secondary sources or digests. You can search a case database for the presence of any word or combinations of words. This allows you to search not only for legal issues and facts but for names of individuals appearing in cases. Thus, you can search for appellate cases written by certain judges or for cases dealing with lower court decisions by certain judges. When presented with a question about possible biases of a certain judge, you can search case law databases to see if his or her name appears.

Other advantages of Lexis Advance and Westlaw include:

- Ability to restrict a full-text search by factors, such as date, author, and jurisdiction
- Ability to locate a case with the name of one party and no case citation
- Ability to hyperlink to an authority cited within the document you are reading
- Ability to instantly cite check a case you are reading by hyperlinking to *Shepard's* or KeyCite

- Ability to copy and paste language or citations into a word-processing document
- Availability of popular materials (especially practice books) to more than one person at a time

On the other hand, Lexis Advance and Westlaw are not without problems. Some of these include the following.

- Although computer search capabilities are continually improving, at times you may have problems with misspelled words, typographical errors, or use of synonyms.
- A tendency to overuse hyperlinks can result in unorganized (and lost) research.
- The use of Lexis Advance and Westlaw can be costly.

Another potential problem with online services stems from the fact that the services contain some unpublished opinions and opinions that are vacated because a higher court grants a hearing. Most of these cases do not appear in printed case reporters. It is absolutely essential that any cite on these services be validated. You should also check the local rules of your court to determine if you can cite unpublished opinions.

Whether you use print or online resources, your legal research strategies are similar. The following is an overview of those strategies.

1. Create a vocabulary list based on your factual problem.
2. Formulate the issue.
3. Use a legal thesaurus and legal dictionary to complete your vocabulary list.
4. Create a research plan before going to a law library or accessing an online site.
5. Determine whether to begin in primary or secondary sources.
6. Take your research terms or vocabulary to indexes.
7. Add additional terms to your vocabulary list as suggested by the indexes.
8. Take notes whether using print or online sources.
9. Organize photocopied or downloaded material.

Read Appendix D for a more detailed overview of research strategies.

10-9 BLOOMBERG LAW

Bloomberg Law, a new legal research site, describes itself as a research system that integrates legal, business, and news content. Bloomberg and its subsidiary Bloomberg BNA have provided legal and financial information and news for many years. Bloomberg Law is a legal research site that provides and integrates law, news, and financial information. While the focus appears to be business related, the site offers extensive case law, complete statutory and regulatory materials, and selected secondary sources. Many of the cases contain headnotes written by Bloomberg staff, and the site offers a feature called BCite to check the history and treatment of case law. Statutory law consists of official versions such as the U.S. Code, Statutes at Large, and Federal Regulations. These are not annotated in the way that Lexis Advance and Westlaw annotate. Secondary sources include most of the BNA publications as well as some additional business-related sources. Bloomberg Law includes an extensive help menu, with tutorial videos, explaining the various features of the site.

Finding It Online

Legal research on the Internet is continually changing. One good website that helps you keep up to date is the website Internet for Lawyers located at http://www.netforlawyers.com/index.htm.

Important training and tutorial resources can be found on the Westlaw and LexisNexis sites. Both provide excellent up-to-date information about their products. Links to these resources can be found on the following research sites:

www.lexis.com

http://www.lexisnexis.com/en-us/products/lexis-advance.page

http://legalsolutions.thomsonreuters.com/law-products/

www.bloomberglaw.com

The Writer's Corner

Dashes, Commas, and Parentheses

When we need to set off information that interrupts a sentence, our general choices are dashes, commas, and parentheses.

The dash adds emphasis
Example: The student—breathless with excitement—eagerly accepted her diploma.

The comma is neutral.
Example: The teacher arranged the tables, chairs, equipment, and boxes.

The parentheses show subordination; they downplay information.
Example: Cory discovered a new bike (worth over $500) when he opened the crate.

Parentheses help with labeling in a series.
Example: To prove that Ruth was negligent, the complaining party must prove that (1) Ruth owed the injured party a duty of care, (2) there was a breach of that duty, (3) Ruth caused the injury, and (4) there are damages.

CITATION MATTERS

ELECTRONIC DATABASES

***THE BLUEBOOK*—Rule 18**

The Internet, Electronic Media, and Other Nonprint Resources

Lexis Advance and Westlaw are large commercial electronic databases. There are other reliable and authoritative commercial databases as well. Rules covering citations to these resources are covered in the following rule.

Rule 18:
- introduction to citation of information found in electronic resources
- commercial electronics databases
- cases
- constitutions and statutes
- legislative, administrative, and executive materials
- secondary materials

CHAPTER SUMMARY

Legal researchers today use legal resource material in electronic format in addition to material in print. This type of research is known as *computer-assisted legal research (CALR).* CALR consists of the use of free Internet websites, fee-based legal databases, such as Lexis Advance and Westlaw.

Lexis Advance and Westlaw offer a variety of methods for searching. Menus, templates, and tables of contents sometimes simplify an online search. An important method of searching these sites is based on Boolean logic. In a Boolean search, referred to as a *terms and connectors search,* the researcher develops a search query based on key words found in the research question and certain connective terms. Lexis Advance and Westlaw both allow natural language or plain English searching. Boolean and natural language searches allow the researcher to conduct full-text searches. A full-text search is a search of the actual documents rather than a search of an index.

Lexis Advance and Westlaw contain extensive amounts of primary and secondary legal research material. In addition to legal research material, a researcher can also access public documents and numerous news sources. Both sites also provide a system for validating research. *Shepard's* is found on Lexis Advance, and KeyCite is found on Westlaw. Recently, Bloomberg Law has entered the world of online research. This site seeks to integrate law with business and financial news and information.

TERMS TO REMEMBER

computer-assisted legal research (CALR)
full-text search
query
key words
Boolean
connectors
document

QUESTIONS FOR REVIEW

1. List the steps in preparing to search online.
2. What is a Boolean search?
3. What is natural language search?
4. What is a full-text search?
5. What types of materials can be found on Lexis Advance?
6. What types of materials can be found on Westlaw?
7. Describe the different types of search methods found on Lexis Advance.
8. Describe the different types of search methods found on Westlaw.
9. What are some of the advantages of searching on Lexis Advance and Westlaw?
10. What are some of the problems with searching on Lexis Advance and Westlaw?

CAN YOU FIGURE IT OUT?

1. Refer to Figure 10-1. If you were looking for the Federal Code of Regulations, which category would be the best to select?
2. Refer to Figure 10-2. If you were doing an advanced search looking for the case, *Betts v. Brady*, which box would be best to use?
3. Refer to Figure 10-3. You are searching for information on the Rico Act dealing with racketeering. You do not want your results to produce references to Puerto Rico. What would your search look like?

TEST YOURSELF (Check Your Answers in Appendix G)

If you have access to Lexis Advance or Westlaw, do the following:

1. With what area of law does 17 U.S.C. §107 deal?
2. What is the subject matter of rule 26.3 of the Federal Rules of Criminal Procedure?
3. What is the name and citation of the U.S. Supreme Court case dealing with redistricting in Texas decided after 2003?

TEST **YOURSELF—**WRITE IT RIGHT Persuasive Fact Patterns

In documents directed to courts, the Statement of Facts should be written such that it attempts to persuade the reader to find for your client. In persuasive legal writing, we take the facts and place the facts and the client in the best light possible. We do not avoid "bad" facts, but we can down play them.

Take a look at the partial Statement of Facts below. Underline the words or phrases where you believe the writer intended to be persuasive. (Check your answers in Appendix G)

Statement of Facts

This wrongful death lawsuit is brought by plaintiff Green after the unfortunate death of decedent Hutchins who was viciously attacked and killed by defendant Baylor's pit bull on January 23, 2008. Genevieve Green and Matthew Hutchins resided at a single family residence owned by Randolf Keen. Robert Baylor lived with his pit bull in the adjacent residence, which was also owned by Keen. On the day of the incident, the pit bull viciously attacked Hutchins while he was simply standing on the sidewalk between the properties.

Prior to this incidence, Green and Hutchins filed for domestic partnership based on the fact that they were both over the age of 62. Green and Hutchins were retired teachers who were dependent on each other for support, however; neither of them was eligible to receive Social Security benefits. Both parties were previously married to spouses who predeceased them. They did not marry because of concerns that Hutchins' children would not accept the marriage. Green was not named as a beneficiary in Hutchins' will instead; everything was left to his children. At the time of Hutchins' death, neither he nor Green had reached the age of 65.

Green maintains that the pit bull was inherently dangerous because of its breed and that there were complaints concerning the dog barking and lunging at other people and animals. The dog also fought with and nearly killed another dog over a bone. She also claims that there was a previous incident where the dog knocked Hutchins down and where the dog lunged and snapped at a stranger. There is no record that either of these incidents was reported to the landlord.

CITATION **EXERCISES**

Use the Citation Matters feature in this chapter to answer this question.

Very simply, what does *Bluebook* rule 18 cover?

FROM **THE WRITER'S CORNER** Dashes, Commas, and Parentheses

1. "The dash ______________ ______________."
2. "The comma is ______________."
3. "The parentheses show ____________; they ______________ ______________."

ASSIGNMENTS AND **ACTIVITIES**

Research Exercises

1. Review problems 1 and 5 in Appendix B and Research Strategies in Appendix D. For each problem, do the following:
   a. Create a vocabulary list of both factual and legal terms.
   b. Review a legal dictionary and legal thesaurus for additional terms.
   c. Create a list of primary and secondary print sources that might be helpful in your research.
   d. Determine whether you would start your research in a primary or secondary source, and explain why.
   e. Explain how your research plan might change if you use Lexis Advance or Westlaw rather than print sources.
2. If you have access to Lexis Advance or Westlaw, answer the following:
   a. What is the title of 6 U.S.C. § 1402?
   b. What is the title of Federal Rules of Criminal Procedure, rule 10?
   c. What is the title and year of the case found at 352 F.2d 945?
   d. What is the citation for the case *United States v. Mancias,* decided by the 8th Circuit Court of Appeals in 2003?
3. Answer the following:
   a. A state has a law providing that in a criminal case a defendant will not be adjudged insane unless he demonstrates that at the time of the crime, he was

afflicted with a mental disease or defect of such severity that he did not know the criminal act was wrong. Does this violate due process under the U.S. Constitution? Find a 2006 case on this point.

b. According to the U.S. Supreme Court, where the parties have a contract that contains an arbitration clause, and where one party claims that the arbitration provision is void for illegality, is the claim to be decided by a court or an arbitrator? Find a case decided sometime after 2004.

4. Shepardize or KeyCite the case at 163 U.S. 537, 16 S.Ct. 1138.
   a. What is the name of the case?
   b. What is the name of the case that overruled it?
   c. If you do not have access to Lexis Advance or Westlaw, try to do the exercises in 1, 2, and 3 on the freely accessible Internet.

Analysis Assignments

5. Review the problems in Appendix B.
   a. Draft queries for finding cases for each of the problems using Boolean logic. Use the Lexis Advance connectors.
   b. Do the same using the Westlaw connectors.
   c. Do the same using natural language.

CASE **PROJECT**

If available to you, use either Lexis Advance or Westlaw to do further research on your case. Do the following.

1. Access cases you have already found. Locate relevant issues in the headnotes of the cases. Using the headnotes, search for other cases in the appropriate jurisdiction.
2. Shepardize or KeyCite cases you found.

chapter **eleven**

COMPUTER-ASSISTED LEGAL RESEARCH (CALR): THE FREELY ACCESSIBLE INTERNET

SKILL OBJECTIVES FOR CHAPTER 11

When you complete chapter 11, you should be able to

- Identify types of legal materials found on the free Internet.
- Distinguish case law and codes found on Lexis Advance and Westlaw from case law and codes found on the free Internet.
- Effectively use online search aids, such as menus, templates, search boxes, and advanced search features.
- Identify and be able to access legal websites that are free and reliable.
- Identify criteria for evaluating legal information found on the Internet.

CHAPTER OUTLINE

From the Desk of W. J. Bryan, Esq.

TO: Research Assistant
FROM: W. J. Bryan
RE: Our Client, Justin Meyers
DATE:

Attached is a citation to an additional case that might apply to the Meyers case, along with citations to several local rules of court that we might need to follow. Please make copies of these for me to read. There is no need to use Lexis Advance or Westlaw (and I do not want to incur the cost of using those services). You should be able to find these on the Internet.

11-1 INTERNET LEGAL RESEARCH

Free Internet access to the electronic version of print materials such as case reporters with summaries and headnotes, annotated codes, and secondary sources such as *American Jurisprudence* is generally limited to fee-based services, such as Westlaw or Lexis Advance. These materials are not found on free websites because ***copyright*** laws protect them. Cases found on free sites do not have the West or Lexis headnotes, and codes do not have case annotations.

copyright
A copyright is a legal protection for the authors of "original works of authorship" such as literary, dramatic, musical, artistic, and certain other works.

On the other hand, the law itself is available. Federal and state constitutions, codes, cases, and regulations can all be located. Although traditional secondary sources are generally not available for free through the Internet, many free websites do provide discussions, explanations, or analysis of the law. Internet sites also provide legal professionals with access to federal and state forms for use in the courts and various government agencies (such as the U.S. Patent Office). Free Internet sites are a valuable legal research tool.

Government agencies, educational institutions, and commercial providers maintain free legal research websites. Like Lexis Advance and Westlaw, some legal websites consist of multiple types of legal materials. For example, a website might provide access to federal and state cases, federal and state codes, as well as a variety of other legal sources. Other sites are limited, such as the site for the U.S. Patent and Trademark Office (www.uspto.gov) that deals exclusively with ***intellectual property*** law. Free Internet sites provide a variety of search methods or features. They also vary in their reliability.

intellectual property
Intangible property including patents, trademarks, trade names, and copyright.

Numerous websites provide legal information. Searching for topics such as "law" or "legal information" on general search engines such as Google or Bing produces countless results. These results range from law school sites to government agencies to lawyers offering free legal advice. Many websites are valuable research tools. However, some are just advertisements, and others are no more than a platform for an individual or group to put forth a personal agenda. Using free Internet legal sources, therefore, requires careful scrutiny on the part of the researcher. This chapter discusses the use of free websites as legal research tools, describes some common search features, and provides an overview of some reliable and helpful websites. The chapter does not cover every website that might prove useful. To fully understand the value of any of the websites provided in this chapter, you will need to actually access the site and spend time exploring it.

11-2 SEARCHING ONLINE LEGAL WEBSITES

Search Features

The creator of the website determines search methods and features for individual websites. However, many sites employ similar methods and search features. Some of the common website features that help online researchers are hyperlinks, templates, tables of contents, search boxes, and advanced search features. Hyperlinks often appear in a menu-type list of items or materials, allowing the researcher to select and link to a desired type of material. Sometimes, hyperlinks appear in a navigation-type bar at the top of a web page. For example, see Figure 11-1 for a copy of a menu list from the website for the Government Publishing Office. This site provides access to numerous types of legal materials. The list of hyperlinks allows you to easily access the page within the website that contains relevant search information.

Like Lexis Advance and Westlaw, many free websites provide templates for searching. Legal professionals commonly refer to legal sources by citation. Templates allow you to retrieve a document with that citation. The template provides a basic format for the citation, requiring the researcher to provide basic information.

Templates simplify the search process when you have a citation to a case or code section and want to retrieve it. Using a template to find a code section or a case allows you to avoid problems caused by incorrect citation formats. See Figures 11-2 and 11-3 for examples of templates used for retrieving cases and codes.

Searching codes and secondary sources is sometimes done by searching the table of contents. The researcher can either browse the full table of contents or conduct a word search within the table of contents. This method of searching often provides narrower results than a full-text search and is therefore more efficient. Browsing a table of contents can also help you find relevant law when you have difficulty identifying the proper key words. See Figure 11-4 for an example of a screen containing a table of contents for the U.S. Code.

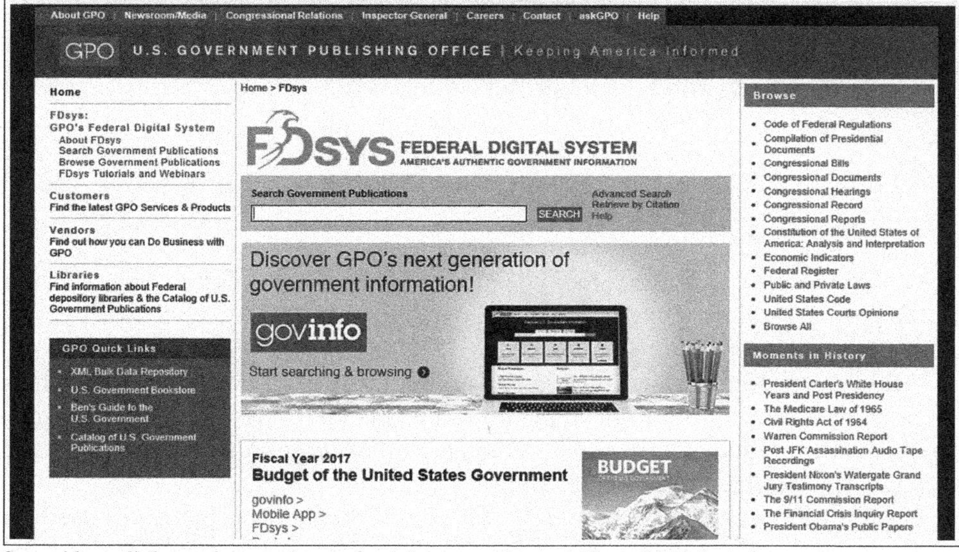

Several hyperlinks on the search page lead the researcher quickly to desired results.

FIGURE 11-1 GPO Federal Digital System from Government Publishing Office

FIGURE 11-2 FindLaw.com Case Template

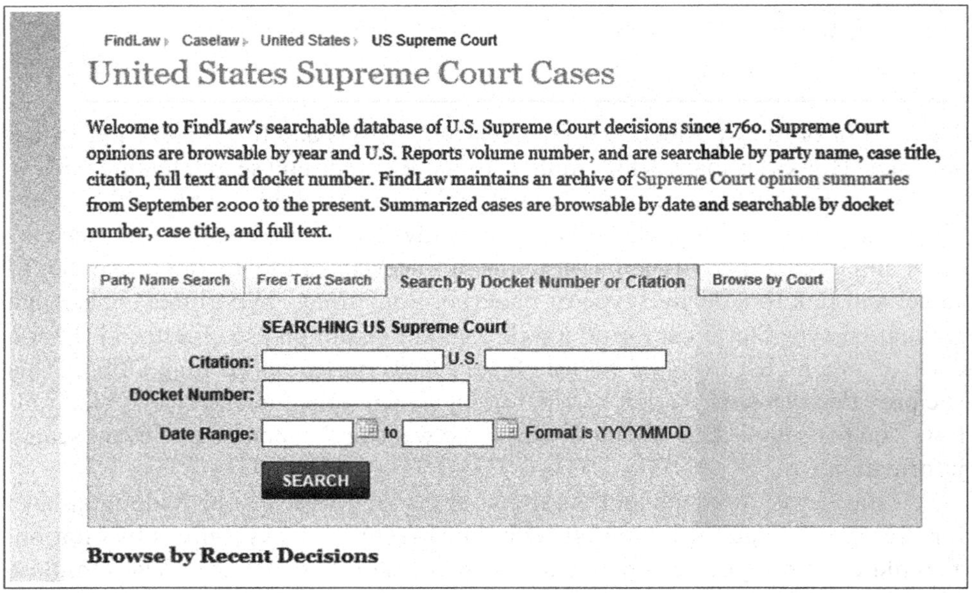

FindLaw › Caselaw › United States › US Supreme Court
United States Supreme Court Cases
Welcome to FindLaw's searchable database of U.S. Supreme Court decisions since 1760. Supreme Court opinions are browsable by year and U.S. Reports volume number, and are searchable by party name, case title, citation, full text and docket number. FindLaw maintains an archive of Supreme Court opinion summaries from September 2000 to the present. Summarized cases are browsable by date and searchable by docket number, case title, and full text.
Party Name Search
Free Text Search
Search by Docket Number or Citation
Browse by Court
SEARCHING US Supreme Court
Citation:
U.S.
Docket Number:
Date Range:
to
Format is YYYYMMDD
SEARCH
Browse by Recent Decisions

The reporter abbreviation (U.S.) is provided. You only need to add the volume and page.

FIGURE 11-3 Search Page Including Code Template

Office of the Law Revision Counsel
UNITED STATES CODE
Search & Browse
Currency and Updating
Classification Tables
Popular Name Tool
Other Tables and Tools
Understanding the Code
Positive Law Codification
Editorial Reclassification
Downloads
The United States Code is a consolidation and codification by subject matter of the general and permanent laws
information, click here.
Search the United States Code
Search
Clear
Title
Section
Jump To:
Go
Browse the United States Code [Current change...]
Front Matter
*Title 1—General Provisions

① A general search box is provided.

② A template is provided if you are looking for a specific U.S. Code section and have the citation.

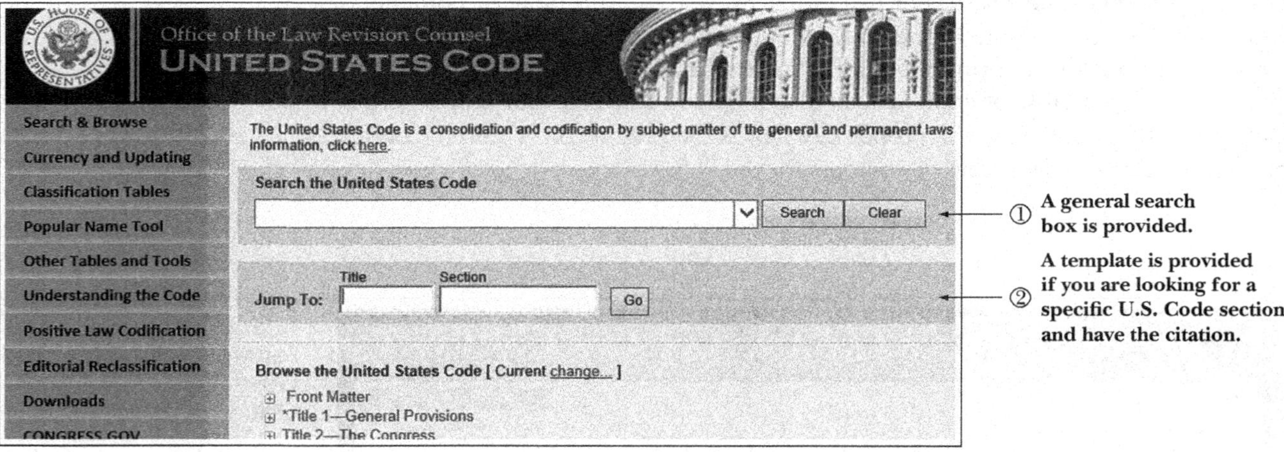

Most websites provide some type of search box that allows the researcher to search part or all of the material on the website. Refer to Figure 11-3 for an example of a simple search box.

In order to conduct a search, you must first identify key words and formulate a search query or question. This type of search is usually based on Boolean logic. This general method of *terms and connectors searching* in Lexis Advance and Westlaw was discussed in Chapter 10.

Although many legal research websites use a search method based on Boolean logic, differences exist among these websites. These websites provide

FIGURE 11-4 Table of Contents for U.S. Code

Selecting a relevant U.S. Code title allows you to continue browsing through the code sections. ①

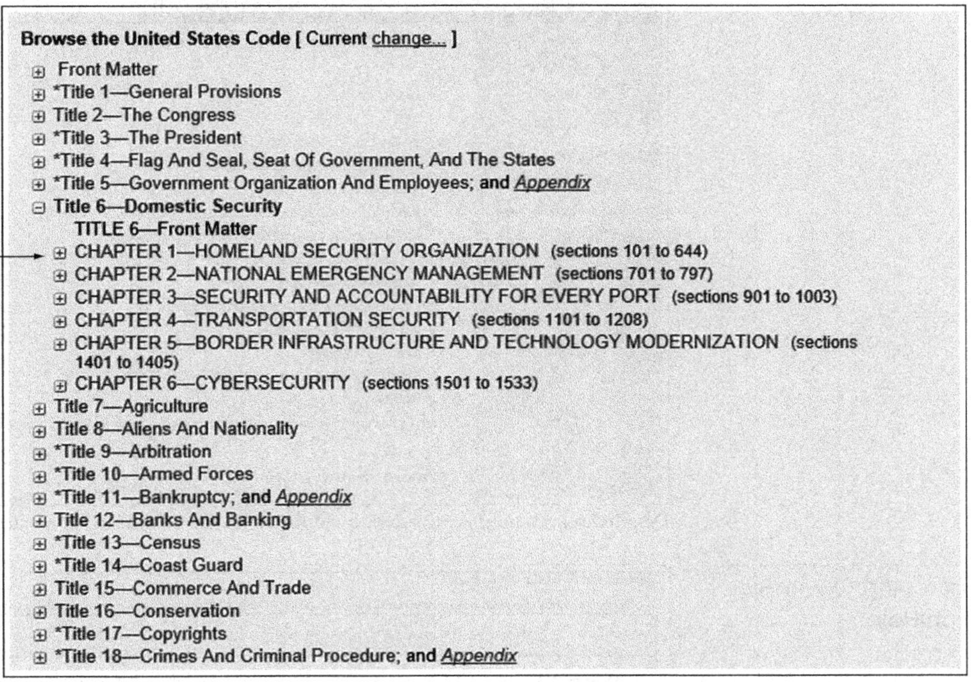

Browse the United States Code [Current change...]

- Front Matter
- *Title 1—General Provisions
- Title 2—The Congress
- *Title 3—The President
- *Title 4—Flag And Seal, Seat Of Government, And The States
- *Title 5—Government Organization And Employees; and Appendix
- Title 6—Domestic Security
  - TITLE 6—Front Matter
  - CHAPTER 1—HOMELAND SECURITY ORGANIZATION (sections 101 to 644)
  - CHAPTER 2—NATIONAL EMERGENCY MANAGEMENT (sections 701 to 797)
  - CHAPTER 3—SECURITY AND ACCOUNTABILITY FOR EVERY PORT (sections 901 to 1003)
  - CHAPTER 4—TRANSPORTATION SECURITY (sections 1101 to 1208)
  - CHAPTER 5—BORDER INFRASTRUCTURE AND TECHNOLOGY MODERNIZATION (sections 1401 to 1405)
  - CHAPTER 6—CYBERSECURITY (sections 1501 to 1533)
- Title 7—Agriculture
- Title 8—Aliens And Nationality
- *Title 9—Arbitration
- *Title 10—Armed Forces
- *Title 11—Bankruptcy; and Appendix
- Title 12—Banks And Banking
- *Title 13—Census
- *Title 14—Coast Guard
- Title 15—Commerce And Trade
- Title 16—Conservation
- *Title 17—Copyrights
- *Title 18—Crimes And Criminal Procedure; and Appendix

instructions and search tips for Boolean searches. It is important to review these instructions. The instructions tell you:

- What connecting terms and symbols can be used in your search query
- Whether connecting words or terms can be abbreviated
- Whether a ***wildcard*** can be substituted for letters within search terms

wildcard
A symbol used in a word that substitutes for any letter; often an asterisk (*)

For example, one website might allow you to search for words or terms within the same sentence and instruct you to use "/s" as an abbreviation for this. Another site might allow you to search for words "near" one another. Many websites also allow you to search for variations of words without typing in every variation. Two characters, the asterisk (*) and the exclamation mark (!), are frequently used as the wildcard or "universal character." See Figure 11-5A for a list of the type of help provided on one site and Figure 11-5B for a list of the connectors that are used on that site.

Some websites use advanced search features to help the researcher construct a search. An advanced search enables you to be very precise in your search. See Figure 11-6 for an example of an Advanced Search screen for the U.S. Code.

One of the most important search features on any website is a help feature that explains how to search on the specific site. Since search features on websites can differ in many ways, always be sure to check this.

A Point to Remember

Before using a search box to find cases or codes, you need to prepare. Analyze your problem, create a list of key words, and consider alternative terms.

FIGURE 11-5A Search Help for the U.S. Code

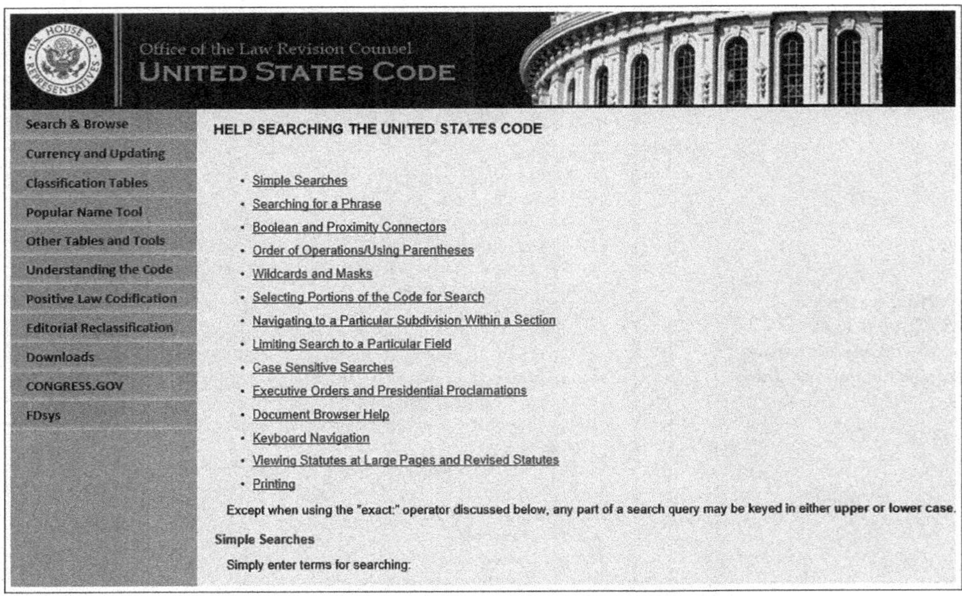

Detailed search help is provided, including help for a Boolean type search.

FIGURE 11-5B Example of Search Help

Boolean and Proximity Connectors

Operators can be specified for more advanced searching, as below. Note that operators can be entered either in lower case or upper case.

Searching for:	Finds documents containing:
wheat adj corn	*wheat* followed immediately by *corn*
wheat and corn	both *wheat* and *corn*
wheat or corn	either *wheat* or *corn*
wheat not corn	*wheat* but not *corn*
wheat before/5 corn	*wheat* followed within 5 words by *corn*
wheat near/5 corn	*wheat* within 5 words of *corn*

After selecting "Boolean and Proximity Connectors" from the list in Figure 11-5A, you are provided with a list and an explanation of the connectors used on this site.

FIGURE 11-6 Example of Advanced Search for U.S. Code

Office of the Law Revision Counsel
UNITED STATES CODE

ADVANCED SEARCH OPTIONS

Search in version: Current

General Search Terms:

Search In: Title Section

+ Also Search In...

Search For: Within: All Fields

+ Also Search For...

Search Clear

Search for references to: Title Section Search Clear

Developmental Deep Reference Searching

Search for references to: Title Section Subsec./Par./Subpar./Etc. Search Clear

11-3 GOVERNMENT WEBSITES (.GOV)

Multiple websites maintained by federal and state governmental agencies provide access to virtually all federal and state primary law. In addition, these sites provide important information about the agency as well as access to forms used by the agency. The following are a few important sites.

www.usa.gov "USA.gov" is the official web portal for the U.S. government. This site provides extensive information about and links to federal agencies, services, and topics. See Figure 11-7A for some of the information available through the homepage of this site. In addition to information about and links to all federal agencies, this site also provides links to state and local government pages. These links can be extremely helpful in researching state and local laws. See Figure 11-7B for an example of local government information that can be accessed.

https://www.gpo.gov/ A good starting point for locating federal law is the website for the Government Publishing Office. This office disseminates information from all three branches of the federal government. By linking to the "Federal Digital System" on the site, you can access extensive online material. A menu on the homepage allows you to easily find and link to the various types of federal law. Refer back to Figure 11-1. Here, you see a menu that leads you to many legal

The official site for the U.S. government.

FIGURE 11-7A USA.gov Homepage

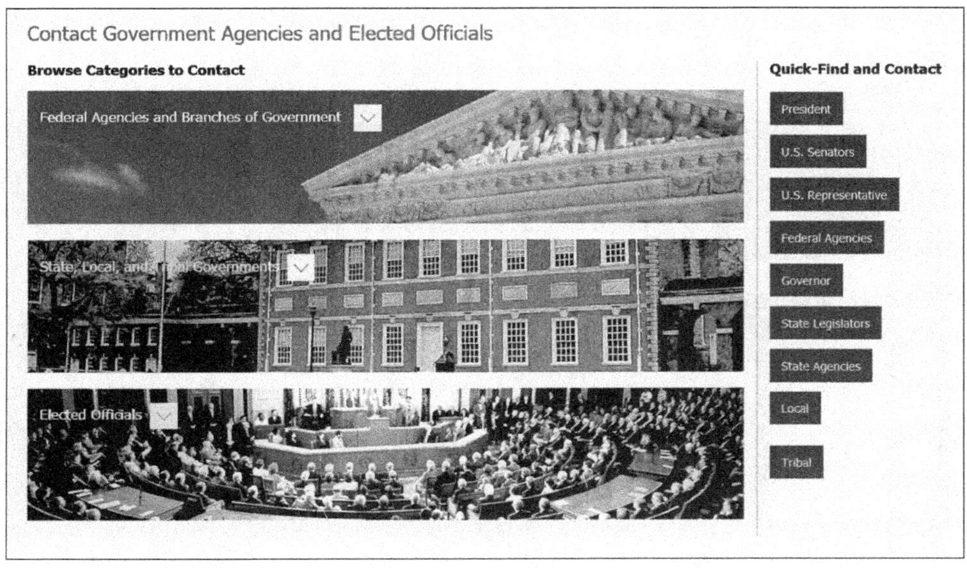

FIGURE 11-7B USA.gov Links to Federal and State Government Information

sources, including the U.S. Codes, the Code of Federal Regulations (C.F.R.), and Supreme Court cases. Through a help menu on the homepage, you can access detailed information about searching on the site. Boolean searching, as used on this site, is explained in detail. The Government has recently introduced a proposed new website entitled "govinfo" that will replace the Federal Digital System. While information and documents are basically the same, the new site will employ a more advanced search engine. The new site is currently located at https://www.govinfo.gov/ See Figure 11-8.

http://www.loc.gov/law/index.php An excellent website for accessing U.S. and international law is the Law Library of Congress. This is a comprehensive site maintained by the Library of Congress. It provides access to vast information, including international, federal, and state primary law. It also provides links to several online law reviews. Also available through this site is access to numerous legislative documents and records. A valuable resource for legal research is the section on "Legal Research Guides." These are short guides on how to conduct various types of legal research (e.g., guides to searching administrative law, foreign and international law, and ***legislative histories***). There is also a beginners research guide. See Figure 11-9.

legislative history
The proceedings that relate to a bill before it becomes law.

www.whitehouse.gov, www.senate.gov, www.house.gov The official websites for the White House, the U.S. Senate, and the U.S. House of Representatives, provide extensive information about the U.S. government and laws as well as links to state and local governments.

www.supremecourt.gov. The official website for the U.S. Supreme Court provides information on the Court itself, direct access to limited Supreme Court documents, and links to collections of Supreme Court cases. Included in the documents provided on the site are transcripts of recent oral arguments, recent slip opinions, and, in pdf format, volumes of the U.S. Reports after 1991 (starting with volume 502). See Figure 11-10.

http://www.uscourts.gov All federal courts maintain websites. Individual federal courts can be accessed through links provided by the website maintained by the Administrative Office of the Courts. In addition to links to all federal courts, the site for the U.S. courts also provides links to all the federal rules as well as various federal forms. An interesting addition to this website is the "Cameras in Courts" feature that allows you to view selected trial court proceedings,

FIGURE 11-8 New Web Source of Government Information from the Government Publishing Office.

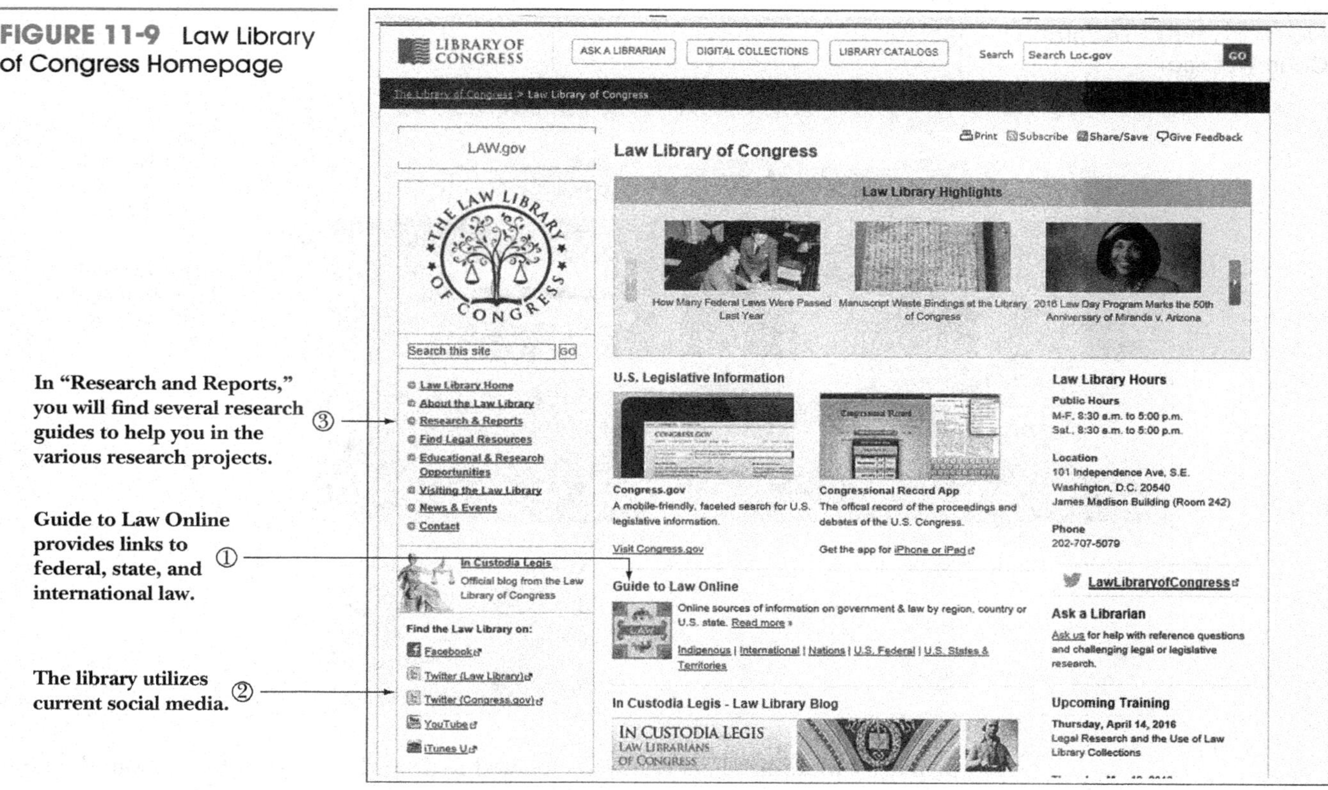

FIGURE 11-9 Law Library of Congress Homepage

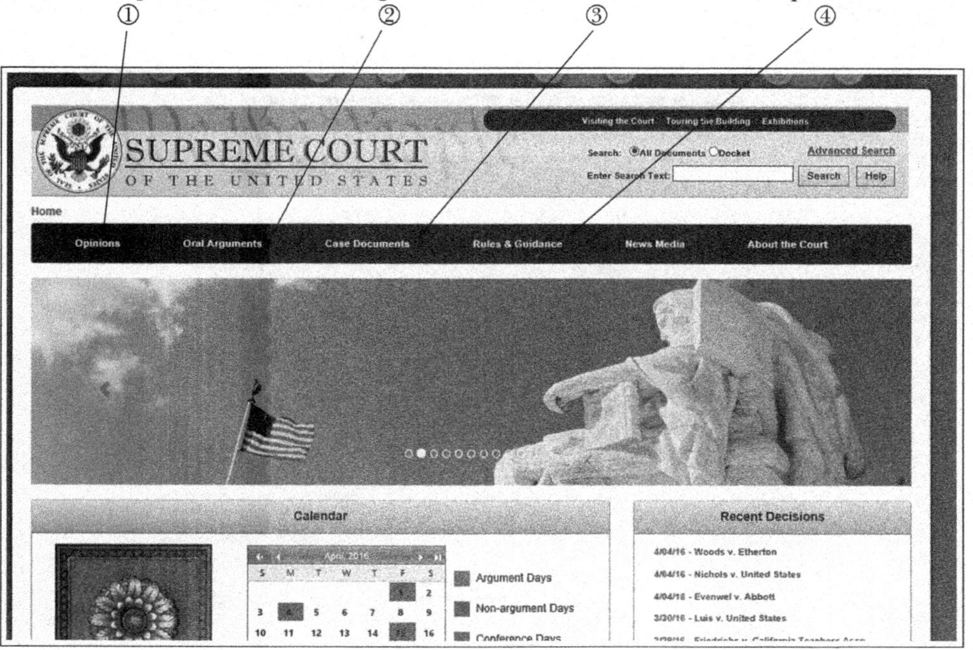

FIGURE 11-10 Website for U.S. Supreme Court

FIGURE 11-11 Federal Court Website

primarily motions. This feature is located in drop-down menu for "About the Federal Courts." See Figure 11-11.

http://www.fjc.gov/ The Federal Judicial Center is the educational and research center for the federal court. On this site, you will find numerous publications dealing with the courts. You will also find information about large class action lawsuits. See Figure 11-12.

FIGURE 11-12 Federal Judicial Center

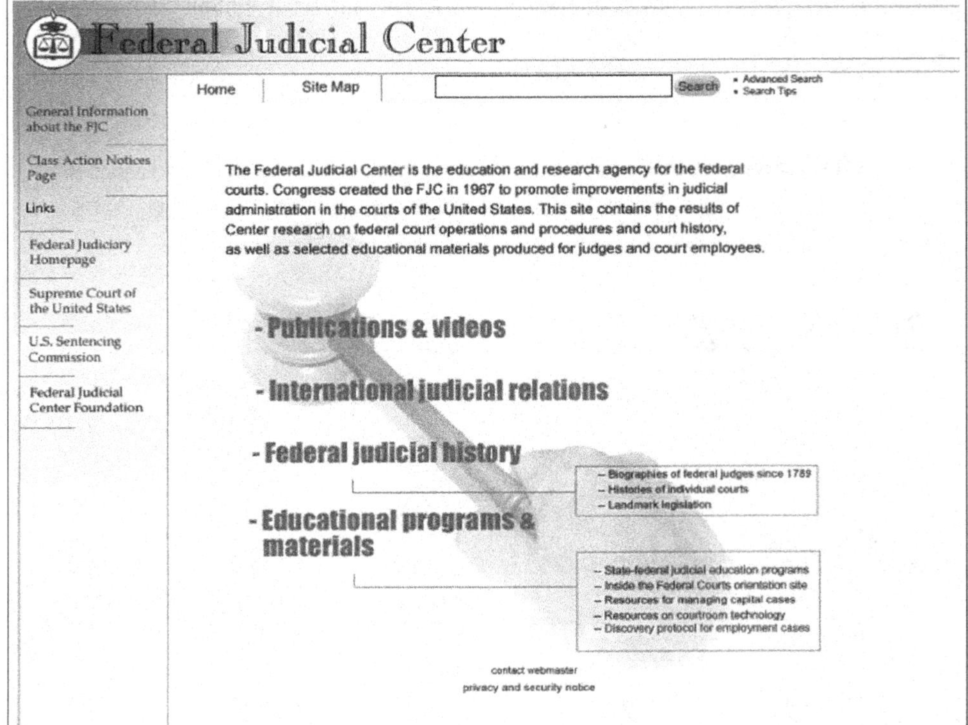

State courts can generally be found through a general search engine, such as Google, or through the homepage for the state. The website www.statelocalgov.net provides links to all state government homepages. From a state's homepage, you can generally find state constitutions, state codes, state cases, and state administrative regulations. State courts may be accessed through the National Center for State Courts at www.ncsc.org.

https://www.pacer.gov/ PACER stands for the Public Access to Court Electronic Records. This site contains electronic copies of documents found in federal court files. This includes appellate court opinions and trial court orders. It also includes legal research memoranda and briefs filed by attorneys. Searching the site is free, although you must first register to use the site. However, a small fee is assessed for actually accessing or downloading documents. (Users are allowed a small minimum without being billed.)

11-4 LAW SCHOOL WEBSITES (.EDU)

Many law school libraries provide excellent information through their websites. Often the sites have links to both federal and state primary law. Many also provide research guides with detailed information about the research process. One well-recognized site follows.

http://www.law.cornell.edu/ This is the site for the Legal Information Institute of Cornell Law School. It is a comprehensive legal portal that provides access to federal and state constitutions, codes, cases, and administrative regulations. In most instances, the databases are searchable using Boolean search methods. The site also contains information about several legal topics, much like a legal encyclopedia. On this site, you can also find an introduction to basic legal citation based on both the ALWD and *The Bluebook*.

The Writer's Corner

Working Words and Noise Words

The most effective sentences use a high percentage of working words. Working words carry the weight of the sentence. The noise words, sometimes referred to as glue words, hold the sentence together.

Example:

"These are the words that carry the weight of the sentence."

This is an 11-word sentence. The working words are underlined. There are four working words and seven noise words. That percentage does not work well. The sentence is "wordy."

Improvement:

"Working words carry the weight of the sentence." The rewritten sentence uses eight words, and five are working words.

Writers should edit looking at the percentage of working words to noise words.

Example:

"The defendant's motion to suppress the evidence was denied by the trial judge."

Again, the working words are underlined in this 13-word sentence. Six of the words are working, and seven are noise.

Improvement:

The trial judge denied the defendant's motion to suppress the evidence. The rewritten sentence uses eleven words, and seven of them are working words.

Notice that this rewritten sentence moves the subject (the trial judge) to the proper place in the sentence. Now the sentence makes better sense. The judge is the "actor" in the sentence. In general, writers want sentences to follow an "actor to action to object" format. The Writer's Corner in Chapter 9 addresses this.

11-5 COMMERCIAL WEBSITES (.COM)

Although you need to be careful when using a commercial website for legal research, several commercial sites provide reliable information.

https://www.justia.com/ This is a comprehensive website providing access to the U.S. Constitution, U.S. codes and regulations, and federal cases, including federal appellate court cases. Federal appellate court cases are categorized by circuit and by the Federal Reporter 2d and 3d series. The site also links to information for many states.

http://lp.findlaw.com/ One of the most well-known commercial websites for legal professionals is FindLaw. FindLaw provides sites for consumers (www.findlaw.com) as well as this site for legal professionals. The site for legal professionals is a comprehensive database of legal materials owned by Thomson Reuters, the same company that owns Westlaw. FindLaw provides access to federal and state constitutions, codes, cases, and administrative rules and regulations. It also provides topical information about many substantive areas of law. Some of the valuable features on FindLaw for Legal Professionals are:

- An annotated version of the U.S. Constitution with a detailed table of contents and hyperlinks to cases that interpret the Constitution. (The U.S. Constitution is annotated by the Congressional Research Service of the Library of Congress and is thus a public document.)
- The U.S. Code, which can be searched or browsed by citation (a template is provided), by key word, by table of contents, or by popular name. Refer back to Figure 11-2.
- The C.F.R., which can be searched by citation (a template is provided) or by key word. (There is also a link to the search tips for the C.F.R. found on https://www.gpo.gov/fdsys/.)
- A searchable version of the Federal Register.
- Links to the Federal Rules of Civil Procedure, Criminal Procedure, and Evidence.
- Supreme Court Cases, which can be retrieved by citation (a template is provided) and by a party name search or a full-text search using key words. Recent cases can also be browsed by year. (FindLaw also provides an explanation of query language, with information about Boolean searching and use of wildcards.)
- U.S. Court of Appeals cases dating from 1994 to 1997, depending on the circuit. The cases can be browsed by date or searched by docket number, by party name, or by a keyword full-text search.
- Selected information from U.S. district courts.
- Links to state codes and cases.
- Information about legal technology and links to popular legal software vendors.
- Information about finding experts in all fields.

http://scholar.google.com/ Google has long been the most popular search engine on the Internet. Using Google, researchers can find numerous legal websites. Google Scholar, a feature on Google, provides direct access to extensive case law. Cases on Google Scholar show page numbers from the official printed versions of the cases, using star pagination. A researcher can also search for relevant law reviews and legal journals. For most law reviews and legal journals, however, the researcher retrieves the title of the journal and a short summary. Accessing the complete text of the secondary source usually requires a fee. However, searching in this way can minimize the time a researcher might need to spend on Lexis Advance and Westlaw and, thus, lead to more cost-effective research. Google Scholar also allows you to search for patents.

www.youtube.com This popular website contains short videos of numerous law-related subjects. You can watch videos of depositions as well as short videos explaining aspects of legal research

A Point to Remember

Most websites have search help that explains the search methods on the site. Often, a list of Boolean connectors used on the site will be provided.

11-6 ORGANIZATIONAL WEBSITES (.ORG)

Numerous organizations maintain websites that provide legal information. The value of the information is often related to the nature of the organization maintaining the site. Two reliable websites are those maintained by the United Nations and the American Bar Association.

http://www.un.org/en/index.html The website for the United Nations, which can be viewed in several languages, provides extensive information on topics such as human rights and international law, including decisions from the International Court of Justice. On a separate website <https://treaties.un.org/>, you find detailed information about numerous treaties.

http://www.americanbar.org/aba.html The American Bar Association is a voluntary and national association of attorneys. Although some of the legal information on the site is accessible only by its members, a great deal of information is available to the public. This site provides information and access to publications dealing with a variety of consumer issues. It also provides information about the legal system, including an overview of the court system, and information about legal careers and education. It also contains links to federal, state, and international laws. (Search for "lawlink" on the American Bar Association web page.)

http://www.plol.org/Pages/Search.aspx The Public Library of Law (plol) offers free access to U.S. Supreme Court and federal appellate court cases, cases from all states dating back to 1997, federal and state statutes, regulations, court rules, and constitutions. While the site is free, registration is required. The Public Library of Law is associated with Fastcase, a commercial site. (Although Fastcase [fastcase.com] is fee based, many state and local bar associations make it available to its members without cost.)

Social Networks The use of social network sites, such as Facebook and Twitter, by government officials and agencies is growing in popularity today. Even the White House has a presence on these sites, providing current news.

11-7 LEGAL BLOGS

Also growing in popularity are legal blogs, discussion sites where individuals post comments and information about various topics. While some of these sites promote personal agendas, some provide valuable legal information. Many legal professional groups sponsor blogs, which are a constant source of current information about specific areas of each group.

http://www.scotusblog.com/ This site, sponsored by Bloomberg Law, provides extensive coverage of the U.S. Supreme Court, including cases and issues before the Court.

See Box 11-1 for an overview of some websites that might help with your research.

BOX 11-1 (FREE) LEGAL WEBSITES: WHERE TO FIND THE LAW

Federal Case Law

Supreme Court

http://www.gpo.gov/fdsys/

http://scholar.google.com/

http://www.supremecourt.gov (PDF versions of recent U.S. Reports

https://www.justia.com/

http://www.plol.org/Pages/Search.aspx

Appellate Court (selected cases)

http://scholar.google.com/

https://www.justia.com/

http://www.plol.org/Pages/Search.aspx

Federal Constitutional and Statutory Law

http://www.loc.gov/law/help/guide.php

http://www.gpo.gov/fdsys

http://www.law.cornell.edu/

http://lp.findlaw.com/

Federal Rules

http://www.law.cornell.edu/

http://www.uscourts.gov/Home.aspx

Federal Regulations

http://www.gpo.gov/fdsys

http://www.law.cornell.edu/

Federal Court Information

http://www.uscourts.gov/Home.aspx

Federal Agency Information

http://www.usa.gov/

http://www.law.cornell.edu/

Portals to Federal and State laws and regulations

http://www.usa.gov/

http://www.loc.gov/law/help/guide.php

http://www.law.cornell.edu/

http://lp.findlaw.com/

https://www.justia.com/

http://www.plol.org/Pages/Search.aspx

11-8 EVALUATING SEARCH RESULTS

Special concerns arise when relying on information obtained through the free Internet. The researcher must ask two critical questions: (1) Who is responsible for the website? and (2) How current is the information on the site? When we use sources such as Lexis Advance and Westlaw, we know that information is supplied by a reliable source. However, anyone can post information on the free Internet. Government sites, law school sites, and sites maintained by reputable legal publishers are the most reliable, when the information is current. Because of the nature of the Internet, outdated information, especially in the form of PDF files, often remains and appears in search results. Even with reliable sites, the currency of information must be checked.

11-9 INTRANETS

If you work in a law firm, you might find that in addition to the Internet, the firm uses an Intranet. Intranets are databases set up and accessible by a specific group, such as a law firm. All members of the firm can access it. If a law firm has several branches in different localities, all of them can access information on an intranet. Intranets also provide the mechanism for setting up e-mail among the various users. Because an intranet is not part of the Internet, some of the security concerns associated with the Internet do not exist. In terms of legal research, intranets provide a vehicle for firms to index and maintain any legal memoranda they prepared. Before researching legal questions, lawyers can check this database to see if the research was done in connection with some other case in the office. Like the Internet, an intranet allows lawyers and their support staff to conduct online discussion groups.

Finding It Online

Legal research on the Internet is continually changing. One good website that helps you keep up to date is the website Internet for Lawyers, located at http://www.netforlawyers.com/index.htm. Another new development is the "Caselaw Access Project," a project of Harvard Law School and Ravel Law to provide free access to all American caselaw.

When you use the Internet for legal research, you will undoubtedly find several favorite sites. Internet browsers, such as Internet Explorer, allow you to "bookmark" these sites and keep the web addresses in a "favorites" file. This gives you easy access to frequently used sites and facilitates your search of the law online.

CITATION MATTERS

INTERNET CITATIONS

***THE BLUEBOOK*—RULE18**

The Internet, Electronic Media, and Other Nonprint Resources

Rule 18 covers a multitude of citation requirements. Legal researchers who use the Internet must pay close attention to the new rules associated with citing to the Internet. A short list of the rules and the coverage of each rule follow.

Rule 18:
- information about the authority being cited
- explanatory phrase indicating which source was used
- provider responsible for the Internet site (if not clear from URL)
- the URL
- a date parenthetical
- order of authorities and parentheticals
- pinpoint citations to Internet sources

CHAPTER SUMMARY

Federal and state primary law is available through numerous free Internet websites. However, editorial enhancements, such as case headnotes and code annotations, are available only through fee-based websites such as Lexis Advance and Westlaw. Limited secondary source material is available without a fee.

Legal websites offer a variety of methods for searching the site. Hyperlinks, templates, and tables of contents sometimes simplify an online search. An important method of searching online legal sources involves the use of Boolean logic. In a Boolean search, sometimes referred to as a *terms and connectors search,* the researcher develops a search query based on the key words found in the research question and certain connective words. Advanced search features facilitate Boolean searches.

Reliability is a key concern with free websites. Reliable free websites are established and maintained by governmental agencies, university law schools, and some commercial enterprises. Various organizations also maintain valuable websites. In addition to free websites, several fee-based sites are available.

TERMS TO REMEMBER

copyright
intellectual property
wildcard
legislative history

QUESTIONS FOR REVIEW

1. Describe the types of law found on the free Internet.
2. Compare and contrast case law found on Lexis Advance and Westlaw with case law found on the free Internet.
3. Compare and contrast codes found on Lexis Advance and Westlaw with codes found on the free Internet.
4. List three major sponsors of websites that provide access to legal materials.
5. Explain how hyperlinks, templates, and tables of contents help researchers.
6. What criteria should be considered in evaluating legal websites?
7. How can free legal websites help a researcher use fee-based sites such as those provided by Lexis Advance and Westlaw?

CAN YOU FIGURE IT OUT?

1. Refer to Figure 11-2. Assume you wanted to retrieve the case *BMW of N. Am. v. Gore,* 517 U.S. 559 (1996). How would you complete the search screen?
2. Refer to Figure 11-3. Assume you wanted to retrieve 18 U.S.C. § 3044. How would you complete the search screen?
3. Refer to Figure 11-4. Which title would you click on if you were looking for a code section dealing with homeland security?
4. Refer to Figure 11-5A. Which item on the list would you select to find information on the use of root expanders in a Boolean search?
5. Refer to Figure 11-5B. Using the connectors in this figure, how would you search for information on free speech?
6. Refer to Figure 11-7A. If you were looking for information from the U.S. Patent Office, what item would you select from the top menu bar?
7. Refer to Figure 11-7B. How would you find local ordinances for your hometown?

TEST YOURSELF (Check Your Answers in Appendix G)

1. What is the title of the case found at 525 U.S. 83 (1998)?
2. What is the general subject matter of 20 U.S.C. § 76i?
3. What is the address of the Texas Eastern District Court?

TEST YOURSELF—WRITE IT RIGHT How to State a Simple Legal Issue

A legal "issue" is a legal question or problem. Lawyers take legal issues to courts for resolution. In very simple terms, an issue has two components: (1) a legal question and (2) the legally relevant facts connected to the legal question. In general, a client brings a problem to a lawyer. The lawyer then finds law that may help resolve the client's problem. It is important that the lawyer frame the client's problem in a way that a judge can easily understand what happened *and* what law may apply to this problem. This is what it means to say that an issue has two components—one factual component and one legal component.

For example, the tort of negligence has four "elements" or four things that a party must prove before damages may be awarded for an act of negligence.

Negligence = duty + breach + causation + damages.

In simple terms, (1) a person may owe a duty to other, (2) if that person breaches that duty, (3) when he is the cause of the accident, and (4) if the injury results in damages—a person may be liable to the injured party.

For example, Tom was driving 45 mph in a 25 mph school zone. He struck a vehicle as he was weaving in and out of traffic in an effort to get to a food truck that was about to close for the day. The vehicle's damage totaled $5,600. There were no physical injuries. The legal question is: Was Tom negligent? To turn this legal question into a legal issue, we need to add in the relevant facts. Think of it this way:

1. Did Tom have a duty to drive safely? Yes.
2. Did Tom breach that duty when he (a) drove 20 miles over the speed limit, (b) was weaving in and out of traffic, (c) in a non-emergency situation?
3. Did Tom cause the vehicle collision? Yes.
4. Did Tom cause damage? Yes.

The issue could be framed like this: Was Tom negligent when he (1) had a duty to drive safely in a school zone, (2) exceeded the speed limit in order to arrive at a food truck before it closed for the day, (c) struck a vehicle while weaving in and out of traffic, and (4) caused damage in the amount of $5,600.

Now, You Try It

(Check your answers in Appendix G)

Facts: Bobby, a 19-year-old college student, was walking down the sidewalk in a busy local public park swinging his new wooden baseball bat. He was not paying attention to other pedestrians. A young mother was trying to strap a child into a baby walker. She was off of the sidewalk and on the grass, in an effort to be out of the way of other pedestrians. She never saw or heard Bobby. As Bobby passed by the young mother, he took a big swing—his follow through struck the woman and broke her arm.

Write the issue, using negligence as the tort. Be sure to use the legally relevant facts.

CITATION EXERCISES

Use the Appendix C to answer these questions. For each of these Bluebook sections, state the topic of coverage:

Example: Bluebook rule 18-7—covers audio recordings

a. *Bluebook* rule 18.2
b. *Bluebook* rule 18.3
c. *Bluebook* rule 18.6

FROM THE WRITER'S CORNER Working Words and Noise Words

1. "The most effective sentences use a high percentage of ____________________ ________________."
2. Underline the working words in this sentence, and then rewrite it: "The defendant was found guilty by the jury."

ASSIGNMENTS AND ACTIVITIES

Analysis Assignment

1. Review case file 1 in Appendix A. Draft queries for finding cases using Boolean logic.
2. Following instructions from your instructor, and working with a partner, select one website described in this chapter. Explore the site and make a presentation to the class about the features on the site.

Online Research Exercises

3. **Statutory Research on the Internet:** Find answers to the following questions using the Internet. Include the site you used to find the answer.
   a. What does 28 U.S.C. § 135 provide?
   b. What does 2 U.S.C. § 135 provide?
   c. Which section of the U.S. Code establishes the Department of Homeland Security?
   d. Where in the U.S. Code do you find the "Drive-by Shooting Prevention Act of 1994"?
   e. Which two constitutional amendments use the term *due process?*
4. **Case Law Research on the Internet:** Find answers to the following questions using the Internet. (Try www.findlaw.com and http://scholar.google.com/.)
   a. What U.S. Supreme Court cases prior to 2004 discuss the law regarding "enemy combatants"?
   b. Which 2003 U.S. Supreme Court case discusses the use of affirmative action in the admission process of a law school?
5. Using either the Law Library of Congress or the Government Publishing Office, find the title of Public Law 109–152. Who initially sponsored the bill?
6. Using Google Scholar, find the title and citation of a *Fordham Law Review* article written in 2010 dealing with *Miranda* warnings.
7. Using a general search engine such as www.google.com, search for information about employment discrimination. You should retrieve from numerous sites. Would any of the first five sites help if you were doing legal research on this issue? Explain. Make a list of legal resources available through this site.

CASE **PROJECT**

Use the Internet to do further research on your case. Do the following.

a. Conduct a general search of the main issues in your case.
b. See if any of the cases or statutes you have found can be located on the Internet.
c. See if the local rules of court for your jurisdiction are on the Internet.
d. See if your local court has a homepage.

chapter **twelve**

BASIC LEGAL WRITING SKILLS

SKILL OBJECTIVES FOR CHAPTER 12

When you complete chapter 12, you should be able to

- Discuss a researcher's initial consideration after completion of the research.
- Create a research outline.
- Explain the purpose of a thesis paragraph.
- Write a thesis paragraph.
- Write a topic sentence.
- Describe the editing and revision process.

CHAPTER OUTLINE

From the Desk of W. J. Bryan, Esq.

TO: Research Assistant
FROM: W. J. Bryan
RE: Our Client, Justin Meyers
DATE:

Now that it has been a few days since you wrote the memorandum in the Meyers case, I would like you to take a final look at it. Proofread it for grammar and style. Edit the content where necessary. The judges who consider these motions are extremely busy. This document must be clear and concise.

12-1 OUTLINE YOUR DOCUMENT BEFORE YOU WRITE

An outline can be a simple list of the headings you plan to use. Think of the outline as a map of your document. As the document unfolds, the headings may change or move around, and that is good. The important thing is that the outline provides a structure for the writer and internal logic or guidance for the reader.

Some of the basic headings rarely change. For example, in an internal memorandum involving the crime of robbery, the headings might look something like this (headings are in bold):

Introduction: A very short snapshot of the case, including any procedural or judicial history.

Statement of Facts: Explain what happened and to whom. Think of this as the "who, what, when, where, and why" used by journalists. Be sure to use all of the key facts and the necessary explanatory facts. A quick review of Sections 2-2 through 2-4 of Chapter 2 might be helpful in figuring out how to sort the facts.

Issue: State the question before the court—"Did the defendant commit robbery when he …."

Rule of Law: State the rule of law—"A prima facie case for the crime of robbery is complete when the following elements are proven by the State: there is a felonious taking, of the personal property of another, from their person or immediate presence, against their will, accomplished by means of force or fear."

Analysis/Application: For the elements listed in the rule of law, provide a simple heading followed by an application of the rule to the facts of the case under consideration. In this instance, if your office represents the state, the headings might look like this:

1. The defendant ripped the victim's purse from her arm while she was removing cash from an ATM.
2. The victim screamed for help as the 6′ 6″ defendant shoved her to the ground and ran.

Conclusion: Provide a simple answer to the issue stated here. "Based on the facts known at this time …"

The basic outline and headings of the document are as follows:

Introduction:
Statement of Facts:
Issue:
Rule of Law:
Analysis/Application:

1. The defendant ripped the victim's purse from her arm while she was removing cash from an ATM.
2. The victim screamed for help as the 6′ 6″ defendant shoved her to the ground and ran.

Conclusion:

When you take the time to create the outline, you ensure that your document will be complete, logical, and easy to follow. Most legal documents follow an easy-to-use format. There is no need to feel as though you must ever start with a blank page.

12-2 BASIC CONSIDERATIONS

Use Topic Sentences

The topic sentence is the writer's initial tool. Even thesis paragraphs need topic sentences. Some sentences serve as transitions from one topic to another or one paragraph to another.

Use Active Voice

Use ***active voice*** whenever possible. Sentences written in active voice usually follow this pattern of construction: subject–verb–object. In other words, open with the actor, move to the action, and then move on to the object of the action. These active voice sentences are very easy to read because they open with a specific actor who then does something to someone.

active voice
Active voice is a tool used by writers to shorten sentences. A sentence written in active voice uses the simple subject–verb–object approach.

Examples:

Active voice:	She soon regretted her actions.
Passive voice:	It was not long before her actions made her sorry that she had done what she had.
Active voice:	Victor kicked the ball.
Passive voice:	The ball was kicked by Victor.
Active voice:	Susan drove the vehicle.
Passive voice:	The vehicle was driven by Susan.

Notice that the active voice sentences are shorter than the passive voice sentences. Check for passive voice while you edit your writing. If you think about it while you are drafting, it will slow you down and you may even lose your thoughts. Most word-processing grammar-check programs help with identifying and correcting passive voice. Notice that the passive voice sentences use too many words. When we edit for passive voice, we also edit out extra words.

Avoid Noise Words

Most sentences contain two types of words—words of "value" and "noise" words. Grammatically correct sentences contain both types of words. The key is to use very few noise words. The noise words help to hold the sentence together, but

they add little to the meaning of the sentence. Editing for noise words is easy. First, count the number of words in the sentence. Second, count the number of noise words. Third, subtract the number of noise words from the total number of words. That provides you with the number of value words. These words are the factually and legally relevant words. Strive to create a much larger proportion of value, or factually and legally relevant, words.
Examples:

> *Poor:* A motion to suppress the confession was brought by the defendant.
> *[There are 11 words in this sentence. The value words are underlined. This sentence has five value words and six noise words.]*
>
> *Better:* The defendant moved to suppress the confession.
> *[There are seven words in this sentence. There are four value words; they are underlined. The noise words are reduced to three. The entire sentence is shortened by four words. This is a better sentence.]*

Use Front-Loaded Sentences

A front-loaded sentence places the important information at the beginning of the sentence. The best practice is to (1) open a sentence with the actor of the sentence, (2) move to the action, and (3) then move on to the object. The "better" sentence in the previous section is crafted in this fashion.

The defendant moved to suppress the confession.

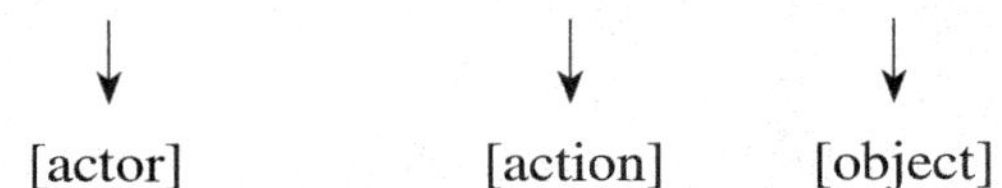

Notice that the "poor" sentence in the previous section is out of order; it does not follow the logical approach of actor first, action second, and object third. Good sentence structure is easy for a reader to follow. A simple way to check your sentence is to read only the value words and skip the noise words. If you try this with the sentence in the example here, the sentence reads: defendant moved suppress confession. This makes sense—it is not grammatically sound, but the reader quickly grasps the content. When you revisit the original sentence—motion to suppress the confession was brought by the defendant—this turns into: motion suppress confession brought defendant. As a writer, you quickly realize that this sentence is out of order. Edit your work using this simple approach.

12-3 KEEP LEGAL WRITING SIMPLE

Use Short Sentences

Keep sentences short. Use 25 words or less as the benchmark of an easily readable sentence. Long sentences become hard to read or even unreadable. As you review your written work, look for sentences that are longer than three lines. Edit them; in most cases, they are too long for your reader to easily follow. Editing may involve cutting the sentence down in size or rewriting it as more than one sentence.

A Point to Remember

Your legal writing is not meant to entertain the reader but rather to inform (predictive writing) or convince (persuasive writing). Many of the tools writers of fiction use to entertain—for example, varying sentence length, creative use of adjectives, and unnecessary words—must be avoided in legal writing. You are writing with a very specific purpose. Stay focused on the purpose of the document and the ultimate audience.

Avoid Unnecessary Words

Keep your legal writing simple. Get to the point, rather than introduce the point. Over the years, somewhere in an English course, we were told to introduce the topic, so we learned to open our sentences with a phrase intended to tell the reader what we were about to do. Edit those phrases and words out of your legal writing. If an introductory phrase adds nothing to the meaning of the sentence, delete it. Examples:

Poor: "Over the years many courts have held that the Fourth Amendment provides protection …."

Better: "The Fourth Amendment provides protection …."

The citations that follow this sentence will show the case precedent for this statement. Extra words do not help. In the example for the "poor" sentence, the reader must trudge through nine words before anything of value is presented. Get to your point, and do it quickly. Readers lose patience with writers who submerge good ideas inside long, poorly worded sentences.

Use Specific, Concrete Terms

The use of specific terminology is essential. Ambiguity arises when vague words invade legal writing. Be as specific as the facts of your situation allow. Use the most important facts to tell a clear story about people. For example, if it was "cold," tell the reader how cold. If the tree was "big," tell the reader it was 50 feet high. If the officer "demanded" something, do not say he "asked" for something. In the following examples, if the writer is describing an accident from the plaintiff's position, the first sentence is poor. However, if the accident is described from the defendant's point of view, the first sentence may be the better choice. Point of view makes a difference.
Examples:

Poor: The defendant's truck moved into the right lane hitting plaintiff's car.

Better: The defendant unexpectedly swerved his Chevrolet Tahoe into plaintiff's lane, seriously injuring the plaintiff and demolishing plaintiff's Ford Focus.

12-4 SENTENCES

Sentences are groups of words expressing a complete thought. This grouping of words must have a noun and a verb. In legal writing, it is best to keep your sentences short and direct. A concise, well-thought-out sentence is easy to read and understand. Long, convoluted sentences are hard to follow and may actually present unwanted ambiguities.

We can learn from case law and statutes, but using their organization and general format may not be the best approach for the legal researcher who is writing to inform (predict) or convince (persuade). Studying well-written and carefully constructed documents can be very helpful.

A Point to Remember

Students are sometimes confused by what might be called the legal "Do as I say, not as I do" approach. The study of law involves reading law, often case law, rather than summaries, discussions, explanations, and factual characterizations written for the court or for clients by legal professionals. Courts structure case opinions to inform or instruct the legal community. Legislatures create statutes to inform all of us about the status of the law. Statutes are often very long and written in a complex format. This is not a signal to you that you should write in this fashion. Similarly, case opinions may not always offer great examples of clear and concise legal writing.

The Role of Topic Sentences

topic sentence
A topic sentence introduces the issues or subissues and connects back to the thesis paragraph.

Most paragraphs begin with a special type of sentence, a ***topic sentence***. A good topic sentence introduces issues or subissues and connects back to the thesis paragraph. It creates unity within the paragraph by summarizing the point made in the paragraph. It forces the writer to articulate clearly. Its function is to set forth the relationship at the very beginning of the paragraph.

Take a look at how the topic sentences work in the argument from the *Caballes* case. As you read, ask yourself if these sentences provide a good road map for the reader.

point heading
The point headings provide the reader with a detailed road map of the legal discussion or argument. Use them to make a *point* you want to stress for the reader. Use point headings in the discussion or argument section.

ARGUMENT

The Fourth Amendment Does Not Require Reasonable Suspicion To Use A Drug-Detection Dog To Sniff The Exterior Of A Vehicle During A Traffic Stop Justified By Probable Cause. [This sentence is the first major ***point heading***.]

1. We begin with a matter that the majority below did not address: the status of canine sniffs under the Fourth Amendment.
2. In *United States v. Place,* 462 U.S. 696 (1983), an officer subjected the defendant's luggage to a canine sniff.
3. The Court has never questioned *Place's* holding that canine sniffs are not searches.
4. In *City of Indianapolis v. Edmond,* 531 U.S. 32 (2000), the Court expressly reaffirmed *Place* with respect to canine sniffs of the exterior of a vehicle.
5. In so ruling, however, *Edmond* reaffirmed *Place's* holding that use of a drug-detection dog to sniff the exterior of a vehicle is not a Fourth Amendment search:

   "It is well established that a vehicle stop at a highway checkpoint effectuates a seizure within the meaning of the Fourth Amendment. The fact that an officer walks a narcotics-detection dog around the exterior of each car at the Indianapolis checkpoints does not transform the seizure into a search. *See United States v. Place,* 462 U.S. 696, 707 (1983). Just as in *Place,* an exterior sniff of an automobile does not require entry into the car and is not designed to disclose any

(*continued*)

information other than the presence or absence of narcotics. Like the dog sniff in *Place,* a sniff by a dog that simply walks around a car is much less intrusive than a typical search. Rather, what principally [makes] these checkpoints [unlawful] is their primary purpose."

6. Because a sniff by a drug-detection dog is not a search, the Illinois Supreme Court erred in holding that reasonable suspicion is required to conduct a sniff of a vehicle already detained on probable cause that a traffic violation occurred.
7. Thus, if Trooper Gillette, when requesting respondent's license and registration, had seen a bag of cocaine or a handgun on the passenger seat, that visual observation would not have been a search and therefore would not have violated the Fourth Amendment.
8. The same result obtains under the actual facts of this case.
9. Two considerations might be advanced to support a contrary result, but neither has merit.
10. It might also be argued that the sniff was unlawful because the dog's arrival at respondent's traffic stop was not inadvertent.
11. For these reasons, conducting a canine sniff during the course of respondent's traffic stop did not violate the Fourth Amendment.

The reader of this document should notice that the author (the advocate) opens with the issue, follows with the legal explanation paragraphs, then uses the rules of law in the legal application paragraphs, and ultimately reaches a conclusion. This approach is one way for you to test your documents. When you pull out the topic sentences, they should provide a logical road map to your legal conclusions.

A Point to Remember

Topic sentences may be added after the paragraph is drafted in a rough format. If you find that writing good topic sentences slows you down or even stops the flow of your writing, add them during the revision process.

In general, avoid placing a citation *in* the topic sentence. Readers are distracted by citations and may miss the actual emphasis of the sentence.

During the revision process, make an outline using only the first sentences, the topic and transition sentences of each paragraph. Review this outline; does it flow? Can you easily follow the information? Topic sentences are a good way to check the internal organization of most legal documents.

These are the topic sentences from the two paragraphs taken from one of the briefs filed in the *Minnesota v. Dickerson* case:

> The Minnesota Supreme Court erred in holding that the police officer who searched respondent exceeded the scope of the protective pat-down search authorized under *Terry v. Ohio.*
>
> The Minnesota Supreme Court also erred in holding that the sense of touch can never provide probable cause to believe that the object felt is contraband.

Both sentences introduce the topic of the paragraph. Each topic sentence is clear and concise.

12-5 PARAGRAPHS IN GENERAL

An effective paragraph is a grouping of related sentences that flow logically and address one idea. It should be clear to the reader why a certain sentence is in a certain paragraph. Good paragraph construction takes time and patience. For each sentence, the writer must ultimately answer the question: Why is *this sentence* in *this paragraph?*

Legal writing, in the discussion section of a ***predictive office memorandum*** or in the argument section of a ***persuasive document*** written to convince a court, generally follows a pattern of legal rule explanation paragraphs, followed by legal rule application paragraphs. Put another way, the rules of law are set out and explained. The following paragraphs apply the rules of law to the client's situation. When a counter argument should be addressed, those paragraphs follow the rule application paragraphs. Good legal writers place their argument before addressing a counter argument. A final paragraph usually reaches a conclusion based on the legal explanation and legal application paragraphs. This organization allows the reader to easily follow the discussion or argument.

predictive office memorandum
A predictive memorandum predicts the outcome of a legal issue, based upon legal research and analysis. This document does not "take sides" or try to convince the reader to adopt a position.

persuasive document
A persuasive document is drafted to persuade the reader to adopt the writer's legal analysis of a specific legal problem. The audience for most persuasive documents is a court (judge).

The following argument was taken from a brief filed with the U.S. Supreme Court in *Illinois v. Caballes,* 543 U.S. 405 (2005). Margin notes are provided to point out various legal writing details and to identify the overall structure of the argument. Notice that the writer opens the argument with a short introduction paragraph.

ARGUMENT

Thesis statement—answer to the issue—used in a point heading.

I. The Fourth Amendment Does Not Require Reasonable Suspicion To Use A Drug-Detection Dog To Sniff The Exterior Of A Vehicle During A Traffic Stop Justified By Probable Cause.

Introduction.

We begin with a matter that the majority below did not address: the status of canine sniffs under the Fourth Amendment. Settled precedent holds that a sniff by a drug-detection dog, in and of itself, is not a search. Given this premise, it does not violate the Fourth Amendment to conduct a canine sniff on the exterior of a vehicle during a traffic stop justified by probable cause.

Rule explanation paragraph.

In *United States v. Place,* 462 U.S. 696 (1983), an officer subjected the defendant's luggage to a canine sniff. *Id.* at 698–99. The dog alerted to the luggage, which later was found to contain cocaine. *Id.* at 699. In considering defendant's challenge to his conviction, this Court noted that if a canine sniff were a Fourth Amendment search, then the seizure of the luggage "could not be justified on less than probable cause." *Id.* at 706. The Court concluded, however, that a sniff by a drug-detection dog is not a search:

> The Fourth Amendment protects people from unreasonable government intrusions into their legitimate expectations of privacy.... A "canine sniff" by a well-trained narcotics detection dog, however, does not require opening the luggage. It does not expose non-contraband items that otherwise would remain hidden from public view, as does, for example, an officer's rummaging through the contents of the luggage. Thus, the manner in which information is obtained through this investigative technique is much less intrusive than a typical search. Moreover, the sniff discloses only the presence or absence of narcotics, a contraband item. Thus, despite the fact that the sniff tells the authorities something about the contents of the luggage, the information obtained is limited. This limited disclosure also ensures that the owner of the property is not subjected to the embarrassment and inconvenience entailed in less discriminate and more intrusive investigative methods.

(*continued*)

Id. at 707. After stating that it was "aware of no other investigative procedure that is so limited both in the manner in which the information is obtained and in the content of the information revealed by the procedure," the Court held that a canine sniff in a public place "does not constitute a 'search' within the meaning of the Fourth Amendment." *Id.*

The Court has never questioned *Place's* holding that canine sniffs are not searches. *See Soldal v. Cook County, Illinois,* 506 U.S. 56, 63 (1992) (noting that *Place* held "that subjecting luggage to a 'dog sniff' did not constitute a search for Fourth Amendment purposes because it did not compromise any privacy interest"); *United States v. Jacobsen,* 466 U.S. 109, 123–24 (1984) (same); *see also Kyllo v. United States,* 533 U.S. 27, 47 (2001) (Stevens, J., dissenting) ("in [*Place*], we held that a dog sniff that discloses only the presence or absence of narcotics does not constitute a search within the meaning of the Fourth Amendment") (internal quotations and citations omitted); *Bond v. United States,* 529 U.S. 334, 341 (2000) (Breyer, J., dissenting) (noting "the accepted police practice of using dogs to sniff for drugs hidden inside luggage").

Rule explanation paragraph.

In *City of Indianapolis v. Edmond,* 531 U.S. 32 (2000), the Court expressly reaffirmed *Place* with respect to canine sniffs of the exterior of a vehicle. *Edmond* considered a challenge to a drug-interdiction checkpoint where vehicles were subjected to a sniff by a drug-detection dog. The Court concluded that the checkpoint violated the Fourth Amendment because it was suspicionless and undertaken for an improper primary purpose. *Id.* at 41–44; *see also Illinois v. Lidster,* 540 U.S., 124 S. Ct. 885, 888 (2004) ("*Edmond* involved a checkpoint at which the police stopped vehicles to look for evidence of drug crimes committed by occupants of those vehicles.")

Rule explanation paragraph.

In so ruling, however, *Edmond* reaffirmed *Place's* holding that use of a drug-detection dog to sniff the exterior of a vehicle is not a Fourth Amendment search:

> It is well established that a vehicle stop at a highway checkpoint effectuates a seizure within the meaning of the Fourth Amendment. The fact that an officer walks a narcotics-detection dog around the exterior of each car at the Indianapolis checkpoints does not *transform* the seizure into a search. *See United States v. Place,* 462 U.S. 696, 707 (1983). Just as in *Place,* an exterior sniff of an automobile does not require entry into the car and is not designed to disclose any information other than the presence or absence of narcotics. Like the dog sniff in Place, a sniff by a dog that simply walks around a car is much less intrusive than a typical search. Rather, what principally [makes] these checkpoints [unlawful] is their primary purpose.

531 U.S. at 40 (emphasis added) (internal quotations and most citations omitted).

Rule explanation paragraph.

Thus, the Fourth Amendment infirmity in *Edmond* was not that a dog sniff transformed a vehicular seizure into a search—the Court made clear that a sniff is not a search—but that the vehicles had been improperly seized in the first place. *Id.* at 40–44.

Because a sniff by a drug-detection dog is not a search, the Illinois Supreme Court erred in holding that reasonable suspicion is required to conduct a sniff of a vehicle already detained on probable cause that a traffic violation occurred. The reason is rooted in long-settled Fourth Amendment doctrine: When police officers, positioned at a lawful vantage point, discover incriminating facts without conducting an additional search or seizure, the discovery causes no intrusion on privacy or security and therefore does not violate the Fourth Amendment. *See Minnesota v. Dickerson,* 508 U.S. 366, 374–75 (1993); *Horton v. California,* 496 U.S. 128, 133 n.5, 141 (1990); *Arizona v. Hicks,* 480 U.S. 321, 325 (1987); *United States v. Hensley,* 469 U.S. 221, 235 (1985); *Michigan v. Long,* 463 U.S. 1032, 1050 (1983); *Illinois v. Andreas,* 463 U.S. 765, 771 (1983).

Rule explanation paragraph.

(*continued*)

Rule application paragraph—notice the shift to the use of the facts of the case—the rule explanation paragraphs above did not mention the facts of the case at issue—the document follows the logical pattern of rule explanation paragraphs followed by rule application paragraphs.

Thus, if Trooper Gillette, when requesting respondent's license and registration, had seen a bag of cocaine or a handgun on the passenger seat, that visual observation would not have been a search and therefore would not have violated the Fourth Amendment. *See Whren v. United States,* 517 U.S. 806, 808–09 (1996) (officer who pulled over vehicle for traffic violations observed bag of crack cocaine in driver's hands); *Hensley,* 469 U.S. at 224 (during investigatory stop of vehicle, officer observed butt of revolver protruding from underneath passenger's seat); *Long,* 463 U.S. at 1036 (during investigatory stop of vehicle, officer discovered bag of marijuana under arm rest). Likewise, if Trooper Graham, upon his arrival at the traffic stop, had smelled marijuana smoke coming from the passenger compartment or the scent of a corpse coming from the trunk, that olfactory observation would not have violated the Fourth Amendment. *See* 1 Wayne R. LaFave, Search and Seizure, § 2.2(a), at 403 (3d ed. 1996).

Rule application paragraph.

The same result obtains under the actual facts of this case. Because there was probable cause to stop respondent for speeding, Troopers Gillette and Graham were entitled to detain and approach respondent's car. The marijuana odors that caused the drug-detection dog to alert were present in the air surrounding the car. Respondent had no legitimate expectation of privacy in the air surrounding his car. *See New York v. Class,* 475 U.S. 106, 114 (1986) ("The exterior of a car, of course, is thrust into the public eye, and thus to examine it does not constitute a 'search.' "). He certainly had no legitimate expectation of privacy in the marijuana odors outside of his car. *See Jacobsen,* 466 U.S. at 123 ("[a] chemical test that merely discloses whether or not a particular substance is cocaine does not compromise any legitimate interest in privacy"); *Place,* 462 U.S. at 707. Thus, the canine sniff of respondent's car entailed no intrusion—more specifically, no intrusion beyond that already effected by its lawful seizure—on respondent's legitimate privacy and possessory interests. *See Dickerson,* 508 U.S. at 375–76. For that reason, the sniff did not violate the Fourth Amendment.

Rule application paragraph—using counter argument—notice that the counter argument follows the rule application paragraphs.

Two considerations might be advanced to support a contrary result, but neither has merit. The first consideration is that Trooper Graham used a dog, rather than his own faculties, to detect the odor of marijuana outside respondent's car. This consideration could not be squared with *Edmond* and *Place,* which held, respectively, that "an exterior sniff of an automobile ... is not designed to disclose any information other than the presence or absence of narcotics," 531 U.S. at 40, and that a canine sniff "disclosing only the presence or absence of narcotics, a contraband item," invades no legitimate privacy interest, 462 U.S. at 707. *See also Jacobsen,* 466 U.S. at 123–24. Thus, it is of no Fourth Amendment moment that Trooper Graham used a dog's superior sense of smell, rather *than his own, to detect the odor of marijuana outside of respondent's vehicle. Compare Kyllo,* 533 U.S. at 38 (use of thermal imaging device "might disclose" intimate details of the home, such as "at what hour each night the lady of the house takes her daily sauna and bath").

It might also be argued that the sniff was unlawful because the dog's arrival at respondent's traffic stop was not inadvertent. *See* Pet. App. 4a ("In *Cox,* we concluded that evidence obtained by a canine sniff was properly suppressed because calling in a canine unit unjustifiably broadened the scope of an otherwise routine traffic stop into a drug investigation.") (citing *Cox,* 202 Ill. 2d at 469, 471, 782 N.E.2d at 280–81). Such a consideration could not be squared with *Horton v. California.* In *Horton,* a police officer searched the defendant's home pursuant to a warrant; the warrant authorized a search for rings stolen during an armed robbery, but not for the weapons used in the robbery. 496 U.S. at 130–31. While conducting the search, the officer discovered the weapons in plain view. *Id.* at 131. The defendant argued that the weapons should have been suppressed because the officer wanted to discover them. This Court disagreed, holding that the Fourth Amendment imposes no "inadvertence" requirement where the police discover incriminating evidence from a lawful vantage point without effecting any additional intrusion on the defendant's legitimate privacy interests. *Id.* at 141–42. Under *Horton,* it does not matter under the Fourth Amendment that Trooper Graham and his dog did not inadvertently stumble upon the scene of respondent's traffic stop.

Rule application paragraph—using counter argument.

For these reasons, conducting a canine sniff during the course of respondent's traffic stop did not violate the Fourth Amendment. The Illinois Supreme Court's contrary ruling should be reversed.

Conclusion.

A Point to Remember

While drafting, try not to slow yourself down worrying about small writing errors. Get your ideas on the screen or page. You must allow time to go back and edit your work. Sometimes valuable ideas are lost because we try to make our first draft absolutely perfect. Draft the document. Go back to edit and proofread.

Construction of a Well-Written Paragraph

Consider the type of analysis to be used in the paragraph before drafting the body of the paragraph. A good paragraph does not assume too much knowledge on the reader's part; it is self-explanatory. Various analytical tools are available to the legal writer. A well-constructed paragraph may use a chronological narration of the facts, or comparison and contrast, or cause and effect to present the information.

The following paragraphs are from the *Minnesota v. Dickerson* decision. Notice the Court's use of detail and simple chronology. Each paragraph opens with a simple topic sentence that sets the scene for the information in the remainder of the paragraph.

On the evening of November 9, 1989, two Minneapolis police officers were patrolling an area on the city's north side in a marked squad car. At about 8:15 p.m., one of the officers observed respondent leaving a 12-unit apartment building on Morgan Avenue North. The officer, having previously responded to complaints of drug sales in the building's hallways and having executed several search warrants on the premises, considered the building to be a notorious "crack house." According to testimony credited by the trial court, respondent began walking toward the police but, upon spotting the squad car and making eye contact with one of the officers, abruptly halted and began walking in the opposite direction. His suspicion aroused, this officer watched as respondent turned and entered an alley on the other side of the apartment building. Based upon respondent's seemingly evasive actions and the fact that he had just left a building known for cocaine traffic, the officers decided to stop respondent and investigate further.

The officers pulled their squad car into the alley and ordered respondent to stop and submit to a pat-down search. The search revealed no weapons, but the officer conducting the search did take an interest in a small lump in respondent's nylon jacket. The officer later testified: "As I pat-searched the front of his body, I felt a lump, a small lump, in the front pocket. I examined it with my fingers and it slid and it felt to be a lump of crack cocaine in cellophane." The officer then reached into respondent's pocket and retrieved a small plastic bag containing one-fifth of one gram of crack cocaine. Respondent was arrested and charged in Hennepin County District Court with possession of a controlled substance.

These paragraphs work because they are well planned. These paragraphs are part of a U.S. Supreme Court opinion. The Court sets the scene for the reader.

The following paragraphs are from an excellent summary of the argument presented to the U.S. Supreme Court in *Frederick v. Morse.* As you read, notice the use of topic sentences, clear language, tone, and general paragraph construction.

> In reversing the district court's grant of summary judgment in favor of the Juneau School Board and Deborah Morse, the Ninth Circuit embraced an unduly narrow reading of this Court's teachings with respect to the free speech rights of public school students. To make very bad matters profoundly worse, the court below fashioned an approach to qualified immunity doctrine that conflicts with this Court's precedents and is dangerously unsettling to thousands of public school educators and administrators across the country. The Ninth Circuit was doubly wrong.
>
> In its teachings with respect to student speech principles, this Court has consistently recognized that public educational institutions possess "special characteristics" that profoundly shape the contextually-sensitive contours of Free Speech doctrine. From its watershed decision in *Tinker,* 393 U.S. 503, through its subsequent decisions in *Fraser,* 478 U.S. 675, and *Kuhlmeier,* 484 U.S. 260, this Court has both protected non-disruptive political speech by students, while respectfully deferring to school administrators' judgments in cabining expression that is inconsistent with the educational function of public schools.
>
> In its First Amendment analysis, the Ninth Circuit fundamentally misconceived the nature and scope of the mission of public education in this country—as elucidated by this Court in both *Fraser* and *Kuhlmeier*—and, at the same time, wildly enlarged the ambit of purportedly political speech. In doing so, the court of appeals substituted its unforgivingly libertarian worldview for the considered judgment of school officials (and school boards) in seeking, consistent with Congress' statutory mandate, to foster and encourage a drug-free student lifestyle. Frederick's banner display not only radically changed the subject from the Olympic Torch Relay ceremony to illegality-promoting, distracting banter, his message itself lay far outside the province of *Tinker*-protected political expression.
>
> To the contrary, as Chief Judge Sedwick rightly concluded, the banner's ambiguous but obtrusive message fell comfortably within the ambit of *Fraser's* focus on promoting appropriate norms of discourse and civility. *Kuhlmeier* likewise supports the school authorities' decision to just say no to respondent's whimsically drug-focused message, inasmuch as the banner—if left undisturbed—could have told not only the high school student body but the larger community that drug-use promotion is openly tolerated within the local public high school. Nothing in law or logic, much less common sense, requires such an extravagant result.
>
> The Ninth Circuit also strayed from this Court's qualified immunity jurisprudence, as embodied in decisions such as *Saucier v. Katz,* 533 U.S. 194 (2001). The court of appeals' conclusion that Deborah Morse, a paradigmatic conscientious educator and administrator, should face a potentially ruinous award for money damages, by virtue of her enforcement actions directed against respondent, cries out for the Court's muscular disapprobation.

12-6 THE THESIS PARAGRAPH

A well-written legal discussion lays a solid foundation for the reader. Before you begin to write, slow down and consider what your reader knows about the problem. You may have worked for many hours and become extremely familiar with all aspects of the problem, but the reader may have little or no knowledge.

A legal discussion or argument should begin with a ***thesis paragraph*** to introduce readers to your client's problem, the legal issues arising from the facts, the rules that govern the issues, and a legal conclusion. This paragraph sets the scene for the reader and provides a short overview of the internal organization of the argument section of a trial brief or the discussion section of a memorandum. If this document will be read by a judge, be sure to request specific relief from the court.

thesis paragraph
The thesis paragraph lays a solid foundation for the reader. This paragraph sets forth the client's problem, states the legal issue, briefly explains the legal rules governing the issues, and states the legal conclusion.

How to Arrange a Thesis Paragraph

1. State the legal issue.
2. Briefly explain the rules of law governing the issues.
3. State the legal conclusion (the thesis).
4. If appropriate, request relief from the court.

The thesis paragraph represents the writer's first opportunity to set the tone and educate the reader and is, therefore, very important. It also outlines the overall organization of the information. Clearly, the thesis paragraph cannot be written until the research is complete and the final analysis is performed.

The following paragraphs are taken from the argument section of the brief for the United States as amicus curiae supporting petitioner in *Minnesota v. Dickerson,* 508 U.S. 366 (1993). Notice that each paragraph follows the format set out in this section.

> I. The Minnesota Supreme Court erred in holding that the police officer who searched respondent exceeded the scope of the protective pat-down search authorized under *Terry v. Ohio. Terry* authorizes a "careful exploration" of a suspect's outer clothing for weapons. 392 U.S. at 16. Officer Rose's brief and limited touching of the pocket of respondent's jacket was an appropriate part of the "careful" examination permitted under *Terry.* Officer Rose did not engage in the sort of prolonged and intrusive manipulation of clothing about which the state supreme court expressed concern. Nor does the record support the suggestion of the state supreme court that Rose made a discrete, conscious decision to continue handling the object in respondent's pocket after concluding that the object was not a weapon. Instead, the officer's act of feeling the object was merely a continuation of a pat-down search indisputably justified at its inception. For that reason the officer's actions are distinguishable from the conduct found to constitute a separate, unauthorized search in *Arizona v. Hicks,* 480 U.S. 321 (1987).

When this paragraph is examined closely, it provides the following:

1. The client's legal issue:
The Minnesota Supreme Court erred in holding that the police officer who searched respondent exceeded the scope of the protective pat-down search authorized under *Terry v. Ohio. Terry* authorizes a "careful exploration" of a suspect's outer clothing for weapons. 392 U.S. at 16.

2. A short explanation of the rule(s) of law:
Terry authorizes a "careful exploration" of a suspect's outer clothing for weapons. 392 U.S. at 16. Officer Rose's brief and limited touching of the pocket of respondent's jacket was an appropriate part of the "careful" examination permitted under *Terry.* Officer Rose did not engage in the sort of prolonged and intrusive manipulation of clothing

about which the state supreme court expressed concern. Nor does the record support the suggestion of the state supreme court that Rose made a discrete, conscious decision to continue handling the object in respondent's pocket after concluding that the object was not a weapon. Instead, the officer's act of feeling the object was merely a continuation of a pat-down search indisputably justified at its inception.

3. The legal conclusion:
   For that reason the officer's actions are distinguishable from the conduct found to constitute a separate, unauthorized search in *Arizona v. Hicks,* 480 U.S. 321 (1987).

II. The Minnesota Supreme Court also erred in holding that the sense of touch can never provide probable cause to believe that the object felt is contraband. This Court has recognized that probable cause can be acquired through senses other than the sense of sight. For example, in *United States v. Johns,* 469 U.S. 478 (1985), the Court held that the "distinct odor of marijuana" provided probable cause to believe that the vehicles from which the odor emanated contained contraband. Moreover, this Court's decision in *Terry* is premised on the ability of police officers to detect concealed firearms by touching the outside of a suspect's clothing. Many lower federal courts have held that the sense of touch may provide probable cause to believe that an item is contraband. In holding to the contrary, the court below mistakenly relied on the differences it perceived between the sense of sight and the sense of touch. Those differences do not warrant a categorical prohibition of the use of the sense of touch to acquire probable cause.

This paragraph also follows a logical format. When examined, it may be separated into the same three components.

1. The client's legal issue:
   The Minnesota Supreme Court also erred in holding that the sense of touch can never provide probable cause to believe that the object felt is contraband.

2. A short explanation of the rule(s) of law:
   This Court has recognized that probable cause can be acquired through senses other than the sense of sight. For example, in *United States v. Johns,* 469 U.S. 478 (1985), the Court held that the "distinct odor of marijuana" provided probable cause to believe that the vehicles from which the odor emanated contained contraband. Moreover, this Court's decision in *Terry* is premised on the ability of police officers to detect concealed firearms by touching the outside of a suspect's clothing. Many lower federal courts have held that the sense of touch may provide probable cause to believe that an item is contraband. In holding to the contrary, the court below mistakenly relied on the differences it perceived between the sense of sight and the sense of touch.

3. The legal conclusion:
   Those differences do not warrant a categorical prohibition of the use of the sense of touch to acquire probable cause.

12-7 OVERVIEW OF PREDICTIVE WRITING

"Predictive writing" is a fancy reference to writing that predicts a legal outcome. The drafter remains neutral; there is no attempt to persuade the reader. The strength or soundness of the rules of law and the application of those rules to a client's situation provide guidance for the reader. These documents are typically drafted in one of several formats; whichever format you choose, the general information is the same.

A simple predictive memorandum may contain the following ***headings***:

headings
Headings provide the reader with a simple road map of the document. Use them to guide the reader through the all the sections of the document.

Facts: short statement of the most relevant facts
Issues: legal question arising from the facts
Brief Answer: simple, direct answer to the legal question (prediction)
Discussion: analysis of the relevant law to the facts

The IRAC method involves a document with four sections.

Issue: the legal question presented by the facts
Rule: the rules of law (constitution, statutes, rules/regulations, and case law)
Analysis: the explanation of the rules of law and the application of the rules to the client's facts
Conclusion: the logical outcome based upon the law used to analyze the facts (prediction)

The CRAC method also involves a document with four sections.

Conclusion: the legal conclusion (often stated in terms of the legal issue)
Rule: the rules of law (constitution, statutes, rules/regulations, and case law)
Analysis: the explanation of the rules of law and the application of the rules to the client's facts
Conclusion: the logical outcome based upon the law used to analyze the facts (prediction)

A predictive memorandum follows. Notice that the Brief Answer takes the place of the thesis paragraph(s).

Sample Predictive Memorandum

Facts

Our client, the Town of Grand View, approved the Jones' application for site development and building permits. Throughout construction of the Jones' home, the Town's only building inspector, David Williams, inspected the Jones' property. Williams' duty was to ensure construction complied with building codes. Williams initialed the Jones' project inspection card, indicating the home's electrical wiring passed inspection. Construction was completed and Williams issued a certificate of occupancy.

The Jones' home caught on fire. The Central Fire District's investigation revealed that the fire started in the home's circuit box, and that the electrical wiring failed to meet building codes. The fire caused over $250,000 in property damage. The Jones' also suffered personal injuries, with medical treatment exceeding $350,000.

The Jones' believe that in response to two letters they sent to the Town manager, complaining about Williams, that Williams acted with corruption or malice in misrepresenting the electric wiring. The first letter complained that Williams failed to appear for four inspections. The second letter complained that Williams failed to appear on time for three more inspections, and that he acted rudely toward the Jones'. The Jones' seek compensation for property damages and personal injuries.

(*continued*)

Questions Presented

I. Is the Town of Grand View immune from liability under Cal. Gov. Code Section 818.8 for misrepresentations made by a public employee?

II. Is the Town's building inspector, Williams, immune from liability for misrepresentation under Cal. Gov. Code Section 822.2 when Williams: (1) made several inspections of the Jones' property, (2) initialed the Jones' inspection card indicating the home's electrical wiring passed inspection, (3) issued a certificate of occupancy, (4) failed to appear on time for seven inspections, and (5) acted rudely toward the Jones'?

Brief Answer

The Town of Grand View is probably immune from liability. Generally, a public entity is not liable for injury resulting from misrepresentations by public employees.

In addition, Williams is probably immune from liability. A public employee is generally immune from liability for his own misrepresentation, unless he or she also acted with corruption, or actual malice. On Williams' facts, a court would almost certainly hold that he committed negligent misrepresentation when he misrepresented the condition of the electrical wiring. However, the court would probably hold that the evidence is insufficient to show Williams acted with corruption or actual malice. The evidence shows that subsequent to the Jones' first letter complaining about Williams, Williams acted rudely toward the Jones, failed to arrive on time to inspections, and misrepresented the safety of the electrical wiring. However, no evidence indicates Williams knew of the letters. Therefore, because evidence of malice is probably insufficient, Williams would probably be immune from liability for misrepresentation.

Discussion

Issue I: The court will almost certainly hold the Town of Grand View immune from liability for Williams' misrepresentation.

California Government Code Section 818.8 provides a governmental entity with immunity from liability for an injury resulting from misrepresentation by an employee. "A public entity is not liable for an injury caused by misrepresentation by an employee of the public entity, whether or not such misrepresentation be negligent or intentional." Cal. Gov. Code § 818.8 (West 20XX). Section 818.8 provides a public entity with immunity from liability for an employee's misrepresentations which result in an interference with a person's financial interests. *Tokeshi v. State,* 217 Cal. App. 3d 999 (1990). In *Tokeshi,* a state employee, instructed plaintiff, Tokeshi, to spray pesticide on his crop. Later, Tokeshi was prohibited from selling his crop due to excess pesticide. The court stated, " 'misrepresentation,' ... applies to interferences with financial ... interests. The Legislature designed Section 818.8 to exempt the governmental entity from this type of liability." *Tokeshi,* 217 Cal. App. 3d at 1005 (citing *Johnson v. State of California,* 69 Cal. 2d 782, 800 (1968)). The court found "plaintiffs' alleged losses are commercial in scope, and therefore the defendants are shielded from liability under the immunity statutes." *Johnson,* 69 Cal. 2d at 801.

The Town of Grand View's case is similar to *Tokeshi* because courts have held that a home is a financial interest. *See Harshbarger v. City of Colton,* 197 Cal. App. 3d 1335 (1998). In *Harshbarger,* "homeowners sued ... after they had to reconstruct their residence because city inspectors allegedly misrepresented and suppressed facts concerning the structure's compliance with the building code." *Tokeshi,* 217 Cal. App. 3d at 1007. The court determined that "misrepresentation immunity barred the action against the public entity because the injury resulted from an interference with the homeowners' financial concerns." *Harshbarger,* 197 Cal. App. 3d at 1342 (*quoted* in *Tokeshi,* 217 Cal. App. 3d at 1007). Similarly, in the Town of Grand View's case, the injuries also resulted from a city inspector who misrepresented a home's compliance with building codes.

(*continued*)

Therefore, since the Jones' personal and financial injuries resulted from the fire caused by Williams' misrepresentation about the Jones' home, a financial interest, the Town of Grand View will almost certainly be immune from liability.

Issue II: The court will probably hold that Williams is immune from liability for misrepresentation.

California Government Code Section 822.2 provides a public employee with limited immunity from liability for his own misrepresentation. "A public employee acting in the scope of his employment is not liable for an injury caused by his misrepresentation be negligent or intentional, unless he is guilty of actual fraud, corruption or actual malice." Cal. Gov. Code § 822.2 (West 20XX). Courts have interpreted Section 822.2 as having three requirements. First, "misrepresentation" was interpreted in the *Schonfeld* case to mean common law deceit. *Schonfeld v. City of Vallejo,* 50 Cal. App. 3d 401, 408 (1975). Second, *Schonfeld* held that where "a plaintiff saw ... the property as to which the alleged misrepresentations were made... he must establish that he was justified in ... relying on the other party...." 50 Cal. App. 3d at 412. Third, courts have interpreted "actual fraud" and "actual malice" as "a conscious intent to deceive, vex, annoy or harm the injured party in his business." *Id.* at 401. Therefore, a public employee is not immune from liability for misrepresentation if the following conditions are satisfied:

1. the employee is guilty of common law deceit;
2. the plaintiff is justified in relying on the employee; and
3. the employee is motivated by corruption, or actual malice.

See id. at 410–12.

A. Williams probably committed common law deceit. When Williams initialed the inspection card he misrepresented the safety of the electrical wiring. Courts have held that negligent misrepresentation is a type of common law deceit.

The court in *Schonfeld* lists four kinds of common law deceit, including negligent misrepresentation. *See id.* at 408. Negligent misrepresentation is, "[t]he assertion, as a fact, of that which is not true, by one who has no reasonable ground for believing it to be true." Cal. Civ. Code, § 1572, subd. 2.

In the Town of Grand View's case, no facts establish Williams knew the electric wiring was unsafe; however, the facts probably establish that Williams committed negligent misrepresentation. As the Town's sole building inspector, Williams had a duty to ensure that construction of the Jones' home complied with all building codes. Furthermore, Williams signed-off on the project's inspection card, indicating that the home's wiring complied with building codes. However, after the fire, the Central Fire District's investigation revealed that the fire started in the main circuit box, which failed to meet any known building codes. Therefore, the court will almost certainly hold that Williams had "no reasonable grounds for believing ... [the electrical wiring was safe] to be true." Cal. Civ. Code, section 1572, subd. 2 (quoted in *Schonfeld,* 50 Cal. App. 3d at 409). This fulfills the requirements for negligent misrepresentation.

B. The Jones' were almost certainly justified in relying on Williams' representations. Williams was the Town's sole building inspector and certified that the Jones' home complied with building codes. Courts have held that a person is justified in relying on the representations of a government employee who holds himself or herself out as an expert.

The court in *Schonfeld* held that where "a plaintiff saw ... the property as to which the ... misrepresentations were made ... he must establish that he ... was justified in not making an inspection or in relying on the other party ...." *Id.* at 412.

(*continued*)

In *Schonfeld,* plaintiff, Schonfeld, invested in a marina after the city manager made representations about the marina's quality. Specifically, one alleged misrepresentation was that the marina was "a first class harbor" and "the best berthing facility in Northern California." *Id.* at 413. The court stated, "[t]he city manager did not hold himself out as an expert on marinas but indicated that the marina was completed according to the city's plans ...." *Id.* The court held that the plaintiff was not justified in relying on the city manager's representations and that the city manager did not commit misrepresentation.

The Town of Grand View's case differs from *Schonfeld.* Williams, the Town's sole building inspector, was supposed to ensure that the Jones' home complied with building codes. In addition, he inspected the Jones' home, initialed the inspection card indicating the electric wiring passed inspection, and issued the certificate of occupancy. Unlike *Schonfeld,* the facts indicate that Williams appears to have held himself out to be an expert in building inspections. Therefore, the court will almost certainly hold that because Williams held himself out to be an expert in building inspections that the Jones' were justified in relying on his representations.

C. The evidence is probably insufficient to indicate Williams was motivated by corruption, or actual malice. Although the Jones' letters indicate that Williams acted rudely after the first letter, no evidence indicates Williams knew about the letters.

In *Schonfeld* the court states, "section 822.2 applies unless, ... a public employee is motivated by corruption or actual malice ...." *Id.* at 411. In *Schonfeld,* the plaintiff alleged that the city manager misrepresented the city's title to the marina. The court held, "There was no evidence from which it could be inferred that the city manager made any representations with the actual malice as required by the statute." *Id.* at 416. This differs from the City of Grand View's case. The Jones' first letter did not complain that Williams acted rudely; however, the second letter did. This may indicate that Williams was angry about the first letter, and in response acted rudely toward the Jones. From Williams' conduct, a court may infer that Williams' misrepresentation was in response to the Jones' letters.

On the other hand, no evidence indicates Williams knew about the letters. If Williams knew about the letters, it is important to find out whether he learned about them before misrepresenting the electric wiring. In addition, knowing if Williams was rude before the first letter could establish that he was not acting rudely in response to the letters, and that the misrepresentation was not in response to the letters.

Therefore, the court will probably hold the evidence is insufficient to infer Williams acted with malicious intent or corruption. Since Section 822.2 provides immunity for misrepresentation without corruption or malicious intent, Williams will probably be immune from liability.

12-8 OVERVIEW OF PERSUASIVE WRITING

Some documents must be persuasive. That is, the document is written so that the reader is persuaded to adopt the writer's point of view. Examples of such documents are trial briefs, appellate briefs, points and authorities in support of motions, declarations, and demand letters. In persuasive writing, every word, phrase, and sentence must be carefully drafted. The writer must consider the impact the document will have on the reader. This goes beyond informative writing.

Set forth in the following are excerpts from briefs filed with the U.S. Supreme Court in the *Minnesota v. Dickerson* case.

This excerpt is from the opening argument section of the brief for the United States as amicus curiae supporting petitioner.

ARGUMENT

I. OFFICER ROSE WAS CONDUCTING A LAWFUL PAT-DOWN SEARCH WHEN HE ACQUIRED PROBABLE CAUSE TO BELIEVE THAT RESPONDENT POSSESSED CONTRABAND.

The Minnesota Supreme Court not only declined as a general matter to recognize a "plain feel" corollary to the "plain view" doctrine; it also held that the crack seized from respondent's pocket would not be admissible under a "plain feel" analysis in any event. The latter holding was based on the court's view that, in the course of determining that the object in respondent's pocket was crack, Officer Rose exceeded the scope of the protective pat-down search authorized under *Terry v. Ohio.* To the contrary, we submit that Officer Rose was acting within the scope of *Terry* when he developed probable cause to believe that respondent was in possession of contraband.

At the outset, we agree with the premise underlying the state court's *Terry* holding: a "plain feel" corollary to the "plain view" doctrine would not authorize a police officer to seize evidence without a warrant if the police officer violated the Fourth Amendment in the course of developing probable cause to support the seizure. An "essential predicate" of a seizure based on "plain feel," like one based on "plain view," is that "the officer did not violate the Fourth Amendment in arriving at the place from which the evidence could be plainly [felt]." *Horton v. California* 469 U.S. 128, 136 (1990). Thus, if a police officer reaches into a suspect's pocket without reasonable suspicion or probable cause and feels an object that the officer knows to be contraband, the seizure of that object cannot be justified on the ground that the seizure was the product of a "plain feel" of the object. In *Sibron v. New York,* 392 U.S. 40, 65 (1968), this Court held that such an intrusion was unlawful, because the intrusion was not justified by reasonable suspicion or probable cause to believe that the suspect had contraband or a weapon in his pocket. The Court therefore ordered suppression of the contraband found in the course of that search.

Officer Rose's conduct, however, was a far cry from the sort of intrusion held to violate the Fourth Amendment in *Sibron.* This was not a case of retroactively justifying a search by what it turned up; rather, because the pat-down search was lawful, the fruits of that search could be considered in determining the lawfulness of Officer Rose's further investigative steps.

This next excerpt is from the opening argument section of the brief filed for the American Civil Liberties Union and the Minnesota Civil Liberties Union as amici curiae in support of respondent.

ARGUMENT

I. THE WARRANTLESS SEARCH OF RESPONDENT'S POCKET CONTRAVENED THE FOURTH AMENDMENT BY EXCEEDING THE SCOPE OF *TERRY*.

A. A *Terry* frisk is limited solely to a narrowly-tailored search for weapons.

In *Terry v. Ohio,* this Court set forth the standard governing pat-downs of temporarily detailed suspects: an officer can only conduct a limited protective search for weapons (a "frisk") when there is "reason to believe that he is dealing with an armed and dangerous individual...." 392 U.S. at 27. Although subsequent cases have extended *Terry's* reach to other contexts, this Court has never deviated from the fundamental rule that a frisk is singularly limited to weapon searches, and thus cannot be conducted simply to locate contraband or evidence of crime.

These principles were reaffirmed in *Ybarra v. Illinois,* 444 U.S. 85, 92–95 (1979): "The *Terry* case created an exception to the requirement of probable cause,"

> an exception whose 'narrow scope' this Court 'has been careful to maintain.' Under that doctrine a law enforcement officer, for his own protection and safety, may conduct a pat-down to find weapons that he reasonably believes or suspects are then in the possession of the person he has accosted. Nothing in *Terry* can be understood to allow a generalized "cursory search for weapons" or, indeed, any search whatever for anything but weapons. *Id.*

Both briefs go on for many pages. Both are convincing. Compare and contrast these two opening arguments.

The Writer's Corner

Edit for Needless Words

The best writers are direct and use concrete terms. The words should "tell" something. That is why good writers strive to fill their sentences with *working words.*

Problematic Expressions	**Improved Expressions**
The phrase "the fact that" should be omitted.	
call his attention to the fact that	remind him
the fact that he had departed	his departure
the fact that he had not won	his loss

The editing process may seem slow and tedious; however, it is necessary. In the following two examples, the problematic expressions are long and lack the directness that is the benchmark of good writing.

Avoid	**Better**
she is a woman who	she
this is a subject that	this subject

Good writing involves placing negatives into positive form. Edit for the word "not."

did not remember	forgot
not helpful	unhelpful
not important	Insignificant

12-9 INITIAL CONSIDERATIONS AFTER COMPLETION OF THE RESEARCH

Before you begin to write, go back to your initial instructions. Did you follow them?

- Did you answer the questions clearly and concisely?
- Did you respond to *all* of the questions?
- Can you honestly tell your supervisor that your research results are accurate, current, and valid?
- Were you as thorough as possible?

If your response to each of these questions is "yes," you are ready to begin the drafting process. After the research is complete, the note-taking and copying are replaced with analysis and writing. The questions and considerations in the next section help organize your writing.

12-10 OVERVIEW OF A LEGAL RESEARCH AND WRITING PROJECT

These questions or considerations help the legal writer focus on the project and recognize problem areas.

1. What exactly is the research project, or what is your goal?
2. Who is the reading audience?
3. What legal issues does the research explore?
4. How will the reading audience benefit from the results of the research?
5. List the most important points you must get across to your audience.
6. List the legal authority that supports each point listed in item number 5.
7. Which citation manual must be followed? (*The Bluebook, A.L.W.D. Citation Manual*)
8. Is there a length restriction? If so, what is it?
9. What is the length of your current draft?
10. When must this project be completed?

These questions help the writer focus and provide structure to the process of research and writing.

12-11 OVERVIEW OF THE EDITING AND REVISION PROCESS

1. Print the document. If time permits, let it sit for a day before you look at it again. Reread your instructions. Have you adequately responded to the initial questions?
2. Look over the document; do not read it, just glance through it.
3. Is the organization of the document readily apparent without actually reading it? If not, go back and work in appropriate point headings.
4. Check to see that each paragraph contains a topic sentence or a sentence that serves as a transition from the previous paragraph.
5. Does the discussion or argument section begin with a thesis paragraph? If not, insert a thesis paragraph now.
6. Make sure each paragraph contains facts or law to support your position.
7. Identify the verbs. Highlight the following: *was, were, is, are, has been, have been, had been, becomes, became, went, did,* and *came.* Where possible, replace these with active verbs. Active verbs create a mental picture of a specific sensation, activity, or sound in the reader's imagination.
8. Place transition words or phrases between sentences and paragraphs where appropriate.
9. Reread the opening of your document. Does it clearly and concisely introduce the topic of your writing? If not, revise or rewrite.
10. Reread the conclusion. Does it clearly and concisely conclude your document? If not, edit or rewrite. When you complete the conclusion, ask yourself if you have created a tone of finality.

Finding It Online

Online Research

This chapter features sections from appellate briefs filed in the case of *Minnesota v. Dickerson*. You can listen to the oral arguments in this case by going to http://www.oyez.org/ (search for *Minnesota v. Dickerson*; or click on Cases, then the year 1992, and scroll for *Minnesota v. Dickerson*). Also, go to www.supremecourtpreview.org. This website is supported by the American Bar Association. It provides a great deal of useful information.

For more information on legal writing, go to the following:

http://press-pubs.uchicago.edu/garner

http://www.bartleby.com/141/ (Elements of Style, William Strunk, Jr.)

http://www.witkin.com/pages/traynor_pages/witkin_on_writing.htm

CITATION MATTERS

USE OF THE ELLIPSIS (OMISSIONS)

***THE BLUEBOOK*—Rule 5.3**

Legal writers often find it useful to use quoted language but may not need all of the sentence or paragraph. The omission of a word or many words is indicated by inserting an ellipsis in place of the omitted word or words. An ellipsis consists of three periods separated by spaces and set off by a space before the first period and after the last period.

For example:

The "core of the judicial system … relies on early disclosure of all the facts."

Omission of words at the end of a quoted sentence is shown by an ellipsis between the last word of the quote and the final punctuation of the quoted sentence.

For example:

The "core of the judicial system … relies on early disclosure …."

Never use an ellipsis to begin a quotation. When language at the beginning of a sentence is deleted, capitalize the first letter of the first word used and place it in square brackets (unless that word is already capitalized).

For example:

"[T]he statute imposes special prohibitions on those speakers who express views on the disfavored subject of race, color, creed, religion or gender."

This is a simple way to alert the reader that the word *The* was not the first word in the quoted sentence. The use of brackets indicates that the writer changed only the case of the letter. This same tool (the square bracket) is used to change a capital letter to lowercase when the writer needs to incorporate a phrase from the beginning of a quoted sentence into one of the writer's own sentences.

For example:

It is true that "[t]he ordinance, even as narrowly construed by the State Supreme Court, is facially unconstitutional …."

In this example, *The* was the first word in the quoted sentence. But the writer needed to incorporate the quoted sentence into a new sentence. By placing the lowercase *t* in square brackets, the writer signals the reader that he or she changed the case of the letter.

CHAPTER SUMMARY

Keep your legal writing clear and concise. Strive to communicate in a straightforward manner. Before you begin to write, go back and check your instructions; have you followed them? Have you responded to all of the questions? Are your answers clear and concise? Is your research accurate, current, and validated? Have you been thorough? Be sure you understand the parameters of your project. Good legal writing opens with a thesis paragraph. Good paragraphs open with topic sentences. The body of a good legal discussion or argument follows a pattern of rule-of-law explanation paragraphs followed by application of the law to the facts paragraphs. Use active voice when possible. Keep your sentences short and avoid the use of unnecessary words. Be specific and always edit your work before passing it along to anyone to review.

TERMS TO REMEMBER

active voice
topic sentence
point heading
predictive office memorandum
persuasive document
thesis paragraph
headings

QUESTIONS FOR REVIEW

1. What is the role of the topic sentence?
2. Why should you use active voice whenever possible?
3. Discuss the purpose and importance of a thesis paragraph.
4. How should a thesis paragraph be arranged?
5. Why should a writer use the "overview of a legal research and writing project" form set forth in Section 12-10 ?

TEST YOURSELF (Check Your Answers in Appendix G)

Rewrite the following sentences. Edit for problems such as passive voice, too many noise words, too-long sentences, and words in the wrong order.

(a) The defendant was reprimanded by the court for his use of inappropriate language.

(b) The statement was made by the witness.

(c) After considerable deliberation, the jury handed down a verdict that has since been held to be invalid by several courts.

TEST YOURSELF—WRITE IT RIGHT Turning Issues into Point Headings for a Predictive Document

Inter office memorandums are often simply designed to inform or predict, rather than to persuade. In most legal writing, we like to see the legal issues turned into clear point headings within the discussion section of the document

For example: Issues Presented

A. Has an unlawful custodial interrogation occurred when an armed police officer questioned the respondent for over two hours in the Principal's office without *Miranda* warnings?

B. Is the respondent's subsequent confession invalid because it is a fruit from the poisonous tree when her confession was not an act of free will and her initial questioning led the police to the crime scene?

These issues contain the legal questions and the legally relevant facts. These issues might become the following point headings in the body of the discussion:

I. A court will likely grant Tara's motion to suppress her confession.

II. Tara's subsequent confession is invalid because it is a fruit of the poisonous tree.

Now, You Try It

(Check your answers in Appendix G)

Write predictive point headings that correspond well to these two issues.

Issues Presented

I. Is Sutter Hills' nuisance claim against Ms. Young for exercising her freedom of expression in displaying a sign in protest of the Iraq War barred by the First Amendment?

II. Is Sutter Hills' restrictive covenant on signs unreasonable, and therefore unenforceable pursuant to California Civil Code Section 1354, where the covenant is arbitrarily enforced against Ms. Young's sign while the American flag at the community hall remains on display?

CITATION EXERCISES

Use Appendix C and the Citation Matters feature in this chapter to answer these questions.

1. State the *Bluebook* rule that explains the use of the ellipsis.
2. What is an ellipsis?
3. When is it appropriate to use an ellipsis?
4. "Never use an ellipsis to begin a ________________."

FROM THE WRITER'S CORNER Edit for Needless Words

1. The best writers use ______________________ and ____________________ terms.
2. Rewrite this sentence: "Ellen did not remember to lock the door."

ASSIGNMENTS AND EXERCISES

Analysis and Writing Assignments

1. Compare and contrast the arguments set forth in the briefs filed with the U.S. Supreme Court in the *Minnesota v. Dickerson* case located in Section 12-8 .
2. Write a factual summary of the Meyers grand jury testimony located in Appendix A.

Online Research Exercises

1. Locate the briefs filed in the *Kyllo* case, 533 U.S. 27 (2001). How many briefs were filed? List each document filed and the party (or interested party) who filed the brief.
2. Read the brief for the petitioner in the *Kyllo* case. Locate one paragraph of at least four sentences. First, type the paragraph as it is in the original. Second, redraft the paragraph using shorter sentences and the other suggestions provided in this chapter.
3. Go to www.supremecourtpreview.org. Open a recent term, for example the 2016–2017 term. Choose a case; click on the merit briefs and read the petitioner's and respondent's briefs on the merits. If the merit briefs are not yet posted (for a very current case), choose two of the amicus briefs. Write a short summary of the facts of the case and the issues before the U.S. Supreme Court. Clearly cite the case you chose for your instructor.

CASE PROJECT

Review the same case you researched in previous chapters. Answer the questions found in Sections 12-9 and 12-10 of this chapter to determine if you are prepared to write, and if so, how you should proceed.

In-Class Small Group Work

1. Review the paragraphs from the summary of the argument found at the end of Section 12-5. For each sentence, do the following:
   a. Count the number of words in each sentence in each paragraph.

      Sentence 1 = _____

      Sentence 2 = _____ and so forth
   b. Count the number of value words versus the number of noise words.

      Sentence 1 = # of value words / # of noise words

      Sentence 2 = # of value words / # of noise words, and so forth
   c. Notice how many of the sentences have far more value words than noise words.
2. Using the same paragraphs as referenced in case project (1), look at the number of sentences that follow the actor to action to object format.

chapter **thirteen**

THE MEMORANDUM OF LAW: PREDICTIVE LEGAL WRITING

SKILL OBJECTIVES FOR CHAPTER 13

When you complete chapter 13, you should be able to

- Explain the purpose of a legal memorandum.
- Describe the format for a memorandum of law.
- Explain the components of a memorandum of law.
- Explain the purpose of each component of a memorandum of law.
- Write a predictive office memorandum.

CHAPTER OUTLINE

From the Desk of W. J. Bryan, Esq.

TO: Research Assistant
FROM: W. J. Bryan
RE: Our Client, Justin Meyers
DATE:

We are still working on pretrial motions in the Meyers case. Your previous memoranda were very helpful. Now I need you to check on a different issue. As you recall from the facts (review the Grand Jury transcript), our client made several statements in the police car while being transported to jail. Please research the law regarding the admissibility of these statements. If we move to suppress the statements, what are our chances of winning?

13-1 INTRODUCTION

As a legal researcher, you understand the importance of locating the cases or codes that answer your legal questions. However, your job as a researcher is not complete until you communicate your findings in an appropriate manner. In earlier chapters, you learned that legal research is performed for different reasons and the results are conveyed to different types of audiences. The result of your research may be conveyed to a layperson or an attorney in an *objective* manner. An objective evaluation or analysis of the case often includes a *prediction* of how a court might rule on the issues of the case. In other cases, it may be conveyed to an attorney or judge not in an objective manner but in an *argumentative* or *persuasive* fashion.

A research assistant does research for a supervising attorney. Initially, the research results are communicated in an objective manner. Ultimately, the research may form the basis of advice given to a client. It may also form the basis of a formal legal document sent to another attorney and to the court.

Documents conveying the results of legal research use various names. A ***memorandum of law*** is a document written in an objective manner where the researcher explains the law governing a specific situation. An ***opinion letter*** is formal correspondence from an attorney to a client or other attorney explaining an attorney's interpretation of the law as applied to a factual situation. Usually, it contains an objective evaluation of the law and the facts. Chapter 16 addresses opinion letters. A ***memorandum of points and authorities*** is a more formal document filed with the court and advocating the client's position. In such a document, the author attempts to persuade the court to follow an interpretation of the law that favors the author's client. A memorandum of points and authorities supports or opposes a motion made in court in connection with a civil or criminal case. A ***trial brief*** is a formal document, filed with the court at the beginning of the trial, in which the author tries to persuade the trial judge to interpret the law in a way that is favorable to the author's client. An ***appellate brief*** is a document filed in a court of appeal in support of or in opposition to an appeal. It contains arguments related to legal errors that may have occurred at trial. This chapter deals with writing in a predictive objective manner for attorneys and clients. The following chapter addresses persuasive documents.

memorandum of law
An objectively written document where the researcher informs the reader of the law governing a specific situation.

opinion letter
Formal correspondence from an attorney to a client or other attorney explaining an attorney's interpretation of the law as applied to a factual situation.

memorandum of points and authorities
A formal document, written in an argumentative or persuasive manner, it is filed with the court, and advocates a certain position.

trial brief
A document filed with the court at the beginning of the trial in which the author is trying to persuade the trial judge to interpret the law in a way that is favorable to the author's client.

appellate brief
A document filed in support of or in opposition to an appeal, containing arguments related to legal errors that may have occurred at trial.

13-2 MEMORANDUM OF LAW

A memorandum of law contains the researcher's initial findings and analysis. This document is included in the client file and is relied upon by the author or by other attorneys. It may form the basis for advice to the client or may serve as the starting point for drafting persuasive documents to be filed with the court. It is important that a memorandum of law be complete and thorough. A research assistant, such as a law clerk or paralegal, often writes the memorandum of law. (It is common to use the phrase *memorandum of law* to describe this type of document, but not always. Lawyers sometimes call this a *memo,* a *legal memorandum,* or even an *interoffice memo.*) It informs the reader, usually an attorney, of the state of the law concerning a certain issue. It contains a legal analysis of the facts and the law and should contain *all* relevant law, even law that does not support your client's position. The analysis in this type of document should include all reasonable arguments and inferences, whether they support your client or not. The researcher, however, often gives an opinion, a prediction, as to what law and what arguments seem to be the strongest. Relevant legal authority must support the opinion. Such a memorandum is a *predictive* memorandum because it strives to predict how a court will rule on the issue.

Attorneys who rely on research assistants depend a great deal on a memorandum of law. A properly researched and written memorandum saves an attorney a great deal of time. Instead of spending hours researching, reading, and analyzing cases and statutes, the attorney can read a memorandum of law summarizing and synthesizing relevant law. Because an attorney may rely exclusively on such a memorandum, it is essential that this document be complete and accurate.

A Point to Remember

If you rely on a memorandum of law found in an office file, always check the date of the memo. Many cases take years before they are completed; a memo found in a file might have been researched years ago. Remember that laws change; if any significant amount of time passed since the memo was written, you must validate and update the research.

Although a memorandum of law is not a court document (meaning it is not filed with a court), it may later form the basis of an opinion letter to a client or a more formal legal memorandum or brief used to convince another attorney or the court of your client's legal position.

13-3 FORMAT FOR A MEMORANDUM OF LAW

There are no absolute formalities for a memorandum of law, although most do follow similar formats. Because this document is likely to be included in a client file, it should contain basic information found in all office memoranda. It should identify the author of the document, the person for whom it is prepared, the date, and the subject matter. The subject matter must always identify the office client so that if the document becomes separated from the file, it can be properly identified. The beginning of a memorandum should look as follows.

Memorandum of Law

To:

From:

Date:

Subject:

The memorandum itself should contain the following components: a concise statement of relevant facts, a statement of the issue(s) or question(s) forming the basis of the research, a discussion of the law and the facts, and a conclusion. There must be a heading for each component. The headings below are in bold typeface. Some writers also use a concise Introduction. This is helpful when the reader is unfamiliar with the subject matter of the memo. For example, a basic template for a memorandum looks like this.

Facts

[State the relevant and explanatory facts. Review Chapter 3 for identifying and writing a concise statement of facts. Remember, you identified these facts before you started your research.]

Issue(s)

[List the legal questions or issues. If you are writing an objective memorandum of law, the supervising attorney probably gave these questions to you. Refer to Chapter 2 for a review of writing issue statements.]

Discussion

[This is the most important part of the memorandum. In this section, you discuss each of the issues, present the authorities you found in your research, and explain or discuss why and how these authorities apply to your factual situation. In discussing your research, you should use the IRAC method. Review Chapters 4 and 6 on using the IRAC method with cases and statutes. Also, do not forget the basic writing techniques discussed in Chapter 12.]

Conclusion

[Although you give a conclusion to each issue you discuss, you may provide a general conclusion summarizing all of your main points. Sometimes, in lieu of a conclusion or in addition to a conclusion, a memorandum contains a section titled "Brief Answer." Place this near the beginning of the memo, immediately following the statement of issues.]

Some attorneys prefer a slightly different order; consider the following

- **Issue**
- **Brief Answer** (This is similar to the conclusion.)
- **Facts**
- **Discussion**

13-4 PREPARING TO WRITE THE MEMORANDUM OF LAW

Whether you realize it or not, you begin preparing to write a memorandum of law the moment you analyze the factual dispute and identify the legal issues. (Recall how and why you do this from Chapters 2.) In doing legal research, you look for relevant law. The determination that law is relevant requires analysis of the law you find to determine if, and how, it applies to your factual situation. You should recall from earlier chapters that this analysis is really a part of the research process. The memorandum of law *communicates* your analysis to the reader in an organized and logical manner.

Prior to writing the "Discussion," it is imperative that you organize your ideas and findings. Making an outline is a good way to do this. An outline for your discussion in a memorandum of law should contain the main points and the law that supports each point in some logical order. Within the memorandum, the topic sentences contain the main points in each paragraph.

In preparing an outline, remember that legal analysis usually follows the IRAC format. Any legal analysis requires identification of the *issue* or question. The *rules of law* follow the issue. These rules of law are located in cases, codes, rules and regulations, and constitutions. Next is the *application* (analysis) of the rules of law to the facts of the case at issue. Finally, a *conclusion* is stated. An important result of making an outline before beginning to write is that it forces you to organize the ideas. Following an outline while you write also encourages organization. There are, of course, different ways to organize the discussion in a memorandum. The following suggestions provide some assistance, but remember they are not the only ways to organize your ideas.

An outline of the research in the Town of Grand View memorandum in Chapter 12 might look like this:

FACTS

Parties

Town of Grand View—Defendant
Mr. and Mrs. Jones (fire damage to home)—Plaintiffs
Inspector Williams—Defendant and employee of Town of Grand View

Issues

Is Town immune from liability? Probably.
Is Inspector immune from liability? Probably.

Discussion

I. The court will probably hold the Town immune from liability

Cal. Gov. Code Section 818.8—provides gov. immunity from liability for an injury resulting from misrepresentation by an employee

Case law: *Tokesi v. State; Johnson v. California; Harshbarger v. City of Colton*

II. The court will probably hold that Inspector is immune from liability for misrepresentation

Cal. Gov. Code Section 822.2—provides a public employee with limited immunity from liability for his misrepresentations

Case law: *Schonfeld v. City of Vallejo*

A. William probably committed common law deceit.
 Schonfeld and Cal. Civ. Code Section 1572
B. The Joneses were justified in relying on the Inspector's representations
 Schonfeld
C. The evidence is insufficient to indicate the Inspector's motivation was corruption or actual malice
 Cal. Gov. Code Section 822.2
 Schonfeld

Organizing a Memorandum

The organization of a memorandum of law often depends on the type of legal authorities controlling your case.

Situations Controlled by Statutory Law

Probably the easiest memorandum to write is one where you must analyze a factual situation and determine whether a particular code section controls the facts. Suppose you need to write a memorandum addressing the following question: Is an off-duty police officer who uses excessive force in making a traffic stop criminally responsible for his acts under the Federal Civil Rights Act?

Organize the memorandum answering this question around the relevant code section, which provides the following:

> Whoever, under color of any law, statute, ordinance, regulation, or custom, willfully subjects any person in any State, Territory, Commonwealth, Possession, or District to the deprivation of any rights, privileges, or immunities secured or protected by the Constitution or laws of the United States, or to different punishments, pains, or penalties, on account of such person being an alien, or by reason of his color, or race, than are prescribed for the punishment of citizens, shall be fined under this title or imprisoned not more than one year, or both; and if bodily injury results from the acts committed in violation of this section or if such acts include the use, attempted use, or threatened use of a dangerous weapon, explosive, or fire, shall be fined under this title or imprisoned not more than ten years, or both; and if death results from the acts committed in violation of this section or if such acts include kidnapping or an attempt to kidnap, aggravated sexual abuse or an attempt to commit aggravated sexual abuse, or an attempt to kill, shall be fined under this title, or imprisoned for any term of years or for life, or both, or may be sentenced to death. 18 U.S.C. § 242.

In this situation, break down the relevant code section into the various elements and then discuss each separately. (Keep in mind that you have already done this type of analysis. As part of the research process, you analyzed the statute to determine if it applied. At this point, you are communicating this analysis in written form. Refer to Chapter 6.)

In the discussion section, you may need to refer to case law interpreting some or all of the elements of the code. In discussing these elements, you can arrange them in the same order that they appear in the code. Alternatively, you can first discuss elements that are obvious and then discuss those that present problems and require a more detailed analysis.

One question that arises occasionally with this type of memorandum is whether you need to discuss every element of the code section. If the code section applies to your facts, then you do need to discuss each element (assuming, of course, that this was the research assignment). If, on the other hand, it is clear to you that the statute does *not* apply, you may only need to discuss those elements that make the statute inapplicable. For example, suppose that a defendant is a private security guard rather than a police officer. The Federal Civil Rights Act requires that one be "acting under color of law." Because a private security guard does not act under color of law, the section is clearly not applicable and it would not be necessary to discuss all the other elements of the code section.

An outline of the predictive memo in this case might look as follows.

Sample Outline

I. Introduction

A. A violation of 18 U.S.C. § 242 requires that a person acting under color of law willfully deprive another of a constitutional right or subject another to different punishments or penalties because of color or race.
B. Facts indicate defendant's actions meet each of the elements.

II. Were Defendant's Actions Under Color of Law? (*This is a statement of the issue.*)

A. 18 U.S.C. § 242 requires that action be under color of law. (*This is the rule of law.*)
B. Defendant was in police uniform.
C. Defendant was performing a regular police function—a traffic stop. (*B. and C. constitute the analysis. Here you apply the facts to the language of the code.*)

III. Was Defendant's Conduct Willful?

A. Code requires that conduct be willful.
B. Defendant's actions were intentional.

IV. Did Defendant Deprive Another of Constitutional Rights?

A. Code requires a deprivation of constitutional rights.
B. A traffic stop is a seizure under the Fourth Amendment to the U.S. Constitution.
C. Defendant's actions, in particular his use of excessive force, were not reasonable as required by the Constitution.

V. Did Defendant Inflict Different Punishment Due to Color or Race?

A. As an alternative to a deprivation of constitutional rights, a violation of 18 U.S.C. § 242 can be based on infliction of different punishments due to color or race.
B. Defendant inflicted extraordinary injury or punishment to victim.
C. Defendant's statements indicate racial bias.

VI. Conclusion

A Point to Remember

During the research process, if you take notes on index cards, using a separate card for each authority, you can arrange these cards according to your outline. Writing your memorandum is much easier.

Situations Controlled by Case Law

cause of action
The basis upon which a lawsuit is brought before the court.

A legal memorandum based on a situation controlled entirely by case law is often more difficult to organize. The organization depends on the research question. One common research task is to determine whether a party has a certain ***cause of action*** entitling that party to some sort of relief (most often money). A cause of action is a set of facts that the law recognizes as entitling a person to relief from the courts. Whether a cause of action exists or not is dependent on the substantive law. Like many code sections, causes of action can be broken down into elements. Relevant case law usually lists (or enumerates) these elements. Organizing this type of memorandum is very similar to organizing a memorandum based on statutory law. Begin by setting out the elements of the cause of action as described in case law. Next discuss each of the elements, bringing in additional case law where needed. Finally, discuss alternative defenses. For example, consider the case described below, Victoria V. v. U Shop Mall.

In this case, the relevant law is the law of negligence. Assume that the law of the state of California controls this situation and your research uncovered the case of *Ann M. v. Pacific Plaza,* found on page 305. In this opinion, the court states what must be shown for a cause of negligence to exist. The court states: "An action in negligence requires a showing that the defendant owed the plaintiff a legal duty, that the defendant breached the duty, and that the breach was a proximate or legal cause of injuries suffered by the plaintiff."

In organizing your research for the memorandum of law regarding the *Victoria V.* case, you could take each of the factors mentioned by the court and discuss them separately, either in the order listed by the court or in any other logical order. Before going on, read the *Ann M.* case found later in this chapter.

Victoria V. v. U Shop Mall

Victoria V. was the victim of a sexual assault in the parking lot of U Shop Mall one evening about 9 p.m. When she entered the shopping center at 6:30 p.m., it was still light outside but Victoria knew that she would shop for several hours and it would probably be dark when she left. Therefore, she parked under a light. Unknown to her, the light was not working.

The shopping center also employs a security guard to patrol its two parking areas, one in front and one in back. It takes the security guard about 30 minutes to patrol each of these. Incidentally, the security guard reported that the parking light was out about 24 hours prior to the assault on Victoria. However, the shopping center did not have any replacement bulbs on hand. Records also indicate that in the past month (before the assault) there were three reports of cars being broken into and items stolen. There was also one report of a mugging of an elderly man that took place in the parking area. Finally, a report of a sexual assault that took place in a shopping center about two miles away was received by the U Shop Mall about two weeks prior to the assault on Victoria. There was no previous report of sexual assault in the U Shop Mall or its parking lot.

Your law firm represents Victoria and wants to file a civil lawsuit against U Shop Mall for its negligence. Your assignment is to research whether such a claim has any merit.

The first part of an outline for your memorandum might look something like this.

Sample Outline

I. Negligence is the basis of Victoria's action.

An action for negligence requires the existence of a legal duty, breach of the duty, and the proximate or legal cause of injuries.

II. Does a landowner have a duty to protect others from criminal attack by third parties?

(This is a statement of the ***issue****. Note that it corresponds to the first element of the cause of action described in B above, i.e., the existence of a legal duty.)*

A. Before a landowner owes a duty to protect a person from criminal attack, the harm must be foreseeable. This requires other similar incidents.

(State the rule of law or holding from the Ann M. *case and from any other authorities that might relate to this issue. At this point, you give the proper cite for your authorities.)*

B. Comparison of facts of *Ann M.* with the facts of *Victoria V.*

(This is the ***analysis****. Because your authorities for this issue consist of case law, your analysis requires that you compare facts of the case law to facts of* Victoria V. *Your outline should list the facts of* Ann M. *that you want to discuss with the facts of the* Victoria V. *case.)*

C. Conclusion.

(Discuss your conclusion on this issue. An objective memorandum may not reach a definitive answer to the issue or question. You might be summarizing the various possibilities.)

III. (Continue with each element of the cause of action and any defenses that may exist.)

Point to Remember

Not all courts follow *The Bluebook* rules for citation. In the *Ann M. v. Pacific Plaza Shopping Center* case, the court uses a format suggested by the *California Style Manual*.

CASE 13-1 *Ann M. v. Pacific Plaza Shopping Center,* 6 Cal. 4th 666, 863 P.2d 207, 25 Cal. Rptr. 2d 137 (1993)

OPINION:

We granted review in this case to determine whether the scope of the duty owed by the owner of a shopping center to maintain common areas within its possession and control in a reasonably safe condition includes providing security guards in those areas. We conclude that, under the facts of this case, the owner did not owe a duty to provide security guards.

I. BACKGROUND:

This case arises out of a civil complaint filed by Ann M. after she was raped at her place of employment. Unless otherwise indicated, the facts as stated herein are not in dispute.

On June 17, 1985, the Original 60 Minute Photo Company, a photo processing service located in a secluded area of the Pacific Plaza Shopping Center (hereafter

(continued)

shopping center), employed Ann M. The shopping center, owned and operated by defendants (hereafter sometimes collectively referred to as Pacific Plaza), is a strip mall located on Garnet Avenue in the Pacific Beach area of San Diego. Approximately 25 commercial tenants occupy the shopping center at any one time.

The lease between the photo store and the shopping center granted the owners of the shopping center the exclusive right to control the common areas. Although the lease gave Pacific Plaza the right to police the common areas, the lease did not purport to impose an obligation to police either common areas or those areas under the exclusive control and management of the tenants. In fact, Pacific Plaza hired no security guards.

At approximately 8 a.m. on June 17, Ann M. opened the photo store for business. She was the only employee on duty. The door was closed but unlocked. The store was equipped with a "drop gate" that was designed to prevent customer access behind the counter, but it had been broken for some period. Shortly after Ann M. opened the store, a man she had never seen before walked in "just like a customer." Ann M. greeted the man, told him that she would assist him shortly, and turned her back to the counter. The man, who was armed with a knife, went behind the counter, raped Ann M., robbed the store, and fled. Police did not apprehend the rapist.

In 1984 and 1985 violent crimes occurred in the census tract in which the shopping center is located. While the record includes some evidence of criminal activity on the shopping center's premises prior to Ann M.'s rape—bank robberies, purse snatchings, and a man pulling down women's pants—there is no evidence that Pacific Plaza had knowledge of these alleged criminal acts. In fact, Pacific Plaza offers uncontroverted evidence that it "is the standard practice of [Pacific Plaza] to note or record instances of violent crime" and that Pacific Plaza's records contain no reference to violent criminal acts in the shopping center prior to Ann M.'s rape.

Ann M. presented evidence that the employees and tenants were concerned about their safety prior to her rape. These concerns centered on the presence of persons described as transients, who loitered in the common areas. One of the employees of the photo store called the police on two different occasions prior to the incident involved herein to complain that she felt threatened by persons loitering outside her employer's store. The photo store ultimately granted this employee permission to bring her dog to work for protection. This employee worked a late night shift, while Ann M. worked during the day. During periodic meetings of the merchants' association, an organization to which all tenants belonged, the tenants voiced complaints about a lack of security in the shopping center and the presence of transients. There is no evidence to indicate, however, that Ann M.'s rapist was one of the loitering transients or that the presence of the transients contributed in any way to Ann M.'s attack.

According to Ann M.'s deposition testimony, the merchants' association invited a security company to address the tenants' concerns at one of its meetings. During that meeting, the security company informed the tenants of different security options and recommended regular walking. Ann M. stated in her deposition that she believed that the merchants' association decided not to hire the security patrols because the cost would be prohibitive. Ann M. further testified that she was told at these meetings that the merchants' association requested that the shopping center provide such patrols. No such patrols occurred. According to the lease, if the shopping center had provided the requested patrols, the tenants would have borne the cost in the form of additional rent. Ultimately, the merchants' association hired a security company to drive by the area three or four times a day instead of arranging for foot patrols. Ann M. was raped sometime thereafter.

After the rape, Ann M. filed a civil complaint for damages in the superior court. She alleged causes of action for negligence against Amapho Corp. (the owner and operator of the photo store), Glen Hutchinson (the president of Amapho Corp.), the shopping center, and La Jolla Development Co. (the corporation employed to manage the shopping center at the time of the rape). Ann M. alleged that the defendants were negligent in failing to provide adequate security to protect her from an unreasonable risk of harm. This specific alleged risk was the presence of transients and the potential for violent confrontation between transients and employees of the shopping center.

Pacific Plaza filed a motion for summary judgment or summary adjudication of issues, claiming that it owed no legal duty to Ann M., primarily because Ann M.'s attack was unforeseeable. Ann M. countered that a duty was owed: the attack was foreseeable because Pacific Plaza permitted transients to congregate in the common areas of the shopping center. Ann M. contended, "[s]ecurity patrols to roust the center's transient population would have provided the [necessary] 'first line of defense' " that Pacific Plaza allegedly had a duty to provide. The trial court granted the motion, finding that Pacific Plaza owed Ann M. no duty of care, and entered judgment in favor of Pacific Plaza.

Ann M. appealed. Following rehearing, the Court of Appeal affirmed the judgment of the trial court, but on different grounds. The Court of Appeal held that Pacific Plaza owed a duty to tenants and their employees to maintain the common areas and leased premises in a reasonably safe condition. This included the duty to take reasonable precautions against foreseeable criminal activity by their persons; however, based on the evidence presented, the Court of Appeal held that no reasonable jury could have concluded that Pacific Plaza acted unreasonably in failing to provide the security patrols that Ann M. claims were necessary.

We granted Ann M.'s petition for review.

II. DISCUSSION

A. Standard of review

Although Ann M.'s complaint is phrased in broader terms, Ann M. concedes that the gravamen of her complaint is that Pacific Plaza's failure to provide security patrols in the common areas constituted negligence. We therefore confine our review to this issue (*Cf. Chern v. Bank of America* (1976) 15 Cal. 3d 866, 873 ["purpose of summary procedure is to penetrate through evasive language and adept pleading and ascertain the existence or absence of triable issues"]; *FPI Development, Inc. v. Nakashima* (1991) 231 Cal. App. 3d 367, 381–382 [pleadings serve as the outer measure of materiality in a summary judgment proceeding].)

An action in negligence requires a showing that the defendant owed the plaintiff a legal duty, that the defendant breached the duty, and that the breach was a proximate or legal cause of injuries suffered by the plaintiff. [emphasis added] (*United States Liab. Ins. Co. v. Haidinger-Hayes, Inc.* (1970) 1 Cal. 3d 586, 594; 6 Witkin, *Summary of Cal. Law* (9th ed. 1988) Torts, § 732, at 60.) On review of a summary judgment in favor of the

(continued)

defendant, we review the record de novo to determine whether the defendant has conclusively negated a necessary element of the plaintiff's case or demonstrated that under no hypothesis is there a material issue of fact that requires the process of trial. (*Molko v. Holy Spirit Assn.* (1988) 46 Cal. 3d 1092, 1107.)

For the reasons discussed below, we conclude that, under the facts of this case, the scope of any duty owed by Pacific Plaza to Ann M. did not include providing security guards in the common areas. Accordingly, we do not address whether Pacific Plaza's failure to provide security guards was a proximate cause of Ann M.'s injuries (*See Nola M. v. University of Southern California* (1993) 16 Cal. App. 4th 421 [hereafter *Nola M.*].)

B. Duty

The existence of a duty is a question of law for the court. (*Isaacs v. Huntington Memorial Hospital* (1985) 38 Cal. 3d 112, 124 [hereafter *Isaacs*]; *Southland Corp. v. Superior Court* (1988) 203 Cal. App. 3d 656, 663.) Accordingly, we determine de novo the existence and scope of the duty owed by Pacific Plaza to Ann M.

It is now well established that California law requires landowners to maintain land in their possession and control in a reasonably safe condition. (Civ. Code, § 1714; *Rowland v. Christian* (1968) 69 Cal. 2d 108.) In the case of a landlord, this general duty of maintenance, which is owed to tenants and patrons, has been held to include the duty to take reasonable steps to secure common areas against foreseeable criminal acts of third parties that are likely to occur in the absence of such precautionary measures. (*Frances T. v. Village Green Owners Assn.* (1986) 42 Cal. 3d 490, 499–501 [hereafter *Frances T.*]; *O'Hara v. Western Seven Trees Corp.* (1977) 75 Cal. App. 3d 798, 802–803 [hereafter *O'Hara*]; *Isaacs, supra*, 38 Cal. 3d at pp. 123–124.)

Pacific Plaza argues that its relationship with Ann M. is insufficient to support the extension to Ann M. of the duty that it owes to its patrons and tenants to take reasonable steps to secure the common areas of its land. Ann M. counters that she is, in effect, Pacific Plaza's invitee and that this status creates a "special relationship" sufficient to support the imposition on Pacific Plaza of a duty to her.

In this state, duties are no longer imposed on an occupier of land solely on the basis of rigid classifications of trespasser, licensee, and invitee. (*Peterson v. San Francisco Community College Dist.* (1984) 36 Cal. 3d 799, 808, fn. 5; *Rowland v. Christian, supra*, 69 Cal. 2d at 119.) The purpose of plaintiff's presence on the land is not determinative. We have recognized, however, that this purpose may have some bearing upon the liability issue. (*Rowland v. Christian, supra*, 69 Cal. 2d at 119.) This purpose therefore must be considered along with other factors weighing for and against the imposition of a duty on the landowner.

We conclude that it is appropriate in this case to apply the rules specifying the duty of a landowner to its tenants and patrons. Ann M.'s reason for being upon Pacific Plaza's land at the time of her attack fully supports this conclusion. As stated above, it is established that a landlord owes a duty of care to its tenants to take reasonable steps to secure the common areas under its control. In this case, Ann M. admittedly was not Pacific Plaza's tenant; her employer was. Nevertheless, in "the commercial context where the tenant generally is not a natural person and must, therefore, act through its employees, it cannot be seriously asserted that a tort duty that a landlord owes to protect the personal safety of its tenant should not extend to its tenant's employees." (*Cf. DeGraf v. Anglo California Nat. Bank* (1939) 14 Cal. 2d 87, 93 ["plaintiff, as manager of the business of a tenant of the building, stood in a position equal to that of an actual tenant thereof"].) Therefore, the issue of the existence and scope of Pacific Plaza's duty to Ann M. is not resolved by the fact that Ann M.'s employer, rather than Ann M. herself, was Pacific Plaza's tenant.

Pacific Plaza next contends that it owed no duty to Ann M. in this case because the crime occurred on property not within its possession and control. While it is true that Ann M. was raped within the tenant's premises, Ann M. alleges that it was Pacific Plaza's failure to adequately maintain the common areas that caused her injury. As a result, she contends that the location of the crime does not necessarily determine the landowner's liability for injuries resulting from criminal acts. (*Frances T., supra*, 42 Cal. 3d at 503; *O'Hara, supra*, 75 Cal. App. 3d at 803.)

In *O'Hara, supra*, 75, Cal. App. 3d 798, a tenant sued her landlord, alleging that it was liable for injuries resulting from her rape inside her apartment. Knowing of several previous rapes of tenants and of conditions indicating a likelihood that the rapist would repeat his attacks, the landlord induced the plaintiff to rent an apartment in the complex without disclosing any of the above information, and by falsely assuring her that the premises were safe and patrolled at all times by professional guards. (at 802.) The landlord also failed to share with the plaintiff knowledge of the suspect's mode of operation and composite drawings of the suspect. (*Ibid.*) The Court of Appeal held that the landlord had a duty to take reasonable precautions to safeguard the common areas against the types of crimes of which it had notice and which were likely to recur if the common areas were not secure. (at 803–804.) Because the landlord's failure to take "reasonable precautions to safeguard the common areas under [its] control could have contributed substantially, as alleged, to [the tenant's] injuries" (at 803), the Court of Appeal reversed the judgment of the trial court with directions to overrule the general demurrer (at 806).

In *Frances T., supra*, 42 Cal. 3d 490, this court adopted the reasoning of the *O'Hara* court and extended it to the context of residential condominiums. We reasoned that a condominium association functions as a landlord in maintaining the common areas of a large condominium complex and, thus, has a duty to exercise care for the residents' safety in those areas under its control. (at 499.) In *Frances T.*, the trial court had sustained the condominium association's demurrer to a unit owner's allegations that it had negligently failed to install adequate lighting in the common areas and was therefore liable for injuries she sustained from a rape that occurred inside her unit. (at 495, 498.) We reversed. Although the rape occurred within the unit and not in a common area, we held that the association owed a duty to the plaintiff on the theory that an exterior condition over which the association had control contributed to the rape. (at 498–503.)

Since the existence of a duty on the part of Pacific Plaza to Ann M. is not precluded in this case either by the lack of a direct landlord-tenant relationship or by the lack of control over the premises where the crime occurred, we turn to the heart of the case: whether Pacific Plaza had reasonable cause to anticipate that criminal conduct such as rape would occur in the shopping center premises unless it provided security patrols in the common areas. For, as frequently

(*continued*)

recognized, a duty to take affirmative action to control the wrongful acts of a third party will be imposed only where such conduct can be reasonably anticipated. (*e.g.*, *Frances T.*, *supra*, 42 Cal. 3d at 501; *Isaacs, supra*, 38 Cal. 3d at 123–124; *Peterson v. San Francisco Community College Dist.*, *supra*, 36 Cal. 3d at 807.)

In this, as in other areas of tort law, foreseeability is a crucial factor in determining the existence of duty. (*Isaacs, supra*, 38 Cal. 3d at 123; *Lopez v. McDonald's Corp.* (1987) 193 Cal. App. 3d 495, 506.) Our most comprehensive analysis to date of the foreseeability required to establish the existence of a business landowner's duty to take reasonable steps to protect its tenants and patrons from third party crime is found in *Isaacs, supra*, 38 Cal. 3d 112.

In *Isaacs*, a doctor affiliated with a private hospital was shot while in one of the hospital's parking lots. The doctor sued the hospital for failure to take reasonable security measures. Although the plaintiff presented evidence of several prior threatened assaults at the nearby hospital emergency room, he presented no evidence of prior assaults in the parking lot where he was shot. The trial court granted the defendant's motion for nonsuit because the plaintiff failed to show that prior similar incidents had occurred on the premises. We granted the petition for review to decide whether the plaintiff might "establish foreseeability other than by evidence of prior similar incidents on [the] premises." (*Isaacs, supra*, 38 Cal. 3d at 120.)

We held that foreseeability, for tort liability purposes, could be established despite the absence of prior similar incidents on the premises. We explained that "foreseeability is determined in light of all the circumstances and not by a rigid application of a mechanical 'prior similars' rule." (*Isaacs, supra*, 38 Cal. 3d at 126.) We also explained that prior similar incidents are "helpful to determine foreseeability but they are not necessary." (at 127.) We further explained that foreseeability should be assessed in light of the "totality of the circumstances," including such factors as the nature, condition and location of the premises. (at 127–129.) We concluded that the totality of the circumstances in *Isaacs* strongly suggested that the foreseeability of an assault in the parking lot should have been presented to the jury. (at 130.)

Since *Issacs* was decided, lower court opinions have questioned the wisdom of our apparent abandonment of the "prior similar incidents" rule. (*See Nola M., supra*, 16 Cal. App. 4th at 438–439.) ["If there is a flaw in our analysis finding the landowner not liable due to lack of causation between alleged security deficiencies and injury, we suggest it may be time for the Supreme Court to reexamine the concept of duty it articulated in [*Isaacs*] in the context of a society which appears unable to effectively stem the tide of violent crime."]; *Onciano v. Golden Palace Restaurant, Inc.* (1990) 219 Cal. App. 3d 385, 396 [conc. & dis. opn. of Woods (Fred), J., following *Isaacs*, but observing that its holding leads to inequity. In addition to judicial criticism, at least one commentator has noted that California is the only jurisdiction to adopt a "totality of the circumstances" rule in the business landowner context. Kaufman, *When Crime Pays: Business Landlords' Duty to Protect Customers from Criminal Acts Committed on the Premises* (1990) 31 S. Tex. L.Rev. 89, 97 [hereafter Kaufman, *When Crime Pays*].

Unfortunately, random, violent crime is endemic in today's society. It is difficult, if not impossible, to envision any locale open to the public where the occurrence of violent crime seems improbable. Upon further reflection and in light of the increase in violent crime, refinement of the rule enunciated in *Isaacs, supra*, 38 Cal. 3d 112, is required. We are not reluctant to revisit the rule announced in *Isaacs* because it was unnecessary for this court to consider the viability of the "prior similar incidents" rule in order to decide the *Isaacs* case: the record contained evidence of prior, violent, third party attacks on persons on the hospital's premises in close proximity to where the attack at issue in that case occurred. *Isaacs, supra*, 38 Cal. 3d at 121.

Moreover, broad language used in *Isaacs* has tended to confuse duty analysis generally in that the opinion can be read to hold that foreseeability in the context of determining duty is normally a question of fact reserved for the jury. *Isaacs, supra*, 38 Cal. 3d at 126, 127, 130. Any such reading of *Isaacs* is in error. Foreseeability, when analyzed to determine the existence or scope of a duty, is a question of law to be decided by the court. *Ballard v. Uribe* (1986) 41 Cal. 3d 564, 572–573, fn. 6; *Lopez v. McDonald's Corp., supra*, 193 Cal. App. 3d at 507, fn. 6.

Turning to the question of the scope of a landlord's duty to provide protection from foreseeable third party crime, we observe that, before and after our decision in *Isaacs*, we have recognized that the scope of the duty is determined in part by balancing the foreseeability of the harm against the burden of the duty to be imposed. (*Isaacs, supra*, 38 Cal. 3d at 125.) " '[I]n cases where the burden of preventing future harm is great, a high degree of foreseeability may be required. [Citation.] On the other hand, in cases where there are strong policy reasons for preventing the harm, or the harm can be prevented by simple means, a lesser degree of foreseeability may be required.' [Citation.]" (*Ibid.*) Or, as one appellate court has accurately explained, duty in such circumstances is determined by a balancing of "foreseeability" of the criminal acts against the "burdensomeness, vagueness, and efficacy" of the proposed security measures. (*Gomez v. Ticor, supra*, 145 Cal. App. 3d at 631.)

While there may be circumstances where the hiring of security guards will be required to satisfy a landowner's duty of care, such action will rarely, if ever, be found to be a "minimal burden." The monetary costs of security guards is not insignificant. Moreover, the obligation to provide patrols adequate to deter criminal conduct is not well defined. "No one really knows why people commit crime, hence no one really knows what is 'adequate' deterrence in any given situation." *7735 Hollywood Blvd. Venture v. Superior Court* (1981) 116 Cal. App. 3d 901, 905. Finally, the social costs of imposing a duty on landowners to hire private police forces are also not insignificant. *See Nola M., supra*, 16 Cal. App. 4th at 437–438. For these reasons, we conclude that a high degree of foreseeability is required in order to find that the scope of a landlord's duty of care includes the hiring of security guards. We further conclude that the requisite degree of foreseeability rarely, if ever, can be proven in the absence of prior similar incidents of violent crime on the landowner's premises. To hold otherwise would be to impose an unfair burden upon landlords and, in effect, would force landlords to become the insurers of public safety, contrary to well-established policy in this state. *See Riley v. Marcus* (1981) 125 Cal. App. 3d 103, 109; *7735 Hollywood Blvd. Venture v. Superior Court, supra*, 116 Cal. App. 3d at 905.)

Turning to the facts of the case before us, we conclude that violent criminal assaults were not sufficiently foreseeable to impose a duty upon Pacific Plaza to provide

(*continued*)

security guards in the common areas. *Cf. Ballard v. Uribe, supra*, 41 Cal. 3d 564, 572–573, fn. 6. First, Pacific Plaza did not have notice of prior similar incidents occurring on the premises. Ann M. alleges that previous assaults and robberies had occurred in the shopping center, but she offers no evidence that Pacific Plaza had notice of these incidents. While a landowner's duty includes the duty to exercise reasonable care to discover that criminal acts are being or are likely to be committed on its land (*Peterson v. San Francisco Community College Dist., supra*, 36 Cal. 3d at 807), Pacific Plaza presented uncontroverted evidence that it had implemented "a standard practice . . . to note or record instances of violent crime" and that Pacific Plaza's records contain no reference to violent criminal acts prior to Ann M.'s rape. Moreover, even assuming that Pacific Plaza had notice of these incidents, Ann M. concedes that they were not similar in nature to the violent assault that she suffered. Similarly, none of the remaining evidence presented by Ann M. is sufficiently compelling to establish the high degree of foreseeability necessary to impose upon Pacific Plaza a duty to provide security guards in the common areas. Neither the evidence regarding the presence of transients nor the evidence of the statistical crime rate of the surrounding area is of a type sufficient to satisfy this burden.

We, therefore, conclude that Pacific Plaza was entitled to summary judgment on the ground that it owed no duty to Ann M. to provide security guards in the common areas.

III. DISPOSITION

The judgment of the Court of Appeal is affirmed.

Lucas, C. J., Kennard, J., Arabian, J., Baxter, J., and George, J., concurred.

The Writer's Corner

Headings in an Internal Memorandum (the Predictive Memorandum)

The headings in an internal memorandum, used to help a reader follow the logic of the document, are often simple statements. They serve as signposts—similar to a road map.

As you already know, most legal writing (including case law) follows the IRAC format.

I = Issue(s) (the legal question)

R = Rule(s) of law

A = Analysis or application of the rule(s) of law to the facts

C = Conclusion

This is the best way to order your research and analysis results.

The headings in an internal memorandum involving a claim of negligence might look like this:

Introduction:

short introduction to the case

Facts:

briefly, using the all of the key and the necessary explanatory facts, explain what happened and to whom

Issue:

state the question—"Was the Defendant negligent when he . . . ."

Rule of Law:

state the rule of law—"The tort of negligence occurs when the following elements are shown": The tortfeasor was under a duty to use due care; the tortfeasor breached that duty of due care; the tortfeasor's act was the actual cause of injuries or damages; or the tortfeasor's act was the proximate case of injuries or damages; and there was actual injury or damage to the complaining party.

Follow each of the headings with an explanation of that specific element of the rule of law.

Analysis/Application:
For each element listed in the rule of law, provide a simple heading followed by an application of the rule to the facts of the client's case. In this instance if your office represents the plaintiff, the headings might look like this:

Defendant owed the plaintiff a duty of care

Defendant breached his duty of care

The defendant's act was the actual cause of

(or)

The defendant's act was the proximate case of

The plaintiff's injuries or damages

Follow each of the headings with an analysis/application of that specific element of the rule of law to the facts of the client's case.

Conclusion: State the legal and factual conclusions you reach after your application of the rule of law to the facts of the case. For the internal memorandum outlined above the headings are:

Introduction:

Facts:

Issue:

Rule of Law:

1. **The tortfeasor was under a duty to use due care**
2. **The tortfeasor breached that duty of due care**
3. **The tortfeasor's act was the actual cause of**

   (or)

4. **The tortfeasor's act was the proximate cause of**
5. **Damages**

Analysis/Application:

1. **Defendant owed the plaintiff a duty of care**
2. **Defendant breached his duty of care**
3. **The defendant's act was the actual cause of injuries or damages**

   (or)

4. **The defendants act was the proximate case of injuries or damages.**
5. **The plaintiff incurred damages**

Conclusion In total, there are 16 headings and point headings in this memo. At first, that may seem like too many. However, when we think about the purpose of the headings we realize they serve as signposts for the reader. The headings guide the reader and keep the reader focused. By writing the headings before drafting the document, it is much easier to compile the research and analysis in a logical—easy-to-read—format. Remember, you are not writing to please yourself; you have an audience.

13-5 WRITING THE MEMORANDUM OF LAW

Statement of Facts

The statement of facts should be a concise statement of all relevant and explanatory facts. The information for this statement comes from the client or from documents found in the client file. You identified key facts before you started the research. However, the results of your research reveal what is or is not a key fact. Therefore, do not write the statement of facts for a memorandum until the research is complete.

Generally, present the facts in one of the following ways.

1. **Chronologically:** A common and easy way of organizing facts in a memorandum of law is in the order in which they occurred chronologically.
2. **By Party:** Another way of organizing the facts is by party. Where multiple parties exist, they may all have their own version of the facts. State each version separately.

3. **According to the Elements of a Cause of Action:** When your memorandum concerns whether a cause of action exists, present the facts in the same order in which you discuss the elements of the cause of action.

See Figure 13-1 for an example of a predictive memo. Read the Facts section.

FIGURE 13-1 Sample Predictive Memorandum of Law

FACTS

Smith signed a job offer acceptance with West Coast Industries in June 20XX. The job offer letter contained a clause stating "[t]his position is terminable at the will of either party." Smith worked for the company for the next four and a half years until January 20XX, when his employment was terminated.

Throughout Smith's employment, he received five performance evaluations. The evaluation system includes ratings of "fully effective" and "commendable." A "fully effective" review is defined as a "[g]ood, solid, consistent performance accomplished in a reliable and professional manner." A "commendable" rating is better than a "fully effective" rating. In Smith's first two annual evaluations, he received "commendable" reviews. In his last three evaluations, he received "fully effective" reviews with an improving trend in performance.

Smith also received three promotions during his employment. He was hired as a Tax Accountant II. Three months after beginning employment, he was promoted to Tax Accountant III. Less than five months later, he was promoted to Tax Supervisor, where he remained for one year and seven months. Finally, he was promoted to Tax Manager, where he remained until termination.

In the fall of 20XX, Gomez, Smith's supervisor, began to examine Smith's punctuality. Smith spoke to the company vice president regarding the tardiness problem. Both men agreed on acceptable guidelines with regard to tardiness.

West Coast Industries has a guideline for the purpose of administering corrective action. The guideline contains suggested steps for corrective action, and the company reserves the right to alter or delete steps of the procedure.

ISSUES

I. Whether a signed job offer constituted an integrated agreement which precludes a subsequent, implied-in-fact employment agreement, where the offer contains a clause stating, "[t]his position is terminable at the will of either party," and where no further at-will employment agreement was signed.

II. Whether an implied-in-fact contract not to terminate Smith's employment but for good cause exists where Smith was employed for four and a half years, received "commendable" and "fully effective" reviews, met with the vice president to determine acceptable guidelines to solve tardiness problems, and where West Coast Industries maintained company guidelines for corrective actions.

DISCUSSION

I. Is Smith precluded from asserting an implied-in-fact employment agreement since he signed a job offer stating his position was terminable at the will of either party?

In order to assert an implied-in-fact employment agreement, Smith must show that the job offer does not preclude subsequent, implied-in-fact agreements. He must show that the

FIGURE 13-1 (continued)

clause in the job offer is merely a statement of California Labor Code section 2922. Generally, if the employment relationship is not reduced to an integrated, written agreement, then language that there is an at-will employment relationship does not establish the relationship as a matter of law. *Walker v. Blue Cross of California*, 4 Cal. App. 4th 985, 993, 6 Cal. Rptr. 2d 184, 189 (1992). Therefore, the clause in question may be a re-statement of section 2922, this creates a rebuttable presumption. *Wilkerson v. Wells Fargo Bank*, 212 Cal. App. 3d 1217, 1225, 261 Cal. Rptr. 185, 189 (1989). Smith can show the clause is a re-statement of section 2922, which creates a presumption that can be rebutted by an implied-in-fact contract. *Id.* Therefore, the clause does not preclude a subsequent implied-in-fact employment agreement.

a. California Labor Code section 2922 creates a rebuttable presumption of "at-will employment."

The rule of law governing employment termination is California Labor Code section 2922. This section states that "[a]n employment, having no specified term, may be terminated at the will of either party on notice to the other." Cal. Lab. Code § 2922 (West 20XX). Consequently, an employer may terminate an employee without just cause. However, section 2922 "creates a presumption which may be superseded by a contract, express or implied, limiting the employer's right to discharge the employee." *Wilkerson*, 212 Cal. App. 3d at 1225, 261 Cal. Rptr. at 189. Therefore, the presumption of "at will employment" created by section 2922 may be overcome by an implied contract to the contrary.

b. The at-will employment clause of Smith's job offer merely restates the California Labor Code section 2922.

Walker helps distinguish which written agreements preclude the possibility of subsequent contracts. *Walker* states that "the employment relationship must be reduced to an integrated written agreement, signed by the employee." 4 Cal. App. 4th at 993, 6 Cal. Rptr. 2d at 189. "Language in the handbook that there is an at-will employment relationship does not establish the nature of the relationship as a matter of law." *Id.* This suggests that an integrated agreement signed by the employee must be present to create an at-will employment that cannot be overcome by a subsequent contract. An integrated agreement is defined as a "final expression of [the parties'] agreement." *Slivinsky v. Watkins,* 221 Cal. App. 3d 799, 804, 270 Cal. Rptr. 585, 588 (1990). In *Slivinsky*, the court held that a signed offer and employment agreement were enough to preclude the creation of a subsequent employment contract. *Id.* at 805, 270 Cal. Rptr. at 588. The signed offer stated that there "will be no agreement expressed or implied, between the Company and Slivinksy for any specific period of employment...." *Id.* The employment agreement used similar language, along with an explicit declaration that employment could be terminated with or without cause. *Id.*

Smith's employment situation can be distinguished from *Slivinsky* in several ways. The clause in the job offer Smith signed is less clear than the clause in Slivinky's offer. This language in *Slivinsky* is specific and manifests an agreement between the parties. Smith's

FIGURE 13-1 (continued)

offer states "[t]his position is terminable at the will of either party." Such a statement requires neither Smith's acceptance, nor agreement thereto. It is merely a statement of a presumed condition present in every employment situation, as set forth by section 2922. Additionally, Slivinsky signed an express employment agreement that there would be no other contract, express or implied, for continuing employment. *Slivinsky,* 221 Cal. App. 3d at 805, 270 Cal. Rptr. at 588. Smith never signed any such agreement. Smith's offer contained no language stating that his employment precluded the existence of an express or implied employment contract. In *Slivinsky,* the court ruled that the writing was intended by the parties as a final expression of their agreement. *Id.* In the case at hand, the offer probably cannot be construed as a final expression of the parties' agreement. The offer is too vague, and does not require explicit acceptance of the clause in question. It follows that the clause in the job offer Smith signed is not an agreement that employment will be exclusively at-will. Hence, the offer does not preclude a subsequent, implied in fact employment agreement.

c. The parol evidence rule probably will not prohibit the introduction of evidence that contradicts the written instrument of the job offer.

West Coast Industries will argue that the parol evidence rule "generally prohibits the introduction of any extrinsic evidence to vary or contradict the terms of an integrated, written instrument." *Wilkerson,* 212 Cal. App. 3d at 1227, 261 Cal. Rptr. at 190. In order to assert this claim, Pacific must show that the offer is an integrated, written instrument. It is undisputed that the offer is a written instrument. However, to be integrated, it must be a "final expression of [the parties'] agreement." *Slivinsky,* 221 Cal. App. 3d at 804, 270 Cal. Rptr. at 586. As formerly explained, it is unlikely that this offer can be construed as a final expression of an agreement. The terms are too vague and indefinite. Additionally, the language does not preclude subsequent employment. Therefore, the parol evidence rule is probably not an issue.

II. Has an implied-in-fact contract not to terminate Smith but for good cause been created?

Smith must prove that the circumstances of his employment created an implied-in-fact agreement requiring Pacific to offer a good cause for his termination. Furthermore, he must show that such an agreement is sufficient to overcome the presumption of section 2922. Several factors may be considered to determine an employment agreement. Such factors include personnel policies, employee's longevity of service, communications by the employer, and practices of the industry. *Miller v. Pepsi-Cola Bottling Co.,* 210 Cal. App. 3d 1554, 1557, 259 Cal. Rptr. 56, 58 (1989). Smith can satisfy many of these factors. Taking into account all of the circumstances of Smith's employment, he might be able to establish an implied-in-fact contract strong enough to overcome the presumption of section 2922.

FIGURE 13-1 (continued)

a. The circumstances of Smith's employment might have created an implied-in-fact agreement that termination requires good cause. This agreement might be sufficient to overcome the presumption of section 2922.

The factors of an employment agreement are defined in *Miller* as "personnel policies. . . , the employee's longevity of service . . . communications by the employer reflecting assurance of continued employment, and practices of the industry. . . ." *Id.* In *Miller*, the appellant based his case on a single job assurance statement at the beginning of his employment, commendations, promotions, and an employment term of 11 years. The court found that no implied contract existed. *Id.* at 1559, 259 Cal. Rptr. at 59.

In *Walker*, the court found the circumstances of the appellant's employment created a triable issue for the existence of an implied-in-fact contract for good cause termination. The factors considered were over 19 years of service, consistent promotions, satisfactory evaluations, and personnel policies. *Smith,*4 Cal. App. 4th at 993, 6 Cal. Rptr. 2d at 189. Many of the factors are present in the case at bar. Smith was employed for four and a half years. Smith also consistently received satisfactory or above satisfactory performance evaluations, and promotions. Finally, Pacific has personnel policies governing the administration of corrective action. These factors are all similar to those in *Walker*. Furthermore, Smith spoke to the vice president of Pacific. This communication set forth "acceptable guidelines" agreeable to both men on the issue of Smith's occasional tardiness. The communication supports the reasonableness in a belief of a good cause termination policy. Since both men agreed on a way to solve the problem, it shows that the company only wants to terminate an employee for a good cause. All of these factors could lead a reasonable person in Smith's position to believe he could only be terminated for a good cause, and would create an implied-in-fact contract.

West Coast Industries will argue that Smith's employment was similar to that in *Miller*. The defense will argue that promotions and salary increases alone "should not change the status of an "at-will" employee to one dischargeable only for "just cause." *Miller,* 210 Cal. App. 3d at 1559, 259 Cal. Rptr. at 58. As stated above, Smith has more than promotions and salary increases to support his position. He has good performance reviews, a company policy that defines steps for corrective actions to be taken, and a communication with the company vice president. The defense will argue that the company policies can be altered at any time to undermine the reasonableness of Smith's belief. However, such an assertion is not problematic for Smith's case. Pacific would not create policies it did not intend to use. The very existence of such policies manifests an intention by the company to only terminate an employee for good cause. The court might find the circumstances create an implied-in-fact contract.

West Coast Industries will distinguish Smith's case from *Foley*. In *Foley* and *Walker*, many of the same factors were presented to support an implied-in-fact contract. However, other factors in *Foley* were "a mandatory seven-step pretermination procedure" and "independent consideration for [Foley's] employment contract." *Miller,* 210 Cal. App. 3d at 1558, 259 Cal. Rptr. at 58. The *Foley* court held that all of these factors create a "reasonable expectation that [the employee] would not be terminated but for good cause." *Walker*, 4

FIGURE 13-1 (continued)

Cal. App. 4th at 993, 6 Cal. Rptr. 2d at 189. This result is distinguishable from the *Walker* case in which the court found that the factors would only create a triable issue of fact. The defense will therefore argue that since Smith's argument lacks consideration and a mandatory termination procedure, Smith could not reasonably expect to be terminated only for good cause. However, the court in *Foley* did not state that all of the factors were required. The court's conclusion in *Walker* set forth factors that were sufficient such that a jury could find an implied-in-fact contract. Hence, the court should rule in favor of Smith on this issue.

CONCLUSION

The language in Smith's job offer should not preclude him from asserting the existence of a subsequent, implied-in-fact contract requiring Pacific to terminate only for good cause. The clause in the offer is a statement of California Labor Code section 2922. It is not an integrated written agreement. The issue of an implied-in-fact contract for good cause termination is less clear than the first issue. Smith's case would be stronger if he had proof of further assurances by his superiors of his job security. However, he does satisfy the factors set forth in *Walker*. Therefore, Smith might be able to prove the existence of an implied-in-fact contract requiring termination to be for a good cause.

Issue Statement

The issue statement is the question you research. Sometimes it is best to start with a very general research question. After researching, you may determine that other questions or issues are also involved. Many research problems have more than one issue. These questions should also be included in the issue statements of your memorandum. Phrase the issue as a question or questions. Review Chapter 2 for a more thorough discussion of identifying and stating the issues.

Read the Issues section of the predictive memo in Figure 13-1.

Discussion

The discussion section in a memorandum is where you explain the results of the research. In this section, you answer the question or questions stated in the issue section. You provide the reasons for your answers. This is *legal analysis*.

Within the discussion, there will probably be several "issues"; these are often subissues raised by the general issue. For example, the main issue in the civil rights violation case described earlier in the chapter is whether the defendant faces criminal responsibility under 18 U.S.C. § 242. In researching this, you discover that you must also answer other questions, such as "Is an off-duty police officer acting under color of authority?" or "Were the victims deprived of any constitutional rights?" In writing the discussion or analysis, you should discuss each issue separately.

Within the memorandum, you can also use point headings to separate the discussion of different issues. Point headings are required in formal argumentative writing. They are similar to chapter titles or titles of various sections within a chapter. Headings not only help the reader stay focused on your ideas but also help you, the writer, stay focused. See Figure 13-1 and note the use of headings in the discussion.

In discussing or analyzing each of your issues, you should follow the IRAC approach discussed in earlier chapters. There are, however, a few additional pointers for using the IRAC approach within a memorandum.

Issue State the issues in your case in the "Issue" section of the memorandum. It is not necessary to restate the question in your analysis. Where there is more than one issue, it is, however, necessary to let the reader know what issue you are discussing. Accomplish this with the use of a point heading or by use of a ***topic sentence*** that lets the reader know the subject of the following paragraph.

topic sentence
A topic sentence introduces the issues or subissues and connects back to the thesis paragraph.

Stating the Rule of Law Take the rule of law from one or more of the primary sources of law (constitution, statutes, rules and regulations, or case law). In stating the rule of law, state the rule and then give the proper citation for the source. At times, the rule of law may be a composite of law from several sources.

The following are examples of the different ways you can state a rule of law.

Case Law

- An off-duty police officer acts under color of authority when the air of official authority pervades the incident. *United States v. Tarpley,* 945 F.2d 806 (5th Cir. 1991).
- In the case of *United States v. Tarpley,* 945 F.2d 806 (5th Cir. 1991), the appellate court held that an off-duty police officer acts under color of authority when the air of official authority pervades the incident.

Statutory Law

- Federal law makes it a crime for anyone acting under color of authority to deprive any person of any constitutional right or to subject that person to different punishments, pains, or penalties, because of that person's race or color. 18 U.S.C. § 242.
- Title 18 § 242 of the U.S. Code makes it a crime for anyone acting under color of authority to deprive any person of any constitutional rights or to subject any person to different punishments, pains, or penalties because of that person's race or color.

This is not an exhaustive list. You may also use direct quotations from the case or statute to confirm the statement of the rule of law. In most cases, state the rule of law in your own words and then use a quotation to verify your statement. You should avoid simply using a quotation without clarification or explanation.

Analysis

The analysis varies depending on whether the rule of law is based on statutory law or on case law. If it is statutory law, your analysis involves breaking the statute down into its elements and applying the language of the law to the facts of your case. If the rule of law comes from case law, analysis involves comparing the facts of the case to your facts. It may also involve applying the reasoning of the case to your facts. In many situations, the analysis involves both statutory and case law.

An example of a Discussion section of a predictive memo follows on page 357.

Conclusion The conclusion is usually the answer to the questions you raised in your statement of the issues. Always state the conclusion, even if you think it is obvious.

An example of a Conclusion section of a predictive memo follows on page 359.

Citing Authorities

Format Citation of legal authorities in any type of legal writing should be in commonly accepted format. Often this means complying with the rules set out in a citation manual. Your state may have its own style manual. If so, you should follow those rules. An attorney may use your memorandum as the basis for the more formal memorandum of points and authorities or trial or appellate brief. If you follow the proper citation rules or your state's style manual, you may find that when you cite a case, it is only necessary to give the official cite. Parallel cites may not be required.

A Point to Remember

If you have photocopied or downloaded important cases or statutes for your research, you might want to attach them to your memorandum. The attorney may want to read important legal authority. Attaching it to your memorandum saves time.

Using Id. and Supra In writing any type of legal memorandum, you occasionally use a shorthand or abbreviated way of citing cases. Once a full citation to a case is used within the memorandum, it is not necessary to use a complete citation each time you refer to it. If the case was the immediately preceding citation, the term *Id.* is substituted for the case name and citation. Thus, the case *United States v. Tarpley,* 945 F.2d 806 (1991) becomes *Id.* If the citation supports a quotation, it then becomes *Id.* at 807. *Id.* is only used when the citation is the immediately preceding citation. If citations to any legal authorities (not just cases) intervene, you cannot use *Id.* The following are accepted shorthand ways of abbreviating this case.

Tarpley, 945 F.2d at 807

945 F.2d at 807

Id. at 807.

Normally when using a shorthand abbreviation, you use the first name of the first party listed in the case name, rather than the second name. Thus, in abbreviating the case name *Smith v. Jones,* you would use *Smith.* However, where the first name is a common one, such as *People* or *United States*, you must use the second name to avoid confusion.

Supra is used for authorities other than cases and statutes. (Although not approved by *The Bluebook,* you see *supra* used with cases by attorneys and judges.) Review Figure 13-1 to see how these terms are used.

Using Quotations Using quotations to emphasize your point can be an effective writing tool. Overuse, on the other hand, distracts the reader. You should keep quotations to a minimum. When a quotation is longer than three or four lines, read it to determine if you really need all of it. Also, incorporate quotations of less than three lines or less than 50 words into the text with quotation marks. Longer quotations are indented on both right and left margins, are single-spaced, and do not use quotation marks. This is a "blocked quote." You saw this tool used in the Argument involving the drug detection dog in Chapters 12. All quotations must be followed by the citation, including the page—this cite to the actual page where the quote is found is a "pin cite."

Conclusion

Every memorandum should have either a conclusion or a brief answer section. Some have both. This is a short summary of your findings. Often it contains a short and concise answer to the questions raised in your issue statement.

A Point to Remember

When you write a memorandum of law, follow the directions of the supervising attorney. When asked to research an issue, research that issue in a complete and objective manner. Do not research an issue that you think is more interesting or something you think is more important. If you are not sure what your supervisor wants, be sure to ask before spending hours researching, analyzing, and writing.

Review Figure 13-2 for another sample of a predictive interoffice memorandum of law.

FIGURE 13-2 Sample Predictive Interoffice Memorandum of Law

To:	Susan Springer, Assistant District Attorney
From:	Research Assistant
Date:	November 2, 20XX
Re:	Prosecution of Mr. David Johnston under California Penal Code Section 186.22(a)

STATEMENT OF ASSIGNMENT

You asked me to re-evaluate the case against David Johnston in order to establish that he meets the requisite elements for participation in a criminal street gang, under section 186.22(a) of the California Penal Code.

FACTS

The People of the State of California charged Mr. David Johnston with participation in a criminal street gang, under section 186.22(a) of the California Penal Code. Mr. Johnston's record shows that he has two prior arrests, one for vandalism in July 2002, and one for theft in September 2001. He was not convicted of either offense. Witness Wilson, a former member of the Rockets gang, will testify under subpoena for the People. His testimony will confirm Mr. Johnston's involvement in the gang.

The San Jose Police received an anonymous tip that two gangs were planning to assemble in San Jose on June 30, 20XX. When Detective Castillo arrived at the scene, two groups of people were gathered around a fight between Peter Davis, the leader of the Rockets, and Andre Soprano, the leader of the Cobras. Both leaders had knives and Soprano was wounded. Castillo was informed by a witness that Davis cut Soprano with a knife. She recognized several people as members of the Rockets and Cobras. Castillo did not recognize the defendant, Johnston. He was not wearing a Rockets jacket, but he was standing in the group Castillo identified as the Rockets. Castillo called for backup and the officers stopped the fight. As the officers approached, Castillo heard the defendant shout, "Stop, Peter! Stop!" Many people ran, but the officers arrested the two fighters and charged them with assault with a deadly weapon. Johnston and several persons known to be gang members were also arrested.

Witness Wilson was a member of the Rockets from 20XX to July 20XX. He claims Johnston was a member when Wilson joined in 2000. Johnston left the gang in October of 20XX, but continues to communicate with Wilson. Johnston is still friends with, and has been seen with, Davis. Wilson believes that Johnston was at the scene of his arrest on June 30, 20XX, to assist Davis. Wilson claims that Davis wanted to affiliate the Rockets with the Cobras and wanted Johnston's help to keep things calm if arguments ensued. Johnston did not have anything to do with the fight, and Wilson heard him say, "Stop, Peter, stop Andre!"

ISSUE

Is David Johnston an active participant in the Rockets criminal street gang according to the California Penal Code, where he was once a member of the Rockets and continues to associate with the members, he has a prior arrest record, and he was recently arrested at the scene of a gang fight?

FIGURE 13-2 (continued)

DISCUSSION

1. Johnston was an active participant in the Rockets gang. The evidence establishes all of the elements for participation in a criminal street gang.

A person actively participates in a criminal street gang, regardless of actual membership, (1) by being more than passively involved, (2) having knowledge of the gang's pattern of criminal activity, and (3) aiding and abetting a felony committed by gang members. David Johnston actively participated in the Rockets gang through his previous membership, his continuous association with the members, his prior arrests on felony charges, and his recent arrest with other gang members at the scene of an alleged assault with a deadly weapon.

A. The California Penal Code provides the requirements for establishing participation in a criminal street gang.

The rule of law governing participation in a criminal street gang in California is found in section 186.22 of the California Penal Code. Under this code section, a person is guilty if he/she "actively participates in any criminal street gang, with knowledge that its members engage in or have engaged in a pattern of criminal gang activity, and who willfully promotes, furthers, or assists in any felonious criminal conduct by members of that gang. . . ." Cal. Penal Code § 186.22 (a) (West 20XX). In order to establish active participation, "it is not necessary for the prosecution to prove that the person devotes all, or a substantial part of his or her time or efforts to the criminal street gang, nor is it necessary to prove that the person is a member of the criminal street gang." Cal. Penal Code § 186.22 (i).

Active participation in a criminal street gang means that a person has involvement with a gang that is "more than nominal or passive." *People v. Castenada*, 23 Cal. 4th 743, 747, 97 Cal. Rptr. 2d 906, 909, 3 P.3d 278, 281 (2000). The defendant does not need to hold a leadership position in the gang in order to actively participate in a gang. *Id.* at 745, 97 Cal. Rptr. 2d at 908, 3 P.3d at 280. *Scales v. United States* articulated the guilty knowledge and intent requirements, holding that "mere association with a group cannot be punished unless there is proof that the defendant knows of and intends to further its illegal aims." *Castenada*, 23 Cal. 4th at 747, 97 Cal. Rptr. 2d at 909, 3 P.3d at 281, citing *Scales v. United States*, 367 U.S. 203 (1961). *People v. Green* further acknowledged that someone who violates section 186.22(a) has also aided and abetted a criminal offense committed by gang members. *Castenada*, 23 Cal. 4th at 747, 97 Cal. Rptr. 2d at 909, 3 P.3d at 283 (citing *People v. Green*, 227 Cal. App. 3d at 703-04, 278 Cal. Rptr. at 151).

B. Johnston actively participated in the Rockets gang with the knowledge that its members engage in a pattern of criminal activity.

In *Castenada*, the defendant was convicted of robbery, attempted robbery, and active participation in Goldenwest, a criminal street gang. *Castenada*, 23 Cal. 4th at 745, 97 Cal. Rptr. 2d at 908, 3 P.3d at 280. The defendant and two others robbed and attempted to rob

FIGURE 13-2 (continued)

victims of their money, watch, and gold chain. *Id.* Police observed the defendant in the presence of gang members seven times. *Id.* at 756, 97 Cal. Rptr. 2d at 908, 3 P.3d at 280. The defendant claimed that he was never initiated into the gang, but just helped out the gang. *Id.* An officer testified that the defendant's numerous contacts and admitted association with the gang indicated his knowledge of the gang's activities. *Id.* Police even warned the defendant that Goldenwest was considered a criminal street gang, but the defendant continued to associate with them. *Id.* at 753, 97 Cal. Rptr. 2d at 914, 3 P.3d at 285. The joint robbery at issue in *Castenada* was sufficient evidence that the defendant promoted, furthered, and assisted felonious criminal conduct of the gang. *Id.* The court ruled that there was enough proof that the defendant actively participated in a criminal street gang within the meaning of section 186.22 (a) of the California Penal Code. *Id.*

In *In re Jose P.*, the defendant was arrested and convicted for robbery, burglary, false imprisonment, and participation in Norteno, a criminal street gang. *In re Jose P.*, 106 Cal. App. 4th 458, 130 Cal. Rptr. 2d 810 (2003). The defendant Jose P. and two other gang affiliates stole two safes from a home and pointed a gun at and put duct tape over the eyes and mouth of the seven-year-old who lived at the home. *Id.* at 462, 130 Cal. Rptr. 2d at 810. Jose P. was convicted of active participation in a criminal street gang. *Id.* at 467, 130 Cal. Rptr. 2d at 816. He admitted to the police that he associated with the Norteno gang, he was contacted in the presence of gang members, and was seen wearing red, the gang's color, at least twice. *Id.* at 468, 130 Cal. Rptr. 2d at 816. He further confessed that if his fellow gang members asked him to do something for them, he would. *Id.* In addition, he was involved in crimes of car theft, attempted robbery, and the robbery in question at trial. *Id.* The evidence was sufficient to prove that the defendant was an active participant in the Norteno gang. *Id.*

Similar to *Castenada* and *In re Jose*, Johnston was seen with the leader of the gang and remains friends with Wilson. He might not have been wearing a jacket on the day of the assault, but it is not necessary to prove that he is currently a member of Rockets, only that he participates more than nominally or passively. *Castenada,* 23 Cal. 4th at 747, 97 Cal. Rptr. 2d at 909, 3 P.3d at 281. Since Johnston was once a member of the Rockets, he has more than "mere association" with the gang. *Castenada*, 23 Cal. 4th at 747, 97 Cal. Rptr. 2d at 909, 3 P.3d at 281, citing *Scales v. United States*, 367 U.S. 203 (1961). His criminal record of multiple arrests shows that he is not someone who remains passively involved. Even if Johnston is no longer a member, he continues to remain friends with members and was arrested at the scene of a crime with gang members. From this evidence, it can be inferred that Johnston continues to have the requisite knowledge of the gang's pattern of criminal activity.

C. Johnston actively participated in the Rockets gang by promoting and assisting in felonious criminal conduct by gang members.

Just as in *Castenada* and *In re Jose*, Johnston was arrested at the scene of a crime with other gang members. Since Johnston was present during an assault with a deadly weapon in order to help out the Rockets gang leader, his involvement was more than nominal or passive. *Castenada,* 23 Cal. 4th at 747, 97 Cal. Rptr. 2d at 909, 3 P.3d at 281.

FIGURE 13-2 (continued)

Scales articulated that a defendant must know of, and intend to further, the gang's illegal aims. *Castenada*, 23 Cal. 4th at 747, 97 Cal. Rptr. 2d at 909, 3 P.3d at 281 (citing *Scales*, 367 U.S. 203 (1961)). In addition, *Green* further acknowledged that a defendant must have aided and abetted a criminal offense committed by gang members. *Castenada*, 23 Cal. 4th at 747, 97 Cal. Rptr. 2d at 909, 3 P.3d at 283 (citing *Green*, 227 Cal. App. 3d at 703–04, 278 Cal. Rptr. at 151). The California Jury Instruction on Culpability for Crime states that one aids and abets the commission of a crime when one: "(1) With knowledge of the unlawful purpose of the perpetrator, and (2) With the intent or purpose of committing or encouraging or facilitating the commission of the crime, and (3) By act or advice aids, promotes, encourages or instigates the commission of the crime. . . ." Mere presence at the scene of a crime which does not itself assist the commission of the crime does not amount to aiding and abetting. The fact that Johnston was at the scene of a gang fight in order to assist the Rockets in becoming affiliated with the Cobras, with knowledge of what might ensue, establishes that he aided and abetted the assault. Since he was no longer a member of the gang, he could have chosen not to attend the event. There is no evidence that he was simply present for peacemaking because a fight broke out and no peacemaking occurred. After the police arrived, Johnston was heard shouting at the gang members to stop fighting. This can be interpreted as attempting to prevent the gang's arrest, not necessarily to stop the assault. Johnston aided the assault when he agreed to be present to help the Rockets gang leader and he did not stop the fight. In addition, his prior arrests might also show his affiliation and attempt to further the gang's illegal aims. *Castenada* , 23 Cal. 4th at 747, 97 Cal. Rptr. 2d at 909, 3 P.3d at 281.

The defense might argue that there is no evidence that his prior arrests were at all related to the gang. In addition, the defense might insist that he was at the scene of his arrest to prevent crime, not to assist in it. The evidence of Johnston's former membership and prior arrests shows his "guilty knowledge" of the gang's activities. *Id.* Furthermore, Johnston's voluntary attendance at the gang fight and his inaction to actually prevent the crime shows that he also has the requisite "guilty intent." *Id.* Johnston had more than passive or nominal knowledge of the gang's activities and he aided in the gang's felonious conduct. *Id.* There seems to be sufficient evidence to suggest that Johnston actively participated in a criminal street gang.

CONCLUSION

A criminal street gang is an ongoing organization of three or more persons, with a common name or symbol, that has as one of its primary activities the commission of enumerated crimes, and whose members engage in a pattern of criminal activity. A person actively participates in a criminal street gang by being more than passively involved, having knowledge of the gang's activities, and aiding in the felonious activity of other members. Johnston actively participated in a criminal street gang.

Finding It Online

For examples of outlining techniques, check the following sites:

https://owl.english.purdue.edu/owl/ (search for outlining)

http://www.lib.jjay.cuny.edu/research/outlining.html

The Internet provides many examples of legal memoranda. To see available documents, do a Google search for "legal memorandum."

CITATION MATTERS

SHORT CITATION FORMAT

***THE BLUEBOOK*—RULE 4**

Legal writing often contains a large number of citations. The "short citation formats" help the reader sort through the citations. This cuts down the amount of repetition for both the writer and the reader.

Probably the most common short citation form is *Id.* Use *id.* when citing the immediately preceding legal authority. This tells the reader that the material originated in the same location as the material cited immediately preceding it.

For example:

> The *Ferber* case upheld a prohibition on the distribution and sale of child pornography, as well as its production, because these acts were "intrinsically related" to the sexual abuse of children in two ways. *New York v. Ferber*, 458 U.S. 747, 759 (1982). First as a permanent record of a child's abuse, the continued circulation itself would harm the child who had participated. *See id.* Second, because the traffic in child pornography was an economic motive for its production, the State had an interest in closing the distribution network.
>
> *Id.* at 760.

In this example of a blocked quote, this alerts the reader that the material in the first sentence is found in the *Ferber* case. Provide the entire citation because this is the first time the case is used. A short format citation follows the second sentence. The "signal" *see* is followed by *id.*, meaning that the writer is asking the reader to look at page 759 in the case (page 759 is listed as the "pinpoint" page in the *Ferber* citation sentence). The *i* in *id.* is lowercase because *id.* is not the first word in the citation sentence. Follow the third sentence with "*Id.* at 760." This tells the reader that this information is located on page 760 of the *Ferber* case.

CHAPTER **SUMMARY**

The legal research process is usually not complete until the results are communicated to another person in either an objective or a persuasive way, depending on the situation. Documents objectively conveying research findings are generally memoranda of law and opinion letters. Documents utilizing a persuasive approach include memoranda of points and authorities, trial briefs, and appellate briefs.

A memorandum of law, usually prepared for an attorney, contains an overview of all of the law related to the research question. It must be accurate and complete. While there are no required formalities for such a document, a memorandum of law should identify the author, the recipient, the date, the subject matter, a statement of the facts, a statement of the issue or issues, a discussion of the relevant law, and a conclusion. Within the discussion, it is common to use the IRAC method of analysis. This includes stating the issue, stating the applicable rule of law (case law, statutory law, or constitutional law), applying the law to the facts, and reaching a conclusion.

TERMS TO **REMEMBER**

memorandum of law
opinion letter
memorandum of points and authorities
trial brief
appellate brief
cause of action
topic sentence

QUESTIONS FOR **REVIEW**

1. Identify and describe the different types of documents used to convey the results of legal research.
2. List other names used to refer to a memorandum of law.
3. What is the purpose of a memorandum of law?
4. Why is it important that a memorandum of law include all law, even that which may be contrary to your client's position?
5. Describe the general format of a memorandum of law.
6. What steps should you follow in preparing to write a memorandum of law?
7. Describe one way of organizing a memorandum where the controlling law is found primarily in statutory law.
8. Describe one way of organizing a memorandum where the controlling law is found primarily in case law.

TEST **YOURSELF** (Check Your Answers in Appendix G)

Using the Predictive Memorandum found in Chapter 12 under Section 12-7, identify the thesis paragraph(s), the rule explanation paragraphs, and the rule application paragraphs.

TEST **YOURSELF**—WRITE IT RIGHT Rule Explanation Paragraphs

The better discussions and arguments use a pattern of *rule explanation paragraphs* followed by rule application paragraphs. Better writers open a discussion, or an argument, with an explanation of the rules of law that she will rely on in the document.

The following three paragraphs are examples of *rule explanation paragraphs*:

A person commits fraud in relation to access devices when he knowingly effects transactions, using access cards issued to other another person, to obtain payment or property with an aggregate value of at least $1,000, within a one-year period, if such transactions affect foreign commerce. 18 U.S.C.A. § 1029(a)(5) (West 2016). Alternatively, the person commits the offense by using unauthorized access devices to obtain anything of value aggregating at least $1,000 within a one-year period. 18 U.S.C.A. § 1029(a)(2). An unauthorized access device is one that is "lost, stolen, expired, revoked, canceled, or obtained with intent to defraud." 18 U.S.C.A. § 1029 (e)(3). An access device is a card or other means of account access that may be used to obtain money or things of value, or to initiate transfers of funds. 18 U.S.C.A. § 1029(e)(1). Conviction under § 1029(a)(5) may result in imprisonment for not more than 15 years for a first-time offender. 18 U.S.C.A. § 1029(c)(1)(A)(ii). Conviction under § 1029(a)(2) may result in imprisonment for not more than 10 years for a first-time offender. 18 U.S.C.A. § 1029(c)(1)(A)(i).

The State may meet the statutory requirement of $1,000 by aggregating the values of payment or property obtained in different transactions, as long as the transactions constitute violations of the same statutory provisions. *United States v. Momeni,* 991 F.2d 493, 495 (9th Cir. 1993) (aggregating unauthorized access card uses at different hotels to meet the $1,000 statutory minimum).

The requirement of an effect on interstate commerce is to be liberally construed so as to jurisdictionally encompass those crimes that meet the minimum statutory requirements set forth in Section 1029. *United States v. Rushdan,* 870 F.2d 1509 1513 (9th Cir. 1989)(holding that possession of out-of-state credit cards affects interstate commerce). An adverse economic effect on a business engaged in interstate commerce is sufficient to constitute an effect on interstate commerce. *United States v. Phillips,* 577 F.2d 495, 501 (9th Cir. 1978) (holding possibility of extortion of interstate corporation to be an effect on interstate commerce). Furthermore, proof of any effect on interstate commerce is sufficient to satisfy the requirement. *United States v. Bagnariol,* 665 F.2d 877 (9th Cir. 1981) (holding that attempted extortion of fictional interstate corporation satisfies interstate commerce requirement).

Notice, the writer *does not use* the *facts of her client's case* in these rule explanation paragraphs. The legally relevant facts are used in rule application paragraphs, and those paragraphs follow the rule explanations.

Now, You Try It

(Check your answers in Appendix G)
Which of the following paragraphs are rule explanation paragraphs?

1. The interstate commerce requirement of § 1029 is also satisfied. Wells Fargo, the issuer of the access devices to Ms. Rhodes, is a corporation engaged in interstate commerce. Thus, the deleterious economic effect caused by Mr. Rhode's crime is sufficient to satisfy the interstate commerce requirement of the statute. *See Phillips,* 577 F.2d at 501.
2. Being an accessory after the fact is a separate and exclusive substantive offense from the offense committed by the principal. *United States v. Taylor,* 322 F.3d 1209, 1212 (9th Cir. 2003) (holding that one convicted as a principal to murder may not also be an accessory after the fact to the same crime). It is not necessary to try or convict the principal in order to convict an accessory after the fact. *United States v. Walker,* 415 F.2d 530, 530 (9th Cir. 1969) (citing *Hiram v. United States,* 354 F.2d 4, 6 n.2 (9th Cir. 1965)) (affirming conviction of accessory after the fact to bank robbery despite the absence of the conviction of the principal).
3. Susan Tan is guilty of being an accessory after the fact to Dylan Rhode's access device fraud. The first of the three elements listed in *Felix-Gutierrez* that the State must prove to establish an offense under 18 U.S.C.A. § 3, that the principal in fact committed an offense against the United States, is established above in the discussion of Mr. Rhode's crime.
4. Various types of conduct may tend to show assistance to prevent or hinder the principal's apprehension under 18 U.S.C.A. § 3. For example, in *Rux,* the court affirmed the accessory after the fact conviction of a defendant who purchased a vehicle for his brother to use to escape from the F.B.I. after committing bank robbery. 412 F.2d at 333. In *Felix-Gutierrez,* the defendant hired a pilot to fly the principal out of the country. 940 F.2d at 1206. In *Hiram,* the court affirmed the defendant's conviction as an accessory after the fact after the defendant traveled with the principal as he evaded the F.B.I. and provided false statements to the F.B.I. regarding the principal after he was arrested. 354 F.2d at 5-6.

CITATION **EXERCISES**

Use Appendix C and the Citation Matters feature in this chapter to answer these questions.

1. State the *Bluebook* rule that explains "short citation format."
2. What is the most common short form citation?
3. List three short-form citations for the following citation:

Mapp v. Ohio, 367 U.S. 643, 647 (1961).

FROM **THE WRITER'S CORNER** Headings in an Internal Memorandum (the Predictive Memorandum)

1. In an internal predictive memorandum, the headings work as ______________ similar to a ___________- ______________.
2. Explain the IRAC format.

ASSIGNMENTS AND **EXERCISES**

Analysis and Writing Exercises

1. Write a predictive memorandum of law based solely on the Victoria V. facts and the *Ann M.* case found in this chapter.
2. Review the hypothetical case of *Speeker v. South Bay County School District* found in Appendix B, Problem 9. Read the authorities cited at the end of the factual background. Use these authorities to write a memorandum of law, addressing the following issues:
   a. Did the school district have the right to suspend Susie for her action?
   b. Assuming that the school district was not justified in its actions, does Susie have a claim under 42 U.S.C. § 1983?

Online Research Exercises

3. Locate: http://bartleby.com/141/

   This is the website where you may access William Strunk Jr.'s *The Elements of Style*. This is the classic reference book for English composition. Open Section: "V. Words and Expressions Commonly Misused." What does this resource say about each of the following:
   a. certainly
   b. very
   c. whom
4. Locate: www.wilbers.com

   This is Stephen Wilbers's *Writing for Business and Pleasure* site. Complete the two 30-second exercises. Be sure to show your instructor the actual exercise and your rewrite.

CASE **PROJECT**

Write a predictive memorandum of law detailing the rights of the parties in the Appendix A hypothetical case you researched in Chapter 12.

Small Group In-Class Project

Using Figure 13-2—the Sample Predictive Memorandum of Law—insert margin notes to identify:

1. the thesis paragraph
2. the rule explanation paragraphs
3. the rule application paragraphs

Discuss the organization of the document and the order of the paragraphs in the memorandum. Your margin notes in the memorandum will help you identify the rule explanation and rule application paragraphs.

chapter **fourteen**

WRITING TO THE COURT: PERSUASIVE WRITING

SKILL OBJECTIVES FOR CHAPTER 14

When you complete chapter 14, you should be able to

- Explain rules of court.
- List and describe common features found in legal memoranda and briefs.
- Describe the purpose of a memorandum of points and authorities.
- Explain how and why declarations are used.
- Describe the purpose of a trial brief.
- Describe the purpose of an appellate brief.
- Write a persuasive memorandum of points and authorities.

CHAPTER OUTLINE

From the Desk of W. J. Bryan, Esq.

TO: Research Associate
FROM: W. J. Bryan
RE: Our Client, Justin Meyers
DATE:

We were served with a memorandum of points and authorities in opposition to our motion to suppress in the Meyers case. Please read the document and the cases cited within it. Then prepare a draft of a reply memorandum of points and authorities. You need to check the rules of court to see how long we have before this needs to be filed. I know it is only a few days.

14-1 INTRODUCTION

In the previous chapter, you saw how the results of legal research are objectively communicated in a memorandum of law. However, when argued to the court, research findings are not presented in an objective manner but rather in a persuasive or argumentative way. The researcher ***advocates*** a position that is most favorable to his or her client. In advocating a position, the researcher tries to convince the court that the law supports the client's position.

advocate
Arguing one side of an issue.

memorandum of points and authorities
Research document filed with the court containing legal analysis of disputed issues occurring in a case pending in court; often used to support or oppose motions.

trial brief
Research document filed with the court prior to trial addressing legal issues in the case.

appellate brief
Research document filed in an appeal addressing the legal issues forming the basis of the appeal.

motion
A request for a court order in connection with a case that is pending in court.

When a researcher writes to the court, formal documents are used and technical rules are followed. The documents used to present a legal argument to the court are ***memoranda of points and authorities***, ***trial briefs***, and ***appellate briefs***. A memorandum of points and authorities is filed when a legal question arises in a case that is pending in court. These memoranda support or oppose a ***motion*** in a case. A trial brief is a document filed at the beginning of a trial. In this document, the attorney presents legal authorities and arguments showing that his or her client should prevail at trial. Trial briefs might also contain legal arguments regarding evidentiary issues that are expected to arise at trial. Appellate briefs are prepared and filed after a case is decided in the trial court. These briefs contain arguments regarding the validity of the trial court judgment.

The following sample memorandum of points and authorities is a simple legal argument written for a court (a judge). The margin notes call out the use of headings, point headings, citation rules and conventions, and organization and structure using rule explanation paragraphs followed by rule application paragraphs.

SAMPLE PERSUASIVE MEMORANDUM OF POINTS AND AUTHORITIES

Introduction

This section provides the reader with a snap shot of what happened and the basis of this party's legal argument.

Notice the use of a short "heading."

As defendant acknowledges, Plaintiff Cheryl Black's action stems from the broken shoulder she suffered when she tripped and fell over a displaced section of concrete located on defendant school grounds. Defendant's motion for summary judgment is based on its claim that the defective condition on defendant's property consisted solely of a ¾-inch displacement between two sections of concrete with no other contributing factors and that the defect is therefore "trivial" as a matter of law. However, the evidence in this case raises triable issues of fact regarding several other factors or conditions that prevent the defect from being trivial as a matter of law.

Facts

On August 19, 20XX, Plaintiff, Cheryl Black has just started working at a BIG SISTERS after-school program located on defendant's school grounds. (Pl. Evid. in Opposition No. 1.) She did not rush and was not in any hurry. (Pl. Evid. in Opposition No. 2.) While walking on school grounds to her assigned building she fell over raised and horribly cracked concrete. (Pl. Evid. in Opposition Nos. 4, 6, & 8; Response to UMF No. 6.) She suffered serious injuries, including a broken shoulder. (Pl. Evid. in Opposition No. 9) Mrs. Black was on the property for the first time the day before the injury, and was unfamiliar with the area where she fell. (Pl. Evid. in Opposition No. 1.) The general area of the injury was a central or "quad" area, bordered by classrooms. (Pl. Evid. in Opposition No. 3.) Mrs. Black recalls that leaves and other debris from trees were located on the concrete near the place of the fall. (Response to UMF No. 6.) The concrete area causing the fall consisted of more than a simple ¾-inch lip. There was a "horrible" crack. (Pl. Evid in Opposition No. 4.) Shortly after the accident, Mrs. Black and her husband went back to the school. She showed him where the fall occurred and he took photographs. This photograph was attached to defendant's moving papers and several were attached to a prior set of answers to interrogatories. (Pl. Evid. in Opposition No. 8; UMF No. 9 & 10.) When they returned, they noticed that the general condition of the school property was poor. In his deposition, Mr. Black described the location of the accident as having displaced concrete, like that caused by tree roots. (Pl. Evid. in Opposition Nos. 5, 6, & 7.) The raised portion of the concrete measured approximately ¾ inch. The jagged, cracked portion is clear in the photographs. (Exhibits A and B to Black Decl.) Mrs. Black was told that because of reduced income, upkeep of school property was suffering and the condition had been poor for some time. She recalls her supervisor and the principal telling her this. (Pl. Evid in Opposition No. 7.)

The Facts section tells a story about people—this is the who, what, when, where, and why section of the brief.

The most important facts (key facts) are used again below in the Argument section.

Again, notice the use of the short "heading."

This is a "cite to the record"—it shows the court where this information is located.

Most of the factual sentences are followed with a cite to the record.

Argument

This simple heading marks the change from facts to legal argument.

I. Summary Judgment Is Improper When a Triable Issue of Material Fact Exists and the Moving Party Is Not Entitled to a Judgment as a Matter of Law.

This is a "point heading"—it makes a legal point.

In making a summary judgment motion, the defendant bears the burden of presenting declarations and evidence that "must either establish a complete defense to plaintiff's action or demonstrate an absence of an essential element of plaintiff's case." *Dolquistv.City of Bellflower* (1987) 196 Cal. App. 3d 261, 266. If the defendant's evidence does this, then before granting summary judgment, the court must also review declarations and evidence submitted by the plaintiff, and if it appears that triable issues of fact exist, denial of the motion is proper. *Id.*; *see also*, Cal. Civ. Proc. Code § 437c.

Proper citation format varies from state to state.

There are several citation manuals.

Many states have their own citation manuals.

The cites in this memorandum of points and authorities adhere to a state citation guide.

To prevail in a summary judgment in an action based on Government Code section 835, defendant must show that *as a matter of law* the property was not in a dangerous condition or that *as a matter of law* defendant did not have actual or constructive notice of the condition. Notice can be either actual or constructive. Cal. Gov. Code § 835.2. Furthermore, the evidence is viewed "most favorably to the plaintiff." Cal. Gov. Code § 830.2.

Always check to see what your state requires—and in some instances you need to check local rules of court.

II. Triable Issues of Fact Exist about the Dangerous Condition of Defendant's Property.

Point heading for the second legal point (issue).

A. Whether a sidewalk defect is trivial is determined by all surrounding circumstances, not solely the size of the defect.

This is a sub-point heading.

The basis of the determination of whether property is in a dangerous condition is the risk of injury, not mathematical measurements, and is generally a question of fact. Gov. Code § 830.2; *Stathoulis v. City of Montebello* (2008) 164 Cal. App. 4th 559, 566–67. A dangerous condition is not trivial as a matter of law unless the

Again, notice that point headings make points.

(continued)

Notice that the code section is cited before the case law.

In general, when there is a code section on point, we address it before we introduce the case law.

This is the proper citation for the code section.

This is the proper use of a pin cite

Under Bluebook rules this is the proper way to show that the information comes from pages 566–67.

(We do not use 566–567.)

In general, the first time a case name is used, the entire cite should accompany the case name.

A lowercase "c" is used here because this is not a U.S. Supreme Court case.

A capital "C" is used when the reference is to the U.S. Supreme Court.

Rule explanation paragraph.

Under Bluebook Rule 5 this is the correct way to "block" and cite a quote of 50 or more words.

This is the proper use of a pin cite.

When the name of the case is in the sentence, you may use this short form of the citation (without the name).

This is the proper way to show that the case quoted or cited another case.

This paragraph and the one above are rule explanation paragraphs.

Rule explanation paragraph.

risk created by the condition was of such a minor, trivial, or insignificant nature in view of the surrounding circumstances that no reasonable person would conclude that the condition created a substantial risk of injury when such property or adjacent property was used with due care in a manner in which it was reasonably foreseeable that it would be used.

CAL. GOV. CODE § 830.2.

Courts have considered numerous cases in which defendant's claim that a sidewalk defect should be considered trivial. Repeatedly, the courts emphasize that size of the defect is not a determining factor. *Stathoulis,* 164 Cal. App. 4th at 566–67. Even the cases cited by defendant reaffirm that rule. For example in *Fielder v. City of Glendale* (1977) 71 Cal. App. 3d 719, the court distinguished a case where a defect was not found trivial. The court stated:

> there were other factors, namely, this was respondent's first sojourn down Lincoln Avenue in this particular direction; the accident occurred at night and the sidewalk was shadowy because of overhead trees; further, the evidence reveals that respondent was walking slowly and apparently did not contribute to the accident in any way.

Id. at 730.

In *Stathoulis*, where the court refused to grant summary judgment (the defect consisted of shallow potholes approximately 1 inch deep in a walkway), the court listed the types of factors or circumstances that should be considered in determining if a defect is trivial. The court, in quoting *Caloroso v. Hathaway* (2004) 122 Cal. App. 4th 922,

927, stated that considerations should include

> whether the walkway had any broken pieces or jagged edges and other conditions of the walkway surrounding the defect, such as whether there was debris, grease, or water concealing the defect, as well as whether the accident occurred at night in an unlighted area or some other condition obstructed a pedestrian's view of the defect.

Stathoulis, 164 Cal. App. 4th at 566.

In addition to broken pieces, jagged edges, and debris, the court in *Stathoulis* also notes that a court should consider "plaintiff's knowledge of the conditions in the area." 164 Cal. App. 4th at 567 (citing *Johnson v. City of Palo Alto* (1962) 199 Cal. App. 2d 148, 152). Another consideration is the use of the property. "One of the factors pertinent to a determination of the question whether the condition of public property is dangerous to the general public, is the use to which that property is put." *Torkelson v. City of Redlands* (1961) 198 Cal. App. 2d 354, 358.

Another relevant case is *Dolquist v. City of Bellflower* (1987) 196 Cal. App. 3d 261. Here the court denied a summary judgment where a woman tripped over a ¼-inch protrusion of steel reinforcement from a concrete parking abutment. Summary judgment was denied even though the plaintiff in *Dolquist* was not carrying anything and was wearing eyeglasses, the weather was dry, the accident occurred in bright daylight, and respondent had no notice of any prior injuries or complaints. *Id.* at 267.

The principal of defendant's school raises the fact that she had no prior complaints. It is well settled that the owner of property with a dangerous condition is charged with constructive notice of defects in the public sidewalk that existed for such a length of time and are of such a character that a reasonable inspection would disclosed them. Cal. Gov. Code § 835.2.

B. The evidence of the circumstances affecting the property in this case creates triable issues of fact regarding its risk of serious harm, and therefore as a matter of law the defect causing Mrs. Black's injuries should not be considered trivial.

Second sub-point heading under the second issue.

This is not a simple case of an individual tripping on an insignificant rise between two sections of concrete, such as in the *Fielder* case cited by defendant. Many of the circumstances surrounding this injury and the condition of defendant's property increase the risk posed here and are of the type listed in *Stathoulis* and *Dolquist* that require a denial of a summary judgment motion. (1) The site of Mrs. Black's fall not only consisted of a rise between two sections of concrete, but the concrete was severely cracked and jagged (see photos and testimony). Thus, the defect itself was more than a simple ¾-inch rise. (2) There was debris in the form of leaves and other tree droppings. Although Mrs. Black was not specific about the exact location of the debris, cases recognize the possibility, if not likelihood, of such matter interfering with the ability of a party to see and judge the nature of a concrete defect. (3) The general condition of the property was poor. (4) Rather than being an open and more visible space, the area was closely bordered by two buildings, (5) Mrs. Black was unfamiliar with the property, having been on the school grounds only once before and not having walked over the area where the fall occurred. These last three factors increase the risk that one defect will not be noticed. (6) The location of the defective condition is a school ground. For the safety of children, maintenance of this area is expected.

This point heading tells the court that the lawyer is shifting to rule application—notice the use the client's name.

The fact that it was a sunny day, that Mrs. Black wore glasses, and that the principal reports no prior complaints should not affect the outcome of this case any more than it did in *Dolquist.*

The nature of the combined ¾-inch rise and cracked, jagged concrete indicates that this was not recent damage to the property, but one that had existed for some time and should have been noticed by defendant with regular inspection.

Government Code section 830 defines a dangerous condition as follows:

"(a) 'Dangerous condition' means a condition of property that creates a substantial (as distinguished from a minor, trivial or insignificant) risk of injury when such property or adjacent property is used with due care in a manner in which it is reasonably foreseeable that it will be used." At the time of her fall, Cheryl Black was walking in a normal, non-rushed manner over an area that provided access to several buildings. She used due care and used the property in a reasonably foreseeable manner. There is no question that plaintiff incurred a substantial injury. This is a foreseeable type of risk to be expected when a condition creates a risk of tripping and falling. Triable issues of fact exist.

Rule application paragraph with a legal conclusion.

III. Liability under Government Code 835 Is Predicated on the Tort of Negligence and Thus Count 1 on the Judicial Council Form Complaint for Premises Liability Applies.

Point heading.

Although liability of a public entity for a dangerous condition on its property must meet the requirements of Government Code section 835, those requirements, as expressly set forth in the statute, are based on the tort of negligence. Under the statute a public entity is under a duty not to knowingly keep its property in a dangerous condition; it breaches that duty when it fails to do this and causes a reasonable person injury or damages. Section 835 and the preceding and subsequent code sections are based on negligent concepts of reasonableness and foreseeability. One section, Government Code section 830.5 mentions the doctrine of res ipsa loquitur, a common negligence concept, as being relevant to some actions under section 835.

Rule explanation paragraph.

Again, notice that the argument begins with a code section and then moves to case law.

(*continued*)

Rule explanation paragraph.

Furthermore, cases dealing with section 835 mention complaints based on negligence. *See Dolquist,* 196 Cal. App. 3d 261. "The complaint alleges among other things that appellant's injuries were proximately caused by respondent's negligence in the ownership, construction, management, maintenance and operation of a dangerous condition on public property." *Id.* at 264; *see also Peters v. City and County of San Francisco* (1953) 41 Cal. 2d 419, 427. Government Code section 835 may *limit* the liability of public entities for their negligence in maintaining property, but it is based on negligence and Count 1—Negligence on the Judicial Council Complaint is therefore appropriate.

Point heading.

IV. Count 2 on the Judicial Council Form Is Based on Willful Failure to Warn, Not on Civil Code section 846.

Rule explanation and application are combined in this paragraph.

Defendant asks for summary adjudication on the issue that Civil Code section 846 does not apply to public entities. Because the Count mentions section 846, a likely intent behind this Count is to cover situations where an owner of recreational property is sued. However, Count 2 is not a cause of action based on section 846. In fact, section 846 specifically states: "Nothing in this section creates a duty of care or ground of liability for injury to person or property." The cause of action is for willful failure to warn of a dangerous condition. Evidence exists that the defendant's property was in a poor condition for some time, thus justifying the Count. Defendant's contention that Count 2 does not apply is unsupported.

The last heading (not a point heading)—the request for relief follows this heading.

Conclusion

For the reasons stated above, the plaintiff respectfully requests the denial of defendant's motion for summary judgment and summary adjudication.

Date: ____________________

Respectfully Submitted,

____

Attorney for Plaintiff

14-2 RULES OF COURT

rules of court
Rules regulating law practice in a particular court or courts.

local rules of court
Procedural rules adopted by an individual court for practice in that specific court.

Documents filed in a court must comply with rules regarding form and content. Most courts have these rules, which are part of their ***rules of court***, sometimes called ***local rules of court***. These rules usually cover such things as acceptable length, citation format, content requirements, and the number of copies that must be submitted. A court may refuse to consider the document when the rules regarding form and content of a memorandum or brief are not followed.

Figure 14-1 contains a copy of one rule from the U.S. Supreme Court regarding briefs that are to be filed in that Court.

14-3 COMMON FEATURES

filed
To become part of the court record.

caption
A caption identifies the parties to the case, the court in which the case is pending, the docket number, and the title of the document.

A memorandum of points and authorities (often referred to by lawyers as "P's and A's"), a trial brief, and an appellate brief contain several common features: a case caption, table of contents, a table of authorities, a statement of facts, a statement of issues or questions presented, an argument, and a conclusion.

Case Caption

In all jurisdictions, any document ***filed*** in a court must contain a case ***caption***. A caption identifies the parties to the case, the court in which the case is pending,

RULE OF COURT FOR THE SUPREME COURT

Rule 24. Briefs on the Merits: In General

1. A brief on the merits for a petitioner or an appellant shall comply in all respects with Rules 33.1 and 34 and shall contain in the order here indicated:

(a) The questions presented for review under Rule 14.1(a). The questions shall be set out on the first page following the cover, and no other information may appear on that page. The phrasing of the questions presented need not be identical with that in the petition for a writ of certiorari or the jurisdictional statement, but the brief may not raise additional questions or change the substance of the questions already presented in those documents. At its option, however, the Court may consider a plain error not among the questions presented but evident from the record and otherwise within its jurisdiction to decide.

(b) A list of all parties to the proceeding in the court whose judgment is under review (unless the caption of the case in this Court contains the names of all parties). Any amended list of parent companies and nonwholly owned subsidiaries as required by Rule 29.6 shall be placed here.

(c) If the brief exceeds five pages, a table of contents and a table of cited authorities is needed.

(d) Citations of the official and unofficial reports of the opinions and orders entered in the case by courts and administrative agencies.

(e) A concise statement of the basis for jurisdiction in this Court, including the statutory provisions and time factors on which jurisdiction rests.

(f) The constitutional provisions, treaties, statutes, ordinances, and regulations involved in the case, set out verbatim with appropriate citation. If the provisions involved are lengthy, their citation alone suffices at this point, and their pertinent text, if not already set out in the petition for a writ of certiorari, jurisdictional statement, or an appendix to either document, shall be set out in an appendix to the brief.

(g) A concise statement of the case, setting out the facts material to the consideration of the questions presented, with appropriate references to the joint appendix, e. g., App. 12, or to the record, e. g., Record 12.

(h) A summary of the argument, suitably paragraphed. The summary should be a clear and concise condensation of the argument made in the body of the brief; mere repetition of the headings under which the argument is arranged is not sufficient.

(i) The argument, exhibiting clearly the points of fact and of law presented and citing the authorities and statutes relied on.

(j) A conclusion specifying with particularity the relief the party seeks.

2. A brief on the merits for a respondent or an appellee shall conform to the foregoing requirements, except that items required by subparagraphs 1(a), (b), (d), (e), (f), and (g) of this Rule need not be included unless the respondent or appellee is dissatisfied with their presentation by the opposing party.

3. A brief on the merits may not exceed the page limitations specified in Rule 33.1(g). An appendix to a brief may include only relevant material, and counsel are cautioned not to include in an appendix arguments or citations that properly belong in the body of the brief.

4. A reply brief shall conform to those portions of this Rule applicable to the brief for a respondent or an appellee, but, if appropriately divided by topical headings, need not contain a summary of the argument.

5. A reference to the joint appendix or to the record set out in any brief shall indicate the appropriate page number. If the reference is to an exhibit, the page numbers at which the exhibit appears, at which it was offered in evidence, and at which it was ruled on by the judge shall be indicated, e. g., Pl. Exh.14, Record 199, 2134.

6. A brief shall be concise, logically arranged with proper headings, and free of irrelevant, immaterial, or scandalous matter. The Court may disregard or strike a brief that does not comply with this paragraph.

FIGURE 14-1 Supreme Court Rule of Court 24

the docket number, and the title of the document. Review Figure 14-5 and identify the caption.

Table of Contents

table of contents
A list of the sections of a document with the page on which they appear within the document.

A ***table of contents*** is a list of the various sections found in the document with the corresponding page. The various sections include, but may not be limited to, the following:

- Table of Authorities
- Statement of Facts
- Issues
- Summary of the Argument
- Argument: Each point heading, and the page on which it appears, is restated under the argument in the table of contents.
- Conclusion
- Signature

A table of contents is generally required for trial briefs and appellate briefs. It is required in a memorandum of points and authorities only if the memorandum exceeds a certain page length. Local rules of court govern this. Some appellate documents may also contain a statement of the case (this is often a summary of the judicial history of the case), jurisdiction statement, corporate disclosure statement, or statement of the standard of review.

See Figure 14-2 for an example of a table of contents from an appellate brief.

Table of Authorities

table of authorities
A list of primary and secondary authorities cited within a memorandum or brief and the page numbers on which they appear.

A ***table of authorities*** contains a list of all legal authorities, primary and secondary, that are cited within the document and the page or pages on which the citation appears. There are several acceptable formats for setting up the table of authorities; a common format follows.

Constitutional Provisions and Statutes

- Cite constitutional provisions in the order where they appear in the Constitution and give all pages on which they appear.
- Cite *U.S. Code* sections in numerical order and give all pages where they appear in the document.
- Cite state code sections (either alphabetically or numerically, depending on how the code is cited) and give all pages where they appear in the documents.
- Cite federal and state regulations.

Case Law

- Cite all cases, listing them alphabetically, and give *all* pages where they appear in the memorandum or brief. Another way to list the case law is to separate the federal and state case law into two lists. When this is done, it is common to follow this format:
- **Under the list of the federal cases,** first list the U.S. Supreme Court cases in alphabetical order; second, follow with the federal circuit court cases in alphabetical order; third, list the miscellaneous reporters (Bankruptcy, Military, etc.) in alphabetical order; and fourth, list the district cases in alphabetical order.
- **Under the list of state cases,** list the state Supreme Court cases in alphabetical order and follow with the state appellate court cases in alphabetical order.

FIGURE 14-2 Table of Contents for Appellate Brief

TABLE OF CONTENTS

ii

FIGURE 14-2 (continued)

TABLE OF CONTENTS--Continued

FIGURE 14-2 (continued)

TABLE OF CONTENTS--Continued

Miscellaneous Sources

- Cite secondary source material and any other source material used (usually alphabetically); include all pages where each source appears.

See Figure 14-3 for an example of a table of authorities. Note how all primary authority is listed first and how the primary authority is organized and labeled.

FIGURE 14-3 Table of Authorities for Appellate Brief

TABLE OF AUTHORITIES

Cases:

Arizona v. Manypenny, 451 U.S. 232 (1981) 13, 35, 36
Barr v. Matteo, 360 U.S. 564 (1959) 30
Bigelow v. Forrest, 76 U.S. 339 (1869) 16
Buck v. Colbath, 70 U.S. 334 (1865) 12, 16
City of Aurora v. Erwin, 706 F.2d 295 (10th Cir. 1983) 47-48
Cleveland C. & c. R.R. v. McClung, 119 U.S. 454 (1886) 21-22
Colorado v. Symes, 286 U.S. 510 (1932) . . . 17, 18, 20, 27, 34
Commonwealth of Pennsylvania v. Newcomer, 618 F.2d 246 (3d Cir. 1980) 33-35
Davis v. South Carolina, 107 U.S. 597 (1882) 14, 16, 25
Ellis v. Railway Clerks, 466 U.S. 435 (1984) 36
Erlenbaugh v. United States, 409 U.S. 239 (1972) 20
Fourco Glass Co. v. Transmirra Prod. Corp., 353 U.S. 222 (1957) 18
Garcia v. United States, 469 U.S. 70 (1984) 6
Gay v. Ruff, 292 U.S. 25 (1934) 12, 15-17, 20
Georgia v. Grady, 10 Fed. Cas. 245 (1876) (No. 5,352) . . 13
Illinois v. Fletcher, 22 F. 776 (N.D. Ill. 1884) 25
In re Debs, 158 U.S. 564 (1895) 45
In re Neagle, 135 U.S. 1 (1890) 13, 14, 49
Jarecki v. Searle & Co., 367 U.S. 303 (1961) 6
Kelly v. Robinson, 479 U.S. __, 107 S.Ct. 353 (1986) 46
Little York Gold-Washing & Water Co. v. Keyes, 96 U.S. 199 (1887) 38
Martin v. Hunter's Lessee, 14 U.S. 304 (1816) 4, 8
Maryland v. Soper (No. 1), 270 U.S. 9 (1926) 2, 18, 20, 23-33, 35, 49

v

FIGURE 14-3 (continued)

TABLE OF AUTHORITIES--Continued

FIGURE 14-3 (continued)

TABLE OF AUTHORITIES--Continued

Verlinden B.V. v. Central Bank of Nigeria,
461 U.S. 480 (1983) 37, 42, 44
Virginia v. Felts, 133 F. 85 (C.C. Va. 1904) 48
Walters v. National Assn. of Radiation Survivors,
473 U.S. 305 (1985) 18
Westfall v. Erwin, 484 U.S. __,
108 S.Ct. 580, 98 L.Ed. 2d 619 (1988) 30, 41
Willingham v. Morgan, 395 U.S. 402 (1969) 14, 23, 28-35, 41
Younger v. Harris, 401 U.S. 37 (1971) 46

United States Constitution and statutes:

U.S. Const. Art. 1, section 8 43
U.S. Const. Art. III, section 2 . . . . 4, 13, 36-40, 42-44
Judiciary Act of 1789, section 25, 1 Stat. 85 7-9
Act of February 4, 1815, ch. 31, section 8, 3 Stat. 198 . . 8-11
Act of March 2, 1833, ch. 57, section 3, 4 Stat. 632 10
Act of March 3, 1863, ch. 81, section 5, 12 Stat. 756 . . 11, 12
Act of July 13, 1866, ch. 184, section 67, 14 Stat. 171 . . . 12
The Internal Revenue Act of June 30, 1864,
ch. 173, section 50, 13 Stat 241 12
Act of May 11, 1866, 14 Stat. 46 11
Act of August 23, 1916, ch. 399, 39 Stat. 532 14-17
28 U.S.C. 2679(b) (Federal Driver's Act) 3, 19
28 U.S.C. 1346 *et seq.* (Federal Tort Claims Act) 19
28 U.S.C. 1442(a)(1). . . . . *passim*
28 U.S.C. 1442(a)(3) 3, 6, 12, 14-17
28 U.S.C. 1442(a)(4) 16
28 U.S.C. 1446(a) 49
28 U.S.C. 1446(a)(4) 41
28 U.S.C. 1446(a)(5) 41

vii

FIGURE 14-3 (continued)

TABLE OF AUTHORITIES--Continued

Miscellaneous authorities:

Like a table of contents, a table of authorities is usually required in trial briefs and appellate briefs. It is generally required in a memorandum of points and authorities only if it exceeds a certain page length. Local rules of court govern this.

A Point to Remember

Not all briefs follow this organization of the case law in the table of authorities. Always check with your supervisor if you are unsure of the format followed in your law office. Sometimes, the case law citations are simply listed in alphabetical order, regardless of the level of the court, as shown in Figure 14-3.

Statement of Facts

court record
Documents and transcripts of proceedings in connection with a case.

declaration
A statement under penalty of perjury containing factual statements.

affidavit
A statement under penalty of perjury sworn to before a notary.

A brief statement of the factual dispute before the court is usually presented in any argumentative document. The facts must be supported in the ***court record*** or in ***declarations*** or ***affidavits*** that are attached to the memorandum or brief. Although facts must always be accurate and truthful, present the statement of facts in a way most favorable to the party filing the memorandum or brief.

This section of the brief follows the table of contents and table of authorities. In this way, the reader has the opportunity to become acquainted with what actually happened before the legal argument begins. (Sometimes the question presented may appear first. In fact, in a brief to the U.S. Supreme Court, place the question presented first, even before the table of contents and table of authorities.) Remember, all legal issues revolve around the facts. Write the facts contained in a brief so that your client is in the best light. This is "slanting the facts to favor your client." *Caution:* Never change the facts, never add facts that do not exist, and never omit damaging facts. Write the facts for the court so that the client is placed in the best possible position. Vocabulary choices and descriptive terms can often produce different pictures of the same event. For example, consider Problem 4 in Appendix A. In describing the facts here, the attorney might state the facts as follows:

> Facing multiple suspects and fearing for his safety, the officer used a reasonable amount of force in order to effect a legal arrest.

On the other hand, the attorney for the victims might characterize the events as follows:

> The officer maliciously, violently, and unreasonably attacked and beat minority individuals, clearly using excessive force in light of the alleged minor infractions.

Downplay or offset damaging facts when possible. Writing an effective factual statement is mastered with practice.

Figure 14-4 contains the beginning sections of the fact statements presented to the U.S. Supreme Court in the *United States v. Virginia* (*VMI*) case. Notice the differences between the Petitioner's statement and the Respondent's statement. Citations to other documents and transcripts are omitted. Also, as you read the appellate brief in Figure 14-5, note how factual statements are supported by references to other materials.

FIGURE 14-4 Petitioner's and Respondent's Statement of Facts in the *Virginia Military Institute* Case

PETITIONER'S STATEMENT OF FACTS

1. The Virginia Military Institute. The Virginia Military Institute (VMI) is a state military college in Lexington, Virginia. Since its founding in 1839, VMI has maintained a policy of admitting only men to its four-year undergraduate degree program. The fourteen other public colleges in Virginia are all coeducational. Approximately 1300 male students are enrolled at VMI.

VMI's mission statement declares that VMI's goal is to produce "citizen-soldiers," described as "educated and honorable men who are suited for leadership in civilian life and who can provide military leadership when necessary." The VMI curriculum includes liberal arts, science and engineering courses, and VMI confers both Bachelor of Arts and Bachelor of Science degrees.

As the district court found, VMI has a strong reputation for producing leaders, and has an exceptionally loyal and powerful alumni network. That network is "enormously influential," especially in the male-dominated fields of engineering, the military, business, and public service in which VMI graduates tend to pursue careers, "VMI alumni overwhelmingly perceive that their VMI educational experience contributed to their obtaining personal goals." VMI enjoys the largest endowment on a per-student basis of any undergraduate institution in the United States.

VMI employs an "adversative" method of character development and leadership training not currently used by any other college-level institution. That method is based on techniques used in "English public schools" and "earlier military training," although it has long been abandoned at the United States military academies. The method "emphasizes physical rigor, mental stress, absolute equality of treatment, absence of privacy, minute regulation of behavior, and indoctrination of values." "As a consequence of completing the rigorous tasks, succeeding, and actually graduating from VMI, VMI cadets have a sense of having overcome almost impossible physical and psychological odds. They have been put through great physical pressures and hazards, and just to have made it yields a feeling of tremendous accomplishment."

VMI's adversative method is implemented through a pervasive military-style system. The system includes the "rat line," which is a seven-month regimen during which first-year cadets, or "rats," are "treated miserably," like "the lowest animal on earth." "Rats" are subjected to a strict system of punishments and rewards that creates "a sense of accomplishment and a bonding to their fellow sufferers and former tormentors." The "rat line" experience is accompanied by "rat training," "a tough physical training program" "designed to foster self-confidence and physical conditioning in fourth classmen [i.e., freshmen] by creating training situations which are stressful enough to show them that they are capable of doing tasks which surpass their previously self-imposed limits."

The "class system" assigns roles to each class of cadets within a hierarchy in order to "cultivate leadership." "After the rat line strips away cadets' old values and behaviors, the class system teaches and reinforces through peer pressure the values and behaviors that VMI exists to promote." VMI's program also includes the "dyke system," an arrangement by which each "rat" is assigned a senior as a mentor to give some "relief from the extreme stress of the rat line." VMI's honor code—providing that a cadet "does not lie, cheat, steal nor tolerate those who do"—provides "the single penalty of expulsion for its violation."

VMI requires cadets to "live within a military framework; they wear the cadet uniform at the Institute, eat most meals in the mess hall, live in a barracks, and regularly take part in parades and drills." "The most important aspects of the VMI educational experience occur in the barracks." There, cadets live at close quarters with one another,

FIGURE 14-4 (continued)

three to five together in stark and unattractive rooms, with poor ventilation, unappealing furniture, windowed doors with no locks and no window coverings. "[A] cadet is totally removed from his social background," and placed in an environment the principal object of which is "to induce stress."

Although VMI has always restricted admission to men, some women "would want to attend [VMI] if they had the opportunity." (Recruitment of women would likely yield a 10% female student body at VMI.) Between 1988 and 1990 VMI received 347 letters from women inquiring about admission, or indicating interest in attending VMI. It is not disputed that some women can succeed within the VMI-type methodology and are capable of doing all of the individual activities required of VMI cadets. The district court expressly found that the VMI methodology "could be used to educate women."

RESPONDENT'S STATEMENT OF FACTS

Petitioner's opening brief presents an incomplete picture of the VMI program and glosses over or contradicts crucial facts found by the courts below. This brief sets forth a more accurate and representative statement of the record and the remedial proceedings below.

A. Mary Baldwin College

Mary Baldwin College (MBC), an historically women's college, was founded in 1842. MBC has responded to the changing role of women in society by expanding its curriculum "to include the new options open to women in business and the professions." MBC has "developed an emphasis on career planning," has "computerized the campus," and has added "new state of the art equipment for its science labs." MBC "is committed to the education of women for a world of expanding opportunity."

MBC enrolls over 700 residential undergraduate students, has a Phi Beta Kappa chapter, is accredited by the Southern Association of Colleges and Schools, and is now ranked first among regional liberal arts colleges in the South. See *U.S. News & World Rep. 141* (Sept. 18, 1995. MBC's 55-acre campus in Staunton, Virginia, includes the facilities of the former Staunton Military Academy, residence halls, classroom buildings, computer and science laboratories, a 40,000-square-foot physical education facility, playing fields, tennis courts, and a swimming pool.

The student-faculty ratio in MBC's residential program is 11 to 1. MBC offers 28 undergraduate majors, including degrees in mathematics, the sciences, business, and the arts, and also offers pre-law and pre-med programs and a joint-degree engineering program with the University of Virginia. MBC is "geared in the direction of trying to encourage women to persist in math and physics."

MBC enjoys "a record of success in developing new programs and operating distinctive and unique programs within the larger traditional undergraduate residential community." For example, MBC has successfully established a unique residential baccalaureate program for academically gifted, high-school-age students tailored to "the academic, emotional and developmental needs of young women."

The Writer's Corner

Point Headings in a Legal Argument Must Make Points

Point headings, in a legal argument, are the reader's guide to the logic of the writer's argument. Each point heading needs to make a point. This is different from the headings in an interoffice memorandum (a predictive memorandum) where the headings may be simple signposts for the audience.

In long documents, the rules of court often require a table of contents. This table is a listing of the point headings. The reader (often a judge) reviews these headings in order to gain an early understanding of the legal argument contained in the memorandum of points and authorities. The point headings should provide a quick tour through the writer's legal positions and legal conclusions.

For example, the point headings for a trial brief are set out below. They provide the reader with a tour of the 11-page argument section of the brief. Other sections include the Introduction, Statement of Facts, Statement of the Issues, and the Conclusion.

Introduction	[section deleted]
Statement of Facts	[section deleted]
Statement of Issues	[section deleted]

Argument

I. The report of Dr. John Mayor does not provide a sufficient basis upon which to base a decision because the report is based on speculation, conjecture, and incomplete medical history.

A. The Board should not rely on reports that are based on conjecture, speculation, or inadequate patient history.

B. Dr. Mayor's medical report is based on conjecture, speculation, and inadequate patient history.

1. Inadequate patient history forms the basis of the report.
2. Dr. Mayor's conclusion is unsupported by the literature mentioned in the report.
3. The report is based on a variety of facts that are speculative and a matter of conjecture.
4. Most importantly, Dr. Mayor's conclusion directly contradicts his deposition testimony.

II. Should the Board not order an additional medical examination, it should find that applicant's injury is work related because an examination of the entire record in this case provides substantial evidence of that conclusion.

A. In determining causation, the Board must consider the entire record, not only the conclusion in an agreed medical report.

B. The evidence in this case provides substantial evidence that applicant's injury is work related.

III. The Defense Presents No Credible Evidence

Conclusion

Notice the use of point headings in the Argument in Figure 14-5.

FIGURE 14-5 Appellate Brief

MORSE v. FREDERICK

On Writ of Certiorari to the United States Court of Appeals for the Ninth Circuit.

Initial Brief: Appellant-Petitioner

KENNETH W. STARR, Counsel of Record

QUESTIONS PRESENTED

Whether the First Amendment allows public schools, at school-sponsored, faculty-supervised events, to prohibit students from displaying messages promoting the use of illegal substances.

Notice that Mr. Starr uses both legal and factual material in the issue.

[The second Issue, Statement of the Case and the Summary of the Argument are not included here.]

(continued)

FIGURE 14-5 (continued)

ARGUMENT

This thesis paragraph sets the scene for this argument.

Under challenge to address declining academic performance in the age of globalization, American public education finds itself—even at a time of war—as a vitally important subject in the unfolding democratic conversation about the Nation's future. The Ninth Circuit's destabilizing decision in this sensitive arena renders all the more daunting the vital task of teachers, administrators, and volunteer school board members in attending holistically to the needs of millions of students entrusted every school day to their charge. In reversing the district court's grant of summary judgment in favor of the Juneau School Board and Deborah Morse, the Ninth Circuit has dramatically altered the legal landscape of public education law in the United States. As to both the First Amendment and the law of qualified immunity, the court of appeals' uncompromisingly libertarian vision is deeply unsettling to public school educators across the country. The decision below is doubly—and dangerously—wrong. The judgment should be reversed.

Notice that this first major point heading responds to the issue.

THE JUNEAU SCHOOL OFFICIALS DID NOT VIOLATE FREDERICK'S FIRST AMENDMENT RIGHTS WHEN THEY DISCIPLINED HIM FOR VIOLATING SCHOOL POLICIES AGAINST PROMOTING ILLEGAL SUBSTANCES AT A SCHOOL ACTIVITY.

A. The "special characteristics" of the school setting require deference for school officials' actions.

Good use of a topic sentence.

Note: you see "short cites" here because this case law was cited earlier in the Summary of the Argument—that is not included here.

Throughout the fifty States (and the District of Columbia), public education serves what this Court long ago described as "a principal instrument in awakening the child to cultural values." *Brown v. Bd. of Educ.,* 347 U.S. 483, 493 (1954). Through government-operated educational institutions, large and small, the vast majority of young Americans are prepared "for later professional training" and for "adjust[ing] normally to [their] environment." *Kuhlmeier,* 484 U.S. at 272 (quoting *Brown,* 347 U.S. at 493). Those who serve as teachers and administrators in this challenging environment are tasked with a weighty and delicate responsibility. In prescribing and controlling student conduct, public educators are inexorably required to balance students' constitutionally-guaranteed liberties with the bedrock duty to educate young minds, including fashioning "the boundaries of socially appropriate behavior." *Fraser,* 478 U.S. at 681. Pursuit of these goals inevitably requires authorities to regulate speech, symbolic and otherwise, in a manner impermissible outside the school setting. *Id.* at 682; *accord Bd. of Educ. v. Earls,* 536 U.S. 822 (2002) (upholding high school's random suspicionless drug testing policy); *Vernonia Sch. Dist. 47J v. Acton,* 515 U.S. 646 (1995) (permitting random drug testing of high school student athletes).

Rule explanation paragraph.

In the First Amendment context, this Court has long emphasized that the rights of students in the public schools "are not automatically coextensive with the rights of adults in other settings." *Fraser,* 478 U.S. at 682 (citing *New Jersey v. T.L.O.,* 469 U.S. 325, 340–42 (1985)). Thus, while students do not "shed their constitutional rights to freedom of speech or expression at the schoolhouse gate," students' rights must be "applied in light of the *special characteristics* of the school environment." *Tinker,* 393 U.S. at 506 (emphasis added). The "uninhibited, robust, and wide-open" free speech in adult discourse, as ordained in *New York Times Co. v. Sullivan,* 376 U.S. 254, 270 (1964), is manifestly different from the latitude accorded to schoolchildren in a "custodial and tutelary" environment. *Vernonia,* 515 U.S. at 655.

Rule explanation paragraph.

As this Court has acknowledged on numerous occasions, the resolution of conflicts arising in the daily operation of school systems "is primarily the responsibility of parents, teachers, and state and local school officials, and not of federal judges." *Kuhlmeier,* 484 U.S. at 273 (citations omitted). Only when a decision to

FIGURE 14-5 (continued)

censor student expression has no valid educational purpose is the First Amendment so "directly and sharply implicate[d]" as to require judicial intervention to protect students' constitutional rights. *Id.* (quoting *Epperson v. Arkansas,* 393 U.S. 97, 104 (1968)). Thus, in discerning the proper doctrinal limitations upon the baseline liberty guaranteed by the Free Speech Clause, a guiding principle unifying this Court's teachings is that "[a] school need not tolerate student speech that is inconsistent with its 'basic educational mission.'" *Id.* at 266 (citing *Fraser,* 478 U.S. at 685). Firmly embedded in this Court's student speech jurisprudence, that overarching principle is the beginning and end of this case.

1. *Tinker* protects speech that does not intrude upon the work of the schools.

The framework for student speech doctrine begins with *Tinker.* In that landmark case, the Court upheld the free speech rights of three students to wear anti-war armbands during the school day as a silent, passive political protest. 393 U.S. at 514. The Court reasoned that wearing black armbands, a traditional sign of mourning, was expressive conduct akin to pure speech, which is entitled to comprehensive protection. *Id.* at 505–06. At the same time, the *Tinker* majority recognized the unique characteristics of a public school and the unavoidable reality that administrators and teachers may suppress student speech, whether in class or out of it, that "intrudes upon the work of the schools or the rights of other students." *Id.* at 508. In the record before it, however, the Court could discern no evidence that the passive wearing of two-inch armbands disrupted school operations. *Id.*

Rule explanation paragraph.

The *Tinker* Court had no occasion to spell out in detail the extent or nature of "disruption" necessary to trigger a school's authority to curtail student speech. The Court described the requisite disruption as "interference, actual or nascent, with the schools' work," which is something more than "undifferentiated fear or apprehension of disturbance." *Id.*Under this standard, if a school administrator reasonably perceives (or forecasts) that a student's expressive conduct is presently interfering (or would eventually interfere) with the school's work, then the administrator is warranted in suppressing the particular expression (or expressive conduct).*Id.* Student speech rising to this level of disruption may occur "in class or out of it" and may "stem[] from time, place, or type of behavior." *Id.* at 513. The Court provided further guidance by distinguishing John Tinker's silent, passive conduct from the disciplinary problems posed by "aggressive, disruptive action or even group demonstrations." *Id.* at 507–08. The *Tinker* Court thus foreshadowed its willingness to approve school intervention when speech is accompanied by antisocial conduct.

Rule explanation paragraph.

Justice Black dissented. He lamented that the broad sweep of the majority decision invited students to "use the schools at their whim as a platform" and that courts, rather than schools, "will allocate to themselves the function of deciding how the pupils' school day will be spent." *Id.* at 517 (Black, J., dissenting). Although his opinion failed to carry the day, Justice Black's plain-spoken words continue to echo through the body of student speech law.

Rule explanation paragraph.

2. *Fraser* permits schools to prohibit student speech that undermines the basic educational mission.

Fraser—the second stage of the student speech decisional trilogy—assured school officials that they retain authority to proscribe student speech that is vulgar, lewd, indecent, obscene, or plainly offensive, even absent a showing of material and substantial disruption to school discipline. 478 U.S. at 683–84. Drawing from *Tinker,* the *Fraser* Court emphasized that inculcating habits and manners of civility—through discouraging offensive language—is "truly the 'work of the schools.'" *Id.* at 683 (quoting *Tinker,* 393 U.S. at 508). To force a school to tolerate indecorous student speech, wrote Chief Justice Burger, "would undermine the school's basic educational mission." *Id.* at 685.

Rule explanation paragraph.

(continued)

FIGURE 14-5 (continued)

Rule explanation paragraph.

Applying this principle, the *Fraser* Court reversed the Ninth Circuit's contrary judgment and upheld a public high school's disciplining a student for delivering a sexually suggestive nominating speech for a student government candidate at a voluntary school assembly. *Id.* That speech referred to the candidate in terms of "an elaborate, graphic, and explicit sexual metaphor," though the speaker's saucy presentation employed neither profanity nor obscenity. *Id.* at 677–78. Under the circumstances, the Court determined that "it was perfectly appropriate for the school to disassociate itself to make the point to the pupils that vulgar speech and lewd conduct is wholly inconsistent with the 'fundamental values' of public school education." *Id.* at 685–86. On that note, the Court embraced Justice Black's broad teaching in *Tinker* that "the Federal Constitution [does not] compel[] ... teachers, parents, and elected school officials to surrender control of the American public school system to public school students." *Id.* at 686 (quoting *Tinker,* 393 U.S. at 526 (Black, J., dissenting)).

Rule explanation paragraph.

Emphasizing that not all types of speech are accorded identical protection, particularly in view of the "special characteristics" of the educational setting, the *Fraser* Court recognized "the marked distinction between the political 'message' of the armbands in *Tinker* and the sexual content of [Matthew Fraser's] speech." *Id.* at 680. The Court acknowledged that some speech is properly subject to age-appropriate restrictions: "[Fraser's sexually explicit] speech could well be seriously damaging to its less mature audience, many of whom were only 14 years old and on the threshold of awareness of human sexuality." *Id.* at 683. In that regard, the *Fraser* Court echoed Justice Stewart's concurrence in *Tinker,* where the Justice from Cincinnati articulated the view that "[a] State may permissibly determine that, at least in some precisely delineated areas, a child—like someone in a captive audience—is not possessed of that full capacity for individual choice which is the presupposition of First Amendment guarantees." *Tinker,* 393 U.S. at 515 (Stewart, J., concurring) (quoting *Ginsburg v. New York,* 390 U.S. 629, 649–50 (1968) (Stewart, J., concurring in result). Significantly for First Amendment analysis, Fraser's ribald electioneering pronouncements fell well below the standards for "obscenity" established in adult contexts. *See, e.g., Miller v. California,* 413 U.S. 15 (1973). The bedrock point from *Tinker* remained: The public education setting has "special characteristics" profoundly informing First Amendment analysis.

Rule explanation paragraph.

Justice Brennan concurred in the judgment. He agreed that, "under certain circumstances, high school students may properly be reprimanded for giving a speech at a high school assembly which school officials conclude disrupted the school's educational mission." *Fraser,* 478 U.S. at 688–89 (Brennan, J., concurring). In dissent, Justice Stevens similarly recognized the appropriateness of disciplining students for expressive conduct that conflicts with a school's educational mission. *Id.* at 691 (Stevens, J., dissenting). He opined that "a school faculty must regulate the content as well as the style of student speech in carrying out its educational mission." *Id.* (Stevens, J., dissenting).

3. *Kuhlmeier* allows student speech restrictions in school-sponsored activities when pursuant to legitimate pedagogical concerns.

Rule explanation paragraph.

Fraser's deferential approach to school officials' First Amendment calibrations was likewise embraced in *Kuhlmeier.* In this final stage of the Court's school speech trilogy, the Court acknowledged that school officials are entitled to exercise pervasive control over the style and content of student speech that reasonably might be perceived to bear the school's imprimatur. 484 U.S. at 273. Regulation of speech viewed as "school-sponsored"—on account of the school lending its name and resources to the activity—is permitted if the curtailment is reasonably related to "legitimate pedagogical concerns." *Id.* Thus, in *Kuhlmeier,* a school properly exercised its discretion in refusing to publish certain student articles on pregnancy and

FIGURE 14-5 (continued)

divorce in a school-funded student newspaper. *Id.* at 276. The Court concluded that suppression of the articles was reasonably related to the tripartite school objectives of (i) protecting the privacy of the individuals referenced in the articles; (ii) shielding younger students from inappropriate subject matter; and (iii) teaching journalistic fairness. *Id.*

The *Kuhlmeier* Court added that "[a] school must also retain the authority to refuse to sponsor student speech that might reasonably be perceived to advocate drug or alcohol use." 484 U.S. at 272. Alluding to *Fraser's* emphasis on upholding schools' "educational mission," the majority recognized that promoting illegal substances was "inconsistent with 'the shared values of a civilized social order.'" *Id.* (quoting *Fraser,* 478 U.S. at 683). Thus, the Court left no doubt that discouraging illegal substance use reflected a legitimate pedagogical concern.

Rule explanation paragraph.

B. The *Tinker-Fraser-Kuhlmeier* trilogy permitted Juneau school officials to discipline Frederick for promoting illegal substances.

The case at hand fits comfortably within the framework of the school speech trilogy. In sharp contrast to Tinker's anti-war armband, Frederick's "bong hits" banner did not involve the passive expression of a political viewpoint. Rather, his slang marijuana reference was part of an antisocial publicity stunt designed to draw attention away from an important (and historic) school activity. The message that Principal Morse, Superintendent Bader, the unanimous School Board, and Chief Judge Sedwick all reasonably gleaned from this banner—and on which the Ninth Circuit proceeded—was that it expressed a positive sentiment about marijuana use. Frederick cannot reasonably contend otherwise. The message was therefore directly contrary to the school's basic educational mission of promoting a healthy, drug-free lifestyle (as expressed in written School Board policies). In the context of a school-sponsored activity, Principal Morse's restriction of this expression was indisputably consistent with an important pedagogical concern. The trilogy—when distilled to its essential principles—stands for the proposition that students have limited free speech rights balanced against the School District's right to carry out its educational mission and to maintain discipline. Under this body of law, Frederick's claim to First Amendment protection falls woefully short.

Rule explanation paragraph.

1. Discouraging use of illegal substances is an undeniably important educational mission.

Preventing teenage drug use is a critical educational mission of our public schools. "That the nature of the concern is important—indeed perhaps compelling—can hardly be doubted." *Vernonia,* 515 U.S. at 661; *see also Lorillard Tobacco Co. v. Reilly,* 533 U.S. 525, 599 (2001) (Souter, J., concurring in part and dissenting in part) ("[F]ew interests are more 'compelling,' than ensuring that minors do not become addicted to a dangerous drug before they are able to make a mature and informed decision as to the health risks associated with that substance . . . ."). While drug abuse remains a serious problem with adults, the severity is even more pronounced with elementary and secondary schoolchildren:

Notice the consistent use of good topic sentences.

Rule explanation paragraph.

> School years are the time when the physical, psychological, and addictive effects of drugs are most severe. Maturing nervous systems are more critically impaired by intoxicants than mature ones are; childhood losses in learning are lifelong and profound; children grow chemically dependent more quickly than

(continued)

FIGURE 14-5 (continued)

adults, and their record of recovery is depressingly poor. And of course the effects of a drug-infested school are visited not just upon the users, but upon the entire student body and faculty, as the educational process is disrupted. *Vernonia,* 515 U.S. at 661–62 (internal citations and quotation marks omitted). Troublingly, "[t]he drug abuse problem among our Nation's youth . . . has only grown worse" in recent years, thus "mak[ing] the war against drugs a pressing concern in every school." *Earls,* 536 U.S. at 834.

Rule explanation paragraph.

In view of this flinty reality, this Court has determined that "'special needs' . . . exist in the public school context" to justify overriding Fourth Amendment privacy interests that would otherwise apply outside the school setting. *Id.* at 843; *Vernonia,* 515 U.S. at 653. Accordingly, the majorities in *Earls* and *Vernonia* upheld random drug testing of students participating in extracurricular activities. 536 U.S. at 837–38; 515 U.S. at 664–65. These precedents once again confirmed that constitutional protections for schoolchildren are inexorably informed (and frequently diluted) by "the special characteristics of the school environment." *Tinker,* 393 U.S. at 506 (emphasis added).

Rule explanation paragraph.

Student free speech rights likewise appropriately yield when it comes to promoting illegal substances. "[T]he single most important factor leading schoolchildren to take drugs . . . [is] peer pressure." *Earls,* 536 U.S. at 840 (Breyer, J., concurring). Impressionable adolescents face strong inducements to use drugs as they are bombarded with pro-drug messages from classmates, adults, and the media. Remaining steadfastly consistent with the drug-free-lifestyle message is therefore particularly important while school is in session. Congress recognized this fact in passing the comprehensive Safe and Drug Free Schools and Communities Act, which supports local schools' drug prevention efforts and requires consistency of message that illegal drugs are "wrong and harmful." 20 U.S.C. § 7114(d)(6).

Rule explanation paragraph.

Consistent with Congress' mandate, thousands of local school boards across the country, much like Juneau's, have addressed the drug problem by crafting policies related to drug-abuse prevention, intervention, treatment, and discipline. Pet. at 17–21. These policies are adopted by duly-elected school board members through a public, deliberative process. The Juneau School Board, for example, is required by statute to develop and periodically review its policies governing student rights and responsibilities. Alaska Admin. Code tit.4, § 07.010. These student conduct rules must substantively and procedurally comply with applicable laws and regulations. *Id.* Through this exercise in constitutional self-government, a common prohibatory theme has emerged: Messages promoting illegal substances are not to be tolerated during school or any school activities. *See* Pet. App. 52a–58a (various anti-drug-message policies adopted in 1985, as revised).

Rule explanation paragraph.

Not surprisingly, lower courts addressing First Amendment challenges to anti-drug school policies had reached a bottom-line consensus—at least prior to Frederick. Several courts had recognized that prohibitions on pro-drug messages are constitutional because such expression is "plainly offensive" under *Fraser* and inconsistent with the mission of schools to promote healthy lifestyles (including by seeking at every turn to combat substance abuse). *See, e.g., Boroff,* 220 F.3d at 471 (upholding ban on Marilyn Manson t-shirts because singer promoted drug use); *Nixon v. N. Local Sch. Dist.,* 383 F. Supp. 2d 965, 971 (S.D. Ohio 2005) ("Examples [of offensive speech under *Fraser*] are speech containing vulgar language, graphic sexual innuendos, or speech that promotes suicide, drugs, alcohol, or murder."); *Barber v. Dearborn Pub. Sch.,* 286 F. Supp. 2d 847, 859 (E.D. Mich. 2003) ("[W]hen student speech is . . . lewd, obscene, or vulgar (including related to alcohol or drugs), school officials may curtail that speech."); *Gano v. Sch. Dist. No. 411,* 674 F. Supp.

FIGURE 14-5 (continued)

796, 798–99 (D. Idaho 1987) (upholding prohibition of t-shirt depicting drunken administrators under *Fraser,* noting that schools have a duty to teach about harmful effects of alcohol).

Other courts have observed that there can be little dispute that messages promoting illegal substances cause disruption within schools. *See Williams v. Spencer,* 622 F.2d 1200, 1205–06 (4th Cir. 1980) (taking judicial notice that messages promoting drug use endanger students' health and safety; prohibiting distribution of underground newspaper containing drug paraphernalia advertisements); *cf. McIntire v. Bethel Sch.,* 804 F. Supp. 1415, 1420–21 (W.D. Okla. 1992) ("Reasonable school officials could forecast that the wearing of clothing bearing a message advertising an alcoholic beverage would substantially disrupt or materially interfere with the teaching of the adverse effects of alcohol and that its consumption by minors is illegal and/or would substantially disrupt or materially interfere with school discipline.").

Rule explanation paragraph.

Still other courts have upheld bans on pro-drug messages in the context of school-sponsored activities. *See Bannon v. Sch. Dist. of Palm Beach County,* 387 F.3d 1208, 1219 (11th Cir. 2004) (approving viewpoint discrimination in school-sponsored speech to forbid pro-drug messages); *Planned Parenthood of S. Nev., Inc. v. Clark County Sch. Dist.,* 941 F.2d 817 (9th Cir. 1991) (permitting school policy banning ads in school publications for tobacco and liquor products); *McCann v. Fort Zumwalt Sch. Dist.,* 50 F. Supp. 2d 918, 920 (E.D. Mo. 1999) (upholding prohibition against school band playing song "White Rabbit" because it might "reasonably be perceived" to advocate the use of illegal drugs).

Rule explanation paragraph.

More broadly, discouraging drug use has been universally recognized and sanctioned by school boards, legislatures, courts (including this Court) as a permissible educational goal. The *Frederick* decision appears to be the first case in American jurisprudence in which any court—federal or state—has stripped public school officials of authority to proscribe pro-drug messages. This Court should remove any lingering doubt whether school authorities, pursuant to their basic educational mission, retain discretion to restrict student speech that is reasonably viewed as promoting or advocating the use of substances that are illegal to minors.

Rule explanation paragraph.

2. Frederick's pro-drug banner interfered with decorum by radically changing the focus of a school activity.

This point heading signals to the reader that the argument is shifting to an application of the rules explained above to the facts of this case.

The *Fraser*-ordained value of preserving decorum in schools likewise stands as a permissible justification for restricting student speech and for which school authorities traditionally are accorded wide discretionary latitude. *See Fraser,* 478 U.S. at 686 ("[M]aintaining security and order in the schools requires a certain degree of flexibility in school disciplinary procedures, and we have respected the value of preserving the informality of the student-teacher relationship." (quoting*T.L.O.,*469 U.S. at 340)). Discipline stemming from the time, place, or manner of a student's expressive conduct in no wise offends the First Amendment when the school has an interest in ensuring that school activities "proceed in an orderly manner." *Fraser,* 478 U.S. at 689 (Brennan, J., concurring in judgment); *cf. Cox v. Louisiana,* 379 U.S. 536, 554 (1965) (recognizing that the rights of free speech and assembly "do not mean that everyone with opinions or beliefs to express may address a group at any public place and at any time.").

Rule application paragraph.

Here, Frederick's "bong hits" banner substantially interfered with a school-sanctioned activity. J.A. 43, Pet. App. 62a. The Olympic Torch Relay was an important community event:

"The arrival of the torch in Juneau is cause for celebration," Gov. Tony Knowles said, "and I urge all Alaskans to embrace the state goal of the Olympic movement—to build a peaceful and better world by educating young people through sport, without discrimination, in the spirit of friendship, solidarity, fair play and mutual understanding."

Rule application paragraph.

(continued)

FIGURE 14-5 (continued)

Notice the repetition of the word "wrong"—this connects back to the thesis paragraph.

See Bingham, supra. At the culminating moment in his high school's welcoming the Olympic Torch Relay, Frederick radically changed the subject. By dividing the audience's attention—and distracting from the purpose that the Juneau School District sought to serve in sanctioning this event—Frederick's expressive conduct warranted the school's uncompromising censure. His message was trebly wrong. It was the wrong message, at the wrong time, and in the wrong place.

3. Principal Morse properly disassociated the school from Frederick's pro-drug banner.

Rule application paragraph.

Fraser, in short, closely fits the facts at hand. But so does the third member of the Court's school speech trilogy. The Ninth Circuit deemed *Kuhlmeier* inapplicable because the school neither sponsored nor endorsed Frederick's banner. Pet. App. 10a–11a. This dismissive conclusion underappreciated *Kuhlmeier's* logical reach.

Rule application paragraph.

Frederick's banner was unfurled in the midst of a highly important "school-sponsored" activity. Pet. App. 34a. By lending its resources to the event and sanctioning student observance during school hours, the School District unwittingly provided Frederick a bully pulpit for his publicity stunt. Frederick's "speech" was not expression in a classroom or hallway. To the contrary, he was situated outside the school with virtually the entire student body watching. At the very moment the school's involvement in the torch relay was at its zenith, Frederick lofted his 14-foot, subject-altering banner for the community (and the world) to see.

Rule application paragraph.

To be sure, reasonable observers might have concluded that the banner's message was so inimical to the school's mission that it did not bear the school's imprimatur. But this could be said of a student who pens a pro-drug article for a school-sponsored newspaper. *Kuhlmeier's* framework still would apply in the latter situation, and thus censoring such an article would be entirely permissible. *See* 484 U.S. at 272 ("A school must also retain the authority to refuse to sponsor student speech that might reasonably be perceived to advocate drug or alcohol use. . . ."). If Ms. Morse had been insouciantly indifferent to Frederick's drug-related banner, many in the community might well have wondered what they are teaching at taxpayer-supported Juneau-Douglas High School. The principal, accordingly, had a powerful pedagogical concern in prohibiting such a mission-compromising expression. Similarly, under *Fraser,* Principal Morse properly determined that it was her responsibility to "disassociate" the school from the banner's pro-drug message, which undermined the school's health and safety educational mission. 478 U.S. at 685–86.

C. Frederick was subject to school disciplinary rules.

Rule application paragraph.

As a student attending a school activity during school hours, Frederick was indisputably under the school's authority. He was standing with the assembled student body, which, as permitted by the administration, had lined both sides of Glacier Avenue directly in front of the school. J.A. 23–24.

Rule application paragraph.

Under these circumstances, the School Board's policies and student handbook left no doubt that Frederick was subject to school disciplinary authority: "Pupils who participate in approved social events and class trips are subject to district rules for student conduct; infractions of those rules will be subject to discipline in the same manner as are infractions of rules during the regular school program." Pet. App. 58a (Juneau Sch. Bd. Policy 5850); *see also* J.A. 100, 103 (defining infractions as including those committed "at school sponsored/sanctioned functions or activities"). The Juneau School District's rules were consistent with common practice and established law. *See generally* 3 James A. Rapp, *Education Law* § 9.03[5][b][i] (2006) ("Authority to discipline students for school related activities extends not only to those occurring on school property but also off school property.").

Based on his findings, Chief Judge Sedwick determined "there is no issue of fact as to whether or not this was a school-sponsored activity." Pet. App. 34a. The Ninth Circuit likewise concluded, simply but decisively: This is a "student speech case," not a "speech on a public sidewalk" case. Pet. App. 5a. Frederick's claim that he was somehow "speaking" in a Jeffersonian public square is entirely refuted by the facts as determined by the two lower courts. And in that school-related context, with its "special characteristics," Frederick was not at liberty to praise, however whimsically, the drug culture and thereby radically change the subject that had brought the student body to that time and place. The First Amendment does not reach nearly so far.

[The argument on the second issue is not included here.]

CONCLUSION

For the foregoing reasons, this Court should reverse the judgment of the Ninth Circuit.

Respectfully submitted,
KENNETH W. STARR, *Counsel of Record,*
RICK RICHMOND, ERIC W. HAGEN, KIRKLAND & ELLIS LLP,
777 South Figueroa Street
34 Floor, Los Angeles, CA 90017
(213) 680-8400
Attorneys for Petitioners
January 16, 2007

FIGURE 14-5 (continued)

Rule application paragraph.

Notice the short, direct closing sentence.

Simple conclusion.

Statement of Issue(s) or Question(s) Presented

This section of a memorandum or brief states in simple terms the legal question or questions before the court. An issue statement sets forth the legal question *and* provides the reader with the most significant facts. The issue is often stated as a question. Remember, it is the question presented to the court for resolution. Sometimes there is only one issue. Other times there are many. Each issue should generally be no more than one sentence. Proper identification and statement of the issues are critical to the success of the parties. Failure to raise all important issues or misstating the issue can result in the court's refusing to consider legal authorities or arguments that might favor your client. Proper identification of the issues obviously must be done before you finish your research and prior to writing a memorandum or brief. Review carefully the section in Chapter 2 dealing with issue statements. The following is the issue statement found in a brief to the Supreme Court in the case of *Paula Jones v. William Clinton:*

Question Presented

Whether a private civil action for damages against the President of the United States, based on events occurring before the President took office, should be permitted to go forward during the President's term of office.

The following are the questions presented in the *VMI* case, mentioned previously.

Petitioner's Question Presented

Whether the Equal Protection Clause permits a State, as one alternative in a primarily coeducational system of higher education, to afford its citizens the option of receiving the acknowledged benefits of single-sex education through methodologies designed by professional educators to accomplish optimal and substantively comparable pedagogical results for both women and men.

Respondent's Questions Presented

1. Whether a State that provides a rigorous military-style public education program for men can remedy the unconstitutional denial of the same

opportunity to women by offering them a different type of single-sex educational program deemed more suited to the typical woman.

2. Whether coeducation is the required remedy in the context of this case.

After reading these questions, can you figure out which party is the petitioner and which is the respondent? What clues do the questions offer?

Summary of Argument

In lengthy memoranda and in appellate briefs, the court requires the parties to include a brief summary of the argument before the argument itself. Figure 14-6 shows three short summaries of the argument in the *Illinois v. Caballas* case (printed in Chapter 3).

Argument

argument
The section of a memorandum or brief containing the legal analysis supporting that party's position on a legal issue.

The ***argument*** is the main part of any memorandum of points and authorities or brief. This is the analysis of law and facts. In the argument section, discuss each issue separately, preferably in the order in which the issues are stated in the "Issue" section of the document. State major points in point headings and then discuss in detail following the point heading. Analyze and cite legal authorities. (Hence the phrase "points and authorities.") Just as with the "Discussion" section of a memorandum of law, outline and analyze the argument prior to the actual writing.

Proper phrasing of the point headings is an important part of the drafting of this section of the document. Remember you are making an argument, not just identifying the issue under discussion. State your position in positive and conclusionary terms. You tell the court how and why it should rule on the issues or questions presented. Refer back to Figure 14-2, the table of contents, and review the point headings found under "Argument." Note how the headings try to persuade the court to rule in a certain way. Also, review the point headings found in the brief in Figure 14-5.

first impression
A case where the legal issue is adjudicated for the first time.

The IRAC method of analysis often forms the basis of the argument just as it does in a discussion. However, in cases that are more complex and in cases of ***first impression***, the argument also includes more analysis of the reasoning behind the law. Most often, a reported case opinion includes a detailed analysis of why the court is ruling the way it is. In writing an argument, the researcher shows how and why this reasoning applies to his or her case. Short quotations from the reported case help to support this.

Conclusion

Every memorandum and brief should contain a conclusion. Sometimes this is a brief summary of the main points. Other times, especially in appellate briefs where the argument contains summaries of the main points, attorneys conclude the legal arguments with this simple paragraph:

For the foregoing reasons, the petitioner requests that the judgment of the lower court be affirmed.

Signature

Any document submitted to the court must contain the signature of the attorney submitting it. Because this is a legal document filed in court, an attorney—not a paralegal or law clerk—must sign it. However, a research associate can do much of the research for a memorandum or brief. Research associates may prepare drafts of the final document for review by the attorney.

FIGURE 14-6 Summaries of the Argument

BRIEF FOR THE RESPONDENT (Caballes)

SUMMARY OF ARGUMENT

Respondent was stopped for speeding, for which the stopping officer decided to issue him a warning. A second officer, apparently in accordance with standard procedure, drove his drug detection dog to the scene and had it sniff the stopped car—even though the sniff could not have disclosed anything relevant to the traffic violation, and the police had no reasonable suspicion of a drug offense. The State argues that the Fourth Amendment did not require any justification for the drug sniff, beyond probable cause to believe that respondent had violated a traffic law.

1. This Court has viewed dog sniffs in particular contexts as imposing only modest burdens on Fourth Amendment interests. Nothing, however, in *United States v. Place, City of Indianapolis v. Edmond*, or any of the Court's other cases establishes the sweeping proposition the State advances here: That use of a trained dog to sniff a locked car trunk requires no individualized justification whatsoever, because it is a "Fourth Amendment non-event."

While dog sniffs are not physically invasive, they do intrude on reasonable privacy interests. Bringing a drug dog to the scene of a traffic stop for the specific purpose of sniffing a motorist's locked trunk is not at all analogous to observing some contraband item in "plain view" during the ordinary course of another investigation. Moreover, using a drug dog during an otherwise routine stop can be intimidating, accusatory and humiliating. Without any substantive limit on when a sniff is permissible, officers' decisions about when to use a dog are open to the reality or perception of discriminatory investigation. And while drug sniffs may in theory be designed to detect only the presence of contraband, in practice they are prone to errors—including, for example, the detection of non-contrab and currency—that will inevitably result in further unjustified invasions of motorists' privacy.

FIGURE 14-6 (continued)

Because investigatory sniffs by drug dogs during routine traffic stops implicate such Fourth Amendment interests, they should not be authorized in the absence of some reasonable, articulable, individualized suspicion of wrong-doing that could be either sharpened or dispelled by the sniff. Requiring that modest level of justification will not interfere with any legitimate investigative activity. It will, however, prevent police from using roving, suspicionless drug sniffs at the scene of routine traffic stops to replace the indiscriminate checkpoints, serving only a general interest in crime control, that this Court specifically disapproved in *Edmond.*

2. The fact that the police had probable cause to stop Caballes for speeding did not authorize them to undertake an investigatory dog sniff, designed solely to prospect for possible evidence of an unrelated offense. Standard Fourth Amendment principles, reflected in *Terry v. Ohio* and many other decisions, require particularized justification not only for the initiation of a non-consensual police encounter, but also for its scope. Those principles apply even when an encounter is justified by probable cause (or, for that matter, even when the police are executing a warrant). They cannot be reconciled with the State's submission that officers who have probable cause to stop a driver for speeding need no further justification to conduct a dog sniff designed to detect illegal drugs. Adopting that standard would be an open invitation to abuse.

The Illinois Supreme Court held only that when officers stop a driver on the highway, they may not take the additional, targeted investigative step of having a dog sniff the car for drugs unless that measure is either reasonably related to the circumstances that justified the initial stop, or otherwise supported by some reasonable suspicion of drug-related wrongdoing. That standard appropriately balances the government's interest in law enforcement against the important personal interests protected by the Fourth Amendment.

FIGURE 14-6 (continued)

BRIEF FOR THE PETITIONER (State of Illinois)

SUMMARY OF ARGUMENT

The Fourth Amendment does not require police to have reasonable suspicion that illegal drugs are present before using a drug-detection dog to sniff the exterior of a vehicle during a legitimate traffic stop. Because the sniff is not a Fourth Amendment search, it requires no independent justification when conducted on a vehicle that has already been detained following an observed traffic violation. That is, a traffic stop justified by probable cause does not lose its legitimacy when a canine sniff occurs during the stop.

In holding otherwise, the Illinois Supreme Court failed to acknowledge settled precedent establishing that canine sniffs are not Fourth Amendment searches. Instead, scrutinizing the sniff of respondent's car under the *Terry* doctrine, the majority invalidated the sniff upon concluding that the officers did not have reasonable suspicion that illegal drugs were present. The majority's analysis erred in two respects. First, the *Terry* doctrine does not govern traffic stops justified by probable cause or canine sniffs that occur during such stops. Second, even if the *Terry* doctrine applied, the sniff of respondent's car still was lawful under the Fourth Amendment because it did not entail any additional intrusion on respondent's legitimate privacy or possessory interests.

FOR THE RESPONDENT

SUMMARY OF THE ARGUMENT (Amicus brief)

The Supreme Court of Illinois correctly held that the Fourth Amendment requires that law enforcement officers have reasonable suspicion that a vehicle contains contraband before using a drug-detection dog to sniff the vehicle during a routine traffic stop. This is true for four reasons. First, suspicionless dog sniffs are not reasonably related in scope to the circumstances that justified the initial stop, when the right of motorists to remain free from arbitrary police interference is balanced against the public interests advanced by the seizure. Such suspicionless sniffs prolong the length and increase the intrusiveness of seizures, without contributing substantially to the interdiction of contraband. In addition, suspicionless sniffs allow unfettered police discretion and present the risk of involuntary consents. Second, requiring reasonable suspicion will reduce the incidence of false positives, a significant problem with drug-detection dogs that results in intrusions upon motorists' Fourth Amendment rights. Third, requiring reasonable suspicion is consistent with this Court's precedents. Fourth, petitioner and its amici are wrong in arguing that suspicionless dog sniffs are justified where police have probable cause to make the traffic stop.

A Point to Remember

A court is obligated to follow authorities that you cite only when those authorities are mandatory authority in your jurisdiction. If you are in a state court, mandatory authority is found in case law from your state courts and constitutional and statutory laws of your state. Only if these do not exist should you use other authorities. If you are in federal court, and the issue is a constitutional or federal one, then cite cases from the U.S. Supreme Court and federal appellate courts from your circuit. Only if these do not exist should you cite cases from other jurisdictions. If you do not cite mandatory authority, the court can ignore your arguments. Review Chapter 3.

14-4 PERSUASION

Persuasion is an important legal tool. A writer must be consistently conscious that an audience must be shown what is important. Repetition can be very persuasive when used well. As you read the appellate brief in Figure 14-5, notice the writer's use of repetition.

The most persuasive writing is clear, concise, and direct. Short, simple sentences work much better than lengthy complicated sentences. Long, complex sentences confuse readers. When we write to persuade, we cannot afford to confuse the reader. Strive to place two or three paragraphs on each page. Short paragraphs allow the reader to take a mental break. If a writer goes on too long in one paragraph, the reader may start to tire of the material or skip it altogether. Break up long paragraphs. Start the second paragraph with a transition word that alerts the reader that the topic did not change.

Many writers work on persuasion as part of the editing process. Once the ideas are out of the mind and on the screen (or page), it may be easier to see where to insert persuasive language. The use of images can be persuasive. This helps the reader visualize the picture the writer is drawing. Think about the image you picture when someone says: "It was like the floodgates opened." Most of us picture something spilling out. Placed in context, this creates a good visual for the reader.

Point headings should be persuasive. Each point heading is an opportunity to highlight something important. Review the point headings from Figure 14-5. These point headings make points. They are persuasive, and they are easy to read. Any point heading that simply directs the reader is a missed opportunity.

THE JUNEAU SCHOOL OFFICIALS DID NOT VIOLATE FREDERICK'S FIRST AMENDMENT RIGHTS WHEN THEY DISCIPLINED HIM FOR VIOLATING SCHOOL POLICIES AGAINST PROMOTING ILLEGAL SUBSTANCES AT A SCHOOL ACTIVITY.

A. The "special characteristics" of the school setting require deference for school officials' actions.

B. The *Tinker–Fraser–Kuhlmeier* trilogy permitted Juneau school officials to discipline Frederick for promoting illegal substances.

1. *Tinker* protects speech that does not intrude upon the work of the schools.
2. *Fraser* permits schools to prohibit student speech that undermines the basic educational mission.
3. *Kuhlmeier* allows student speech restrictions in school-sponsored activities when pursuant to legitimate pedagogical concerns.

C. Frederick was subject to school disciplinary rules

14-5 MEMORANDUM OF POINTS AND AUTHORITIES

As mentioned previously, a memorandum of points and authorities is a document filed with a court where the author argues for or against a legal position on a matter. This type of document is often filed in support of or in opposition to a motion. A motion is a request for an order from the court in either criminal or civil cases. A motion involves an attorney making a request in connection with a pending case, such as a motion to dismiss a case, a motion for summary judgment, or a motion to suppress evidence that was obtained illegally. A memorandum of points and authorities contains an argument based on the law and the facts of the case.

Unlike a memorandum of law, the object of a memorandum of points and authorities is not to present an objective and thorough treatment of the law. In this document, attorneys advocate their client's position in a matter before the court. Although it is an ethical violation to misstate either the law or the facts, attorneys generally try to present the material in a way that is most favorable to their clients.

Even though the purpose is different, in many ways a memorandum of points and authorities resembles a memorandum of law. It generally contains a statement of facts, a statement of issues, legal analysis, and a conclusion. In lieu of a discussion, however, a memorandum of points and authorities contains an argument. Within this argument, the attorney sets forth the points he or she is making and then gives the legal authorities for these points. The IRAC method of analysis is used within the argument, just as it is in a discussion. The points are usually set out in point headings that precede each section of the argument.

We use memoranda of points and authorities in adversary proceedings, and, therefore, each side has the opportunity to submit a memorandum to the court. Memoranda are filed as follows.

Memorandum of Points and Authorities in Support of the Motion This is the first memorandum filed by the ***moving party***, the party making the motion. In this motion, the party, who may be the plaintiff or the defendant in the action, sets forth the legal argument for the court to grant the motion. This memorandum contains a caption, statement of facts, statement of issues, argument, conclusion, and attorney signature. It may also include a table of contents and a table of authorities if it is lengthy.

moving party
The party making a motion.

Memorandum of Points and Authorities in Opposition to the Motion This motion is filed by the responding party within strict time limits set by law. In this memorandum, the responding party tries to accomplish two goals: (1) set forth the strongest argument in support of his or her position and (2) refute arguments set forth by the moving party. This document may or may not include a statement of facts and a statement of issues. If the responding party is satisfied with the statements set forth in the opening memorandum, it is not necessary to repeat them.

Reply Memorandum The moving party generally has the opportunity to file a reply memorandum, again within very strict time limits. This document replies to points raised in the responding memorandum.

In addition to rules regarding time limits for filing, many courts have rules regarding the maximum number of pages allowable in the memorandum of points and authorities.

14-6 DECLARATIONS

Always support the statement of facts in a memorandum or brief with evidence in the court record. When parties file a memorandum of points and authorities, they often use declarations or affidavits, rather than live testimony, to present the facts to the court. A declaration is a statement made under penalty of perjury. An affidavit is also a statement made under penalty, but it is sworn to before a notary.

Facts contained in a declaration take on a tone quite different from those in a fact statement in a memorandum or brief. The person having firsthand knowledge of the facts makes the declaration. It may be the client's words, or it might be an attorney's statement. This is the declarant's story. A declaration often reads like a narrative of the *events from the client's point of view*. Even though it may be the client's story, and even though the client may sign it, it is still drafted by the attorney or the attorney's associate. A well-written declaration may be a powerful tool when combined with a motion. The following is an example of a declaration written in support of a request for a temporary restraining order in a family law matter:

Example

Declaration of Alma Steinman:

1. I am the plaintiff in the above-entitled action.
2. On July 3, 2010, my husband, the Defendant, Robert Steinman, arrived at my home about 11:45 p.m. drunk and angry. At that time, we had been separated and living apart for almost one year. That night he yelled horrible things at me. The children were in their rooms but they could hear him. He said things like, "You will pay for everything you have done," and "I will make sure you never leave me."
3. When I tried to close the door he pushed me to the floor and began slapping me and punching me. I was screaming and crying. Our oldest child, Marcy, called 911 for help. The police came and took my husband away.
4. Since that day he has called my office and home at least six times every day. He continues to threaten me. Some of his threats are really violent. He told me on August 19 that he would "kill me" if I see another man. I am very afraid of him.

I declare that the foregoing is true and correct under penalty of perjury.

You can see that this simple declaration in the client's own words is a powerful statement, much more so than the statement of facts in the memorandum itself. See Figure 14-7 for an example of a declaration by an attorney prepared in connection with a motion.

In some cases, support for facts presented in a memorandum of points and authorities originates in deposition testimony rather than in declarations or affidavits. A deposition is an out-of-court proceeding where attorneys question a witness. Each witness swears to tell the truth under penalty of perjury, and a written transcript of the questions and answers is prepared.

14-7 TRIAL AND ARBITRATION BRIEFS

A trial brief is a document filed with the trial court, usually immediately prior to the start of the trial. The purpose of this document is to establish the legal support for the party's claims or defenses at trial. A second purpose is to present legal argument for evidentiary issues that a party anticipates will arise during trial. For

FIGURE 14-7 Declaration in Opposition to Motion

IN THE SUPERIOR COURT OF THE STATE OF CALIFORNIA
IN AND FOR THE COUNTY OF SANTA CLARA

THE PEOPLE OF THE STATE OF CALIFORNIA, Plaintiff, vs. RANDOLPH RAMBEAUX, Defendant.	Case No. 196239 DECLARATION OF MARK B. HAMES IN OPPOSITION TO MOTION TO DISMISS Date: November 20, 2015 Time: 9:00 a.m. Dept: 2

I, Mark Hames, do declare as follows:

1. I am a Supervising Deputy District Attorney as to the prosecution and preliminary examination of the above-entitled case;
2. On or about May 1, 2015, I received a call from the then attorney for the defendant, to resolve a Penal Code §1275 source of bail issue. As I was not available, I asked to take up the matter on May 2, 2015, as we would both be in Judge Phillips' department for preliminary examination;
3. On May 2, 2015 at 8:30 a.m. counsel and I appeared in Judge Phillips' department. We both advised the court in chambers that we were trying to resolve a Penal Code §1275 issue. These discussions lasted approximately 30 minutes at which time the court took the bench and the preliminary examination started;
4. During the course of the Penal Code §1275 discussions Judge Phillips stated that he had viewed the complaint and prior history and was "inclined" to raise the bail;
5. Thereafter, defendant's counsel made his CCP §170.6 for the first time, it was denied as being untimely;
6. Throughout the preliminary examination, neither counsel nor the defendant stated or implied that Judge Phillips had previously represented the defendant in 1990.
7. Throughout the preliminary examination, Judge Phillips did not state or imply that he had represented the defendant almost 16 years ago.

I declare, under penalty of perjury, that the above is true and correct, and that this declaration was executed in San Jose, California on November 12, 2015.

MARK B. HAMES
Supervising Deputy District Attorney

example, in a medical malpractice case, the defendant, a doctor, might want to be assured that the plaintiff does not present any evidence relating to the doctor's insurance. In a trial brief filed before the case begins, the doctor's attorneys can present legal authorities supporting such a request. Trial briefs can also provide legal support for jury instructions.

In many jurisdictions, trial briefs are not required but are filed only when attorneys anticipate that legal questions will arise during trial. If a trial brief is filed, it is for the benefit of the judge. If a jury is trying the case, the jurors never see the document. Furthermore, because there are no requirements that a party file a trial brief, the plaintiff is not necessarily the first one to file such a document. It is possible for both parties to file a trial brief simultaneously or for the defendant to file first. In any event, if one party has filed a brief, the other will often respond to the issues that are raised. The court might even ask the attorneys to do this.

arbitration
An out-of-court proceeding where parties submit a dispute to a neutral person for resolution.

Today, many cases go to ***arbitration*** rather than to trial. Arbitration is an out-of-court proceeding that takes place before a neutral party. This neutral party,

arbitration brief
A document submitted in an arbitration proceeding addressing the legal issues in the arbitration.

an arbitrator, hears evidence from both parties and makes a decision. In an arbitration proceeding, parties may file ***arbitration briefs***, which are similar to trial briefs and serve the same purposes.

14-8 APPELLATE BRIEFS

Upon appeal of a trial court decision, the parties are required to file briefs with the reviewing court. The initial brief, filed by the party who appeals, is the *brief for the petitioner*. The brief filed by the other party is the *brief for the respondent*. The petitioner, or appellant, also files a reply brief. In the opening, or petitioner's brief, the appealing party describes legal errors that it contends occurred at trial. These form the basis for the legal issues in the brief that contains legal argument supporting these contentions. The respondent's brief answers these contentions, arguing that no legal errors occurred or, if they did, they were harmless and do not justify a reversal. In the reply brief, the petitioner answers points raised in the respondent's brief. Like a memorandum of points and authorities, an appellate brief is a persuasive document. In addition, as with memoranda of points and authorities, strict time limits govern the filing dates for each brief.

A Point to Remember

Be careful not to confuse parties in an appellate brief. Often the appellant is the petitioner. This is not the same as the plaintiff at the trial level. The petitioner, or appellant, may be either the plaintiff or the defendant.

Appellate briefs generally contain the following sections: Table of Contents, Table of Authorities, Statement of Facts, Statement of the Case, Issues or Questions Presented, Argument, and Conclusion. A statement of the case, which is usually not included in a memorandum of points and authorities or a trial brief, is a brief summary of the procedural history of the case. In substance, an appellate brief is very similar to a memorandum of points and authorities. The respondent's brief may or may not contain a statement of facts, a statement of the case, or an issue statement. If the respondent accepts the statements of the petitioners, there is no need to repeat it. Reply briefs generally do not contain any of the above.

Writing an appellate brief requires one step not usually required for a memorandum of points and authorities or for a trial brief. Because the appellate brief deals with what happened at trial, frequent mention is made of testimony or documents from the lower court. When this happens, reference or citation to the testimony or documents must be made in the brief. Pursuant to an appeal, two types of records are prepared—a ***clerk's transcript*** and a ***reporter's transcript***. The clerk's transcript consists of all the documents filed in the case or introduced at trial as exhibits. The pages are bound and numbered. The reporter's transcript contains a verbatim record of oral proceedings.

clerk's transcript
Copies of all documents filed in a case and compiled by the clerk of the court at a party's request.

reporter's transcript
A verbatim record of oral proceedings in a case.

A reference to the clerk's transcript in a brief may look like this:

> On September 15, 1998, plaintiff filed a complaint accusing defendant of having violated the Civil Rights Act and asking for damages. (CT 7–12)

A reference to the reporter's transcript in a brief may look like this:

> During trial, the judge denied plaintiff's request to admit a videotape of the incident. (RT 125)

Another requirement that is unique to appellate briefs is a color-coded cover. Appellate court rules dictate the color of a cover for the particular brief.

14-9 ROLE OF THE RESEARCH ASSOCIATE

Any legal memorandum or brief filed in court must bear the signature of an attorney rather than of a paralegal or law clerk. This does not mean, however, that research associates play no role in the preparation of a legal memorandum or brief; indeed, the opposite is often true. Tasks performed by paralegals and law clerks include researching the legal issues, drafting memoranda of law explaining their research findings, reviewing and summarizing transcripts that are connected to the proceeding, and cite-checking and proofreading the final document. Occasionally, a research associate prepares a draft of a memorandum of points and authorities or brief for the attorney. Review Box 14-1 for examples of how two research associates helped in the preparation of a memorandum of points and authorities.

BOX 14.1 CLOSE-UP WITH GERALD UELMEN, ATTORNEY—CONSTITUTIONAL LAW SCHOLAR—PROFESSOR OF LAW

Professor Uelmen, who often uses research associates, provides the following insights and advice about legal research and writing.

The *key* to good research is thoroughness. All research must be updated and current. Researchers must use the most current sources available. The research project must be complete. A complete research project includes the "bad news" as well as the law that supports the client's interests. Thorough research of the counterarguments and weaknesses is necessary.

Professor Uelman advises researchers to strive for clarity. Clarity is an essential element of good writing. Researchers must have a clear idea of where they are going *during* the research process. This initial focus enables the researcher to produce a writing that is clear and well-reasoned. When doing his own research, much of his initial effort is through the Lexis service. He often supplements his computer-assisted legal research with various printed materials.

At the time of this interview, Professor Uelmen was one of several defense attorneys working on the Marijuna Club cases in federal court in San Francisco, California. The attorneys divided up the issues, with Professor Uelmen focusing on four issues. Law student volunteers performed the initial research and provided memos to Professor Uelmen, which he then transformed into an argument, which, as a portion of the Memorandum of Points and Authorities, was filed with the federal court.

Professor Uelmen is former dean of the School of Law at Santa Clara University. His publications include *Lessons from the Trial: The People v. O. J. Simpson*; *Disorderly Conduct: Verbatim Excerpts from Actual Cases*; *Supreme Folly*; and *Drug Abuse and the Law: Cases, Text, Materials*. He has litigated many high-profile cases; his former clients include O. J. Simpson and Christian Brando.

Online Research

For examples of briefs and arguments written for the court, there may be no better sources than Lexis and Westlaw. Both databases offer the user the opportunity to view the briefs submitted to the U.S. Supreme Court over the past few decades. In addition, in newsworthy litigation the pleadings and briefs are often available through these resources. This may be the best way to fully understand the arguments made by both parties in a case before the U.S. Supreme Court.

Note: The transcripts of the oral arguments may be available.

Findlaw provides the pleadings and briefs on some current cases.

The archives include a wide variety of documents.

http://lp.findlaw.com/ (Link to "Legal News" and then look for "Featured Legal Documents.")

The 7th Circuit provides a great deal of very useful information. Check the website at www.ca7.uscourts.gov/ (look under "Rules and Guides").

CITATION MATTERS

USE OF PINPOINT CITATIONS

***THE BLUEBOOK*—RULE B17.1.2 (FROM THE BLUEPAGES) AND RULE 4**

Legal writers use pinpoint citations to direct the reader to the exact page where the information cited to is located. This allows a reader to go directly to the relevant portion of a case, book, article, or periodical. Pinpoint citations also direct readers to specific subdivisions of a document or a statute. These pinpoint citations are widely used by good legal writers.

For example:

Ashcroft v. Free Speech Coalition, 535 U.S. 234, 241 (2002).

This citation includes the pinpoint to page 241 of the *Ashcroft* decision. This citation follows material taken from page 241. All quotes must be followed by a citation that includes a pinpoint cite, unless the material quoted from is not paginated. This is probably the most widely used type of pinpoint citation. Rule 3.2 illustrates how to use pinpoint citations for books, law review articles, the *Congressional Record,* the *United States Code,* and more.

The use of *id.*is not limited to quotations. Any time material is borrowed, even general ideas, citations must be used. The audience of a legal document expects to see well-chosen and properly cited law.

CHAPTER **SUMMARY**

Research memoranda written for the courts are persuasive or argumentative documents where an attorney advocates a position favorable to the client. These documents, which include a memorandum of points and authorities, a trial brief, and an appellate brief, are formal documents that must adhere to technical rules of form and content. Rules govern such things as length, content, citation format, and filing deadlines. Rules of court contain guidelines and rules about form and content.

Research documents filed in court have several common features. These include a case caption, a table of contents, a table of authorities, a statement of facts, a statement of issues or questions presented, an argument, a conclusion, and a signature. A table of contents and a table of authorities are often not required in short documents.

When legal issues arise in a pending case, those issues are addressed in a memorandum of points and authorities prepared by the attorneys for the disputing parties. These memoranda support or oppose a motion. Trial briefs analyze legal issues anticipated to arise at trial. These include substantive issues in the case as well as anticipated evidentiary problems. Appellate briefs analyze legal questions that form the basis of an appeal. All documents filed in court must bear the signature of an attorney rather than a paralegal or law clerk. However, research associates often help in the preparation of these documents by (1) researching the law, (2) preparing research memoranda, (3) drafting memoranda of points and authorities or briefs for attorney review, (4) summarizing and reviewing transcripts of hearings or trials that are relevant to the issues, (5) checking cites, and (6) proofreading the final document to be filed with the court.

TERMS TO **REMEMBER**

advocate
memorandum of points and authorities
trial brief
appellate brief
motion
rules of court
local rules of court
filed
caption
table of contents
table of authorities
court record
declaration
affidavit
argument
first impression
moving party
arbitration
arbitration brief
clerk's transcript
reporter's transcript

QUESTIONS FOR **REVIEW**

1. Briefly describe the three types of research documents submitted to a court.
2. How do rules of court affect research documents?
3. What is the difference between a table of contents and a table of authorities?
4. What are point headings, and how are they used in an argument?
5. What types of documents usually require a table of contents and a table of authorities?
6. What is the significance of the court record, declarations, and affidavits to research documents?
7. Why must an attorney and not a paralegal or a law clerk sign a memorandum or brief that is filed with the court?
8. Describe the three types of memoranda of points and authorities.
9. Compare and contrast a memorandum of law with a memorandum of points and authorities.
10. Compare and contrast a trial brief with an appellate brief.

TEST **YOURSELF** (Check Your Answers in Appendix G)

Using the first four pages of Figure 14-5, identify the persuasive techniques used by the author of that appellate brief.

TEST **YOURSELF**—WRITE IT RIGHT Rule Application Paragraphs

The better discussions and arguments use a pattern of rule explanation paragraphs followed by rule *application paragraphs*. Better writers open a discussion, or an argument, with an explanation of the rules of law that she will rely on in the document. Once the rules are explained, a writer should move on to the *application* of the rules to the facts of the case at hand.

The following three paragraphs are examples of *rule application paragraphs*. The author uses law and facts and she reaches conclusions.

1. Dylan Rhodes committed fraud in relation to access devices under the meaning of 18 U.S.C.A. § 1029(a)(5). Mr. Rhodes used access devices belonging to another person, his recently deceased mother. The MasterCard and ATM card he took were registered in Sandra Rhodes' name and were not authorized for use by any other person. Only two days after Ms. Rhodes' death, her son used the ATM card to clear out her Wells Fargo checking account of $758. On the same date, he made a purchase of $600 at Mario's jewelers using the MasterCard. These actions constitute using access devices issued to another person to obtain payment and property valued at $1,358, above the statutory minimum. 18 U.S.C.A. § 1029(a)(5). Because

both transactions are violations of § 1029(a)(5), use of access device issued to another person, the values may be aggregated under the holding of *Momeni.* 991 F.2d at 495. Furthermore, because the purchase and withdrawal occurred on the same day, they are within the statutory time limit of one year. *Id.*

2. The interstate commerce requirement of § 1029 is also satisfied. Wells Fargo, the issuer of the access devices to Ms. Rhodes, is a corporation engaged in interstate commerce. Thus, the deleterious economic effect caused by Mr. Rhodes' crime is sufficient to satisfy the interstate commerce requirement of the statute. *See Phillips,* 577 F.2d at 501.
3. Alternatively, it can be argued that Mr. Rhodes' is guilty of violating § 1029(a)(2), fraudulent use of so-called "unauthorized" access devices. However, the statutory definition of an unauthorized access device, one that is "lost, stolen, expired, revoked, canceled, or obtained with intent to defraud," 18 U.S.C.A. § 1029(e)(3), is not as descriptive of the access device Mr. Rhodes used as the language in § 1029(a)(5), which prohibits use of an access device issued to another person. 18 U.S.C.A. § 1029(a)(5). Here, the cards in question were issued to another person, Mr. Rhodes' late mother. Thus, it is more appropriate to charge him with violating § 1029(a)(5) because it is more descriptive of his actual conduct.

Each paragraph uses rules that were explained earlier in the discussion or argument. Here the rules are applied to the facts of the current case. This involves a weaving of rules (law) and facts. The writer also reaches conclusions in these rule application paragraphs.

Now, You Try It

(Check your answers in Appendix G)

1. For each paragraph above, underline the factual application.
2. For each paragraph above, highlight the rules (the use of law). Note that the paragraphs include conclusions, so highlight the conclusions in another color.

FROM **THE WRITER'S CORNER** (Point Headings in a Legal Argument Must Make Points)

1. In long documents, the rules of court often require a ______________ of ______________. This table is a listing of the ______________ ______________.
2. Point headings in a legal argument are the reader's guide to the ______________ of the writer's ______________.

CITATION EXERCISES

Use the Citation Matters feature in this chapter to answer these questions.

1. What is a pinpoint citation?
2. State the *Bluebook* rule that explains the use of pinpoint citations.
3. Explain what "647" means in the following citation: *Mapp v. Ohio*, 367 U.S. 643, 647 (1961).

ASSIGNMENTS AND **EXERCISES**

Analysis and Writing Exercises

1. After comparing and contrasting the summaries of the arguments in the *Illinois v. Caballas* case (Figure 14-6), explain the theory of the case for each party. (Think of the "theory of the case" as the foundation of the argument.)
2. Prepare a table of authorities for the memorandum in Figure 14-5.
3. Prepare a table of contents for the memorandum in Figure 14-5.

CASE **PROJECT**

You may recall reviewing a "Case File" in Section 2-8 of Chapter 2. The following is the case file for your new client. Follow your teacher's instructions for the content and format of the document you will draft. Notice that the years are in the form of 20XX. Your teacher will explain the dates you will use for this project.

MEMO TO RESEARCH ASSOCIATE

From: Assistant U.S. Attorney
To: Research Associate
Re: Potential Criminal Complaint (*U.S. v. Baylor*)
Date:

I recently received a file from the F.B.I. involving the commission of a credit card/ access card fraud and need you to research some questions and prepare a memo. Very briefly, the case involves a young man who used ATM and credit cards belonging to his deceased mother. Unfortunately, this individual appears to have fled the country, and prosecution against him at this time is unlikely. However, the investigation into this matter shows that the young man's girlfriend (Melyssa Baylor) willingly accepted and kept property acquired with the credit card and assisted her boyfriend in evading arrest. I am not filing charges for receiving stolen property because I cannot establish that she knew the ring was stolen when she first accepted it. However, I would like to file charges against her for being an accessory after the fact. I am attaching a copy of an application for a search warrant in which the investigating F.B.I. agent details the facts of this case and his justification for searching the Baylor residence. I am also attaching a copy of the search warrant and the return of the warrant. The return of the warrant lists the items that were found during the search of the Baylor residence.

Please review these documents and review the federal statutes dealing with accessory after the fact and credit card fraud. Do some preliminary research regarding our charging Ms. Baylor with being an accessory after the fact. There should be ample case law related to this issue, but it would be a good idea to get an overview of this offense by checking some sources such as *Am. Jur.*or*A.L.R.* (The federal jury instructions might also provide some help.) There may be many issues in this case. We will need to prove the elements of this offense as listed in the code. One of those elements requires that we prove that the underlying felony also occurred. At this point, I would like you to concentrate on the following questions:

1. Can we meet the requirement of the accessory statute requiring that the accused had knowledge that someone had committed a federal offense?
2. Does it matter that we cannot find Baylor's boyfriend to arrest and prosecute him for the underlying felony?
3. Can we support the element of the underlying felony requiring that the property obtained by fraud be valued at $1,000 or more?

I have scheduled a tentative meeting time on February 3 for us to discuss your preliminary findings. Until then, limit your research to the above questions. If you identify any other potential problems, make a note of them, but do not spend time researching these. When we meet on February 3 we will discuss the issues. I would expect a memo on February 12.

Your affiant, Bryan Jergen, has been an agent with the F.B.I. for eleven years. For the past five years I have been assigned to work in the unit investigating White Collar Crimes. Part of my responsibilities with that Unit includes the investigation of credit card fraud. During the past five years I have been involved in the investigation of over one hundred cases involving credit card fraud. In approximately 80 percent of those cases I was the lead investigator.

On November 15, 20XX, I was contacted by Martin Jankovich, an investigator employed by Citibank. I have worked with Investigator Jankovich in more than fifteen investigations, including credit card fraud and bank robbery. He has always proved to be a reliable and thorough investigator and has always provided this department with reliable information. On November 15, 20XX, Investigator Jankovich

(*continued*)

informed me of an investigation he had conducted related to a suspected credit card fraud perpetrated by one Benjamin Creighton. He believes that Benjamin Creighton used the ATM card and Citibank MasterCard belonging to Terry Creighton, his mother, two days after her death. His investigation resulted in the following factual findings.

A review of records of Citibank showed that Terry Creighton maintained a checking account with Citibank as well as having a Citibank MasterCard. Terry Creighton was issued an ATM card for use with the checking account. Both the checking account and the credit card were in Terry Creighton's name alone. No one else was authorized to access the account or use the credit card. On July 26, 20XX, the ATM card was used to withdraw a sum of $758 from the checking account, bringing its balance to zero. In addition, on the same date, the credit card was used to purchase an item of jewelry at Mario's Jewelers. The item price was $600 plus tax for a total of $648. Between August 2, 20XX, and August 5, 20XX, three checks were submitted to Citibank drawn against the checking account owned by Terry Creighton. The checks were signed by Ms. Creighton and dated July 20, 20XX. Although the checking account had no funds at the time the checks were presented for payment, the checks were paid pursuant to the "overdraft protection" covering Ms. Creighton's account. Regular credit card billing statements were sent to Ms. Creighton in August, September, and October of 20XX. No payment was received. Statements showing the balance owed on the overdraft protection were also sent during these months. No payment was received.

Employees of Citibank attempted to personally contact Ms. Creighton regarding the overdue accounts. In the course of such attempts, employees telephoned Ms. Creighton at numbers provided to Citibank by Creighton. These telephone numbers included both a home telephone and a work telephone number. The home telephone number was disconnected. Contact was made with individuals at the work telephone number on or about November 2, 20XX. Citibank was advised that Ms. Creighton had died suddenly on July 24, 20XX. Because of the usage of both the ATM card and credit card after July 24, 20XX, the matter was referred to Martin Jankovich, a bank investigator. Investigator Jankovich provided me with copies of business records from Citibank verifying the above information, and I personally verified the contents of these records.

Investigator Jankovich stated as soon as the matter was referred to him on November 2, 20XX, he again contacted Ms. Creighton's employer and spoke with Ellen Rivera, an employee believed to be a close friend of Terry Creighton. Ms. Rivera stated that Terry Creighton was divorced and lived with her twenty-four-year-old son, Benjamin, in a rented home. Benjamin was the only known relative of Ms. Creighton. Ms. Creighton often complained about her son, who was unemployed and often in minor trouble with the law. Ms. Rivera did not know the specifics of his legal troubles. Ms. Rivera was able to provide Investigator Jankovich with a cellular phone number for Benjamin Creighton. She also told Investigator Jankovich that Ms. Creighton often spoke about a new girlfriend of her son. She had hoped that the girlfriend would "straighten out" her son. Ms. Creighton had mentioned that the young woman and her son had talked about marriage. The girlfriend's name was Melyssa Baylor. Ms. Rivera was also able to provide Investigator Jankovich with a photograph of Benjamin Creighton that Ms. Creighton had kept on her desk.

On or about November 5, 20XX, Investigator Jankovich contacted the owner of Mario's Jewelers regarding the Citibank MasterCard charge. After reviewing his records, Mario Battaglia, the owner of Mario's, recalled the transaction. The transaction involved the purchase of a diamond engagement ring. The purchaser of the ring had been in the store on several prior occasions with a young woman looking at rings. Mr. Battaglia described the purchaser as having physical characteristics similar to that of Benjamin Creighton. At this point, Investigator Jankovich showed Battaglia the photograph of Benjamin Creighton provided by Ellen Rivera, and Battaglia positively identified him as the purchaser of the ring. Battaglia also stated that he sold the ring for $600 because he was closing his business. He gave the purchaser a written appraisal stating that the value of the ring was $1,200. Prior to the sale, the ring was offered at $1,050.

Investigator Jankovich then managed to locate contact information for Melyssa Baylor. On November 10, 20XX, he had a telephone conversation with her during which he inquired about the whereabouts of Benjamin Creighton. He also asked about the engagement ring. Ms. Baylor stated that Benjamin Creighton had stayed with her from August 15, 20XX, through October 30, 20XX, but that he had left on October 30, 20XX, and she had not heard from him since then. She denied any knowledge concerning the ring. She also denied that she had ever been in a jewelry store with Creighton looking at rings. After this conversation, Investigator Jankovich approached various neighbors of Ms. Baylor. One neighbor, Mildred Delmonico, told Investigator Jankovich that within the last week she had seen Melyssa wearing a diamond engagement ring.

At this point, Investigator Jankovich contacted the F.B.I. and the case was referred to this affiant. I obtained the California driver's license for Benjamin Creighton and compared the picture on the driver's license with the photo obtained from Ellen Rivera. The pictures appeared to be of the same individual. On November 17, 20XX, I contacted Ellen Rivera, Mario Battaglia, and Mildred Delmonico. They all confirmed the facts related to me by Investigator Jankovich. Mario Battaglia provided a further description of the ring. It was a round solitaire of approximately 0.4 carats, set in white gold.

Also on November 17, 20XX, I contacted Melyssa Baylor. After I identified myself as an agent of the F.B.I., she refused to have any discussion with me. For the past seventeen months Melyssa Baylor has lived at 786 Hightower Dr., San Jose, California.

Based on the foregoing investigation and upon my experience, I believe that the diamond ring purchased by fraudulent use of a credit card is located at the premises at 786 Hightower Dr., San Jose, California. Because of its value, it is not likely that the parties have disposed of the ring. It is my opinion based on my experience that other indicia of the ring is also located on the premises including the appraisal and photographs. It is also my belief, based on my experience, that letters or other documentation indicating the present location of Benjamin Creighton is likely to be found on the premises.

chapter **fifteen**

MOTION PRACTICE: RESEARCH AND WRITING ISSUES

CHAPTER OUTLINE

15-1 Introduction

15-2 Nature and Purpose of Motions
General Purpose of a Motion
General Motion Procedure
Motions Made in Civil Cases
Motions Made in Criminal Cases

15-3 Research Issues in Motion Practice
Identify the Basis or Grounds for Granting the Motion
Researching Procedural Issues for a Motion
Inconsistent Local Rules of Court

15-4 Writing Issues in Motion Practice
The Memorandum of Points and Authorities
Affidavits, Declarations, and the Statement of Facts
Other Supporting Documents
Using Forms

SKILL OBJECTIVES FOR CHAPTER 15

When you complete chapter 15, you should be able to

- Describe the general purpose of motions.
- Describe the general procedures for motions.
- Identify some common civil motions.
- Identify some common criminal motions.
- Explain the importance of the grounds or basis for the granting of a motion.
- Conduct research that identifies the procedural requirements for motions.
- Explain the importance of local rules of court to research related to any motion.
- Describe the general content and explain the importance of affidavits and declarations.
- List some supporting documents that must accompany a memorandum of points and authorities in support of a motion.
- Draft a document using forms.

From the Desk of W. J. Bryan, Esq.

TO: Research Associate
FROM: W. J. Bryan
RE: Our Client, Justin Meyers
DATE:

We were served with a memorandum of points and authorities in opposition to our motion to suppress in the Meyers case. Please read the document and the cases cited within it. Then prepare a draft of a reply memorandum of points and authorities. You need to check the rules of court to see when this needs to be filed. I know it is only a few days.

15-1 INTRODUCTION

Chapter 14 discussed persuasive legal writing and the types of documents included in this category of legal writing. One of those documents is the memorandum of points and authorities, a common document often ***filed*** in trial courts. A memorandum of points and authorities is generally required in connection with ***motions*** made by attorneys. A motion is a request for an order from the court. In almost all cases, this request deals with issues in a pending case.

filed
Made part of the court record.

motion
A request for an order from the court.

When judges consider whether to grant or deny a motion, they must consider requirements of the specific motion. Consider the case of Justin Meyers. The issue for the motion to suppress is whether an illegal search and seizure occurred. If a judge finds that it did, the judge will probably grant the motion to suppress the evidence. However, if Meyers's attorney made a motion to dismiss the case, rather than just suppress the evidence, the judge would deny the motion, even if he or she found an illegal search and seizure. This is because a motion to dismiss a criminal case is not justified under these facts. To prepare an effective and persuasive memorandum of points and authorities, therefore, you must be familiar with the nature and specific requirements of the motion. This chapter introduces you to the general nature of some common motions and the specific research and writing issues that arise when preparing a memorandum of points and authorities in connection with a motion.

15-2 NATURE AND PURPOSE OF MOTIONS

General Purpose of a Motion

A motion is a request for an order from a court, usually in connection with an existing case. Motions occur in both civil and criminal cases and are common at all stages of the court process: before trial, during trial, and after trial. Court cases rarely progress from beginning to end without some problems arising. The problems vary. Sometimes one side needs to continue a trial date and needs a court order to do this. Other times, one of the parties believes that the case has no merit and should not go to trial. In most instances, the attorneys handling the case can resolve these problems between themselves. Sometimes they cannot, and an order from a judge is required. To obtain this order, one party makes a motion. Therefore, the general purpose of a motion is to seek an order that is related to the case from the court. Although you need to research the law related to specific motions, a basic knowledge of some of the common types of motions helps the research process and provides a starting point for this research.

General Motion Procedure

Similar proceedings occur in most motions. Pretrial motions, those motions made before trial, and post-trial motions, those made after trial, generally involve the following steps:

moving party
The party making a motion.

affidavit
A statement under penalty of perjury sworn to before a notary.

declaration
A statement under penalty of perjury containing factual statements.

responding party
The party opposing a motion.

1. After obtaining a hearing date from the court, the ***moving party*** serves the opposing side with a memorandum of points and authorities along with supporting documents describing the motion and notifying the other side of the time, date, and place of a hearing on the motion, and ***affidavits*** or ***declarations*** stating the factual basis for the motion. For some motions, additional documents are required.
2. The ***responding party*** serves and files a memorandum of points and authorities and affidavits or declarations opposing the motion.
3. The moving party files and serves a reply memorandum.
4. A brief court hearing occurs where the judge hears arguments from the attorneys.
5. The judge issues an order.

Motions Made in Civil Cases

Primarily, the Federal Rules of Civil Procedure and the case law that interprets these rules govern motions made in civil cases in federal courts. Motions are also subject to local rules of court. State codes, case law, and state and local rules of court govern motions in state court. The following is a list and brief description of some motions made in federal courts. The federal rule of civil procedure that governs each motion is included. Similar motions arise in state courts. Many of these motions are subject to strict time limits. Some motions require special documents. A discussion of these documents occurs later in the chapter.

pleading
The formal written allegations filed with the court by both sides to a lawsuit; claims and defenses are clearly set out so that both parties are placed on notice of the position of the opposing party.

demurrer
A state-court pleading comparable to a motion to dismiss the complaint.

jurisdiction
The power or authority to act in a certain situation; the power of a court to hear cases and render judgments.

venue
The geographical area in which a case should be tried.

service
Proper delivery of papers to a party affected by a legal proceeding.

Motions Regarding the Pleadings Several motions are directed toward the ***pleadings*** in a civil case. Pleadings include complaints, answers, counterclaims, cross-claims, third-party complaints, and responses. Motions affecting these documents include motions to amend a pleading (Rule 15) or to strike a pleading or portion of a pleading (Rule 12). Motions can also be made requesting a more definite statement if a complaint is vague and uncertain (Rule 12). (In some state courts, a ***demurrer*** rather than this motion raises this issue.) A motion for a judgment on the pleadings occurs when the pleadings are insufficient (Rule 12). Motions to dismiss a case are made when a party challenges ***jurisdiction***, ***venue***, improper ***service***, or the legal basis of the claim (Rule 12).

Discovery Motions Discovery is an important aspect of all civil cases. It is also a source of many problems resulting in motions. The most common motion is a motion to compel further discovery, made when one party believes the other party is not disclosing discoverable information or documents. Motions for protective orders are also frequently heard. In this motion, a party asks the court to limit discovery. Discovery motions often require special documents and are frequently subject to local rules of court (Rules 26–37).

Summary Judgment Motions A motion for summary judgment is one of the most important motions made in civil cases in both federal court (Rule 56) and state court. This motion, raised by either a plaintiff or a defendant, requests that the court render a judgment for the moving party before trial. The court grants this motion when the moving party establishes that no disputes over material factual issues exist. The moving party establishes this by affidavits or declarations and supporting documents. Supporting documents often include discovery responses from the responding party to the motion. Drafting these affidavits or declarations is an important part of this motion. In some courts, the parties must also file a ***statement of undisputed material facts***. A discussion of these documents occurs later in the chapter.

statement of undisputed material facts
A statement required in a summary judgment motion in which the moving party lists facts that are not in dispute.

Motion for Judgment as a Matter of Law After a party has presented his or her case before a jury but before the jury decides the case, a court has the power to take the case away from the jury and to render judgment itself. A party requests that a court do this in a motion for judgment as a matter of law (Rule 50). The court grants this motion when it finds that no reasonable jury would believe that there is legally sufficient evidence to support a different decision. A trial judge may review his initial denial of the motion after trial. If granted, such a motion overturns the jury verdict.

Motion for a New Trial If a court finds that a verdict or judgment was based on legal error or jury misconduct, it can grant a new trial if the aggrieved party makes a motion for a new trial (Rule 59).

Motion for Relief from Judgment or Order This motion is also known as a motion to set aside a default. It is granted if the court finds the judgment (or default) was entered because of very specific reasons, including mistake, inadvertence, surprise, excusable neglect, fraud, and misrepresentation (Rule 60).

Motions Made in Criminal Cases

Motions made in criminal cases in federal court are governed by the Federal Rules of Criminal Procedure, case law, and, in some instances, protections under the U.S. Constitution. The following is a list of some of the common motions filed in criminal cases, along with a reference to the governing federal rule of criminal procedure. The list is not exhaustive.

Motion for Change of Venue When a defendant believes that a fair trial is impossible in the court where the criminal case was filed, he or she may move for a change of venue. The defendant must establish more than unfavorable publicity. He or she must show undue prejudice (Rule 21).

Motion to Suppress Evidence To prevent the use of evidence obtained in violation of the defendant's constitutional rights, a party may move to suppress the evidence. In federal courts, this usually involves a defendant's claim of a violation of his or her Fourth, Fifth, or Sixth Amendment rights. This motion often involves many complex legal questions. Extensive case law addresses the substantive issues. Rules 12 and 41 address some of the procedural aspects of the rule.

Discovery Motions Discovery in criminal cases is very different from discovery in civil cases. Discovery in criminal cases does not involve the same technical methods. Both sides in criminal cases, however, are required to disclose certain information to the other side. If this is not done, then either the prosecution or the defense can make a motion asking the court for an order requiring disclosure. Rule 16 provides some guidance for this motion.

Motion to Dismiss A defendant can move to dismiss the case for a number of different reasons. These include a lack of jurisdiction by the court and an insufficiency in the indictment process.

Motion for Judgment of Acquittal This motion is a defendant's request that the judge, and not a jury, render a judgment of ***acquittal***. At trial, at the end of the prosecution's case or after all evidence is introduced, a party may move for

acquittal
A "not guilty" verdict.

judgment of acquittal. A court grants this motion if it decides the evidence is insufficient to support a decision (Rule 29).

Motion for New Trial As with civil cases, if the court finds that there was an error in law or jury misconduct, it can grant this motion. An additional ground for this motion in criminal cases is newly discovered evidence (Rules 29 and 33).

15-3 RESEARCH ISSUES IN MOTION PRACTICE

Identifying the Basis or Grounds for Granting the Motion

Preparing a motion requires that you research the law dealing with the basis or grounds for granting or denying the specific motion. For most motions, who will ultimately prevail in the case is not an issue. For example, in the Meyers case, whether the court should grant the motion to suppress evidence does not depend on whether the judge believes that Meyers is guilty of the crime. Your research for a motion must focus on the basis or grounds for the motion.

When an attorney makes a motion, he or she has a very specific purpose or request. Should evidence be excluded from trial? Should a continuance be granted? Should the case be dismissed? Before granting or denying a motion, the court must determine that it has a legal basis for the action it takes. Sometimes this is included in the rule or code section that describes the motion. For example, consider the language in Rule 60 of the Federal Rules of Civil Procedure dealing with a civil motion to set aside a default judgment.

RULE 60. RELIEF FROM A JUDGMENT OR ORDER

(b) Grounds for Relief from a Final Judgment, Order, or Proceeding. On motion and just terms, the court may relieve a party or its legal representative from a final judgment, order, or proceeding for the following reasons:

(1) mistake, inadvertence, surprise, or excusable neglect;
(2) newly discovered evidence that, with reasonable diligence, could not have been discovered in time to move for a new trial under Rule 59(b);
(3) fraud (whether previously called intrinsic or extrinsic), misrepresentation, or misconduct by an opposing party;
(4) the judgment is void;
(5) the judgment has been satisfied, released or discharged, it is based on an earlier judgment that has been reversed or vacated; or applying it prospectively is no longer equitable; or
(6) any other reason that justifies relief.

Rule 60 sets out very specific grounds for the granting of this motion. However, the interpretation of these grounds may require case law research. Terms like *mistake* or *excusable neglect* require court interpretation. Checking all notes of decision found in an annotated version of the rules of court or codes is important.

Consider the following situation: Reed, a former business partner, sues Smythe for breach of contract. After he is served, Smythe talks to Reed, telling him that he believes the lawsuit has no basis, but, in any case, he has no money or assets, and any judgment would be uncollectable. He also tells Reed that he is very ill and has a condition that may be terminal. Reed, feeling sorry for Smythe, tells him not to worry about the lawsuit. Smythe does not consult a lawyer and does not file an answer to the complaint. Reed obtains a default judgment for $1 million. Shortly after, Smythe wins $10 million in the lottery. He also learns that his medical condition was not as serious as the doctors first told him. He now wants to make a motion to set aside the default judgment for $1 million. He has substantial evidence that he did not breach the contract with Reed. Should the court grant Smythe's motion? The memorandum of points and authorities supporting Smythe's motion will not focus on the contract issues in the case. Even if Smythe has clear evidence that no breach of contract occurred, he still might not prevail on his motion. A memorandum of points and authorities must focus on why Smythe did not respond to the complaint, not whether he has a good case.

Motions for a Judgment Some motions in both civil and criminal cases ask the court to grant a judgment without a full trial. In civil cases, these include motions for summary judgment and motions for judgment as a matter of law. In a criminal case, this includes the motion for a judgment of acquittal. In these motions, the court is concerned with the substantive issues in the cases. However, the court does not decide the motion on which party has the *best* evidence. These motions depend on whether the responding party to the motion has *any* admissible evidence that would support a judgment in his or her favor. The rule or code section describing the motion often specifies a ***standard of review***, that is, the standard by which the court must review the evidence in ruling on the motion.

standard of review
The criteria a court uses to review the merits of a motion or appeal.

A memorandum of points and authorities in support of any motion should contain an analysis of the legal basis for the motion. If the motion specifies a standard of review that the court must use, the memorandum must analyze that standard. In motions for a judgment, the memorandum must also contain an analysis of the substantive issues in the case. See Figure 15-1 for an example of a memorandum of points and authorities in support of a motion for summary judgment.

Researching Procedural Issues for a Motion

In addition to researching the legal basis for a motion, procedural issues are evaluated. Procedural issues include requirements related to the format of the memorandum of points and authorities, time limits for filing the motion, time limits for submitting opposing and reply memoranda, and service requirements. Some of these requirements are found in the rule or code section describing the motion. For example, Rule 60 of the Federal Rules of Civil Procedure, described earlier, requires that the motion be filed within a reasonable time and in some situations not more than one year after the default judgment. Often, procedural requirements are found in local rules of court and are most easily located on the court's website. For example, consider the following local rule of court relating to motions from the U.S. District Court for the Northern District of California.

RULE 7-2. NOTICE AND SUPPORTING PAPERS

(a) Time. Except as otherwise ordered or permitted by the assigned Judge or these Local Rules, and except for motions made during the course of a trial or hearing, all motions must be filed, served, and noticed in writing on the motion calendar of the assigned Judge for hearing not less than 35 days after service of the motion.

FIGURE 15-1
Memorandum of Points and Authorities in Support of Motion for Summary Judgment

Michael Thomas
State Bar Number 341
Thomas and Gomez
892 First Street
San Diego, California 92103
(619) 123-4567
thomas@gomez.com

Attorney for the Defendant

SUPERIOR COURT OF THE STATE OF CALIFORNIA

COUNTY OF SAN DIEGO

MISSION HILLS HOMEOWNERS	)	NO. CIV-3654
ASSOCIATION,	)	
Plaintiff,	)	MEMORANDUM OF POINTS AND AU-
vs.	)	THORITIES IN SUPPORT OF DEFEN-
GLORIA JENNINGS,	)	DANT'S MOTION FOR SUMMARY
Defendant	)	JUDGMENT, OR IN THE ALTERNATIVE,
	)	SUMMARY ADJUDICATION.
	)	
	)	
	)	

Now into court, through undersigned counsel, comes Defendant Gloria Jennings, who moves for summary judgment, or in the alternative, summary adjudication, as follows, and asks this Court to grant this motion after due proceedings.

FIGURE 15-1 (continued)

STATEMENT OF THE FACTS

In March of 2007, Defendant Gloria Jennings's nephew was killed in Iraq while honorably serving in the military. Distraught and heartbroken over her loss, Jennings decided to peacefully and respectfully express her opposition to the war. She erected a sixteen square foot sign that displays two sets of numbers. These numbers correspond to the number of military and civilian casualties incurred during the war in Iraq. No words are displayed on the sign and the Defendant took no measures to explain the sign's meaning to the public. Jennings placed the sign so that it was visible from her neighbor's property and from the community center. Jennings knew that the placement of the sign would gain added meaning because of the nearby military base and the American flag flying over the community center. The sign did not have any words because the sign represented all of those who have died and can no longer speak for themselves.

"The Mission Hills Restrictions" are recorded with the Recorder of San Diego County. Section 3.02(h) of this declaration states, in pertinent part: "No signs whatsoever, including but without limitation, commercial, political, and similar signs, visible from neighboring property, shall be erected or maintained upon any private area…." Jennings's sign caused a slight increase in traffic through the area as motorists slow down to view the sign. In May 2007, three notices were sent to Jennings informing her that the sign violated Section 3.02(h) and demanded that the sign be removed. Jennings has not removed the sign to date.

QUESTIONS PRESENTED

1. Is the Plaintiff's nuisance action barred under the Free Speech clause of the First Amendment because disallowing the sign serves no essential governmental interest as the sign is relatively small, only contains two sets of numbers and no words, and the presence of the sign merely created an increase in neighborhood traffic?
2. Is the restrictive covenant of the Mission Hills Subdivision unreasonable, and therefore unenforceable because the covenants only restrict certain types of signs, and are therefore arbitrary, and because the covenant restricting the use of signs abridges the vital public policy of permitting free speech?

FIGURE 15-1 (continued)

STANDARD FOR SUMMARY JUDGMENT

A defendant may move for summary judgment in any action if she contends that the action is without merit. Cal. Code of Civ. Proc. § 437c. When making such a motion supporting affidavits or declarations should be submitted by a person who has personal knowledge of facts and is competent to testify to the matters stated in the affidavit or declaration. *Id.* The affidavit or declaration must contain admissible evidence. *Id.* The purpose of this motion is to provide a method for the court to determine is a trial is warranted, despite allegations that appear in the pleading. *Aguilar v. Atlantic Richfield Co.,* 25 Cal. 4th 826, 843 (2001). In other words, are there disputed material facts requiring a trial. A genuine issue of material fact exists "if, and only if, the evidence would allow a reasonable trier of fact to find the underlying fact in favor of the party opposing the motion in accordance with the applicable standard of proof." *Id.* at 845.

ARGUMENT

I. <u>THIS TORT ACTION IS BARRED BY THE FIRST AMENDMENT'S FREE SPEECH CLAUSE BECAUSE THE DEFENDANT'S SIGN CONSTITUTES SYMBOLIC SPEECH AND THERE IS NO SIGNIFICANT STATE INTEREST TO JUSTIFY THIS INFRINGEMENT.</u>

Jennings's sign is symbolic speech that is entitled to First Amendment protection because Jennings intended the sign to express her opposition to the war, and this message was received and understood by others. By enforcing the restrictive covenant and forcing Jennings to remove the sign, California, through it's judiciary, would infringe Jennings's constitutional rights. There is no governmental interest that justifies abridging Jennings's right to free speech. The only negative impact is a slight increase in traffic through her neighborhood. The court should not allow mere inconvenience to trample the fundamental right of free speech.

A. <u>Judicial action in this case constitutes state action for the purposes of the First and Fourteenth Amendments.</u>

The First Amendment protects an individual's freedom of speech from government intervention. U.S. Const. amend. I. It states that "Congress shall make no law. . . . abridging the freedom of speech. . . ." *Id.* This protection extends to the states through the Fourteenth Amendment: "no state shall make or enforce any law which shall abridge the privileges or immunities of citizens of the United States. . . ." U.S. Const. amend. XIV § 1. Therefore, the First Amendment provides protection for freedom of speech and the Fourteenth Amendment prohibits states from making laws that curtail this individual "privilege." *Id.*

The Constitution protects individual liberties from governmental intrusion. In order to possess a constitutional claim, the government, not an individual, must

FIGURE 15-1 (continued)

take some action that infringes upon a personal freedom. This dichotomy was discussed by the Supreme Court in *Shelley v. Kraemer*, 334 U.S. 1 (1948). This case addressed a private restrictive covenant prohibiting property ownership by minorities. *Id.* at 5. The Court stated that the agreement could only be enforced through "judicial enforcement by state courts of the restrictive terms of the agreements." *Id.* at 13–14. Enforcement of the agreements necessarily entailed actions by the state through it's judiciary. Thus, the judicial enforcement of the restrictive covenant constituted state action that was entitled to constitutional protection.

Just as in *Shelley*, Jennings contends that the restrictive covenant abridges her constitutional rights. If the court hears this case, then it will be taking state action, because the court would be enforcing the restrictive covenant against Jennings. Therefore, constitutional analysis under the First Amendment is appropriate.

B. <u>The Defendant's sign is symbolic speech protected by the First Amendment because Defendant intends to communicate a specific message, and the message is received and understood by others.</u>

1. Symbolic Speech is protected under the First Amendment.

While most associate "speech" with the spoken word, the Court extends First Amendment protection to certain expressive acts. *Spence v. Washington*, 418 U.S. 405, 411 (1974). These expressive acts are called symbolic speech. However, the Court does not "accept the view that an apparently limitless variety of conduct can be labeled 'speech' whenever the person engaging in the conduct intends to . . . express a message." *United States v. O'Brien,* 391 U.S. 367, 376 (1968). The Court in *Spence v. Washington* set the standard for determining if expressive activity constitutes symbolic speech. *Spence,* 418 U.S. at 405. The Defendant was convicted under a Washington statute prohibiting unlawful use of the American flag when he attached a peace symbol to a flag which hung outside his apartment. *Id.* The Court found that expressive activity is speech (1) when the act intends to express a particularized message, and (2) when the act is likely to be understood by others. *Id.* at 415. These factors were met in *Spence* and the Court reversed the conviction.

2. Jennings's sign is symbolic speech because it expresses a specific message and is understood by others.

In a case strikingly similar to Jennings's, the Supreme Court in *Ladue v. Gilleo* held that a city ordinance that restricted the placement of signs on private property violated the Defendant's free speech rights. 512 U.S. 43 (1994). The City of Ladue, in an attempt to "minimize visual clutter," prohibited all signs except those that fell within certain categories. *Id.* at 54. In analyzing the signs as a medium of

FIGURE 15-1 (continued)

expression, the court stated: "displaying a sign in one's own residence often carries a message quite distinct from placing the sign somewhere else . . . A sign advocating "Peace in the Gulf" in the front lawn of a retired general or decorated war veteran may provoke a different reaction than the same sign in a 10-year-old child's bedroom. . . ." *Id.* at 56. The Court indicates that the mere placement of a sign on one's property may express a particularized message. This message may gain added meaning through the context in which it is placed.

In *Texas v. Johnson*, the Court found that burning the American flag was expressive conduct protected by the First Amendment. 491 U.S. 397, 399 (1989). The Defendant burned the flag during a political demonstration protesting the Reagan administration. *Id.* The Court again relied on the context in which the act was executed to determine if the act was protected symbolic speech. "Johnson burned the American flag as part ... of a political demonstration that coincided with the convening of the Republican Party and its renomination of Ronald Reagan . . . . a more powerful statement of symbolic speech . . . couldn't have been made at that time." *Id.* at 406. The *Johnson* Court concluded that "Johnson's burning of the flag was conduct 'sufficiently imbued with elements of communication' to implicate the First Amendment." *Johnson,* 491 U.S. at 406 (quoting *Spence v. Washington*, 418 U.S. 405, 409 (1974)).

By applying these principles to Jennings's sign, it is evident that the *Spence* two part test is satisfied. First, Jennings intended "to convey a particularized message." *Spence,* 418 U.S. at 415. Jennings's nephew was killed while honorably serving in the military. Distraught over her loss, Jennings placed the sign on her property to respectfully display her opposition to the war. Jennings intentionally placed the sign such that it was visible from the neighbor's property and the community center. *See* Haley Deposition at 3. She also erected the sign knowing that it would be near an American flag and a military base. *See* Haley Deposition at 6. By placing the sign in proper context, as did the courts in *Ladue* and *Johnson,* the sign's communicative power is apparent. By placing the sign on her property, Jennings is intentionally conveying to the community that she is experiencing the tragedy of war, and that she is opposed to the government's involvement in Iraq. The sign is powerful expressive conduct designed to express Jennings's "particularized message." *Spence,* 418 U.S. at 415.

FIGURE 15-1 (continued)

Second, Jennings's message is understood by others. Ben's death was reported in the *Empire News Guardian*, a weekly newsletter distributed to all residents of Mission Hills. Hames Deposition at 3. Therefore, members of the community were aware of Jennings's loss. While Jennings's sign did not include words indicating what the numbers referred to, the casualty figures were readily available in the media. Also, Jennings had conversations with her neighbors regarding her opposition to the war. Hames Deposition at 3. Since her neighbors were aware of Jennings's views, they would assume the sign had something to do with the war. Therefore, the second part of the *Spence* test is satisfied and the sign constitutes symbolic speech.

C. <u>State action to disallow the sign is unconstitutional because it serves no significant state interest.</u>

While the sign is symbolic speech, the Supreme Court limits constitutional protection for some types of symbolic speech. *See United States v. O'Brien*, 391 U.S. 367 (1968). Generally, state action prohibiting expressive speech is permissible if there is a government interest that sufficiently justifies the regulation. In *O'Brien*, the Court held that Defendant's act of burning his selective service registration card was not afforded First Amendment protection. *Id.* at 370. There was a sufficient government interest in ensuring the preservation of the certificates.

Defendants were suspended from school for wearing black armbands to protest the Vietnam War in *United States v. Tinker*, 393 U.S. 503 (1968). The Court found that the armbands were symbolic speech and did not find any substantial governmental interest sufficient to waive First Amendment protection. It held that the school "must be able to show that its action was caused by something more than a mere desire to avoid the discomfort and unpleasantness that always accompany an unpopular viewpoint." *Id.* at 509.

In Jennings's case, no sufficient government interest is served by enforcing the restrictive covenant. The only negative impact on the community is the slight increase in traffic. As *Tinker* holds, the desire to avoid the display of an unpopular or uncomfortable viewpoint is not enough to deny extension First Amendment protection. *Id.*

FIGURE 15-1 (continued)

II. THE RESTRICTIVE COVENANT IS UNREASONABLE, AND THEREFORE UNENFORCEABLE BECAUSE THE RESTRICTION IS ARBITRARY, VIOLATES A FUNDAMENTAL PUBLIC POLICY, AND IMPOSES A BURDEN ON THE USE OF THE LAND THAT OUTWEIGHS ANY BENEFIT.

Jennings merely wants to express her views in a peaceful and respectful manner. The sign is not obscene and is not excessively large. Jennings looked across the street and saw the American flag flying above the community center, and thought that it was reasonable that she be able to express her ideas too. However, the restrictive covenant unjustly and unreasonably strips her of this right. The restriction is unreasonable, and conflicts with the inherent right of free expression.

California Civil Code Section 1354 deals with the enforceability of restrictive covenants. It states that "the covenants and restrictions in the declaration shall be enforceable as equitable servitudes, unless unreasonable. . . ." Cal. Civ. Code § 1354 (West 2007). The rules governing equitable servitudes generally require a purchaser of property to have actual notice of the restrictions. *Narstedt v. Lakeside Village Condominium Association*, 8 Cal. 4th 361, 375, 33 Cal. Rptr. 2d 63, 71, 878 P.2d 1275, 1283 (1994). However, "the inclusion of covenants and restrictions in the declaration recorded with the county recorder provides sufficient notice to permit the enforcement of such recorded covenants and restrictions as equitable servitudes." *Id.* at 379, 33 Cal. Rptr. 2d at 73, 878 P.2d at 1285. The Mission Hills Restrictions were recorded in June 1996, they meet the requirements of equitable servitudes and fall under the control of Section 1354.

The California Supreme Court held that restrictive covenants that are recorded with the county recorder are "presumed to be reasonable" and the burden of proving otherwise is upon the challenging party. *Id.* at 379, 33 Cal. Rptr. 2d at 73, 878 P.2d at 1285. A party may show that the restriction is unreasonable by proving the restriction is "arbitrary, imposes burdens on the use of lands it affects that substantially outweigh the restriction's benefits. . . . , or violates a fundamental public policy." *Id.* at 382, 33 Cal. Rptr. 2d at 75, 878 P.2d at 1287. In analyzing the reasonableness of a restriction, the evaluation must be made "not by reference to facts that are specific to the objecting homeowner, but by reference to the common interest development as

FIGURE 15-1 (continued)

a whole."*Id.* at 386, 33 Cal. Rptr. 2d at 78, 878 P.2d at 1290. The enforcement of the restriction "must be fair and applied uniformly." *Id.* Therefore, a party may overcome a restriction's presumptive validity by establishing that the restriction is (1) arbitrary, (2) violates public policy, or (3) its burdens outweigh the benefits as applied to the community as a whole.

A. The restrictive covenant is arbitrary, and therefore unreasonable, because it bears no rational relationship to the protection, preservation, operation, or purpose of the land and it is not evenly applied.

In *Dolan King v. Rancho Santa Fe Association*, a community association sought to enforce its restrictive covenant to prevent a resident from making certain additions to her home. 81 Cal. App. 4th 965, 97 Cal. Rptr. 2d 280 (2000). The association sought to "preserv[e] the character" of the community by restricting the appearance of its resident's homes. *Id.* at 970, 97 Cal. Rptr. 2d 280, 283. Dolan King asserted that the restriction was arbitrary because of its subjective guidelines. The California Supreme Court stated that "a restriction is arbitrary when it bears no rational relationship to the protection, preservation, operation, or purpose of the affected land." *Narstedt,* 8 Cal.4th at 381, 33 Cal. Rptr. 2d at 75, 878 P.2d at 1287. Here, the court determined that maintaining a community that is artistically pleasing is not arbitrary because it bears a relationship to preserving the value of the homeowner's property.

In *Liebler v. Point Loma Tennis Club*, a condominium owner challenged a restriction that excluded nonresident owners from using the community's recreational facilities. 40 Cal. App. 4th 1600, 47 Cal. Rptr. 2d 783 (1995). Liebler, who owned property but did not reside in the development, used the development's tennis court in violation of the restriction. The California Supreme Court held that the restriction was not arbitrary because "there were valid reasons why members of a tennis-oriented residential condominium might choose to restrict access to their private tennis courts." *Id.* at 1611, 47 Cal. Rptr. 2d at 788–789. Hence, the restriction was related to the "operation" and "purpose" of the development.

The Mission Hills restrictive covenant limiting the use of certain signs is arbitrary because there is no rational reason to justify its enforcement. Section 3.02(H) strictly prohibits the use of certain kinds of signs, including "commercial, political,

FIGURE 15-1 (continued)

and similar signs." Mission Hills Restrictions, § 3.02H. There is no articulated reason why the community is attempting to restrict these types of signs. The restrictions have no relationship to the "protection, preservation, operation or purpose" of the land. *Narstedt,* 8 Cal. 4th at 381, 33 Cal. Rptr. 2d at 75, 878 P.2d at 1287. First, the restriction does not serve to increase security in the area. Second, there is no evidence indicating that a sign would cause any deterioration to the property or surrounding properties, and, thus, does not affect the "preservation" of the community. Third, a sign, at most, has a negligible effect on the operation of the land. Finally, the purpose of the land is to provide a means of shelter and enjoyment. The presence of a sign will in no way affect the "purpose" of the land.

The Mission Hills restrictions must be "fair and uniformly applied." *Narstedt,* 8 Cal. 4th at 386, 33 Cal. Rptr. 2d at 78, 878 P.2d at 1290. The Mission Hills community center bears an American flag the same size as Jennings's sign. It is wholly arbitrary to prohibit residents in the community from expressing their views through the use of a sign, while at the same time allowing the Homeowner's Association to express its views through the use of a flag. The restrictions, therefore, are not "uniformly applied." Thus, the restrictive covenant is arbitrary because there is no rational explanation for it, and it is not uniformly applied to the whole community.

B. <u>The restrictive covenant violates the fundamental public policy of free speech.</u>

As discussed in detail in Issue I above, the restrictive covenant violates Jennings's constitutionally protected right to freedom of expression. The Supreme Court addressed this issue in *Ladue v. Gilleo,* in which the City of Ladue enacted an ordinance prohibiting the display of any sign on residential property. 512 U.S. 43 (1994). The Court described that "a special respect for individual liberty in the home has been a part of our culture and our law; that principle has special resonance when the government seeks to constrain a person's ability to speak there." *Id.* at 58. The Mission Hills restrictive covenant attempts to constrain Jennings's ability to express her views through the use of her property. The covenant violates public policy because it violates the U.S. Constitution, and, therefore, is unreasonable.

FIGURE 15-1 (continued)

C. The restrictive covenant is unreasonable because the harmful effects of enforcement outweigh any possible benefits.

The benefits of enforcing this restriction are few, if any. The use of signs does not reduce the security of the area, nor does it inhibit those in the surrounding properties from using and enjoying their property. There is no evidence before the court that the use of signs will decrease property values. While the benefits are few, the burdens are great. Enforcing this restriction will infringe on one of the strongest and most important privileges in our society. The restriction serves to deny Jennings a fundamental medium to peacefully and respectfully express her views. By balancing these considerations, it is evident that the burden of infringing on the freedom of speech far outweighs the slight inconvenience of the sign.

CONCLUSION

Ms. Jennings respectfully submits that the Mission Hills restrictive covenant infringes on her First Amendment rights of free speech. The sign constitutes symbolic speech because she intends to convey a particularized message and this message is received by others. The restriction is also unreasonable because it is arbitrary, violates the fundamental public policy of free speech, and its burdens outweigh any benefits. Ms. Jennings simply wants to respectfully and peacefully express her views, and this right should not be discarded because of a few extra cars on a street.

Respectfully Submitted,

Dated:

(signature line)

Attorney for Defendant

Inconsistent Local Rules of Court

The relationship between federal or state rules and local rules of court deserves special attention. At times, a federal or state rule regarding procedural issues may be inconsistent with a local rule of court. Local rules of court may also be inconsistent from district to district. Even if you find the answer to a procedural research question in federal or state rules, you must always check the local rules of court to determine if a different rule applies in the specific court. In most cases, you need to follow the procedure found in the local rule of court.

15-4 WRITING ISSUES IN MOTION PRACTICE

The Memorandum of Points and Authorities

Rules of Court A memorandum of points and authorities filed in support of or in opposition to a motion must comply with the rules of court. In federal court, the federal rules of civil and criminal procedures as well as local rules of court contain numerous provisions relating to the format of the memorandum. In state court, state rules of court as well as local rules of court do the same. Rules specify requirements for captions, signatures, page length, and citations. You may even find rules that dictate the type of font and the type of paper required. Review the following two local rules of one U.S. District Court.

RULE 7-2. NOTICE AND SUPPORTING DOCUMENTS

(b) Form. In one filed document not exceeding 25 pages in length, a motion must contain:

(1) On the first page in the space opposite the caption and below the case number, the noticed hearing date and time;

(2) In the first paragraph, notice of the motion including date and time of hearing;

(3) In the second paragraph, a concise statement of what relief or Court action the movant seeks; and

(4) In the succeeding paragraphs, the points and authorities in support of the motion—in compliance with Civil L.R. 7-4(a).

(c) Proposed Order. Unless excused by the Judge who will hear the motion, each motion must be accompanied by a proposed order.

(d) Affidavits or Declarations. Each motion must be accompanied by affidavits or declarations pursuant to Civil L.R. 7-5.

RULE 7-4. BRIEF OR MEMORANDUM OF POINTS AND AUTHORITIES.

(a) Content. In addition to complying with the applicable provisions of Civil L.R. 3-4, a brief or memorandum of points and authorities filed in support, opposition or reply to a motion must contain:

(1) On the first page in the space opposite the caption and below the case number, the noticed hearing date and time;

(2) If in excess of 10 pages, a table of contents and a table of authorities;

(3) A statement of the issues to be decided;

(4) A succinct statement of the relevant facts; and

(5) Argument by the party, citing pertinent authorities.

(b) Length. Unless the Court expressly orders otherwise pursuant to a party's request made prior to the due date, briefs or memoranda filed with opposition papers may not exceed 25 pages of text and the reply brief or memorandum may not exceed 15 pages of text.

Affidavits, Declarations, and the Statement of Facts

For most pretrial motions, evidence is not presented at a court hearing. Instead, evidence is presented to the court through affidavits or declarations and attached documents. Both affidavits and declarations are testimony made under penalty of perjury. An affidavit is sworn to before a notary. A declaration is not. Some courts require the use of affidavits for motions. Others allow either affidavits or declarations. Affidavits and declarations are drafted in the first person by an individual who has personal knowledge of the facts stated. These documents must contain admissible evidence; if they do not, a challenge is appropriate. Review Chapter 14 for the importance of using persuasive techniques in drafting these documents.

When preparing the statement of facts in the memorandum of points and authorities, you should cite the relevant portion of any affidavit, declaration, or other document that supports the fact. Furthermore, facts should not be included in the statement of facts unless some evidence is submitted to the court establishing the fact. Read Figure 15-2 for an example of a declaration that might accompany the memorandum of points and authorities in Figure 15-1, the memorandum of points and authorities in support of a motion for summary judgment. Also, review Figure 15-1. Read the statement of facts in the document. Note the references to the declaration of Gloria Jennings.

FIGURE 15-2
Declaration of Gloria Jennings

I, Gloria Jennings, declare as follows:

1. I am the defendant in the above entitled action. I have personal knowledge of the facts set forth below and if called upon to testify could and would testify competently thereto.
2. In March 20XX, my nephew was tragically killed in Iraq, while proudly serving his country as a member of the military.
3. Subsequently, to memorialize his service and that of all individuals serving in the armed forces, I created a 16 square foot sign displaying two sets of numbers corresponding to the number of military and civilian casualties incurred during the war in Iraq.
4. No other words, signs, or symbols appear on the sign. A photograph of this sign is attached hereto as Exhibit A.
5. I erected the sign on property that I own, which property is subject to restrictions recorded with the Recorder of San Diego County. Said restrictions prohibit any signs, including political and similar signs that are visible from neighboring property. Said property is also located in close proximity to a military base.
6. The sign is visible to neighboring property and although minimal traffic increase has occurred, the sign has not interfered with the peaceful enjoyment of any neighbor's property.
7. The sign is intended solely as an expression of my concern regarding military casualties in the war in the Mideast and for that reason I have not removed it.

I declare under penalty of perjury under the laws of the state of California that the foregoing is true and correct. Executed this 23rd day of December, 20XX at San Diego, California.

____
Gloria Jennings

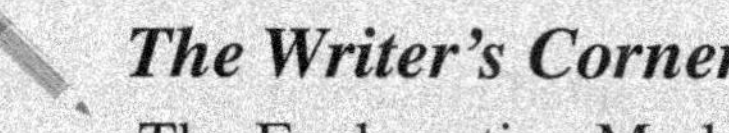

The Writer's Corner

The Exclamation Mark

In formal legal writing, there is little need for the exclamation mark. Use this tool after commands or exclamations.

Example:

Stop!

Fire!

What a great party!

Exclamation marks do not add persuasion. Reserve the use of this tool for informal writing.

Other Supporting Documents

In addition to the memorandum of points and authorities, motions require several other documents. The moving party to a motion is required to provide written notice of the time, place, and nature of the motion. This form is called a ***notice of motion***. The factual basis for or against the motion is generally presented to the court in the form of an affidavit. Chapter 14 contained examples of affidavits and explained how they involve persuasion. In addition, the affidavits must contain facts that show the presence or absence of facts related to the basis or grounds for the motion. For example, consider the hypothetical situation of Smythe and Reed described earlier in the chapter. In an affidavit in support of his motion to set aside the default judgment, Smythe must state the facts that would convince a judge that the default occurred because of one of the reasons stated in Rule 60.

notice of motion
A document describing a motion and containing the date, time, and place of a hearing on that motion.

Motions such as discovery motions or motions for summary judgment sometimes have additional written requirements. For example, consider the following federal local rule of court regarding the discovery motion to compel a further response to a discovery request.

RULE 37-2. FORM OF MOTIONS TO COMPEL

In addition to complying with applicable provisions of Civil L.R. 7, a motion to compel further responses to discovery requests must set forth each request in full, followed immediately by the objections and/or responses thereto. For each such request, the moving papers must detail the basis for the party's contention that it is entitled to the requested discovery and must show how the proportionality and other requirements of Fed. R. Civ. Pro. 26(b)(2) are satisfied.

interrogatories
A method of discovery used in civil cases consisting of written questions from one party to another requiring a response in a timely manner.

deposition
An out-of-court oral questioning of a witness or party in a case by an attorney; answers to questions are under oath, and a written or video transcript is prepared.

If a party makes a motion to compel a further response to ***interrogatories*** or to questions in a ***deposition***, that party must submit a document with the motion listing each question to which a response was given, the objection or response to the question, and then the basis for requesting an additional response.

Summary judgment motions sometimes require a document called a statement of undisputed facts. The California Rules of Court describe this document and provide a format that must be used.

RULE 3.1350. MOTION FOR SUMMARY JUDGMENT OR SUMMARY ADJUDICATION

d) Separate statement in support of motion

The Separate Statement of Undisputed Material Facts in support of a motion must separately identify each cause of action, claim, issue of duty, or affirmative defense, and each supporting material fact claimed to be without dispute with respect to the cause of action, claim, issue of duty, or affirmative defense. In a two-column format, the statement must state in numerical sequence the undisputed material facts in the first column followed by the evidence that establishes those undisputed facts in that same column. Citation to the evidence in support of each material fact must include reference to the exhibit, title, page, and line numbers.

b) Format for separate statements

Supporting and opposing separate statements in a motion for summary judgment must follow this format:

Supporting statement:

Moving Party's Undisputed Material Facts and Supporting Evidence:	**Opposing Party's Response and Supporting Evidence:**
1. Plaintiff and defendant entered into a written contract for the sale of widgets. Jackson declaration, 2:17-21; contract, Ex. A to Jackson declaration.	
2. No widgets were ever received. Jackson declaration, 3:7-21.	

Opposing statement:

Moving Party's Undisputed Material Facts and Alleged Supporting Evidence:	**Opposing Party's Response and Evidence:**
1. Plaintiff and defendant entered into a written contract for the sale of widgets. Jackson declaration, 2:17-21; contract, Ex. A to Jackson declaration.	Undisputed.
2. No widgets were ever received. Jackson declaration, 3:7-21.	Disputed. The widgets were received in New Zealand on August 31, 2001. Baygi declaration, 7:2-5.

When drafting a document such as this, you must first consider the grounds for a motion for summary judgment, namely that there are no disputes of material issues of fact and the moving party is entitled to judgment as a matter of law. To prepare a document such as this, you first need to identify the elements of the cause of action. Research the substantive law of the case to accomplish this. You must then review the facts of your client's case. The relevant facts for this document depend on whether you represent the moving party or the responding party and whether you represent the plaintiff or the defendant in the action. In choosing the relevant facts, though, the question is always the same: "What facts do I need to prevail on the motion?" (Review Chapter 2.)

Using Forms

In drafting supporting documents, attorneys often rely on forms. Recall from Chapter 7 that form books are an important secondary source for researchers. In the past, the Federal Rules of Civil Procedure contained an Appendix of Forms, including forms used in motion practice. This is no longer the case, though. You must use your basic research skills to locate and adapt proper forms. Legal professionals must know how to use and adapt them to their specific cases.

15-5 THE INTERNET AND MOTION PRACTICE

Today, the Internet plays a vital role in many law and motion matters and its use is controlled by various federal, state, and local rules that must be researched. Many attorneys file and serve papers electronically. Filing electronically is not always simple. You may need to search a court's website to find instructions to do this. Court rules may dictate who can do this, the proper format documents to be filed, and when filing is deemed to take place. Documents are not generally filed in a traditional "Microsoft Word" format. Special requirements usually exist. Court rules often proscribe dates when responses and replies to motion papers must be filed. For example, a response to a motion may be required to be filed 10 days prior to the scheduled court hearing. If the clerk's office at the court closes at 4 p.m., it must be filed before that time. However, when filing electronically a different rule might be followed. This needs to be researched. Likewise, service rules often change when service is done electronically. Again, this may need to be researched. One relatively new practice in some courts is to issue a "tentative ruling" in the case the day before the motion is set for hearing. This ruling is generally published on the court's website and accessed there by the attorneys. The purpose behind this, of course, is to eliminate unnecessary court hearings. However, parties are still entitled to appear and argue their case—provided they follow certain notice requirements. If you are working on a motion where tentative rulings are posted, you need to be able to find these requirements. Today, many ancillary research tasks can result.

See Box 15-1 for a general research and writing checklist for motion practice.

BOX 15-1 RESEARCH AND WRITING CHECKLIST FOR MOTION PRACTICE

Research Tasks

- ✔ Locate rules of court governing motions in general
- ✔ Locate the Rule or code section governing the specific motion and determine the grounds for the motion as well as any special requirements
- ✔ Research case law dealing with the specific grounds for the motion
- ✔ Research case law dealing with the more general area of law in dispute
- ✔ Locate relevant forms in practice or form books

Writing Tasks

- ✔ Draft Memorandum of Points and Authorities
- ✔ Draft necessary affidavits or declarations
- ✔ Draft supplemental documents required by law
- ✔ Draft Proposed Order

Finding It Online

Local rules of court play an important role in motion practice. Local rules of court are usually found on a court's website. To find a court's website, the following sites are helpful:

Federal courts

www.uscourts.gov

State courts

www.ncsc.org/

www.govengine.com/

www.statelocalgov.net/

CITATION MATTERS

CITING AND ABBREVIATING COURT AND LITIGATION DOCUMENTS

THE BLUEBOOK—RULE B17 AND TABLE BT1

The statement of facts in a persuasive memorandum or brief must contain citations to authority for the factual assertion. Declarations, affidavits, transcripts, and numerous other court documents contain that authority. These citations should not include abbreviations unless the meaning is clear. Enclosing the citation to the court document in parentheses is an option. It also includes a period at the end of the citation, and if parentheses are used, the period is included in the parentheses.

For example:

> Defendant drove a motorcycle at a high rate of speed, weaving in and out of traffic. (Jones Aff. 4.) *or*

> Defendant drove a motorcycle at a high rate of speed, weaving in and out of traffic. Jones Aff.4.

Numerous abbreviations for words found in court documents appear in Table BT1. Some of those abbreviations include the following:

Affidavit	Aff.
Brief	Br.
Complaint	Compl.
Declaration	Decl.
Defendant's	Def.'s
Deposition	Dep.
Memorandum	Mem.
Petition	Pet.
Points and Authorities	P. & A.
Summary	Summ.
Testimony	Test.
Transcript	Tr.

CHAPTER **SUMMARY**

Motions are requests for an order from the court and occur in both civil and criminal cases. The types of motions vary, but procedures in pretrial and post-trial motions are similar. After a court date is set, moving and responding documents are filed, a brief court hearing occurs and the judge issues an order. The Federal Rules of Civil Procedure and case law primarily govern federal court motions in civil cases. The Federal Rules of Criminal Procedure, the Constitution, and case law govern motions in criminal cases. Local rules of court also play an important role. State codes, case law, and state and local rules of court govern motions in state court.

Research for a motion should focus on the grounds or basis for granting the motion. The rule explaining the motion will state the grounds or basis for granting the motion. The question of who will ultimately prevail in the action is not relevant unless the motion is one for summary judgment or judgment as a matter of law. Procedural issues related to the motion must also be researched. These procedural rules are usually very technical and are often found in local rules of court. At times local rules of court are inconsistent with the federal and state law. Most often, for procedural rules in motions, the local rules control.

In addition to the memorandum of points and authorities, documents in support of or in opposition to a motion include affidavits or declarations. These documents, created under penalty of perjury, contain the factual basis for the motion. They must also contain admissible evidence. A moving party to a motion also prepares a notice of motion, a document describing the motion and the time, place, and date of the hearing. A proposed order is also often required. Some motions, such as summary judgment motions and discovery motions, have specific documents that accompany the moving and responding papers. In drafting many of these documents, attorneys rely on forms found in privately published form books.

TERMS TO **REMEMBER**

filed
motion
moving party
affidavit
declarations
responding party
pleadings
demurrer
jurisdiction
venue
service
statement of undisputed material facts
acquittal
standard of review
notice of motion
interrogatories
deposition

QUESTIONS FOR **REVIEW**

1. What is the general purpose of motions?
2. Describe the general procedures for motions.
3. What are some common motions in civil cases?
4. What are some common motions in criminal cases?
5. Explain the importance of the grounds or basis for granting a motion.
6. Describe the research sources for determining the procedural requirements for motions.
7. What is the importance of local rules of court to research related to any motion?
8. What is the purpose of an affidavit or declaration in relationship to motions?
9. List some supporting documents that accompany a memorandum of points and authorities in support of a motion.
10. Explain the role of the Internet in motion practice.

CAN YOU **FIGURE IT OUT?**

1. Review Figure 15-1. What type of motion is made here? What are the statutory grounds for the motion?

TEST **YOURSELF** (Check Your Answers in Appendix G)

1. Assume that you are filing a motion to dismiss for lack of jurisdiction in the U.S. District Court for the Eastern District of Texas. You want to file electronically. Under the local rules, in what format must the documents be? Cite the specific local rule that governs.

TEST **YOURSELF**—WRITE IT RIGHT Effective Use of Point Headings

Point headings are important legal writing tools. Effective point headings guide a reader through an argument or a discussion. They allow the reader to understand if rule explanation paragraphs will follow or if rule application paragraphs will follow. You worked with rule explanation and rule application point headings in previous chapters.

The partial argument below includes the *major* point heading (in bold) for the second section of the document. Under this point heading, there should be three sub-point headings that will help alert the reader to what is coming next.

The sub-point headings are listed here:

Susan Tan became an accessory after the fact to Dylan Rhodes' fraud when she allowed him to stay with her for over two months despite knowing of his crime against the United States, kept the ring he fraudulently obtained for her, and knowingly lied to investigators about his whereabouts.

An individual is an accessory after the fact under 18 U.S.C.A. § 3, if she receives, relieves, comforts, or assists the perpetrator of a crime against the United States with knowledge that the crime has been committed and the intent to prevent the perpetrator's apprehension.

It is not necessary to try or convict the principal to a federal offense in order to convict the accessory after the fact to the offense.

NOW, YOU TRY IT:

Figure out where in the document these sub-point headings should be placed.

II. Susan Tan is an accessory after the fact to Dylan Rhodes' access card fraud because she assisted him within the meaning of 18 U.S.C.A. Section 3 with the intent to prevent his apprehension by lying to investigators about his whereabouts and denied knowledge of the ring later found in her home. [major point heading]

Being an accessory after the fact is a separate and exclusive substantive offense from the offense committed by the principal. *United States v. Taylor,* 322 F.3d 1209, 1212 (9th Cir. 2003) (holding that one convicted as a principal to murder may not also be an accessory after the fact to the same crime). It is not necessary to try or convict the principal in order to convict an accessory after the fact. *United States v. Walker,* 415 F.2d 530, 530 (9th Cir. 1969) (citing *Hiram v. United States,* 354 F.2d 4, 6 n.2 (9th Cir. 1965)) (affirming conviction of accessory after the fact to bank robbery despite the absence of the conviction of the principal). Here, therefore, it is immaterial to the conviction of Ms. Tan that Mr. Rhodes has yet to be apprehended. She may be tried as an accessory after the fact to his access device fraud, although he is not available to stand trial.

An accessory after the fact to a federal crime is one who, knowing that an offense against the United States has been committed, receives, relieves, comforts, or assists the perpetrator to prevent or hinder his apprehension. 18 U.S.C.A. § 3 (West 2016). In order to convict the defendant of being an accessory after the fact, the State must prove the following elements: (1) the principal committed an offense against the United States; (2) the accessory had knowledge of the commission of such offense; and (3) the accessory assisted the principal in avoiding apprehension. *United States v. Felix-Gutierrez,* 940 F.2d 1200, 1206 (9th Cir. 1991).

The accessory must have knowledge of the principal's commission of every material element of the underlying offense, but is not required to know that those elements establish an offense against the United States. *United States v. Graves,* 143 F.3d 1185, 1186 (9th Cir. 1998) (reversing accessory conviction for lack of knowledge that the principal was a convicted felon in addition to possessing a firearm). This requirement of knowledge does not extend to knowledge of jurisdictional requirements of the underlying offense. *Felix-Gutierrez,* 940 F.2d at 1207. Knowledge that the principal committed an offense may be shown entirely through circumstantial evidence. *United States v. Rux,* 412 F.2d 331, 333 (9th Cir. 1969) (holding reasonable inference of knowledge of the robbery from defendant's behavior to be sufficient to convict accessory after the fact).

Various types of conduct may tend to show assistance to prevent or hinder the principal's apprehension under 18 U.S.C.A. § 3. For example, in *Rux,* the court affirmed the accessory after the fact conviction of a defendant who purchased a vehicle for his brother to use to escape from the F.B.I. after committing bank robbery. 412 F.2d at 333. In *Felix-Gutierrez,* the defendant hired a pilot to fly the principal out of the country. 940 F.2d at 1206. In *Hiram,* the court affirmed the defendant's conviction as an accessory after the fact after the defendant traveled with the principal as he evaded the F.B.I. and provided false statements to the F.B.I. regarding the principal after he was arrested. 354 F.2d at 5-6.

An accessory convicted under the statute is subject to a term of imprisonment not more than half of the maximum sentence imposed on the principle. 18 U.S.C.A. § 3. Thus, an accessory after the fact to the commission of access device fraud under 18 U.S.C.A. § 1029(a)(5) faces a maximum sentence of seven and one half years.

Susan Tan is guilty of being an accessory after the fact to Dylan Rhodes' access device fraud. The first of the three elements listed in *Felix-Gutierrez* that the State must prove to establish an offense under 18 U.S.C.A. § 3, that the principal in fact committed an offense against the United States, is established above in the discussion of Mr. Rhodes' crime.

The second element, that the accessory knew that an offense against the United States was committed, is satisfied as well. *Graves* requires that the accessory have knowledge of every material element of Mr. Rhodes' offense, 143 F.3d at 1186, and Ms. Tan satisfies this requirement. First, it is reasonable to infer that she was aware that Mr. Rhodes was illegally using his dead mother's access devices. Because he lived with her for over two months, beginning soon after his mother died, it is exceedingly unlikely that she was unaware of his mother's death. Furthermore, the F.B.I. uncovered credit card statements in the deceased mother's name within Ms. Tan's home. Second, evidence shows that she knew that he used the illegal access devices to obtain property valued over $1,000. The F.B.I. also discovered the appraisal signed by Mario Battaglia, stating the value of Ms. Tan's diamond ring, $1,200, and credit card statements corresponding with that purchase in the mother's name. Last, under *Felix-Gutierrez*, Ms. Tan does not need to have knowledge of the jurisdictional element of the offense, the effect on interstate commerce.940 F.2d at 1207. Thus, Ms. Tan has the requisite knowledge under 18 U.S.C.A. § 3 to be an accessory after the fact.

Ms. Tan also satisfies the third and final element of the crime, assisting the principal in avoiding apprehension by the legal authorities. Ms. Tan's conduct is well in line with the precedent case law holding accessories liable under 18 U.S.C.A. § 3. In *Rux,* the accessory bought a car to facilitate the principal's escape from the F.B.I. 412 F.2d at 333. In *Felix-Gutierrez,* the accessory hired a pilot to assist the principal in fleeing the country. 940 F.2d at 1206. Similarly, here, Ms. Tan purchased a plane ticket for Mr. Rhodes to flee investigation for his crimes. When the F.B.I. searched her home, they uncovered documents relating to Ms. Tan's purchase of an Alaska Airlines ticket for Mr. Rhodes. It is no stretch to infer that Ms. Tan purchased this ticket in order to assist Mr. Rhodes' attempt to flee from justice.

CITATION **EXERCISES**

Use the Citation Matters feature in this chapter to answer these questions.

1. What do *Bluebook* rule B17 and Table BT1 cover?
2. "The statement of facts in a persuasive memorandum or brief must contain ____________________________ ______________________________________."
3. "Plaintiff waved at the people in the SUV. (Kobel Dep. 14.)" Explain what (Kobel Dep. 14) means.

FROM **THE WRITER'S CORNER** The Exclamation Mark

1. In formal legal writing, there is little need for the ____________________ ____________________.
2. Identify which of the following would most likely take an exclamation point (identify all terms you think need an exclamation point):

Halt.

Wow.

It was a gigantic explosion.

Connor is a little dog.

Run.

ASSIGNMENTS AND **EXERCISES**

RESEARCH EXERCISES

1. Find and summarize local rules of court regarding summary judgment motions for your local federal and state trial courts.
2. Locate and copy a form in a form book for an order after a motion.

ONLINE RESEARCH

1. Under the Federal Rules of Civil Procedure (not local rules), how much notice of a motion must be given?
2. Can a civil motion be served on the other party electronically?
3. In a criminal case, what rule governs motions and what motions must be made before trial?

WRITING EXERCISES

4. Consider the Smythe case described in Section 15-3. Draft an affidavit or declaration that Smythe might file in support of motion to set aside his default.

ANALYSIS ASSIGNMENTS

5. Consider the Smythe case described in Section 15-3. Based on Rule 60, should the court grant the motion?

CASE **PROJECT**

Review the case file at the beginning of this chapter. Check the local rules of court for your local state and federal trial courts. What requirements are there for a discovery motion in a criminal case? How do these requirements differ from the requirements for a civil discovery motion to compel discovery?

chapter **sixteen**

LEGAL CORRESPONDENCE

SKILL OBJECTIVES FOR CHAPTER 16

When you complete chapter 16, you should be able to

- Write a business letter using standard business letter format.
- Describe the different types of general correspondence that law firms use.
- List and describe the type of information contained in a case summary.
- Summarize a case file.
- Describe the content and tone of an opinion letter.
- Draft an opinion letter based on provided facts.
- Describe the content and tone of a demand letter.
- Draft a demand letter based on provided facts.

CHAPTER OUTLINE

From the Desk of W. J. Bryan, Esq.

TO: Research Assistant
FROM: W. J. Bryan
RE: Our Client, Justin Meyers
DATE:

I recently received an offer from the prosecutor allowing Meyers to plead guilty to involuntary manslaughter rather than murder, provided that he does so before the motion to suppress is decided by a judge. I discussed this matter with our client and gave him my evaluation and opinion in the matter. I want to follow this up with a letter setting out the arguments for and against his accepting this offer and my recommendation. Please check my calendar and schedule a time when I can discuss this with you. You will write a draft of the letter. I will review and sign it.

16-1 INTRODUCTION

An important type of legal writing is the business letter. The efficient functioning of any law office depends on this communication method. Letters are used to communicate with other lawyers, clients, and the courts. They serve many different purposes. In some instances, business letters are used to communicate factual information. For example, if documents are sent to a court for filing, a letter provides the court with a description of the documents and instructions for filing. This letter is called a ***transmittal letter*** or ***cover letter*** and is fairly simple. Simple business letters set up or confirm appointments or court dates, request information from a client, or confirm conversations. Correspondence that is more complex involves the legal issues in a case. Sometimes correspondence includes a *summary* of a legal position, providing the reader with an objective explanation of the law. For example, an attorney might write a letter to a client (especially an insurance company) summarizing the legal position of an opposing party who made a motion in court. Other times, the correspondence includes not only an explanation of the law but also a legal opinion regarding the client's rights or obligation. This letter is known as an ***opinion letter*** and is a type of predictive writing. Letters also initiate settlement of a case. Such a letter utilizes persuasive techniques to encourage an opposing party to settle a case, either by paying a sum of money or by taking some other action. This is known as a ***demand letter*** because it demands that some action be taken by the person to whom it is directed. All letters, regardless of how simple or how complex, must look professional, be grammatically correct, and be clear and understandable.

transmittal letter
A letter sent with documents or other items, explaining the nature of the documents or items as well as directions to the recipient for any actions to be taken with the documents or items; also referred to as a cover letter.

cover letter
A letter sent with documents or other items, explaining the nature of the documents or items as well as directions to the recipient for any actions to be taken with the documents or items; also referred to as a transmittal letter.

opinion letter
Formal correspondence from an attorney to a client or other attorney explaining an attorney's interpretation of the law as applied to a factual situation.

demand letter
Formal correspondence from an attorney to a party or other attorney demanding that action be taken or requesting a settlement of a claim or dispute.

In addition to formal business letters, today's law office sees correspondence exchanged through e-mail and fax. Even though this results in instant communication and has some definite advantages, e-mail and fax present numerous potential problems.

This chapter discusses the different types of legal correspondence.

16-2 BUSINESS LETTER FORMAT

Legal correspondence follows the standard format for any type of business letter. It includes the following:

1. Name and address of the sender
2. The date

The Writer's Corner

Keep Things Simple

Avoid using three or four words when one or two will do.

Too Many Words	**Keeping It Simple**
by reason of	because of
with respect to	on
in accordance with	under, by
for the reason that	because
prior to	before
in the event that	if
subsequent to	after
with reference to	about
inasmuch as	since
in favor of	for
with a view to	To

When you edit your work, remember the key is to keep it simple. Long sentences are easy to write, but they are difficult to read.

3. Special mailing or delivery methods
4. The inside address
5. A reference line
6. The salutation
7. The body
8. The closing
9. The signature block
10. Notations of enclosures, initials of preparer, and notation of copies sent

Letterhead and Date

The name and address of the sender are normally in a letterhead, preprinted on office stationery. In the case of a large law firm, the letterhead usually includes the name of the firm as well as the name of all attorneys in the firm. A paralegal's name may or may not be included, depending on the law of the state and the policy of the office. The date is shown below the letterhead.

Special Mailing or Delivery Methods

Below the date, a notation is made of special types of mailing or delivery methods. Legal correspondence may be sent using certified mail or overnight delivery. These methods may have legal consequences. Today it is common to send correspondence first by fax, followed by first-class mail. Indicate this in the letter.

Inside Address and Reference Line

The inside address contains the name, title, and address of the person to whom the correspondence is sent. Following the inside address is a reference line describing the subject matter of the legal correspondence. A reference line serves two purposes. It allows the recipient to know immediately what the letter concerns. If the recipient is another law office, an insurance company, or other business, this allows the person opening the mail to attach the letter to the office file before giving it to the named recipient. Also, should the letter ever be separated from your file (this happens in busy law offices, especially when attorneys remove documents from files), anyone finding it knows where it belongs. The information on the reference line varies. The most obvious is your client's name. However, that may not be very helpful to recipients of the letter, especially if they represent someone else. It is, therefore, preferable to include not only your client's name but also the name of the client to whom the letter is sent. If legal correspondence is a response to other letters that contain client names or file numbers, reference these in your letter. Such a reference line might read as follows:

Re: Victoria V. v. U Shop Mall

Your File No.: A12345

Salutation

The salutation in a letter from the law office is formal. Unless some special relationship exists between you and the recipient, avoid the use of first names and use the terms "Mr." and "Ms." If the communication is sent to an unknown person, such as the clerk of the court, the person's title can be used—for example:

Dear Mr. Smith:

Dear Clerk:

Body

The body of the letter depends on the purpose of the letter. Some of the more common purposes are discussed in the following sections. However, regardless of the purpose, always keep the tone professional and businesslike. Avoid slang and never use contractions (such as *didn't* instead of *did not*). Be concise and to the point. Know what you want to say before you begin writing. Start with the end in mind.

Closing and Signature Block

The closing is very simple in a business letter. The phrases "Sincerely," "Sincerely yours," and "Very truly yours" are most commonly used. The signature block includes the name of the person sending the correspondence and his or her title. If you work as a paralegal, you may sometimes sign letters on your own behalf. If so, always indicate your title following your name (such as "Paralegal" or "Legal Assistant"). In many cases, however, you draft letters on behalf of your supervising attorney. In such a case, the attorney's name and signature appear at the end of the letter.

Closing Notations

When a letter is sent under an attorney's signature, but has been prepared by a secretary or paralegal, a notation is made showing the initials of the attorney followed by the initials of the secretary or paralegal. For example:

WR: ybf

If documents are enclosed, that is also noted at the end of the letter, along with the number of documents enclosed, and looks as follows:

Enclosure

Enclosures (2)

With any legal correspondence, the question of who receives copies is important. In addition to the named recipient, the client sometimes receives copies of the legal correspondence. This lets the client know what is happening on the case. However, before sending copies to the client, always check with the attorney. If legal correspondence is sent in connection with a pending lawsuit and multiple attorneys are involved in the case, copies of correspondence between two of the attorneys are usually sent to all of the attorneys, especially if the matter relates to any time deadlines, court appearances, or other action pertaining to the case. Such closing notations look as follows:

CC: Donald Best

See Figure 16-1 and note the various parts of a business letter.

William Rose
Attorney at Law
349 Sixth Street
New York, NY 10027
Tel. (212) 453-2314 Fax. (212) 453-5566
www.roselaw.com

January 12, 20XX

Ms. Gloria Wright
765 Westwood St.
New York, N.Y. 10024

Re: 767 Westwood St. lease

Dear Ms. Wright:

This letter is a follow-up to our discussion yesterday, January 13, 20XX, regarding your lease of the property located at 767 Westwood St. Based on our conversation, I have drafted a proposed lease. A copy of that document is attached. I am also sending a copy of this letter and the attachment to your business partner, Donald Best.

Please confirm as soon as possible that the lease conforms to our discussion and meets your requirements. We can then finalize this part of your negotiations with the property owner. Please call me as soon as possible after reviewing this letter; my direct line is (212) 496-9125.

Sincerely,

William Rose
Attorney at Law

WR:ybf

Enclosure

CC: Donald Best

FIGURE 16-1 Example of a Confirmation Letter

16-3 GENERAL CORRESPONDENCE

Effectively operating a law office requires constant correspondence with clients, opposing attorneys, the courts, and miscellaneous parties. Four types of letters regularly found in a law office file include confirming letters, appointment letters, cover or transmittal letters, and information letters.

Confirmation Letters

In order to avoid misunderstandings, confirming letters are sent to confirm an oral (usually telephone) conversation. Confirmation letters are sent to confirm the following:

1. Substantive agreements relating to the case (e.g., in a family law matter, parties may agree to a child visitation schedule)
2. Agreements regarding the due date of any document, especially if it concerns an extension
3. Agreements setting or changing a court date, deposition, or other legal proceeding
4. Any conversation that might need verification at a later date

Confirmation letters may serve several purposes. Primarily, of course, the reason is to avoid misunderstandings that sometimes result from oral communications. They are also necessary because of the way that law firms operate. Reassignment of office files is common, and attorneys and paralegals may leave one firm and join another. The result is that the new attorney or paralegal has no way of knowing what agreements their predecessors reached unless some written memorandum or letter is contained in the file. Refer to Figure 16-1 for an example of a confirmation letter.

Appointment Letters

When a person is represented by an attorney, all notices from the courts or other attorneys in the case are sent to the attorney—not the client. This is true even when the notice requires that the client appear in court or at some other legal proceeding. The attorneys are obligated to notify their clients of the time, date, and place of any appearance or appointment. Although such notice can be given by telephone, an appointment letter should also be sent. The letter should clearly set forth the essential information, such as time, date, and place. Describe the place completely; if the client is to appear in court, the letter should give the address of the court, not just a reference to the "district court." Furthermore, always make certain that you have some way of confirming that the client received the letter and will appear as directed. Either ask the client to call you to confirm his or her appearance or call the client at some future date. See Figure 16-2 for an example of an appointment letter.

Cover or Transmittal Letters

A cover letter explains documents that are sent. A cover letter should state exactly what documents accompany the letter and what the recipient is to do with the documents, and any due dates for a response. In other words, is the recipient to review the documents, sign the documents, file the documents, or record the documents? The cover letter should also describe any expected response. Do you want the recipient to sign the documents and return them to

WILLIAMS & SMITH
Attorneys at Law
666 First Street
The Filmore Building, 16th Floor
San Diego, CA 92104
Tel. (619) 444-2316 Fax. (619) 444-5693
www.jwslaw.com

April 12, 20XX

Mr. Howard Jones
234 Baywood St.
San Diego, CA 92103

Re: Purchase of property at 213 Shoreline Blvd., San Diego, CA

Dear Howard:

As we discussed during our phone conversation on April 11, 20XX, I write to confirm our meeting on May 6, 20XX at 11:00 a.m. at my office located on the 16th Floor of the The Filmore Building, 666 First Street, San Diego, CA 92104. Thomas Ganines, a partner here at the firm, will join us.

Please bring all documents connected to the purchase of the property located at 213 N. Shoreline Blvd., San Diego, CA 92103.

Should you need additional information, please call Roberta Norris, my legal assistant, at (619) 444-7878. If you need to change the date or time of the meeting, please inform us as soon as possible.

Sincerely,

Sharon R. Williams
Attorney at Law

SRW:rln

CC: Thomas Ganines

FIGURE 16-2 Example of Appointment Letter

you? If so, are the documents due by a certain date? Do you want the court to file the documents and return copies to you? If you want copies returned to you, enclose a self-addressed stamped envelope. Many courts will not return documents unless you do this.

Information Letters

A letter requesting or conveying information may be used to obtain information from a client, a witness, or some other third party. Sometimes the information sought is solely related to a specific case. For example, in an automobile accident case, you might need a client to provide copies of all medical bills. Other times, the information is more general. For example, you have a client who wants to obtain a zoning variance for a piece of real estate, and you need to know whether the local regulating agency has any specific forms or guidelines to follow. The most difficult part about preparing a letter requesting information is identifying the party who has the information. This may take some preliminary work on your part.

In addition to requesting information, letters convey information. This might involve advising a client about the status of his or her case or responding to an inquiry from another attorney. In all cases, be sure that you understand the information to be conveyed before writing any letter. If you are in doubt, check your facts.

16-4 CASE SUMMARIES

Information letters are common in law firms that handle claims covered by insurance. In these instances, insurance companies not only are responsible for any ultimate judgment or settlement but also bear the expense of litigation. These companies expect to receive periodic reports or summaries of the litigation. Case summaries must be prepared. In complex cases, case summaries are also routinely prepared to help the attorney handling the litigation. Case summaries are an important type of legal writing.

The purpose of a summary of any document or information is to inform the reader of the main ideas found in the summarized documents or data. The summary replaces the multiple pages found in the original data. Recall the case briefs (summaries) discussed in Chapter 4. These briefs contain the main ideas found in the case opinion. By reading a case brief, the reader knows what is in the case opinion without having read the entire case opinion. Also, recall from Chapter 14 that when a memorandum of points and authorities exceeds a certain length, many courts demand a summary of the argument be included in the memorandum.

A summary of any document requires that the writer extract the main points or ideas. A good way to begin this process is by looking for topic sentences in each paragraph of the document. Well-written topic sentences provide the main topic of the paragraph.

A case summary involves reviewing and summarizing the factual basis supporting the case as well as summarizing all of the documents found in a case file. One way of summarizing the factual basis of a case is to prepare a chronology of events. The chronology is often prepared in a column format with the following information:

Date	Event	Source of Information	Comments

Summarizing documents is similar. The main topics from documents include the date the document was prepared, the type of document (e.g., a complaint, a motion, or a letter), the parties who wrote or received copies of the documents as well as any parties mentioned within the document, the main ideas or topics found within the document (e.g., if it is a memorandum of points and authorities, a summary should include a summary of the argument and all authorities cited within it), and finally any comments (e.g., a note that one document conflicts with another). Such a summary might be organized as follows:

Date	Type of Document	Parties	Content	Comments

Before preparing any case summary, you should know the specific purpose of the summary. This affects both the information contained in the summary and the organization of the summary.

A Point to Remember

When preparing a case summary, do not just describe the case. The summary must contain the main topics or ideas found in the case. The summary may replace the entire case file.

16-5 OPINION LETTER

An opinion letter analyzes a particular factual situation in light of existing law and offers a legal opinion to the reader. For example, consider the Meyers case development as set forth in the note at the beginning of this chapter. The prosecutor offered a plea bargain if Meyers pleads guilty immediately. Rather than a murder charge that might involve a life sentence, the prosecutor agreed to accept a plea of involuntary manslaughter, a charge that carries much less jail time. However, Meyers must drop his motions to suppress evidence. Before deciding whether to accept this offer, Meyers would undoubtedly rely on the advice and opinion of his attorney. The attorney must evaluate the chances of the judge granting the motions as well as evaluating what might happen at a trial. This evaluation requires the attorney to analyze both the facts and the law. Based on those evaluations, the attorney makes recommendation or gives his opinion to Meyers. Even though such opinions are discussed with the client, an attorney might also want to include this information in a written *opinion* letter to the client.

Tone

Opinion letters often respond to an inquiry of a party who has a dispute with another party and is trying to determine what course of action to take. When an attorney recommends a specific course of action, he or she must first predict how a court would resolve the dispute. Only based on this prediction can an attorney advise a client. Predictions, of course, are never 100% accurate, and this must be conveyed to the recipient of an opinion letter. When writing the legal analysis in an opinion letter, you use the predictive writing techniques described in Chapter 13.

Fact Statement

Figure 16-3 shows an example of an opinion letter. In this letter, attorney Birk-Ramiriz is responding to a client, Frank Bennett, who has a dispute with a neighbor over the height of a fence. Like most opinion letters, the analysis and recommendations are based on the facts related to the attorney by the client. Note that prior to analyzing the law and giving an opinion, the attorney is careful to relate the facts that were provided and to limit any opinion to those facts.

Analysis

Following the statement of the facts is an explanation and analysis of the law and a prediction of a probable outcome. An opinion letter requires that you do legal research and analysis. Earlier chapters discussed these skills. However, remember that in writing such a letter, you are not writing it for an attorney or other legal

FIGURE 16-3 Example of an Opinion Letter

JANET BIRK-RAMIRIZ
Attorney at Law
573 Second Ave. Suite 234
San Jose, CA 95110
Tel. (408) 555-1234 Fax. (408) 555-2345
jbr@online.com www.jbrlaw.com

July 31, 2XXX

VIA FAX AND FIRST CLASS MAIL

Frank Bennett
3085 Monteverde Dr.
Cupertino, CA 94123

Re: Fence Dispute

Dear Mr. Bennett:

This letter is in response to your recent inquiry regarding a dispute you have with your neighbor over a fence. The facts you related to me are as follows. Your neighbor recently tore down a six-foot-high split rail fence located on the boundary between your two homes, and erected a brick fence measuring ten feet high in its place. This new fence blocks your view of neighboring hills. You also informed me that you have a history of problems with your neighbor, dating back over ten years. In the past, your neighbor has trampled on your flowers, thrown garbage in your yard and on several occasions shouted loud obscenities to you and your wife. Last summer, while you were on a two week vacation, evidently your neighbor called the police complaining that your car was parked on the street where it remained during your vacation. You now want to know if you can force your neighbor to tear down the brick fence and if you are entitled to any monetary damages because of your neighbor's conduct. Pursuant to your request I have researched the matter. My findings and opinions are dependent on the facts you presented being complete and accurate.

California law contains a specific provision regarding "spite fences." This provision, section 841.4 of the California Civil Code, provides as follows:

> Any fence or other structure in the nature of a fence unnecessarily exceeding 10 feet in height maliciously erected or maintained for the purpose of annoying the owner or occupant of adjoining property is a private nuisance. Any owner or occupant of adjoining property injured either in his comfort or the enjoyment of his estate by such nuisance may enforce the remedies against its continuance prescribed in Title 3, Part 3, Division 4 of this code.

Under this section you must show (1) that the fence exceeds 10 feet in height, (2) that the height is unnecessary, and (3) that it was maliciously erected. The facts related to me indicate that the fence is 10 feet high. The code section applies to fences that *exceed* 10 feet. You must obtain exact measurements of the height of the fence. Even if the fence does not exceed 10 feet, other legal theories may apply to your case. Before spending time researching this, however, I advise that you obtain exact measurements. Assuming that the fence exceeds 10 feet, even by a small amount, I believe you have strong evidence of a malicious motive on the part of your neighbor. Your neighbor's past conduct provides a history of ill will and bad feelings and is strong evidence of his intent in building this fence. In fact, there is a California case from the court of appeals, *Griffin v. Northridge* (1944) 67 Cal. App. 2d 69 that closely parallels your situation. The court held that conduct such as has occurred in your case, is strong evidence of malicious intent. For your information, I am including a copy of this case.

If your neighbor will not voluntarily remove the fence, you can file a lawsuit and ask the court to order the removal of the fence. Alternatively, you may ask for money damages. At this point, if you wish to proceed further, I suggest that you call me and set up an appointment to discuss the next action to take.

Sincerely,

Janet Birk-Ramiriz
Attorney at Law

JBK:hen

Enclosure (1)

BOX 16-1 OPINION LETTER CHECKLIST

- ✔ State all facts upon which the opinion is based.
- ✔ Explain the relevant law.
- ✔ Explain how the law applies to the given facts.
- ✔ State opinion or conclusion.

professional. Try to avoid legal jargon. (Avoid jargon in any legal writing, but it is particularly important to do so here.) When writing an opinion letter, you often need to decide whether to include legal citations to cases or statutes. Practice differs on this point. Some attorneys believe that clients do not understand citations, so including them in a letter is unnecessary or possibly confusing. However, other attorneys are so used to citing law that they automatically include citations. There is an additional consideration. A copy of an opinion letter is included in the office client file. Should an attorney or other legal professional review the file and read the opinion letter, it is very helpful to have citations for authorities mentioned in the letter.

Conclusion

Finally, the letter provides the client with possible courses of actions or recommendations. Sometimes the letter expresses an opinion about the party's rights and obligations. Other times it recommends possible action that the party can take. Because an opinion letter gives legal advice, an attorney must always sign it. A paralegal cannot sign this type of letter.

See Figure 16-3 for an example of an opinion letter. See Box 16-1 for a checklist for an opinion letter.

16-6 DEMAND LETTER

A demand letter generally seeks resolution of a dispute or settlement of some matter, utilizing persuasive writing techniques. Sometimes it requests (or demands) that a party stop certain conduct (e.g., creating a nuisance or infringing on a patent) or comply with an existing obligation (e.g., payment of money owed). Other times a demand letter is sent in the hopes of settling an existing or potential lawsuit (e.g., a claim resulting from an automobile accident). Regardless of the reason for the letter, most demand letters include (1) a statement of facts establishing that the client has a legitimate legal claim, (2) a discussion of the law showing the legal basis for a cause of action, (3) an itemization of damages, and (4) a demand for a specific settlement.

Tone

The tone used in demand letters varies considerably. In some cases, the letter may be as harsh as the name suggests. For example, if your client in a divorce case advises you that the separated spouse (who is unrepresented by an attorney) is harassing your client at work, you might send a letter *demanding* that the behavior stop immediately. Likewise, if money is owed to your client on an overdue promissory note, a demand letter might demand immediate payment. On the other hand, some demand letters are much more conciliatory in their tone, especially when the attorney is attempting to reach a monetary settlement in a case.

(Demand letters are frequently sent to insurance companies for this purpose.) All demand letters intend to be persuasive. The object of the letter is to convince the recipient of the letter to do something.

Fact Statement

The statement of facts in a demand letter is a critical part of the letter. If the reader does not accept your version of the facts, there may be little reason to settle a case. The persuasive nature of the demand letter begins here. If possible, more than your own client's statement should support facts stated in a demand letter. Support for the facts giving rise to the claim is found in the following sources: witness statements, police reports, investigative reports, documents, photographs, and statements made by the opposing party. In writing the factual background in a demand letter, identify the source of all facts. In many instances, the letter should include verifying documents or photographs.

Analysis

The legal analysis also uses persuasive techniques. Chapter 14 describes these techniques. Here controlling statutory and case law is discussed and applied to the stated facts.

Damages and Injuries

Like the statement of facts, the itemization of damages and description of injuries require verification. Copies of medical bills or other out-of-pocket expenses should be included with the letter. Verification of any personal or property damage should also be included. Medical reports, photographs, and property appraisals are commonly included.

The Demand or Offer to Settle

A demand letter concludes with a clear statement of the action requested or offer of settlement. Generally, time limits for compliance or acceptance are also included. See Figure 16-4 for an example of a demand letter. The demand letter is based on the case *Victoria V. v. U Shop Mall* and the *Ann M.* case found in Chapter 13.

16-7 FAX AND E-MAIL

Most legal correspondence still arrives by mail. However, fax and e-mail correspondence offer speed in communicating and email especially is often favored by attorneys. There are, however, some concerns when using a fax machine or e-mail to transmit a letter. Confidentiality is a concern. Sending information via fax or e-mail does not ensure any degree of confidentiality because anyone can be on the receiving end. Many lawyers add a paragraph to any information they transmit by fax or e-mail asserting the confidentiality of the matter. Such a paragraph might read as follows:

> **Caution—Confidential**
>
> The document transmitted to you may contain information protected by attorney–client privilege. It is intended only for the person to whom it is addressed. If you have received this facsimile in error, please notify us immediately and destroy the document.

FIGURE 16-4 Example of Demand Letter

Roberta Jenkins
Attorney at Law
156 Oak St.
Central City, CA 91111
Tel. 510 555-1212 Fax. 510 555-2121

January 5, 20XX

Thomas Lord
Claims Adjuster
Goodhands Insurance Co.
78 Woodland Rd.
Central City, CA 96111

Re: Victoria V. v. U Shop Mall

Dear Mr. Lord:

I am writing on behalf of my client Victoria V., regarding her claim for personal injuries against your client U Shop Mall. The injuries were incurred when my client was assaulted on your client's premises on June 15, 20XX. I was advised by U Shop Mall that your company insures the mall and that all correspondence in this matter should be directed to you. After reviewing the statements of parties and witnesses and after examining various documents, I conclude that liability of your client is clear and that an early settlement in this matter is in everyone's best interests. The following information provides substantial justification for our offer of settlement.

Factual Basis
My client, Victoria V., was sexually assaulted in your client's parking lot at approximately 9 p.m. on June 15 of last year by an unknown assailant. The details of this event are found in a Central City Police Report dated June 16 of last year. The police report contains statements of Ms. V. as well as statements of two witnesses who observed an individual running from the scene and who assisted Ms. V. immediately after the assault. The report also contains a statement from a security guard employed by your client as well as the manager of the U Shop Mall. The statements from the witness substantiate the attack and resulting injuries. The statement from your employee, the security guard, confirms that the light in the parking lot was not operating. His statement also confirms that he reported this defective and dangerous condition several days prior to June 15. He also indicated that it takes him approximately 30 minutes to patrol the parking lot. The statement from your manager confirms that your client had prior notice of criminal acts on its premises and on nearby premises. He even admits, "I was afraid something like this would happen." A copy of the police report including all relevant statements is attached to this letter.

Legal Basis
The law in this jurisdiction is clear. Landowners owe a duty to maintain their premises in a reasonably safe condition. Cal. Civ. Code § 1714. This includes a duty to protect against criminal assaults by third parties when the landowner has knowledge that prior attacks have occurred. *Ann. M. v. Pacific Plaza Shopping Center*, 6 Cal. 4th 666 (1993). In this case, the facts prove that your client had such knowledge. Prior criminal acts occurred on the premises and on nearby premises. Your own client admits that he feared something like this would happen. Your client therefore had a duty to protect my client against attacks and breached that duty by failing to repair lights and by failing to provide adequate security guards.

Injuries and Damages
As a result of your client's negligence my client suffered severe physical and psychological injuries. She was treated at Central City Hospital where she was admitted. She also saw Dr. B. Feldon for her physical injuries and received therapy from Dr. K. Gordon, a psychiatrist. Copies of medical reports from Dr. Feldon and Dr. Gordon are attached to this letter. As the medical reports indicate, Ms. V. suffered numerous contusions and abrasions, as well as lumbar strain. She continues to have back pain. The emotional distress was severe and post traumatic stress syndrome may continue for the remainder of her life. To date Ms. V.'s medical expenses are as follows:

Central City Hospital	$10,569
Dr. Feldon	$ 1,250
Dr. Gordon	$2,400

It is anticipated that therapy will be needed for at least an additional six months, at a cost of $4,500. Copies of medical bills are enclosed.

In addition to medical expenses, Ms. V. was unable to work for 2 months. She has a management position at A & B Enterprises and her income is $120,000 per year. She lost approximately $40,000 in income.

Settlement Offer
In view of the clear liability and the nature and extent of the injuries and damages, my client is agreeable to settling this matter for the sum of $250,000. I believe this to be fair and reasonable and hope to hear from you soon. The offer will remain open for 30 days.

Sincerely,

Roberta Jenkins
Attorney at Law

RJ:op

Enclosures (3)

cc: Victoria V.

However, this serves little purpose if the receiver is not an attorney or is not otherwise bound by an ethical standard of behavior. Faxing and e-mail are not safe with highly confidential or sensitive material.

E-mail presents additional problems. Because law offices need to keep copies of correspondence that is sent and received, e-mail cannot be used without making hard copies of messages sent and received. Because of the informal nature of e-mail, sometimes there is a tendency to forget that a communication from a law office is business correspondence. Always carefully read and review all e-mail before sending. Always be aware of, and follow, any office policy regarding use of e-mail or fax.

BASIC E-MAIL ETIQUETTE

1. Do not send an e-mail when you are upset or angry.
2. Make the subject line meaningful.
3. The reply all option often creates e-mail clutter (and unanticipated consequences.)
4. Avoid the bcc field.
5. Compress large attachments when possible.
6. Be concise.
7. Review before sending the e-mail.
8. Pick up the phone if you have a lot to communicate or if you need to go back and forth several times.
9. Let senders know their e-mail was received.
10. Ask prior to sending huge attachments.
11. Writing in all caps is the equivalent of shouting on the screen.
12. Be very cautious about using color typeface.

A Point to Remember

Opinion letters and demand letters should generally be signed by an attorney. If signed by a paralegal or other non-attorney, it may constitute the unauthorized practice of law.

Finding It Online

Several government agencies are responsible for providing opinions on a variety of topics. Two such agencies are the U.S. Department of Labor and the Federal Trade Commission. Find several of their opinion letters online at the following sites:

https://www.dol.gov/ (search for "opinion letters" to find letters issued by the Department of Labor)

https://www.ftc.gov/enforcement/cases-proceedings (opinion letters issued by the Federal Trade Commission)

CITATION MATTERS

THE USE OF BRACKETS WITHIN QUOTATIONS

***THE BLUEBOOK*—Rule 5.2**

Use brackets when a letter needs to be changed from lower to uppercase, or vice versa.

1. Substituted letters (possibly to change tense)
2. Words (possibly to correct agreement or provide clarification)
3. Other inserted material

The Bluebook provides an excellent example:

> [P]ublic confidence in the [adversary] system depend[s upon] full disclosure of all the facts, within the framework of the rules of evidence.

In this example, a lowercase *p* was capitalized, and *adversary* and *supon* were added to make the sentence read well.

When there is a significant error in the original quote, place [sic] directly following the mistake.

> The Court noted that the judgment were [sic] not necessarily harsh, given the circumstances under which the crime was committed.

CHAPTER SUMMARY

Law offices routinely use business letters for numerous purposes. Regardless of the purpose, these letters follow standard business letter format and contain the name, address, and other contact information of the sender; the date; a notation of special delivery methods; an inside address; a reference line; a salutation; the body of the letter; a closing; a signature block; and a notation of enclosures or copies. Use letters for routine law office procedures such as confirming information, setting appointments, and conveying or requesting information. Cover or transmittal letters are used when documents are transmitted. In addition to routine office proceedings, attorneys use two special types of letters, opinion letters and demand letters. Write opinion letters to clients to explain and analyze a legal problem. Opinion letters contain an opinion of the client's rights and obligations or a recommendation for a course of action. Demand letters demand specific action from a party or to offer to settle a dispute.

TERMS TO REMEMBER

transmittal letter
cover letter
opinion letter
demand letter

QUESTIONS FOR REVIEW

1. What are the components of a standard business letter?
2. Can a paralegal's name be included in an office letterhead?
3. What is a cover or transmittal letter?
4. Describe situations in which an information letter might be used.
5. What is the purpose of a case summary?
6. What is an opinion letter?
7. List the components of an opinion letter.
8. What is a demand letter?
9. List the component parts of a demand letter.
10. Describe some problems in using fax and e-mail as methods of legal correspondence.

TEST YOURSELF—WRITING IT RIGHT Turning Issues into Major Point Headings

Well-written issues are easily turned into well-written point headings. There should be a direct connection between the major point headings and the issue statements. In general, the number of issues determines the number of major point headings. This organization helps the reader follow the writer's reasoning.

Consider the following two issues:

1. Did Dylan Rhodes commit access card fraud within the meaning of 18 U.S.C.A § 1029 when he used his deceased mother's Wells Fargo-issued access devices to obtain property, including an engagement ring and money from her accounts, all with an aggregate value greater than $1,000?
2. Is Susan Tan an accessory after the fact to Mr. Rhode's commission of access card fraud because she knowingly lied to investigators about Mr. Rhode's whereabouts and denied knowledge of the ring that was later seized in her home?

Now, consider the following two point headings that connect to these issues:

I. Dylan Rhodes committed access card fraud within the meaning of 18 U.S.C.A § 1029 when he used his deceased mother's Wells Fargo-issued access devices to obtain property, including an engagement ring and money from her accounts, all with an aggregate value greater than $1,000.

II. Susan Tan is an accessory after the fact to Dylan Rhode's access card fraud because she assisted him within the meaning of 18 U.S.C.A. Section 3 with the intent to prevent his apprehension by lying to investigators about his whereabouts and denied knowledge of the ring later found in her home.

In these two examples, the writer turned the question from the issue into a statement. Notice that the facts used in the issue are also used in the point heading. This sort of repetition is helpful and can be persuasive.

Now, You Try It

(Check your answers in Appendix G)

Write the point headings that should follow the issues below:

1. Does res ipsa loquitur apply without the need for expert testimony when common knowledge is sufficient to infer negligence from Mr. Smith's burn injuries sustained while unconscious during a routine surgery where his treating physicians are unable to provide a non-negligent explanation or evidence of an unpreventable cause?
2. Does Mr. Smith's action for medical malpractice expire under the statute of limitations one year from the date he discovered his burn injuries March 29, 2015, or one year from the second opinion visit with the plastic surgeon who suggested legal counsel?

CITATION EXERCISES

Use the Citation Matters feature in this chapter to answer these questions.

1. State the *Bluebook* rule that explains the use of brackets.
2. Brackets are helpful when you quote and you need to change very small things in a sentence in order to make the sentence read well. You might begin your quote with only part of the original sentence. Show this by changing the lower case to the upper case.

Original: "There remains steady public confidence in the system depending upon full disclosure of all the facts … ." When you only need a portion of that quote and you need to add some clarity, this rewrite may be the result: "[P]ublic confidence in the [adversary] system depend[s upon] full disclosure of all the facts … ."

1. Explain what "[P]" from the previous sentence tells a reader. (What was changed?)
2. Explain what "depend[s upon]" tells a reader. (What was changed?)

FROM THE WRITER'S CORNER Keep Things Simple

1. Avoid using three or four words when ________ or ____________ will do.
2. When you edit your work, the key is to ____________ it _________________.

ASSIGNMENTS AND EXERCISES

Analysis and Writing Exercises

1. Mr. and Mrs. Robert Smith contacted a lawyer with the following issue: Their son, Jeffrey, turned 18 four months ago. He is a senior in high school, living at home, and will graduate in five months. He has a part-time job at a local fast-food restaurant and earns approximately $400 per month, most of which he spends on his car and entertainment. He is not married. Jeffrey has become a problem for Mr. and Mrs. Smith. He refuses to follow house rules and stays out

extremely late. He is causing a great deal of stress at home. The Smiths are demanding that Jeffrey find another place to live, but they want to know if they will be responsible for his support, and if so, how long this duty exists. Assume that the following Family Code section applies in your state:

> Subject to this division, the father and mother of a minor child have an equal responsibility to support their child in the manner suitable to the child's circumstances.
>
> The duty of support imposed herein continues as to an unmarried child who has attained the age of 18 years, is a full-time high school student, and who is not self-supporting, until the time the child completes the 12th grade or attains the age of 19 years, whichever occurs first. (Family Code §3.456)

Based on this code section, write a draft of an opinion letter to the Smiths regarding their obligation to support Jeffrey.

2. Refer to Figure 16-4. Assume that your client, Frank Bennett, contacts your office and tells you that he hired a contractor to measure the fence in question. He presents you with a written report from the contractor, James Hammer, stating that precise measurements were taken and the fence measures 10 feet, 2 inches. James Hammer is a licensed general contractor. Write a demand letter to Mr. Bennett's neighbors, Paul and Marie Vista, demanding that he tear down the fence and pay Mr. Bennett the sum of $5,000 to cover the cost of having the fence measured and for damages destroying your client's view. The Vistas live at 3087 Monteverde Dr.
3. Consider the following facts: Because of uninsured medical expenses, Dora Speckles incurred credit card charges of several thousand dollars. She was also unable to work for several months and was unable to pay the credit card bill. Once her health was restored, Dora found employment in a small business office. However, she was still unable to make payments on the credit card account. The credit card company eventually turned the account over to Collect 'R Else Collection Agency. The collection agency learned of Dora's employment and telephoned her there to demand payment on the account. Dora advised the agency that she was not allowed to receive any nonemergency personal calls and requested that the collection agency not call her at work. Nevertheless, the collection agency continued to call her once a day. After two weeks, Dora was fired. Her employer told her she was terminated because of all the personal telephone calls. Dora worked as a receptionist for the Allied Title Company, earning $500 per week. After losing her job, Dora became very depressed, although she cannot afford to obtain medical treatment for this condition. After being unemployed for two months, Dora has finally found another job. Fearing that the collection agency will learn of this employment, Dora sought legal advice. Your law firm has agreed to represent Dora and advised her that she has remedies under the Fair Debt Collection Practices Act.

Draft a letter to the Collect 'R Else Collection Agency demanding that it have no further direct contact with Dora, either at home or any place of employment. Also, demand damages for their past conduct in accordance with the Fair Debt Collection Practices Act. The relevant portions of the act are set forth as follows:

Fair Debt Collection Practices Act:

Communication in connection with debt collection [15 U.S.C. §1692c]

(a) COMMUNICATION WITH THE CONSUMER GENERALLY. Without the prior consent of the consumer given directly to the debt collector or the express permission of a court of competent jurisdiction, a debt collector may not communicate with a consumer in connection with the collection of any debt—
   1. at any unusual time or place or a time or place known or which should be known to be inconvenient to the consumer. In the absence of knowledge of circumstances to the contrary, a debt collector shall assume that the convenient time for communicating with a consumer is after 8 o'clock antimeridian and before 9 o'clock postmeridian, local time at the consumer's location;
   2. if the debt collector knows the consumer is represented by an attorney with respect to such debt and has knowledge of, or can readily ascertain, such attorney's name and address, unless the attorney fails to respond within a reasonable period of time to a communication from the debt collector or unless the attorney consents to direct communication with the consumer; or
   3. at the consumer's place of employment if the debt collector knows or has reason to know that the consumer's employer prohibits the consumer from receiving such communication.

(b) COMMUNICATION WITH THIRD PARTIES. Except as provided in section 804, without the prior consent of the consumer given directly to the debt collector, or the express permission of a court of competent jurisdiction, or as reasonably necessary to effectuate a postjudgment judicial remedy, a debt collector may not communicate, in connection with the collection of any debt, with any person other than a consumer, his attorney, a consumer reporting agency if otherwise permitted by law, the creditor, the attorney of the creditor, or the attorney of the debt collector.

Civil liability [15 U.S.C. §1692k]

(c) Except as otherwise provided by this section, any debt collector who fails to comply with any provision of this title with respect to any person is liable to such person in an amount equal to the sum of—

1. any actual damage sustained by such person as a result of such failure;
2. (A) in the case of any action by an individual, such additional damages as the court may allow, but not exceeding $1,000.

Online Research Exercises

4. Access the websites for the Department of Labor and the Federal Trade Commission found in the Online Legal Research feature. Select one opinion letter from each source and write a summary of the letters.
5. Using a general Internet search engine, find examples of different types of business letters.

Appendix A

RESEARCH CASE FILES

MEYERS CASE FILE *Sample Instructions for Memorandum on This Case File*

Unless instructed otherwise by your teacher, you are asked to write a memorandum following these instructions. The chapters in the text introduced you to the Meyers case from the perspective of the defendant and his attorney. For this assignment you are asked to approach the case from the court's perspective. This memo is directed to a judge and will be used to support her ruling on a motion. She has already decided how she will rule. Because of the specific request of the judge, this memo should be persuasive rather than predictive.

This case is set in a fictional state. You are asked to use federal primary sources in your final memo. You can also assume that the state of New Brunswick follows criminal procedural rules found in the Federal Rules of Criminal Procedure.

You are asked to do your initial research using print resources. Once you find appropriate primary sources, you can download and/or read them online. Although we live in a technological world, attorneys still use print sources for research. Practice in doing this is essential to developing the skills you will need as an attorney. You must also "validate" any authority you use in your memo. (This means you must either Shepardize or KeyCite the authorities—this should be done online.)

As usual, this memo must be typed and double spaced, with the pages numbered. Please use 12-point font. The memo should include a heading, question presented, statement of the facts, discussion, conclusion, and recommendation(s). (For this assignment we are omitting the brief answer.) Using a 12-point font and 1-inch margins, please keep the paper to no more than 10 pages. The following items are due as follows:

The educational goals of this assignment are:

1. To gain or improve the following skills:
   - Skill in research (federal sources);
   - Skill in validating sources;
   - Skill in legal citation;
   - Skill in organizing a multi-issue memorandum;
   - Skill in synthesizing and explaining clearly a complex series of rules;
   - Skill in analogical reasoning (contrasting favorably and distinguishing); and
   - Skill in using persuasive writing.

(continued)

2. To gain additional practice in the following skills, which you used in prior assignments
   - Skill in identifying legal issues arising in a client's case;
   - Skill in combining rules from statutes with rules from cases when writing a rule explanation;
   - Skill in anticipating and responding to opposing arguments;
   - Skill in outlining the elements of legal rules;
   - Skill in thinking and writing in the classic IRAC paradigm: issue, rules, application, conclusion;
   - Skill in drafting issue statements;
   - Skill in applying legal rules to the facts of a given case;
   - Skills in writing thesis paragraphs; and
   - Skills in writing and using topic sentences and thesis statements in the context of a legal office memo.

If you have any questions about the memo, please let me know.

NEW BRUNSWICK SUPERIOR COURT
LOS DIABLOS COUNTY

MEMORANDUM

TO: Research Assistant
FROM: Judge Melissa Grant
DATE: January 22, 20XX

RE: State of New Brunswick v. Meyers

Justin Meyers is charged with first degree murder. His attorney recently made a motion to suppress evidence and to suppress statements made to police. The evidence consists of a bloody handkerchief found in the course of a search pursuant to a search warrant. The statements in question are those made in the police vehicle while Meyers was being transported to jail, after being arrested for possession of drugs.

Both the prosecution and the defense submitted the motion on the search warrant and Grand Jury testimony. A copy of the warrant and the transcript of the testimony are attached. No other evidence was submitted in support of or in opposition to the motion. The defense based the motion on the contention that both the search and the statements were obtained in violation of the U.S. Constitution.

After reviewing all the facts in this case, under no circumstances do I want to suppress this evidence. Such a ruling could destroy the prosecutor's case. However, this case will be closely scrutinized, and I need to write an opinion that clearly justifies my decision. My ruling will be based on the fact that the search and subsequent statements were NOT obtained in violation of the U.S. Constitution. I want you to limit your research to federal law.

I need you to research this motion and write a memorandum providing me with the law and arguments that will support my ruling in favor of the prosecution.

Please prepare a memorandum that analyzes the legal and factual issues raised by the motion to suppress.

CIRCUIT COURT STATE OF NEW BRUNSWICK
COUNTY OF LOS DIABLOS

In the Matter of the Search of:

The person of JUSTIN MEYERS, further described as a male Caucasian, 5′10″, 175 pounds, brown hair, brown eyes, D.O.B. 5/27/1980; and

The premises at 24870 Lake View Place, Apartment 17, Centerville, and further described as a two-bedroom apartment in a four story apartment complex bearing the name, "Lake View Apartments," including all containers, rooms and other parts therein; and also including a detached parking area and storage compartment designated as belonging to the resident of Apartment 17.

SEARCH WARRANT

TO: Any sheriff, policeman or peace officer in the county of Los Diablos:

Affidavit(s) having been made before me by Matthew A. Alonza who has reason to believe that on the person of JUSTIN MEYERS, or on the premises known as "Lake View Apartments," Apartment 17 located at 24870 Lake View Place, Centervile in the County of Los Diablos there is now concealed a certain person or property, namely:

Cocaine, and cocaine paraphernalia including milk sugar, scales and other weighing devices, balloons, condoms, paper bindles, measuring devices, miniature spoons, short straws; articles tending to establish and document sales of cocaine including U.S. currency, buyer lists, seller lists, and recordations of sales including personal computers; articles of personal property tending to establish the identity of person in control of the premises, vehicles, storage areas and containers being searched including company receipts, rent receipts, address mail and keys.

I am satisfied that the affidavit(s) and any record testimony establish probable cause to believe that the person or property so described is now concealed on the person or premises above-described and establish grounds for the issuance of this warrant.

YOU ARE HEREBY COMMANDED to search on or before June 16, 20XX (not to exceed 10 days) the person or place named above for the person or property specified, serving this warrant and making the search in the daytime—6:00 A.M. to 10:00 P.M.

☐ at anytime in the day or night

as I find reasonable cause has been established and if the person or property be found there to seize same, leaving a copy of this warrant and receipt for the person or property taken, and prepare a written inventory of the person or property seized and promptly return this warrant to as required by law.

Dated: June 7, 20XX

____________________ ____________________

Name and Title of Judge Signature of Judge

PEOPLE OF THE STATE OF NEW BRUNSWICK, COUNTY OF LOS DIABLOS, Plaintiff, vs. JUSTIN MEYERS, Defendant	Case No.: 07-7507 TRANSCRIPT OF GRAND JURY PROCEEDING

Dated this 3rd day of December, 20XX

Questioning by Deputy District Attorney Margaret Yow of witness Matthew A. Alonza:

Q. Please state your name and occupation.

A. Matthew Alan Alonza, Detective with the Los Diablos County Sheriff's Department.

Q. How long have you been so employed?

A. I have been employed by the Sheriff's Department for 15 years. I have been a detective for the last 7 years.

Q. Are you assigned to a specific unit within the Sheriff's Department?

A. Yes.

Q. What unit is that?

A. The narcotics investigation unit.

Q. How long have you been assigned to that unit?

A. For 3 years.

Q. And before that what was your assignment within the Department.

A. Well, I have had several different assignments. I started as a sheriff's deputy assigned to traffic patrol. As a sheriff's deputy I was also assigned to the jails and to court security. After about 4 years I became a sergeant and then in another two years I was promoted to detective. As a detective I am involved in investigating numerous types of crimes, including burglaries, assaults, including domestic violence, a variety of theft crimes, sex offenses, and homicides.

Q. What is your educational background?

A. I have a Bachelor's Degree in Administration of Justice.

Q. Have you taken any police investigation courses?

A. Of course. Some courses were included in my undergraduate degree program, but since that time I have taken various courses at the state college as well as attending numerous seminars offered by various police agencies.

Q. And did any of these courses cover crime scene investigation.

A. Yes, several courses covered this.

Q. Now, as a member of the sheriff's department, I assume that you investigated numerous crime scenes.

A. That is correct.

Q. And have any of these investigations involved the execution of search warrants?

A. Yes

Q. Can you estimate how many involved search warrants?

A. Many. I couldn't give you a specific number.

Q. Detective Alonza, I would like to direct your attention to a search warrant that you served on June 10 of this year. I have here a copy of a search warrant identified as people's exhibit A. I would ask you to examine this and state whether you have seen this search warrant prior to today.

A. Yes, I have seen this.

Q. Is this a copy of a search warrant that you served?

A. Yes it is.

Q. And this search warrant allows you to search the apartment occupied by the accused, Justin Meyers. Is that correct?

A. Yes it is.

Q. And did you participate in the execution or search pursuant to this warrant?

A. Yes I did.

Q. In general this warrant allows you to search the apartment of Mr. Meyers for cocaine or cocaine paraphernalia, along with any evidence showing that Mr. Meyers was engaged in the sale of cocaine. Is that correct?

A. Yes it is.

Q. And this warrant also allows you to search and seize any evidence that tends to prove that Mr. Meyers was the occupant or resident of the premises identified in the search warrant?

A. Yes it does.

Q. Now on June 10 of this year you searched Mr. Meyers pursuant to this search warrant. Is that correct?

A. Yes.

Q. When you served that search warrant was Mr. Meyers present in the apartment?

A. Yes, he was.

Q. During your search, did you find evidence showing that Justin Meyers occupied the premises?

A. Yes we did.

Q. Please describe this.

A. Well, we found utility bills addressed to Mr. Meyers at the apartment address. We were also able to access a personal computer on the premises that clearly belonged to Mr. Meyers.

Q. During your search, did you find evidence of cocaine possession or sale?

A. Yes, we did. We found drugs and scales in the living and kitchen areas.

Q. Would you describe Mr. Meyer's apartment.

A. As you enter the apartment you walk into a living area with an attached kitchen toward the back. To the left was a short hallway leading to two bedrooms. Off one bedroom was a bathroom.

Q. Please describe how the bedrooms were furnished.

A. One room was furnished as a typical bedroom and the other was furnished as an office.

(continued)

Q. Now, the bedroom furnished as an office—did it contain a bed?

A. No.

Q. Was Mr. Meyer's the sole occupant of this apartment?

A. Yes.

Q. And what led you to this conclusion?

A. A number of factors. There was only one bed. The clothing in the closet was all the same size. And when we checked with the manager of the apartment he told us that Mr. Meyer's was the only person on the rental agreement and he had never seen anyone else in the apartment on any regular basis.

Q. While serving the search warrant marked as exhibit A, did you search all the rooms in the apartment?

A. Of course.

Q. While searching the room used as a bedroom, did you find anything unusual?

A. Yes.

Q. Please describe.

A. The first thing I noticed was a photograph on the top of the accused's dresser. The photo showed 5 people all smiling and huddled together. One of the individuals in the photo was the accused, Justin Meyers. Another of the individuals appeared to be a young woman, Nadine Bostick, who was reported missing approximately 2 weeks earlier. Foul play was suspected in her disappearance and a small task force from our department was assigned to her case.

Q. Were you on the task force?

A. No.

Q. To your knowledge was the accused a suspect in her disappearance?

A. No, he was not.

Q. Would you have known if he was a suspect?

A. Probably. We are a relatively small department.

Q. After noticing the photograph, what did you do?

A. I continued searching the dresser and closet for drugs.

Q. And did you find anything?

A. I didn't find drugs, but I did find a handkerchief with dried blood on it. The handkerchief was in the pocket of a jacket hanging in the closet.

Q. What did you do with this?

A. I placed it in a plastic container and seized it.

Q. Why did you take the handkerchief?

A. Well, there were a few reasons. I thought it might have traces of cocaine on it. I thought maybe that the accused might have used it to wipe off some of the paraphernalia we found. But I was also suspicious of the bloody rag. It just seemed strange. I guess in the back of my mind I was thinking about the young woman in the photograph. I was suspicious.

Q. What made you suspicious, then?

A. I don't know, but I have been a police officer for over 15 years and I do not believe in coincidences. We had a woman who had disappeared, a known drug dealer and a bloody handkerchief. I just thought there might be some connection.

Q. Did you ask the accused about the handkerchief?

A. Yes, as soon as I finished searching the bedroom I returned to the living room, where the accused was detained by another officer. He was handcuffed, sitting on the sofa and I showed him the handkerchief and asked him where the blood came from.

Q. What did he say?

A. He said he must have had a bloody nose. He didn't remember.

Q. Did you ask him anything else?

A. Yes, I asked him if he knew Nadine Bostick.

Q. And what did he say?

A. He said he had met her once—she was a friend of a friend.

Q. Did you ask him anything else?

A. Yes, I continued to ask him about Nadine. He looked very nervous to me, and I told him if he knew anything about her disappearance he should let us know. He told me that he didn't know anything.

Q. What did you do next?

A. We placed Mr. Meyers under arrest and put him in the patrol car to transport him to the jail.

Q. Did you read Mr. Meyers his *Miranda* Rights?

A. Yes. We read his rights as soon as we placed him under arrest.

Q. And what did he say.

A. He said he wanted a lawyer.

A. While you were transporting him to the jail, did you engage in any further conversations.

Q. Yes. The defendant asked us if we had any leads in Nadine's disappearance. This made us all very cautious and I then asked the defendant why he wanted to know.

A. He responded that he was just curious and hoped that she was o.k.

Q. Was anything else said?

A. Yes. I told the defendants that Nadine's parents were devastated at her disappearance and if he knew anything that could lead to finding her, he should let us know. He then said that with the time that has gone by, didn't we all think that she was probably dead. At this point I told him that we hoped she was not, but if she was, her parents deserved to know this so that they could give her a proper burial and find some peace in their lives. The defendant hesitated for a moment and then said that if he were investigating the case he would look in the Diablo Dam near the picnic area known as Cedar Point. I asked him why he would do this and he then said that he didn't want to talk about this anymore until he had a lawyer.

Q. What did you do in response to the statements of the defendant?

A. I immediately contacted the head of the task force. The next morning they had a team of divers at the location mentioned by the defendant. After a few hours they found her body.

Q. What did you do with the bloody handkerchief?

A. I took it to our crime lab and asked them to run DNA tests to check the blood against Nadine's.

Q. And did they do this?

A. Yes.

Q. What did they report to you?

(continued)

A. They reported that Nadine's DNA matched the DNA of the blood on the handkerchief.

Q. How long did it take for you to receive these test results?

A. I think it was a few weeks.

Q. And where was the accused during this time?

A. Well, he had been arrested for the sale of drugs and was in jail on that charge.

ROPER CASE FILE *Memorandum*

TO: Research Attorneys
FROM: Terry Mason, Attorney
DATE: June 30, 20XX
RE: Roper v. City of San Jose

I need your immediate assistance. I am in the middle of trial in the Roper matter and just completed presenting my evidence in support of our claim for damages against the city based on the negligence of the police department. At the end of my case the defendant made a motion claiming that we did not present evidence to support our claim of negligence. This motion will be granted and our case will be dismissed if the judge finds that no evidence supports the necessary elements of our cause of action or if an affirmative defense exists. The judge will base his decision on the evidence we presented. The relevant parts of the transcript are attached. The judge has given us a few days to submit a memorandum of points and authorities in opposition to a motion for nonsuit, the title of the document you are writing. (The defendant will simultaneously be submitting a memorandum of points and authorities in support of the motion.)

Please research the issues raised by the motion and prepare a memorandum in opposition to the motion. The memorandum should contain:

- Caption page with attorney information and document title
- Introduction
- Statement of Facts
- Questions Presented
- Argument, including point headings
- Conclusion
- Date and counsel's student identification number on last page

Thanks!

SUPERIOR COURT FOR SANTA CLARA COUNTY STATE OF CALIFORNIA
Charlotte Roper,
Plaintiff,

vs.

CITY OF SAN JOSE,
Defendant

Case No.: 2010CV-1245

TRIAL TRANSCRIPT

Day 4 June 30, 20XX

Direct Examination of Charlotte Roper by Attorney Mason

Question: Would you please state your name and address for the record?
Answer: Charlotte Roper, 4987 Applewood Court, San Jose.
Question: What kind of residence is this?
Answer: It's a single family home in a residential area.
Question: How long have you lived at that address?
Answer: About 4 years.
Question: So you were living there on January 2, 20XX?
Answer: Yes.
Question: On January 2, 20XX, did anything unusual occur at your residence?
Answer: Yes. I had gone out shopping in the early afternoon and when I returned I found that someone had broken into my house.
Question: And how could you tell that someone had broken in?
Answer: Well, when I walked in I noticed that the place was a mess. Lamps were overturned, pillows were on the floor. Then I looked in the bedroom and found clothes all over the place. Dresser drawers were open. It was a mess. But the really scary part was when I went into the kitchen and saw several knives laid out on the table. I always keep the knives in a drawer.
Question: Was anything missing?
Answer: No.
Question: What did you do after you looked in the kitchen?
Answer: I called the police.
Question: Was this San Jose Police Department?
Answer: Yes.
Question: And what did they say or do?
Answer: They sent out an officer—Officer Benjamin Bright.
Question: And when did he arrive at your apartment?
Answer: About 45 minutes after I called.

(continued)

Question:	What did you do during that time?
Answer:	I was extremely upset so I called a neighbor, Angela Marino, who lives just a few doors away. She came right over and stayed with me until the officer arrived.
Question:	And what did you two do?
Answer:	Well we didn't do much because I didn't want to touch anything. We just sat on the sofa and waited. Angela told me that I should hire some private security for protection. I said I would think about it.
Question:	And what happened when the officer arrived?
Answer:	Not much, he asked me a few questions and said he would make a report. Since nothing was taken, and since I didn't see anyone, he doubted that anything could be done. He did tell me that these break-ins were often the result of young kids who had nothing better to do.
Question:	How did you react to this?
Answer:	I told the officer I didn't think that this was the result of young kids. I explained to him that there was a man who lived in neighborhood who looked and acted really weird. He often hung around and watched me work in the yard. I noticed him slowly walking past my house looking at the windows on three or four occasions. One time I was sure he was looking in a side window from my driveway. I really thought it might be him but Officer Bright told me that even if it was, he was harmless. His exact words were "these guys just like to look, they are harmless enough."
Question:	Do you know the neighbor's name?
Answer:	Yes. It's John Hough.
Question:	Did an occasion arise when you had to call the police again?
Answer:	Yes. On January 11, 20XX, I called the San Jose Police Department again because I saw someone in my backyard. I was sure it was Hough. Officer Bright came by again, this time within five minutes of my call. By the time he arrived, though, there was no one in the backyard. Officer Bright listened patiently, but he told me that these "peeping Tom-types" are "not dangerous" and she should not "lose sleep over this."
Question:	What was your response to this?
Answer:	Well I wasn't convinced. After the first incident, Angela tried to convince me to hire some private security. She even gave me a card for an agency that she had used at work.
Question:	Do you remember the name of this agency?
Answer:	Yes. SecurityPlus. I even called them after the first break-in to discuss the possibility of hiring them. I spoke to the head of the agency, a woman named Laura Holt. Ms. Holt told me she had a great deal of experience and had been a police officer for several years before starting her own company.
Question:	Did you hire her agency?
Answer:	Well, I was still thinking about it when I noticed Hough in my backyard. I mentioned this to Officer Bright when he came out. He was very adamant that this was just a waste of money. He said he knew the agency and they were not very good. He assured me that it was not necessary to hire the agency. He explicitly said that he would personally make sure that nothing happened to me. He

was sure that Hough was harmless, but that to make sure he would run a rap sheet and make sure Hough had no serious offenses. He also said he would pay a visit to Mr. Hough. As he was leaving her house, he was called to an emergency and he did not speak with Mr. Hough that day. The next day the Officer did stop by but Hough did not answer the door. A few days later, on January 15, 20XX, I saw Officer Bright talking to Hough on his front porch. Officer Bright stopped by to talk to me after he talked to Hough. He said Hough denied everything. However, he told me he understood how worried and upset I felt, and so he stopped by every other day to check on me after his shift ended.

Question: Did you experience any other disturbing events?

Answer: Yes. On January 20, 20XX, I began receiving phone calls of a disturbing nature. The caller did not speak. All I could hear was heavy breathing and strange laughter. The calls persisted for five days. Again I called the police and spoke to Officer Bright. He told me that "calls like this are common and usually stop," if I would stop answering the phone. He told me if the calls continued, the police could work with the phone company to check the source of the calls or I could change my phone number. I again mentioned the private security, but Officer Bright seemed insistent that it was just a waste of time.

Question: Can you tell us what happened on January 29, 20XX?

Answer: Yes. This is very difficult. On January 29, 20XX, Hough broke a window and entered my home. I was beaten and stabbed in the thigh and upper arm by my assailant.

Question: Were you able to identify your assailant?

Answer: Yes. It was John Hough.

Question: And have you recovered from your injuries?

Answer: I guess physically I have somewhat recovered. I still have scars on my leg and arm and occasional pain and stiffness in my leg. However, I am still extremely distressed by the whole experience. I am seeing a therapist, but I cannot sleep and I am always nervous. I am thinking about selling my house because the memories are so terrible.

Attorney Mason: I have no further questions.

Judge: Mr. Robertson, do you wish to cross examine?

Attorney Robertson: Just a few questions, your Honor.

Cross-Examination of Charlotte Roper by Attorney Kevin Robertson

Question: Good afternoon, Ms. Robertson. I have just a few questions. Have you lived in San Jose for very long?

Answer: Yes—for almost 35 years.

Question: Then you are familiar with the city?

Answer: Yes.

Question: You know that this is a very large city?

Answer: Yes.

(continued)

Question: And you know that many crimes are committed every day?
Answer: Yes.
Question: And you know that the police department cannot provide you with 24 hour protection?
Answer: Well, of course.
Question: And you understood this when you first called SecurityPlus?
Answer: Yes. That's why I called them.
Question: When you called the security company, did you discuss cost?
Answer: Yes.
Question: I imagine they are pretty expensive, aren't they?
Answer: You have no idea.
Question: I imagine the cost made you think twice about hiring them.
Answer: Yes. I am not a rich woman.
Mr. Robertson: That's all I have. Thank you Ms. Roper.
Judge Praeder: Redirect counsel?
Mr. Mason: Yes, Your Honor.
Question: Ms. Roper, why did you not hire the security company?
Answer: Because Officer Bright told me not to. He assured me that he could keep me safe and I trusted him.
Mr. Mason: Thank you, Ms. Roper. That's all I have.
Judge Praeder: Call your next witness counsel
Mr. Mason: I call Officer Benjamin Bright. Your Honor, I am calling this witness as a hostile witness, pursuant to section 776 of the Evidence Code.
Judge Praeder: I assume there is no objection. You may proceed counselor.

Direct Examination of Officer Benjamin Bright by Attorney Terry Mason

Mr. Mason:
Question: Please state your name and occupation.
Answer: Officer Benjamin Bright. I am an officer with the San Jose Police Department.
Question: Do you recall Charlotte Roper?
Answer: Yes.
Question: When did you first have contact with her?
Answer: May I refer to my notes?
Question: Yes.
Answer: I first saw her on January 2, 20XX.
Question: What was the reason for this contact?
Answer: Ms. Roper had called the police department complaining of a break-in.
Question: And did you respond to this call?
Answer: Yes, I went to her home to take a report.
Question: What did you observe when you arrived at her home?

Answer: The house was a mess. Someone had really trashed it.

Question: What advice did you give Ms. Roper after viewing her residence on January 2, 20XX?

Answer: I suggested that she have all of her locks changed—because she was not sure how the person got into the house. It was possible someone had a key, but it was also possible she left a door or window open or unlocked.

Question: Did you have any other suggestions?

Answer: Yes.

Question: What were those suggestions?

Answer: I suggested that she check all of the window locks, to make sure they still locked properly.

Question: Okay, anything else?

Answer: Yes, I thought she should consider purchasing a stun gun.

Question: How did Ms. Roper react to your suggestion about the gun?

Ans'wer: She said she could not imagine herself owning or using any sort of gun. But she did think she could get additional dead bolts installed.

Question: Was this all of the advice you gave her?

Answer: Well, I explained that most of these types of incidents are random and only occur once.

Question: Did you also tell her that these sorts of intruders were almost always harmless?

Answer: I probably said something like that.

Question: Well, it didn't turn out that way this time did it?

Bright's Counsel: Objection. There is no …

Question: All right. I will move on. Officer Bright, did you tell Ms. Roper that 'guys that do this sort of thing—just like to look—they are pretty harmless?'

Answer: I probably said something like that. Hey look, they usually are harmless.

Question: That has been your experience, Officer Bright?

Answer: Yes.

Question: Did Ms. Roper mention that she thought the intruder might be a neighbor, a John Hough.

Answer: Yes.

Question: Did you follow up and investigate the neighbor?

Answer: No.

Question: Why not?

Answer: Because, I did not have enough to go on.

Question: That is your professional opinion?

Answer: Yes.

Question: How long have you been a police officer?

Answer: Six years.

Question: Isn't it true, officer, that you have access to an individual's rap sheet without having to have probable cause?

(continued)

Answer: Yes.

Question: And isn't it true, Officer, that Megan's Law in California requires registry of all convicted sex offenders?

Answer: Yes.

Question: When did you next meet Charlotte Roper?

Answer: May I consult my notes?

Counsel for Roper: Yes.

Answer: I next met her on January 11, 20XX.

Question: Why did you go to her residence?

Answer: Ms. Roper called 911 to report that someone was in her backyard. Specifically, she identified the person as a neighbor John Hough.

Question: What did your investigation turn up?

Answer: I arrived at the Roper residence about 5 or 6 minutes after her call was received by 911. I walked all around her home. There was no longer anyone there.

Question: Did you believe someone had been there?

Answer: I believe she thought she saw someone.

Question: You saw no evidence that anyone had trespassed into the backyard.

Answer: No, but the area where Ms. Roper thought she saw someone is on a concrete patio, so there would not be footprints or anything. Nothing appeared to be disturbed.

Question: Did you tell Ms. Roper that these "peeping Tom-types are not dangerous and she should not lose sleep over this."

Answer: Yes, I was trying to help her calm down. And it is true, these guys are usually harmless.

Question: Why did you feel that she needed to calm down?

Answer: Well, she was clearly upset about this and the earlier break in. Now, there was nothing specific to connect the two events. And no one but Ms. Roper saw anyone in the backyard. I thought her imagination might be getting the best of her, because of the earlier break in.

Question: Do you recall Ms. Roper mentioning that she was thinking of hiring a security company?

Answer: I have a vague recollection of this.

Question: Do you have a vague recollection of what you told her?

Mr. Robertson: Objection, Your Honor. There is no need for this sarcasm.

Mr. Mason: Sorry, Your Honor. I will rephrase the question. Do you recall what you told her?

Answer: I think I told her that it would probably be very expensive and a waste of time. Unless she were to have around the clock protection, the security company wouldn't do her any good. I hated to see her taken advantage of.

Question: Did Ms. Roper show you a business card from Security Plus?

Answer: Yes.

Question: You were familiar with this agency, weren't you officer?

Answer: Yes.

Question: Isn't it true that you used to work with Laura Holt when she was with San Jose P.D.?

Answer: Yes.

Question: And isn't it true that she filed a complaint against you for sexual harassment?

Answer: Yes.

Question: And isn't it true that as a result of this you lost a promotion opportunity and were officially reprimanded.

Answer: Yes, but that's not why I told Ms. Roper not to hire the agency. They could not have done any good.

Question: O.K. officer, let's get back to January 11.

Question: Did you investigate this incident?

Answer: Yes.

Question: What did you do?

Answer: I told Ms. Roper that I would pay a visit to her neighbor, Mr. John Hough.

Question: And did you?

Answer: Well, yes, but not that day.

Question: Why not?

Answer: Because as I was leaving the Roper residence I got an emergency call and had to answer that call immediately. But, I did go by the Hough residence the next day.

Question: Did you speak with Mr. Hough at that time?

Answer: No, because he was not home.

Question: Did you follow up?

Answer: On January 12, 20XX, I did stop by his residence. But he was not home, or he did not answer the door. I left my card with a note to call me in his mailbox.

Question: Did he call you?

Answer: No.

Question: When is the next time you say Ms. Roper?

Answer: I stopped by her home on January 13, 20XX.

Question: Did she call you or 911?

Answer: No.

Question: Then, why did you go to her home?

Answer: I just wanted to check on her and let her know the Police care about her. I thought it would make her feel better.

Question: And did it, did it make her feel better?

Answer: Yes, I think so. She seemed more at ease when I left.

Question: What did you do while you were there?

Answer: I checked her doors and windows and walked around the perimeter of the home. I did not see anything amiss.

Question: When is the next time you returned to the Roper residence?

Answer: I stopped by two days later.

Question: Why?

(continued)

Answer:	I was trying to reassure her that we were there for her. I stopped by every other day on my way home from work, after my shift ended.
Question:	When was the last time you stopped by the Roper residence?
Answer:	January 28, 20XX.
Question:	Were you still in uniform when you stopped by?
Answer:	Yes.
Question:	Were you in a marked car?
Answer:	No.
Question:	Okay, lets go back to Hough. Did you speak with him?
Answer:	Yes.
Question:	Tell me about that conversation.
Answer:	I went to his home on January 15, 20XX. I asked him about his whereabouts on January 2nd and 11th.
Question:	What did he say?
Answer:	He said he was probably home alone during the timeframes I mentioned.
Question:	Did you believe him?
Counsel Bright:	Objection.
Question:	I will move on. Did Mr. Hough offer any other information?
Answer:	He said whoever thought she saw him was probably just some paranoid middle aged woman.
Question:	Would you describe Charlotte Roper as a paranoid, middle aged woman?
Answer:	I don't know about "paranoid" but she is middle aged.
Question:	Did Mr. Hough's reference to a 'paranoid middle aged woman' concern you?
Answer:	Not at that time.
Question:	After this incident did you run any sort of background check on Mr. Hough?
Answer:	No.
Question:	Why not?
Answer:	I just did not see that it was necessary.
Question:	Did Ms. Roper tell you about the heavy breathing phone calls?
Answer:	Yes.
Question:	Did you have any advice for her?
Answer:	I told her to alert the phone company and have them work with the San Jose Police Department to have the caller tracked.
Question:	Did that happen?
Answer:	I don't think so.
Question:	Did you see Ms. Roper on January 28, 20XX?
Answer:	Yes.
Question:	Under what circumstances?

Answer:	She had been attacked and managed to get away from her assailant and call the police. I was one of the officer's who responded.
Question:	Was she able to tell you who did it?
Answer:	Yes.
Question:	And it was John Hough, wasn't it?
Answer:	Yes.
Question:	And did you run a background check at this point?
Answer:	Yes.
Question:	And what did it show?
Answer:	Mr. Hough was a convicted sex offender.
Question:	And just when was he convicted?
Answer:	Which time?
Question:	All the times.
Answer:	He was first convicted in 2000 and then again in 2004.
Question:	Was he required to register as a sex offender?
Answer:	Yes.
Question:	And to his knowledge was he registered in January of 20XX?
Answer:	Yes.
Mr. Mason:	No further questions.
Judge Praeder:	Do you have any other witnesses, counselor?
Mr. Mason:	No, Your Honor.
Judge Praeder:	Mr. Robertson you may call your first witness.
Mr. Robertson:	Before doing that, Your Honor, I have a motion to make.
Judge Praeder:	Well, in that case I guess we better excuse the jury.
	Ladies and gentlemen the lawyers and I have some matters to take up that will not require your presence. You are therefore excused. It's almost lunch time, so why don't you come back at 2 P.M.
	All right, counselor, let's hear your motion.
Mr. Robertson:	Your Honor, I am asking the court to dismiss this case. I do not believe that the plaintiff has produced any evidence to support her claim for negligence by the police department.
Judge Praeder:	Counselors, I am not going to rule on this motion until I receive Memoranda of Points and Authorities from each of you. I will give each of you until Monday morning to submit a memorandum. Mr. Robertson, I assume that you are challenging whether the police department has any duty to Ms. Roper based on a failure to investigate, so as to the negligence issue, concentrate on this.

BAYLOR CASE FILE *Memo to Research Associate*

FROM: Assistant U.S. Attorney
TO: Research Associate
RE: Potential Criminal Complaint (U.S. v. Baylor)
DATE: January 25

I have recently received a file from the F.B.I. involving the commission of a credit card/access card fraud and need you to research some questions and prepare a memo. Very briefly, the case involves a young man who used ATM and credit cards belonging to his deceased mother. Unfortunately, this individual appears to have fled the country and prosecution against him at this time is unlikely. However, the investigation into this matter shows that the young man's girl friend (Melyssa Baylor) willingly accepted and kept property acquired with the credit card and assisted her boyfriend in evading arrest. I am not filing charges for receiving stolen property because I cannot establish that she knew the ring was stolen when she first accepted it. However, I would like to file charges against her for being an accessory after the fact. I am attaching a copy of an application for a search warrant in which the investigating F.B.I. agent details the facts of this case and his justification for searching the Baylor residence. I am also attaching a copy of the search warrant and the return of the warrant. The return of the warrant lists the items that were found during the search of the Baylor residence.

Please review these documents and review the federal statutes dealing with accessory after the fact and credit card fraud. Do some preliminary research regarding our charging Ms. Baylor with being an accessory after the fact. There should be ample case law related to this issue, but it would be a good idea to get an overview of this offense by checking some sources such as *Am. Jur.* or *A.L.R.* (The federal jury instructions might also provide some help.) There may be many issues in this case. We will need to prove the elements of this offense as listed in the code. One of those elements requires that we prove that the underlying felony also occurred. At this point I would like you to concentrate on the following questions:

1. Can we meet the requirement of the accessory statute requiring that the accused had knowledge that someone had committed a federal offense?
2. Does it matter that we cannot find Baylor's boyfriend to arrest and prosecute him for the underlying felony?
3. Can we support the element of the underlying felony requiring that the property obtained by fraud be valued at $1,000 or more?

I have scheduled a tentative meeting time on February 3 for us to discuss your preliminary findings. Until then, limit your research to the above questions. If you identify any other potential problems make a note of them, but do not spend time researching these. When we meet on February 3 we will discuss the issues. I would expect a memo on February 12.

AO106 (Rev. 7/87) Affidavit for Search Warrant

UNITED STATES DISTRICT COURT

NORTHERN DISTRICT OF CALIFORNIA

In the Matter of the Search of
(Name, address or brief description of person, property or premises to be

The Person of Melyssa Baylor and
The Premises at 786 Hightower Drive, San Jose, California

APPLICATION AND AFFIDAVIT FOR SEARCH WARRANT

Case Number: cr-00897

I, Bryan Jergen being duly sworn depose and say:

I am a(n) Agent of the Federal Bureau of Investigation ___ and have reason to believe
Official Title

that ✓ on the person of or ✓ on the property or premises known as (name, description and/or location)

Melyssa Baylor and 786 Hightower Drive, San Jose, California

in the Northern District of California

there is now concealed a certain person or property, namely (describe the person or property to be seized)

a diamond ring, documentation related to the fraudulent purchase of said ring, documentation showing the location of one Benjamin Creighton

which is (state one or more bases for search and seizure set forth under Rule 41(b) of the Federal Rules of Criminal Procedure)

contraband and evidence of a crime

concerning a violation of Title 18 United States code, Section(s) 1029

The facts to support a finding of Probable Cause are as follows:

Included in the Statement of Probable Cause attached as an addendum hereto and incorporated by reference herein.

Continued on the attached sheet and made a part hereof: ✓ Yes No

Signature of Affiant

Sworn to before me and subscribed in my presence,

November 25, 20xx at San Jose, California
Date City and State

CLARA DARROW, MAGISTRATE
Name and Title of Judicial Officer

Signature of Judicial Officer

Your affiant, Bryan Jergen, has been an agent with the Federal Bureau of Investigation for 11 years. For the past five years I have been assigned to work in the unit investigating white collar crimes. Part of my responsibilities with that unit includes the investigation of credit card fraud. During the past five years I have been involved in the investigation of over 100 cases involving credit card fraud. In approximately 80% of those cases I was the lead investigator.

On November 15, 20XX, I was contacted by Martin Jankovich, an investigator employed by Citibank. I have worked with Investigator Jankovich in more than 15 investigations, including credit card fraud and bank robbery. He has always proved to be a reliable and thorough investigator and has always provided this department with reliable information. On November 15, 20XX, Investigator Jankovich informed me of an investigation he had conducted related to a suspected credit card fraud perpetrated by one Benjamin Creighton. He believes that Benjamin Creighton used the ATM card and Citibank Mastercard belonging to Terry Creighton, his mother, two days after her death. His investigation resulted in the following factual findings.

A review of records of Citibank showed that Terry Creighton maintained a checking account with Citibank as well as having a Citibank Mastercard. Terry Creighton was issued an ATM card for use with the checking account. Both the checking account and the credit card were in Terry Creighton's name alone. No one else was authorized to access the account or use the credit card. On July 26, 20XX, the ATM card was used to withdraw the sum of $758 from the checking account, bringing its balance to zero. In addition on the same date, the credit card was used to purchase an item of jewelry at Mario's Jewelers. The item price was $600 plus tax for a total of $648.00. Between August 2, 20XX and August 5, 20XX, three checks were submitted to Citibank drawn against the checking account owned by Terry Creighton. The checks were signed by Ms. Creighton and dated July 20, 20XX. Although the checking account had no funds at the time the checks were presented for payment, the checks were paid pursuant to the "overdraft protection" covering Ms. Creighton's account. Regular credit card billing statements were sent to Ms. Creighton in August, September, and October of 20XX. No payment was received. Statements showing the balance owed on the overdraft protection were also sent during these months. No payment was received.

Employees of Citibank attempted to personally contact Ms. Creighton regarding the overdue accounts. In the course of such attempts, employees telephoned Ms. Creighton at numbers provided to Citibank by Creighton. These telephone numbers included both a home telephone and work telephone number. The home telephone number was disconnected. Contact was made with individuals at the work telephone number on or about November 2, 20XX, Citibank was advised that Ms. Creighton had died suddenly on July 24, 20XX. Because of the usage of both the ATM card and credit card after July 24, 20XX, the matter was referred to Martin Jankovich, a bank investigator. Investigator Jankovich provided me with copies of business records from Citibank verifying the above information and I personally verified the contents of these records.

Investigator Jankovich stated as soon as the matter was referred to him on November 2, 20XX, he again contacted Ms. Creighton's employer and spoke with Ellen Rivera, an employee believed to be a close friend of Terry Creighton. Ms. Rivera stated that Terry Creighton was divorced and lived with her 24-year-old son, Benjamin, in a rented home. Benjamin was the only known relative of Ms. Creighton. Ms. Creighton often complained about her son, who was unemployed and often in minor trouble with the law. Ms. Rivera did not know the specifics of his legal troubles. Ms. Rivera was able to provide Investigator Jankovich with a cellular phone number for Benjamin Creighton. She also told Investigator Jankovich that Ms. Creighton often spoke about a new girlfriend of her son. She had hoped that the girlfriend would "straighten out" her son. Ms. Creighton had mentioned that the young woman and her son had talked about marriage. The girlfriend's name was Melyssa Baylor. Ms. Rivera was also able to provide Investigator Jankovich with a photograph of Benjamin Creighton that Ms. Creighton had kept on her desk.

On or about November 5, 20XX, Investigator Jankovich contacted the owner of Mario's Jewelers regarding the Citibank Mastercard charge. After reviewing his records, Mario Battaglia, the owner of Mario's, recalled the transaction. The transaction involved the purchase of a diamond engagement ring. The purchaser of the ring had been in the store on several prior occasions with a young woman looking at rings. Mr. Battaglia described the purchaser as having physical characteristics similar to that of Benjamin Creighton. At this point, Investigator Jankovich showed Battaglia the photograph of Benjamin Creighton provided by Ellen Rivera and Battaglia positively identified him as the purchaser of the ring. Battaglia also stated that he sold the ring for $600 because he was closing his business. He gave the purchaser a written appraisal stating that the value of the ring was $1200. Prior to the sale, the ring was offered at $1050.00.

Investigator Jankovich then managed to locate contact information for Melyssa Baylor. On November 10, 20XX, he had a telephone conversation with her during which he inquired about the whereabouts of Benjamin Creighton. He also asked about the engagement ring. Ms. Baylor stated that Benjamin Creighton had stayed with her from August 15, 20XX, through October 30, 20XX, but that he had left on October 30, 20XX, and she had not heard from him since then. She denied any knowledge concerning the ring. She also denied that she had ever been in a jewelry store with Creighton looking at rings. After this conversation, Investigator Jankovich approached various neighbors of Ms. Baylor. One neighbor, Mildred Delmonico, told Investigator Jankovich that within the last week she had seen Melyssa wearing a diamond engagement ring.

At this point, Investigator Jankovich contacted the F.B.I. and the case was referred to this affiant. I obtained the California driver's license for Benjamin Creighton and compared the picture on the driver's license with the photo obtained from Ellen Rivera. The pictures appeared to be of the same individual. On November 17, 20XX, I contacted Ellen Rivera, Mario Battaglia and Mildred Delmonico. They all confirmed the facts related to me by Investigator Jankovich. Mario Battaglia provided a further description of the ring. It was a round solitaire of approximately .4 carats, set in white gold.

Also on November 17, 20XX, I contacted Melyssa Baylor. After I identified myself as an agent of the F.B.I., she refused to have any discussion with me. For the past 17 months Melyssa Baylor has lived at 786 Hightower Dr., San Jose, California.

Based on the foregoing and upon my experience, I believe that the diamond ring purchased by fraudulent use of a credit card is located at the premises at 786 Hightower Dr., San Jose, California. Because of its value, it is not likely that the parties have disposed of the ring. It is my opinion based on my experience that other indicia of the ring is also located on the premises including the appraisal and photographs. It is also my belief, based on my experience, that letters or other documentation indicating the present location of Benjamin Creighton is likely to be found on the premises.

AO 93 (Rev. 5/85) Search Warrant

United States District Court

FOR THE NORTHERN DISTRICT OF CALIFORNIA

In the Matter of the Search of
(Name, address or brief description of the person or property to be searched))

The Person of Melyssa Baylor
The Premises at 786 Hightower Drive, San Jose, California

SEARCH WARRANT

CASE NUMBER: cr-00897

TO: Agent Bryan Jergen, Federal Bureau of Investigation and any Authorized Officer of the United States

Affidavit(s) having been made before me by Agent Bryan Jergen who has reason to
Affiant

believe that ☑ on the person of or ☑ on the premises know as (name, description and/or location)
Melyssa Baylor and 786 Hightower Drive, San Jose, California

in the Northern District of California there is now concealed a certain person or property, namely (describe the person or property)
a diamond ring, documentation related to the fraudulent purchase of said ring, documentation showing the location of one Benjamin Creighton

I am satisfied that the affidavit(s) and any record testimony establish probable cause to believe that the person or property so described is now concealed on the person or premises above-described and establish grounds for the issuance of this warrant.

YOU ARE HEREBY COMMANDED to search on or before December 5, 20XX
Date
(not to exceed 10 days) the person or place named above for the person or property specified, serving this warrant and making the search (in the daytime--6:00 A.M. to 10:00 P.M.) (at any time in the day or night as I find reasonable cause has been established), and if the person or property be found there to seize same, leaving a copy of this warrant and receipt for the person or property taken, and prepare a written inventory of the person or property seized and promptly return this warrant to CLARA DARROW, Magistrate
U.S. Judge or Magistrate
as required by law.

November 25, 20XX at San Jose, California
Date and Time Issued City and State

CLARA DARROW, MAGISTRATE
Name and Title of Judicial Officer

[signature]
Signature of Judicial Officer

AO 93 (Rev. 2/90) Search Warrant

RETURN

DATE WARRANT RECEIVED	DATE AND TIME WARRANT EXECUTED	COPY OF WARRANT AND RECEIPT FOR ITEMS LEFT WITH
November 27, 20XX	November 27, 20XX, 11:00 a.m.	Melyssa Baylor

INVENTORY MADE IN THE PRESENCE OF

CLARA DARROW, MAGISTRATE

INVENTORY OF PERSON OR PROPERTY TAKEN PURSUANT TO THE WARRANT

1. one diamond ring
2. copy of appraisal of diamond ring signed by Mario Battaglia
3. copies of credit card billing statements from Citibank in the name of Terry Creighton for account number 4987 5789 0009 8987, for the months of September and October.
4. copies of a credit card statement in the name of Melyssa Baylor for an airline ticket on Alaska Air in the amount of $378.00 dated November 5, 20XX

CERTIFICATION

I swear that this inventory is true and detailed account of the person or property taken by me on the warrant.

Subcribed, sworn to, and returned before me this date.

U.S. Judge or Magistrate Date

RAMBEAUX CASE FILE *Case Summary*

BACKGROUND:

Randy Rambeaux, a San Diego city police officer, is facing both civil liability and criminal charges as a result of injuries he caused during a traffic stop. Although he is accused of using excessive force, Rambeaux claims he acted in self-defense and always used an appropriate amount of force. The incident occurred as follows:

Rambeaux, who was not on duty at the time, observed a pickup truck with a defective tail light. He was, however, still in uniform since he had just completed his shift. After observing the truck, Rambeaux pulled up alongside the truck (Rambeaux was operating his own motorcycle), and motioned for the truck to pull over. The pickup pulled over to the side of the road and stopped. At this point there is some disagreement as to what happened. The accounts of the incident have been taken from a police report filed by Rambeaux, depositions of various parties, and statements from witnesses. However, uncontroverted is the fact that the driver of the truck suffered a severe blow to his head, resulting in a serious brain injury from which he has not recovered. One passenger in the truck has also been injured.

The following information was obtained from police reports and depositions of the parties:

POLICE REPORT

On March 21 of last year, San Diego Police Officer Randy Rambeaux stopped a 1989 Ford pickup truck with a camper shell, license, 123 ABC, because of defective brake lights. When he approached the vehicle, Rambeaux saw numerous individuals crowded together in the camper shell. Rambeaux states that he ordered these individuals out of the vehicle. None of the individuals obeyed the officer's request. The request was repeated and still no one obeyed. Believing that the individuals might not understand English, Officer Rambeaux opened the driver's door, placed his hand on the arm of the driver (later identified as Jose Alcosta), and gestured for him to exit the vehicle. Alcosta resisted, and more force was used to remove him from the vehicle. Fearing attack from the other passengers, Rambeaux removed his baton for self-protection. When Alcosta was pulled from the vehicle, he stumbled and fell, injuring himself. After Alcosta fell, suspect #2, Roberto Alcosta, jumped out of the vehicle. He slipped on the street, scraping his arms and legs. It was later determined that all passengers in the vehicle were in this country illegally. Both Alcostas were taken to San Diego County Hospital so that their injuries could be treated. The individuals in the camper shell, who were all under 18 years of age, were taken to county child protective services.

DEPOSITION SUMMARY OF ROBERTO ALCOSTA (TAKEN THROUGH AN INTERPRETER)

Jose Alcosta is a citizen of Mexico who decided to come to the United States. Jose is 19 years old and has worked in construction in Mexico. Roberto is his 17-year-old brother. They lived a life of poverty in Mexico and hoped to find a better life in California. Friends told them that they could find work in California. Neither speaks English.

On the date of the incident, he recalls the following: The Alcosta family came across the border in a Ford pickup truck with a camper shell. At some point in time, police stopped their vehicle. The officer appeared to be saying something to them, but it was in English and they did not understand. Alcosta told the officer in Spanish that he did not understand him. The officer then grabbed Jose Alcosta and dragged him out of the vehicle. He then hit him repeatedly with a baton. Roberto Alcosta attempted to come to the aid of his brother and was grabbed and thrown to the ground by the officer. Jose suffered a severe blow to the head, a broken right arm, and internal injuries requiring the removal of his spleen. He has not recovered from the head injury. Roberto suffered numerous contusions and abrasions, but no broken bones.

DEPOSITION SUMMARY OF ROCK MACMILLAN, CHIEF OF POLICE

Chief MacMillan testified that it is highly unusual for off-duty police to make traffic stops and they are not encouraged to do so. Chief MacMillan also testified that the following is San Diego office policy regarding the use of force: Police officers are allowed to use reasonable force to effect an arrest or defend themselves. This includes the use of their baton or gun where appropriate. In the past year, the department has received twenty-six citizen complaints of excessive force. Fourteen of these complaints concerned arrests of illegal aliens. Of the twenty-six complaints made, the department determined that only two had any merit. In both cases, the officers involved received reprimands.

The police department investigated the Rambeaux matter. Police talked to one witness who told them that Rambeaux ordered the driver and passengers out of the vehicle. Then, without giving them a chance to exit, he reached into the vehicle and pulled the driver out, throwing him on the ground. He drew his baton and struck the driver, saying, "Why don't you guys go back where you came from?"

Other evidence consists of a video showing Rambeaux pulling Jose Alcosta from the car and hitting him with a baton. The video also shows the officer pushing Roberto Alcosta to the ground. There is no sound on the video.

DEPOSITION SUMMARY OF RANDY RAMBEAUX

Officer Rambeaux took the Fifth Amendment when deposed.

In addition to the depositions and police report, other discovery (mostly record production) revealed the following about the officer:

Randy Rambeaux is a ten-year veteran with the police department. He is married and has three children, ages 4, 7, and 13. He graduated from UCLA with a degree in criminal justice. He graduated cum laude. He had a minor in psychology. He has received two commendations for his work as a police officer. One of the commendations revolved around an incident where he went into a burning building and saved a young child. The child was Latino. On two prior occasions complaints have been made against Rambeaux for use of excessive force. One incident involved two African-American teenagers. The other involved Anglo teenagers. These two incidents were investigated by the department, which found that there was insufficient evidence against Rambeaux to take any action. Both incidents occurred five years ago.

Following your instructor's directions, draft a memorandum addressing the following questions:

1. Is Rambeaux criminally responsible for his actions under 18 U.S.C. § 242?
2. Is Rambeaux civilly liable under 42 U.S.C. § 1983?
3. Is the Rambeaux's employer, the city, liable under 42 U.S.C. § 1983?

CASE V. SPEND LESS FOODS MATTER *Selected Case File Documents*

Cort Case filed a complaint for wrongful termination against Spend Less Foods. Subsequently, Spend Less Foods made a motion to dismiss the case. The motion was denied. Following are excerpts from a deposition of Cort Case and from the declaration of Boss Hoggs, a Spend Less Foods employee, filed with the motion to dismiss. Assume that Cort Case claims that the drug tests violated his right to privacy under both a state and federal law. He specifically claims that he had the right to use marijuana for a physical condition.

RESEARCH QUESTION:

Assume that you work for attorney W. J. Bryan, who wants to evaluate the case for possible settlement. Prepare a memorandum of law analyzing Case's position on both the state and federal claim of privacy. Assume that this case occurs in your state.

EXCERPT FROM DEPOSITION OF PLAINTIFF, CORT CASE

Questioning by W. J. Bryan, Esq., attorney for Spend Less Food Stores:

Q. Please state your name and address for the record.

A. Cort Case; 784 Willow St., Centerville.

Q. How long have you lived at that address?

A. I think it's been about 4 years. I can't remember exactly.

Q. What was your previous address?

A. I can't remember.

Q. What is your date of birth?

A. May 4, 1968.

Q. Are you currently employed?

A. No.

Q. Who was your last employer?

A. Spend Less Food Stores.

Q. What was your position with Spend Less?

A. I worked in the warehouse, mostly loading and unloading heavy merchandise.

Q. Were you ever required to operate a forklift?

A. This was not my responsibility, but on one or two occasions I helped out and did this.

Q. Were you operating a forklift on January 29, 20XX?

A. Yes, the regular operator was on a break and my supervisor asked me to load some items on a shelf in the store.

Q. And on January 29, 20XX did the fork lift strike a child while you were driving it?

A. No.

Q. No? You were not involved in an accident on January 29, 20XX?

A. Yes, I was involved in an accident, but the child ran into me. I didn't run into her.

Q. Within 24 hours preceding this accident, had you consumed any alcohol?

A. No.

Q. Within 24 hours preceding this accident had you taken any medication?

A. Only what my physician has prescribed for me.

Q. And what was that?

A. Marijuana—I have frequent back aches from my job and the only thing that ever seemed to help was marijuana.

Q. And where did you acquire this marijuana?

Objection by Mr. Darrow: Objection, irrelevant. Do not answer the question.

Q. O.k. I'll withdraw the question. Mr. Case, did you submit to drug testing following this incident?

A. Yes.

Q. And you are aware that the results showed the presence of marijuana in your system.

A. Yes.

Q. Is there any reason to think that the test results were not accurate?

A. No.

Q. Did you tell the technician who conducted the test that you had a prescription for marijuana?

A. Yes.

Q. Did you have any verification of this?

A. Yes.

Q. What was that?

A. I keep a copy of the prescription.

Q. Did you show that to the lab tech?

A. Yes.

Q. You do realize, however, that possession of marijuana is illegal under federal law? Mr. Darrow: Objection, argumentative and irrelevant. Mr. Case, don't answer the question.

Declaration of Boss Hoggs in Support of Motion to Dismiss

I, Boss Hoggs, declare as follows:

1. I am employed by defendant, Spend Less Food Stores, as a supervising manager, and have been so employed 10 years.
2. In my capacity as manager I have supervised Cort Case, plaintiff in the above entitled action, for a period of 4 years immediately prior to February 15, 20XX.
3. During that period of time, Cort Case worked in the warehouse of Spend Less Foods and was responsible for loading and unloading merchandise. As part of his responsibilities he was occasionally required to drive a small forklift through the store aisles.
4. At the time of his hiring Spend Less Foods did not have any drug testing policy in effect. Two years ago, though, a policy was implemented by the store. The drug policy provided that all employees engaged in dangerous activities could be tested for illegal drugs at any time, without notice. Any employee found to have illegal drugs was subject to immediate termination. However, if any employee could show a valid physician's prescription for any drug, the presence of that drug in his system would remain confidential with the testing laboratory and would not be grounds for any disciplinary proceedings at work.
5. On January 29, 20XX, while operating a forklift within the Spend Less Foods Store, Cort Case hit a small child with the vehicle.
6. Immediately after the incident, I spoke to Cort Case who told me that he did not see the child. At the time I observed that plaintiff Case seemed to demonstrate some signs of intoxication. His speech was slightly slurred and he seemed somewhat incoherent. I reported this to my immediate supervisor and together we agreed that Smith should submit to chemical testing for alcohol and/or drugs.
7. A test was performed at Drug Testing Laboratories and they reported to us that marijuana was present in Mr. Case's system.
8. As a result, Cort Case was terminated on February 15, 20XX.

I declare the foregoing to be true under penalty of perjury.
Executed on April 27, 20XX.

Appendix B

RESEARCH AND WRITING PROBLEMS BASED ON SHORT STATED FACT PATTERNS

PROBLEM 1

People v. Baxter

In a busy shopping mall, Baxter grabs a bag of merchandise from Simpson. Simpson gives chase. In the course of the chase, Simpson has a heart attack and dies. With what crimes, if any, should Baxter be charged?

PROBLEM 2

Flowers v. Mitchells

Peggy Mitchells is an aspiring fiction writer. She responds to a contest in a national magazine, *Sixteen,* and submits a short story. The short story is based on a teenage experience of Peggy revolving around a conflict with another girl, Tiffany Flowers, over a boy. In the short story, which is written in the first person, Peggy describes Tiffany as a "slut." Unfortunately, Peggy did not change Tiffany's name in the story. Tiffany has sued both Peggy and the magazine for libel.

Are Peggy and the magazine liable to Tiffany for damages?

PROBLEM 3

Anystate v. Sutter

Sutter, a hospital, and Anystate, an insurance provider, signed a contract regarding health care services. The contract contained a provision requiring binding arbitration in the event of a dispute. Anystate claims that the contract was void and unenforceable and filed a lawsuit for declaratory relief and for rescission. Sutter filed an answer. Soon after the answer was filed, Anystate petitioned the court to require Sutter to submit to binding-arbitration. Sutter claims that Anystate waived the arbitration provision by (1) claiming that the contract was void and unenforceable and by (2) filing a lawsuit in court.

Is Sutter correct?

1. Assume the contract is governed by state law.
2. Assume the contract is governed by federal law and the Federal Arbitration Act.

PROBLEM 4

Drummond v. Jergins

Drummond, a customer in a bar, gets into a heated discussion with the bartender (Bob) over politics. Bob gets very angry and throws a glass of scotch at Drummond, splashing him in the face with the alcohol. The alcohol causes severe burning of Drummond's eyes. Bob then asks Bouncer Bill to eject Drummond from the bar. Bill grabs Drummond, dislocating Drummond's arm. Drummond sues Joe Jergins, the owner of the bar, for $100,000 for the damage to his eyes and his arm. Bob, the bartender, had worked for Jergins for only two weeks, during which time there were no complaints. Jergins did a background check of Bob before hiring him and found nothing to suggest he had violent tendencies. Is Jergins liable for the injuries claimed by Drummond?

PROBLEM 5

Matter of Estate of Starr

Marjorie Starr had one natural child, a daughter, Evelyn Starr, and one foster child, Anthony Dilman. Anthony became her foster child when he was sixteen years old. Marjorie's daughter Evelyn left home when she turned eighteen and contacted her mother only when she needed money. Anthony, on the other hand, remained at home until he completed college. When Marjorie developed a terminal illness, Anthony moved back home and became her primary caregiver. Marjorie was dependent on Anthony for the last two years of her life. During this time, Evelyn rarely called and never visited.

When Anthony was twenty-seven, Marjorie died. She left no will, but surprisingly left an estate valued in excess of $2 million. Evelyn claims the entire estate as the sole child. Anthony has made a claim contending that there was an equitable adoption. Pretrial discovery indicates the following facts: Marjorie and Anthony had a very close relationship from the time he first came to live with Marjorie. While in high school, Marjorie attended mother–son events with him and always referred to him as *my boy*. She wore a "mother's ring" with the birthstones of both Evelyn and Anthony. However, Anthony was never formally adopted, nor were any attempts made to adopt. Anthony always kept his own name.

Does Anthony have a legitimate claim against the estate?

PROBLEM 6

Owens v. Adams

Adams saw an advertisement on the Internet for the sale of a "wooded real estate lot." This was the only property advertised on this site. The lot was offered at $50,000, and interested parties were asked to e-mail the owner. Adams, who was familiar with the property in question, e-mailed the owner (Owens) as follows.

To: owens@aol.com

Re: Purchase of wooded real estate lot as seen on www.woodedlot.com

I am interested in your lot and hereby offer to purchase the property at $45,000, all cash, with the sale to close in 30 days.

M. Adams

Owens responded as follows:

To: madams@yahoo.com

Re: Offer to purchase lot

I will sell you the land at $47,500.

Owens

Adams replied immediately:

To: owens@aol.com

Re: Offer to purchase lot

Great! We have a deal

☺

Two weeks later, after doing considerable legal research on the Internet, Adams backed out of the deal, claiming that the transaction did not meet the requirements of the statute of frauds.

Is Adams correct?

PROBLEM 7

People v. Barker

While on routine traffic patrol, police officer Matthew Dillon spotted Sonny Barker driving a late model white Mercedes automobile. Barker was well known to the police department and was suspected of being a drug dealer, although he had never been convicted of any drug offenses. Barker appeared to be obeying all traffic laws. Officer Dillon then noted that the vehicle did not have current registration tags and decided to stop the car, hoping that he might just see something related to the drug dealing. After stopping the vehicle, Dillon asked to see Barker's driver's license and the car registration. Barker could not produce either his license or the car's registration. Barker told Dillon that the car belonged to his mother. Dillon checked on Barker's driver's license and the car license. There were no warrants and the car had not been reported as stolen. He then asked Barker if he could search the car. Barker said yes. Dillon looked in the glove box and found the following: Barker's wallet, a little over one ounce of what looked like marijuana, and a piece of paper with the following writing—sbarker@digicom.com ("doobie"). Officer Dillon then reached under the front seat and found a large quantity of marijuana in a clear plastic bag. At this point he arrested Barker.

Later, Officer Dillon, who happens to be a computer fanatic and recognized the writing on the paper as being an Internet e-mail address, accessed the e-mail of S. Barker (*doobie* being the password). Dillon used his own computer to do this. Barker's e-mail contained the following message, "Sold latest shipment of maryjane for a cool million; deposited your share in your mutual fund account at Citibank. Love, Ma."

Based on all of the information here, Sonny was charged with possession for sale.

The following issues have been raised in the criminal case.

1. Was the original stop good?
2. Was the search of the car good?
3. Was the officer's accessing Sonny's e-mail proper?
4. How should the court resolve these issues?

PROBLEM 8

Su v. KILR

KILR, a local radio station, sponsored a "treasure chest" type contest. The station had buried a treasure ($5,000) and periodically gave clues as to its location. The first one to find the treasure won the money. Steven Shriver heard a clue and was sure he knew the location of the money. However, several clues had been given over a period of time and Shriver was fairly certain that other people would also be able to figure out the clues. In order to get to the treasure first, Shriver therefore ignored the posted speed limits and was travelling 40 mph in a 25 mph zone (largely a residential neighborhood). When Shriver was about five blocks from the "treasure site," he noticed a police car behind him signaling him to pull over.

Instead of pulling over, Shriver increased his speed to 50 mph. The police followed. Shriver kept increasing his speed, as did the police car following him. A high-speed chase ensued for about three blocks, at which time Shriver ran a stop sign, colliding with another car and injuring the driver of that car. The injured party, Sally Su, has sued Shriver, KILR Radio Station, and Metro City Police Department for her injuries.

Su is a 35-year-old computer programmer. She is married and has two children. As a result of the accident, she suffered a cervical strain and was unable to work for three weeks following the accident. She did not have her seat belt on at the time of the accident.

Shriver is a nineteen-year-old college student. He was uninsured at the time of the accident.

Analyze the liability of the following parties:

(a) KILR Radio Station
(b) Metro City Police Department

PROBLEM 9

Facts and Law Provided

Susie Speeker is a student at Oliver Wendell Holmes High School, located in South Bay County School District. South Bay County is a small community and has only one high school. Recently Susie Speeker was suspended from school by Principal Pat Strickland for her involvement with drugs. The factual background is as follows.

For several months the high school has had a special program directed at promoting the health of students. One of the topics stressed in this program is the harmful effects of drug use. In May of last year, the community of South Bay sponsored a community-wide health fair held in a city park. Various private and public community entities were invited to set up informational booths at the fair. There was no fee for participating, nor did any of the participants have any voice in the organization or operation of the fair. South Bay High School was invited to have a booth and they agreed to do so. At the booth, volunteers from the school (mostly teachers) agreed to disseminate material on a number of health issues, including the use of drugs.

The school administration and various teachers at Oliver Wendell Holmes High School encouraged students to attend the fair and promised "extra credit" if they attended the fair. Attendance would be verified by students signing an attendance sheet to be kept at the school-sponsored booth.

Susie Speeker attended the fair with her parents and older brother. The Speeker family believes that marijuana should be legalized for compassionate use by those who suffer from different illnesses. Susie's mother is a breast cancer survivor and her experiences led to this belief. At the fair, Susie held a sign which read, "Be compassionate, legalize marijuana for medical purposes." Susie was photographed carrying the sign by another Oliver Wendell Holmes student who worked on the school newspaper. The picture of Susie, with the sign, was published in the school paper. Principal Pat Strickland saw the picture and after a brief meeting with Susie and her parents, suspended Susie from school for ten days pursuant to a school policy that allows suspension for students who "use, advocate or promote the use of any illegal drug at a school function." Susie and her parents appealed the suspension to the South Bay County School District, which upheld the suspension.

As a result of the suspension, Susie claims to have suffered ridicule and harassment from other students and faculty, causing great emotional damage. She also claims that as a result of her suspension, her grades have suffered and this may have a long-term effect of jeopardizing her college choices.

Susie has filed a lawsuit in federal district court claiming a violation of her civil rights under 42 U.S.C. § 1983.

Analyze the following questions:

1. Did the school district have the right to suspend Susie for her action?
2. Assuming that the school district was not justified in its actions, does Susie have a claim under 42 U.S.C. §1983?

In writing the memorandum use the following authorities:

Morse v. Frederick, 541 U.S. 393, 127 S.Ct. 2618, 168 L. Ed. 2d 290 (2007)

Tinker v. Des Moines Independent Community School Dist., 393 U.S. 503, 89 S.Ct. 733, 21 L. Ed. 2d 731 (1969)

U.S. Constitution Amend. 1

42 U.S.C. §1983

The majority opinions from the two cases are included in Appendix H.

Appendix C

LEGAL CITATION

CONTENTS:

I. BASIC INDEX TO THE TWENTIETH EDITION OF *THE BLUEBOOK*

When Citing	Check Bluebook Page	Rule/Table
A.L.R. Annotation	168	Rule 16.7.6
American Jurisprudence (Am. Jur.)	23, 155	Rule 15.8
Books	149–158	Rule 15
Brackets	83–84	Rule 5.2
Briefs	113–115	Rule 10.8.3
States and the District of Columbia	233–306	T.1
Capitalization	91–93	Rule 8
Case History	109–111	Rule 10.7

When Citing	Check Bluebook Page	Rule/Table
Case Names	96–102	Rule 10.2
Constitution, The	118–119	Rule 11
Corpus Juris Secundum (C.J.S.)	155	Rule 15.8
Dictionaries	155	Rule 15.8
Dissenting Opinions	107	Rule 10.6
Federal Judicial and Legislative Materials	233–248	T.1
Federal Rules	130	Rule 12.9.3
Footnotes	72–74	Rule 3.2
Internet Sources	178–189	Rule 18
Introductory Signals	58–60	Rule 1.2
Law Review Articles	159–171	Rule 16
Lexis	186, 134	Rule 18.3, Rule 12.10
Looseleaf Services	190–192	Rule 19
Model Codes	131–133	Rule 12.9.4 & 12.9.5
Newspapers	163–164	Rule 16.6
Official Reporters	15–18, 102–104, 233–306	B10-17, Rule 10.3, T.1
Pages	67–70	Rule 3.2
Parenthetical Explanation of Authorities	107–108, 128–129	Rule 10.6, 12.7, 12.8,
Pending and Unreported Cases	111–113	Rule 10.8.1
Periodical Abbreviations (Law Reviews)	510–511	T.13
Periodicals	159–171	Rule 16
Pinpoint Citations	23, 72–74, 115–117	B15.2, Rule 3.2, 10.8.3
Quote Marks	82–86	Rule 5
Restatements	132	Rule 12.9.4
Short Citation Forms	78–81	Rule 4
State Cases	248–306	T.1
Statutes	120–134	Rule 12
Treatises	149–155	Rule 15
Uniform Acts	131–133	Rule 12.9.4
United States Supreme Court Cases	94, 233	Rule 10, T.1
Westlaw	186, 134	Rule 18.3, Rule 12.10

II. BASIC CITATION REFERENCE GUIDE

This citation information is taken from *The Bluebook: A Uniform System of Citation* (Harvard 20th ed. 2015).

Learning to cite correctly and consistently is essential. *The Bluebook* is a reference manual. It has more citation rules than you will ever need to learn. However, this tool is indispensable. The "rules" and "conventions" are all here. It takes patience to become familiar with *The Bluebook*. Take the time to look through this tool before you need to find answers quickly. The index to *The Bluebook* is excellent: Use it.

Note: Many states have a legal style or citation manual. Check with your instructor for your state guidelines.

A. CASE LAW

***The Bluebook*, Rule 10**

United States Supreme Court Case Law

Most case citations follow this basic format:

Name	Volume	Reporter	Page	Year
Miranda v. Arizona,	384	U.S.	436	(1966)

Miranda v. Arizona is the name of the case. Case names are underlined or italicized. This makes them easy to see on the page.

The *Miranda* case is located in volume 384 of the *United States Reports*. The *United States Reports* is the official reporter for U.S. Supreme Court cases. It is "official" because it is published by the U.S. government. The proper abbreviation for this reporter is: U.S.

In volume 384, the *Miranda* case is located at page 436. The case was decided in 1966. The year is placed in parentheses.

This information allows anyone looking at the citation to locate the actual decision.

All U.S. Supreme Court cases are located in print form in three separate reporters, published by three different publishers. The full citation for the *Miranda* case is as follows:

Miranda v. Arizona, 384 U.S. 436, 86 S. Ct. 1602, 16 L. Ed. 2d 694 (1966).

86 S. Ct. 1602 and 16 L. Ed. 2d 694 are referred to as *parallel citations*.

A Point to Remember

When you refer to or "cite" a case, be sure to provide your reader with a complete citation. Use the name, volume, reporter, page number, year, and if necessary, the parallel citations.

GO TO: *The Bluebook*, Table 1

State Case Law

State cases are cited much the same as Supreme Court cases. Sometimes, though, states have their own citation rules that provide alternative ways of citing.

For example, in the state of California, either of the following citations is correct for a California case.

Long Beach v. Superior Court, 64 Cal. App. 3d 65, 134 Cal. Rptr. 468 (1976).

or

Long Beach v. Superior Court (1976) 64 Cal. App. 3d 65, 134 Cal. Rptr. 468.

In California and other states, there is an unofficial publisher of state case law. In the citation here, Cal. Rptr. is the abbreviation for the California Reporter, published by West Publishing. 134 Cal. Rptr. 468 is the parallel citation.

Sometimes, you will see references to "regional reporters". The regional reporter abbreviations follow.

Atlantic Reporter	A.2d
North Eastern Reporter	N.E.2d
North Western Reporter	N.W.2d
Pacific Reporter	P.2d
Southern Reporter	So. 2d
South Eastern Reporter	S.E.2d
South Western Reporter	S.W.2d

The 2d following the regional reporter abbreviation indicates that each of these reporters is in the second series.

A Point to Remember

Most legal sources follow the general format of

Title
Volume
Book or Reporter (abbreviated)
Page
Year

When you are looking at an unfamiliar citation, try to identify these elements. This will enable you to understand the various citations you come across in your legal studies.

GO TO: *The Bluebook*, Table 1

B. UNITED STATES CONSTITUTION

***The Bluebook*, Rule 11**

The Fourteenth Amendment to the U.S. Constitution is written as follows:
U.S. Const. amend. XIV.
If you want to indicate a certain section of the Amendment you add: § 1
The full citation looks like this:
U.S. Const. amend. XIV, § 1.

C. UNITED STATES CODE (STATUTES)

***The Bluebook*, Rule 12**

The *United States Code* is cited in the following manner:

Number of Code Title	Code	Section Cited	Date
28	U.S.C.	§ 1291	(XXXX)

The proper cite is 28 U.S.C. § 1291 (XXXX).

***The Bluebook*, Rule 12.5**

The Bluebook on pages 126–127 provides guidance on citations to statutes found on electronic media and online sources.

D. FEDERAL RULES OF COURT

***The Bluebook*, Rule 12.9.3**

Fed. R. Civ. p. 26
Fed. R. Crim. p. 6
Fed. R. Evid. 301

E. STATE CODES (STATUTES)

***The Bluebook*, Table 1**—this table displays the proper format for state rules of court also

A statute citation must show

1. the numbers of the statutory topic,
2. the abbreviated name of the publication,
3. the specific statute or section of the statute, and
4. the year of the publication.

Examples

Ariz. Rev. Stat. Ann. § ## (XXXX)	Arizona Revised Statutes Annotated
Cal. Educ. Code § ## (XXXX)	California Education Code
Conn. Gen. Stat. § ## (XXXX)	Connecticut General Statutes
Ind. Code § ## (XXXX)	Indiana Code

F. INTERNET SOURCES, ELECTRONIC MEDIA, AND OTHER NON-PRINT SOURCES

***The Bluebook*, Rule 18**

The Bluebook on pages 164–170 provides guidance on citations to the Internet, electronic media, and other non-print sources.

Note that *The Bluebook* **requires** the citation and use of printed sources when available.

Rule 18.1 Basic Citation Forms [provided for the following]

authenticated or official documents
unaltered scanned copies of print source
documents for which print copy is practically unavailable
electronic version improving reader access to source also available in print
online-only sources
subheadings linked from main page of website
dynamic webpages, such as blogs
online source requiring form, query, or unwieldy URL
online source that preserves original pagination, such as a PDF
commercial electronic databases
electronic storage media
microform collections

films and broadcasts
commercial audio recordings
non-commercial recordings
podcasts

Rule 18.2 The Internet

General Internet Citation Principles - 18.2.1
Direct Citations to Internet Sources - 18.2.2
Parallel Citations to Internet Sources - 18.2.3

Rule 18.3 Commercial Electronic Databases

Rule 18.4 CD-ROM and Other Electronic Storage Media

Rule 18.5 Microform

Microform Collections Reproducing Preexisting Materials Rule 18.5.1
Microform Collections Containing Original materials Rule 18.5.2

Rule 18.6 Films, Broadcasts, & Noncommercial Video Materials
Rule 18.7 Audio Recordings
Commercial Recordings Rule 18.7.1
Noncommercial Recordings Rule 18.7.2
Podcasts and Recordings Available Online Rule 18.7.3

Rule 18.8 Short Citation Forms

G. SECONDARY RESOURCES

***The Bluebook*—Rules 15, 16, 17, and 18**

Books, Periodical Materials, and Other Secondary Sources

Examples of two general legal encyclopedias:

15 Am. Jur. 2d *Civil Rights* § 18 (1983)
23 C.J.S. Contracts § 33 (1977)

H. SHORT CITATION FORMAT

***The Bluebook*, Rule 4**

Legal writing often contains a large number of citations. The "short citation formats" help the reader sort through the citations. This cuts down the amount of repetition for both the writer and the reader.

Probably the most common short citation form is "*Id.*" Use *id.* when citing the immediately preceding legal authority. This tells the reader that the material originated in the same location as the material cited immediately preceding it.

For example:

> The *Ferber* case upheld a prohibition on the distribution and sale of child pornography, as well as its production, because these acts were "intrinsically related" to the sexual abuse of children in two ways. *New York v. Ferber*, 458 U.S. 747, 759 (1982). First as a permanent record of a child's abuse, the continued circulation itself would harm the child who had participated. *See id.* Second, because the traffic in child pornography was an economic motive for its production, the State had an interest in closing the distribution network.
> *Id.* at 760.

In this example of a blocked quote, this alerts the reader that the material in the first sentence is found in the *Ferber* case. Provide the entire citation because this is the first time the case is used. A short format citation follows the second sentence. The "signal" *see* is followed by *id.*, meaning that the writer is asking the reader to look at page 759 in the case (page 759 is listed as the "pinpoint" page in the *Ferber* citation sentence). The *i* in *id.* is lowercase because *id.* is not the first word in the citation sentence. Follow the third sentence with "*Id.* at 760." This tells the reader that this information is located on page 760 of the *Ferber* case.

Short Forms in Court Documents and Legal Memoranda

The Bluebook, The Bluepages—B10.2, B12.2, B15.1

The Bluepages at B10.2, B12.2, and B15.1 offers a good list of short forms for cases, constitutions, statutes and regulations, and books, pamphlets, and other nonperiodic materials. For example, acceptable short form citations for *Ashcroft v. Free Speech Coalition*, 535 U.S. 234, 245 (2002) are the following:

Free Speech Coalition, 535 U.S. at 245.
535 U.S. at 245.

I. PINPOINT CITATIONS

The Bluebook, B10.1.2 (from the Bluepages) and Rule 4

Legal writers use pinpoint citations to direct the reader to the exact page where the information cited to is located. This allows a reader to go directly to the relevant portion of a case, book, article, or periodical. Pinpoint citations also direct readers to specific subdivisions of a document or a statute. These pinpoint citations are widely used by good legal writers.

For example:

Ashcroft v. Free Speech Coalition, 535 U.S. 234, 241 (2002).

This citation includes the pinpoint to page 241 of the *Ashcroft* decision. This citation follows material taken from page 241. All quotes must be followed by a citation that includes a pinpoint cite, unless the material quoted from is not paginated. This is probably the most widely used type of pinpoint citation. Rule 3.2 illustrates how to use pinpoint citations for books, law review articles, the *Congressional Record*, the *United States Code*, and more.

J. QUOTATIONS

The Bluebook, Rule 5

When you quote, you must alert the reader that you are using quoted language. Usually this means you must use quote marks. A citation must follow a quote. This citation lets the reader know where the borrowed material originated. Quotations of 50 words or more are blocked. A blocked quote is single spaced and indented on the left and right margins. No quote marks are used with a blocked quotation.

K. SIGNALS

Signals serve a variety of purposes. Signals indicate support, suggest comparisons, indicate contradictions, or indicate background material. When there is no signal, the cited authority is the source of the quoted material. A common introductory signal is "*See.*" When the signal *see* is placed in front of the cited authority, it means that the cited authority clearly supports the proposition found in the quoted language.

Introductory Signals

***The Bluebook*, Rule 1.2**

The purpose of a signal is to alert the reader to something. Signals are used to show support, suggest a comparison, indicate a contradiction, and indicate background materials. These signals must be italicized. However, when a signal is used as a verb in a sentence, it is not italicized.

Examples of signals:

- ***No signal***—indicates the cited authority (a) directly states the proposition, (b) shows the source of quoted language, or (c) identifies the authority cited in the text.
- ***E.g.,***—is used to show that the cited material states the proposition presented in the sentence; other materials also state the same proposition, but a citation to them is not helpful or is not necessary. This signal is often used in combination with other signals, for example: *See, e.g.,*.
- ***See***—is used instead of "no signal" when the proposition presented is not *exactly* stated by the authority cited but clearly follows from it. This signal alerts the reader that there is an *inferential step* between the proposition and the cited authority.
- ***See Also***—is used to show that the cited authority is additional support for the proposition presented.
- ***Cf.***—is used when the writer needs the reader to understand that the cited authority provides material that is analogous with the main proposition.
- ***Compare***—is used to show that comparison of the authorities offers support for the proposition presented. Parenthetical explanations often follow these authorities.

Examples of signals that indicate a *contradiction:*

- ***Contra***—is used to show that the cited authority *states* the contrary of the proposition.
- ***But see***—is used to show that the cited authority *supports* a position that is contrary to the writer's main position.

Example of a signal that indicates *background material:*

- ***See generally***—is used to show that the cited authority offers background information related to the proposition.

Example of a signal used as a *verb:*

- *See Wisconsin v. Mitchell,* 508 U.S. 476 (1993). (*See* used as a signal.)
- See *Wisconsin v. Mitchell,* 508 U.S. 476 (1993) for an explanation of what made the statute at issue unconstitutionally overbroad. (*See* used as a verb.)

GO TO: *The Bluebook*, Rule 1.2

Information on the order of signals is found in *The Bluebook* at Rule 1.3

L. THE ELLIPSIS (OMISSIONS)

***The Bluebook*, Rule 5.3**

Legal writers often find it useful to use quoted language but may not need all of the sentence or paragraph. Indicate the omission of a word or many words by inserting an ellipsis in place of the omitted word or words. An ellipsis consists of three periods separated by spaces and set off by a space before the first period and after the last period.

For example:

> The "core of the judicial system … relies on early disclosure of all the facts."
> The "core of the judicial system … relies on early disclosure … ."

Never use an ellipsis to begin a quotation. When language at the beginning of a sentence is deleted, capitalize the first letter of the first word used and place it in brackets (unless that word is already capitalized).

For example:

> "[T]he statute imposes special prohibitions on those speakers who express views on the disfavored subject of race, color, creed, religion or gender."

This is a simple way to alert the reader that the word *The* was not the first word in the quoted sentence. The use of brackets indicates that the writer changed only the case of the letter. This same tool (the bracket) is used to change a capital letter to lowercase when the writer needs to incorporate a phrase from the beginning of a quoted sentence into one of the writer's own sentences.

For example:

> It is true that "[t]he ordinance, even as narrowly construed by the State Supreme Court, is facially unconstitutional … ."

In this example, *The* was the first word in the quoted sentence. However, the writer needed to incorporate the quoted sentence into a new sentence. By placing the lowercase *t* in brackets, the writer signals the reader that he or she changed the case of the letter.

Appendix D

RESEARCH STRATEGIES: AN OVERVIEW

CREATE THE VOCABULARY LIST

Every fact pattern provides an initial vocabulary or terminology list. Sort the terms into two lists: one factual and the other legal.

As you review what you know, some terms are easily placed into your vocabulary list. At this point, do not worry too much about which list a certain fact actually belongs on; just pull out the key terminology. Some terms or concepts may seem to be both legal and factual. Do not let that confuse you. Your research will help you separate the legal from the factual.

From personal experience you may want to add terms or phrases. The important thing is that you have a list of words and phrases identified before you even consider going to the law library. If case law research becomes important, other facts will be important when you begin to compare and contrast the facts of your client's case and the facts of the reported decisions your research produces. You now have a list of terms to take to an index.

FORMULATE THE ISSUE

Attempt to articulate the legal issue. Remember, a well-written legal issue contains the cause of action (or legal problem) and the key facts. However, rather than attempting to write a formal issue statement at this early stage of the research, just ask a simple question.

Your initial research will clarify the cause of action. Once the elements of the cause of action are known, you will be better able to determine which of the facts are most important. This initial research also helps you to articulate the issue in a more formal format, that is, a format acceptable to send to the court. For now, keep it simple and remain focused on the research project.

USE THE LEGAL DICTIONARY AND THESAURUS

Once the initial vocabulary list is complete, take a few moments to consult a legal dictionary and a legal thesaurus. These resources expand your research list. That is, you will have a larger list of terms to take to the indexes of the legal research resources.

With this list of terms you are ready to begin work in the indexes. The questions become "Which set of books?" and "Which index?"

CREATE A RESEARCH PLAN BEFORE GOING TO THE LAW LIBRARY

Before going to the law library, sit down and consider where to begin the research. Make a list of books or sets of books you plan to review. Break that list into primary sources and secondary sources.

Most states have a state legal encyclopedia. This can be a good starting place when you know very little about the topic you are researching. Pleading and practice guides provide good examples. These secondary resources provide the researcher with a foundation to perform the research in primary sources. Once the vocabulary list and a list of library resources are prepared, you are ready to begin the initial research.

TAKE YOUR RESEARCH TERMS/ VOCABULARY TO THE INDEXES

Step One

Determine which resource to attack first. Take a moment to look the set over. Notice how much information is on the spine of every volume. Notice that some of the volumes may say "Index" on them. This is a good sign. It means that in addition to a large comprehensive index at the end of the set, there is also a topical index for each topic.

Step Two

Locate the index for the set. The comprehensive index is usually at the end of the set of books. In most instances, the index is a large multivolume set. Sometimes these indexes are called "Descriptive Word Indexes" or "General Index." They are arranged alphabetically. Begin to methodically look up your vocabulary words and phrases. An early understanding of the cause of action provides an overall understanding of the materials you will locate.

EFFECTIVE USE OF THE INDEX VOLUMES

As you look at the index pages, you may locate terms that are not on your initial list, but look interesting. Add them to your list and pursue them.

Legal researchers must be armed with as many vocabulary terms as possible. With this expanded vocabulary list you are ready to begin the actual research in the sources you have chosen.

WHEN TO BEGIN THE RESEARCH IN PRIMARY SOURCES

Although your first inclination may be to begin all research in primary sources, this may not always be the best choice. Remember: Primary sources contain the law, not a discussion or explanation of the law. Primary sources are often annotated, but this information is usually a brief summary of case law, not an explanation or discussion written to educate or inform the reader.

Primary sources are a good place to begin research when you are familiar with the area of law to be researched and you are familiar with the vocabulary involved in the factual situation. In such cases, you may not need to perform foundation research.

Remember to begin with the terms directly produced by the initial fact pattern. However, you may need to expand the list of terms through a dictionary, thesaurus, and various indexes. As the list expands and becomes more complex, your understanding of the terminology may diminish. Good legal researchers work to expand their vocabulary. Take the time to understand all terminology before beginning the research.

With a good foundation of basic vocabulary and a clear legal issue, you are prepared to begin research in the statutes. You will have already used the index to look for terms; while searching for terms, you must begin to make a list of codes that may be applicable to your fact pattern. Methodically, list the code section names and numbers. When the initial list is complete, begin to locate and read the statutes you identified from the index.

In addition to a general index, usually a multivolume set located at the end of the set of books you are researching, there may be an index located at the end of the specific subject within the set of books. For example, if you know your topic is summary judgment motions, and you know that the general information on these motions is found in the civil procedure section of the state code, you could go to the last volume of the civil procedure sections of the state code to find the index to just the civil procedure statutes. This allows the researcher to limit or pinpoint the research. Think of this as a way to filter out other references that may be irrelevant.

WHEN TO BEGIN RESEARCH IN SECONDARY SOURCES

The set you choose to work in reflects how much prior knowledge you bring to the research situation. Legal encyclopedias, *American Law Reports*, and law review articles often provide a great deal of basic information. When a researcher knows very little about the topic, this is a good place to begin to build a research foundation.

Caution: When performing state-specific research, if possible, use your state's legal encyclopedia and try to find articles and *American Law Reports* annotations that include your state. If your issue is federal, you may want to look at the *American Law Reports Federal* edition and search out law review articles that focus on federal issues.

If your topic is somewhat narrow and you must search for case law, consider using the appropriate digest. The digest provides narrow topics listed in alphabetical order. Following each topic are references to specific cases. These references are often referred to as *annotations*.

The specialty sets and pleading and practice sets work well when the researcher is focused and understands the basic vocabulary associated with the topic to be researched.

Make a list of potential resources to be reviewed. Prioritize the list. Start with the set you feel will provide the most efficient path to your answers. Make sure you have thought about what you already know and what you need to know. Remember: Your goal is to locate relevant primary law.

Another approach to locating background information is to locate and read an *American Law Reports* annotation (article). There may even be a specialty set appropriate to your research situation.

As you can see, there are several places to begin your research. With practice, you will develop preferences for certain resources over other, less user-friendly resources. Do not lose sight of the research plan. Create a plan and follow it until you have good reason to believe that the initial plan is not producing reliable results.

TAKE NOTES WHEN WORKING WITH PRINTED MATERIALS

Finding the law is a good starting point. Try not to go too far into the research without slowing down and checking the validity of your research results. In addition, make sure you have the most current information available.

Use *Shepard's* to update and validate your research. *Shepard's* is available in print and on Lexis Advance. Shepardize any case or statute you feel you may rely on. Do not forget that you may Shepardize law review articles and *A.L.R.* annotations.

Westlaw offers a similar service called KeyCite; this is also introduced in Chapter 9. These services are designed to be used in addition to *Shepard's*.

TAKE NOTES WHEN WORKING WITH PRINTED MATERIALS

ORGANIZATION AND ATTENTION TO DETAIL	
Get ready to take notes.	You need pencils, pens, underliners, self-adhesive notes, and paperclips.
Be prepared to take notes.	Get your materials out and ready; be organized at each step of the research process.
Think about the paper you will use.	Loose leaf paper? Bound tablet? Large index cards? Adhesive notes?

Loose leaf paper is easy to shuffle and organize later. It is also easy to misplace. These pages may look a lot like the other notes in your notebooks.

A bound tablet will keep everything in one place but does not provide much flexibility when shuffling becomes necessary. At some point it becomes necessary to organize the notes in a logical order. Remember: Your research results may not proceed in the same order you will eventually write up your memorandum or brief.

Large index cards, sometimes color-coded, prove useful because of their versatility. Many researchers color-code their issues. All research on a specific issue is placed, for example, on blue 5 × 7 cards. On the back of each card, the researcher notes the date the research is performed, the source of the data, and any personal notes. It is easy later to shuffle and organize by color. Sometimes a researcher places each case reviewed on a separate card. The notes on each statute are also noted on separate cards. This makes later organization much easier.

Self-adhesive notes are small, come unstuck, and are easily misplaced. Consider using them only in addition to other resources.

Work toward establishing a personal preference. Consider the nature of your research. If you plan to take a good number of written notes, maybe index cards or loose leaf paper will provide you with the ability to easily organize and rearrange your results. Try several approaches and work toward finding a note-taking process that is comfortable and reliable.

TAKE NOTES AND RECORD RESULTS WHEN WORKING WITH ONLINE OR CD-ROM MATERIALS

Instead of making handwritten notes from the screen during online research, consider printing or downloading the relevant information. Some handwritten notes may be necessary, however: keep in mind that the database in which you are researching may be quite expensive and note taking is time consuming.

When working with CD-ROM products, the time element is not critical. Still, you may want to take minimal notes while you print and download the most useful data. Be sure that you note why you printed the material and how you plan to use it.

ORGANIZATION OF PHOTOCOPIED OR DOWNLOADED MATERIALS

Organization of Materials

In the process of legal research, you will photocopy and download many documents, probably too many. It is critical that you organize these documents *as you acquire them*. Staple pages that belong together; do not paperclip them. On the reverse side of every document copied or printed, note the date you acquired the material, the reason you copied it, the source and the issue(s) it pertains to. Over days or weeks of research, you *will* forget why you copied materials and where they originated. You may also find that some of the documents you copy in the early stages of research may not be as relevant as they seemed at the time you copied them. The date notation may help you place perspective on the data.

Create folders or files. Organize the materials issue by issue or separate the documents into groups of case law and statutes. If you organize from the very beginning, the process of creating the written document is made much easier.

Appendix E

CASE BRIEFING PRACTICE

The following case briefs have one or more sections incomplete. Read the cases and complete the briefs. The majority opinions for the cases are found in Appendix H.

Brendlin v. California, 551 U.S. 249 (2007)

JUDICIAL HISTORY

After petitioner was charged with possession and manufacture of methamphetamine in state court, he made a motion to suppress evidence obtained from a search of his person and a search of the vehicle in which he was a passenger. The motion was denied by the trial court. Petitioner then pled guilty and appealed the ruling on the motion. The California Court of Appeals reversed the denial of the motion. The California Supreme Court reversed the Court of Appeals decision and reinstated the conviction. The U.S. Supreme Court granted certiorari.

FACTS

[To be completed]

ISSUE

When a police officer makes a traffic stop, is a passenger seized within the meaning of the Fourth Amendment?

RULES

Delaware v. Prouse, 440 U.S. 648 (1979) and *Whren v. United States,* 517 U.S. 806 (1996) A traffic stop entails a Fourth Amendment seizure of the driver "even though the purpose of the stop is limited and the resulting detention quite brief."

United States v. Mendenhall, 446 U.S. 544 (1980) Where the actions of police or a suspect are ambiguous, a seizure of the suspect occurs if "in view of all the circumstances surrounding the incident, a reasonable person would have believed he was not free to leave."

Florida v. Bostick, 501 U.S. 429 (1991) and *California v. Hodari D.,* 499 U.S. 621 (1991) When a person voluntarily submits to police, whether a seizure occurs is measured by asking whether a reasonable person would feel free to decline the officer's requests or otherwise terminate the encounter.

ANALYSIS

Although the issue here is one of first impression, dicta in *Prouse* and *Whren* suggest that the Court has long believed that passengers and drivers should be treated

(continued)

the same in determining whether a traffic stop results in a seizure. In these cases the Court clearly ruled that even a brief traffic stop results in a Fourth Amendment seizure of the driver. In reaching this conclusion, the Court described the petitioner driver as an occupant rather than as a driver, suggesting that the ruling should apply to all occupants of the vehicle, not just the driver.

The Court further resolved the issue here by applying the tests stated in *Mendenhall, Bostick* and *Hodari* and asking whether a reasonable person in petitioner Brendlin's position when the car stopped would have believed himself free to terminate the encounter between the police and himself. The Court believed that no reasonable person would believe this. It is not reasonable for passengers to believe that once a car is stopped passengers would be allowed to move about freely.

CONCLUSION

[To be completed]

Elk Grove Unified School District v. Newdow, 542 U.S. 1 (2004)

JUDICIAL HISTORY

Respondent filed a complaint against petitioner in the federal district court on his own behalf and on behalf of his minor daughter, alleging that school recitation of the Pledge of Allegiance violates the First Amendment. The District Court ruled that the Pledge of Allegiance is constitutional and dismissed the complaint. Respondent appealed and the federal appellate court reversed holding that as a parent, respondent had standing to sue and that the school district's policy violated the First Amendment. After the appellate court ruling, the mother of the child filed a petition to intervene or dismiss the complaint. The school district filed a petition for writ of certiorari in the Supreme Court and the Court granted a hearing.

FACTS

Students of Petitioner school district, including Respondent's daughter, recite the Pledge of Allegiance each day in class. Respondent, who is an atheist, objects to this practice because of the words "under God." Respondent is divorced from his daughter's mother. The parents share physical custody of their daughter; however, the mother has sole legal custody.

ISSUES

1. Does a parent who has joint physical custody but no legal custody have standing to sue a school district on behalf of his daughter, or on his own behalf, where the school district's policy requires the recitation of the Pledge of Allegiance?
2. Does a school district's policy requiring recitation of the Pledge of Allegiance violate the First Amendment?

RULES

[To be completed]

ANALYSIS

[To be completed]

CONCLUSION

The Supreme Court reversed the Court of Appeals decision because it found that under California state law a father who has no legal custody does not have standing to sue on behalf of his daughter. The Court also found that Respondent had no standing to sue on his own behalf because the school district's policy did not affect his rights. Because the Court found no standing, it did not address the second issue, the constitutionality of the school district's policy regarding the Pledge of Allegiance.

Marshall v. Marshall, 546 U.S. 1165 (2006)

JUDICIAL HISTORY

[To be completed]

FACTS

Petitioner, Vicki Marshall, aka Anna Nicole Smith, was the surviving spouse of Howard Marshall. Respondent E. Pierce Marshall was the son of decedent J. Howard Marshall. J. Howard Marshall's will left no provision for his surviving spouse, although she claimed that he told her he would provide for her in a "catch all" trust. Petitioner and Respondent were parties to a Texas state court action regarding the validity of the will when petitioner filed an action for bankruptcy in California. Respondent filed a claim for a debt in the bankruptcy court alleging that petitioner had defamed him by saying that he engaged in forgery, fraud and overreaching to gain control of his father's assets. Petitioner counterclaimed that respondent had tortiously interfered with the execution of the will, causing decedent to omit petitioner from the will.

ISSUE

Does a tort action involving the enforceability of a will, which is the subject of a state probate action, fall within the "probate exception" to federal court jurisdiction?

RULES

Ankenbrandt v. Richards, 504 U. S. 689 (1992) The "domestic relations" exception to federal jurisdiction is limited in scope and does not apply to a tort action between parent and child where the court would have jurisdiction based on diversity.

28 U.S.C. §1334 Federal district courts have jurisdiction in bankruptcy cases and related proceedings.

Markham v. Allen, 326 U.S. 490 (1946) Federal courts have jurisdiction to hear lawsuits to determine the rights of creditors, legatees, heirs and other claimants, so long as the federal court does not interfere with the probate proceedings.

ANALYSIS

Among longstanding limitations on federal jurisdiction which would otherwise be proper are the "domestic relations" and "probate" exceptions. These exceptions are not found expressly stated in federal law, but are derived from historical jurisdiction of the English courts. Nothing in Article III of the U.S. Constitution prohibits

(continued)

jurisdiction in such matters. The Court in this case acknowledged that while such exceptions are recognized, the exceptions are limited by case law, in particular, *Ankenbrandt v. Richards*, a 1992 case dealing with the domestic relations exception. In *Ankenbrandt* a lawsuit was filed on behalf of children against their father for damages for sexual abuse. The action was filed in federal court based on diversity. The Supreme Court found that this was an exception to the domestic relations exception which applied only to divorce and support proceedings. The Court analogized the *Marshall* situation to that in *Ankenbrandt* and found that there was no reason to treat the probate exception any differently than the domestic relations one. If a tort action was proper in the domestic relations case, it should also be proper in the probate action.

The Court also reasoned that this result is supported by both 28 U.S.C. § 1334, which gives the federal district courts jurisdiction in bankruptcy cases and related proceedings and the earlier case of *Markham v. Allen*, 326 U.S. 490 (1946). In *Markham*, the Court stated that the probate exception applied only where the claim in bankruptcy does not interfere with the probate proceedings or assume general jurisdiction of the probate or control of the property in the custody of the state court. Although, the Court in *Marshall* found this language somewhat confusing, it did find that in *Marshall*, the actions of the bankruptcy court did not interfere with the probate proceedings and that therefore federal jurisdiction was proper.

CONCLUSION

The Court held that the bankruptcy court did have jurisdiction and reversed and remanded the case to the Ninth Circuit Court of Appeals so that it could review the case on its merits.

San Diego v. Roe, 543 U.S. 77 (2004)

JUDICIAL HISTORY

Roe brought suit in District Court claiming the termination violated his First Amendment right to free speech. District court granted summary judgment in favor of the City of San Diego. The Court of Appeals reversed. The Supreme Court granted a writ of certiorari.

FACTS

Respondent, John Roe, a San Diego police officer, made a sexually explicit video and sold it on the adults-only section of eBay. He also sold an official SDPD police uniform and various other materials. Roe's activity was discovered by his supervisor, a police sergeant, who reported it to police authorities. An investigation by SDPD's internal affairs department concluded with a report that Roe's conduct violated department policies including conduct unbecoming an officer, outside employment, and immoral conduct. Roe was ordered to stop the sales. Roe failed to follow this order and Roe was dismissed from the police force.

ISSUE

[To be completed]

RULES

Connick v. Myers, 461 U.S. 138 (1983) Public employees have a First Amendment right to speak on matters of public concern.

United States v. Treasury Employees, 513 U.S. 454 (1995) (NTEU) Government employees have a First Amendment right to speak or write on their own time on topics unrelated to their employment, absent some governmental justification "far stronger than mere speculation."

Pickering v. Board of Ed. of Township High School Dist. 205, Will Cty., 391 U.S. 563 (1968) The court shall balance an employee's right to engage in speech with the government employer's right to protect its own legitimate interests in performing its mission.

ANALYSIS

The Court noted that the proper test to be applied in this action is based on the *Connick* and *Pickering* cases. *Pickering* adopted a balancing test, requiring the court to evaluate restraints on a public employee's speech with the interests of an employee as a citizen, in commenting upon matters of public concern. But *Pickering* did not hold that any and all statements by a public employee were entitled to balancing. A threshold inquiry is whether the speech touches on a matter of public concern.

Although the boundaries of public concern are not well drawn, cases make it clear that public concern is something that is a subject of legitimate news interest, or touch on matters of public concern such as comments about the President. The Court stated that the court of appeals erred when it concluded that Respondent's actions were a matter of public concern. Historically, First Amendment protections have been applied to off-duty employees whose writings or speech contributed substantially to literature or art. Respondent's activities here did not do this. On the contrary, his use of a uniform and law enforcement references were injurious to his employer. The Court concluded that Roe's expression does not qualify as a matter of public concern under any view of the public concern test. His speech was detrimental to the mission and functions of the employer and of no benefit to the community. As a result he failed the threshold test and the *Pickering* balancing test did not come into play.

CONCLUSION

[To be completed]

Appendix F
SUPPLEMENTAL CASES

Ohio v. Robinette, 519 U.S. 33 (1996)

Cancellier v. Federated Department Stores, 672 F.2d 1312 (9th Cir. 1981)

Richards v. Wisconsin, 520 U.S. 385 (1997)

Marshall v. Marshall, 546 U.S. 1165 (2006)

City of San Diego v. Roe, 543 U.S. 77 (2004)

Elk Grove School District v. Newdow, 542 U.S. 1 (2004)

Brendlin v. California, 551 U.S. 249 (2007)

Tinker v. Des Moines School Dist., 393 U.S. 503 (1969)

Morse v. Frederick, 551 U.S. 393 (2007)

Ohio v. Robinette, 519 U.S. 33 (1996)

OPINION: CHIEF JUSTICE REHNQUIST delivered the opinion of the Court.

We are here presented with the question whether the Fourth Amendment requires that a lawfully seized defendant must be advised that he is "free to go" before his consent to search will be recognized as voluntary. We hold that it does not.

This case arose on a stretch of Interstate 70 north of Dayton, Ohio, where the posted speed limit was 45 miles per hour because of construction. Respondent Robert D. Robinette was clocked at 69 miles per hour as he drove his car along this stretch of road, and was stopped by Deputy Roger Newsome of the Montgomery County Sheriff's office. Newsome asked for and was handed Robinette's driver's license, and he ran a computer check which indicated that Robinette had no previous violations. Newsome then asked Robinette to step out of his car, turned on his mounted video camera, issued a verbal warning to Robinette, and returned his license.

At this point, Newsome asked, "One question before you get gone: Are you carrying any illegal contraband in your car? Any weapon of any kind, drugs, anything like that?" App. To Brief for Respondent 2 [internal quotation marks omitted]. Robinette answered "no" to these questions, after which Deputy Newsome asked if he could search the car. Robinette consented. In the car, Deputy Newsome discovered a small amount of marijuana and, in a film container, a pill which was later determined to be methylenedioxymethamphetamine (MDMA). Robinette was then arrested and charged with knowing possession of a controlled substance, MDMA, in violation of Ohio Rev. Code Ann. § 2925.11(A) (1993).

Before trial, Robinette unsuccessfully sought to suppress this evidence. He then pleaded "no contest," and was found guilty. On appeal, the Ohio court of appeals reversed, ruling that the search resulted from an unlawful detention. The Supreme Court of Ohio, by a divided vote, affirmed. 73 Ohio St. 3d 65, 653 N.E.2d 695 (1995). In its opinion, that court established a bright-line prerequisite for consensual interrogation under these circumstances:

"The right, guaranteed by the federal and Ohio Constitutions, to be secure in one's person and property requires that citizens stopped for traffic offenses be clearly informed by the detaining officer when they are free to go after a valid detention, before an officer attempts to engage in a consensual interrogation. Any attempt at consensual interrogation must be preceded by the phrase 'At this time you legally are free to go' or by words of similar import." *Id.*, at 650–651, 653 N.E. 2d at 696.

We granted certiorari, 516 U.S. ____ (1996), to review this *per se* rule, and we now reverse.

We must first consider whether we have jurisdiction to review the Ohio Supreme Court's decision. Respondent contends that we lack such jurisdiction because the Ohio decision rested upon the Ohio Constitution, in addition to the Federal Constitution. Under *Michigan v. Long*, 463 U.S. 1032 (1983), when "a state court decision fairly appears to rest primarily on federal law, or to be interwoven with the federal law, and when the adequacy and independence of any possible state law ground is not clear from the face of the opinion, we will accept as the most reasonable explanation that the state court decided the case the way it did because it believed that federal law required it to do so." *Id.*, at 1040–1041. Although the opinion below mentions Article I, Section 14 of the Ohio Constitution in passing (a section which reads identically to the Fourth Amendment), the opinion clearly relies on federal law nevertheless. Indeed, the only cases it discusses or even cites are federal cases, except for one state case which itself applies the federal constitution.

Our jurisdiction is not defeated by the fact that these citations appear in the body of the opinion, while, under Ohio law, "the Supreme Court speaks as a court only through the syllabi of its cases." *See Ohio v. Gallagher*, 425 U.S. 257, 259 (1976). When the syllabus, as here, speaks only in general terms of "the federal and Ohio Constitutions," it is permissible for us to turn to the body of the opinion to discern the grounds for decision. *Zacchini v. Scripps-Howard Broadcasting Co.*, 433 U.S. 562, 566 (1977).

Respondent Robinette also contends that we may not reach the question presented in the petition because the Supreme Court of Ohio also held, as set out in the syllabus (1): "When the motivation behind a police officer's continued detention of a person stopped for a traffic violation is not related to the purpose of the original, constitutional stop, and when that continued detention is not based on articulable facts giving rise to a suspicion of some separate illegal activity justifying an extension of the detention, the continued detention constitutes an illegal seizure," 73 Ohio St. 3d at 650, 653 N.E.2d at 696.

In reliance on this ground, the Supreme Court of Ohio held that when Newsome returned to Robinette's car and asked him to get out of the car, after he had determined in his own mind not to give Robinette a ticket, the detention then became unlawful.

Respondent failed to make any such argument in his brief in opposition to certiorari. *See* this Court's Rule 15.2. We believe the issue as to the continuing legality of the detention is a "predicate to an intelligent resolution" of the question presented, and therefore "fairly included therein." This Court's rule 14.1. (a); *Vance v. Terrazas*, 444 U.S. 252, 258–259, n. 5 (1960). The parties have briefed this issue, and we proceed to decide it.

We think that under our recent decision in *Whren v. United States*, 517 U.S. _____ (1996) (decided after the Supreme Court of Ohio decided the present case), the subjective intentions of the officer did not make the continued detention of respondent illegal under the Fourth Amendment. As we made clear in *Whren*, " 'the fact that [an] officer does not have the state of mind which is hypothecated by the reasons which provide the legal justification for the officer's action does not invalidate the action taken as long as the circumstances, viewed objectively, justify that action'... Subjective intentions play no role in ordinary, probable-cause Fourth Amendment analysis." *Id.*, at (slip op. at 6–7) (quoting *Scott v. United States*, 436 U.S. 128, 138 (1978)). And there is no question that, in light of the admitted probable cause to stop Robinette for speeding, Deputy Newsome was objectively justified in asking Robinette to get out of the car, subjective thoughts notwithstanding.*See Pennsylvania v. Mimms*, 434 U.S. 106, 111, n. 6 (1977). ("We hold ... that once a motor vehicle has been lawfully detained for traffic violation, the police officers may order the driver to get out of the vehicle without violating the Fourth Amendment's proscription of unreasonable searches and seizures.")

We now turn to the merits of the question presented. We have long held that the "touchstone of the Fourth Amendment is reasonableness." *Florida v. Jimeno*, 500 U.S.

248, 250 (1991). Reasonableness, in turn is measured in objective terms by examining the totality of the circumstances.

In applying this test we have consistently eschewed bright-line rules, instead emphasizing the fact-specific nature of the reasonableness inquiry. Thus, in *Florida v. Royer*, 460 U.S. 491 (1983), we expressly disavowed any "litmus-paper test" or single "sentence or ... paragraph ... rule," in recognition of the "endless variations in the facts and circumstances" implicating the Fourth Amendment. *Id.*, at 506. Then in *Michigan v. Chesternut*, 486 U.S. 567 (1988), when both parties urged "bright-line rules applicable to all investigatory pursuits," we rejected both proposed rules as contrary to our "traditional contextual approach." *Id.*, at 572–573. And again, in *Florida v. Bostick*, 501 U.S. 429 (1991), when the Florida Supreme Court adopted a per se rule that questioning aboard a bus always constitutes a seizure, we reversed, reiterating that the proper inquiry necessitates a consideration of "all the circumstances surrounding the encounter." *Id.*, at 439.

We have previously rejected a per se rule very similar to that adopted by the Supreme Court of Ohio in determining the validity of a consent to search. In *Schneckloth v. Bustamonte*, 412 U.S. 218 (1973), it was argued that such a consent could not be valid unless the defendant knew that he had a right to refuse the request. We rejected this argument: "While knowledge of the right to refuse consent is one factor to be taken into account, the government need not establish such knowledge as the *sine qua non* of an effective consent." *Id.*, at 227. And just as it "would be thoroughly impractical to impose on the normal consent search the detailed requirements of an effective warning," *Id.*, at 231, so too would it be unrealistic to require police officers to always inform detainees that they are free to go before a consent to search may be deemed voluntary.

The Fourth Amendment test for a valid consent to a search is that the consent be voluntary, and "voluntariness is a question of fact to be determined from all the circumstances," *Id.*, at 248–249. The Supreme Court of Ohio having held otherwise, its judgment is reversed, and the case is remanded for further proceedings not inconsistent with this opinion.

It is so ordered.

CONCUR: JUSTICE GINSBURG, concurring in the judgment.

Robert Robinette's traffic stop for a speeding violation on an interstate highway in Ohio served as a prelude to a search of his automobile for illegal drugs. Robinette's experience was not uncommon in Ohio. As the Ohio Supreme Court related, the sheriff's deputy who detained Robinette for speeding and then asked Robinette for permission to search his vehicle "was on drug interdiction patrol at the time." 73 Ohio St. 3d 650, 651, 653 N.E. 2d 695, 696 (1995). The deputy testified in Robinette's case that he routinely requested permission to search automobiles he stopped for traffic violations. *Ibid.* According to the deputy's testimony in another prosecution, he requested consent to search in 786 traffic stops in 1992, the year of Robinette's arrest. *State v. Retherford*, 93 Ohio App. 3d 586, 594, n. 3, 639 N.E. 2d 498, 503 n. 3, *dism'd*, 69 Ohio St. 3d 1488, 635 N.E. 2d 43 (1994).

From their unique vantage point, Ohio's courts observed that traffic stops in the State were regularly giving way to contraband searches, characterized as consensual, even when officers had no reason to suspect illegal activity. One Ohio appellate court noted: "Hundreds, and perhaps thousands of Ohio citizens are being routinely delayed in their travels and asked to relinquish to uniformed police officers their right to privacy in their automobiles and luggage, sometimes for no better reason than to provide an officer the opportunity to 'practice' his drug interdiction technique." 932 Ohio App. 3d at 594, 639 N.E. 2d, at 503 (footnote omitted).

Against this background, the Ohio Supreme Court determined, and announced in Robinette's case, that the federal and state constitutional rights of Ohio citizens to be secure in their persons and property called for the protection of a clear-cut instruction to the State's police officers: An officer wishing to engage in consensual interrogation of a motorist at the conclusion of a traffic stop must first tell the motorist that he or she is free to go. The Ohio Supreme Court described the need for its first—tell-then-ask rule this way:

"The transition between detention and a consensual exchange can be so seamless that the untrained eye may not notice that it has occurred...."

"Most people believe that they are validly in a police officer's custody as long as the officer continues to interrogate them. The police officer retains the upper hand and the accouterments of authority. That the officer lacks legal license to continue to detain them is unknown to most citizens, and a reasonable person would not feel free to walk away as the officer continues to address him."

"While the legality of consensual encounters between police and citizens should be preserved, we do not believe that this legality should be used by police officers to turn a routine traffic stop into a fishing expedition for unrelated criminal activity. The Fourth Amendment to the federal Constitution and Section 14, Article I of the Ohio Constitution exist to protect citizens against such an unreasonable interference with their liberty." 73 Ohio St. 3d at 654–655, 653 N.E. 2d at 698–699.

Today's opinion reversing the decision of the Ohio Supreme Court does not pass judgment on the wisdom of the first-tell-then-ask rule. This Court's opinion simply clarifies that the Ohio Supreme Court's instruction to police officers in Ohio is not, under this Court's controlling jurisprudent the command of the Federal Constitution. *See ante*, at 5–6. The Ohio Supreme Court invoked both the Federal Constitution and the Ohio Constitution without clearly indicating whether state law, standing alone, independently justified the court's rule. The ambiguity in the Ohio Supreme Court's decision renders this Court's exercise of jurisdiction proper under *Michigan v. Long*, 463 U.S. 1032, 1040–1042 (1983), and this Court's decision on the merits is consistent with the Court's "totality of the circumstances" Fourth Amendment precedents, *see ante*, at 5. I therefore concur in the Court's judgment.

I write separately, however, because it seems to me improbable that the Ohio Supreme Court understood its first-tell-then-ask rule to be the Federal Constitution's mandate for the Nation as a whole. "[A] State is free as a matter of its own law to impose greater restrictions on police activity than those this Court holds to be necessary upon federal constitutional standards." *Oregon v. Haas*, 420 U.S. 714, 719. But ordinarily, when a state high court grounds a rule of criminal procedure in the Federal Constitution, the court thereby signals its view that the Nation's Constitution would require the rule in all 50 States. Given this Court's decisions in consent-to-search cases such as *Schneckloth v. Bustamonte*, 412 U.S. 218 (1973), and *Florida v. Bostick*, 501 U.S. 429 (1991), however, I suspect that the Ohio Supreme Court may not have homed in on the implication ordinarily to be drawn from a state court's reliance on the Federal constitution. In other words, I question whether the Ohio court thought of the strict rule it announced as a rule for the governance of police conduct not only in Miami County, Ohio, but also in Miami, Florida.

The first-tell-then-ask rule seems to be a prophylactic measure not so much extracted from the text of any constitutional provision as crafted by the Ohio Supreme Court to reduce the number of violations of textually guaranteed rights. In *Miranda v. Arizona*, 384 U.S. 436 (1966), this Court announced a similarly motivated rule as a minimal national requirement without suggesting that the text of the Federal Constitution required the precise measures the Court's opinion set forth. *See id.*, at 467 ("The *Miranda* exclusionary rule... sweeps more broadly than the Fifth Amendment itself"). Although all parts of the United States fall within this Court's domain, the Ohio Supreme Court is not similarly situated. That court can declare prophylactic rules governing the conduct of officials in Ohio, but it cannot command the police forces of sister States. The very ease with which the Court today disposes of the federal leg of the Ohio Supreme Court's decision strengthens my impression that the Ohio Supreme Court saw its rule as a measure made for Ohio, designed to reinforce in that State the right of the people to be secure against unreasonable searches and seizures.

The Ohio Supreme Court's syllabus and opinion, however, were ambiguous. Under *Long*, the existence of ambiguity regarding the federal- or state-law basis of a state court decision will trigger this Court's jurisdiction. *Long* governs even when, all things considered, the more plausible reading of the state court's decision may be that the state court did not regard the Federal Constitution alone as a sufficient basis for its ruling. Compare

Arizona v. Evens, 514 U.S. _____ (1995) (slip op., at 4–7), with *id.*, at _____ (slip op., at 10–11) (GINSBURG, J., dissenting).

It is incumbent on a state court, therefore, when it determines that its State's laws call for protection more complete than the Federal constitution demands, to be clear about its ultimate reliance on state law. Similarly, a state court announcing a new legal rule arguably derived from both federal and state law can definitively render state law an adequate and independent ground for its decision by a simple declaration to that effect. A recent Montana Supreme Court opinion on the scope of an individual's privilege against self-incrimination includes such a declaration:

"While we have devoted considerable time to a lengthy discussion of the application of the Fifth Amendment to the United States constitution, it is to be noted that this holding is also based separately and independently on [the defendant's] right to remain silent pursuant to Article II, Section 25 of the Montana Constitution." *State v. Fuller*, _____ Mont. _____ 915 P.2d 809, 816, *cert. denied*, 519 U.S. _____ (1996).

An explanation of this order meets the Court's instruction in *Long* that "if the state court decision indicates clearly and expressly that it is alternatively based on bona fide separate, adequate, and independent grounds, [this Court] will not undertake to review the decision." *Long*, 463 U.S. at 1041.

On remand, the Ohio Supreme Court may choose to clarify that its instructions to law-enforcement officers in Ohio find adequate and independent support in state law, and that in issuing these instructions, the court endeavored to state dispositively only the law applicable in Ohio. *See Evans*, 514 U.S. at _____ (slip op., at 8–12) (GINSBURG, J., dissenting). To avoid misunderstanding, the Ohio Supreme Court must itself speak with the clarity it sought to require of its State's police officers. The efficacy of its endeavor to safeguard the liberties of Ohioans without disarming the State's police can then be tested in the precise way Our Federalism was designed to work. *See e.g., Kaye, State Courts at the Dawn of a New Century: Common Law Courts Reading Statutes and Constitutions*, 70 N.Y.U.L. Rev. 1, 11–18 (1995); Linda, *First Things First: Rediscovering the States' Bills of Rights*, 9 U. Ballet. L. Rev. 379, 392–396 (1980).

Cancellier v. Federated Department Stores, 672 F.2d 1312 (9th Cir. 1981)

Prior History:

Appeal from the United States District Court for the Northern District of California.

Opinion:

The plaintiffs below and appellants here, Philip D. Cancellier, John W. Costello, and Zelma Smith Ritter, are former employees of I. Magnin, the defendant below and cross-appellant here. They won a jury verdict in the district court totaling $1.9 million, plus court-awarded attorneys' fees of $400,000, on their claims under the Age Discrimination in Employment Act (ADEA), 29 U.S.C. §§ 621–634 (1976 & Supp. II 1978) and pendent state claims. They appeal denial of their motions for reinstatement and for an injunction against I. Magnin. I. Magnin cross-appeals the judgment primarily on grounds of improper ADEA instructions, use of a general verdict, and an erroneous award of compensatory and punitive damages for breach of the implied covenant. We affirm.

I. Facts:

Plaintiffs-appellants are former executives of I. Magnin. Cancellier was vice president for stores and operations. Costello was divisional merchandise manager for accessories. Ritter was a buyer of sportswear. In early 1978 they were terminated after having been employed at I. Magnin for twenty-five, seventeen, and eighteen years, respectively. In July 1979 they brought this action in the United States District Court for the Northern District of California alleging that their terminations violated the ADEA. They sought back pay, liquidated damages, reinstatement to their former positions, and an injunction against further age discrimination at I. Magnin. Appellants also raised claims under California law for breach of employment contract and breach of the implied covenant of good faith and fair dealing. Costello sought additional relief claiming fraud in connection with a promise of future employment at I. Magnin.

After a six-week trial the jury returned general verdicts in favor of Cancellier in the amount of $800,000, Costello in the amount of $600,000, and Ritter in the amount of $500,000. The jury also returned verdicts in favor of I. Magnin on Costello's fraud claims. Both sides appeal. For convenience, I. Magnin's cross-appeal is discussed first.

II.

I. Magnin's Cross-Appeal

A. ADEA "Determining Factor" Standard

The ADEA makes it unlawful for an employer to discharge any individual because of such individual's age. 29 U.S.C. § 623(a) (1976). In *Kelly v. American Standard, Inc.*, 640 F.2d 974, 984–85 (9th Cir. 1981), this court set out the requirements for a proper jury instruction on age discrimination. We adopted the "determining factor" test established in *Laugesen v. Anaconda*, 510 F.2d 307, 317 (6th Cir. 1975), and restated as a "but for" test in *Loeb v. Textron*, 600 F.2d 1003, 1019 (1st Cir. 1979). We rejected the argument that plaintiff must prove age was the sole factor in his discharge, and upheld a jury instruction stating that plaintiff has the burden of proving that one of the reasons he was terminated was because of his age, and that he should prevail if this factor "made a difference" in determining whether the plaintiff was retained or discharged.

The essence of a proper jury instruction under *Kelly* is that it requires the jury to focus on the marginal effect of the age factor. Age need not be the sole factor in a discharge or other discriminatory practice. Conversely, it is not enough that age discrimination be present or even that it figure in the decision to fire; age must "make a difference" between termination and retention of the employee in the sense that, but for the presence of age discrimination, the employee would not have been discharged.

Here the district judge instructed the jury that "age must be a determining factor in an employer's personnel policies or practices before violation of the Act occurs." The district judge completely failed to give any guidance as to the meaning of "determining factor" in lawsuits under the ADEA, or to refer to the *Laugesen* and *Loeb* test we adopted in *Kelly v. American Standard, Inc.* This was error. The words "determining factor" are not self-explanatory. In general, fair application of the Act requires the trial judge to formulate precisely what employer conduct the ADEA redresses and what employer conduct it leaves undisturbed. Because the attribute with which the statute is concerned comes to each of us in time, it will inevitably be present in a multitude of employee discharges. It will be a factor in many and a determining factor in some. It is only this last group that can obtain relief under the ADEA, even though, in the broad sense, it aims to benefit the entire aged employment force.

However, a careful reading of the transcript and record convinces us that in this case the instruction does not require reversal. Giving it was harmless error. There is little or no indication in the proceedings that the outcome would have changed if the *Kelly* jury instruction had been given. This case was not decided by a hairsbreadth. There was ample evidence that consideration of age "made a difference" in the termination of Cancellier, Costello, and Ritter. Moreover, it was conceded at oral argument that the challenged instruction was fashioned by the judge from language submitted by I. Magnin. While we are extremely reluctant to affirm verdicts based on jury instructions different from those approved in *Kelly* or their equivalent, we find that on the facts of this case refusing a new trial is consistent with substantial justice. Fed.R.Civ.P. 61; *Ginsburg v. Ginsburg*, 276 F.2d 94, 96 n.2 (9th Cir. 1960); 7 J. Moore & J. Lucas, Moore's Federal Practice P 61.11 & n.1a (2d ed. 1979). The instruction approved in *Kelly* adequately protects against mistaken inferences either that age must be the sole factor in the discharge, or that age may be less than a "but for" cause of the discharge. It is strongly preferred. Here, however, we find the error harmless.

B. Use of General Verdict

I. Magnin contends that the district court committed reversible error by using simple general verdict forms without requiring special interrogatories or any breakdown of the verdict by source of damages. Thus, I. Magnin contends, the possibility of punitive damages not recoverable under the ADEA in this lawsuit or of duplicative damages in the pendent state claims requires a new trial.

Submission of special interrogatories is a matter committed to the discretion of the district judge. Fed.R.Civ.P. 49(b); *Monsma v. Central Mutual Insurance Co.*, 392 F.2d 49 (9th Cir. 1968); 5A J. Moore & J. Lucas, Moore's Federal Practice P 49.04 & n.3 (2d ed. 1981). A jury generally is not required to itemize the components that enter into an award of damages. *Neal v. Saga Shipping Co.*, 407 F.2d 481, 489 (5th Cir.), *cert. denied*, 395 U.S. 986, 89 S. Ct. 2143, 23 L. Ed. 2d 775 (1969), cited in *Frito-Lay, Inc. v. Local 137, International Brotherhood of Teamsters*, 623 F.2d 1354, 1365 (9th Cir. 1980), *cert. denied*, 449 U.S. 1013, 101 S. Ct. 571, 66 L. Ed. 2d 472 (1981), and *cert. denied*, 449 U.S. 1112, 101 S. Ct. 922, 66 L. Ed. 2d 841 (1981) (district court sitting as trier of fact not required to itemize damage award).

When state claims for breach of the implied covenant of good faith and fair dealing are joined to claims of age discrimination under the ADEA, however, review of jury verdicts presents special difficulty to appellate courts. A general verdict may conceal punitive damages which may not be allowed under the ADEA. If the state claims are flawed, the entire verdict may have to be reversed. For these reasons, a separate verdict for each claim and a separate verdict on punitive damages is strongly preferred.

Nevertheless, failure to submit special interrogatories was not an abuse of discretion. The amounts awarded here are consistent with a reasonable award on the ADEA and pendent state claims. We find no reversible error. I. Magnin's claim that it is impossible to tell which plaintiffs prevailed on which of their claims is unpersuasive. The court submitted general verdict forms in favor of the defendant on each claim. The jury returned general verdict forms in favor of I. Magnin on Costello's fraud claim and Costello's negligent misrepresentation claim; clearly, all other claims were resolved in favor of the plaintiffs. The verdict is clear as to which plaintiffs prevailed on which claims.

C. Tort Damages for Breach of the Implied Covenant

Breach of the Implied Covenant

I. Magnin contends that a claim for breach of the implied covenant under the circumstances here is contrary to California law. The contention is without merit.

California law recognizes an implied covenant of good faith and fair dealing in certain contracts that neither party will do anything to deprive the other of the benefit of the contract. *See, e.g., Gruenberg v. Aetna Insurance Co.*, 9 Cal.3d 566, 578, 108 Cal.Rptr. 480, 510 P.2d 1032 (1973) (*en banc*); *Comunale v. Traders & General Insurance Co.*, 50 Cal.2d 654, 658, 328 P.2d 198 (1958). California courts have recently applied the duty created by the implied covenant to the situation where the employee alleges no more than long service and the existence of personnel policies or oral representations showing an implied promise by the employer not to act arbitrarily in dealing with its employees. Such claims sound in both contract and tort and may give rise to emotional distress damages and punitive damages. *Pugh v. See's Candies, Inc.*, 116 Cal.App.3d 311, 171 Cal.Rptr. 917 (1981); *Cleary v. American Air Lines*, 111 Cal.App.3d 443, 168 Cal.Rptr. 722 (1980) (alternative holding). *See Tameny v. Atlantic Richfield Co.*, 27 Cal.3d 167, 179 n.12, 164 Cal.Rptr. 839, 610 P.2d 1330 (1980) (dicta). Cf. Note, Defining Public Policy Torts in At-Will Dismissals, 34 Stan.L.Rev. 153 (1981) (arguing against application of implied covenant to employment context).

Preemption

The ADEA does not preempt the award of tort damages on pendent state claims. *Kelly v. American Standard, Inc.*, 640 F.2d 974, 983 (9th Cir. 1981) (upholding emotional distress damages under state age discrimination statute). The award of tort damages on state claims here did not duplicate ADEA relief. Plaintiffs' ADEA claims were based on age discrimination in firing. Plaintiffs' contract and covenant claims were based on I. Magnin's obligation not to deal arbitrarily or unfairly in terminating plaintiff's employment, an obligation created by I. Magnin's personnel policies and the fact of long service by the employee. Punitive and emotional distress damages for this violation, unavailable under the ADEA, do not duplicate the ADEA award for back pay, lost benefits, and liquidated damages. While the wisdom of allowing open-ended state claims for breach of the implied covenant to coexist with ADEA claims whose financial redress Congress has carefully limited to specific damage elements, *see* 29 U.S.C. § 626(b) (1976); *Kelly v. American Standard, Inc.*, 640 F.2d at 983, is arguable, it is for Congress, not us, to decide whether state common law remedies trench too closely on the federal scheme. Pendent jurisdiction, of course, is a doctrine of discretion. We recognize that in appropriate circumstances dismissal of the state claims without prejudice is proper. *United Mineworkers v. Gibbs*, 383 U.S. 715, 726–27, 86 S. Ct. 1130, 1139, 16 L. Ed. 2d 218 (1966). Such circumstances may exist, for example, where the trial judge finds that the state issues predominate in terms of the comprehensiveness of the remedy sought, or that there is a sufficient likelihood of jury confusion in treating divergent legal theories of relief to justify separating state and federal claims. *Id.*

Punitive Damages

A jury may award punitive damages if it finds by a preponderance of the evidence that defendant was guilty of malice, oppression, or fraud. Cal.Civ.Code § 3294 (West 1981); *Egan v. Mutual of Omaha Insurance Co.*, 24 Cal.3d 809, 819, 169 Cal.Rptr. 691, 620 P.2d 141 (1979). It is a question for the jury whether defendant's conduct was fraudulent, malicious, or oppressive. *Id.* at 821, 169 Cal.Rptr. 691, 620 P.2d 141. The evidence before the jury adequately supported a finding against I. Magnin on the issue of punitive damages.

D. Other Alleged Errors

I. Magnin's additional claims of error are without merit. A thorough review of the record below establishes that the trial was fairly and properly conducted.

III.

Appeal of Cancellier, Costello, and Ritter

A. Reinstatement and Injunction

The ADEA provides that "in any action brought to enforce (the Act) the court shall have jurisdiction to grant such legal or equitable relief as may be appropriate ... including without limitation judgments compelling employment, reinstatement or promotion...." 29 U.S.C. § 626(b) (1976). Reinstatement is not a mandatory remedy; it lies within the discretion of the trial court after careful consideration of the particular facts of the case. *Combes v. Griffin Television, Inc.*, 421 F. Supp. 841, 846 (W.D.Okl.1976). Ordinarily a verdict for plaintiff on the age discrimination claim is res judicata on plaintiff's equitable reinstatement claim. *Cleverly v. Western Electric Co.*, 450 F. Supp. 507, 511 (W.D.Mo.1978), aff'd, 594 F.2d 638 (8th Cir. 1979). However, courts have refused to grant reinstatement where the employer continued a reduction in force for permissible business reasons, *id.*, or where discord and antagonism between the parties made it preferable to fashion relief from other available remedies, *Combes v. Griffin Television, Inc., supra*, at 846–47.

Damages in lieu of reinstatement may be awarded in addition to liquidated damages. However, the value of reinstatement is often speculative. Thus, availability of a substantial liquidated damages award may be a proper consideration in denying additional damages in lieu of reinstatement. *Loeb v. Textron, Inc.*, 600 F.2d 1003, 1021–23 (1st Cir. 1979).

The trial judge in this case denied reinstatement because he found evidence of acrimony in the record and because he was "fully satisfied that (the verdict) has made the plaintiffs whole." Clerk's Record 124. The court noted the testimony of an I. Magnin officer who referred to plaintiff Ritter as a "cancer." I. Magnin's numerous attacks during the trial on plaintiffs' abilities support the trial judge's conclusion that plaintiffs and I. Magnin could no longer "co-exist in a business relationship that would be productive to the consumer, community or to the business itself." Clerk's Record 125. By virtue of his position in conducting the trial, the judge was peculiarly well-situated to observe the demeanor of plaintiffs and defendants in making this determination. Moreover, in view of the substantial verdict the judge did not abuse his discretion in finding that it had made the plaintiffs whole.

Like the reinstatement remedy, injunctive relief is available under the ADEA when appropriate. The trial judge found that the $2.3 million judgment against I. Magnin, including attorneys' fees, was sufficient to discourage I. Magnin from practicing age discrimination in the future. This finding was not an abuse of discretion.

B. Attorneys' Fees on Appeal

A grant of fees on appeal is within the discretion of the appellate court. *Kelly v. American Standard, Inc.*, 640 F.2d 974, 986 (9th Cir. 1981). Although plaintiffs did not prevail on their reinstatement and injunction claims, an award of fees on appeal in some amount is appropriate to reflect successful defense of the verdict below. *See id.; Cleverly v. Western Electric Co.*, 594 F.2d 638, 642 (8th Cir. 1979) (fees awarded to plaintiff denied reinstatement). We remand to the district court for a determination of the proper amount.

IV.

Conclusion

While the instructions approved in *Kelly v. American Standard, Inc., supra*, and separate verdict forms for each claim, as well as a separate verdict form for punitive damages, are preferred, the trial judge did not commit reversible error in instructing the jury on "determining factor" under the ADEA, in using a general verdict, or in allowing tort damages on pendent state claims. Nor was denial of plaintiffs' motions for reinstatement and for injunctive relief against continuing age discrimination at I. Magnin an abuse of discretion. Plaintiffs are entitled to reasonable attorneys' fees in light of the outcome on appeal. The judgment of the district court is affirmed.

AFFIRMED.

Richards v. Wisconsin,
520 U.S. 385 (1997)

STEVENS, J., delivered the opinion for a unanimous Court.

In *Wilson v. Arkansas*, 514 U.S. 927, 131 L. Ed. 2d 976, 115 S. Ct. 1914 (1995), we held that the Fourth Amendment incorporates the common law requirement that police officers entering a dwelling must knock on the door and announce their identity and purpose before attempting forcible entry. At the same time, we recognized that the "flexible requirement of reasonableness should not be read to mandate a rigid rule of announcement that ignores countervailing law enforcement interests," *id.* at 934, and left "to the lower courts the task of determining the circumstances under which an unannounced entry is reasonable under the Fourth Amendment." *Id.* 936.

In this case, the Wisconsin Supreme Court concluded that police officers are never required to knock and announce their presence when executing a search warrant in a felony drug investigation. In so doing, it reaffirmed a pre-*Wilson* holding and concluded that *Wilson* did not preclude this *per se* rule. We disagree with the court's conclusion that the Fourth Amendment permits a blanket exception to the knock-and-announce requirement for this entire category of criminal activity. But because the evidence presented to support the officers' actions in this case establishes that the decision not to knock and announce was a reasonable one under the circumstances, we affirm the judgment of the Wisconsin court.

I.

On December 31, 1991, police officers in Madison, Wisconsin obtained a warrant to search Steiney Richards' hotel room for drugs and related paraphernalia. The search warrant was the culmination of an investigation that had uncovered substantial evidence that Richards was one of several individuals dealing drugs out of hotel rooms in Madison. The police requested a warrant that would have given advance authorization for a "no-knock" entry into the hotel room, but the magistrate explicitly deleted those portions of the warrant.

The officers arrived at the hotel room at 3:40 A.M. Officer Pharo, dressed as a maintenance man, led the team. With him were several plainclothes officers and at least one man in uniform. Officer Pharo knocked on Richards' door and, responding to the query from inside the room, stated that he was a maintenance man. With the chain still on the door, Richards cracked it open. Although there is some dispute as to what occurred next, Richards acknowledges that when he opened the door he saw the man in uniform standing behind Officer Pharo. He quickly slammed the door closed and, after waiting two or three seconds, the officers began kicking and ramming the door to gain entry to the locked room. At trial, the officers testified that they identified themselves as police while they were kicking the door in. When they finally did break into the room, the officers caught Richards trying to escape through the window. They also found cash and cocaine hidden in plastic bags above the bathroom ceiling tiles.

Richards sought to have the evidence from his hotel room suppressed on the ground that the officers had failed to knock and announce their presence prior to forcing entry into the room. The trial court denied the motion, concluding that the officers could gather from Richards' strange behavior when they first sought entry that he knew they were police officers and that he might try to destroy evidence or to escape. *Id.* at 54. The judge emphasized that the easily disposable nature of the drugs the police were searching for further justified their decision to identify themselves as they crossed the threshold instead of announcing their presence before seeking entry. *Id.* at 55. Richards appealed the decision to the Wisconsin Supreme Court and that court affirmed. 201 Wis. 2d 845, 549 N.W.2d 218 (1996).

The Wisconsin Supreme Court did not delve into the events underlying Richards' arrest in any detail, but accepted the following facts: "On December 31, 1991, police executed a search warrant for the motel room of the defendant seeking evidence of the felonious crime of Possession with Intent to Deliver a Controlled Substance in violation of Wis. Stat. Section 161.41 (lm) (1991–92). They did not knock and announce prior to their entry. Drugs were seized." *Id.* at 849, 549 N.W.2d at 220.

Assuming these facts, the court proceeded to consider whether our decision in *Wilson* required the court to abandon its decision in *State v. Stevens*, 181 Wis. 2d 410, 511 N.W.2d 591 (1994), *cert. denied*, 515 U.S. 1102 (1995), which held that "when the police have a search warrant, supported by probable cause, to search a residence for evidence of delivery of drugs or evidence of possession with intent to deliver drugs, they necessarily have reasonable cause to believe exigent circumstances exist" to justify a no-knock entry. 201 Wis. 2d at 852, 549 N.W.2d at 221. The court concluded that nothing in *Wilson's* acknowledgment that the knock-and-announce rule was an element of the Fourth Amendment "reasonableness" requirement would prohibit application of a *per se* exception to that rule in a category of cases. 201 Wis. 2d at 854–855, 549 N.W.2d at 220. In reaching this conclusion, the Wisconsin court found it reasonable—after considering criminal conduct surveys, newspaper articles, and other judicial opinions—to assume that all felony drug crimes will involve "an extremely high risk of serious if not deadly injury to the police as well as the potential for the disposal of drugs by the occupants prior to entry by the police." *Id.* at 847–848, 549 N.W.2d at 219. Notwithstanding its acknowledgment that in "some cases, police officers will undoubtedly decide that their safety, the safety of others, and the effective execution of the warrant dictate that they knock and announce," *id.* at 863, 549 N.W.2d at 225, the court concluded that exigent circumstances justifying a no-knock entry are always present in felony drug cases. Further, the court reasoned that the violation of privacy that occurs when officers who have a search warrant forcibly enter a residence without first announcing their presence is minimal, given that the residents would ultimately be without authority to refuse the police entry. The principal intrusion on individual privacy interests in such a situation, the court concluded, comes from the issuance of the search warrant, not the manner in which it is executed. *Id.* at 864–865, 549 N.W.2d at 226. Accordingly, the court determined that police in Wisconsin do not need specific information about dangerousness, or the possible destruction of drugs in a particular case, in order to dispense with the knock-and-announce requirement in felony drug cases.

Justice Abrahamson concurred in the judgment because, in her view, the facts found by the trial judge justified a no-knock entry. *Id.*, at 866–868, 549 N.W.2d at 227. Specifically, she noted that Richards' actions in slamming the door when he saw the uniformed man standing behind Officer Pharo indicated that he already knew that the people knocking on his door were police officers. Under these circumstances, any further announcement of their presence would have been a useless gesture. *Id.* at 868–869, n3, 549 N.W.2d at 228. While agreeing with the outcome, Justice Abrahamson took issue with her colleagues' affirmation of the blanket exception to the knock-and-announce requirement in drug felony cases. She observed that the constitutional reasonableness of a search has generally been a matter left to the court, rather than to the officers who conducted the search, and she objected to the creation of a blanket rule that insulated searches in a particular category of crime from the neutral oversight of a reviewing judge. *Id.* at 868–875, 549 N.W.2d at 228–230.

II.

We recognized in *Wilson* that the knock-and-announce requirement could give way "under circumstances presenting a threat of physical violence," or "where police officers have reason to believe that evidence would likely be destroyed if advance notice were given." 514 U.S. at 936. It is indisputable that felony drug investigations may frequently involve both of these circumstances. The question we must resolve is whether this fact justifies dispensing with case-by-case evaluation of the manner in which a search was executed.

The Wisconsin court explained its blanket exception as necessitated by the special circumstances of today's drug culture, 201 Wis. 2d at 863–866, 549 N.W.2d at 226–227, and the State asserted at oral argument that the blanket exception was reasonable in "felony drug cases because of the convergence in a violent and dangerous form of commerce of weapons and the destruction of drugs." Tr. of Oral Arg. 26. But creating exceptions to the knock-and-announce rule based on the "culture" surrounding a general category of criminal behavior presents at least two serious concerns.

First, the exception contains considerable over-generalization. For example, while drug investigation frequently does pose special risks to officer safety and the preservation of evidence, not every drug investigation will pose these risks to a substantial degree. For example, a search could be conducted at a time when the only individuals present in a residence have no connection with the drug activity and thus will be unlikely to threaten officers or destroy evidence. Or the police could know that the drugs being searched for were of a type or in a location that made them impossible to destroy quickly. In those situations, the asserted governmental interests in preserving evidence and maintaining safety may not outweigh the individual privacy interests intruded upon by a no-knock entry. Wisconsin's blanket rule impermissibly insulates these cases from judicial review.

A second difficulty with permitting a criminal-category exception to the knock-and-announce requirement is that the reasons for creating an exception in one category can, relatively easily, be applied to others. Armed bank robbers, for example, are, by definition, likely to have weapons, and the fruits of their crime may be destroyed without too much difficulty. If a *per se* exception were allowed for each category of criminal investigation that included a considerable—albeit hypothetical—risk of danger to officers or destruction of evidence, the knock-and-announce element of the Fourth Amendment's reasonableness requirement would be meaningless.

Thus, the fact that felony drug investigations may frequently present circumstances warranting a no-knock entry cannot remove from the neutral scrutiny of a reviewing court the reasonableness of the police decision not to knock and announce in a particular case. Instead, in each case, it is the duty of a court confronted with the question to determine whether the facts and circumstances of the particular entry justified dispensing with the knock-and-announce requirement.

In order to justify a "no-knock" entry, the police must have a reasonable suspicion that knocking and announcing their presence, under the particular circumstances, would be dangerous or futile, or that it would inhibit the effective investigation of the crime by, for example, allowing the destruction of evidence. This standard—as opposed to a probable cause requirement—strikes the appropriate balance between the legitimate law enforcement concerns at issue in the execution of search warrants and the individual privacy interests affected by no-knock entries. *Cf. Maryland v. Buie*, 494 U.S. 325, 337, 108 L. Ed. 2d 276, 110 S. Ct. 1093 (1990) (allowing a protective sweep of a house during an arrest where the officers have "a reasonable belief based on specific and articulable facts that the area to be swept harbors an individual posing a danger to those on the arrest scene"); *Terry v. Ohio*, 392 U.S. 1, 30, 20 L. Ed. 2d 889, 88 S. Ct. 1868 (1968) (requiring a reasonable and articulable suspicion of danger to justify a pat-down search). This showing is not high, but the police should be required to make it whenever the reasonableness of a no-knock entry is challenged.

III.

Although we reject the Wisconsin court's blanket exception to the knock-and-announce requirement, we conclude that the officers' no-knock entry into Richards' hotel room did not violate the Fourth Amendment. We agree with the trial court, and with Justice Abrahamson, that the circumstances in this case show that the officers had a reasonable suspicion that Richards might destroy evidence if given further opportunity to do so. The judge who heard testimony at Richards' suppression hearing concluded that it was reasonable for the officers executing the warrant to believe that Richards knew, after opening the door to his hotel room the first time, that the men seeking entry to his room were the police. Once the officers reasonably believed that Richards knew who they were, the court concluded, it was reasonable for them to force entry immediately given the disposable nature of the drugs. *Id.* at 55.

In arguing that the officers' entry was unreasonable, Richards places great emphasis on the fact that the magistrate who signed the search warrant for his hotel room deleted the portions of the proposed warrant that would have given the officers permission to execute a no-knock entry. But this fact does not alter the reasonableness of the officers' decision, which must be evaluated as of the time they entered the hotel room. At the time the officers obtained the warrant, they did not have evidence sufficient, in the judgment of the magistrate, to justify a no-knock warrant. Of course, the magistrate could not have anticipated in every particular the circumstances that would confront the officers when they arrived at Richards' hotel room. These actual circumstances—petitioner's apparent recognition of the officers combined with the easily disposable nature of the drugs—justified the officers' ultimate decision to enter without first announcing their presence and authority.

Accordingly, although we reject the blanket exception to the knock-and-announce requirement for felony drug investigations, the judgment of the Wisconsin Supreme Court is affirmed.

It is so ordered.

NOTICE: This opinion is subject to formal revision before publication in the preliminary print of the United States D. C. 20543, of any typographical or other formal errors, in order that corrections may be made before the preliminary print goes to press.

Marshall v. Marshall, **546 U.S. 1165 (2006)**

ON WRIT OF CERTIORARI TO THE UNITED STATES COURT OF APPEALS FOR THE NINTH CIRCUIT

[May 1, 2006]

Justice Ginsburg delivered the opinion of the Court.

In *Cohens v. Virginia*, Chief Justice Marshall famously cautioned: "It is most true that this Court will not take jurisdiction if it should not: but it is equally true, that it must take jurisdiction, if it should.... We have no more right to decline the exercise of jurisdiction which is given, than to usurp that which is not given." 6 Wheat. 264, 404 (1821). Among longstanding limitations on federal jurisdiction otherwise properly exercised are the so-called "domestic relations" and "probate" exceptions. Neither is compelled by the text of the Constitution or federal statute. Both are judicially created doctrines stemming in large measure from misty understandings of English legal history. *See, e.g.*, Atwood, Domestic Relations Cases in Federal Court: Toward a Principled Exercise of Jurisdiction, 35 Hastings L. J. 571, 584–588 (1984); *Spindel v. Spindel*, 283 F. Supp. 797, 802 (EDNY 1968) (collecting cases and commentary revealing vulnerability of historical explanation for domestic relations exception); Winkler, The Probate Jurisdiction of the Federal Courts, 14 Probate L. J. 77, 125–126, and n. 256 (1997) (describing historical explanation for probate exception as "an exercise in mythography"). In the years following Marshall's 1821 pronouncement, courts have sometimes lost sight of his admonition and have rendered decisions expansively interpreting the two exceptions. In *Ankenbrandt v. Richards*, 504 U.S. 689 (1992), this Court reined in the "domestic relations exception." Earlier, in *Markham v. Allen*, 326 U. S. 490 (1946), the Court endeavored similarly to curtail the "probate exception."

Nevertheless, the Ninth Circuit in the instant case read the probate exception broadly to exclude from the federal courts' adjudicatory authority "not only direct challenges to a will or trust, but also questions which would ordinarily be decided by a probate court in determining the validity of the decedent's estate planning instrument." 392 F. 3d 1118, 1133 (2004). The Court of Appeals further held that a State's vesting of exclusive jurisdiction over probate matters in a special court strips federal courts of jurisdiction to entertain any "probate related matter," including claims respecting "tax liability, debt, gift, [or] tort." *Id.*, at 1136. We hold that the Ninth Circuit had no warrant from Congress, or from decisions of this Court, for its sweeping extension of the probate exception.

I

Petitioner, Vickie Lynn Marshall (Vickie), also known as Anna Nicole Smith, is the surviving widow of J. Howard Marshall II (J. Howard). Vickie and J. Howard met in October 1991. After a courtship lasting more than two years, they were married on June 27, 1994. J. Howard died on August 4, 1995. Although he lavished gifts and significant sums of money on Vickie during their courtship and marriage, J. Howard did not include anything for Vickie in his will. According to Vickie, J. Howard intended to provide for her financial security through a gift in the form of a "catch-all" trust.

Respondent, E. Pierce Marshall (Pierce), one of J. Howard's sons, was the ultimate beneficiary of J. Howard's estate plan, which consisted of a living trust and a "pourover" will. Under the terms of the will, all of J. Howard's assets not already included in the trust were to be transferred to the trust upon his death.

Competing claims regarding J. Howard's fortune ignited proceedings in both state and federal courts. In January 1996, while J. Howard's estate was subject to ongoing proceedings in Probate Court in Harris County, Texas, Vickie filed for bankruptcy under Chapter 11 of the Bankruptcy Code, 11 U.S.C. §1101 *et seq.*, in the United States Bankruptcy Court for the Central District of California. *See* 275 B.R. 5, 8 (CD Cal. 2002). In June 1996, Pierce filed a proof of claim in the federal bankruptcy proceeding, *id.*, at 9; see 11 U.S.C. §501, alleging that Vickie had defamed him when, shortly after J. Howard's death, lawyers representing Vickie told members of the press that Pierce had engaged in forgery, fraud, and overreaching to gain control of his father's assets. 275 B.R., at 9. Pierce sought a declaration that the debt he asserted in that claim was not dischargeable in bankruptcy.*Ibid.*[1] Vickie answered, asserting truth as a defense. She also filed counterclaims, among them a claim that Pierce had tortiously interfered with a gift she expected. *Ibid.;* see App. 23–25. Vickie alleged that Pierce prevented the transfer of his father's intended gift to her by, among other things: effectively imprisoning J. Howard against his wishes; surrounding him with hired guards for the purpose of preventing personal contact between him and Vickie; making misrepresentations to J. Howard; and transferring property against J. Howard's expressed wishes. *Id.*, at 24.

Vickie's tortious interference counterclaim turned her objection to Pierce's claim into an adversary proceeding. *Id.*, at 39; see Fed. Rule Bkrtcy. Proc. 3007. In that proceeding, the Bankruptcy Court granted summary judgment in favor of Vickie on Pierce's claim and, after a trial on the merits, entered judgment for Vickie on her tortious interference counterclaim. *See* 253 B.R. 550, 558–559 (2000). The Bankruptcy Court also held that both Vickie's objection to Pierce's claim and Vickie's counterclaim qualified as "core proceedings" under 28 U.S.C. §157, which meant that the court had authority to enter a final judgment disposing of those claims. See 257 B.R. 35, 39–40 (2000). The court awarded Vickie compensatory damages of more than $449 million—less whatever she recovered in the ongoing probate action in Texas—as well as $25 million in punitive damages. *Id.*, at 40.

Pierce filed a post-trial motion to dismiss for lack of subject-matter jurisdiction, asserting that Vickie's tortious interference claim could be tried only in the Texas probate proceedings. *Id.*, at 36. The Bankruptcy Court held that "the 'probate exception' argument was waived" because it was not timely raised. *Id.*, at 39. Relying on this Court's decision in *Markham*, the court observed that a federal court has jurisdiction to "adjudicate rights in probate property, so long as its final judgment does not undertake to interfere with the state court's possession of the property." 257 B.R., at 38 (citing *Markham*, 326 U. S., at 494).

Meanwhile, in the Texas Probate Court, Pierce sought a declaration that the living trust and his father's will were valid. 392 F. 3d, at 1124–1125. Vickie, in turn, challenged the validity of the will and filed a tortious interference claim against Pierce, *ibid.*, but voluntarily dismissed both claims once the Bankruptcy Court entered its judgment, *id.*, at 1128. Following a jury trial, the Probate Court declared the living trust and J. Howard's will valid. *Id.*, at 1129.

Back in the federal forum, Pierce sought district-court review of the Bankruptcy Court's judgment. While rejecting the Bankruptcy Court's determination that Pierce had forfeited any argument based on the probate exception, the District Court held that the exception did not reach Vickie's claim. 264 B.R. 609, 619–625 (CD Cal. 2001). The Bankruptcy Court "did not assert jurisdiction generally over the probate proceedings… or take control over [the] estate's assets," the District Court observed, *id.*, at 621, "[t]hus, the probate exception would bar federal jurisdiction over Vickie's counterclaim only if such jurisdiction would 'interfere' with the probate proceedings," *ibid.* (quoting *Markham*, 326 U. S., at 494). Federal jurisdiction would not "interfere" with the probate proceedings, the District Court concluded, because: (1) success on Vickie's counterclaim did not necessitate any declaration that J. Howard's will was invalid, 264 B.R., at 621; and

[1]Among debts not dischargeable in bankruptcy, see 11 U.S.C. §523(a), are those arising from "willful and malicious injury by the debtor," §523(a)(6).

(2) under Texas law, probate courts do not have exclusive jurisdiction to entertain claims of the kind asserted in Vickie's counterclaim, *id.*, at 622–625.

The District Court also held that Vickie's claim did not qualify as a "core proceedin[g] arising under title 11, or arising in a case under title 11." 28 U.S.C. §157(b)(1); see 264 B.R., at 625–632. A bankruptcy court may exercise plenary power only over "core proceedings." *See* §157(b)–(c).[2] In non-core matters, a bankruptcy court may not enter final judgment; it has authority to issue only proposed findings of fact and conclusions of law, which are reviewed *de novo* by the district court. *See* §157(c)(1). Accordingly, the District Court treated the Bankruptcy Court's judgment as "proposed[,] rather than final," and undertook a "comprehensive, complete, and independent review of" the Bankruptcy Court's determinations. 264 B.R., at 633.

Adopting and supplementing the Bankruptcy Court's findings, the District Court determined that Pierce had tortiously interfered with Vickie's expectancy. Specifically, the District Court found that J. Howard directed his lawyers to prepare an *inter vivos* trust for Vickie consisting of half the appreciation of his assets from the date of their marriage. *See* 275 B.R., at 25–30, 51–53. It further found that Pierce conspired to suppress or destroy the trust instrument and to strip J. Howard of his assets by backdating, altering, and otherwise falsifying documents, arranging for surveillance of J. Howard and Vickie, and presenting documents to J. Howard under false pretenses. See *id.*, at 36–50, 57–58; see also 253 B.R., at 554–556, 559–560. Based on these findings, the District Court awarded Vickie some $44.3 million in compensatory damages. 275 B.R., at 53–57. In addition, finding "overwhelming" evidence of Pierce's "willfulness, maliciousness, and fraud," the District Court awarded an equal amount in punitive damages. *Id.*, at 57–58.

The Court of Appeals for the Ninth Circuit reversed. The appeals court recognized that Vickie's claim "does not involve the administration of an estate, the probate of a will, or any other purely probate matter." 392 F. 3d, at 1133. Nevertheless, the court held that the probate exception bars federal jurisdiction in this case. In the Ninth Circuit's view, a claim falls within the probate exception if it raises "questions which would ordinarily be decided by a probate court in determining the validity of the decedent's estate planning instrument," whether those questions involve "fraud, undue influence[, or] tortious interference with the testator's intent." *Ibid.*

The Ninth Circuit was also of the view that state-court delineation of a probate court's exclusive adjudicatory authority could control federal subject-matter jurisdiction. In this regard, the Court of Appeals stated: "Where a state has relegated jurisdiction over probate matters to a special court and [the] state's trial courts of general jurisdiction do

---

[2]"Core proceedings include, but are not limited to—

"(A) matters concerning the administration of the estate;

"(B) allowance or disallowance of claims against the estate or exemptions from property of the estate, and estimation of claims or interests for the purposes of confirming a plan under chapter 11, 12, or 13 of title 11 but not the liquidation or estimation of contingent or unliquidated personal injury tort or wrongful death claims against the estate for purposes of distribution in a case under title 11;

"(C) counterclaims by the estate against persons filing claims against the estate;

"(D) orders in respect to obtaining credit;

"(E) orders to turn over property of the estate;

"(F) proceedings to determine, avoid, or recover preferences;

"(G) motions to terminate, annul, or modify the automatic stay;

"(H) proceedings to determine, avoid, or recover fraudulent conveyances;

"(I) determinations as to the discharge ability of particular debts;

"(J) objections to discharges;

"(K) determinations of the validity, extent, or priority of liens;

"(L) confirmations of plans;

"(M) orders approving the use or lease of property, including the use of cash collateral;

"(N) orders approving the sale of property other than property resulting from claims brought by the estate against persons who have not filed claims against the estate;

"(O) other proceedings affecting the liquidation of the assets of the estate or the adjustment of the debtor-creditor or the equity security holder relationship, except personal injury tort or wrongful death claims; and

"(P) recognition of foreign proceedings and other matters under chapter 15 of title 11." 28 U.S.C.A. §157(b)(2) (1993 ed. and July 2005 Supp.).

not have jurisdiction to hear probate matters, then federal courts also lack jurisdiction over probate matters." *Id.*, at 1136. Noting that "[t]he [P]robate [C]ourt ruled it had exclusive jurisdiction over all of Vickie['s] claims, " the Ninth Circuit held that "ruling... binding on the United States [D]istrict [C]ourt." *Ibid.* (citing *Durfee v. Duke*, 375 U. S. 106, 115–116 (1963)).

We granted certiorari, 545 U. S. _____ (2005), to resolve the apparent confusion among federal courts concerning the scope of the probate exception. Satisfied that the instant case does not fall within the ambit of the narrow exception recognized by our decisions, we reverse the Ninth Circuit's judgment.

II

In *Ankenbrandt v. Richards*, 504 U. S. 689 (1992), we addressed both the derivation and the limits of the "domestic relations exception" to the exercise of federal jurisdiction. Carol Ankenbrandt, a citizen of Missouri, brought suit in Federal District Court on behalf of her daughters, naming as defendants their father (Ankenbrandt's former husband) and his female companion, both citizens of Louisiana. *Id.* at 691. Ankenbrandt's complaint sought damages for the defendants' alleged sexual and physical abuse of the children. *Ibid.* Federal jurisdiction was predicated on diversity of citizenship. *Ibid.* (citing 28 U.S.C. §1332). The District Court dismissed the case for lack of subject-matter jurisdiction, holding that Ankenbrandt's suit fell within "the 'domestic relations' exception to diversity jurisdiction." 504 U. S., at 692. The Court of Appeals agreed and affirmed. *Ibid.* We reversed the Court of Appeals' judgment. *Id.*, at 706–707.

Holding that the District Court improperly refrained from exercising jurisdiction over Ankenbrandt's tort claim, *id.*, at 704, we traced explanation of the current domestic relations exception to *Barber v. Barber*, 21 How. 582 (1859). *See Ankenbrandt*, 504 U. S., at 693–695. In *Barber*, the Court upheld federal-court authority, in a diversity case, to enforce an alimony award decreed by a state court. In dicta, however, the *Barber* Court announced—without citation or discussion—that federal courts lack jurisdiction over suits for divorce or the allowance of alimony. 21 How., at 584–589; see *Ankenbrandt*, 504 U. S., at 693–695.

Finding no Article III impediment to federal-court jurisdiction in domestic relations cases, *id.*, at 695–697, the Court in *Ankenbrandt* anchored the exception in Congress' original provision for diversity jurisdiction, *id.*, at 698–701. Beginning at the beginning, the Court recalled:

> "The Judiciary Act of 1789 provided that 'the circuit courts shall have original cognizance, concurrent with the courts of the several States, of *all suits of a civil nature at common law or in equity, where the matter in dispute exceeds*, exclusive of costs, the sum or value of *five hundred dollars*, and... an alien is a party, or the suit is *between a citizen of the State where the suit is brought, and a citizen of another State*.'" *Id.*, at 698 (quoting Act of Sept. 24, 1789, §11, 1 Stat. 78; emphasis added in *Ankenbrandt*).

The defining phrase, "all suits of a civil nature at common law or in equity," the Court stressed, remained in successive statutory provisions for diversity jurisdiction until 1948, when Congress adopted the more economical phrase, "all civil actions." 504 U. S., at 698; 1948 Judicial Code and Judiciary Act, 62 Stat. 930, 28 U.S.C. §1332.

The *Barber* majority, we acknowledged in *Ankenbrandt*, did not expressly tie its announcement of a domestic relations exception to the text of the diversity statute. 504 U. S., at 698. But the dissenters in that case made the connection. They stated that English courts of chancery lacked authority to issue divorce and alimony decrees. Because "the jurisdiction of the courts of the United States in chancery is bounded by that of the chancery in England," *Barber*, 21 How., at 605 (opinion of Daniel, J.), the dissenters reasoned, our federal courts similarly lack authority to decree divorces or award alimony, *ibid.* Such relief, in other words, would not fall within the diversity statute's original grant of jurisdiction over "all suits of a civil nature at common law or in equity." We concluded in *Ankenbrandt* that "it may be inferred fairly that the jurisdictional limitation recognized by the *[Barber]* Court rested on th[e] statutory basis" indicated by the dissenters in that case. 504 U. S., at 699.

We were "content" in *Ankenbrandt* "to rest our conclusion that a domestic relations exception exists as a matter of statutory construction not on the accuracy of the historical justifications on which [the exception] was seemingly based." *Id.*, at 700. "[R]ather," we relied on "Congress' apparent acceptance of this construction of the diversity jurisdiction provisions in the years prior to 1948, when the statute limited jurisdiction to 'suits of a civil nature at common law or in equity.' " *Ibid.* (quoting 1 Stat. 78). We further determined that Congress did not intend to terminate the exception in 1948 when it "replace[d] the law/equity distinction with the phrase 'all civil actions.' " 504 U. S., at 700. Absent contrary indications, we presumed that Congress meant to leave undisturbed "the Court's nearly century-long interpretation" of the diversity statute "to contain an exception for certain domestic relations matters." *Ibid.*

We nevertheless emphasized in *Ankenbrandt* that the exception covers only "a narrow range of domestic relations issues." *Id.*, at 701. The *Barber* Court itself, we reminded, "sanctioned the exercise of federal jurisdiction over the enforcement of an alimony decree that had been properly obtained in a state court of competent jurisdiction." 504 U. S., at 702. Noting that some lower federal courts had applied the domestic relations exception "well beyond the circumscribed situations posed by *Barber* and its progeny," *id.*, at 701, we clarified that only "divorce, alimony, and child custody decrees" remain outside federal jurisdictional bounds, *id.*, at 703, 704. While recognizing the "special proficiency developed by state tribunals... in handling issues that arise in the granting of [divorce, alimony, and child custody] decrees," *id.*, at 704, we viewed federal courts as equally equipped to deal with complaints alleging the commission of torts, *ibid.*

III

Federal jurisdiction in this case is premised on 28 U.S.C. §1334, the statute vesting in federal district courts jurisdiction in bankruptcy cases and related proceedings. Decisions of this Court have recognized a "probate exception," kin to the domestic relations exception, to otherwise proper federal jurisdiction. *See Markham v. Allen*, 326 U. S., at 494; see also *Sutton v. English*, 246 U. S. 199 (1918); *Waterman* v. *Canal-Louisiana Bank & Trust Co.*, 215 U. S. 33 (1909). Like the domestic relations exception, the probate exception has been linked to language contained in the Judiciary Act of 1789.

Markham, the Court's most recent and pathmarking pronouncement on the probate exception, stated that "the equity jurisdiction conferred by the Judiciary Act of 1789... , which is that of the English Court of Chancery in 1789, did not extend to probate matters." 326 U. S., at 494. See generally Nicolas, Fighting the Probate Mafia: A Dissection of the Probate Exception to Federal Jurisdiction, 74 S. Cal. L. Rev. 1479 (2001). As in *Ankenbrandt*, so in this case, "[w]e have no occasion... to join the historical debate" over the scope of English chancery jurisdiction in 1789, 504 U. S., at 699, for Vickie Marshall's claim falls far outside the bounds of the probate exception described in *Markham.* We therefore need not consider in this case whether there exists any uncodified probate exception to federal bankruptcy jurisdiction under §1334.[3]

---

[3]We note that the broad grant of jurisdiction conferred by §1334(b) is subject to a mandatory abstention provision applicable to certain state law claims. Section 1334(c)(2) provides:

"Upon timely motion of a party in a proceeding based upon a State law claim or State law cause of action, related to a case under title 11 but not arising under title 11 or arising in a case under title 11, with respect to which an action could not have been commenced in a court of the United States absent jurisdiction under this section, the district court shall abstain from hearing such proceeding if an action is commenced, and can be timely adjudicated, in a State forum of appropriate jurisdiction."

That provision is, in turn, qualified: "Non-core proceedings under section 157(b)(2)(B) of title 28, United States Code, shall not be subject to the mandatory abstention provisions of section 1334(c)(2)." §157(b)(4). Because the Bankruptcy Court rejected Pierce's motion for mandatory abstention as untimely, 257 B.R. 35, 39 (CD Cal. 2000), we need not consider whether these provisions might have required abstention upon a timely motion.

In *Markham*, the plaintiff Alien Property Custodian[4] commenced suit in Federal District Court against an executor and resident heirs to determine the Custodian's asserted rights regarding a decedent's estate. 326 U. S., at 491–492. Jurisdiction was predicated on §24(1) of the Judicial Code, now 28 U.S.C. §1345, which provides for federal jurisdiction over suits brought by an officer of the United States. At the time the federal suit commenced, the estate was undergoing probate administration in a state court. The Custodian had issued an order vesting in himself all right, title, and interest of German legatees. He sought and gained in the District Court a judgment determining that the resident heirs had no interest in the estate, and that the Custodian, substituting himself for the German legatees, was entitled to the entire net estate, including specified real estate passing under the will.

Reversing the Ninth Circuit, which had ordered the case dismissed for want of federal subject-matter jurisdiction, this Court held that federal jurisdiction was properly invoked. The Court first stated:

> "It is true that a federal court has no jurisdiction to probate a will or administer an estate.... But it has been established by a long series of decisions of this Court that federal courts of equity have jurisdiction to entertain suits 'in favor of creditors, legatees and heirs' and other claimants against a decedent's estate 'to establish their claims' so long as the federal court does not interfere with the probate proceedings or assume general jurisdiction of the probate or control of the property in the custody of the state court." 326 U. S., at 494 (quoting *Waterman*, 215 U. S., at 43).

Next, the Court described a probate exception of distinctly limited scope:

> "[W]hile a federal court may not exercise its jurisdiction to disturb or affect the possession of property in the custody of a state court,... it may exercise its jurisdiction to adjudicate rights in such property where the final judgment does not undertake to interfere with the state court's possession save to the extent that the state court is bound by the judgment to recognize the right adjudicated by the federal court." 326 U. S., at 494.

The first of the above-quoted passages from *Markham* is not a model of clear statement. The Court observed that federal courts have jurisdiction to entertain suits to determine the rights of creditors, legatees, heirs, and other claimants against a decedent's estate, "so long as the federal court does not *interfere with the probate proceedings*." *Ibid.* (emphasis added). Lower federal courts have puzzled over the meaning of the words "interfere with the probate proceedings," and some have read those words to block federal jurisdiction over a range of matters well beyond probate of a will or administration of a decedent's estate. *See, e.g., Mangieri v. Mangieri*, 226 F. 3d 1, 2–3 (CA1 2000) (breach of fiduciary duty by executor); *Golden ex rel. Golden v. Golden*, 382 F. 3d 348, 360–362 (CA3 2004) (same); *Lepard v. NBD Bank*, 384 F. 3d 232–237 (CA6 2004) (breach of fiduciary duty by trustee); *Storm v. Storm*, 328 F. 3d 941, 943–945 (CA7 2003) (probate exception bars claim that plaintiff's father tortiously interfered with plaintiff's inheritance by persuading trust grantor to amend irrevocable *inter vivos* trust); *Rienhardt v. Kelly*, 164 F. 3d 1296, 1300–1301 (CA10 1999) (probate exception bars claim that defendants exerted undue influence on testator and thereby tortiously interfered with plaintiff's expected inheritance).

We read *Markham*'s enigmatic words, in sync with the second above-quoted passage, to proscribe "disturb[ing] or affect[ing] the possession of property in the custody of a state court." 326 U. S., at 494. True, that reading renders the first-quoted passage in part

---

[4]Section 6 of the Trading with the Enemy Act, 40 Stat. 415, 50 U.S.C. App., authorizes the President to appoint an official known as the "alien property custodian," who is responsible for "receiv[ing],... hold[ing], administer[ing], and account[ing] for" "all money and property in the United States due or belonging to an enemy, or ally of enemy... ." The Act was originally enacted during World War I "to permit, under careful safeguards and restrictions, certain kinds of business to be carried on" among warring nations, and to "provid[e] for the care and administration of the property and property rights of enemies and their allies in this country pending the war." *Markham v. Cabell*, 326 U. S. 404, 414, n. 1 (1945) (Burton, J., concurring) (quoting S. Rep. No. 113, 65th Cong., 1st Sess., p. 1 (1917)).

redundant, but redundancy in this context, we do not doubt, is preferable to incoherence. In short, we comprehend the "interference" language in *Markham* as essentially a reiteration of the general principle that, when one court is exercising *in rem* jurisdiction over a *res*, a second court will not assume *in rem* jurisdiction over the same *res*. *See, e.g., Penn General Casualty Co. v. Pennsylvania ex rel. Schnader*, 294 U. S. 189, 195–196 (1935); *Waterman*, 215 U. S., at 45–46. Thus, the probate exception reserves to state probate courts the probate or annulment of a will and the administration of a decedent's estate; it also precludes federal courts from endeavoring to dispose of property that is in the custody of a state probate court. But it does not bar federal courts from adjudicating matters outside those confines and otherwise within federal jurisdiction.

A

As the Court of Appeals correctly observed, Vickie's claim does not "involve the administration of an estate, the probate of a will, or any other purely probate matter." 392 F. 3d, at 1133. Provoked by Pierce's claim in the bankruptcy proceedings, Vickie's claim, like Carol Ankenbrandt's, alleges a widely recognized tort. *See King v. Acker*, 725 S. W. 2d 750, 754 (Tex. App. 1987); Restatement (Second) of Torts §774B (1977) ("One who by fraud, duress or other tortious means intentionally prevents another from receiving from a third person an inheritance or gift that [s]he would otherwise have received is subject to liability to the other for loss of the inheritance or gift."). Vickie seeks an *in personam* judgment against Pierce, not the probate or annulment of a will. *Cf. Sutton*, 246 U. S., at 208 (suit to annul a will found "supplemental to the proceedings for probate of the will" and therefore not cognizable in federal court). Nor does she seek to reach a *res* in the custody of a state court. *See Markham*, 326 U. S., at 494.

Furthermore, no "sound policy considerations" militate in favor of extending the probate exception to cover the case at hand. *Cf. Ankenbrandt*, 504 U. S., at 703. Trial courts, both federal and state, often address conduct of the kind Vickie alleges. State probate courts possess no "special proficiency... in handling [such] issues." *Cf. id.*, at 704.

B

The Court of Appeals advanced an alternate basis for its conclusion that the federal courts lack jurisdiction over Vickie's claim. Noting that the Texas Probate Court "ruled it had exclusive jurisdiction over all of Vickie Lynn Marshall's claims against E. Pierce Marshall," the Ninth Circuit held that "ruling... binding on the United States [D]istrict [C]ourt." 392 F. 3d, at 1136. We reject that determination.

Texas courts have recognized a state-law tort action for interference with an expected inheritance or gift, modeled on the Restatement formulation. *See King*, 725 S. W. 2d, at 754; *Brandes v. Rice Trust, Inc.*, 966 S. W. 2d 144, 146–147 (Tex. App. 1998).[5] It is clear, under *Erie R. Co. v. Tompkins*, 304 U. S. 64 (1938), that Texas law governs the substantive

[5]Texas appellate courts have on occasion held claims of tortious interference with an expected inheritance "barred" by a prior probate court judgment, apparently applying ordinary principles of preclusion. *See, e.g., Thompson v. Deloitte & Touche*, 902 S. W. 2d 13, 16 (Tex. App. 1995) (final probate court judgment bars claim of tortious interference with inheritance expectancy because probate court "necessarily found that [the decedent] signed the will with testamentary capacity, and that it reflected his intent, was not the result of coercion or undue influence, and was valid"); *Neill v. Yett*, 746 S. W. 2d 32, 35–36 (Tex. App. 1988) (complaint alleging fraud and tortious interference with inheritance expectancy, filed more than two years after will was admitted to probate, was barred by both the statute of limitations and the final probate judgment, and failed to state the elements of the claim). Neither *Thompson* nor *Neill* questions the Texas trial courts' subject-matter jurisdiction over the claims in question.

Pierce maintains that *Thompson*, *Neill*, and other Texas decisions support his contention that preclusion principles bar Vickie's claim. See Brief for Respondent 36–38. Vickie argues to the contrary. See Brief for Petitioner 42 n. 30 (urging that preclusion does not apply because (1) Vickie's claim was not litigated to final judgment in the Texas probate proceedings; (2) having presented her claim in the Bankruptcy Court years before she joined the Texas will contest, Vickie was not obliged to present her claim in the Texas proceedings; (3) the Bankruptcy Court's judgment preceded the Probate Court judgment; and (4) the Texas Probate Court did not have before it important evidence). See also Tex. Rule Civ. Proc. 97; *Ingersoll-Rand Co. v. Valero Energy Corp.*, 997 S. W. 2d 203, 206–207 (Tex. 1999). The matter of preclusion remains open for consideration on remand. See *infra*, at 18.

elements of Vickie's tortious interference claim. It is also clear, however, that Texas may not reserve to its probate courts the exclusive right to adjudicate a transitory tort. We have long recognized that "a State cannot create a transitory cause of action and at the same time destroy the right to sue on that transitory cause of action in any court having jurisdiction." *Tennessee Coal, Iron & R. Co. v. George*, 233 U. S. 354, 360 (1914). Jurisdiction is determined "by the law of the court's creation and cannot be defeated by the extraterritorial operation of a [state] statute... , even though it created the right of action." *Ibid.* Directly on point, we have held that the jurisdiction of the federal courts, "having existed from the beginning of the Federal government, [can] not be impaired by subsequent state legislation creating courts of probate." *McClellan v. Carland*, 217 U. S. 268, 281 (1910) (upholding federal jurisdiction over action by heirs of decedent, who died intestate, to determine their rights in the estate (citing *Waterman*, 215 U. S. 33)).

Our decision in *Durfee v. Duke*, 375 U. S. 106 (1963), relied upon by the Ninth Circuit, 392 F. 3d, at 1136, is not to the contrary. *Durfee* stands only for the proposition that a state court's final judgment determining *its own* jurisdiction ordinarily qualifies for full faith and credit, so long as the jurisdictional issue was fully and fairly litigated in the court that rendered the judgment. See 375 U. S., at 111, 115. At issue here, however, is not the Texas Probate Court's jurisdiction, but the federal courts' jurisdiction to entertain Vickie's tortious interference claim. Under our federal system, Texas cannot render its probate courts exclusively competent to entertain a claim of that genre. We therefore hold that the District Court properly asserted jurisdiction over Vickie's counterclaim against Pierce.

IV

After determining that Vickie's claim was not a "core proceeding," the District Court reviewed the case *de novo* and entered its final judgment on March 7, 2002. 275 B.R., at 5–8. The Texas Probate Court's judgment became final on February 11, 2002, nearly one month earlier. App. to Pet. for Cert. 41. The Court of Appeals considered only the issue of federal subject-matter jurisdiction. It did not address the question whether Vickie's claim was "core"; nor did it address Pierce's arguments concerning claim and issue preclusion. 392 F. 3d, at 1137. These issues remain open for consideration on remand.

* * *

For the reasons stated, the judgment of the Court of Appeals for the Ninth Circuit is reversed, and the case is remanded for further proceedings consistent with this opinion.

It is so ordered.

City of San Diego, California v. John Roe, 543 U.S. 77 (2004)

ON PETITION FOR WRIT OF CERTIORARI
TO THE UNITED STATES COURT OF APPEALS
FOR THE NINTH CIRCUIT

No. 03–1669. Decided December 6, 2004

PER CURIAM. The city of San Diego (City), a petitioner here, terminated a police officer, respondent, for selling videotapes he made and for related activity. The tapes showed the respondent engaging in sexually explicit acts. Respondent brought suit alleging, among other things, that the termination violated his First and Fourteenth Amendment rights to freedom of speech. The United States District Court for the Southern District of California granted summary judgment to the City. The Court of Appeals for the Ninth Circuit reversed.

The petition for a writ of certiorari is granted, and the judgment of the Court of Appeals is reversed.

I

Respondent John Roe, a San Diego police officer, made a video showing himself stripping off a police uniform and masturbating. He sold the video on the adults-only section of eBay, the popular online auction site. His user name was "Codestud3@aol.com," a word play on a high priority police radio call. 356 F. 3d 1108, 1110 (CA9 2004). The uniform apparently was not the specific uniform worn by the San Diego police, but it was clearly identifiable as a police uniform. Roe also sold custom videos, as well as police equipment, including official uniforms of the San Diego Police Department (SDPD), and various other items such as men's underwear. Roe's eBay user profile identified him as employed in the field of law enforcement.

Roe's supervisor, a police sergeant, discovered Roe's activities when, while on eBay, he came across an official SDPD police uniform for sale offered by an individual with the username "Codestud3@aol.com." He searched for other items Codestud3 offered and discovered listings for Roe's videos depicting the objectionable material. Recognizing Roe's picture, the sergeant printed images of certain of Roe's offerings and shared them with others in Roe's chain of command, including a police captain. The captain notified the SDPD's internal affairs department, which began an investigation. In response to a request by an undercover officer, Roe produced a custom video. It showed Roe, again in police uniform, issuing a traffic citation but revoking it after undoing the uniform and masturbating.

The investigation revealed that Roe's conduct violated specific SDPD policies, including conduct unbecoming of an officer, outside employment, and immoral conduct. When confronted, Roe admitted to selling the videos and police paraphernalia. The SDPD ordered Roe to "cease displaying, manufacturing, distributing or selling any sexually explicit materials or engaging in any similar behaviors, via the internet, U. S. Mail, commercial vendors or distributors, or any other medium available to the public." 356 F. 3d, at 1111 (internal quotation marks omitted). Although Roe removed some of the items he had offered for sale, he did not change his seller's profile, which described the first two videos he had produced and listed their prices as well as the prices for custom videos. After discovering Roe's failure to follow its orders, the SDPD—citing Roe for the added violation of disobedience of lawful orders—began termination proceedings. The proceedings resulted in Roe's dismissal from the police force.

Roe brought suit in the District Court pursuant to Rev. Stat. §1979, 42 U.S.C. §1983, alleging that the employment termination violated his First Amendment right to free speech. In granting summary judgment to the City, the District Court decided that Roe had not demonstrated that selling official police uniforms and producing, marketing, and selling sexually explicit videos for profit qualified as expression relating to a matter of "public concern" under this Court's decision in *Connick v. Myers*, 461 U. S. 138 (1983).

In reversing, the Court of Appeals held Roe's conduct fell within the protected category of citizen commentary on matters of public concern. Central to the Court of Appeals' conclusion was that Roe's expression was not an internal workplace grievance, took place while he was off-duty and away from his employer's premises, and was unrelated to his employment. 356 F. 3d, at 1110, 1113–1114.

II

A government employee does not relinquish all First Amendment rights otherwise enjoyed by citizens just by reason of his or her employment. *See, e.g., Keyishian v. Board of Regents of Univ. of State of N. Y.*, 385 U. S. 589, 605–606 (1967). On the other hand, a governmental employer may impose certain restraints on the speech of its employees, restraints that would be unconstitutional if applied to the general public. The Court has recognized the right of employees to speak on matters of public concern, typically matters concerning government policies that are of interest to the public at large, a subject on which public employees are uniquely qualified to comment. *See Connick, supra; Pickering v. Board of Ed. of Township High School Dist. 205, Will Cty.*, 391 U. S. 563 (1968). Outside of this category, the Court has held that when government employees speak or write on their own time on topics unrelated to their employment, the speech can have First Amendment protection, absent some governmental justification "far stronger than mere speculation" in regulating it. *United States v. Treasury Employees*, 513 U. S. 454, 465, 475 (1995) *(NTEU)*. We have little difficulty in concluding that the City was not barred from terminating Roe under either line of cases.

A

In concluding that Roe's activities qualified as a matter of public concern, the Court of Appeals relied heavily on the Court's decision in *NTEU*. 356 F. 3d, at 1117. In *NTEU* it was established that the speech was unrelated to the employment and had no effect on the mission and purpose of the employer. The question was whether the Federal Government could impose certain monetary limitations on outside earnings from speaking or writing on a class of federal employees. The Court held that, within the particular classification of employment, the Government had shown no justification for the outside salary limitations. The First Amendment right of the employees sufficed to invalidate the restrictions on the outside earnings for such activities. The Court noted that throughout history public employees who undertook to write or to speak in their spare time had made substantial contributions to literature and art, *NTEU*, *supra*, at 465, and observed that none of the speech at issue "even arguably [had] any adverse impact" on the employer. *Ibid*.

The Court of Appeals' reliance on *NTEU* was seriously misplaced. Although Roe's activities took place outside the workplace and purported to be about subjects not related to his employment, the SDPD demonstrated legitimate and substantial interests of its own that were compromised by his speech. Far from confining his activities to speech unrelated to his employment, Roe took deliberate steps to link his videos and other wares to his police work, all in a way injurious to his employer. The use of the uniform, the law enforcement reference in the Web site, the listing of the speaker as "in the field of law enforcement," and the debased parody of an officer performing indecent acts while in the course of official duties brought the mission of the employer and the professionalism of its officers into serious disrepute. 356 F. 3d, at 1111 (internal quotation marks omitted).

The Court of Appeals noted the City conceded Roe's activities were "unrelated" to his employment. *Id*., at 1112, n. 4. In the context of the pleadings and arguments, the proper interpretation of the City's statement is simply to underscore the obvious proposition that Roe's speech was not a comment on the workings or functioning of the SDPD. It is quite a different question whether the speech was detrimental to the SDPD. On that score the City's consistent position has been that the speech is contrary to its regulations and harmful to the proper functioning of the police force. The present case falls outside the protection afforded in *NTEU*. The authorities that instead control, and which are considered below, are this Court's decisions in *Pickering, supra, Connick, supra*, and the decisions which follow them.

B

To reconcile the employee's right to engage in speech and the government employer's right to protect its own legitimate interests in performing its mission, the *Pickering* Court adopted a balancing test. It requires a court evaluating restraints on a public employee's speech to balance "the interests of the [employee], as a citizen, in commenting upon matters of public concern and the interest of the State, as an employer, in promoting the efficiency of the public services it performs through its employees." 391 U. S., at 568; *see also Connick, supra*, at 142.

Underlying the decision in *Pickering* is the recognition that public employees are often the members of the community who are likely to have informed opinions as to the operations of their public employers, operations which are of substantial concern to the public. Were they not able to speak on these matters, the community would be deprived of informed opinions on important public issues. See 391 U. S., at 572. The interest at stake is as much the public's interest in receiving informed opinion as it is the employee's own right to disseminate it.

Pickering did not hold that any and all statements by a public employee are entitled to balancing. To require *Pickering* balancing in every case where speech by a public employee is at issue, no matter the content of the speech, could compromise the proper functioning of government offices. *See Connick*, 461 U. S., at 143. This concern prompted the Court in *Connick* to explain a threshold inquiry (implicit in *Pickering* itself) that in order to merit *Pickering* balancing, a public employee's speech must touch on a matter of "public concern." 461 U. S. at 143 (internal quotation marks omitted).

In *Connick*, an assistant district attorney, unhappy with her supervisor's decision to transfer her to another division, circulated an intra office questionnaire. The document solicited her co-workers' views on, *inter alia*, office transfer policy, office morale, the need for grievance committees, the level of confidence in supervisors, and whether employees felt pressured to work in political campaigns. *See id.*, at 141.

Finding that—with the exception of the final question—the questionnaire touched not on matters of public concern but on internal workplace grievances, the Court held no *Pickering* balancing was required. 461 U. S., at 141. To conclude otherwise would ignore the "common-sense realization that government offices could not function if every employment decision became a constitutional matter." *Id.*, at 143. *Connick* held that a public employee's speech is entitled to *Pickering* balancing only when the employee speaks "as a citizen upon matters of public concern" rather than "as an employee upon matters only of personal interest." 461 U. S. at 147.

Although the boundaries of the public concern test are not well-defined, *Connick* provides some guidance. It directs courts to examine the "content, form, and context of a given statement, as revealed by the whole record" in assessing whether an employee's speech addresses a matter of public concern. *Id.*, at 146–147. In addition, it notes that the standard for determining whether expression is of public concern is the same standard used to determine whether a common-law action for invasion of privacy is present. *Id.*, at 143, n. 5. That standard is established by our decisions in *Cox Broadcasting Corp. v. Cohn*, 420 U. S. 469 (1975), and *Time, Inc. v. Hill*, 385 U. S. 374, 387–388 (1967). These cases make clear that public concern is something that is a subject of legitimate news interest; that is, a subject of general interest and of value and concern to the public at the time of publication. The Court has also recognized that certain private remarks, such as negative comments about the President of the United States, touch on matters of public concern and should thus be subject to *Pickering* balancing. *See Rankin v. McPherson*, 483 U. S. 378 (1987).

Applying these principles to the instant case, there is no difficulty in concluding that Roe's expression does not qualify as a matter of public concern under any view of the public concern test. He fails the threshold test and *Pickering* balancing does not come into play.

Connick is controlling precedent, but to show why this is not a close case it is instructive to note that even under the view expressed by the dissent in *Connick* from four Members of the Court, the speech here would not come within the definition of a matter of public concern. The dissent in *Connick* would have held that the entirety of the questionnaire circulated by the employee "discussed subjects that could reasonably be expected to be of interest to persons seeking to develop informed opinions about the manner in which... an elected official charged with managing a vital governmental agency, discharges his responsibilities." 461 U. S. at 163 (opinion of Brennan, J.). No similar purpose could be attributed to the employee's speech in the present case. Roe's activities did nothing to inform the public about any aspect of the SDPD's functioning or operation. Nor were Roe's activities anything like the private remarks at issue in *Rankin*, where one coworker commented to another co-worker on an item of political news. Roe's expression was widely broadcast, linked to his official status as a police officer, and designed to exploit his employer's image.

The speech in question was detrimental to the mission and functions of the employer. There is no basis for finding that it was of concern to the community as the Court's cases have understood that term in the context of restrictions by governmental entities on the speech of their employees.

The judgment of the Court of Appeals is *Reversed.*

NOTICE: This opinion is subject to formal revision before publication in the preliminary print of the United States Reports. Readers are requested to notify the Reporter of Decisions, Supreme Court of the United States, Washington, D. C. 20543, of any typographical or other formal errors, in order that corrections may be made before the preliminary print goes to press.

Elk Grove Unified School District v. Newdow, 542 U.S. 1 (2004)

ON WRIT OF CERTIORARI TO THE UNITED STATES COURT OF APPEALS FOR THE NINTH CIRCUIT

[June 14, 2004]

JUSTICE STEVENS delivered the opinion of the Court.

Each day elementary school teachers in the Elk Grove Unified School District (School District) lead their classes in a group recitation of the Pledge of Allegiance. Respondent, Michael A. Newdow, is an atheist whose daughter participates in that daily exercise. Because the Pledge contains the words "under God," he views the School District's policy as a religious indoctrination of his child that violates the First Amendment. A divided panel of the Court of Appeals for the Ninth Circuit agreed with Newdow. In light of the obvious importance of that decision, we granted certiorari to review the First Amendment issue and, preliminarily, the question whether Newdow has standing to invoke the jurisdiction of the federal courts. We conclude that Newdow lacks standing and therefore reverse the Court of Appeals' decision.

I

"The very purpose of a national flag is to serve as a symbol of our country," *Texas v. Johnson*, 491 U. S. 397, 405 (1989), and of its proud traditions "of freedom, of equal opportunity, of religious tolerance, and of good will for other peoples who share our aspirations," *id.*, at 437 (STEVENS, J., dissenting). As its history illustrates, the Pledge of Allegiance evolved as a common public acknowledgement of the ideals that our flag symbolizes. Its recitation is a patriotic exercise designed to foster national unity and pride in those principles.

The Pledge of Allegiance was initially conceived more than a century ago. As part of the nationwide interest in commemorating the 400th anniversary of Christopher Columbus' discovery of America, a widely circulated national magazine for youth proposed in 1892 that pupils recite the following affirmation: "I pledge allegiance to my Flag and the Republic for which it stands: one Nation indivisible, with Liberty and Justice for all."[1] In the 1920's, the National Flag Conferences replaced the phrase "my Flag" with "the flag of the United States of America."

In 1942, in the midst of World War II, Congress adopted, and the President signed, a Joint Resolution codifying a detailed set of "rules and customs pertaining to the display and use of the flag of the United States of America." Chapter 435, 56 Stat. 377. Section 7 of this codification provided in full:

> "That the pledge of allegiance to the flag, 'I pledge allegiance to the flag of the United States of America and to the Republic for which it stands, one Nation indivisible, with liberty and justice for all', be rendered by standing with the right hand over the heart;

---

[1]J. Baer, The Pledge of Allegiance: A Centennial History, 1892–1992, p. 3 (1992) (internal quotation marks omitted). At the time, the phrase "one Nation indivisible" had special meaning because the question whether a State could secede from the Union had been intensely debated and was unresolved prior to the Civil War. See J. Randall, Constitutional Problems Under Lincoln 12–24 (1964). See also W. Rehnquist, Centennial Crisis: The Disputed Election of 1876, p. 182 (2004).

> extending the right hand, palm upward, toward the flag at the words 'to the flag' and holding this position until the end, when the hand drops to the side. However, civilians will always show full respect to the flag when the pledge is given by merely standing at attention, men removing the headdress. Persons in uniform shall render the military salute."*Id.*, at 380.

This resolution, which marked the first appearance of the Pledge of Allegiance in positive law, confirmed the importance of the flag as a symbol of our Nation's indivisibility and commitment to the concept of liberty.

Congress revisited the Pledge of Allegiance 12 years later when it amended the text to add the words "under God." Act of June 14, 1954, ch. 297, 68 Stat. 249. The House Report that accompanied the legislation observed that, "[f]rom the time of our earliest history our peoples and our institutions have reflected the traditional concept that our Nation was founded on a fundamental belief in God." H. R. Rep. No. 1693, 83d Cong., 2d Sess., p. 2 (1954). The resulting text is the Pledge as we know it today: "I pledge allegiance to the Flag of the United States of America, and to the Republic for which it stands, one Nation under God, indivisible, with liberty and justice for all." 4 U.S.C. §4.

II

Under California law, "every public elementary school" must begin each day with "appropriate patriotic exercises." Cal. Educ. Code Ann. §52720 (West 1989). The statute provides that "[t]he giving of the Pledge of Allegiance to the Flag of the United States of America shall satisfy" this requirement. *Ibid.* The Elk Grove Unified School District has implemented the state law by requiring that "[e]ach elementary school class recite the pledge of allegiance to the flag once each day."[2] Consistent with our case law, the School District permits students who object on religious grounds to abstain from the recitation. See *West Virginia Bd. of Ed. v. Barnette*, 319 U. S. 624 (1943).

In March 2000, Newdow filed suit in the United States District Court for the Eastern District of California against the United States Congress, the President of the United States, the State of California, and the Elk Grove Unified School District and its superintendent.[3] App. 24. At the time of filing, Newdow's daughter was enrolled in kindergarten in the Elk Grove Unified School District and participated in the daily recitation of the Pledge. Styled as a mandamus action, the complaint explains that Newdow is an atheist who was ordained more than 20 years ago in a ministry that "espouses the religious philosophy that the true and eternal bonds of righteousness and virtue stem from reason rather than mythology." *Id.*, at 42, 53. The complaint seeks a declaration that the 1954 Act's addition of the words "under God" violated the Establishment and Free Exercise Clauses of the United States Constitution,[4] as well as an injunction against the School District's policy requiring daily recitation of the Pledge. *Id.*, at 42. It alleges that Newdow has standing to sue on his own behalf and on behalf of his daughter as "next friend." *Id.*, at 26, 56.

The case was referred to a Magistrate Judge, whose brief findings and recommendation concluded, "the Pledge does not violate the Establishment Clause." *Id.*, at 79. The District Court adopted that recommendation and dismissed the complaint on July 21, 2000. App. to Pet. for Cert. 97. The Court of Appeals reversed and issued three separate decisions discussing the merits and Newdow's standing.

---

[2]Elk Grove Unified School District's Policy AR 6115, App. to Brief for United States as Respondent Supporting Petitioners 2a.

[3]Newdow also named as defendants the Sacramento Unified School District and its superintendent on the chance that his daughter might one day attend school in that district. App. 48. The Court of Appeals held that Newdow lacks standing to challenge that district's policy because his daughter is not currently a student there. *Newdow v. U.S. Congress*, 328 F. 3d 466, 485 (CA9 2003) (*Newdow III*). Newdow has not challenged that ruling.

[4]The First Amendment provides in relevant part that "Congress shall make no law respecting an establishment of religion, or prohibiting the free exercise thereof." U. S. Const., Amdt. 1. The Religion Clauses apply to the States by incorporation into the Fourteenth Amendment.

See *Cantwell v. Connecticut*, 310 U. S. 296, 303 (1940).

In its first opinion the appeals court unanimously held that Newdow has standing "as a parent to challenge a practice that interferes with his right to direct the religious education of his daughter." *Newdow v. U.S. Congress*, 292 F. 3d 597, 602 (CA9 2002) (*Newdow I*). That holding sustained Newdow's standing to challenge not only the policy of the School District, where his daughter still is enrolled, but also the 1954 Act of Congress that had amended the Pledge, because his "injury in fact" was "fairly traceable" to its enactment. *Id.*, at 603–605. On the merits, over the dissent of one judge, the court held that both the 1954 Act and the School District's policy violate the Establishment Clause of the First Amendment. *Id.*, at 612.

After the Court of Appeals' initial opinion was announced, Sandra Banning, the mother of Newdow's daughter, filed a motion for leave to intervene, or alternatively to dismiss the complaint. App. 82. She declared that although she and Newdow shared "physical custody" of their daughter, a state-court order granted her "exclusive legal custody" of the child, "including the sole right to represent [the daughter's] legal interests and make all decision[s] about her education" and welfare. *Id.*, at 82, 2–3. Banning further stated that her daughter is a Christian who believes in God and has no objection either to reciting or hearing others recite the Pledge of Allegiance, or to its reference to God. *Id.*, at 83, 4. Banning expressed the belief that her daughter would be harmed if the litigation were permitted to proceed, because others might incorrectly perceive the child as sharing her father's atheist views. *Id.*, at 85, 10. Banning accordingly concluded, as her daughter's sole legal custodian, that it was not in the child's interest to be a party to Newdow's lawsuit. *Id.*, at 86. On September 25, 2002, the California Superior Court entered an order enjoining Newdow from including his daughter as an unnamed party or suing as her "next friend." That order did not purport to answer the question of Newdow's Article III standing. *See Newdow v. U.S. Congress*, 313 F. 3d 500, 502 (CA9 2002) (*Newdow II*).

In a second published opinion, the Court of Appeals reconsidered Newdow's standing in light of Banning's motion. The court noted that Newdow no longer claimed to represent his daughter, but unanimously concluded that "the grant of sole legal custody to Banning" did not deprive Newdow, "as a noncustodial parent, of Article III standing to object to unconstitutional government action affecting his child." *Id.*, at 502–503. The court held that under California law Newdow retains the right to expose his child to his particular religious views even if those views contradict the mother's, and that Banning's objections as sole legal custodian do not defeat Newdow's right to seek redress for an alleged injury to his own parental interests. *Id.*, at 504–505.

On February 28, 2003, the Court of Appeals issued an order amending its first opinion and denying rehearing en banc. *Newdow v. U.S. Congress*, 328 F. 3d 466, 468 (CA9 2003) (*Newdow III*). The amended opinion omitted the initial opinion's discussion of Newdow's standing to challenge the 1954 Act and declined to determine whether Newdow was entitled to declaratory relief regarding the constitutionality of that Act. *Id.*, at 490. Nine judges dissented from the denial of en banc review. *Id.*, at 471, 482. We granted the School District's petition for a writ of certiorari to consider two questions: (1) whether Newdow has standing as a noncustodial parent to challenge the School District's policy, and (2) if so, whether the policy offends the First Amendment. 540 U. S. 945 (2003).

III

In every federal case, the party bringing the suit must establish standing to prosecute the action. "In essence the question of standing is whether the litigant is entitled to have the court decide the merits of the dispute or of particular issues." *Warth v. Seldin*, 422 U. S. 490, 498 (1975). The standing requirement is born partly of "'an idea, which is more than an intuition but less than a rigorous and explicit theory, about the constitutional and prudential limits to the powers of an unelected, unrepresentative judiciary in our kind of government.'" *Allen v. Wright*, 468 U. S. 737, 750 (1984) (quoting *Vander Jagt v. O'Neill*, 699 F. 2d 1166, 1178–1179 (CADC 1983) (Bork, J., concurring)).

The command to guard jealously and exercise rarely our power to make constitutional pronouncements requires strictest adherence when matters of great national significance are at stake. Even in cases concededly within our jurisdiction under Article III, we abide by "a series of rules under which [we have] avoided passing upon a large part of all the constitutional questions pressed upon [us] for decision." *Ashwander v. TVA*, 297 U. S. 288, 346 (1936) (Brandeis, J., concurring). Always we must balance "the heavy obligation to exercise jurisdiction," *Colorado River Water Conservation Dist. v. United States*, 424 U. S. 800, 820 (1976), against the "deeply rooted" commitment "not to pass on questions of constitutionality" unless adjudication of the constitutional issue is necessary, *Spector Motor Service, Inc. v. McLaughlin*, 323 U. S. 101, 105 (1944). *See also Rescue Army v. Municipal Court of Los Angeles*, 331 U. S. 549, 568–575 (1947).

Consistent with these principles, our standing jurisprudence contains two strands: Article III standing, which enforces the Constitution's case or controversy requirement, *see Lujan v. Defenders of Wildlife*, 504 U. S. 555, 559–562 (1992); and prudential standing, which embodies "judicially self-imposed limits on the exercise of federal jurisdiction," *Allen*, 468 U. S., at 751. The Article III limitations are familiar: The plaintiff must show that the conduct of which he complains has caused him to suffer an "injury in fact" that a favorable judgment will redress. *See Lujan*, 504 U. S., at 560–561. Although we have not exhaustively defined the prudential dimensions of the standing doctrine, we have explained that prudential standing encompasses "the general prohibition on a litigant's raising another person's legal rights, the rule barring adjudication of generalized grievances more appropriately addressed in the representative branches, and the requirement that a plaintiff's complaint fall within the zone of interests protected by the law invoked." *Allen*, 468 U. S., at 751. *See also Secretary of State of Md. v. Joseph H. Munson Co.*, 467 U. S. 947, 955–956 (1984). "Without such limitations—closely related to Art. III concerns but essentially matters of judicial self-governance—the courts would be called upon to decide abstract questions of wide public significance even though other governmental institutions may be more competent to address the questions and even though judicial intervention may be unnecessary to protect individual rights." *Warth*, 422 U. S., at 500.

One of the principal areas in which this Court has customarily declined to intervene is the realm of domestic relations. Long ago we observed that "[t]he whole subject of the domestic relations of husband and wife, parent and child, belongs to the laws of the States and not to the laws of the United States." *In re Burrus*, 136 U. S. 586, 593–594 (1890). *See also Mansell v. Mansell*, 490 U. S. 581, 587 (1989) ("[D]omestic relations are preeminently matters of state law"); *Moore v. Sims*, 442 U. S. 415, 435 (1979) ("Family relations are a traditional area of state concern"). So strong is our deference to state law in this area that we have recognized a "domestic relations exception" that "divests the federal courts of power to issue divorce, alimony, and child custody decrees." *Ankenbrandt v. Richards*, 504 U. S. 689, 703 (1992). We have also acknowledged that it might be appropriate for the federal courts to decline to hear a case involving "elements of the domestic relationship," *id.*, at 705, even when divorce, alimony, or child custody is not strictly at issue:

> "This would be so when a case presents 'difficult questions of state law bearing on policy problems of substantial public import whose importance transcends the result in the case then at bar.' Such might well be the case if a federal suit were filed prior to effectuation of a divorce, alimony, or child custody decree, and the suit depended on a determination of the status of the parties." *Id.*, at 705–706 (quoting *Colorado River*, 424 U. S., at 814).

Thus, while rare instances arise in which it is necessary to answer a substantial federal question that transcends or exists apart from the family law issue, *see, e.g., Palmore v. Sidoti*, 466 U. S. 429, 432–434 (1984), in general it is appropriate for the federal courts to leave delicate issues of domestic relations to the state courts.[5]

---

[5]Our holding does not rest, as THE CHIEF JUSTICE suggests, *see post*, at 2–5, on either the domestic relations exception or the abstention doctrine. Rather, our prudential standing analysis is informed by the variety of contexts in which federal courts decline to intervene because, as *Ankenbrandt v. Richards*, 504 U. S. 689 (1992), contemplated, the suit "depend[s] on a determination of the status of the parties," *id.*, at 706. We deemed it appropriate to review the dispute in *Palmore* because it "raise[d] important federal concerns arising from the Constitution's commitment to eradicating discrimination based on race." 466 U. S., at 432. In this case, by contrast, the disputed family law rights are entwined inextricably with the threshold standing inquiry. THE CHIEF JUSTICE in this respect, see *post*, at 3, misses our point: The *merits* question undoubtedly transcends the domestic relations issue, but the *standing* question surely does not.

As explained briefly above, the extent of the standing problem raised by the domestic relations issues in this case was not apparent until August 5, 2002, when Banning filed her motion for leave to intervene or dismiss the complaint following the Court of Appeals' initial decision. At that time, the child's custody was governed by a February 6, 2002, order of the California Superior Court. That order provided that Banning had "'*sole* legal custody as to the rights and responsibilities to make decisions relating to the health, education and welfare of'" her daughter. *Newdow II*, 313 F. 3d, at 502. The order stated that the two parents should "'consult with one another on substantial decisions relating to'" the child's "'psychological and educational needs,'" but it authorized Banning to "'exercise legal control'" if the parents could not reach "'mutual agreement.'" *Ibid.*

That family court order was the controlling document at the time of the Court of Appeals' standing decision. After the Court of Appeals ruled, however, the Superior Court held another conference regarding the child's custody. At a hearing on September 11, 2003, the Superior Court announced that the parents have "joint legal custody," but that Banning "makes the final decisions if the two... disagree." App. 127–128.[6]

Newdow contends that despite Banning's final authority, he retains "an unrestricted right to inculcate in his daughter—free from governmental interference—the atheistic beliefs he finds persuasive." *Id.*, at 48, 78. The difficulty with that argument is that Newdow's rights, as in many cases touching upon family relations, cannot be viewed in isolation. This case concerns not merely Newdow's interest in inculcating his child with his views on religion, but also the rights of the child's mother as a parent generally and under the Superior Court orders specifically. And most important, it implicates the interests of a young child who finds herself at the center of a highly public debate over her custody, the propriety of a widespread national ritual, and the meaning of our Constitution.

The interests of the affected persons in this case are in many respects antagonistic. Of course, legal disharmony in family relations is not uncommon, and in many instances that disharmony poses no bar to federal-court adjudication of proper federal questions. What makes this case different is that Newdow's standing derives entirely from his relationship with his daughter, but he lacks the right to litigate as her next friend. In marked contrast to our case law on *jus tertii, see, e.g., Singleton v. Wulff*, 428 U. S. 106, 113–118 (1976) (plurality opinion), the interests of this parent and this child are not parallel and, indeed, are potentially in conflict.[7]

Newdow's parental status is defined by California's domestic relations law. Our custom on questions of state law ordinarily is to defer to the interpretation of the Court of Appeals for the Circuit in which the State is located. *See Bishop v. Wood*, 426 U. S. 341, 346–347 (1976). In this case, the Court of Appeals, which possesses greater familiarity with California law, concluded that state law vests in Newdow a cognizable right to influence his daughter's religious upbringing. *Newdow II*, 313 F. 3d, at 504–505. The court based

[6]The court confirmed that position in a written order issued January 9, 2004:

"The parties will have joint legal custody defined as follows: Ms. Banning will continue to make the final decisions as to the minor's health, education, and welfare if the two parties cannot mutually agree. The parties are required to consult with each other on substantial decisions relating to the health, education and welfare of the minor child, including... psychological and educational needs of the minor. If mutual agreement is not reached in these areas, then Ms. Banning may exercise legal control of the minor that is not specifically prohibited or is inconsistent with the physical custody." App. to Reply Brief for United States as Respondent Supporting Petitioners 12a.

Despite the use of the term "joint legal custody"—which is defined by California statute, *see* Cal. Fam. Code Ann. §3003 (West 1994)—we see no meaningful distinction for present purposes between the custody order issued February 6, 2002, and the one issued January 9, 2004. Under either order, Newdow has the right to consult on issues relating to the child's education, but Banning possesses what we understand amounts to a tie breaking vote.

[7]"There are good and sufficient reasons for th[e] prudential limitation on standing when rights of third parties are implicated—the avoidance of the adjudication of rights which those not before the Court may not wish to assert, and the assurance that the most effective advocate of the rights at issue is present to champion them." *Duke Power Co. v. Carolina Environmental Study Group, Inc.*, 438 U. S. 59, 80 (1978). Banning tells us that her daughter has no objection to the Pledge, and we are mindful in cases such as this that "children themselves have constitutionally protectible interests." *Wisconsin v. Yoder*, 406 U. S. 205, 243 (1972) (Douglas, J., dissenting). In a fundamental respect, "[i]t is the future of the student, not the future of the parents," that is at stake. *Id.*, at 245.

its ruling on two intermediate state appellate cases holding that "while the custodial parent undoubtedly has the right to make ultimate decisions concerning the child's religious upbringing, a court will not enjoin the noncustodial parent from discussing religion with the child or involving the child in his or her religious activities in the absence of a showing that the child will be thereby harmed." *In re Marriage of Murga*, 103 Cal. App. 3d 498, 505, 163 Cal. Rptr. 79, 82 (1980). *See also In re Marriage of Mentry*, 142 Cal. App. 3d 260, 268–270, 190 Cal. Rptr. 843, 849–850 (1983) (relying on *Murga* to invalidate portion of restraining order barring noncustodial father from engaging children in religious activity or discussion without custodial parent's consent). Animated by a conception of "family privacy" that includes "not simply a policy of minimum state intervention but also a presumption of parental autonomy," 142 Cal. App. 3d, at 267–268, 190 Cal. Rptr., at 848, the state cases create a zone of private authority within which each parent, whether custodial or noncustodial, remains free to impart to the child his or her religious perspective.

Nothing that either Banning or the School Board has done, however, impairs Newdow's right to instruct his daughter in his religious views. Instead, Newdow requests relief that is more ambitious than that sought in *Mentry* and *Murga*. He wishes to forestall his daughter's exposure to religious ideas that her mother, who wields a form of veto power, endorses, and to use his parental status to challenge the influences to which his daughter may be exposed in school when he and Banning disagree. The California cases simply do not stand for the proposition that Newdow has a right to dictate to others what they may and may not say to his child respecting religion. *Mentry* and *Murga* are concerned with protecting "'the fragile, complex interpersonal bonds between child and parent,'" 142 Cal. App. 3d, at 267, 190 Cal. Rptr., at 848, and with permitting divorced parents to expose their children to the "'diversity of religious experiences [that] is itself a sound stimulant for a child,'" *id.*, at 265, 190 Cal. Rptr., at 847 (citation omitted). The cases speak not at all to the problem of a parent seeking to reach outside the private parent-child sphere to restrain the acts of a third party. A next friend surely could exercise such a right, but the Superior Court's order has deprived Newdow of that status.

In our view, it is improper for the federal courts to entertain a claim by a plaintiff whose standing to sue is founded on family law rights that are in dispute when prosecution of the lawsuit may have an adverse effect on the person who is the source of the plaintiff's claimed standing. When hard questions of domestic relations are sure to affect the outcome, the prudent course is for the federal court to stay its hand rather than reach out to resolve a weighty question of federal constitutional law. There is a vast difference between Newdow's right to communicate with his child—which both California law and the First Amendment recognize—and his claimed right to shield his daughter from influences to which she is exposed in school despite the terms of the custody order. We conclude that, having been deprived under California law of the right to sue as next friend, Newdow lacks.[8]

The judgment of the Court of Appeals is reversed.

It is so ordered.

JUSTICE SCALIA took no part in the consideration or decision of this case.

> NOTICE: This opinion is subject to formal revision before publication in the preliminary print of the United States Reports. Readers are requested to notify the Reporter of Decisions, Supreme Court of the United States, Washington, D. C. 20543, of any typographical or other formal errors, in order that corrections may be made before the preliminary print goes to press.

---

[8]Newdow's complaint and brief cite several additional bases for standing: that Newdow "at times has himself attended—and will in the future attend—class with his daughter," App. 49, 80; that he "has considered teaching elementary school students in [the School District]," *id.*, at 65, 120; that he "has attended and will continue to attend" school board meetings at which the Pledge is "routinely recited," *id.*, at 52, 85; and that the School District uses his tax dollars to implement its Pledge policy, *id.*, at 62–65. Even if these arguments suffice to establish Article III standing, they do not respond to our prudential concerns. As for taxpayer standing, Newdow does not reside in or pay taxes to the School District; he alleges that he pays taxes to the District only "indirectly" through his child support payments to Banning. Brief for Respondent Newdow 49, n. 70. That allegation does not amount to the "direct dollars-and-cents injury" that our strict taxpayer-standing doctrine requires. *Doremus v. Board of Ed. of Hawthorne*, 342 U. S. 429, 434 (1952).

Brendlin v. California, 551 U.S. 249 (2007)

ON WRIT OF CERTIORARI TO THE SUPREME COURT OF CALIFORNIA

[June 18, 2007]

JUSTICE SOUTER delivered the opinion of the Court.

When a police officer makes a traffic stop, the driver of the car is seized within the meaning of the Fourth Amendment. The question in this case is whether the same is true of a passenger. We hold that a passenger is seized as well and so may challenge the constitutionality of the stop.

I

Early in the morning of November 27, 2001, Deputy Sheriff Robert Brokenbrough and his partner saw a parked Buick with expired registration tags. In his ensuing conversation with the police dispatcher, Brokenbrough learned that an application for renewal of registration was being processed. The officers saw the car again on the road, and this time Brokenbrough noticed its display of a temporary operating permit with the number "11," indicating it was legal to drive the car through November. App. 115. The officers decided to pull the Buick over to verify that the permit matched the vehicle, even though, as Brokenbrough admitted later, there was nothing unusual about the permit or the way it was affixed. Brokenbrough asked the driver, Karen Simeroth, for her license and saw a passenger in the front seat, petitioner Bruce Brendlin, whom he recognized as "one of the Brendlin brothers." *Id.*, at 65. He recalled that either Scott or Bruce Brendlin had dropped out of parole supervision and asked Brendlin to identify himself.[1]

Brokenbrough returned to his cruiser, called for backup, and verified that Brendlin was a parole violator with an outstanding no-bail warrant for his arrest. While he was in the patrol car, Brokenbrough saw Brendlin briefly open and then close the passenger door of the Buick. Once reinforcements arrived, Brokenbrough went to the passenger side of the Buick, ordered him out of the car at gunpoint, and declared him under arrest. When the police searched Brendlin incident to arrest, they found an orange syringe cap on his person. A pat down search of Simeroth revealed syringes and a plastic bag of a green leafy substance, and she was also formally arrested. Officers then searched the car and found tubing, a scale, and other things used to produce methamphetamine.

Brendlin was charged with possession and manufacture of methamphetamine, and he moved to suppress the evidence obtained in the searches of his person and the car as fruits of an unconstitutional seizure, arguing that the officers lacked probable cause or reasonable suspicion to make the traffic stop. He did not assert that his Fourth Amendment rights were violated by the search of Simeroth's vehicle, *cf. Rakas v. Illinois*, 439 U. S. 128 (1978), but claimed only that the traffic stop was an unlawful seizure of his person. The trial court denied the suppression motion after finding that the stop was lawful and Brendlin was not seized until Brokenbrough ordered him out of the car and formally arrested him. Brendlin pleaded guilty, subject to appeal on the suppression issue, and was sentenced to four years in prison.

The California Court of Appeal reversed the denial of the suppression motion, holding that Brendlin was seized by the traffic stop, which they held unlawful. 8 Cal. Rptr. 3d 882 (2004) (officially depublished). By a narrow majority, the Supreme Court of California reversed. The State Supreme Court noted California's concession that the officers had no reasonable basis to suspect unlawful operation of the car, 38 Cal. 4th 1107, 1114, 136 P. 3d

[1]The parties dispute the accuracy of the transcript of the suppression hearing and disagree as to whether Brendlin gave his name or the false name "Bruce Brown." App. 115.

845, 848 (2006),[2] but still held suppression unwarranted because a passenger "is not seized as a constitutional matter in the absence of additional circumstances that would indicate to a reasonable person that he or she was the subject of the peace officer's investigation or show of authority," *id.*, at 1111, 136 P. 3d, at 846. The court reasoned that Brendlin was not seized by the traffic stop because Simeroth was its exclusive target, *id.*, at 1118, 136 P. 3d, at 851, that a passenger cannot submit to an officer's show of authority while the driver controls the car, *id.*, at 1118–1119, 135 P. 3d, at 851–852, and that once a car has been pulled off the road, a passenger "would feel free to depart or otherwise to conduct his or her affairs as though the police were not present," *id.*, at 1119, 136 P. 3d, at 852. In dissent, Justice Corrigan said that a traffic stop entails the seizure of a passenger even when the driver is the sole target of police investigation because a passenger is detained for the purpose of ensuring an officer's safety and would not feel free to leave the car without the officer's permission. *Id.*, at 1125, 136 P. 3d, at 856.

We granted certiorari to decide whether a traffic stop subjects a passenger, as well as the driver, to Fourth Amendment seizure, 549 U. S. _____ (2007). We now vacate.

II

A

A person is seized by the police and thus entitled to challenge the government's action under the Fourth Amendment when the officer, " 'by means of physical force or show of authority,' " terminates or restrains his freedom of movement, *Florida v. Bostick*, 501 U. S. 429, 434 (1991) (quoting *Terry v. Ohio*, 392 U. S. 1, 19, n. 16 (1968)), "*through means intentionally applied*," *Brower v. County of Inyo*, 489 U. S. 593, 597 (1989) (emphasis in original). Thus, an "unintended person… [may be] the object of the detention," so long as the detention is "willful" and not merely the consequence of "an unknowing act." *Id.*, at 596; *cf. County of Sacramento v. Lewis*, 523 U. S. 833, 844 (1998) (no seizure where a police officer accidentally struck and killed a motorcycle passenger during a high-speed pursuit). A police officer may make a seizure by a show of authority and without the use of physical force, but there is no seizure without actual submission; otherwise, there is at most an attempted seizure, so far as the Fourth Amendment is concerned. *See California v. Hodari D.*, 499 U. S. 621, 626, n. 2 (1991); *Lewis, supra*, at 844, 845, n. 7.

When the actions of the police do not show an unambiguous intent to restrain or when an individual's submission to a show of governmental authority takes the form of passive acquiescence, there needs to be some test for telling when a seizure occurs in response to authority, and when it does not. The test was devised by Justice Stewart in *United States v. Mendenhall*, 446 U. S. 544 (1980), who wrote that a seizure occurs if "in view of all of the circumstances surrounding the incident, a reasonable person would have believed that he was not free to leave," *id.*, 554 (principal opinion). Later on, the Court adopted Justice Stewart's touchstone, *see, e.g., Hodari D., supra*, at 627; *Michigan v. Chesternut*, 486 U. S. 567, 573 (1988); *INS v. Delgado*, 466 U. S. 210, 215 (1984), but added that when a person "has no desire to leave" for reasons unrelated to the police presence, the "coercive effect of the encounter" can be measured better by asking whether "a reasonable person would feel free to decline the officers' requests or otherwise terminate the encounter," *Bostick, supra*, at 435–436; *see also United States v. Drayton*, 536 U. S. 194, 202 (2002).

The law is settled that in Fourth Amendment terms a traffic stop entails a seizure of the driver "even though the purpose of the stop is limited and the resulting detention quite brief." *Delaware v. Prouse*, 440 U. S. 648, 653 (1979); *see also Whren v. United States*, 517 U. S. 806, 809–810 (1996). And although we have not, until today, squarely answered the question whether a passenger is also seized, we have said over and over in dicta that during a traffic stop an officer seizes everyone in the vehicle, not just the driver.

---

[2]California conceded that the police officers lacked reasonable suspicion to justify the traffic stop because a "'vehicle with an application for renewal of expired registration would be expected to have a temporary operating permit.' " 38 Cal. 4th, at 1114, 136 P. 3d, at 848 (quoting Brief for Respondent California in No. S123133 (Sup. Ct. Cal.), p. 24).

See, e.g., Prouse, supra, at 653 ("[S]topping an automobile and detaining its occupants constitute a 'seizure' within the meaning of [the Fourth and Fourteenth] Amendments"); *Colorado v. Bannister*, 449 U. S. 1, 4, n. 3 (1980) (*per curiam*) ("There can be no question that the stopping of a vehicle and the detention of its occupants constitute a 'seizure' within the meaning of the Fourth Amendment"); *Berkemer v. McCarty*, 468 U. S. 420, 436–437 (1984) ("[W]e have long acknowledged that stopping an automobile and detaining its occupants constitute a seizure" (internal quotation marks omitted)); *United States v. Hensley*, 469 U.S. 221, 226 (1985) ("[S]topping a car and detaining its occupants constitute a seizure"); *Whren, supra*, at 809–810 ("Temporary detention of individuals during the stop of an automobile by the police, even if only for a brief period and for a limited purpose, constitutes a 'seizure' of 'persons' within the meaning of [the Fourth Amendment]").

We have come closest to the question here in two cases dealing with unlawful seizure of a passenger, and neither time did we indicate any distinction between driver and passenger that would affect the Fourth Amendment analysis. *Delaware v. Prouse* considered grounds for stopping a car on the road and held that Prouse's suppression motion was properly granted. We spoke of the arresting officer's testimony that Prouse was in the back seat when the car was pulled over, see 440 U. S., at 650, n. 1, described Prouse as an occupant, not as the driver, and referred to the car's "occupants" as being seized, *id.*, at 653. Justification for stopping a car was the issue again in *Whren v. United States*, where we passed upon a Fourth Amendment challenge by two petitioners who moved to suppress drug evidence found during the course of a traffic stop. See 517 U. S., at 809. Both driver and passenger claimed to have been seized illegally when the police stopped the car; we agreed and held suppression unwarranted only because the stop rested on probable cause. *Id.*, at 809–810, 819.

B

The State concedes that the police had no adequate justification to pull the car over, see n. 2, *supra*, but argues that the passenger was not seized and thus cannot claim that the evidence was tainted by an unconstitutional stop. We resolve this question by asking whether a reasonable person in Brendlin's position when the car stopped would have believed himself free to "terminate the encounter" between the police and himself. *Bostick, supra*, at 436. We think that in these circumstances any reasonable passenger would have understood the police officers to be exercising control to the point that no one in the car was free to depart without police permission.

A traffic stop necessarily curtails the travel a passenger has chosen just as much as it halts the driver, diverting both from the stream of traffic to the side of the road, and the police activity that normally amounts to intrusion on "privacy and personal security" does not normally (and did not here) distinguish between passenger and driver. *United States v. Martinez-Fuerte*, 428 U. S. 543, 554 (1976). An officer who orders one particular car to pullover acts with an implicit claim of right based on fault of some sort, and a sensible person would not expect a police officer to allow people to come and go freely from the physical focal point of an investigation into faulty behavior or wrongdoing. If the likely wrongdoing is not the driving, the passenger will reasonably feel subject to suspicion owing to close association; but even when the wrong doing is only bad driving, the passenger will expect to be subject to some scrutiny, and his attempt to leave the scene would be so obviously likely to prompt an objection from the officer that no passenger would feel free to leave in the first place. *Cf. Drayton, supra*, at 197–199, 203–204 (finding no seizure when police officers boarded a stationary bus and asked passengers for permission to search for drugs).[3]

---

[3]Of course, police may also stop a car solely to investigate a passenger's conduct. *See, e.g., United States v. Rodriguez-Diaz*, 161 F. Supp. 2d 627, 629, n. 1 (Md. 2001) (passenger's violation of local seatbelt law); *People v. Roth*, 85 P. 3d 571, 573 (Colo. App. 2003) (passenger's violation of littering ordinance). Accordingly, a passenger cannot assume, merely from the fact of a traffic stop, that the driver's conduct is the cause of the stop.

It is also reasonable for passengers to expect that a police officer at the scene of a crime, arrest, or investigation will not let people move around in ways that could jeopardize his safety. In *Maryland v. Wilson*, 519 U. S. 408 (1997), we held that during a lawful traffic stop an officer may order a passenger out of the car as a precautionary measure, without reasonable suspicion that the passenger poses a safety risk. *Id.*, at 414–415; *cf. Pennsylvania v. Mimms*, 434 U. S. 106 (1977) (*per curiam*) (driver may be ordered out of the car as a matter of course). In fashioning this rule, we invoked our earlier statement that " '[t]he risk of harm to both the police and the occupants is minimized if the officers routinely exercise unquestioned command of the situation.' " *Wilson, supra*, at 414 (quoting *Michigan v. Summers*, 452 U. S. 692, 702–703 (1981)). What we have said in these opinions probably reflects a societal expectation of " 'unquestioned [police] command' " at odds with any notion that a passenger would feel free to leave, or to terminate the personal encounter any other way, without advance permission. *Wilson, supra*, at 414.[4]

Our conclusion comports with the views of all nine Federal Courts of Appeals, and nearly every state court, to have ruled on the question. *See United States v. Kimball*, 25 F. 3d 1, 5 (CA1 1994); *United States v. Mosley*, 454 F. 3d 249, 253 (CA3 2006); *United States v. Rusher*, 966 F. 2d 868, 874, n. 4 (CA4 1992); *United States v. Grant*, 349 F. 3d 192, 196 (CA5 2003); *United States v. Perez*, 440 F. 3d 363, 369 (CA6 2006); *United States v. Powell*, 929 F. 2d 1190, 1195 (CA7 1991); *United States v. Ameling*, 328 F. 3d 443, 446–447, n. 3 (CA8 2003); *United States v. Twilley*, 222 F. 3d 1092, 1095 (CA9 2000); *United States v. Eylicio-Montoya*, 70 F. 3d 1158, 1163–1164 (CA10 1995); *State v. Bowers*, 334 Ark. 447, 451–452, 976 S. W. 2d 379, 381–382 (1998); *State v. Haworth*, 106 Idaho 405, 405–406, 679 P. 2d 1123, 1123–1124 (1984); *People v. Bunch*, 207 Ill. 2d 7, 13, 796 N. E. 2d 1024, 1029 (2003); *State v. Eis*, 348 N. W. 2d 224, 226 (Iowa 1984); *State v. Hodges*, 252 Kan. 989, 1002–1005, 851 P. 2d 352, 361–362 (1993); *State v. Carter*, 69 Ohio St. 3d 57, 63, 630 N. E. 2d 355, 360 (1994) *(per curiam); State v. Harris*, 206 Wis. 2d 243, 253–258, 557 N. W. 2d 245, 249–251 (1996). And the treatise writers share this prevailing judicial view that a passenger may bring a Fourth Amendment challenge to the legality of a traffic stop. *See, e.g.*, 6 W. LaFave, Search and Seizure §11. 3(e), pp. 194, 195, and n. 277 (4th ed. 2004 and Supp. 2007) ("If either the stopping of the car, the length of the passenger's detention thereafter, or the passenger's removal from it are unreasonable in a Fourth Amendment sense, then surely the passenger has standing to object to those constitutional violations and to have suppressed any evidence found in the car which is their fruit" (footnote omitted)); 1 W. Ringel, Searches & Seizures, Arrests and Confessions §11:20, p. 11–98 (2d ed. 2007) ("[A] law enforcement officer's stop of an automobile results in a seizure of both the driver and the passenger").[5]

C

The contrary conclusion drawn by the Supreme Court of California, that seizure came only with formal arrest, reflects three premises as to which we respectfully disagree. First, the State Supreme Court reasoned that Brendlin was not seized by the stop because Deputy Sheriff Brokenbrough only intended to investigate Simeroth and did not direct a show of authority toward Brendlin. The court saw Brokenbrough's "flashing lights [as] directed at the driver," and pointed to the lack of record evidence that Brokenbrough "was even aware [Brendlin] was in the car prior to the vehicle stop." 38 Cal. 4th, at 1118, 136 P. 3d, at 851. But that view of the facts ignores the objective *Mendenhall* test of what a reasonable passenger would understand. To the extent that there is anything ambiguous in the show of force (was it fairly seen as directed only at the driver or at the car and its occupants?),

---

[4]Although the State Supreme Court inferred from Brendlin's decision to open and close the passenger door during the traffic stop that he was "awar[e] of the available options," 38 Cal. 4th 1107, 1120, 136 P. 3d845, 852 (2006), this conduct could equally be taken to indicate that Brendlin felt compelled to remain inside the car. In any event, the test is not what Brendlin felt but what a reasonable passenger would have understood.

[5]Only two State Supreme Courts, other than California's, have stood against this tide of authority. *See People v. Jackson*, 39 P. 3d 1174, 1184–1186 (Colo. 2002) (en banc); *State v. Mendez*, 137 Wash. 2d 208, 222–223, 970 P. 2d 722, 729 (1999) (en banc).

the test resolves the ambiguity, and here it leads to the intuitive conclusion that all the occupants were subject to like control by the successful display of authority. The State Supreme Court's approach, on the contrary, shifts the issue from the intent of the police as objectively manifested to the motive of the police for taking the intentional action to stop the car, and we have repeatedly rejected attempts to introduce this kind of subjectivity into Fourth Amendment analysis. *See, e.g., Whren*, 517 U. S., at 813 ("Subjective intentions play no role in ordinary, probable-cause Fourth Amendment analysis"); *Chesternut*, 486 U. S., at 575, n. 7 ("[T]he subjective intent of the officers is relevant to an assessment of the Fourth Amendment implications of police conduct only to the extent that that intent has been conveyed to the person confronted"); *Mendenhall*, 446 U. S., at 554, n. 6 (principal opinion) (disregarding a Government agent's subjective intent to detain Mendenhall); cf. *Rakas*, 439 U. S., at 132–135 (rejecting the "target theory" of Fourth Amendment standing, which would have allowed "any criminal defendant at whom a search was directed" to challenge the legality of the search (internal quotation marks omitted)).

California defends the State Supreme Court's ruling on this point by citing our cases holding that seizure requires a purposeful, deliberate act of detention. See Brief for Respondent 9–14. But *Chesternut, supra*, answers that argument. The intent that counts under the Fourth Amendment is the "intent [that] has been conveyed to the person confronted," *id.*, at 575, n. 7, and the criterion of willful restriction on freedom of movement is no invitation to look to subjective intent when determining who is seized. Our most recent cases are in accord on this point. In *Lewis*, 523 U. S. 833, we considered whether a seizure occurred when an officer accidentally ran over a passenger who had fallen off a motorcycle during a high-speed chase, and in holding that no seizure took place, we stressed that the officer stopped Lewis's movement by accidentally crashing into him, not "through means intentionally applied." *Id.*, at 844 (emphasis deleted). We did not even consider, let alone emphasize, the possibility that the officer had meant to detain the driver only and not the passenger. Nor is *Brower*, 489 U. S. 593, to the contrary, where it was dispositive that "Brower was meant to be stopped by the physical obstacle of the roadblock—and that he was so stopped." *Id.*, at 599. California reads this language to suggest that for a specific occupant of the car to be seized he must be the motivating target of an officer's show of authority, see Brief for Respondent 12, as if the thrust of our observation were that Brower, and not someone else, was "meant to be stopped." But our point was not that Brower alone was the target but that officers detained him "through means intentionally applied"; if the car had had another occupant, it would have made sense to hold that he too had been seized when the car collided with the roadblock. Neither case, then, is at odds with our holding that the issue is whether a reasonable passenger would have perceived that the show of authority was at least partly directed at him, and that he was thus not free to ignore the police presence and go about his business.

Second, the Supreme Court of California assumed that Brendlin, "as the passenger, had no ability to submit to the deputy's show of authority" because only the driver was in control of the moving vehicle. 38 Cal. 4th, at 1118, 1119, 136 P. 3d, at 852. But what may amount to submission depends on what a person was doing before the show of authority: a fleeing man is not seized until he is physically overpowered, but one sitting in a chair may submit to authority by not getting up to run away. Here, Brendlin had no effective way to signal submission while the car was still moving on the roadway, but once it came to a stop he could, and apparently did, submit by staying inside.

Third, the State Supreme Court shied away from the rule we apply today for fear that it "would encompass even those motorists following the vehicle subject to the traffic stop who, by virtue of the original detention, are forced to slow down and perhaps even come to a halt in order to accommodate that vehicle's submission to police authority." *Id.*, at 1120, 136 P. 3d, at 853. But an occupant of a car who knows that he is stuck in traffic because another car has been pulled over (like the motorist who can't even make out why the road is suddenly clogged) would not perceive a show of authority as directed at him or his car. Such incidental restrictions on freedom of movement would not tend to affect an individual's "sense of security and privacy in traveling in an automobile." *Prouse*, 440 U. S., at 662. Nor would the consequential blockage call for a precautionary rule to avoid the kind of "arbitrary and oppressive interference by [law] enforcement officials with the privacy and personal security of individuals" that the Fourth Amendment was intended to limit. *Martinez-Fuerte*, 428 U. S., at 554.[6]

Indeed, the consequence to worry about would not flow from our conclusion, but from the rule that almost all courts have rejected. Holding that the passenger in a private car is not (without more) seized in a traffic stop would invite police officers to stop cars with passengers regardless of probable cause or reasonable suspicion of anything illegal.[7] The fact that evidence uncovered as a result of an arbitrary traffic stop would still be admissible against any passengers would be a powerful incentive to run the kind of "roving patrols" that would still violate the driver's Fourth Amendment right. *See, e.g., Almeida-Sanchez v. United States*, 413 U. S. 266, 273 (1973) (stop and search by Border Patrol agents without a warrant or probable cause violated the Fourth Amendment); *Prouse, supra*, at 663 (police spot check of driver's license and registration without reasonable suspicion violated the Fourth Amendment).

* * *

Brendlin was seized from the moment Simeroth's car came to a halt on the side of the road, and it was error to deny his suppression motion on the ground that seizure occurred only at the formal arrest. It will be for the state courts to consider in the first instance whether suppression turns on any other issue. The judgment of the Supreme Court of California is vacated, and the case is remanded for further proceedings not inconsistent with this opinion.

It is so ordered.

Tinker v. Des Moines School Dist., 393 U.S. 503 (1969)

MR. JUSTICE FORTAS delivered the opinion of the Court.

Petitioner John F. Tinker, 15 years old, and petitioner Christopher Eckhardt, 16 years old, attended high schools in Des Moines, Iowa. Petitioner Mary Beth Tinker, John's sister, was a 13-year-old student in junior high school.

In December 1965, a group of adults and students in Des Moines held a meeting at the Eckhardt home. The group determined to publicize their objections to the hostilities in Vietnam and their support for a truce by wearing black armbands during the holiday season and by fasting on December 16 and New Year's Eve. Petitioners and their parents had previously engaged in similar activities, and they decided to participate in the program.

The principals of the Des Moines schools became aware of the plan to wear armbands. On December 14, 1965, they met and adopted a policy that any student wearing an armband to school would be asked to remove it, and if he refused he would be suspended until he returned without the armband. Petitioners were aware of the regulation that the school authorities adopted.

---

[6]California claims that, under today's rule, "all taxi cab and bus passengers would be 'seized' under the Fourth Amendment when the cab or bus driver is pulled over by the police for running a red light." Brief for Respondent 23. But the relationship between driver and passenger is not the same in a common carrier as it is in a private vehicle, and the expectations of police officers and passengers differ accordingly. In those cases, as here, the crucial question would be whether a reasonable person in the passenger's position would feel free to take steps to terminate the encounter.

[7]Compare *Delaware v. Prouse*, 440 U. S. 648, 663 (1979) (requiring "at least articulable and reasonable suspicion" to support random, investigative traffic stops), and *United States v. Brignoni-Ponce*, 422 U. S. 873, 880–884 (1975) (same), with *Whren v. United States*, 517 U. S. 806, 810 (1996) ("[T]he decision to stop an automobile is reasonable where the police have probable cause to believe that a traffic violation has occurred"), and *Atwater v. Lago Vista*, 532 U. S. 318, 354 (2001) ("If an officer has probable cause to believe that an individual has committed even a very minor criminal offense in his presence, he may, without violating the Fourth Amendment, arrest the offender").

On December 16, Mary Beth and Christopher wore black armbands to their schools. John Tinker wore his armband the next day. They were all sent home and suspended from school until they would come back without their armbands. They did not return to school until after the planned period for wearing armbands had expired—that is, until after New Year's Day.

This complaint was filed in the United States District Court by petitioners, through their fathers, under 1983 of Title 42 of the United States Code. It prayed for an injunction restraining the respondent school officials and the respondent members of the board of directors of the school district from disciplining the petitioners, and it sought nominal damages. After an evidentiary hearing the District Court dismissed the complaint. It upheld the constitutionality of the school authorities' action on the ground that it was reasonable in order to prevent disturbance of school discipline. 258 F. Supp. 971 (1966). The court referred to but expressly declined to follow the Fifth Circuit's holding in a similar case that the wearing of symbols like the armbands cannot be prohibited unless it "materially and substantially interfere[s] with the requirements of appropriate discipline in the operation of the school." *Burnside v. Byars*, 363 F.2d 744, 749 (1966).

On appeal, the Court of Appeals for the Eighth Circuit considered the case en banc. The court was equally divided, and the District Court's decision was accordingly affirmed, without opinion. 383 F.2d 988 (1967). We granted *certiorari*. 390 U.S. 942 (1968).

I

The District Court recognized that the wearing of an armband for the purpose of expressing certain views is the type of symbolic act that is within the Free Speech Clause of the First Amendment. *See West Virginia v. Barnette*, 319 U.S. 624 (1943); *Stromberg v. California*, 283 U.S. 359 (1931). *Cf. Thornhill v. Alabama*, 310 U.S. 88 (1940); *Edwards v. South Carolina*, 372 U.S. 229 (1963); *Brown v. Louisiana*, 383 U.S. 131 (1966). As we shall discuss, the wearing of armbands in the circumstances of this case was entirely divorced from actually or potentially disruptive conduct by those participating in it. It was closely akin to "pure speech" which, we have repeatedly held, is entitled to comprehensive protection under the First Amendment. *Cf. Cox v. Louisiana*, 379 U.S. 536, 555 (1965); *Adderley v. Florida*, 385 U.S. 39 (1966).

First Amendment rights, applied in light of the special characteristics of the school environment, are available to teachers and students. It can hardly be argued that either students or teachers shed their constitutional rights to freedom of speech or expression at the schoolhouse gate. This has been the unmistakable holding of this Court for almost 50 years. In *Meyer v. Nebraska*, 262 U.S. 390 (1923), and *Bartels v. Iowa*, 262 U.S. 404 (1923), this Court, in opinions by Mr. Justice McReynolds, held that the Due Process Clause of the Fourteenth Amendment prevents States from forbidding the teaching of a foreign language to young students. Statutes to this effect, the Court held, unconstitutionally interfere with the liberty of teacher, student, and parent. *See also Pierce v. Society of Sisters*, 268 U.S. 510 (1925); *West Virginia v. Barnette*, 319 U.S. 624 (1943); *McCollum v. Board of Education*, 333 U.S. 203 (1948); *Wieman v. Updegraff*, 344 U.S. 183, 195 (1952) (concurring opinion); *Sweezy v. New Hampshire*, 354 U.S. 234 (1957); *Shelton v. Tucker*, 364 U.S. 479, 487 (1960); *Engel v. Vitale*, 370 U.S. 421 (1962); *Keyishian v. Board of Regents*, 385 U.S. 589, 603 (1967); *Epperson v. Arkansas*, ante, p. 97 (1968). In *West Virginia v. Barnette, supra*, this Court held that under the First Amendment, the student in public school may not be compelled to salute the flag. Speaking through Mr. Justice Jackson, the Court said:

> "The Fourteenth Amendment, as now applied to the States, protects the citizen against the State itself and all of its creatures—Boards of Education not excepted. These have, of course, important, delicate, and highly discretionary functions, but none that they may not perform within the limits of the Bill of Rights. That they are we are not to strangle the free mind at its source and teach youth to discount important principles of our government as mere platitudes." 319 U.S., at 637.

On the other hand, the Court has repeatedly emphasized the need for affirming the comprehensive authority of the States and of school officials, consistent with fundamental constitutional safeguards, to prescribe and control conduct in the schools. *See Epperson v. Arkansas, supra*, at 104; *Meyer v. Nebraska, supra*, at 402. Our problem lies in the area where students in the exercise of First Amendment rights collide with the rules of the school authorities.

II

The problem posed by the present case does not relate to regulation of the length of skirts or the type of clothing, to hair style, or deportment. *Cf. Ferrell v. Dallas Independent School District*, 392 F.2d 697 (1968); *Pugsley v. Sellmeyer*, 158 Ark. 247, 250 S. W. 538 (1923). It does not concern aggressive, disruptive action or even group demonstrations. Our problem involves direct, primary First Amendment rights akin to "pure speech."

The school officials banned and sought to punish petitioners for a silent, passive expression of opinion, unaccompanied by any disorder or disturbance on the part of petitioners. There is here no evidence whatever of petitioners' interference, actual or nascent, with the schools' work or of collision with the rights of other students to be secure and to be let alone. Accordingly, this case does not concern speech or action that intrudes upon the work of the schools or the rights of other students.

Only a few of the 18,000 students in the school system wore the black armbands. Only five students were suspended for wearing them. There is no indication that the work of the schools or any class was disrupted. Outside the classrooms, a few students made hostile remarks to the children wearing armbands, but there were no threats or acts of violence on school premises.

The District Court concluded that the action of the school authorities was reasonable because it was based upon their fear of a disturbance from the wearing of the armbands. But, in our system, undifferentiated fear or apprehension of disturbance is not enough to overcome the right to freedom of expression. Any departure from absolute regimentation may cause trouble. Any variation from the majority's opinion may inspire fear. Any word spoken, in class, in the lunchroom, or on the campus, that deviates from the views of another person may start an argument or cause a disturbance. But our Constitution says we must take this risk, *Terminiello v. Chicago*, 337 U.S. 1 (1949); and our history says that it is this sort of hazardous freedom—this kind of openness—that is the basis of our national strength and of the independence and vigor of Americans who grow up and live in this relatively permissive, often disputatious, society.

In order for the State in the person of school officials to justify prohibition of a particular expression of opinion, it must be able to show that its action was caused by something more than a mere desire to avoid the discomfort and unpleasantness that always accompany an unpopular viewpoint. Certainly where there is no finding and no showing that engaging in the forbidden conduct would "materially and substantially interfere with the requirements of appropriate discipline in the operation of the school," the prohibition cannot be sustained. *Burnside v. Byars, supra*, at 749.

In the present case, the District Court made no such finding, and our independent examination of the record fails to yield evidence that the school authorities had reason to anticipate that the wearing of the armbands would substantially interfere with the work of the school or impinge upon the rights of other students. Even an official memorandum prepared after the suspension that listed the reasons for the ban on wearing the armbands made no reference to the anticipation of such disruption. On the contrary, the action of the school authorities appears to have been based upon an urgent wish to avoid the controversy which might result from the expression, even by the silent symbol of armbands, of opposition to this Nation's part in the conflagration in Vietnam. It is revealing, in this respect, that the meeting at which the school principals decided to issue the contested regulation was called in response to a student's statement to the journalism teacher in one of the schools that he wanted to write an article on Vietnam and have it published in the school paper. (The student was dissuaded.)

It is also relevant that the school authorities did not purport to prohibit the wearing of all symbols of political or controversial significance. The record shows that students in some of the schools wore buttons relating to national political campaigns, and some even wore the Iron Cross, traditionally a symbol of Nazism. The order prohibiting the wearing of armbands did not extend to these. Instead, a particular symbol—black armbands worn to exhibit opposition to this Nation's involvement in Vietnam—was singled out for prohibition. Clearly, the prohibition of expression of one particular opinion, at least without evidence that it is necessary to avoid material and substantial interference with schoolwork or discipline, is not constitutionally permissible.

In our system, state-operated schools may not be enclaves of totalitarianism. School officials do not possess absolute authority over their students. Students in school as well as out of school are "persons" under our Constitution. They are possessed of fundamental rights which the State must respect, just as they themselves must respect their obligations to the State. In our system, students may not be regarded as closed-circuit recipients of only that which the State chooses to communicate. They may not be confined to the expression of those sentiments that are officially approved. In the absence of a specific showing of constitutionally valid reasons to regulate their speech, students are entitled to freedom of expression of their views. As Judge Gewin, speaking for the Fifth Circuit, said, school officials cannot suppress "expressions of feelings with which they do not wish to contend." *Burnside v. Byars, supra*, at 749.

In *Meyer v. Nebraska, supra*, at 402, Mr. Justice McReynolds expressed this Nation's repudiation of the principle that a State might so conduct its schools as to "foster a homogeneous people." He said:

> "In order to submerge the individual and develop ideal citizens, Sparta assembled the males at seven into barracks and intrusted their subsequent education and training to official guardians. Although such measures have been deliberately approved by men of great genius, their ideas touching the relation between individual and State were wholly different from those upon which our institutions rest; and it hardly will be affirmed that any legislature could impose such restrictions upon the people of a State without doing violence to both letter and spirit of the Constitution."

This principle has been repeated by this Court on numerous occasions during the intervening years. In *Keyishian v. Board of Regents*, 385 U.S. 589, 603, MR. JUSTICE BRENNAN, speaking for the Court, said:

> "'The vigilant protection of constitutional freedoms is nowhere more vital than in the community of American schools.' *Shelton v. Tucker*, [364 U.S. 479,] at 487. The classroom is peculiarly the 'marketplace of ideas.' The Nation's future depends upon leaders trained through wide exposure to that robust exchange of ideas which discovers truth 'out of a multitude of tongues, [rather] than through any kind of authoritative selection.'"

The principle of these cases is not confined to the supervised and ordained discussion which takes place in the classroom. The principal use to which the schools are dedicated is to accommodate students during prescribed hours for the purpose of certain types of activities. Among those activities is personal intercommunication among the students. This is not only an inevitable part of the process of attending school; it is also an important part of the educational process. A student's rights, therefore, do not embrace merely the classroom hours. When he is in the cafeteria, or on the playing field, or on the campus during the authorized hours, he may express his opinions, even on controversial subjects like the conflict in Vietnam, if he does so without "materially and substantially interfer[ing] with the requirements of appropriate discipline in the operation of the school" and without colliding with the rights of others. *Burnside v. Byars, supra*, at 749. But conduct by the student, in class or out of it, which for any reason—whether it stems from time, place, or type of behavior—materially disrupts classwork or involves substantial disorder or invasion of the rights of others is, of course, not immunized by the constitutional guarantee of freedom of speech. *Cf. Blackwell v. Issaquena County Board of Education*, 363 F.2d 749 (C. A. 5th Cir. 1966).

Under our Constitution, free speech is not a right that is given only to be so circumscribed that it exists in principle but not in fact. Freedom of expression would not truly exist if the right could be exercised only in an area that a benevolent government has provided as a safe haven for crackpots. The Constitution says that Congress (and the States) may not abridge the right to free speech. This provision means what it says. We properly read it to permit reasonable regulation of speech-connected activities in carefully restricted circumstances. But we do not confine the permissible exercise of First Amendment rights to a telephone booth or the four corners of a pamphlet, or to supervised and ordained discussion in a school classroom.

If a regulation were adopted by school officials forbidding discussion of the Vietnam conflict, or the expression by any student of opposition to it anywhere on school property except as part of a prescribed classroom exercise, it would be obvious that the regulation would violate the constitutional rights of students, at least if it could not be justified by a showing that the students' activities would materially and substantially disrupt the work and discipline of the school. *Cf. Hammond v. South Carolina State College*, 272 F. Supp. 947 (D.C. S. C. 1967) (orderly protest meeting on state college campus); *Dickey v. Alabama State Board of Education*, 273 F. Supp. 613 (D.C. M. D. Ala. 1967) (expulsion of student editor of college newspaper). In the circumstances of the present case, the prohibition of the silent, passive "witness of the armbands," as one of the children called it, is no less offensive to the Constitution's guarantees.

As we have discussed, the record does not demonstrate any facts which might reasonably have led school authorities to forecast substantial disruption of or material interference with school activities, and no disturbances or disorders on the school premises in fact occurred. These petitioners merely went about their ordained rounds in school. Their deviation consisted only in wearing on their sleeve a band of black cloth, not more than two inches wide. They wore it to exhibit their disapproval of the Vietnam hostilities and their advocacy of a truce, to make their views known, and, by their example, to influence others to adopt them. They neither interrupted school activities nor sought to intrude in the school affairs or the lives of others. They caused discussion outside of the classrooms, but no interference with work and no disorder. In the circumstances, our Constitution does not permit officials of the State to deny their form of expression.

We express no opinion as to the form of relief which should be granted, this being a matter for the lower courts to determine. We reverse and remand for further proceedings consistent with this opinion.

Reversed and remanded.

Morse v. Frederick, 551 U.S. 393 (2007)

ON WRIT OF CERTIORARI TO THE UNITED STATES COURT OF APPEALS FOR THE NINTH CIRCUIT

[JUNE 25, 2007]

CHIEF JUSTICE ROBERTS delivered the opinion of the Court.

At a school-sanctioned and school-supervised event, a high school principal saw some of her students unfurl a large banner conveying a message she reasonably regarded as promoting illegal drug use. Consistent with established school policy prohibiting such messages at school events, the principal directed the students to take down the banner. One student—among those who had brought the banner to the event—refused to do so. The principal confiscated the banner and later suspended the student. The Ninth Circuit held that the principal's actions violated the First Amendment, and that the student could sue the principal for damages.

Our cases make clear that students do not "shed their constitutional rights to freedom of speech or expression at the schoolhouse gate." *Tinker v. Des Moines Independent*

Community School Dist., 393 U. S. 503, 506 (1969). At the same time, we have held that "the constitutional rights of students in public school are not automatically coextensive with the rights of adults in other settings," *Bethel School Dist. No. 403 v. Fraser*, 478 U.S. 675, 682 (1986), and that the rights of students "must be 'applied in light of the special characteristics of the school environment.' " *Hazelwood School Dist. v. Kuhlmeier*, 484 U.S. 260, 266 (1988) (quoting *Tinker*, *supra*, at 506). Consistent with these principles, we hold that schools may take steps to safeguard those entrusted to their care from speech that can reasonably be regarded as encouraging illegal drug use. We conclude that the school officials in this case did not violate the First Amendment by confiscating the prodrug banner and suspending the student responsible for it.

I

On January 24, 2002, the Olympic Torch Relay passed through Juneau, Alaska, on its way to the winter games in Salt Lake City, Utah. The torchbearers were to proceed along a street in front of Juneau-Douglas High School (JDHS) while school was in session. Petitioner Deborah Morse, the school principal, decided to permit staff and students to participate in the Torch Relay as an approved social event or class trip. App. 22–23. Students were allowed to leave class to observe the relay from either side of the street. Teachers and administrative officials monitored the students' actions.

Respondent Joseph Frederick, a JDHS senior, was late to school that day. When he arrived, he joined his friends (all but one of whom were JDHS students) across the street from the school to watch the event. Not all the students waited patiently. Some became rambunctious, throwing plastic cola bottles and snowballs and scuffling with their classmates. As the torchbearers and camera crews passed by, Frederick and his friends unfurled a 14-foot banner bearing the phrase: "BONG HiTS 4 JESUS." App. to Pet. for Cert. 70a. The large banner was easily readable by the students on the other side of the street.

Principal Morse immediately crossed the street and demanded that the banner be taken down. Everyone but Frederick complied. Morse confiscated the banner and told Frederick to report to her office, where she suspended him for 10 days. Morse later explained that she told Frederick to take the banner down because she thought it encouraged illegal drug use, in violation of established school policy. Juneau School Board Policy No. 5520 states: "The Board specifically prohibits any assembly or public expression that... advocates the use of substances that are illegal to minors... ." *Id.*, at 53a. In addition, Juneau School Board Policy No. 5850 subjects "[p]upils who participate in approved social events and class trips" to the same student conduct rules that apply during the regular school program. *Id.*, at 58a.

Frederick administratively appealed his suspension, but the Juneau School District Superintendent upheld it, limiting it to time served (8 days). In a memorandum setting forth his reasons, the superintendent determined that Frederick had displayed his banner "in the midst of his fellow students, during school hours, at a school-sanctioned activity." *Id.*, at 63a. He further explained that Frederick "was not disciplined because the principal of the school 'disagreed' with his message, but because his speech appeared to advocate the use of illegal drugs." *Id.*, at 61a.

The superintendent continued:

> "The common-sense understanding of the phrase 'bong hits' is that it is a reference to a means of smoking marijuana. Given [Frederick's] inability or unwillingness to express any other credible meaning for the phrase, I can only agree with the principal and countless others who saw the banner as advocating the use of illegal drugs. [Frederick's] speech was not political. He was not advocating the legalization of marijuana or promoting a religious belief. He was displaying a fairly silly message promoting illegal drug usage in the midst of a school activity, for the benefit of television cameras covering the Torch Relay. [Frederick's] speech was potentially disruptive to the event and clearly disruptive of and inconsistent with the school's educational mission to educate students about the dangers of illegal drugs and to discourage their use." *Id.*, at 61a–62a.

Relying on our decision in *Fraser, supra*, the superintendent concluded that the principal's actions were permissible because Frederick's banner was "speech or action that intrudes upon the work of the schools." App. to Pet. for Cert. 62a (internal quotation marks omitted). The Juneau School District Board of Education upheld the suspension.

Frederick then filed suit under 42 U.S.C. §1983, alleging that the school board and Morse had violated his First Amendment rights. He sought declaratory and injunctive relief, unspecified compensatory damages, punitive damages, and attorney's fees. The District Court granted summary judgment for the school board and Morse, ruling that they were entitled to qualified immunity and that they had not infringed Frederick's First Amendment rights. The court found that Morse reasonably interpreted the banner as promoting illegal drug use—a message that "directly contravened the Board's policies relating to drug abuse prevention." App. to Pet. for Cert. 36a–38a. Under the circumstances, the court held that "Morse had the authority, if not the obligation, to stop such messages at a school-sanctioned activity." *Id.*, at 37a.

The Ninth Circuit reversed. Deciding that Frederick acted during a "school-authorized activit[y]," and "proceed[ing] on the basis that the banner expressed a positive sentiment about marijuana use," the court nonetheless found a violation of Frederick's First Amendment rights because the school punished Frederick without demonstrating that his speech gave rise to a "risk of substantial disruption." 439 F. 3d 1114, 1118, 1121–1123 (2006). The court further concluded that Frederick's right to display his banner was so "clearly established" that a reasonable principal in Morse's position would have understood that her actions were unconstitutional, and that Morse was therefore not entitled to qualified immunity. *Id.*, at 1123–1125.

We granted certiorari on two questions: whether Frederick had a First Amendment right to wield his banner, and, if so, whether that right was so clearly established that the principal may be held liable for damages. 549 U. S. _____ (2006). We resolve the first question against Frederick, and therefore have no occasion to reach the second.[1]

II

At the outset, we reject Frederick's argument that this is not a school speech case—as has every other authority to address the question. See App. 22–23 (Principal Morse); App. to Pet. for Cert. 63a (superintendent); *id.*, at 69a (school board); *id.*, at 34a–35a (District Court); 439 F. 3d, at 1117 (Ninth Circuit). The event occurred during normal school hours. It was sanctioned by Principal Morse "as an approved social event or class trip," App. 22–23, and the school district's rules expressly provide that pupils in "approved social events and class trips are subject to district rules for student conduct." App. to Pet. for Cert. 58a. Teachers and administrators were interspersed among the students and charged with supervising them. The high school band and cheerleaders performed. Frederick, standing among other JDHS students across the street from the school, directed his banner toward the school, making it plainly visible to most students. Under these circumstances, we agree with the superintendent that Frederick cannot "stand in the midst of his fellow students, during school hours, at a school-sanctioned activity and claim he is not at school." *Id.*, at 63a. There is some uncertainty at the outer boundaries as to when courts should apply school-speech precedents, *see Porter v. Ascension Parish School Bd.*, 393 F. 3d 608, 615, n. 22 (CA5 2004), but not on these facts.

---

[1]JUSTICE BREYER would rest decision on qualified immunity without reaching the underlying First Amendment question. The problem with this approach is the rather significant one that it is inadequate to decide the case before us. Qualified immunity shields public officials from money damages only. *See Wood v. Strickland*, 420 U. S. 308, 314, n. 6 (1975). In this case, Frederick asked not just for damages, but also for declaratory and injunctive relief. App. 13. JUSTICE BREYER'S proposed decision on qualified immunity grounds would dispose of the damages claims, but Frederick's other claims would remain unaddressed. To get around that problem, JUSTICE BREYER hypothesizes that Frederick's suspension—the target of his request for injunctive relief—"may well be justified on non-speech-related grounds." *See post*, at 9. That hypothesis was never considered by the courts below, never raised by any of the parties, and is belied by the record, which nowhere suggests that the suspension would have been justified solely on non-speech-related grounds.

III

The message on Frederick's banner is cryptic. It is no doubt offensive to some, perhaps amusing to others. To still others, it probably means nothing at all. Frederick himself claimed "that the words were just nonsense meant to attract television cameras." 439 F. 3d, at 1117–1118. But Principal Morse thought the banner would be interpreted by those viewing it as promoting illegal drug use, and that interpretation is plainly a reasonable one.

As Morse later explained in a declaration, when she saw the sign, she thought that "the reference to a 'bong hit' would be widely understood by high school students and others as referring to smoking marijuana." App. 24. She further believed that "display of the banner would be construed by students, District personnel, parents and others witnessing the display of the banner, as advocating or promoting illegal drug use"—in violation of school policy. *Id.*, at 25; see *ibid.* ("I told Frederick and the other members of his group to put the banner down because I felt that it violated the [school] policy against displaying... material that advertises or promotes use of illegal drugs").

We agree with Morse. At least two interpretations of the words on the banner demonstrate that the sign advocated the use of illegal drugs. First, the phrase could be interpreted as an imperative: "[Take] bong hits ..."—a message equivalent, as Morse explained in her declaration, to "smoke marijuana" or "use an illegal drug." Alternatively, the phrase could be viewed as celebrating drug use—"bong hits [are a good thing]," or "[we take] bong hits"—and we discern no meaningful distinction between celebrating illegal drug use in the midst of fellow students and outright advocacy or promotion. *See Guiles v. Marineau*, 461 F. 3d 320, 328 (CA2 2006) (discussing the present case and describing the sign as "a clearly pro-drug banner").

The pro-drug interpretation of the banner gains further plausibility given the paucity of alternative meanings the banner might bear. The best Frederick can come up with is that the banner is "meaningless and funny." 439 F. 3d, at 1116. The dissent similarly refers to the sign's message as "curious," *post*, at 1, "ambiguous," *ibid.*, "nonsense," *post*, at 2, "ridiculous," *post*, at 6, "obscure," *post*, at 7, "silly," *post*, at 12, "quixotic," *post*, at 13, and "stupid," *ibid.* Gibberish is surely a possible interpretation of the words on the banner, but it is not the only one, and dismissing the banner as meaningless ignores its undeniable reference to illegal drugs.

The dissent mentions Frederick's "credible and uncontradicted explanation for the message—he just wanted to get on television."*Post*, at 12. But that is a description of Frederick's *motive* for displaying the banner; it is not an interpretation of what the banner says. The *way* Frederick was going to fulfill his ambition of appearing on television was by unfurling a pro-drug banner at a school event, in the presence of teachers and fellow students.

Elsewhere in its opinion, the dissent emphasizes the importance of political speech and the need to foster "national debate about a serious issue," *post*, at 16, as if to suggest that the banner is political speech. But not even Frederick argues that the banner conveys any sort of political or religious message. Contrary to the dissent's suggestion, see *post*, at 14–16, this is plainly not a case about political debate over the criminalization of drug use or possession.

IV

The question thus becomes whether a principal may, consistent with the First Amendment, restrict student speech at a school event, when that speech is reasonably viewed as promoting illegal drug use. We hold that she may.

In *Tinker*, this Court made clear that "First Amendment rights, applied in light of the special characteristics of the school environment, are available to teachers and students." 393 U. S., at 506. *Tinker* involved a group of high school students who decided to wear black armbands to protest the Vietnam War. School officials learned of the plan and then adopted a policy prohibiting students from wearing armbands. When several students nonetheless wore armbands to school, they were suspended. *Id.*, at 504. The students sued, claiming that their First Amendment rights had been violated, and this Court agreed.

Tinker held that student expression may not be suppressed unless school officials reasonably conclude that it will "materially and substantially disrupt the work and discipline of the school." *Id.*, at 513. The essential facts of *Tinker* are quite stark, implicating concerns at the heart of the First Amendment. The students sought to engage in political speech, using the armbands to express their "disapproval of the Vietnam hostilities and their advocacy of a truce, to make their views known, and, by their example, to influence others to adopt them." *Id.*, at 514. Political speech, of course, is "at the core of what the First Amendment is designed to protect." *Virginia v. Black*, 538 U. S. 343, 365 (2003). The only interest the Court discerned underlying the school's actions was the "mere desire to avoid the discomfort and unpleasantness that always accompany an unpopular viewpoint," or "an urgent wish to avoid the controversy which might result from the expression." *Tinker*, 393 U. S., at 509, 510. That interest was not enough to justify banning "a silent, passive expression of opinion, unaccompanied by any disorder or disturbance." *Id.*, at 508.

This Court's next student speech case was *Fraser*, 478 U. S. 675. Matthew Fraser was suspended for delivering a speech before a high school assembly in which he employed what this Court called "an elaborate, graphic, and explicit sexual metaphor." *Id.*, at 678. Analyzing the case under *Tinker*, the District Court and Court of Appeals found no disruption, and therefore no basis for disciplining Fraser. 478 U. S., at 679–680. This Court reversed, holding that the "School District acted entirely within its permissible authority in imposing sanctions upon Fraser in response to his offensively lewd and indecent speech." *Id.*, at 685.

The mode of analysis employed in *Fraser* is not entirely clear. The Court was plainly attuned to the content of Fraser's speech, citing the "marked distinction between the political 'message' of the armbands in *Tinker* and the sexual content of [Fraser's] speech." *Id.*, at 680. But the Court also reasoned that school boards have the authority to determine "what manner of speech in the classroom or in school assembly is inappropriate." *Id.*, at 683. *Cf. id.*, at 689 (Brennan, J., concurring in judgment) ("In the present case, school officials sought only to ensure that a high school assembly proceed in an orderly manner. There is no suggestion that school officials attempted to regulate [Fraser's] speech because they disagreed with the views he sought to express").

We need not resolve this debate to decide this case. For present purposes, it is enough to distill from *Fraser* two basic principles. First, *Fraser*'s holding demonstrates that "the constitutional rights of students in public school are not automatically coextensive with the rights of adults in other settings." *Id.*, at 682. Had Fraser delivered the same speech in a public forum outside the school context, it would have been protected. *See Cohen v. California*, 403 U. S. 15 (1971); *Fraser, supra*, at 682–683. In school, however, Fraser's First Amendment rights were circumscribed "in light of the special characteristics of the school environment." *Tinker, supra*, at 506. Second, *Fraser* established that the mode of analysis set forth in *Tinker* is not absolute. Whatever approach *Fraser* employed, it certainly did not conduct the "substantial disruption" analysis prescribed by *Tinker, supra*, at 514. *See Kuhlmeier*, 484 U. S., at 271, n. 4 (disagreeing with the proposition that there is "no difference between the First Amendment analysis applied in *Tinker* and that applied in *Fraser*," and noting that the holding in *Fraser* was not based on any showing of substantial disruption).

Our most recent student speech case, *Kuhlmeier*, concerned "expressive activities that students, parents, and members of the public might reasonably perceive to bear the imprimatur of the school." 484 U. S., at 271. Staff members of a high school newspaper sued their school when it chose not to publish two of their articles. The Court of Appeals analyzed the case under *Tinker*, ruling in favor of the students because it found no evidence of material disruption to classwork or school discipline. 795 F. 2d 1368, 1375 (CA8 1986). This Court reversed, holding that "educators do not offend the First Amendment by exercising editorial control over the style and content of student speech in school-sponsored expressive activities so long as their actions are reasonably related to legitimate pedagogical concerns." *Kuhlmeier, supra*, at 273.

Kuhlmeier does not control this case because no one would reasonably believe that Frederick's banner bore the school's imprimatur. The case is nevertheless instructive because it confirms both principles cited above. *Kuhlmeier* acknowledged that schools may regulate some speech "even though the government could not censor similar speech outside the school." *Id.*, at 266. And, like *Fraser*, it confirms that the rule of *Tinker* is not the only basis for restricting student speech.[2]

Drawing on the principles applied in our student speech cases, we have held in the Fourth Amendment context that "while children assuredly do not 'shed their constitutional rights... at the schoolhouse gate,'... the nature of those rights is what is appropriate for children in school." *Vernonia School Dist. 47J v. Acton*, 515 U. S. 646, 655–656 (1995) (quoting *Tinker, supra*, at 506). In particular, "the school setting requires some easing of the restrictions to which searches by public authorities are ordinarily subject." *New Jersey v. T. L. O.*, 469 U. S. 325, 340 (1985). *See Vernonia, supra*, at 656 ("Fourth Amendment rights, no less than First and Fourteenth Amendment rights, are different in public schools than elsewhere... "); *Board of Ed. of Independent School Dist. No. 92 of Pottawatomie Cty. v. Earls*, 536 U. S. 822, 829–830 (2002) ("'special needs' inhere in the public school context"; "[w]hile schoolchildren do not shed their constitutional rights when they enter the schoolhouse, Fourth Amendment rights... are different in public schools than elsewhere; the 'reasonableness' inquiry cannot disregard the schools' custodial and tutelary responsibility for children" (quoting *Vernonia*, 515 U. S., at 656; citation and some internal quotation marks omitted).

Even more to the point, these cases also recognize that deterring drug use by schoolchildren is an "important—indeed, perhaps compelling" interest. *Id.*, at 661. Drug abuse can cause severe and permanent damage to the health and well-being of young people:

> School years are the time when the physical, psychological, and addictive effects of drugs are most severe. Maturing nervous systems are more critically impaired by intoxicants than mature ones are; childhood losses in learning are lifelong and profound; children grow chemically dependent more quickly than adults, and their record of recovery is depressingly poor. And of course the effects of a drug-infested school are visited not just upon the users, but upon the entire student body and faculty, as the educational process is disrupted." *Id.*, at 661–662 (citations and internal quotation marks omitted).

Just five years ago, we wrote: "The drug abuse problem among our Nation's youth has hardly abated since *Vernonia* was decided in 1995. In fact, evidence suggests that it has only grown worse." *Earls, supra*, at 834, and n. 5.

The problem remains serious today. See generally 1 National Institute on Drug Abuse, National Institutes of Health, Monitoring the Future: National Survey Results on Drug Use, 1975–2005, Secondary School Students (2006). About half of American 12th graders have used an illicit drug, as have more than a third of 10th graders and about one-fifth of 8th graders. *Id.*, at 99. Nearly one in four 12th graders has used an illicit drug in the past month. *Id.*, at 101. Some 25% of high schoolers say that they have been offered, sold, or given an illegal drug on school property within the past year. Dept. of Health and Human Services, Centers for Disease Control and Prevention, Youth Risk Behavior Surveillance—United States, 2005, 55 Morbidity and Mortality Weekly Report, Surveillance Summaries, No. SS–5, p. 19 (June 9, 2006).

Congress has declared that part of a school's job is educating students about the dangers of illegal drug use. It has provided billions of dollars to support state and local drug-prevention programs, Brief for United States as *Amicus Curiae* 1, and required that

---

[2]The dissent's effort to find inconsistency between our approach here and the opinion in *Federal Election Commission v. Wisconsin Right to Life, Inc.*, 551 U. S. _____ (2007), *see post*, at 12 (opinion of STEVENS, J.), overlooks what was made clear in *Tinker*, *Fraser*, and *Kuhlmeier*: student First Amendment rights are "applied in light of the special characteristics of the school environment." *Tinker*, 393 U. S., at 506. *See Fraser*, 478 U. S., at 682; *Kuhlmeier*, 484 U. S., at 266. And, as discussed above, *supra*, at 8, there is no serious argument that Frederick's banner is political speech of the sort at issue in *Wisconsin Right to Life*.

schools receiving federal funds under the Safe and Drug-Free Schools and Communities Act of 1994 certify that their drug prevention programs "convey a clear and consistent message that... the illegal use of drugs [is] wrong and harmful." 20 U.S.C. §7114(d)(6) (2000 ed., Supp. IV).

Thousands of school boards throughout the country—including JDHS—have adopted policies aimed at effectuating this message. See Pet. for Cert. 17–21. Those school boards know that peer pressure is perhaps "the single most important factor leading schoolchildren to take drugs," and that students are more likely to use drugs when the norms in school appear to tolerate such behavior. *Earls*, *supra*, at 840 (BREYER, J., concurring). Student speech celebrating illegal drug use at a school event, in the presence of school administrators and teachers, thus poses a particular challenge for school officials working to protect those entrusted to their care from the dangers of drug abuse.

The "special characteristics of the school environment," *Tinker*, 393 U. S., at 506, and the governmental interest in stopping student drug abuse—reflected in the policies of Congress and myriad school boards, including JDHS—allow schools to restrict student expression that they reasonably regard as promoting illegal drug use. *Tinker* warned that schools may not prohibit student speech because of "undifferentiated fear or apprehension of disturbance" or "a mere desire to avoid the discomfort and unpleasantness that always accompany an unpopular viewpoint." *Id*., at 508, 509. The danger here is far more serious and palpable. The particular concern to prevent student drug abuse at issue here, embodied in established school policy, App. 92–95; App. to Pet. for Cert. 53a, extends well beyond an abstract desire to avoid controversy.

Petitioners urge us to adopt the broader rule that Frederick's speech is proscribable because it is plainly "offensive" as that term is used in *Fraser*. See Reply Brief for Petitioners 14–15. We think this stretches *Fraser* too far; that case should not be read to encompass any speech that could fit under some definition of "offensive." After all, much political and religious speech might be perceived as offensive to some. The concern here is not that Frederick's speech was offensive, but that it was reasonably viewed as promoting illegal drug use.

Although accusing this decision of doing "serious violence to the First Amendment" by authorizing "viewpoint discrimination,"*post*, at 2, 5 (opinion of STEVENS, J.), the dissent concludes that "it might well be appropriate to tolerate some targeted viewpoint discrimination in this unique setting," *post*, at 6–7. Nor do we understand the dissent to take the position that schools are required to tolerate student advocacy of illegal drug use at school events, even if that advocacy falls short of inviting "imminent" lawless action. *See post*, at 7 ("[I]t is possible that our rigid imminence requirement ought to be relaxed at schools"). And even the dissent recognizes that the issues here are close enough that the principal should not be held liable in damages, but should instead enjoy qualified immunity for her actions. *See post*, at 1. Stripped of rhetorical flourishes, then, the debate between the dissent and this opinion is less about constitutional first principles than about whether Frederick's banner constitutes promotion of illegal drug use. We have explained our view that it does. The dissent's contrary view on that relatively narrow question hardly justifies sounding the First Amendment bugle.

* * *

School principals have a difficult job, and a vitally important one. When Frederick suddenly and unexpectedly unfurled his banner, Morse had to decide to act—or not act—on the spot. It was reasonable for her to conclude that the banner promoted illegal drug use—in violation of established school policy—and that failing to act would send a powerful message to the students in her charge, including Frederick, about how serious the school was about the dangers of illegal drug use. The First Amendment does not require schools to tolerate at school events student expression that contributes to those dangers.

The judgment of the United States Court of Appeals for the Ninth Circuit is reversed, and the case is remanded for further proceedings consistent with this opinion.

It is so ordered.

Appendix G

ANSWER KEY TO "TEST YOURSELF" AND "TEST YOURSELF—WRITING IT RIGHT"

CHAPTER 1

Test Yourself:

1. en banc—all the members of a court deciding a case, rather than a select few.

   petitioner—an individual who files a petition in court; the individual making a request of a court.

   percuriam—an appellate or Supreme Court opinion from the entire court rather than written by one justice.

2. (a) State law controls the charge of possession of drugs. The legality of the search is controlled by both federal and state laws. The legality of searches and seizures is governed by the U.S. Constitution, but states can also regulate this area. However, the state cannot deprive an individual of any rights guaranteed under the U.S. Constitution.

   (b) The lawsuit should be filed in California because the incident occurred in that state. It could be filed in a state court because this is the type of action normally within the jurisdiction of states. However, because the parties are citizens of different states, the action could also be filed in a U.S. district court, if the damages exceed $75,000. Regardless of the court, California state law applies to the case.

3. The drug laws were state laws. The defendant was charged with violation of Ohio state law (Ohio Rev. Code Ann. § 2925.22(A)). The majority opinion of the Supreme Court case decided the search and seizure question using the U.S. Constitution. It did this because it was reviewing the action of the Ohio Supreme Court whose decision was based on the U.S. Constitution.

4. Legal Guides:

   Guide to Law Online: Criminal Justice System

   Guide to Law Online: Elections

   Guide to Law Online: Enron (Legal Aspects)

   Guide to Law Online: Law Reviews Online

Guide to Law Online: Legal Services
Guide to Law Online: Indians of North America
Guide to Law Online: Terrorism
Guide to Law Online: U.S. Lists
Guide to Law Online: United States Legal System

Test Yourself—Writing It Right

1. The Blackhawks won the game.
2. Crosby shot the puck.
3. The Judge read the jury verdict.
4. A response must be filed with the court 60 days after the Order is served.

CHAPTER 2

Test Yourself:

Answers will differ slightly. Read Problem 9 in Appendix B—(*Speeker v. Oliver Wendell High School*) and the case of *Morse v. Frederick* in Appendix F.

a. **Fact Chart:**

Relevant Facts

Speeker's high school was invited to maintain a booth at a local health fair.

Students were given extra credit by the school for attending the health fair.

At the health fair, Speeker held up a sign advocating the legalization of marijuana for medicinal purposes.

Speeker was suspended from school for violating the school policy on drugs.

Explanatory Facts

Speeker's high school had programs stressing the harm of drugs.

Speeker was photographed holding the sign, and the picture was published in a school paper.

Legally Insignificant Facts

Speeker attends Oliver Wendell Holmes High School.

Speeker attended the fair with her parents and brother.

Speeker's mother is a breast cancer survivor.

b. The legal issue is whether Speeker's First Amendment right of free speech was violated when she was suspended from school for advocating the compassionate use of marijuana for medicinal purposes at a school-sanctioned health fair.

c. The legal issue in the *Morse v. Frederick* case is whether a high school student's First Amendment rights were violated when he was suspended from school for displaying a sign promoting the use of marijuana at an off-campus location for an event sponsored by the school.

Relevant Facts

At a school-sponsored and sanctioned event, a school principal saw students holding a banner advocating the use of drugs.

The principal asked students to take down the banner, but one student (Frederick) refused.

The principal confiscated the banner and latter suspended the student.

Explanatory Facts

On the day of the incident, the Olympic Torch Relay passed through the town where the parties lived.

The Torch Relay was during the school day, and students were supervised by instructors and administrators.

Legally Insignificant Facts

Fredericks was late for school the day of the parade.

Fredericks was a senior at Juneau-Douglas High School.

Test Yourself—Writing It Right

1. Tomas created the attack plan.
2. The Judge examined the juvenile defendant.
3. The lawyer's opening statement contained three factual misstatements.
4. The office served the Request for Production of Document three months ago

CHAPTER 3

Test Yourself:

1. *Ash v. Tyson Foods, Inc.,* 549 U.S. 1181 (2007)
   Domino's Pizza, Inc. v. McDonald, 546 U.S. 470 (2006)
   Newman v. Piggie Park Enterprises, 390 U.S. 400 (1968)
   a. Speeker and her family were attending a community-wide health fair at which the harmful nature of drugs was stressed.

      Morse: Frederick and friends attended a parade honoring the carriers of the Olympic torch.
   b. Speeker is a high school student who was promised extra credit by her teachers for attending the health fair.

      Morse: Student attendance at the parade was sponsored by the school.
   c. Speeker was suspended from school for holding a sign reading "Be compassionate, legalize marijuana for medical purposes."

      Morse: Frederick was suspended from school for holding a sign reading "Bong hits 4 Jesus" and for refusing to put the sign down when ordered to do so by school officials.

Test Yourself—Writing It Right

1. Here, it can be inferred that Smith would have formally adopted Kilmer earlier in his lifetime "but for" her husband's unwillingness to consent. As spousal consent is required in the adoption process, Smith was legally estopped from formally adopting Kilmer.
2. Admittedly, her husband's unwillingness to consent does not alone satisfy the requirement that a legal barrier "must have continued throughout the joint lifetimes of the" claimant and deceased. *In reJoseph*, 17 Cal. 4th 203, 207 (1998). However, Smith was offered only a small window of opportunity to adopt Kilmer following her husband's death and her debilitating cancer. This satisfies the but-for legal barrier requirement of Cal. Prob. Code section 6454.

CHAPTER 4

Test Yourself:

Judicial History: The District Court granted Summary Judgment for the School Board and Morse. The Ninth Circuit reversed. The United States Supreme Court granted certiorari.

Issue(s): Whether Frederick had a First Amendment right to wield his banner, and if so, whether that right was so clearly established that the principal may be held liable for damages.

RULES

(*Note:* the Court cites many other cases, but it is these three cases upon which it appears to rely most heavily.)

Tinker v. Des Moines Independent Community School Dist., 393 U.S. 503, 506 (1969): "Our cases make clear that students do not 'shed their constitutional right to freedom of speech or expression at the schoolhouse gate.'"

Bethel School Dist. No. 403 v. Fraser, 478 U.S. 675, 682 (1986): "[W]e have held that 'the constitutional rights of students in public school are not automatically coextensive with the rights of adults in other settings… .'"

Hazelwood School Dist. v. Kuhlmeier, 484 U.S. 260, 266 (1988): "[T]he rights of students 'must be applied in light of the special characteristics of the school environment.'"

Conclusion: "We conclude that the school officials in this case did not violate the First Amendment by confiscating the pro-drug banner and suspending the student responsible for it."

Test Yourself—Writing It Right

Every person who, under color of any statute, ordinance, regulation, custom, or usage, of any State or Territory or the District of Columbia

- subjects, or causes to be subjected
- any citizen of the United States or other person within the jurisdiction thereof
- to the deprivation of any rights, privileges, or immunities secured by the Constitution and laws
- shall be liable to the party injured in an action at law, suit in equity, or other proper proceeding for redress
- except that in any action brought against a judicial officer for an act or omission taken in such officer's judicial capacity
- injunctive relief shall not be granted unless a declaratory decree was violated or declaratory relief was unavailable

CHAPTER 5

Test Yourself:

1. 6 U.S.C.A. § 111 establishes the Department of Homeland Security and states the mission and responsibilities of the organization.

2. Federal Rule of Civil Procedure rule 61 deals with harmless error, providing that harmless error is not grounds for new trial, setting aside a verdict, or judgment; the court must disregard harmless errors.
3. U.S. Const. art. 2 § 4 states that "the President, Vice President, and all Civil Officers of the United States, shall be removed from Office on Impeachment for and Conviction of, Treason, Bribery, or other high Crimes and Misdemeanors."
4. 18 U.S.C. § 521 defines a criminal street gang.
5. Federal Rule of Civil Procedure 7 describes the types of pleadings and motions for federal courts

Using an Online Resource

6. 8 C.F.R. § 232.2 deals with examination in the United States of alien applicants for benefits under the immigration laws and other aliens.
7 The Safe Schools Act of 1994 is found in Pub. L. 103-227, title VII, Mar. 31, 1994, 108 Stat. 204 (20 U.S.C. 5961 et seq.) (Short title, see 20 U.S.C. 5961(a)
8. Using the U.S. Constitution, Analysis and Interpretation, locate the section on the Fifth Amendment right to an indictment by a Grand Jury. Footnote 4 contains a reference to an 1884 case. What is the case, and what was the holding of the case?

   This provision applies only in federal courts and is not applicable to the States, either as an element of due process or as a direct command of the Fourteenth Amendment. *Hurtado v. California* , 110 U.S. 516 (1884);

Test Yourself—Writing It Right

Introduction: Attached is the deposition summary you requested in the Adams matter. Mr. Adams appears to have strong evidence to support his claim that the City is overcharging him for fees associated with the use of the sidewalk in front of his café.

CHAPTER 6

Test Yourself:

1. The statutory requirements for a copyright are:
   a. there must be an original work of authorship and
   b. the work must be fixed in a tangible medium of expression and
   c. the work must be able to be perceived, reproduced, or communicated and
   d. the work must not consist of an idea, procedure, process, system, method of operation, concept, principle, or discovery.
2. a. The statutory requirements for a conspiracy are
      1. two or more persons
      2. conspiring to commit any offense against the United States or
      3. conspiring to defraud the United States or any agency thereof.

   b. H and W have committed a conspiracy. H and W are two persons, by hiding their assets they were conspiring to defraud the bankruptcy court, a federal agency. *See U.S. v. Stern*, 186 F. 854 (E.D.Pa.1911) affirmed 193 F. 888, 114 C.C.A. 102.

Test Yourself—Writing It Right

Our client, Jill Thompson, is a 16-year-old girl charged as an accessory to murder. As a result of her initial custodial interrogation, the police were able to locate the crime scene and ultimately link Jill to the murder through physical evidence.

Police discovered a body located in a ditch, and investigation revealed animosity and fights between Jill's boyfriend and the decedent. Jill's boyfriend revealed to police that he and Jill were at the mall together the night of the decedent's death.

The following morning, an officer questioned Jill in the Principal's office during school. The doors to the officer remained locked throughout the interrogation session. Jill explicitly stated that she wanted to return to class and that she wanted to call her parents. The officer did not allow Jill to call her parents. The officer told Jill that if she did not cooperate, she could "go down to juvenile hall." Jill was allowed to use a restroom that was within eyesight of the Principal's office.

After locating the crime scene following Jill's interrogation, the police discovered physical evidence linking Jill and her boyfriend to the murder. Police arrested Jill after her boyfriend stated that she was present when the killing occurred. Jill begged the police officers to allow her parents to accompany her as she was being arrested, but the officers refused her request. She requests that the court grant her a motion to suppress all of the statements she made to law enforcement officers.

CHAPTER 7

Test Yourself:

1. 49 Am. Jur. 2d Landlord and Tenant § 907
2. 45 A.L.R. Fed. 2d 1 (Border Search or Seizure of Traveler's Laptop Computer, or Other Personal Electronic or Digital Storage Device)
3. Leonard Chazen and Leonard Ross, *Harvard Law Review*,
   Vol. 83, No. 8 (Jun., 1970), pp. 1820–1841
   Up to 20 channels.
4. Criminal Instruction 2.07 Is titled "Statement by Defendant."

Test Yourself—Writing It Right

Discussion

A person commits fraud in relation to access devices when he knowingly effects transactions, using access cards issued to other another person, to obtain payment or property with an aggregate value of at least $1,000, within a one-year period, if such transactions affect foreign commerce. **CITATION NEEDED HERE.** Alternatively, the person commits the offense by using unauthorized access devices to obtain anything of value aggregating at least $1,000 within a one-year period. **CITATION NEEDED HERE.** An unauthorized access device is one that is "lost, stolen, expired, revoked, canceled, or obtained with intent to defraud." **CITATION NEEDED HERE.** An access device is a card or other means of account access that may be used to obtain money or things of value, or to initiate transfers of funds. **CITATION NEEDED HERE.** Conviction may result in imprisonment for not more than 15 years for a first-time offender. **CITATION NEEDED HERE.** Conviction may also result in imprisonment for not more than 10 years for a first-time offender. **CITATION NEEDED HERE.**

The state may meet the statutory requirement of $1,000 by aggregating the values of payment or property obtained in different transactions, as long as the transactions constitute violations of the same statutory provisions. **CITATION NEEDED HERE.**

CHAPTER 8

Test Yourself:

1. a. Child Custody ⊶ 558 *Abuse, Neglect, or Abandonment of Child*
   b. Federal Courts ⊶ 198 *Arbitration*
   c. Negligence ⊶ 1085 *Breach of Duty*
2. *U.S. v. Smith*, 459 F.3d 1276 (11th Cir. 2006)

Test Yourself—Writing It Right

1. Underlined topic sentences.

Summary of Argument

<u>In reversing the district court's grant of summary judgment in favor of the Juneau School Board and Deborah Morse, the Ninth Circuit embraced an unduly narrow reading of this Court's teachings with respect to the free speech rights of public school students.</u> To make very bad matters profoundly worse, the court below fashioned an approach to qualified immunity doctrine that conflicts with this Court's precedents and is dangerously unsettling to thousands of public school educators and administrators across the country. The Ninth Circuit was doubly wrong.

<u>In its teachings with respect to student speech principles, this Court has consistently recognized that public educational institutions possess "special characteristics" that profoundly shape the contextually sensitive contours of Free Speech doctrine.</u> From its watershed decision in *Tinker,* 393 U.S. 503, through its subsequent decisions in *Fraser,* 478 U.S. 675, and *Kuhlmeier,* 484 U.S. 260, this Court has protected nondisruptive political speech by students, while respectfully deferring to school administrators' judgments in cabining expression that is inconsistent with the educational function of public schools.

<u>In its First Amendment analysis, the Ninth Circuit fundamentally misconceived the nature and scope of the mission of public education in this country—as elucidated by this Court in both *Fraser* and *Kuhlmeier.*</u> At the same time, it wildly enlarged the ambit of purportedly political speech. In doing so, the court of appeals substituted its unforgivingly libertarian worldview for the considered judgment of school officials (and school boards) in seeking, consistent with Congress' statutory mandate, to foster and encourage a drug-free student lifestyle. Frederick's banner display not only radically changed the subject from the Olympic Torch Relay ceremony to illegality-promoting, distracting banter, his message itself lay far outside the province of *Tinker*-protected political expression.

<u>To the contrary, as Chief Judge Sedwick rightly concluded, the banner's ambiguous but obtrusive message fell comfortably within the ambit of Fraser's focus on promoting appropriate norms of discourse and civility.</u> *Kuhlmeier* likewise

supports the school authorities' decision to just say no to respondent's whimsically drug-focused message, inasmuch as the banner—if left undisturbed—could have told not only the high school student body but the larger community that drug-use promotion is openly tolerated within the local public high school. Nothing in law or logic, much less common sense, requires such an extravagant result.

The Ninth Circuit also strayed from this Court's qualified immunity jurisprudence, as embodied in decisions such as *Saucier v. Katz*, 533 U.S. 194 (2001). The court of appeals' conclusion that Deborah Morse, a paradigmatic conscientious educator and administrator, should face a potentially ruinous award for money damages, by virtue of her enforcement actions directed against respondent, cries out for the Court's muscular disapprobation.

As a threshold matter, for reasons already adumbrated, the court of appeals fell into error as a matter of substantive First Amendment law. With that foundation removed, the edifice of potential personal liability for money damages entirely collapses. Even assuming arguendo, however, that Principal Morse was in constitutional error in enforcing the School Board's anti-drug-message policies, the Ninth Circuit was still mistaken in its articulation and application of qualified immunity principles. Under this Court's objective test, immunity doctrine provides a shield from civil damages suits unless "it is obvious that no reasonably competent officer would have concluded" that the actions at issue were constitutional at the time they were undertaken. *Malley v. Briggs,* 475 U.S. 335, 341 (1986).

Principal Morse abundantly satisfies that objective standard. Responsible for maintaining order and proper decorum at a celebratory gathering of more than 1,000 high school students, the principal was confronted with a flagrant, inherently disruptive violation of a written school policy proscribing pro-illegal-drug messages. She responsibly took the appropriate action to ensure that the Olympic Torch Relay event was not further disrupted by Frederick's pro-drug banner. Nor does the fact that Frederick was not physically on school grounds at the time of the banner display exempt him from school discipline. At the pivotal moment when engaging in his expressive conduct, Frederick was a student participating in a school activity during school hours. A reasonable principal could well have believed that enforcing a well-established policy against promoting illegal substances at a non-classroom school activity was entirely lawful, and indeed required by School Board mandate. By doing so, the principal acted entirely reasonably. Accordingly, her conduct should, under this Court's body of qualified immunity jurisprudence, be fully immunized from judicial condemnation.

2. List of topic sentences:

In reversing the district court's grant of summary judgment in favor of the Juneau School Board and Deborah Morse, the Ninth Circuit embraced an unduly narrow reading of this Court's teachings with respect to the free speech rights of public school students.

In its teachings with respect to student speech principles, this Court has consistently recognized that public educational institutions possess "special characteristics" that profoundly shape the contextually sensitive contours of Free Speech doctrine.

In its First Amendment analysis, the Ninth Circuit fundamentally misconceived the nature and scope of the mission of public education in this country—as elucidated by this Court in both *Fraser* and *Kuhlmeier*.

To the contrary, as Chief Judge Sedwick rightly concluded, the banner's ambiguous but obtrusive message fell comfortably within the ambit of Fraser's focus on promoting appropriate norms of discourse and civility.

The Ninth Circuit also strayed from this Court's qualified immunity jurisprudence, as embodied in decisions such as Saucier v. Katz, 533 U.S. 194 (2001).

As a threshold matter, for reasons already adumbrated, the court of appeals fell into error as a matter of substantive First Amendment law.

Principal Morse abundantly satisfies that objective standard.

CHAPTER 9

Test Yourself:

1. Shepardize *United States v. Bramblett*, 348 U.S. 503 (1955).
   a. **What are the parallel cites?**
   99 L. Ed. 594, 75 S. Ct. 504, 1955 U.S. LEXIS 975 (1955)
   b. **What are the lower court citations for this case?**
   120 F. Supp. 857, 231 F.2d 489
   c. **Give all parallel cites for the case that overruled *Bramblett*.**
   514 U.S. 695
   131 L. Ed. 2d 779
   115 S. Ct. 1754
   d. **What is the full name of the *Bramblett* case?**
   United States v. Bramblett
   e. **What is the citation for the case from the Eighth Circuit that questioned *Bramblett*?**
   U.S. v. Raether, 940 F. Supp. 1485
   f. **What is the citation for an A.L.R. annotation where the case is mentioned?**
   102 A.L.R. Fed. 742, sec. 2 or
   111 A.L.R. Fed.295, secs. 2, 16
   (*Note:* this answer may change.)
2. *Bowers v. Hardwick*, 478 U.S. 186 (1986) was overruled by *Lawrence v. Texas,* 539 U.S. 558.

Test Yourself—Writing It Right

Mr. Ralph Smith was injured when a City bus struck him. The bus turned on a red light without stopping before turning. Mr. Smith was in the intersection, on a "walk" signal with about 21 seconds left to cross the street when he was struck.

Mr. Smith suffered a broken hip and a broken arm. He may need more surgery and he also needs physical therapy. Mr. Smith cannot pay his medical bills.

CHAPTER 10

Test Yourself:

1. 17 U.S.C. §107 deals with fair use of copyright material.
2. Rule 26.3 of the Federal Rules of Criminal Procedure deals with mistrials.
3. *League of United Latin American Citizens v. Perry*, 548 U.S. 399, 126 S. Ct. 2594 (2006)

Test Yourself—Writing It Right

Statement of Facts

This wrongful death lawsuit is brought by plaintiff Green after the unfortunate death of decedent Hutchins who was viciously attacked and killed by defendant Baylor's aggressive pit bull on January 23, 2016. Genevieve Green and Matthew Hutchins resided at a single family residence owned by Randolf Keen. Robert Baylor lived with his pit bull in the adjacent residence, which was also owned by Keen. On the day of the incident, the pit bull viciously attacked Hutchins while he was simply standing on the sidewalk between the properties.

Prior to this attack, Green and Hutchins filed for domestic partnership based on the fact that they were both over the age of 62. Green and Hutchins were retired teachers who were dependent on each other for support, however; neither of them was eligible to receive Social Security benefits. Both parties were previously married to spouses who predeceased them. They did not marry because of concerns that Hutchins' children would not accept the marriage. Green was not named as a beneficiary in Hutchins' will instead; everything was left to his children. At the time of Hutchins' death, neither he nor Green had reached the age of 65.

Green maintains that the pit bull was inherently dangerous because of its breed and that there were complaints concerning the dog barking and lunging at other people and animals. The dog also fought with and nearly killed another dog over a bone. She also claims that there was a previous incident where the dog knocked Hutchins down and where the dog lunged and snapped at a stranger. There is no record that either of these incidents was reported to the landlord.

CHAPTER 11

Test Yourself:

1. *Minnesota v. Carter*, 525 U.S. 83 (1998)
2. 20 U.S.C. § 76i deals with the John F. Kennedy Center for the Performing Arts.
3. What is the address of the Texas Eastern District Court?
   The court has several divisions:
   Jack Brooks Federal Building and United States Courthouse
   300 Willow Street
   Beaumont, TX 77701

   Ward R. Burke United States Courthouse
   104 North Third Street
   Lufkin, TX 75901

Sam B. Hall, Jr. Federal Building and United States Courthouse
100 East Houston Street
Marshall, TX 75670-4144

Federal Building
101 East Pecan Street, 1st Floor
Sherman, TX 75090

Sherman Division
Plano Office
7940 Preston Road
Plano, TX 75024

United States Courthouse and Post Office
500 North State Line Avenue, 3rd Floor
Texarkana, TX 71854-5957

William M. Steger Federal Building and United States Courthouse
211 West Ferguson Street, Room 106
Tyler, TX 75702

United States Courthouse
7940 Preston Road
Plano, TX 75024

Test Yourself—Writing It Right

Was Bobby negligent when (1) he knew he had a duty to behave in a safe manner, (2) he breached that duty when he was carelessly walking on a busy sidewalk swinging a wooden bat, (3) his actions caused the broken arm, and (4) the young mother has $6,800 in medical bills?

CHAPTER 12

Test Yourself:

1. The court reprimanded the defendant for use of inappropriate language.
2. The witness made the statement.
3. Several courts invalidated the jury verdict.

Test Yourself—Writing It Right

Predictive Point Headings:

I. Ms. Young's display of the sign is expressive conduct protected under the Free Speech Clause of the First Amendment.
II. The Restrictive Covenant is unreasonable, and therefore unenforceable.

CHAPTER 13

Test Yourself:

Brief Answer

The Town of Grand View is probably immune from liability. Generally, a public entity is not liable for injury resulting from misrepresentations by public employees.

In addition, Williams is probably immune from liability. A public employee is generally immune from liability for his own misrepresentation, unless he or she also acted with corruption, or actual malice. On Williams' facts, a court would almost certainly hold that he committed negligent misrepresentation when he misrepresented the condition of the electrical wiring. However, the court would probably hold that the evidence is insufficient to show Williams acted with corruption or actual malice. The evidence shows that subsequent to the Jones' first letter complaining about Williams, Williams acted rudely toward the Jones, failed to arrive on time to inspections, and misrepresented the safety of the electrical wiring. However, no evidence indicates Williams knew of the letters. Therefore, because evidence of malice is probably insufficient, Williams would probably be immune from liability for misrepresentation.

Discussion

Issue I: The court will almost certainly hold the Town of Grand View immune from liability for Williams' misrepresentation.

California Government Code Section 818.8 provides a governmental entity with immunity from liability for an injury resulting from misrepresentation by an employee. "A public entity is not liable for an injury caused by misrepresentation by an employee of the public entity, whether or not such misrepresentation be negligent or intentional." Cal. Gov. Code § 818.8 (West 20XX). Section 818.8 provides a public entity with immunity from liability for an employee's misrepresentations that result in an interference with a person's financial interests. *Tokeshi v. State,* 217 Cal. App. 3d 999 (1990). In *Tokeshi,* a state employee, instructed plaintiff, Tokeshi, to spray pesticide on his crop. Later, Tokeshi was prohibited from selling his crop due to excess pesticide. The court stated, "'misrepresentation,' … applies to interferences with financial … interests. The Legislature designed Section 818.8 to exempt the governmental entity from this type of liability." *Id.* at 1005 citing *Johnson v. State of California,* 69 Cal. 2d 782, 800 (1968). The court found "plaintiffs' alleged losses are commercial in scope, and therefore the defendants are shielded from liability under the immunity statutes." *Id.* at 801.

The Town of Grand View's case is similar to *Tokeshi* because courts have held that a home is a financial interest. *See Harshbarger v. City of Colton,* 197 Cal. App. 3d 1335 (1998). In *Harshbarger,* "homeowners sued … after they had to reconstruct their residence because city inspectors allegedly misrepresented and suppressed facts concerning the structure's compliance with the building code." *Tokeshi,* 217 Cal. App. 3d at 1007. The court determined that "misrepresentation immunity barred the action against the public entity because the injury resulted from an interference with the homeowners' financial concerns." *Harshbarger,* 197 Cal. App. 3d at 1342, *quoted in Tokeshi,* 217 Cal. App. 3d at 1007. Similarly, in the Town of Grand View's case, the injuries also resulted from a city inspector who misrepresented a home's compliance with building codes.

Therefore, since the Jones' personal and financial injuries resulted from the fire caused by Williams' misrepresentation about the Jones' home, a financial interest, the Town of Grand View will almost certainly be immune from liability.

Issue II: The court will probably hold that Williams is immune from liability for misrepresentation.

California Government Code Section 822.2 provides a public employee with limited immunity from liability for his own misrepresentation. "A public employee acting in the scope of his employment is not liable for an injury caused by his misrepresentation be negligent or intentional, unless he is guilty of actual fraud, corruption or actual malice." Cal. Gov. Code § 822.2 (West 20XX). Courts have interpreted Section 822.2 as having three requirements. First, "misrepresentation" was interpreted in the *Schonfeld* case to mean common law deceit. *Schonfeld v. City of Vallejo,* 50 Cal. App. 3d 401, 408 (1975). Second, *Schonfeld* held that where "a plaintiff saw … the property as to which the alleged misrepresentations were made … he must establish that he was justified in … relying on the other party… ." *Schonfeld,* 50 Cal. App. 3d at 412. Third, courts have interpreted "actual fraud" and "actual malice" as "a conscious intent to deceive, vex, annoy or harm the injured party in his business." *Id.* at 401. Therefore, a public employee is not immune from liability for misrepresentation if the following conditions are satisfied:

1. the employee is guilty of common law deceit; and
2. the plaintiff is justified in relying on the employee; and
3. the employee is motivated by corruption, or actual malice.
   See id. at 410–412.

A. Williams probably committed common law deceit. When Williams initialed the inspection card, he misrepresented the safety of the electrical wiring. Courts have held that negligent misrepresentation is a type of common law deceit.

The court in *Schonfeld* lists four kinds of common law deceit, including negligent misrepresentation. *See id.* at 408. Negligent misrepresentation is, "[t]he assertion, as a fact, of that which is not true, by one who has no reasonable ground for believing it to be true." Ca. Civ. Code, § 1572, subd. 2.

In the Town of Grand View's case, no facts establish Williams knew the electric wiring was unsafe; however, the facts probably establish that Williams committed negligent misrepresentation. As the Town's sole building inspector, Williams had a duty to ensure that construction of the Jones' home complied with all building codes. Furthermore, Williams signed off on the project's inspection card, indicating that the home's wiring complied with building codes. However, after the fire, the Central Fire District's investigation revealed that the fire started in the main circuit box, which failed to meet any known building codes. Therefore, the court will almost certainly hold that Williams had "no reasonable grounds for believing … [the electrical wiring was safe] to be true." Ca. Civ. Code, section 1572, subd. 2, *quoted in Schonfeld,* 50 Cal. App. 3d at 409. This fulfills the requirements for negligent misrepresentation.

B. The Jones were almost certainly justified in relying on Williams' representations. Williams was the Town's sole building inspector and certified that the Jones' home complied with building codes. Courts have held that a person is justified in relying on the representations of a government employee who holds himself or herself out as an expert.

The court in *Schonfeld* held that where "a plaintiff saw … the property as to which the … misrepresentations were made … he must establish that he … was justified in not making an inspection or in relying on the other party… ." *Id.* at 412.

In *Schonfeld,* plaintiff, Schonfeld, invested in a marina after the city manager made representations about the marina's quality. Specifically, one alleged misrepresentation was that the marina was "a first class harbor" and "the best berthing facility in Northern California."*Id.* at 413. The court stated, "[t]he city manager did not hold himself out as an expert on marinas but indicated that the marina was completed according to the city's plans… ." *Id.* The court found that the plaintiff was not justified in relying on the city manager's representations and that the city manager did not commit misrepresentation.

The Town of Grand View's case differs from *Schonfeld.* Williams, the Town's sole building inspector, was supposed to ensure that the Jones' home complied with building codes. In addition, he inspected the Jones' home, initialed the inspection card indicating the electric wiring passed inspection, and issued the certificate of occupancy. Unlike *Schonfeld,* the facts indicate that Williams appears to have held himself out to be an expert in building inspections. Therefore, the court will almost certainly hold that because Williams held himself out to be an expert in building inspections that the Jones' were justified in relying on his representations.

C. The evidence is probably insufficient to indicate Williams was motivated by corruption, or actual malice. Although the Jones' letters indicate that Williams acted rudely after the first letter, no evidence indicates Williams knew about the letters.

In *Schonfeld* the court states, "section 822.2 applies unless, … a public employee is motivated by corruption or actual malice… ." *Id.* at 411. In *Schonfeld,* plaintiff, Schonfeld, alleged that the city manager misrepresented the city's title to the marina. The court held, "there was no evidence from which it could be inferred that the city manager made any representations with the actual malice as required by the statute." *Id.* at 416. This differs from the City of Grand View's case. The Jones' first letter did not complain that Williams acted rudely; however, the second letter did. This may indicate that Williams was angry about the first letter, and in response acted rudely toward the Jones. From Williams' conduct, a court may infer that Williams' misrepresentation was in response to the Jones' letters.

On the other hand, no evidence indicates Williams knew about the letters. If Williams knew about the letters, it is important to find out whether he learned about them before misrepresenting the electric wiring. In addition, knowing if Williams was rude before the first letter could establish that he was not acting rudely in response to the letters, and that the misrepresentation was not in response to the letters.

Therefore, the court will probably hold the evidence is insufficient to infer Williams acted with malicious intent or corruption. Since Section 822.2 provides immunity for misrepresentation without corruption or malicious intent, Williams will probably be immune from liability.

Test Yourself—Writing It Right

Paragraphs 2 and 4 are rule explanation paragraphs. The others are rule application paragraphs.

CHAPTER 14

Test Yourself:

Using the first four pages of Figure 14-5, identify the persuasive techniques used by the author of that appellate brief.

1. The author chooses his words very carefully. For example, the first sentence (of the thesis paragraph) explains how important this case is.
2. In the first four pages, there is repetition of the idea that Ninth Circuit's decision is "wrong" and that opposing counsel's argument is "wrong."
3. Use of terms and phrases such as:
   - destabilizing
   - sensitive
   - vital
   - dramatically
   - legal landscape
   - doubly—and dangerously—wrong

   all help to paint images for the reader.
4. The author uses clear, direct sentences.
5. The point headings make points. They are easy to understand.
6. The topic sentences are effective—clear, concise, and direct.
7. The rule explanation paragraphs open with clear rules of law followed by citations.

Test Yourself—Writing It Right

1. Dylan Rhodes committed fraud in relation to access devices under the meaning of 18 U.S.C.A. § 1029(a)(5).Mr. Rhodes used access devices belonging to another person, his recently deceased mother. The MasterCard and ATM card he took were registered in Sandra Rhodes' name and were not authorized for use by any other person. Only two days after Ms. Rhodes' death, her son used the ATM card to clear out her Wells Fargo checking account of $758. On the same date, he made a purchase of $600 at Mario's jewelers using the MasterCard. These actions constitute using access devices issued to another person to obtain payment and property valued at $1,358, above the statutory minimum. 18 U.S.C.A. § 1029(a)(5). Because both transactions are violations of § 1029(a)(5), use of access device issued to another person, the values may be aggregated under the holding of *Momeni.* 991 F.2d at 495. Furthermore, because the purchase and withdrawal occurred on the same day, they are within the statutory time limit of one year. *Id.*
2. The interstate commerce requirement of § 1029 is also satisfied. Wells Fargo, the issuer of the access devices to Ms. Rhodes, is a corporation engaged in interstate commerce. Thus, the deleterious economic effect caused by Mr. Rhodes' crime is sufficient to satisfy the interstate commerce requirement of the statute. *See Phillips,* 577 F.2d at 501.
3. Alternatively, it can be argued that Mr. Rhodes is guilty of violating § 1029(a)(2), fraudulent use of so-called "unauthorized" access devices. However, the statutory definition of an unauthorized access device, one that is "lost, stolen, expired, revoked, canceled, or obtained with intent to defraud," 18 U.S.C.A. § 1029(e)(3), is not as descriptive of the access device Mr. Rhodes used as the language in § 1029(a)(5), which prohibits use of an access device issued to another person. 18 U.S.C.A. § 1029(a)(5). Here, the cards in question were issued to another person, Mr. Rhodes' late mother. Thus, it is more appropriate to charge him with violating § 1029(a)(5) because it is more descriptive of his actual conduct.

CHAPTER 15

Test Yourself:

1. LOCAL RULE CV-7 Searchable PDF format
   Here, the Brief Answer serves the purpose of the thesis paragraph(s).
   Rule Explanation Paragraph.
   Rule Application Paragraph.
   Conclusion.
   Rule Application Paragraph.
   Rule Application Paragraph.
   Rule Application Paragraph.
   Rule Application Paragraph.
   Rule Application Paragraph.
   Rule Application Paragraph.
   Counter-argument Paragraph.
   Conclusion.

Test Yourself—Writing It Right

Susan Tan is an accessory after the fact to Dylan Rhodes' access card fraud because she assisted him within the meaning of 18 U.S.C.A. Section 3 with the intent to prevent his apprehension by lying to investigators about his whereabouts and denied knowledge of the ring later found in her home.

A. **It is not necessary to try or convict the principal to a federal offense in order to convict the accessory after the fact to the offense.**

Being an accessory after the fact is a separate and exclusive substantive offense from the offense committed by the principal. *United States v. Taylor,* 322 F.3d 1209, 1212 (9th Cir. 2003) (holding that one convicted as a principal to murder may not also be an accessory after the fact to the same crime). It is not necessary to try or convict the principal in order to convict an accessory after the fact. *United States v. Walker,* 415 F.2d 530, 530 (9th Cir. 1969) (citing *Hiram v. United States,* 354 F.2d 4, 6 n.2 (9th Cir. 1965)) (affirming conviction of accessory after the fact to bank robbery despite the absence of the conviction of the principal). Here, therefore, it is immaterial to the conviction of Ms. Tan that Mr. Rhodes has yet to be apprehended. She may be tried as an accessory after the fact to his access device fraud, although he is not available to stand trial.

B. **An individual is an accessory after the fact under 18 U.S.C.A. § 3, if she receives, relieves, comforts, or assists the perpetrator of a crime against the United States with knowledge that the crime has been committed and the intent to prevent the perpetrator's apprehension.**

An accessory after the fact to a federal crime is one who, knowing that an offense against the United States has been committed, receives, relieves, comforts, or assists the perpetrator to prevent or hinder his apprehension. 18 U.S.C.A. § 3 (West 2016). In order to convict the defendant of being an accessory after the fact, the State must prove the following elements: (1) the principal committed an offense against the United States, (2) the accessory had knowledge of the commission of such offense, and (3) the accessory assisted the principal in avoiding apprehension. *United States v. Felix-Gutierrez,* 940 F.2d 1200, 1206 (9th Cir. 1991).

The accessory must have knowledge of the principal's commission of every material element of the underlying offense, but is not required to know that those elements establish an offense against the United States. *United States v. Graves,* 143 F.3d 1185, 1186 (9th Cir. 1998) (reversing accessory conviction for lack of knowledge that the principal was a convicted felon in addition to possessing a firearm). This requirement of knowledge does not extend to knowledge of jurisdictional requirements of the underlying offense. *Felix-Gutierrez,* 940 F.2d at 1207. Knowledge that the principal committed an offense may be shown entirely through circumstantial evidence. *United States v. Rux,* 412 F.2d 331, 333 (9th Cir. 1969) (holding reasonable inference of knowledge of the robbery from defendant's behavior to be sufficient to convict accessory after the fact).

Various types of conduct may tend to show assistance to prevent or hinder the principal's apprehension under 18 U.S.C.A. § 3. For example, in *Rux,* the court affirmed the accessory after the fact conviction of a defendant who purchased a vehicle for his brother to use to escape from the F.B.I. after committing bank robbery. 412 F.2d at 333. In *Felix-Gutierrez,* the defendant hired a pilot to fly the principal out of the country. 940 F.2d at 1206. In *Hiram,* the court affirmed the defendant's conviction as an accessory after the fact after the defendant traveled with the principal as he evaded the F.B.I. and provided false statements to the F.B.I. regarding the principal after he was arrested. 354 F.2d at 5-6.

An accessory convicted under the statute is subject to a term of imprisonment not more than half of the maximum sentence imposed on the principle. 18 U.S.C.A. § 3. Thus, an accessory after the fact to the commission of access device fraud under 18 U.S.C.A. § 1029(a)(5) faces a maximum sentence of seven and one half years.

C. **Susan Tan became an accessory after the fact to Dylan Rohodes' fraud when she allowed him to stay with her for over two months despite knowing of his crime against the United States, kept the ring he fraudulently obtained for her, and knowingly lied to investigators about his whereabouts.**

Susan Tan is guilty of being an accessory after the fact to Dylan Rhodes' access device fraud. The first of the three elements listed in *Felix-Gutierrez* that the State must prove to establish an offense under 18 U.S.C.A. § 3, that the principal in fact committed an offense against the United States, is established above in the discussion of Mr. Rhodes' crime.

The second element, that the accessory knew that an offense against the United States was committed, is satisfied as well. *Graves* requires that the accessory have knowledge of every material element of Mr. Rhodes' offense, 143 F.3d at 1186, and Ms. Tan satisfies this requirement. First, it is reasonable to infer that she was aware that Mr. Rhodes was illegally using his dead mother's access devices. Because he lived with her for over two months, beginning soon after his mother died, it is exceedingly unlikely that she was unaware of his mother's death. Furthermore, the F.B.I. uncovered credit card statements in the deceased mother's name within Ms. Tan's home. Second, evidence shows that she knew that he used the illegal access devices to obtain property valued over $1,000. The F.B.I. also discovered the appraisal signed by Mario Battaglia, stating the value of Ms. Tan's diamond ring, $1,200, and credit card statements corresponding with that purchase in the mother's name. Last, under *Felix-Gutierrez,* Ms. Tan does not need to have knowledge of the jurisdictional element of the offense, the effect on interstate commerce.940 F.2d at 1207. Thus, Ms. Tan has the requisite knowledge under 18 U.S.C.A. § 3 to be an accessory after the fact.

Ms. Tan also satisfies the third and final element of the crime, assisting the principal in avoiding apprehension by the legal authorities. Ms. Tan's conduct is well in line with the precedent case law holding accessories liable under 18 U.S.C.A. § 3. In *Rux,* the accessory bought a car to facilitate the principal's escape from the F.B.I. 412 F.2d at 333. In *Felix-Gutierrez,* the accessory hired a pilot to assist the principal in fleeing the country. 940 F.2d at 1206. Similarly, here, Ms. Tan purchased a plane ticket for Mr. Rhodes to flee investigation for his crimes. When the F.B.I. searched her home, they uncovered documents relating to Ms. Tan's purchase of an Alaska Airlines ticket for Mr. Rhodes. It is no stretch to infer that Ms. Tan purchased this ticket in order to assist Mr. Rhodes' attempt to flee from justice.

CHAPTER 16

Test Yourself—Writing It Right

I. Res ipsa loquitur probably applies without the need for expert testimony when common knowledge is sufficient to infer negligence from Mr. Smith's burn injuries sustained while unconscious during a routine surgery where his treating physicians are unable to provide a non-negligent explanation or evidence of an unpreventable cause.

II. Mr. Smith's action for medical malpractice probably expires under the statute of limitations one year from March 29, 2015, because that was the date he was aware of both the burn injuries and potential negligence.

Appendix H

U.S. COURT SYSTEM

THE FEDERAL COURT SYSTEM

The U.S. Constitution provides for the establishment of a Supreme Court and such inferior courts as Congress may establish. Today, the federal court structure consists of trial courts (primarily the U.S. district courts, but also various specialized courts), appellate courts (U.S. courts of appeals), and one Supreme Court. The courts are arranged much like a pyramid, with the Supreme Court at the top, the courts of appeals in the middle, and the district courts at the bottom. See Figure App H-1.

U.S. DISTRICT COURTS

In exercising its power to establish lower courts, Congress divided the United States into more than ninety separate districts and established federal district courts for each of the districts. These districts obviously do not parallel state lines, and many states have more than one district located within their boundaries. In addition, district courts exist for the District of Columbia, Guam, Puerto Rico, the

FIGURE H-1 Court Structure

Virgin Islands, and the Northern Mariana Islands. The number of judges assigned to each district depends on the needs of the individual courts and is influenced by the population of the district as well as by the federal budget. The U.S. district courts are referred to by the geographical region they serve—for example, the U.S. District Court for the Northern District of California.

original jurisdiction
The power to hear and try a case first.

District courts are courts of ***original jurisdiction,*** or more simply, trial courts. Original jurisdiction means the power to hear and determine the case first. Most federal cases begin in a district court. If you work in a law office, you will probably deal with the district court (or its state equivalent) more than the higher courts. If the case is in a federal court, this is the court where you file papers in connection with lawsuits and where trials take place. The role of a trial court, such as the federal district court, is to resolve disputes between parties. The process of resolving a dispute often involves a proceeding called a trial. At a trial, the parties present evidence supporting their position. Presiding over the trial is a judge who rules on all legal issues that arise during the trial. Depending on the type of case, a jury may also be involved in the trial process. A jury is responsible for resolving questions or disputes regarding factual matters. If there is no jury, then the judge determines these factual issues. Resolving disputes in a trial court involves two separate steps. First, the court must determine the facts of the dispute; second, it must apply the appropriate law to those facts

federal jurisdiction
The power of federal a court to hear cases and render judgments.

diversity of citizenship
A basis for federal jurisdiction of a lawsuit based on the fact that plaintiffs and defendants are residents of different states or nations.

U.S. district courts are federal courts and, therefore, they are allowed to hear cases only where ***federal jurisdiction*** exists. In criminal cases, federal jurisdiction exists when the crime is a violation of federal law. In civil cases, federal jurisdiction usually occurs when the dispute revolves around the U.S. Constitution or some federal law. Federal jurisdiction also exists when the United States is a party to the action or when the action is between residents of different states and the amount in dispute exceeds $75,000. This is known as ***diversity of citizenship.***

Certain kinds of federal cases are heard not in the district courts but rather in specialized trial courts, which include the following.

- Bankruptcy courts—courts handling bankruptcy proceedings
- U.S. Court of International Trade—a court that handles cases involving international trade and custom duties
- U.S. Claims Court—a court that hears suits against the federal government for money damages in numerous civil matters
- U.S. Tax Court—a court that handles controversies between taxpayers and the Internal Revenue Service (IRS) involving underpayment of federal taxes.

After the events of September 11, 2001, the existence of a specialized court, the Foreign Intelligence Surveillance Court, became better known. This court was created in 1978 for the purpose of issuing search warrants against suspected foreign enemies. The court consists of eleven district court judges appointed by the chief justice of the Supreme Court. Warrants issued by this court are not entitled to all of the protections surrounding warrants in normal criminal cases.

U.S. COURTS OF APPEALS

Thirteen federal jurisdictions make up the intermediate appellate level of the federal court system. The United States is divided into twelve separate geographical appellate areas, called circuits. In addition, one appellate court has national jurisdiction to hear appeals in patent, copyright, and trademark cases as well as all appeals from the U.S. Claims Court and the U.S. Court of International Trade.

Cases heard in a court of appeals are normally heard by a three-judge panel that decides the case by a majority vote. Occasionally a case is heard by the entire panel of justices assigned to the particular circuit court. When this happens, the court is said to be sitting ***en banc***. The total number of justices assigned to each court of appeals differs from court to court and depends on caseload and budgetary constraints. A U.S. court of appeals is referred to by number, for example, the U.S. Court of Appeals for the Sixth Circuit (or sometimes the Sixth Circuit Court of Appeals).

en banc
A situation in which all judges on a court hear and decide a matter, rather than a smaller panel of judges.

As the name suggests, a U.S. court of appeals is primarily a court of ***appellate jurisdiction,*** that is, a court of review. In our legal system, parties in most cases have the right to have an appellate court review what happened at the trial court. The one major exception to this occurs in criminal trials, where the prosecutor cannot appeal a "not guilty" verdict because of the constitutional right against double jeopardy. The purpose of appellate review is to guarantee that parties receive a fair trial. The appellate judges do not review the case to see if they agree with the outcome at the trial court. They review what happened at the trial court to make sure that the trial was fair.

appellate jurisdiction
The power of a court to hear and decide an appeal.

When a case is appealed, transcripts of the trial court proceedings and documents are prepared. These transcripts are sent to the appellate court so that the judges can review what happened in the trial court. Sometimes these transcripts are called the ***record.*** The attorneys in the case also submit written ***appellate briefs,*** documents that explain the factual and legal basis for and against the appeal.

record
Copies of documents and oral transcripts of a court proceeding.

appellate briefs
A document filed in support or in opposition to an appeal, containing arguments related to legal errors that may have occurred at trial.

In exercising its appellate jurisdiction, the court examines the record to determine whether any substantial legal errors were committed that denied the appealing party (the appellant) a fair trial. Legal errors consist of a number of different things, including erroneously admitted or excluded evidence and improper jury instructions. ***Jury instructions*** are statements of law read to the jury at the end of the trial. These statements of law must relate to the evidence that has been admitted at trial. If the court of appeals determines that the trial judge made an error in interpreting or applying the law, the court of appeals would be justified in reversing the decision if it found that the error was significant.

jury instructions
Statements of the law read to the jury at the end of trial.

In reviewing a case, the appellate court can do a number of different things. Obviously, it can ***affirm*** or uphold the trial court's decision (which, incidentally, is what happens in most cases). Just as obviously, it can ***reverse***, or change, the trial court's decision. It can also reverse and ***remand***, that is, send the case back to the trial court for a retrial with instructions regarding the procedure to be followed.

affirm
To uphold; in connection with an appeal to uphold the lower court's decision

reverse
To change

remand
To send back

THE U.S. SUPREME COURT

The U.S. Supreme Court, located in Washington, D.C., consists of nine justices, one of whom serves as the chief justice. Usually, when the Court hears cases, all nine of the justices participate in the case, each one having an equal vote in the decision.

The Supreme Court is primarily a court of review. It exercises appellate jurisdiction. It hears cases from the lower federal courts. It can also hear cases that originated in the state courts if the case involves a constitutional issue or a question of federal law. If the issues in the case relate only to state law, then the Supreme Court has no authority to hear the case. In most instances, the Supreme Court has discretionary power to review cases. It often exercises that power in cases of major importance or in cases where the lower courts are in disagreement regarding the law to be applied.

The Supreme Court cannot hear every case brought to it. Parties desiring a hearing before the Supreme Court usually file a document known as a ***petition for writ of certiorari.*** In this petition, the parties set out their reasons for requesting

petition for writ of certiorari
A request for a hearing in the Supreme Court.

FIGURE APP H-2 Map of the Circuit and District Courts

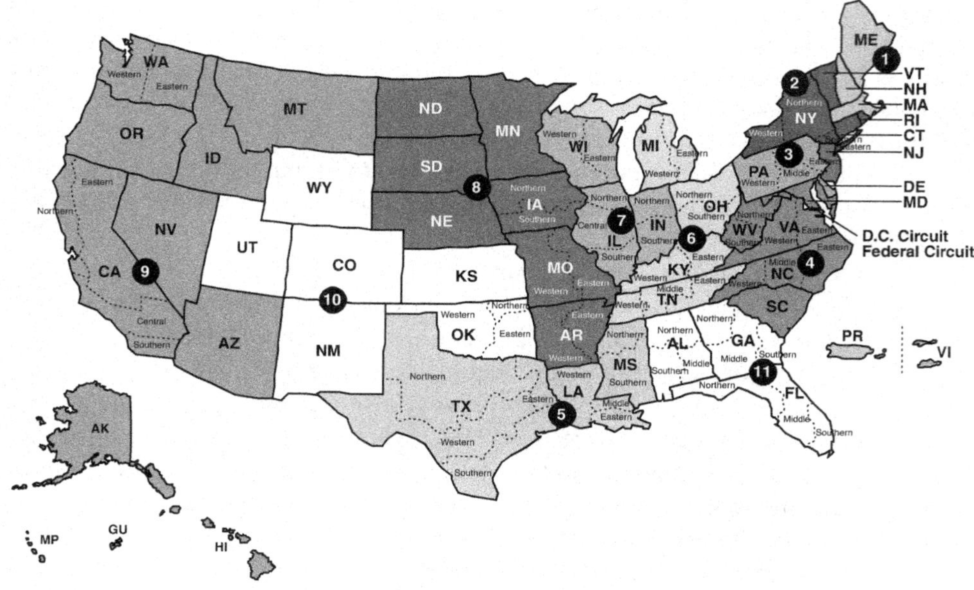

a hearing. The Court then votes on whether to grant the hearing. At least four of the justices must vote to hear the case or grant the petition for writ of *certiorari*. If the Court does grant certiorari, then it considers the merits of the case. A majority vote determines the outcome of the case. If the Court does not grant *certiorari*, the lower court's decision stands. If the Court agrees to hear a case on its merits, its decision is binding on all lower courts in the United States.

While the Supreme Court, like the appellate courts, is primarily a court of review, it has original jurisdiction in certain types of cases. Article III, Section 2, of the U.S. Constitution provides:

> In all cases affecting ambassadors, other public ministers and consuls, and those in which a state shall be a party, the Supreme Court shall have original jurisdiction. In all other cases before mentioned [Art. III Section 2.1] the Supreme Court shall have appellate jurisdiction, both as to law and fact, with such exception, and under such regulations as the Congress shall make.
>
> See Figure App H-2 for a map of the federal circuit and district courts.

To read more about the U.S. Courts go to www.uscourts.gov.

STATE COURT SYSTEMS

State court systems are established and organized according to state law. The various state systems resemble the federal system. All states have trial courts and courts of review. Some states, like the federal system, have three tiers of courts: trial courts, intermediate appellate courts, and a court of last review. Other states maintain a two-tiered system of courts: trial courts and one level of appellate courts. The function of trial courts and appellate courts is similar to that of their federal counterparts, although the names of the various courts are often different. For example, trial courts are sometimes called superior courts, municipal courts, circuit courts, city courts, surrogate courts, and even supreme courts. Furthermore, some states have more than one level of trial court. For information and links to the state courts go to www.ncsc.org.

Glossary

A

Acquittal A "not guilty" verdict

Active Voice Active voice is a tool used by writers to shorten sentences; a sentence written in active voice uses the simple subject–verb–object approach

Administrative Procedures Procedures used by agencies and boards

Advocate Arguing one side of an issue

Affidavit A statement under penalty of perjury sworn to before a notary

Affirm To uphold; in connection with an appeal to uphold the lower court's decision

Affirmative Defenses Defenses raised by the defendant in the answer; reasons why the plaintiff should not recover even if all of the allegations of the complaint are true

Amend To change

Annotated A brief summary of a statute or a case added to explain or clarify

Appeal Review of a lower court decision

Appellant One who appeals

Appellate Brief A document filed in support of or in opposition to an appeal, containing arguments related to legal errors that may have occurred at trial

Appellee Party in an appeal who did not file the appeal

Arbitration An out-of-court proceeding where parties submit a dispute to a neutral person for resolution

Arbitration Brief A document filed in an arbitration proceeding addressing the legal issues in the arbitration

Argument The section of a memorandum or brief containing legal analysis supporting that party's position on a legal issue

B

Bill Proposed legislation

Bill of Rights First ten amendments to the U.S. Constitution

Binding Authority Another term for mandatory authority

Boolean A special logic used in computerized legal research; utilizes the use of connective words

Brief A written document that might contain a summary of the facts, issues, rules, and analysis used by a court and a comparison with a client's facts; a case brief is a short summary of a published case

C

Caption A caption identifies the parties to the case, the court in which the case is pending, the docket number, and the title of the document

Case Brief A short summary of a reported case

Case Law A collection of reported cases

Case Law Reporters Sets of published volumes of cases decided by various courts

Case Reporters Books that contain case decisions from the courts

Cause of Action The basis upon which a lawsuit may be brought before the court

Century Digest Part of the American Digest System; contains case annotations from the year 1658 to 1896

Citators Research materials used to update or "validate" legal authorities

Cited Authority The authority you are Shepardizing (updating and validating)

Citing Authority Authorities you are referred to when you Shepardize

Civil Law The area of law dealing with private disputes between parties

Clerk's Transcript Copies of all documents filed in a case and compiled by the clerk of the court at a party's request

Code A topical organization of statutes

Code Books Books that contain codes or statutes

Common Law Body of law developed through the courts

Computer-Assisted Legal Research (CALR) Legal research done with the use of a computer; includes the use of CD-ROM, online services such as Lexis, Westlaw, the Internet, and intranets

Concurrent Jurisdiction Jurisdiction or power exercised by two different entities

Connectors Words such as *and* or *or* used in a search query to show the relationship between key words or terms

Copyright A copyright is a legal protection for the authors of "original works of authorship" such as literary, dramatic, musical, artistic, and certain other works

Court Record Documents and transcripts of proceedings in connection with a case

Cover Letter A letter sent with documents or other items, explaining the nature of the documents or items as well as directions to the recipient for any actions to be taken with the documents or items; also referred to as a *transmittal letter*

Criminal Law The area of law dealing with prosecution and defense of crimes

D

Database Compilation of electronically stored information

Decennial Digest Updates to the *Century Digest,* now published every five years

Decision The formal written resolution of a case; it explains the legal and factual issues, the resolution of the case, and the law used by the court in reaching its resolution

Declaration A statement under penalty of perjury containing factual statements

Demand Letter Formal correspondence from an attorney to a party or other attorney demanding that action be taken or requesting a settlement of a claim or dispute

Demurrer A state-court pleading comparable to a motion to dismiss the complaint

Deposition An out-of-court oral questioning of a witness or party in a case by an attorney; answers to questions are under oath, and a written or video transcript is prepared

De-publish In rare instances, a court will decide a case and write and release a decision; however, before it is published in the official reporter, the court decides not to publish some or all of the case decision; a de-published case cannot be used as precedent

Descriptive Word Index An alphabetical listing of words describing the topics contained in a book or a set of books; refers the researcher to the volume and page where the topic is discussed

Dictum Reasoning or a comment by the court that is not essential to the outcome (the holding) of the decision. Dictum (the plural is dicta) is nonbinding on other courts

Digest An index to reported cases, arranged by subject; a short summary of cases is provided

Digest Topics Topics included in an index (digest) to reported case law, arranged by subject

Document An identifiable item located in a database; can refer to a case or a single code section

Double Jeopardy Clause in the U.S. Constitution that generally prevents the government from trying a person more than once for the same offense

E

Editorial Enhancements Helpful information included in many unofficial publications; the enhancements assist the researcher to understand the material. Most official publications have little or no editorial enhancements

Electronic Search Query Words that constitute a search request when using electronically stored data, that is, information on the Internet or on a CD-ROM

Elements The components of a cause of action or of a statute

Express Powers Powers given to the federal government that are expressly stated in the Constitution

F

Federal Reporter The set containing all of the federal appellate decisions

Federal Rules Decisions The set containing federal opinions, decisions, and rulings involving the Federal Rules of Civil Procedure and the Federal Rules of Criminal Procedure

Federal Supplement The set containing the cases argued and determined in the U.S. District Courts, the U.S. Court of International Trade, and the rulings of the Judicial Panel on Multidistrict Litigation

Federalism A system of government in which the people are regulated by both federal and state governments

Filed To become part of the court record

First Impression A case where the legal issue has not previously been decided

Forms of Pleading and Practice Form books containing forms for use in connection with litigation

Full-text Search Legal research method utilized in computer-assisted legal research, in which all documents in a database are searched for certain words

G

General Digest Updates to the Decennial Digest

Good Law Law that is still in effect or valid and can be cited as authority

H

Heading A heading provides the reader with a road map of the document. Use it to guide the reader through the document. A major point heading also serves at the thesis statement and answer to the issue

Headnote Editorial enhancement added to the front material of a case; useful summary of most of the legal topics addressed in the case

Holding The legal principle to be taken from the court's decision

Hornbook Name given to books published by West that are a type of treatise; commonly used by law students

I

Implied Powers Power to make all laws that are necessary and proper for carrying into execution any of the stated or express powers of the government

Index A list of words and phrases that reflect the topics covered in the book

Intellectual Property Intangible property, including patents, trademarks, trade names, and copyright

Interrogatories A method of discovery used in civil cases consisting of written questions from one party to another to which a response is required in a timely manner

Intranet A secure database set up and accessible by a specific group, such as a law firm

J

Judicial History The legal (courtroom) history of a case

Jurisdiction The power or authority to act in a certain situation; the power of a court to hear cases and render judgments

Jury Instructions Statements of the law read to the jury at the end of trial

K

Key Numbers A research aid unique to the West Group materials; these numbers allow a researcher to quickly access specific material in a digest

Key Words Words that describe important aspects of a research question

L

Law Library A library dedicated to legal resource material

Law Review A type of legal periodical published by law schools containing articles on different legal topics

Lawyers' Edition LexisNexis publishes this unofficial (nongovernment) printing of all U.S. Supreme Court case law

Legal Analysis The process of analyzing facts and legal issues in light of existing constitutional, statutory, or case law

Legal Citations Special abbreviations used to describe resource material

Legal Dictionary A dictionary defining and explaining legal terms

Legal Encyclopedia A collection of legal information arranged alphabetically by topic; a secondary source of the law

Legal Error Application of law to a case in a mistaken way

Legal Issue A question that must be decided by a court

Legal Thesaurus A book providing synonyms for legal words

Legislative History The proceedings that relate to a bill before it becomes law

Legislative Intent The purpose of the legislature in passing a law

Lexis A computer-assisted legal research service

Local Rules of Court Procedural rules adopted by an individual court for practice in that specific court

Looseleaf Service Legal material published in a binder format, regularly supplemented with replacement pages

M

Mandatory Authority Case law that must be followed by a court

Memorandum of Law An objectively written document where the researcher informs the reader of the law governing a specific situation

Memorandum of Points and Authorities A formal document, written in an argumentative or persuasive manner, filed with the court, and advocating a certain position

Model Codes A collection of sample laws, created for the states to adopt in whole or in part; help to create uniformity in law

Motion A request for an order from the court

Motion for Summary Judgment A request that the trial court decide the case without a trial

Moving Party The party making a motion

N

Notice of Motion A document describing a motion and containing the date, time, and place of a hearing on that motion

Nutshell Series Condensed versions of hornbooks

O

Official Citation This is the citation to the official publication of case law for a particular jurisdiction (this is usually a government publication); the official citation includes the name of the case, volume number in which the case is located, the first page of the case, and the year of the decision

Official Reporters Sets of case law published by the government or the designee of the government

Opinion A decision is sometimes referred to as an *opinion*

Opinion Letter Formal correspondence from an attorney to a client or other attorney explaining an attorney's interpretation of the law as applied to a factual situation

P

Parallel Citations Many case citations include references to unofficial publications as well as the official citation. These additional references are parallel citations; simply stated, you may find the exact case in more than one publication

Periodical Legal material, published at regular intervals, consisting of magazines, journals, and law reviews

Persuasive Authority Nonbinding case law that is nevertheless considered by a court

Persuasive Document A persuasive document is drafted to persuade the reader to adopt the writer's legal analysis of a specific legal problem. The audience for most persuasive documents is a court (judge)

Petition for Writ of Certiorari A request for a hearing in the Supreme Court

Petitioner The person who files a petition with the court

Pleading and Practice Guides Secondary sources providing sample pleadings and general practice advice; available in most states and for some federal practice areas

Pleadings The formal written allegations filed with the court by both sides to a lawsuit; claims and defenses are clearly set out so that both parties are placed on notice of the position of the opposing party

Pocket Part A removable supplement; includes all changes or additions to the material contained in the hardbound volume

Point Headings Point headings provide the reader with a road map of the document. Use them to make a point you want to stress for the reader

Positive Law Codes that were enacted into law by Congress

Practice Books Books for use in federal and state legal practice; these often contain discussions of an area of law and provide forms needed for practice in that legal area

Precedent The example set by the decision of an earlier court for similar cases or similar legal questions that arise in later cases

Predictive Office Memorandum A predictive memorandum predicts the outcome of a legal issue, based upon legal research and analysis. This document does not "take sides" or try to convince the reader to adopt a position

Preempt To assume sole responsibility to regulate

Prefatory Material Material found in the front of a book or a set of books, describing such matters as the purpose of the book and directions for using the book

***Prima Facie* Case** On first view or on its face; for example, the plaintiff presented a strong *prima facie* case for establishing the negligence of the defendant

Primary Authority The resources that provide the actual law; laws are found in constitutions, statutes, case law, and some administrative materials

Primary Source A work that contains the law itself

Private Laws Laws enacted by Congress that affect only selected individuals

Public Law Laws enacted by Congress that affect the public in general

Q

Query Words that constitute a search request when using CD-ROM or online materials

Questions Presented A statement of the legal issue presented to the court for resolution

R

Rationale The reasoning or explanation for the court's ultimate resolution of a case

Real Party in Interest A party who has a true interest in the action

Regional Reporters A set of published volumes of cases by courts in specific regions of the United States; for example, the *Pacific Reporter* or the *North Eastern Reporter*

Remand To send back

Repeal To undo; to declare a law no longer in effect

Reported Case A published judicial decision

Reporter's Transcript A verbatim record of oral proceedings in court prepared by the court reporter

Responding Party (Respondent) The party who answers the petitioner's petition

Reverse To change

Rules of Court Procedural rules adopted by all courts regulating practice in the court

S

Secondary Source A tool used to understand the law; one such tool is a legal encyclopedia that explains the law

Service Proper delivery of papers to a party affected by a legal proceeding

Session Laws Laws from state legislatures, published in chronological order

Shepardize To check the validity of a citation in one of the *Shepard's* citations

Shepard's System used to update, validate, and expand research results

Slip Law First publication of a law; usually in pamphlet form

Specialized Reporters Collections of cases grouped by specific topics rather than by level of court or jurisdiction

Standard of Review The criteria a court uses to review the merits of a motion or appeal

Stare Decisis "It stands decided"; another term for *precedent*

Statement of Undisputed Material Facts A statement required in a summary judgment motion in which the moving party lists facts that are not in dispute

Statutory Law Law enacted through the legislative process

Statutory Requirements Various requirements or elements of a statute that must be met before the statute applies to a situation

Strategy A well-thought-out plan or approach to a project

Style Manual A manual illustrating the proper citation format for a particular state

Superseded Replaced

Supplemented Kept up to date

Supremacy Clause Clause in the U.S. Constitution providing that the U.S. Constitution is the supreme law of the land

Supreme Court Reporter Printed by West, this is an unofficial publication of all U.S. Supreme Court case law

T

Table of Abbreviations A common feature of legal publications containing an explanation of all abbreviations found in the book

Table of Authorities A list of primary and secondary authorities cited within a memorandum or brief and the page numbers on which they appear

Table of Cases A common feature of legal publications containing the names of all cases cited in the book or document

Table of Contents A list of the sections of a document with the page on which they appear within the document

Table of Statutes A common feature of legal publications containing a list of all statutes or codes that are referenced in the book or document

Thesis Paragraph The thesis paragraph lays a solid foundation for the reader. This paragraph sets forth the client's problem, states the legal issue, briefly explains the legal rules governing the issues, and states the legal conclusion

Topic and Key Number System used by the West Group to integrate its various primary and secondary resource materials

Topic Sentence A topic sentence introduces the issues or subissues and connects back to the thesis paragraph

Topical Index An index arranged by subject-matter topics

Transaction Forms Books that contain forms for use in connection with business and personal transactions

Transmittal Letter A letter sent with documents or other items, explaining the nature of the documents or items as well as directions to the recipient for any actions to be taken with the documents or items; also referred to as a *cover letter*

Treatise Either one book or a multivolume series of books dealing with one legal topic

Trial A court proceeding before a judge or jury wherein each side presents evidence of the facts that form the basis for the lawsuit or the defense to the lawsuit

Trial Brief A document submitted to the court; the trial brief contains a statement of facts, the issues, the party's legal argument, and the conclusion

Trial Court Where cases originate and where the factual dispute is resolved at trial

U

Uniform Laws Similar laws that are enacted by the legislatures of different states (i.e., Uniform Commercial Code); intended to create uniformity in the law

Uniform System of Citation A reference manual; contains the rules for proper citation format; often called *The Bluebook*

United States Reports Official publication of all U.S. Supreme Court case law; published by the federal government

Unofficial Publication Material not published by a government entity or a government designee

Unofficial Reporters Collections of printed decisions that are not government publications or sanctioned by government

V

Validate To verify that an authority is still good law

Venue The geographical area in which a case should be tried

W

Westlaw A computer-assisted legal research service

Wildcard A symbol used in a word that substitutes for any letter; often an asterisk (*)

Writ of Habeas Corpus An order directing the release of one who is in custody

Writ of Mandate Order from higher court to lower court to take some action

Credits

Chapter 1 **Figure 1-2** p. 9: "Westlaw Directory" from the website of Westlaw Online Dictionary. Copyright © by Thomson Reuters; pp. 11–13: Based on The Bluebook: A Uniform System of Citation, 20e; p. 15: From Duncan v. Louisiana 391 U.S. 145 (1968), Supreme Court.

Chapter 2 **Figure 2-2** pp. 30–33: From U.S. Supreme Court, by the Supreme Court of the United States; p. 25: From George w. Bush, et al., petitioners v. Albert gore, jr., et al. On writ of certiorari to the Florida Supreme Court, by the Supreme Court of the United States, 2000; pp. 26–28: From U.S. Supreme Court, by the Supreme Court of the United States; p. 34: From The Bluebook—Rule 15.8, Published by Bluebook, © 2015.

Chapter 3 **Case 3-1** pp. 68–70: From Supreme Court of the United States; **Figure 3-2** pp. 41–42: From Rules of the Supreme Court of the United States, Supreme Court of Illinois; **Figure 3-3** pp. 43–45: From Supreme Court of the United States; **Figure 3-4** pp. 46–49 From Supreme Court Reporter. Copyright © by Thomson Reuters; **Figure 3-5** pp. 50–58: From Lawyers Edition, Published by LexisNexis Legal Department; pp. 72–74: From The Bluebook—Rule 8,10, Published by Bluebook. © 2015.

Chapter 4 **Case 4-1** pp. 83–87: From U.S. Supreme Court, by the Supreme Court of the United States; **Case 4-2** pp. 89–95: From Cases Adjudged in the Supreme Court, by the Supreme Court of the United States; pp. 88–89: From U.S. Supreme Court, by the Supreme Court of the United States; pp. 96–97: From Cases Adjudged in the Supreme Court, by the Supreme Court of the United States; p. 100: From The Bluebook—Rule 5, Published by Bluebook.

Chapter 5 **Figure 5-1** pp. 108–109: From Preamble, U.S. Constitution. Copyright © by Thomson Reuters. **Table 1-1** pp. 114–115: From Code of Federal Regulations, U.S. Government Publishing Office (GPO); **Figure 5-2** pp. 112–113: From Public Law pp. 103–322, Library of Congress; **Figure 5-3** p. 117: From Office of the Law Revision Council United States Code, U.S. Supreme Court; **Figure 5-4** pp. 118–119: From The Bluebook—Rule B8.2, Published by LexisNexis Legal Department; **Figure 5-5** p. 124: From the Constitution of the United States, U.S. National Archives and Records Administration; **Figure 5-6** p. 125: From The United States Code, United States House of Representatives; **Figure 5-7** p. 127: From The United States Code, United States House of Representatives; **Figure 5-8** p. 128: From Office of the Law Revision Council United States Code; **Figure 5-9A** p. 129: From Rules of the Supreme Court of the United States, U.S. Supreme Court; **Figure 5-9B** p. 129: From Office of the Law Revision Council United States Code; **Figure 5-9C** p. 130: From Office of the Law Revision Council United States Code; **Figure 5-10A** p. 131: From Federal Digital System America's Authentic Government Information, U.S. Government Publishing Office; **Figure 5-10B** p. 131: From Federal Digital System America's Authentic Government Information, U.S. Government Publishing Office; p. 123: From Deprivation of Rights Under Color of Law, United States Codes. Published by United States House of Representatives; p. 107: From Constitution of the United States, U.S. National Archives and Records Administration; pp. 110–111: From Rules of the Supreme Court of the United States, U.S. Supreme Court; p. 133: From The Bluebook—Rule 11, Published by Bluebook.

Chapter 6 **Figure 6-1** p. 147: Reprinted with permission of Thomson Reuters; **Box 6-1** pp. 149–150: From United States Codes, Office of the Law Revision Counsel; **Case 6-1** pp. 156–159: From United States Court of Appeals, Fifth Circuit, United States Court of Appeals, Fifth Circuit; **Figure 6-2** p. 148: From Thomson Reuters Westlaw Online Legal Research. Copyright © by Thomson Reuters; **Figure 6-3** pp. 152–153: From U.S.C.C.A.N. Copyright © by Thomson Reuters; **Box 6-3** p. 155: Joanne B Hames, Yvonne Ekern, *Legal Research, Analysis, and Writing*, 6e, © 2018, Pearson Education, Inc., New York, NY; **Box 6-4** p. 155: Joanne B Hames, Yvonne Ekern, *Legal Research, Analysis, and Writing*, 6e, © 2018, Pearson Education, Inc., New York, NY; **Figure 6-4** p. 162: From Bearing Arms, Second Amendment. Published by Library of Congress; **Figure 6-5** p. 163: From Federal Digital System America's Authentic Government Information, Government Publishing Office; **Figure 6-6** p. 163: From Library of Congress; p. 143: Rule 47 Motion and Supporting

Affidavits from United States Codes, Office of the Law Revision Counsel; p. 144: From Accessory after the Fact, United States Codes, Office of the Law Revision Counsel; p. 144: From Deprivation of Rights Under Color of Law, United States Codes, Office of the Law Revision Counsel; pp. 163–164: From The Bluebook—Rule 18, Published by Bluebook; p. 165: From Subject Matter of Copyright: In General, United States Codes, Office of the Law Revision Counsel; p. 165: From Conspiracy to Commit Offense or to Defraud United States, United States Codes, Published by Office of the Law Revision Counsel; p. 167: From Civil Action for Deprivation of Rights, United States Codes, Published by Office of the Law Revision Counsel; p. 168: From Budget Contents and Submission to Congress, United States Codes, Office of the Law Revision Counsel; p. 168: From Amendment V, U.S. National Archives and Records Administration; pp. 168–169: From Amendment XIV, U.S. National Archives and Records Administration.

Chapter 7 **Figure 7-1** p. 173: From U.S.C.C.A.N. Copyright © by Thomson Reuters; **Box 7-1** p. 178: Joanne B Hames, Yvonne Ekern, *Legal Research, Analysis, and Writing,* 6e, © 2018, Pearson Education, Inc., New York, NY; **Figure 7-2** p. 174: From U.S.C.C.A.N. Copyright © by Thomson Reuters; **Figure 7-3** p. 175: From U.S.C.C.A.N. Copyright © by Thomson Reuters; **Figure 7-4** p. 177: From American Jurisprudence, 2d. Copyright © 1998–2014 by Thomson Reuters; **Figure 7-5** pp. 179–180: From American Law Reports, Federal, 2d (ALR® Series). Copyright © 2005–2014 by Thomson Reuters; **Figure 7-6** pp. 185–186: Restatement, Second, Torts. Copyright © 1965 by the American Law Institute. Reproduced with permission. All rights reserved; **Figure 7-7** p. 188: From Law Reviews Online, Library of Congress; **Figure 7-8** p. 188: © 2015 Google Inc. All rights reserved. Google and the Google Logo are registered trademarks of Google Inc.; **Figure 7-9** p. 189: From 9.1 Section 1983 Claim—Introductory Instruction, U.S. Courts for the ninth Circuit; p. 190: From The Bluebook—Rules 15, 16, 17, and 18, Published by Bluebook; p. 192: Joanne B Hames, Yvonne Ekern, *Legal Research, Analysis, and Writing,* 6e, © 2018, Pearson Education, Inc., New York, NY.

Chapter 8 **Figure 8-1** p. 196: From Thomson Reuters. Copyright © by Thomson Reuters; **Figure 8-2** p. 197: Reprinted with Permission of Thomson Reuters; **Figure 8-3** p. 198: From Thomson Reuters. Copyright © by Thomson Reuters; **Figure 8-4** p. 200: From Thomson Reuters. Copyright © by Thomson Reuters; **Figure 8-5** p. 204: Reprinted with permission of Thomson Reuters; **Figure 8-6A** p. 204: From Thomson Reuters. Copyright © by Thomson Reuters; **Figure 8-6B** p. 204: From Thomson Reuters. Copyright © by Thomson Reuters; **Figure 8-7A** p. 205: From Thomson Reuters. Copyright © by Thomson Reuters; **Figure 8-7B** p. 205: From Thomson Reuters. Copyright © by Thomson Reuters; p. 207: From The Bluebook—Rule 15, Published by Bluebook.

Chapter 9 **Figure 9-1** p. 214: Reprinted with permission of LexisNexis Legal Department; **Figure 9-2** p. 216: Reprinted with permission of LexisNexis Legal Department; **Figure 9-3** p. 217: Reprinted with permission of LexisNexis Legal Department; **Figure 9-4** pp. 220–221: Reprinted with permission of LexisNexis Legal Department; **Figure 9-5** p. 222: Reprinted with permission of LexisNexis Legal Department; **Figure 9-6** p. 224: Reprinted with permission of LexisNexis Legal Department; **Figure 9-7** p. 224: Reprinted with permission of LexisNexis Legal Department; **Figure 9-8A** p. 225: Reprinted with permission of LexisNexis Legal Department; **Figure 9-8B** p. 225: Reprinted with permission of LexisNexis Legal Department; **Figure 9-9** p. 227: From Thomson Reuters. Copyright © by Thomson Reuters; **Figure 9-10** p. 227: From Thomson Reuters. Copyright © by Thomson Reuters; **Figure 9-11** p. 227: From Thomson Reuters. Copyright © by Thomson Reuters; pp. 229–230: From The Blue Book-Rule 1.2, Published by Bluebook.

Chapter 10 **Figure 10-1** p. 238: From LexisNexis Legal Department; **Figure 10-2** p. 241: From LexisNexis Legal Department; **Figure 10-3** p. 241: From Thomson Reuters. Copyright © by Thomson Reuters; **Figure 10-4** p. 242: From LexisNexis Legal Department; **Figure 10-5** p. 242: From LexisNexis Legal Department; **Figure 10-6** p. 243: From LexisNexis Legal Department; **Figure 10-7** p. 245: From LexisNexis Legal Department; **Figure 10-8** p. 247: From Thomson Reuters. Copyright © by Thomson Reuters; **Figure 10-9** p. 247: From Thomson Reuters. Copyright © by Thomson Reuters; **Figure 10-10** p. 248: From Thomson Reuters. Copyright © by Thomson Reuters; p. 251: From The Bluebook—Rule 18, Published by Bluebook.

Chapter 11 **Figure 11-1** p. 257: From U.S. Government Publishing Office; **Figure 11-2** p. 258:

ɔmson Reuters. Copyright © by Thomson .s; **Figure 11-3** p. 258: From United States .ɛ by United States House of Representatives; .igure 11-4 p. 259: From United States Code by United States House of Representatives; **Figure 11-5A** p. 260: From United States Code by United States House of Representatives; **Figure 11-5B** p. 260: From United States Code by United States House of Representatives; **Figure 11-6** p. 260: From United States Code by United States House of Representatives; **Figure 11-7A** p. 261: From U.S. Government by U.S. General Services Administration; **Figure 11-7B** p. 261: From U.S. Government by U.S. General Services Administration; **Figure 11-8** p. 262: From United States Government Publishing Office (GPO); **Figure 11-9** p. 263: From Law Library of Congress; **Figure 11-10** p. 263: From U.S. Supreme Court; **Figure 11-11** p. 264: From U.S. Courts; **Figure 11-12** p. 264: From Federal Judicial Centre; p. 269: From The Bluebook—Rule 18, Published by Bluebook.

Chapter 12 pp. 278–279: Based on Illinois v. Caballes, 543 U.S. 405 (2005), by U.S. Supreme Courts; pp. 280–283: Based on Illinois v. Caballes, 543 U.S. 405 (2005), by U.S. Supreme Courts; p. 283: From Minnesota v. Dickerson 508 U.S. 366 (1993) Opinion, by U.S. Supreme Courts; p. 284: From Facts and Case Summary - Morse v. Frederick 551 U.S., 127 S. Ct. 2618 (2007), by U.S. Supreme Courts; pp. 291–292: Based on Minnesota v. Dickerson 508 U.S. 366 (1993), U.S. Supreme Courts; p. 286: Based on Minnesota v. Dickerson, 508 U.S. 366 (1993), by U.S. Supreme Courts; p. 294: From The Bluebook—Rule 5.3, Published by Bluebook.

Chapter 13 **Case 13-1** pp. 305–312: From Ann M. v. Pacific Plaza Shopping Center (1993), by U.S. Supreme Courts; p. 304: Based on Victoria V. – Premises Liability for Criminal Act of Third Party, U.S. Supreme Courts; p. 302: From 18 U.S. Code § 242, by U.S. Supreme Courts; p. 304: From Ann M. v. Pacific Plaza Shopping Center (1993), by the Supreme Court of California; p. 325: From The Bluebook—Rule 4, Published by Bluebook.

Chapter 14 **Figure 14-1** p. 335: From Rules of the Supreme Court of the United States, by U.S. Supreme Court; **Figure 14-2** pp. 337–339: From U.S. Court of Appeals, by Kenneth Rosenblatt; p. 333: From Government Code Section 835–835.4 by California State Legislature; p. 366: From The Bluebook—Rule B8.2, by Bluebook.

Chapter 15 **Figure 15-1** pp. 378–387: From Mission Hills Homeowners Association v. Gloria Jennings, No: Civ - 3654, by California Courts; **Figure 15-2** p. 389: From Mission Hills Homeowners Association v. Gloria Jennings, No: Civ - 3654, by California Courts; p. 376: From Federal Rules Of Civil Procedure, by The Committee of Judiciary House Of Representatives; p. 377: From Civil Local Rules, by U.S. Supreme Court; p. 388: From Civil Local Rules, by U.S. Supreme Court; p. 388: From Civil Local Rules, by U.S. Supreme Court; p. 390: From Civil Local Rules, by U.S. Supreme Court; p. 391: From 2016 California Rules of Court, by Judicial Council of California.

Chapter 16 p. 411: From The Bluebook—Rule 5.2, Published by Bluebook; p. 413: From Family Code Section 3900–3902, by California State Legislature; pp. 413–414: From Rules of the Supreme Court of the United States, by U.S. Supreme Court.

Index

F

G

H

I

M